LAY ANALYSIS
Life Inside the Controversy

Robert S. Wallerstein, M.D.

LAY ANALYSIS
Life Inside the Controversy

Robert S. Wallerstein

Routledge
Taylor & Francis Group
New York London

First Published by The Analytic Press, Inc.

This edition published 2012 by Routledge

Routledge
Taylor & Francis Group
711 Third Avenue
New York, NY 10017

Routledge
Taylor & Francis Group
27 Church Road, Hove
East Sussex BN3 2FA

First issued in paperback 2014

Routledge is an imprint of the Taylor and Francis Group, an informa business

Index by Leonard S. Rosenbaum

Library of Congress Cataloging-in-Publication Data

Wallerstein, Robert S.
    Lay analysis : life inside the controversy / Robert S. Wallerstein
        p.   cm.
    Includes bibliographical references and index.
    ISBN: 0-88163-285-6
    1. Welch, Bryant, 1946-   —Trials, litigation, etc. 2. American Psychoanalytic Association—Trials, litigation, etc.
3. International Psycho-Analytical Association—Trials, litigation, etc. 4. Lay analysis (Psychoanalysis)—Law and legislation--United States. 5. Lay analysis (Psychoanalysis)—History. I. Title.
KF228.W413W35   1998   98-46417
150.19′5′0801—dc21   CIP

ISBN 13: 978-0-88163-285-9 (hbk)
ISBN 13: 978-1-138-00542-6 (pbk)

To my beloved grandchildren, Jonah, Hannah, Benjamin, Alexei, and Nicole, from their proud and admiring grandfather.

I believe that to solve any problem that has never been solved before, you have to leave the door ajar. You have to permit the possibility that you do not have it exactly right.

Richard P. Feynman
The Meaning of It All: Thoughts of a Citizen Scientist

Contents

Preface
The Conception of This Book

As of this writing (1995–1996), psychoanalysis as a science and profession is almost exactly 100 years old. Sigmund Freud's defining *Studies on Hysteria*, written in collaboration with Josef Breuer, bears the publication dates, 1893–1895. Even prior to that, Freud had published a number of forerunner papers on hypnotism and suggestion over the years 1888 to 1892 (*Standard Edition*, Vol. 1), and over the decade of the 1890s he published a variety of early psychoanalytic papers on hysteria, on phobias and obsessions, on neurasthenia and "anxiety neurosis," on the "neuro-psychoses of defence," on sexuality, on forgetting, and on screen memories (*Standard Edition*, Vol. 3). Together, these early publications in the decade of the 1890s limned the outlines of this daring new science of the mind and established the fundaments of a professional practice designed to ameliorate and reverse the mental and emotional ills to which the mind is subject. Over the succeeding decades, until his death at 83 in 1939, Freud progressively enlarged and also substantially altered both his theory of the development and functioning of the mind and his technique for therapeutically addressing its ills. By the time of his death he left, in his *Gesammelte Werke*, a corpus of work he had singlehandedly created, which, if no further contributions were to be made by any others, would still by itself constitute an adequate enough theory of normal and abnormal mental functioning and a viable enough mental healing technique. In all, Freud's labors spanned just a few years short of the first half-century of psychoanalysis.

My own entry into psychiatric residency training with the explicit intention to become a psychoanalyst was in January 1949, just a few years after the start of the second half-century of psychoanalytic work. At that point I began to read the psychoanalytic literature, beginning with Freud, after an initial orientation via a first book by an author other than Freud, *Psychotherapy in Medical Practice* (1942), by Maurice Levine, the psychoanalyst chairman of the psychoanalytically infused Department of Psychiatry of the University of Cincinnati Medical School. My career in psychoanalysis thus has spanned almost precisely the second half of this hundred-year history of the discipline, and it has been my fate to have been active in organizational psychoanalysis throughout my professional lifetime and to have been centrally drawn into its major educational, scientific, and professional preoccupations over that time span. Dominant among these issues, and ramifying into every aspect of our organized educational, scientific, and professional concerns, has been the question of "lay analysis" that is, the education for and practice of psychoanalysis by nonphysicians — an issue that for me emerged not just as a guild concern for control of access to this endeavor scientifically and professionally, but far more as a question of the very nature of psychoanalysis as a discipline. How I mean this I shall work to clarify over the course of this book.

To set the framework, my involvement with this issue within the American Psychoanalytic Association was a somewhat serendipitous conse-quence of my becoming established, during the decade of my psychoanalytic candidacy in the 1950s, as one of the pioneering generation of empirical researchers into the processes and outcomes of psychoanalysis and the derived psychoanalytic psychotherapies (in the work of the Psychotherapy Research Project of The Menninger Foundation), which led to my being immediately invited, when I became a member of the American in 1960, to membership on its newly established Committee on Training for Research, created in 1958 as the first and sole avenue for the authorized psychoanalytic training of nonphysicians under the auspices of the American—non-physicians who were academic scholars (primarily psychologists), to be trained for careers of psychoanalytic research. My involvement in this committee is a central thread in my narrative.

In the International Psychoanalytical Association (IPA), my involve-ment was a consequence, a quarter-century later, in 1985, of my becoming President of the IPA in July of that year. This was just a few months after the filing of a class-action lawsuit against the American by four clinical psychologists, on behalf of a declared class of several thousand, alleging an illegal conspiracy, in violation of the Sherman Anti-Trust Act, to deprive nonphysicians in America of access to training for the clinical practice of this prestigious and remunerative profession. The IPA was also named as a defendant in this suit for permitting its American component organization to engage in these unfair practices. The lawsuit persisted actively over a three-and-a-half-year period until its settlement by agreement between the contending parties in October 1988, and it was clearly the central administrative and intellectual concern of my four-year presidency of the IPA, from 1985 through 1989. Over the course of that lawsuit I was party to all the negotiations and was one of very few individuals privy to the seemingly endless meetings, briefings, negotiating sessions, telephone conferences, letters, documents, legal briefs, depositions, and the like—one of the very few who can claim an insider's perspective on that complexly crisscrossing and always very contentious process.

Obviously, many lifetime professional experiences and relationships have helped shape the manner of my responses to this issue of lay analysis and to the many events in which I participated that transpired around this issue. In that sense, this book is a personal scientific memoir that I trust is at the same time a history of interest and value to the psychoanalytic community. In this context I should state that as far as I am consciously aware, I came first to these concerns with lay analysis as a relative tabula rasa. The son of a physician who practiced internal medicine over his lifetime, I entered into medicine with the expectation of a similar career, perhaps more academically and research focused, and when I first came to psycho-analysis out of residency training, first in internal medicine and then in psychiatry, lay analysis was no issue for me at all. I had till then lived comfortably with the notion that psychoanalysis, being a special psycho-logical treatment for at least some of the mental and emotional disorders within the purview of psychiatry, itself a specialty within medicine, was properly the province of physicians.

Now, after close to a half-century of psychiatric and psychoanalytic training and practice and of absorption organizationally with what Freud (1926b) called *The Question of Lay Analysis*, and of gradually crystallizing my own perspectives on the central meanings of this issue for the unique identity of psychoanalysis as both science and profession, I have undertaken to chronicle the intertwining of two main stories. The first is the story of this question of "lay analysis" from its beginnings, which go back to the earliest days of psychoanalysis itself, to the seemingly inexorable split, which started in the teens of this century, between Freud's (and generally, the European) openness of psychoanalysis to interested adherents from all intellectual routes, and the contrary, American, concern to limit psychoanalysis to the properly (i.e., medically) trained and qualified, and from there to the continuing controversy in the field until its (one hopes) final resolution with the alteration in the Regional Association status of the American Psychoanalytic Association within the International, voted at the IPA Congress in Montreal in August 1987, and the subsequent settlement of the lawsuit against the American and the IPA in October 1988.

The second story is what I have called my personal scientific memoir in organized psychoanalysis. This starts with my entry into psychiatry in 1949, but is built around this special focus on the inside story (my inside story) of my involvement in this issue of nonmedical analysis, through the vicissitudes of the struggles over this issue within the American over the decades of the 60s, 70s, and 80s, and merges finally into the joint struggles of the American and the International as they sought to accommodate their disparate views into a common response to the challenges of the lawsuit.

This accounting is thus very much my own eyewitness account of the events in which I was an inside participant, and therefore my truth. I fully realize that my interpretations of reasons, causes, and meanings will not be shared by all who were involved with me in the events described, whether among the analyst defendants or the psychologist plaintiffs. I offer in this context an apposite opinion from the United States Supreme Court (*Gertz v. Robert Welch, Inc.*, 418 US 323, 339–40, 1974): "Under the First Amendment there is no such thing as a false idea. However pernicious an opinion may seem, we depend for its correction not on the conscience of judges and juries but on the competition of other ideas." In this spirit, my account may stimulate others of the various protagonists in these dramas to offer their histories and their interpretations; to me, the issues involved are so fundamental to the nature of our discipline, to its identity and its place among the various avenues of intelligence of humankind, that it deserves no less than the fullest and most multisided accounting.

Acknowledgments

This book is a history, the story, within psychoanalysis, of the contentious issue of nonmedical or "lay" analysis that bedeviled the discipline from the time the issue first arose in 1910 until its resolution three quarters of a century later. I have woven into it my personal scientific history focused around my own close involvement as a central protagonist in the recorded events for the almost half-century of my own career in psychoanalysis. The many protagonists involved in the lawsuit—its precursors, its course, and its aftermath—that is, in the central drama of the volume, are described in their varying roles, as I experienced them, throughout the book, and are listed alphabetically in the volume's reference list. I trust that my appreciation of each of them becomes clear in the reading. They have collectively fashioned the story.

But the writing of the narrative chronicled here required the assistance of many more. Pearl King, Hon. Archivist of the British Psychoanalytical Society, and Allan B. Barns, Archives Assistant, spent hours guiding my search of the early archives of the British Society, which include all the archival material of the International Psychoanalytical Association (IPA) that had accumulated there up to the conclusion of Ernest Jones's successive presidencies of the IPA in 1949. Wolfgang Lederer translated into English the German language letters that I drew upon from that archival material. Adam Limentani, Hon. Archivist of the IPA, provided me with his (then still unpublished) *Brief History of the International Psychoanalytical Association* (1996) and guided me through the sequence of relevant Bulletins of the IPA upon which I drew.

Helen Fischer, Administrative Director of the American Psychoanalytic Association (APsaA), retrieved and provided the reports that I had made, as Chair of the American's Committee on Training for Research, to its Board on Professional Standards (BOPS) during the 1960s, and she led me as well to other relevant APsaA reports. Homer Curtis, as Chair of the BOPS Committee on Prerequisites for Training (1975–1981), provided the detailed committee minutes recorded by Paula Bernstein, its Secretary, as well as his own reports to BOPS over that time span. Kenneth Calder, Richard Isay, and Vann Spruiell similarly provided their reports as Chairs of the three successor committees to the Curtis committee. And Herbert Schlesinger provided documents from his personal files which had been prepared during his unofficial liaison services between the American and the plaintiffs over the course of the lawsuit.

Lester Luborsky recounted to me his personal tribulations in seeking full clinical psychoanalytic training through both the American and the British Associations in the late 1940s. Martin and Maria Bergmann, representatives of the first generation of nonphysicians who sought and patched together unofficial clinical psychoanalytic training in the late 1940s, afforded me extended interviews covering their professional life histories and the details of the conditions under which they and others obtained that unofficial (and surreptitious) psychoanalytic training at that time. Frederic J. Levine provided me his historical manuscript covering the rise of independent psychoanalytic institutes in the United States outside the framework of the American over the post-World War II decades.

There were still others. Nathan Hale and Riccardo Steiner, as historians of psychoanalysis, provided valuable consultations on the issues and problems involved in this kind of enterprise. The book title I owe to Fred Pine, who discussed with me a variety of possibilities. Charles Hanly provided me a very helpful update (in August 1994) of the various events in the aftermath of the settlement of the lawsuit covering the period during which I was no longer in the loop of those privy to all the correspondence and executive discussion of these issues. And Anton Kris provided an English translation of a paragraph from the 1993 Grubrich-Simitis book detailing Freud's attitudes towards America and Americans.

The manuscript was entered into the word processor by Barbara Lehman with diligence, accuracy, and expeditiousness. All correspondence relating to it has been handled by Ali Anderson. And special thanks are due The Analytic Press, to its Managing Director, Paul E. Stepansky, who undertook the book with great enthusiasm, to his colleague John Kerr who joined in the support, and to Nancy J. Liguori, Senior Production Manager, who so effectively guided the production process. The index was carefully done by Leonard Rosenbaum.

The description of events and the views expressed in this volume are based on the search of the IPA Archives, the study of the relevant published scientific literature, and the many documents that originated with me or came to me when I was president of the IPA between 1985 and 1989, when so many of the events described in this book took place. The IPA has not formally reviewed the manuscript and is, of course, not responsible for its contents. What remains to be stated is my great gratitude for a lifetime marital and intellectual partnership with my wife, Judy. She has shared with me every aspect of my involvement in the events recorded here, in all the thinking that guided my participation and decision making. And, of course, none of this impressive array of credits and thanks can absolve me of my own full responsibility for the descriptions and interpretations recorded here.

I end this list of acknowledgments on a sad note. On October 6, during the period when this book was going to press, Joseph Sandler died after a sudden and short illness. He was a very dear personal friend and brilliant colleague for over thirty years, a true comrade-in-arms in all my struggles depicted in this volume, and he contributed a generous endorsement to the book jacket.

The Origins of the Question
of Lay Analysis
The Development in Europe

I began the preface to this book with the statement that as of this writing, psychoanalysis is approximately 100 years old. James Strachey traced the origin of the word itself to that same time in the mid-1890s. In his introductory note to Freud's "Heredity and the Aetiology of the Neuroses" (1896a), he stated:

> This paper [published first in French] and the next one, the second on the neuropsychoses of defence (1896b), were sent off to their respective publishers on the same day, February 5, 1896, as Freud reported to Fliess in a letter the day after (Freud, 1950, Letter 40 [Masson, 1985, p. 170]). The French paper was published at the end of March, some six weeks before the other, and it consequently has priority over it for the first published appearance of the word "psycho-analysis" (p. 151) [p. 142].

The quotation from that paper reads as follows:

> As regards the second class of major neuroses, hysteria and obsessional neurosis, the solution of the aetiological problem is of surprising simplicity and uniformity. I owe my results to a new method of psycho-analysis, Josef Breuer's exploratory procedure; it is a little intricate, but it is irreplaceable, so fertile has it shown itself to be in throwing light upon the obscure paths of unconscious ideation [Freud, 1896a, p. 151].

Strachey had even more assiduously traced the precursor designation to a point actually three years earlier. In the paper "The Neuro-Psychoses of Defence" (1894), Freud had written, "In the third form of hysteria, which we have demonstrated by means of a psychical analysis" (p. 47), and in a footnote to this phrase, Strachey added, "The term 'to analyse' had already appeared in the 'Preliminary Communication' [*Studies on Hysteria*], 1893, *Standard Ed.* 2, 7. . . . 'Psychoanalysis' first appears in the French paper on the aetiology of the neuroses (1896a)" (p. 47).

Quite currently, two authors have marked this same centennial dating of psychoanalysis, but from broader perspectives. Horacio Etchegoyen in his 1993 address to the 38th Congress of the International Psychoanalytical Association in Amsterdam began by stating,

> We may agree with Strachey . . . that the word "psychoanalysis" appears for the first time in L'heredité et l'etiologie des névroses (Freud, 1896a) written for the *Revue de Neurologie*; however, there is no doubt that the transition from associative coercion to psychoanalysis was slow and gradual. This is evident from the final case histories of the *Studies on Hysteria* . . . , in which Freud comes increasingly to realize that forgetting is substantially bound up with resistance to remembering. The conceptual step, on the other hand, is clear-cut; from coercion with the application of the hands to free association. It is, therefore, a sufficiently close approximation to say that psychoanalysis has now been in existence for a century, divided into two halves by Freud's death [1993, p. 1109].

Martin Bergmann in his even earlier (December 1991) address at the Fall Meeting of the American Psychoanalytic Association in New York had put it as follows:

> Let us turn back to September 21, 1897, when Freud informed Wilhelm Fliess that he had lost faith in his "neurotica" [his theory of the traumatic origin of the neuroses] (Masson, 1985, p. 264). This day may well be the birthday of psychoanalysis. It is one of the glorious moments in the history of psychoanalysis. . . . At this historical juncture the concept of unconscious psychic reality as determining much of human behavior became central to psychoanalysis (Freud, 1900, pp. 610, 613; 1913b, p. 159) [1993, pp. 934–935].

There is of course a difference in emphasis between the statements of Etchegoyen and Bergmann; to Etchegoyen the defining event is Freud's discovery of the method of free association, while to Bergmann it is the recognition of the role of the dynamic unconscious in powering human behavior.

From these beginnings Freud embarked on his psychoanalytic career with a decade of work that he later called (1914) his period of "splendid isolation." In that paper, Freud referred to this period somewhat whimsically as follows:

> Like Robinson Crusoe, I settled down as comfortably as possible on my desert island. When I look back to those lonely years, away from the pressures and confusions of to-day, it seems like a glorious heroic age. My "splendid isolation" was not without its advantages and charms. I did not have to read any publications, nor listen to any ill-informed opponents; I was not subject to influence from any quarter; there was nothing to hustle me. I learnt to restrain speculative tendencies and to follow the unforgotten advice of my master, Charcot: to look at the same things again and again until they themselves begin to speak [1914, p. 22].

In his introduction to the *Minutes of the Vienna Psychoanalytic Society* (Nunberg and Federn, 1962), Herman Nunberg described Freud's feelings during that period quite differently, and probably more accurately.

> It is commonly known that from the very beginning Freud's new ideas were not well received by the medical profession; he was severely criticized by his colleagues, hated, and ostracized. Even some of his old friends deserted him. Thus he became a lonesome man. But he was a sociable man as well; he could be a great and faithful friend. . . . He loved to have people around him with whom he could communicate and exchange ideas. The loneliness into which he was driven—like all men who are ahead of their times—oppressed him; he would often say that the analyst should not be isolated, but, on the contrary, he should associate with others and exchange ideas and experiences with them. In a letter to his friend Wilhelm Fliess he wrote that Fliess was his "Publicum," his audience. He needed a sounding board. When he realized that Fliess ceased to follow his ideas, he suffered intensely; finally the friendship broke up [1962, p. xix].

It was not until 1902 that a small group clustered around Freud and began to meet weekly in Freud's apartment as the Psychological Wednesday Evenings. When this loose circle gradually transformed itself into the Vienna Psychological Society, the tradition of the Wednesday evening meetings continued as a Society function, and in 1910 the meetings, having by then considerably enlarged, were moved from Freud's apartment to the

College of Physicians (pp. xviii–xix). Nunberg went on to ask of this initial group:

> Who were the men who formed the Wednesday Evening Group, and why did they become psychoanalysts? On the one hand there was a group of men in search of new ideas and of a leader, and on the other hand there was a lonely man who had made important new discoveries and wished to share them with others. . . . The group was heterogeneous; it consisted of physicians, educators, writers and others. In short, its members represented a cross-section of the intellectuals at the beginning of the century. Different as they were in their backgrounds and personalities, they were held together by their common discontent with the conditions that prevailed in psychiatry, education, and other fields dealing with the human mind [p. xx]. . . . At the outset they formed an almost harmonious group. Each member showed intense interest in the topic under discussion, whether it was a clinical case, a poet or artist and his work, a teacher, a pupil, or a criminal. Papers were read, books and magazine articles were reviewed, and a variety of problems discussed: biology, animal psychology, psychiatry, sociology, mythology, religion, art and literature, education and criminology, even the association and psychogalvanic experiments [p. xxii].

As is clear from the above, this initial group of "intellectuals" comprised both physicians and nonphysicians. Of the 22 listed in the book's Notes on the Members of the Psychological Wednesday Evening Society, 16 were physicians (including specialists in surgery and physiotherapy) and six were not. These six included an eminent musicologist, a teacher, a publisher, and, best known today, Otto Rank, with no designated formal education, who was from the start the salaried secretary who recorded the minutes of these meetings (pp. xxxiii–xxxvii). Freud, for his part, welcomed the rallying of this cluster of gifted intellectuals to his new doctrines, no doubt for the reasons spelled out so poignantly by Nunberg, and from the start made no distinction between those who came from clinical medicine and those who did not—and he spent his lifetime thereafter propagating this position, to which he lent the enormous weight of his personal authority within the gradually enlarging psychoanalytic world.

Then how and why did the question of lay analysis become so contentious and divisive an issue for psychoanalysis? I begin the accounting of this issue with the year 1910, marked for our purposes by two events, seemingly totally unrelated, and widely separated geographically. The one, in Europe, was the publication of the paper "'Wild' Psycho-Analysis," Freud's initial cry of alarm that the psychoanalytically untrained, in this case a physician claiming an expertise in our field that he did not have,[1] would impart pseudoanalytic advice that could be hurtful to the patient. Freud considered this, however well-meaning, very deplorable, and it was just this kind of happening which was occurring often enough as our nascent science began to gain some adherents, and at least in certain educated circles, some credibility, that impelled Freud and his followers, as he stated in this paper, to establish the International Psychoanalytical Association in that very same year (1910) at the Second Psychoanalytical Congress, at Nuremberg, with Carl Jung installed as its first president. And it was for the same reasons that a few years later, after the defections of Stekel and Adler and Jung over the three-year span from 1910 to 1913, Freud created the famous Committee of the seven ring holders to try to guarantee the stability of his central psychoanalytic doctrines, as well as the loyalty and the capacity of those who carried the psychoanalytic imprimatur.

The other event in 1910, this one in America, was the issuance by the Carnegie Foundation of the famed Flexner report, that startling expose of the shocking state of medical education in the United States, with its widespread proliferation of so-called medical schools that were little more than diploma mills, converting the dollars of the students into quick degrees. Even the best organized schools were found to be sadly deficient in full-time faculty and in basic science education, and with only Johns Hopkins approaching the then standard of excellence of the German medical schools. The hue and cry raised by this devastating critique in both the medical and the wider supporting public world led to an extraordinarily rapid sea change in American medicine. About half the existing medical schools were driven to close their doors over the following decade and the remainder were moved to emulate the Hopkins model and to shake down into the approximately 100 class A medical schools in the nation by the 1930s. The watchword was to exorcise the charlatans from the therapeutic activity and to make the proper medical degree, from the now fully upgraded schools, the hallmark of proper training and competence in the healing arts.

---

[1] In this paper, Freud made one of his earliest references to the need for *specific training* in the theory and technique of psychoanalysis in order to qualify as a proper practitioner: "It is not enough, therefore, for a physician to know a few of the findings of psycho-analysis; he must also have familiarized himself with its technique if he wishes his medical procedure to be guided by a psycho-analytic point of view. This technique cannot yet be learnt from books, and it certainly cannot be discovered independently without great sacrifices of time, labour and success. Like other medical techniques, it is to be learnt from those who are already proficient in it" (1910, p. 226).

From these very disparate sets of circumstances, beginning in 1910, two diverging developmental paths can be traced for organized institutional psychoanalysis. One was in the Central European heartland, where Freud lived and was personally so enormously influential, and the other in America, where as early as the teens of the century, and in considerably larger numbers after World War I, some doctors became interested in psychoanalysis, went to Europe for variable periods of personal analysis and some rudiments of training, and then returned to establish the new science in North America under the early leadership of A. A. Brill (actually Austrian-born) and C. P. Oberndorf, and with help from Ernest Jones, a temporary missionary to Canada and the United States. The much larger numbers, of course, were with Freud in Europe; the Americans were no more than 20% of the world numbers in the IPA as late as 1930.

Of course, the European development was heavily determined by Freud's personal career, and the openness of Freud's early emerging psychoanalytic circle to physicians and nonphysicians alike was an all but inevitable aspect of the circumstances within which psychoanalysis came into being in Europe. As already stated, Freud's new doctrines were not at all welcomed by the established medical or academic worlds. In later years, Freud jokingly said that people used to treat him like a freshly painted wall; nobody dared to touch him (Nunberg and Federn, 1962, p. xix). This was in considerable part a reflection of the scandalous sexual nature of his theories of psychopathology and psychotherapy with their focus on the role of infantile sexuality in the genesis of neurotic illness—and this in Victorian turn-of-the-century Vienna. Added to this, of course, was the more or less official anti-Semitism of Freud's Vienna within the Austro-Hungarian Empire, which blocked Freud in his lifelong yearnings for recognition in the university and medical worlds.

Despite Freud's growing worldwide fame, in fact, he was only a Privatdozent and then a Professor Extraordinarius at the University of Vienna, both actually peripheral titles equivalent to low-ranking clinical faculty appointments here in America. Although he is known to have given various courses of university lectures, the only recorded series was that given over the academic years, 1915–1917, in the midst of the first World War (Freud, 1916–1917, Strachey's introduction, p. 5), the series of weekly lectures on the fundamentals of psychoanalysis which is the famous sequence of the 28 Introductory Lectures (1916–1917). But for the most part, psychoanalysis had to exist and grow in Vienna, and throughout the European continent, outside of academia, outside of organized medicine, and in its early days, often in the face of active medical and public opprobrium, as but a private-practice activity carried out by those who were drawn to it. When the first organized psychoanalytic training institute was formed by Max Eitingon and his colleagues in Berlin in 1920, it was, again, a private night school carried on the tired energies of part-time men and women, after daytimes of clinical practice. To this growing psychoanalytic activity Freud welcomed those who came. The majority of them were physicians drawn mostly from a sterile diagnostic neurology that was devoted largely to establishing differential diagnoses between such disorders as multiple sclerosis and the florid hysterical illnesses with their strange sensory and motor dysfunctions, for neither of which—multiple sclerosis nor grand hysteria—did the neurologists have anything curative to offer. From this they were drawn to the new field of psychoanalysis with its heady promise of treatment and cure, at least for the psychogenically ill.

But would-be psychoanalysts also came from a great array of nonmedical fields, starting with the very first membership roster recorded for the Psychological Wednesday Evenings (Nunberg and Federn, 1962, pp. xxxiii–xxxvii). Among the next generation of prominent students of the new science, Victor Tausk and Hanns Sachs came from law, Robert Waelder from theoretical physics, Ernst Kris was an art historian, Siegfried Bernfeld an educator, and Ella Sharpe an English professor. (Parenthetically, I should note that clinical psychology, the largest present disciplinary source of nonmedical psychoanalysts, did not yet exist as a distinct profession at that time.) Additionally, we are all familiar with how many of those who created the field of child analysis came from pedagogy, mostly elementary and preschool teaching, starting with Anna Freud, or had an incomplete university education like Melanie Klein, or had even less formal education than that, like Erik Erikson who had been an itinerant artist. To Freud, once they were immersed in their own analyses and acculturated to the analytic activity, with the informal consultations with each other that characterized the training of that early period, and once they became participants in the Vienna Psychoanalytic Society, they all became psychoanalysts equally, and Freud did not differentiate between those medically trained or not. It was those who were not psychoanalytically equipped in this way that Freud considered laymen to analysis, whether or not they were physicians.

It was in Freud's (1913a) introduction to Pfister's *The Psychoanalytic Method*, a book by one of the very first laymen to practice psychoanalysis, that Strachey in his note said Freud made his earliest published plea in favor of the full recognition of nonmedical psychoanalysts. In that introduction, Freud stated:

> The only question is whether the practice of psycho-analysis
> may not have as its prerequisite a medical training, from which
> the educator and the pastoral worker must remain debarred, or
> whether there may be other considerations which are opposed
> to the suggestion that the technique of psycho-analysis should

be confided to any but a doctor's hands. I confess that I can see no ground for any such reservation. The practice of psycho-analysis calls much less for medical training than for psychological instruction and a free human outlook. The majority of doctors are not equipped to practice psycho-analysis and have completely failed to grasp the value of that therapeutic procedure. The educator and the pastoral worker are bound by the standards of their profession to exercise the same consideration, care and restraint as are usually practiced by the doctor, and apart from this their association with young people perhaps makes them better fitted to understand these young people's mental life. But in both cases the only guarantee of the harmless application of the analytic procedure must depend on the personality of the analyst [1913, pp. 330–331].

Freud did add a caveat to this statement, one he made at greater length in his full-length statement on this issue in *The Question of Lay Analysis* (1926b), that of the continued place he felt for the physician consultant: "Where a case borders upon mental abnormality, the analytic educator will be bound to make himself familiar with the most necessary psychiatric knowledge, and furthermore to call a doctor into consultation when the diagnosis and prognosis of the disturbance appear doubtful. In a number of cases it will only be possible to achieve success if there is collaboration between the educator and the doctor" (p. 331). This whole issue of the place of lay analysis burst beyond the bounds of psychoanalytic discourse and erupted into public controversy when Newton Murphy, an American physician whom Freud had sent to Theodor Reik, one of his most gifted younger nonmedical colleagues,[2] became dissatisfied with his analysis and proffered legal charges against Reik, alleging a breach of an Austrian law against "quackery"—a law which made it illegal for a person without a medical degree to treat patients (Gay, 1988, p. 490; Strachey's note, Freud, 1926b, p. 180). Freud's response to this suit was stated by Strachey as follows:

Freud at once intervened energetically. He argued the position privately with an official of high standing, and went on to compose the present pamphlet [*The Question of Lay Analysis*, 1926b] for immediate publication. He began writing it at the end of June; it was in print before the end of July, and was

---

[2] Reik's doctoral dissertation in Vienna (1912) in psychology was the first *psychoanalytic* doctoral thesis ever. It was a study of artistic creativity in Flaubert's *Temptation of St. Anthony* (Sherman, 1988).

published in September. Partly, perhaps, as a result of his intervention, but partly because the evidence was unsatisfactory, the Public Prosecutor stopped the proceedings after a preliminary investigation [1926b, p. 180].[3]

It is worth citing Freud's central argument in his book in considerable detail because it is critical to the thesis I am building of the implications of this controversy for my own perspective upon its fundamental meaning for the nature and the identity of psychoanalysis as a field. Both Jones (1957) and Peter Gay (1988) in their biographies of Freud spoke to this point. Jones put it this way: "It has sometimes been thought that Freud's crusade in favor of lay analysis sprang from resentment at the scurvy way in which he had for so many years been treated by the medical profession. In my opinion there is very little truth in this suggestion; what mainly influenced him was the wish for a *broader outlook on psychoanalysis* than could be expected from doctors alone" (p. 288; italics added). Gay's statement was, "his early texts made plain that Freud's defense of lay analysts did not arise from the need for special pleading in their behalf. It followed naturally from what he perceived to be the *essential nature of psychoanalysis*. Freud had a high stake in lay analysis years before Theodor Reik came into conflict with the Austrian law" (p. 492; italics added).

The centerpiece of Freud's argument in elucidation of this "broader outlook on psychoanalysis" and of its "essential nature" is perhaps best summarized in an oft-repeated quotation from the postscript to *The Question of Lay Analysis* written a year later (1927) in response to the many commentaries this book elicited from psychoanalysts around the world. There he said:

I have assumed as axiomatic something that is still violently disputed in the discussion. I have assumed, that is to say, that psycho-analysis is not a specialized branch of medicine. I cannot see how it is possible to dispute this. Psycho-analysis is a part of psychology; not of medical psychology in the old sense, not

---

[3] Though Strachey (and Jones in his Freud biography) stated that the case never came to trial, and Reik likewise denied that it had, Murray Sherman (1988) stated that there actually was one. He stated that a cable to *The New York Times* dated May 25, 1927, described the court proceedings in a daylong trial. Though the complainant was supported by Professor Wagner-Jauregg, a foe of Freud's (who incidentally won the Nobel Prize that very year for the malaria treatment of neurosyphilis), Freud was able to convince the court to decide in Reik's favor. The other two leading lay analysts in Freud's circle, Otto Rank and Hanns Sachs, were never charged under the Austrian law. Nominally, all the nonmedical members of the Vienna Society were under the supervision of medical members.

of the psychology of morbid processes, but simply of psychology. It is certainly not the whole of psychology, but its substructure and perhaps even its entire foundation. The possibility of its application to medical purposes must not lead us astray [p. 252].

Freud had made exactly this point in a letter he wrote to Paul Federn in March 1926, prior to writing *The Question of Lay Analysis*: "the battle for lay analysis must be fought out at some time or other. Better now than later. As long as I live, I shall do everything in my power to prevent psychoanalysis from being swallowed up by medicine" (Freud, 1926a). That sentiment was reiterated in somewhat different form in another famous quotation from the postscript to the book: "I only want to feel assured that the therapy will not destroy the science" (Freud, 1926b, p. 254).

For the therapeutic practice of this psychoanalysis one of course needed rigorous training (as then defined). Freud put it thus:

Preparation for analytic activity is by no means so easy and simple. The work is hard, the responsibility great. But anyone who has passed through such a course of instruction, who has been analyzed himself, who has mastered what can be taught to-day of the psychology of the unconscious, who is at home in the science of sexual life, who has learnt the delicate technique of psycho-analysis, the art of interpretation, of fighting resistances and of handling the transference—anyone who has accomplished all this *is no longer a layman in the field of psychoanalysis*. He is capable of undertaking the treatment of neurotic disorders, and will be able to achieve in that field whatever can be required from this form of therapy [p. 228].

Put most succinctly, Freud declared: "I lay stress on the demand that *no one should practice analysis who has not acquired the right to do so by a particular training*. Whether such a person is a doctor or not seems to me immaterial" (p. 233). On the other hand, those not so trained are the true laymen in the field, or in Freud's harsher language, quacks. He said: "A quack is anyone who undertakes a treatment without possessing the knowledge and capacities necessary for it" (p. 230), and somewhat snidely: "Doctors form a preponderating contingent of quacks in analysis. They very frequently practice analytic treatment without having learnt it and without understanding it" (p. 230). Overall, Freud had proposed even before laying out his argument in detail: "It may perhaps turn out that in this instance the patients are not like other patients, that the laymen are not really laymen, and that the doctors have not exactly the qualities which one has a right to expect of doctors and on which their claims should be based" (p. 184).

For the proper practice of this psychoanalysis, Freud laid out his utopian vision of a school for psychoanalysis.

> If—which may sound fantastic today—one had to found a college of psycho-analysis, much would have to be taught in it which is also taught by the medical faculty: alongside of depth-psychology, which would always remain the principal subject, there would be an introduction to biology, as much as possible of the science of sexual life, and familiarity with the symptomatology of psychiatry. On the other hand, analytic instruction would include branches of knowledge which are remote from medicine and which the doctor does not come across in his practice; the history of civilization, mythology, the psychology of religion and the science of literature. Unless he is well at home in these subjects, an analyst can make nothing of a large amount of his material. By way of compensation, the great mass of what is taught in medical schools is of no use to him for his purposes [p. 246].[4]

Because such a "college of psycho-analysis" could not be envisioned in the foreseeable future, Freud did acknowledge that "people who have had a preliminary education in medicine are the best material for future analysts. We have a right to demand, however, that they should not mistake their preliminary education for a complete training" (p. 257). And he balanced this statement by the warning that a "medical education appears to me to be an arduous and circuitous way of approaching the profession of analysis. No doubt it offers an analyst much that is indispensable to him. But it burdens him with too much else of which he can never make use, and there is a danger of its diverting his interest and his whole mode of thought from the understanding of psychical phenomena" (p. 252).

Freud, however, was never as fanatically one-sided on this issue as some of those who advocated alongside him. He did provide a threefold special place for the physician specialist. The first was on issues of proper differential diagnosis: "I allow—no, I insist—that in every case which is under consideration for analysis the diagnosis shall be established by a doctor. For the greater number of neuroses which occupy us are fortunately

---

[4] It is just this utopian vision of Freud's which inspired my efforts to create within the University of California system just such a preparatory college for psychoanalysis, as a five-year doctoral-level program leading to a Doctor of Mental Health degree. This effort lasted 13 years and graduated some nine classes before it was aborted, a story that I chronicle in its proper place in this book.

of a psychogenic nature and give no grounds for pathological suspicions. Once the doctor has established this, he can confidently hand over the treatment to a lay analyst" (p. 243). The second place was in regard to supervening somatic symptoms: "There is a further contingency, again, in which the analyst has to ask the doctor's help. In the course of an analytic treatment, symptoms—most often physical symptoms—may appear about which one is doubtful whether they should be regarded as belonging to the neurosis or whether they should be related to an independent organic illness that has intervened. The decision on this point must once again be left to a doctor" (p. 243). And the third place was in the arena we today call psychosomatic: "I also share the view that all those problems which relate to the connection between psychical phenomena and their organic, anatomical and chemical foundations can be approached only by those who have studied both, that is, by medical analysts. It should not be forgotten, however, that this is not the whole of psycho-analysis" (p. 257). The last phrase clearly relates to Freud's constant fear lest psychoanalysis, with all its ramifying vistas for the understanding of the human condition, be simply "swallowed up by medicine . . . to find its last resting-place in a text-book of psychiatry, under the heading 'Methods of Treatment'" (p. 248).

But Freud also knew that not all of his colleagues, even within his own Vienna circle, agreed with him on this issue, and he stated in this same book that "a good proportion of my medical colleagues do not agree with me on this and are in favour of doctors having an exclusive right to the analytic treatment of neurotics" (p. 239). Of all the major European leaders in psychoanalysis, Ernest Jones, one of the seven ring holders, but the only one not from the Central European heartland, played the most pivotal role in articulating his own and in orchestrating the worldwide psychoanalytic response to Freud's manifesto; this was in his various roles as the editor of the *International Journal of Psycho-Analysis,* as the dominant figure in the very influential British Psychoanalytical Society, and as the major European link with the American analysts, who were so uniformly antagonistic to Freud on this issue.

Jones in his biography of Freud quotes his own September 23, 1926 letter to Freud about the newly published book:

> The thing I think you have settled beyond all doubt is that it would be very injurious to our movement to forbid lay analysis. There will be lay analysts, and there must be because we need them. . . . The wider question of how far we should aim at making analysis an independent profession, having only certain links with the medical one, is extraordinarily interesting, and I find there is much to say about it. In all probability, however, it will not be settled by us, but by fate [Jones, 1957, p. 293].

The same cautious note was struck by Jones in the book review he wrote, published in the *International Journal* in the very next year. He characterized the book as having three elements, "first, an exposition, which is quite up to the author's usual standard of excellence; secondly, an argument, which has several features of imperfection; and thirdly, a vision, which is the most remarkable and interesting part of the whole book" (1927, p. 86). The "vision" was discerned as that of "psycho-analysis constituting itself into a totally independent discipline, forming thus a profession by itself" (p. 92). This, and the linked concept of the "college of psychoanalysis," though Jones declared it to bristle with both theoretical and practical difficulties, certainly did "capture the imagination" (p. 92); "It all sounds very much like Zukunftsmusik [music for the future]. But after all the main thing is the idea" (p. 92).

The bulk of the review had a more negative cast, however. Jones gave several examples of what he considered to be Freud's one-sided partiality in his arguments on behalf of lay analysis which Jones called polemical, exaggerated, and, to a considerable extent, unsubstantiated. In addition, the difficulties in the way of implementing Freud's vision, Jones said, were "glossed over, simplified, or left altogether unmentioned, to an extent that will leave many analysts unsatisfied and only desirous of a fuller exposition" (p. 86). Jones also offered his view of the reasons for Freud's one-sided approach: "Professor Freud was probably concerned to put his case forcibly because of an intense conviction that any alternative would seriously imperil the future development of psycho-analysis. He gives very weighty grounds, which we shall consider below, for this conviction. A second, less obvious motive would appear to lie in a certain animus against the medical profession" (p. 89).[5] But at the end, Jones, contrapuntally, strove to present a more upbeat overview: "To sum up our impression of the main argument. It is presented with Professor Freud's usual skill and cleverness, but it contains nothing new, it omits much of importance, and it is unmistakably partial. Nevertheless, in spite of these deficiencies the conclusions reached may be perfectly sound; we may reasonably hope that a more extensive discussion will lead to a definite decision as to their validity" (p. 92).

Jones did try to provide this more extensive discussion through publishing later in that same year (1927), in the *International Journal*, an array of 26 solicited position statements in response to Freud's book, from

---

[5] This statement about "a certain animus" against the medical profession is at considerable variance with Jones's later statement, already quoted, in his 1957 biography of Freud (published 30 years later) that Freud's crusade about lay analysis did *not* spring from resentment against the medical profession, but had more fundamental roots in Freud's conception of the essential nature of psychoanalysis as a discipline.

every major center of organized psychoanalytic activity, including four from America (Jones et al., 1927, pp. 174–283, 392–401). Jones's own contribution to this worldwide symposium was the first, the longest (24 pages), and the most exhaustively reasoned, and is the only one to be cited in any detail. He began by acknowledging that 40% of the members of the British Psychoanalytical Society were nonmedical, but balanced this with the statement that nonetheless, "We cannot escape from some relation with medicine, and the only question is what is this to be" (p. 178). After adducing a range of considerations regarding this issue of lay analysis, Jones came to the conclusion that, to that point, "enough has perhaps been said to establish two propositions: first, that it is undesirable for lay analysts to engage in independent practice, and secondly, that there needs to be a definite selection [by medical analysts] of the cases judged suitable for treatment at their hands" (p. 183).

Following this, Jones went on to state that there seemed to be three general opinions among his colleagues on this issue, namely: "(1) only medically qualified analysts should conduct psycho-analyses, (2) it is irrelevant whether the analyst is medically qualified or not, and (3) it is desirable that most analysts be medically qualified, but there is no good reason why selected lay persons should not conduct analyses under certain definite conditions. The first two of these may fairly be termed extreme views, and I have no hesitation in rejecting them both, for reasons that are here expounded" (pp. 183–184). Here Jones clearly staked out his own middle position on this issue, while indicating that he felt Freud's position— the second—to be extreme.[6] Jones went on then to indicate why he rejected the two opposed, "extreme," positions. About the value of lay analysts he said, "It seems to me, in short, that advance in the science of psycho-analysis would be seriously impeded if all lay workers were excluded. I am speaking here not only of the matter of practice, of the number of skillful practitioners in analysis we should lose by excluding the laity but of the more important question of losing the contributions they can and do make to our knowledge" (pp. 184–185). And about the counterpart value of the strong tie to medicine, he said that psychoanalysis becoming a truly independent profession

> would wrench the knowledge of psychopathology more and more from the medical profession, for the better it succeeded the more would psychical affections be regarded as "non-medical." . . . This would stifle the hope of those who look

---

[6] In his Freud biography Jones (1957) complained about, "Freud's suspicion that I was opposed to lay analysis. He could never understand midway positions, such as mine was and is" (pp. 294–295).

forward to steady improvement in the psychological education of the medical profession as a whole. We know not only that most neurotics first consult a general physician, and presumably always will do so, but—what is perhaps even more important—that the part played by psychical factors in organic disease is immensely greater than is now at all widely recognized; if one makes a general survey it becomes quite doubtful whether the general practitioner has more to do with psychical or with physical factors in his daily work" (p. 187).

Jones was also mindful, however, of the adamant American opposition to the recognition of lay analysts and in regard to this he said:

> Our American colleagues fear that their only hope [of avoiding "pseudo-scientific charlatans"] is to unite psycho-analysis, as a special branch, with an already established profession, i.e., medicine, and when they take the view that the conditions in America are so different from those in Europe that psycho-analysis there should be *confined* to the medical profession, with some resentment against those European analysts who actively force the opposite solution on them against their better judgement, I must say that I find it harder to disagree with them than do some Europeans with less experience of that interesting Continent [p. 192].

The solution that Jones proposed for this dilemma was that of national autonomy:

> I hold definitely that in regard to the present question the various national groups should be accorded a high degree of autonomy. If such a group, which should be in the best position to judge the particular requirements and conditions of their country, came to a definite decision in one direction, then any attempts on the part of any others of the International Association to override this and force a contrary decision on them (e.g. by training analysts from the first country which the Training Committee of that country regard as undesirable) can only lead to friction between the groups and act in the long run deleteriously on the interests of psycho-analysis as a whole [p. 198].

As good a summary as any of Jones's complicated and often fence-straddling views on this subject was given by Lewis A. Kaplan (1986), attorney for the American Psychoanalytic Association during the lawsuit against it on Sherman Anti-Trust grounds during the mid-80s, as part of his brief to the court in support of the motion for a summary judgment to dismiss the complaint.

> Ernest Jones, later Freud's biographer, favored lay analysis under carefully limited conditions, but argued that lay analysts should not engage in independent practice. [Jones et al., 1927, pp. 181–182]. He contended that diagnosis—in his view, a medical function—often can be made "only during and by means of the analysis itself" [pp. 182–183]. And he believed that analysts ordinarily should be medical doctors because eliminating the requirement of medical qualification would discourage doctors from becoming analysts, would tend to drive a wedge between medicine and psychoanalysis despite their mutual concern with the care of the mentally afflicted, would stifle improvement in the psychological education of the medical profession, would deprive analysts of adequate medical contact, and would stultify progress in psychoanalysis by divorcing it from the biological sciences [pp. 183–198]. In sum, he contended that both the patients' interest in the best possible care, and the public and professional interests in the advancement of medicine and psychoanalysis, warranted restricting the independent practice of psychoanalysis to medical doctors and restricting psycho-analytic training to medical doctors with comparatively few exceptions [Kaplan, 1986, p. 20].

After Jones, 25 additional position statements followed—nine from Vienna, seven from Berlin, four from America (all in New York), two from Britain (in addition to Jones), two from Budapest, and one from Holland—perhaps roughly reflecting the distribution of psychoanalysts around the world in 1927? Ten were strongly supportive of Freud's position, and 11 equally strongly opposed. Three of the 25 supported Jones's "midway" position and one simply never made clear how he stood. Expectedly, all four Americans were adamant in their opposition, while the two other British were two of the three who supported Jones's middle position. The Vienna and Berlin groups were quite split, pro and con, while the Hungarians unreservedly supported Freud. As far as I could tell only four of the 25 (Carl Muller-Braunschweig, Theodor Reik, Hanns Sachs, and Robert Waelder) were themselves lay analysts, and they all supported Freud wholeheartedly.

Among the 25, I single out two for special citation: Oberndorf for his eloquent statement of the negative American position, and Franz Alexander of Berlin for his equally impassioned and visionary statement, going even beyond Freud in his defense of the need for the lay analyst. In addition, for single points of emphasis Geza Roheim of Budapest and Paul Schilder of Vienna are notable. Oberndorf expressed clearly the American concern lest quacks and cults, those he called "the correspondence school psycho-analysts who operate in America" (Jones et al., 1927, p. 206) invade the medical field, just as the osteopaths and the chiropractors were doing, with the consequence that an "ill-trained, uneducated, irresponsible group [would be given] free to play at battledore and shuttlecock with a term [psychoanalysis] representing one of the greatest efforts in thinking of the present century" (p. 206). This he felt to be a special risk for psychoanalysis: "Psycho-analysis is a method peculiarly adaptable to the customary procedure of quacks, since it does not admit the presence of a critical third party, and is particularly available since it does not involve any physical interference with the patient in connection with which demonstrable injury might be attributed and damages claimed" (p. 205). He also averred that, "In my analytical experience—extending over a period of fifteen years—I cannot recall a single case where in the evaluation of symptoms I have not been compelled to fall back upon medical training and a knowledge of the functioning of the body in health and in disease" (p. 204).

Alexander, in his defense of Freud, made a vigorous counterattack. He began with the statement that "it would seem to be self-evident that for a training in psycho-analysis—the science of the mental personality—a course of study in those branches of knowledge embraced by mental science must be more useful than a preliminary medical training, which up to the present has sadly neglected the psychological aspect of human nature" (pp. 224–225). And he followed with, "As Freud has said emphatically, when confronted with certain morbid symptoms, they [physicians] are merely laymen, while the lay analyst is a specialist. It is in stressing this acknowledged evil that psycho-analysis will find the best means of exercising a salutary influence on the whole development of medicine" (p. 226).

From there Alexander went on to advance his major claim: "It seems to us, then, that we have actually almost a stronger reason for advancing the claim that psycho-analysts shall have a complete medical training, the contrary claim that the medical man should have a psycho-analytical training. From the standpoint of principle, therefore, the two claims are at least equally justified" (p. 227). Then even further, "We must, therefore, consider both the lay analyst and the physician without psycho-analytical training as *transitory phenomena of our age* which have arisen as the necessary consequences of the one-sided medical therapeutics and science of the present day (p. 227) ... and of these two [the layman in psychology and the psycho-analyst who is a layman] the latter does far less mischief than the former" (p. 229). This brought Alexander to his climax.

> At present psycho-analysis needs medicine less than medicine psycho-analysis ... a knowledge of the structure and function

of the psychical apparatus shall be as fundamental and as indispensable a part of the future as knowledge of the anatomy and physiology of the body. Psycho-analysis can never be merged with medicine as a special subject, as a branch of therapeutics: it can only enter it in its entirety as a *half* of equal importance. The science of personality and the knowledge of the body will stand side by side as two parts of the whole, equal in value and complementary to one another. . . . At present, however, we still have the lay analyst with us, and just because he is unhampered by academic medicine with its authoritative support and its apsychological—indeed anti-psychological—attitude, he is frequently more capable of psychological understanding than the analyst with a medical training [pp. 229–230].

Surely this is a utopian vision of an unrealized future when all physicians would be psychoanalytically educated and the "need" for the lay analyst would no longer exist.

The two others from this same 1927 debate whom I mention are Geza Roheim, the first anthropologist analyst, who made a special plea for lay analysis in order to ensure the future of the important arena of "applied analysis," and Paul Schilder, who opted to let the marketplace, that is, the consumer, decide this contentious issue: "Anyone who seeks healing belongs to the physician. Anyone who desires or needs to be educated belongs to the educator. He who seeks consolation, to the pastor. The adult generally decides for himself to which group he belongs" (pp. 246–247). Schilder, however, does not mention that it is in precisely this realm of mental healing or education or consolation that the prospective patient-student-supplicant may have the greatest difficulty in making this decision, absent expert guidance. And who is the expert to be? This again brings us back to the issue of medical and/or lay analysis.

Freud was accorded the right of response to this sequence of commentaries on his book, published in a later issue of the *International Journal* that year (in Jones et al., 1927) and published as well as the Postscript to the book itself in the *Standard Edition* (1926). Comments from that postscript have already been cited in my quotations from Freud's book and will not be repeated. Final remarks on this issue were then made by Max Eitingon in his capacity as Chairman of the International Training Commission (ITC) of the International Association, an organ recently formed to effect uniform training standards amongst all the IPA component organizations. Eitingon's summation of this multisided debate was expressed as follows:

What conditions are to be imposed on candidates who aspire to train as practising analysts? In the discussion the desirability has so far never seriously been questioned—on the contrary it has in general been more or less expressly emphasized—of such candidates having a preliminary training in medicine, which should be as good as possible. On the other hand it is admitted on all sides [editorial note: not by the Americans] that a whole series of psychoneuroses, and precisely those which come within the true sphere of psycho-analysis as a therapy, can be successfully treated not only by physicians, but by trained non-medical practitioners, provided only that they are thoroughly instructed in analysis [in Jones et al., 1927, p. 399].

Eitingon's concern in this was clearly for the thoroughness of the psychoanalytic training, for medical and nonmedical aspirants alike. He concluded with what he called a utopian question: "Is it altogether utopian to suggest that what we have to aim at, if this is to be a more ideal state of affairs in the future, is that the practising analyst's plan of procedure and training should be so framed as to substitute for the co-operation of non-medical analyst and physician the combination in a single person of an equally good analytical and medical training?" (p. 400) thus echoing Alexander's identically utopian vision.

I conclude this chapter with retrospective comments on Freud's 1926 book and the 1927 26-party debate concerning it, made by Jones (1957) and Gay (1988) in their Freud biographies and by Kurt Eissler (1965) in his entire book devoted to this subject. Jones, in a statement most revealing of his own intense ambivalence about this issue, stated quite dismissively, "Freud . . . painted a seductive, and indeed grandiose, picture of a new and quite independent profession, and wanted to initiate it by opening the doors wide to lay analysts drawn from various sources" (p. 289). His own hurt feelings were openly expressed in the statement already quoted, that Freud "could never understand midway positions, such as mine was and still is" (pp. 294–295). Gay, also a major Freud biographer, but unlike Jones, not a protagonist himself in the 1926–27 debates, could maintain a somewhat more objective perspective. He stated: "Freud was so intent on his case that he did not hesitate to question his opponents' motives; resistance to lay analysis, he charged, was really resistance to analysis in general. Considering the stature, and the arguments, of psychoanalysts on the other side of the question, this verdict seems facile and tendentious" (p. 493).

Gay then stated his own perspective more fully.

By the mid-1920s . . . analysts in France, Britain, and, most audibly, the United States, were heard to mutter that far too many self-appointed therapists were trying to live off, and managing to subvert, whatever prestige psychoanalysis had managed to amass. . . . Whoever was responsible for this chaos, real psychoanalysts must decisively distance themselves from all charlatans. Freud's foreign "pupils" going back home to practice, were beginning to think about the rewards of respectability and to construct professional establishments to safeguard them. In that enterprise, lay analysts were likely to figure as distracting, possibly embarrassing, intruders [p. 494]. . . . Not unexpectedly, Freud discovered the true villains in the piece to be the Americans. Certainly American psychoanalysts were the most intransigent opponents of lay analysis anywhere [p. 497].[7]

Apropos the American position, Jones (1957) had said that Freud "would never admit . . . that the opposition of American analysts to lay

---

[7] Riccardo Steiner in a personal communication (November 1, 1995) indicated that he felt that the uncompromising American opposition to Freud's position on the question of lay analysis was, in turn, intensified in reaction to Freud's widely known and often quoted antipathy to everything American. As an example, in a letter to Ernest Jones, dated September 25, 1924, Freud wrote, "What is the use of Americans, if they bring no money? They are not good for anything else. My attempt at giving them a chief in the person of Frink, which has so sadly miscarried, is the last thing I will ever do for them, had I to live the one hundred years you set down for the incorporation of psychoanalysis into Psychiatry" (Paskauskas, 1993, p. 552). These same anti-American sentiments were stated by Freud (1930) in an introduction to a special issue of an American journal. This one-and-a-half-page statement is actually nothing but an anti-American diatribe.

It seems to me that the popularity of the name of psychoanalysis in America signifies neither a friendly attitude to the thing itself nor any specially wide or deep knowledge of it . . . the contributions to our science from that vast country are exiguous and provide little that is new. Psychiatrists and neurologists make frequent use of psychoanalysis as a therapeutic method but as a rule they show little interest in its scientific problems and its cultural significance. Quite particularly often we find in American physicians and writers a very insufficient familiarity with psycho-analysis, so that they know only its terms and a few catch-words—though this does not shake them in the certainty of their judgement. . . . they make a hotch-potch out of psycho-analysis and other elements and quote this procedure as evidence of their broad-mindedness, whereas it only proves their lack of judgement [pp. 254–255].

In a recent book, Ilse Grubrich-Simitis (1993) reports and cites a three-page section omitted from the publication of the 1927 Postscript (*Standard Edition*, Vol. 20, p. 258, between the next-to-last and last paragraphs). In a summary of that citation provided to me by Anton Kris, Freud ascribes what he considered to be the American failure to hold a deep interest in psychoanalysis to the shallowness of the American character, its cultural deficiency, the emphasis on time-is-money, and the defectiveness of the American superego, which can so readily be bought off by business interests. Peter Gay in his Freud biography (1988) devoted eight pages (562–570) to a detailed documentation of Freud's violently disparaging and demeaning statements about America and Americans, mostly cited from letters (and therefore less circumspect than what he actually allowed to be published), like the letter to Jones I have analysis was to a considerable extent a part of the struggle of various learned professions in America to secure respect and recognition for expert knowledge and the training needed to acquire it" (p. 297). Eissler, an emigré Viennese analyst who became a central figure in the New York Psychoanalytic Society during the post–World War II period, and a powerful supporter of Freud on this issue, wrote *Medical Orthodoxy and the Future of Psychoanalysis* (1965), a book of nearly 600 pages, advocating Freud's position to the American psychoanalytic world. The reader is referred to his book for its very detailed historical recounting of this issue to that date.

Here I want only to cite one statement in which Eissler averred the fundamental importance of this question of lay analysis but unhappily— from my perspective—did a disservice in comparing it to religious doctrinal disputation rather than, more appropriately, to the broad intellectual issue of the essential nature of psychoanalysis as a major avenue of intelligence of human mental life.

> From the historical study, one obtains the impression that the question of lay analysis is more than merely a matter of administration or organization. Behind what may appear to the outsider as a cut-and-dry issue of bureaucracy, there rest differences of conception, outlook, almost, one might say, of philosophy, which make the question of lay analysis—however academic it may be at present in the United States—a very worthwhile subject of inquiry on theoretical grounds.
>
> For obvious reasons, a comparison (which I hesitate to make, for it may be easily misunderstood and turned against psychoanalysis) with religious issues, say of the Christian churches, comes to mind. Such was the controversy between Homoiousianism and Homoousianism, which to the outsider may even seem to be nothing but a quibble about a letter, yet it covered vast differences of doctrine [p. 48].

---

cited from the Paskauskas volume. Here are some additional samples: (to Jones), "Yes, America is gigantic, but a gigantic mistake" (p. 563); (to Rank), "the only rational kind of conduct appropriate for a stay among these savages: to sell your life as dearly as possible. . . . It has often seemed to me that analysis suits Americans as a white shirt suits a raven" (p. 563); (to Max Schur), "This race is destined to extinction. They can no longer open their mouths to speak; soon they won't be able to do so to eat" (p. 567). For further documentation of Freud's virulent anti-American attitudes and for speculation about its psychodynamic roots, see Mahony, 1993.

The Confrontation from America
and the "1938 Rule"

I have used the year 1910—for our purposes, marked in Europe by the publication of Freud's "'Wild' Psycho-analysis" and in America by the issuance of the Flexner report on the deplorable state of American medical education—to signal the origin of the differing organizational and educational paths taken in the historical development of psychoanalysis on the two sides of the Atlantic. The alarming issue emerging in psychoanalysis at the time was that of the growth of a wild, pseudoanalysis, so well described in Freud's paper. The European response to this pending crisis of credibility for the new profession was traced in the preceding chapter; the creation of the International Psychoanalytical Association in 1910 to promote commitment to shared standards of professional practice, the subsequent creation of the committee of the seven ring holders to authoritatively promulgate the proper confines of psychoanalytic doctrine, and then, most decisively, the organization of proper psychoanalytic institutes, the first established by Eitingon and his colleagues as early as 1920 in Berlin, with the delineation then of the requisite training standards. From the very beginning, these standards consisted of the still-extant tripartite structure of personal (training) analysis, an appropriate sequence of theoretical and clinical seminars on both the theory and technique of psychoanalysis, and the satisfactory conduct of supervised analyses with carefully selected cases.

The American response to the same problem was different. It was to restrict eligibility for psychoanalytic practice to those whose preliminary training in the healing arts met the standards promulgated nationwide in the wake of the Flexner report, namely, those individuals who had completed medical school and a psychiatric residency in the now upgraded American medical education system, and could thus be trusted to travel to Europe to learn psychoanalysis properly and to return to America to practice and to

23

teach.[1] In that period, the first two decades following the 1910 Flexner report, almost the entire number of psychoanalysts in America was clustered in the four cities of New York, Boston, Philadelphia, and the Washington-Baltimore area, with an overall majority in New York City. Both the American and the New York Psychoanalytic Society were organized already in 1911, but New York did not inaugurate its formal institute training program until three decades later, in 1940. Societies were organized in Boston and Baltimore-Washington, both in 1914, but organized institute training not until 1933 in each; Chicago was the first where society and training institute were organized almost contemporaneously, in 1931 and 1932.

Thus the logic of the early development of psychoanalysis in America. With training for the practice of psychoanalysis something to be acquired on an extended sojourn in Europe, either within the earliest formal training structure of Berlin, or more commonly, in the somewhat later organized Vienna orbit, but with the period of personal analysis either with Freud himself or with a colleague to whom Freud referred the American applicant, the control that the first generation of American analysts—Brill and Oberndorf and their colleagues—could exert over training qualifications and standards was in restriction to the medically qualified. They felt equally mindful as Freud and his confrères that the new science and therapy of psychoanalysis should be in the hands of the properly psychoanalytically trained; but mindful also of the morass of pseudomedical charlatanism from which the Flexner report had aroused the nation into long-overdue corrective action, they believed, oppositely from Freud but as strongly, that the integrity of psychoanalysis could only be safeguarded within the now increasingly respectable and scientific medical orbit.

With my own psychoanalytic life centered on the West Coast, in California, I have more access to this early period of turmoil as it expressed itself here, probably two decades or so later than, but no doubt comparable in character to, the earlier period on the East Coast. The historian of psycho-analysis Nathan Hale (1993) has chronicled the free-wheeling and irresponsible atmosphere in which psychoanalytic ideas were taking hold during those earliest days on the West Coast.

---

[1] It must be remembered that at that time, the teens and 20s of the century, psychiatry was the only functioning mental health profession in the private practice arena. Clinical psychology did not yet exist as an independent profession, and clinical social work, while an already emergent activity, was essentially limited to work in social agencies with the most disadvantaged, especially the immigrant poor. The same point, incidentally, about the divergent responses to the problem of wild analysis, establishing formal training institutes in Europe, and restricting access to practice in America, was made by Phyllis Tyson (1994) in an article on the history of nonmedical training under the auspices of the American Psychoanalytic Association, written for *The American Psychoanalyst* (the newsletter of the American).

You must remember that psychoanalysis was introduced to America partly on the wave of a craze for religious sponsored healing in 1908 and 1909, a development that unnerved Freud on his American visit. In the 1920s Americans enthusiastically repeated to themselves the formula of the French therapist Coué: that every day and in every way they were getting better and better. In Los Angeles, a Mrs. Wilshire, clothed in Grecian robes, plied a self taught psychoanalysis. In 1923, André Triton, the most notorious American lay analyst, who gilded his toenails for cocktail parties, wrote an introduction to some writings of Freud's he had pirated and published, to Freud's intense irritation. And Freud and the European analysts, among them Rank and Ferenczi . . . sent back half trained laymen to set up practice in America [p. 2].

Lee Shershow (1986) documented the early psychoanalytic history specifically in Los Angeles for the fortieth anniversary celebration of the Los Angeles Psychoanalytic Society and Institute. He also referred to Mary Wilshire, a self-styled Jungian psychoanalyst who would greet her patients in flowing Greek robes during the mid-20s. Sometime after (in 1927) a group of Americans, mostly trained in Vienna, established a psychoanalytic study group; the initial five members, Thomas Libbin, Margaret Monk Libbin, David Brunswick, and Mr. and Mrs. Jerome Lockenbrook, were all nonphysicians. It wasn't until 1934 that Ernst Simmel, the first European medical analyst, came to Los Angeles, encouraged to come by A. A. Brill in New York, in order to "put Los Angeles on the psychoanalytic map" (p. 5). But Simmel turned out to be "too encouraging" to lay analysts and also naive and gullible about people. For example, "There was a man named Montgomery who appeared on Simmel's doorstep and said he had a letter from A. A. Brill and was an analyst. Simmel was, apparently, a naive man and said fine, and Montgomery went into practice. Then, to make a long story short, it turned out that Montgomery wanted to train people to be analysts by having them hide in the closet of his office while he was doing analysis. That was his idea of supervision; so they would hear how he did it" (p. 6). Montgomery was finally induced to leave town, and when Simmel called Brill it turned out that Brill had never heard of the man. Thus the scene against which the medical analysts in America were reacting in tightening orthodoxy.

Still another powerful determination fed into this American struggle to keep psychoanalysis in this country in medical hands. Whether explicitly thought out in terms of the long-range goals sought and the full array of consequences that subsequently eventuated, or simply an inherent aspect of the intent to keep the mental healing activity in the safe hands of those felt to be properly medically qualified, in retrospect it seems that an even broader strategy in regard to the relationship of psychoanalysis to the larger body of psychiatry and medicine was deliberately evolved and pursued. This was that psychoanalysis in America should follow a different path than the proud and lonely isolation it had in Europe. It was to penetrate into the receptive soil of American psychiatry, in effect, to capture academic psychiatry and become its prevailing psychological theory under the banner of dynamic psychiatry or psychodynamics, and thus to be firmly planted in the midst of medicine, the medical school, and, at least via this route, the university as well. Here I speak not specifically of the university-based psychoanalytic institute, which was a subsequent development in time, but of the more basic effort to transform the departments of psychiatry in the various medical schools and teaching hospitals of our nation into bulwarks of psychodynamic thinking and practice.

This story, the success of this effort, in the sense of the radical transformation of American psychiatry which reached its high-water mark through the decades of the 1950s and 1960s, in which in one after another of the major departments of psychiatry in the country, the retiring chairman, characteristically an Adolf Meyer-trained psychobiological psychiatrist,[2] was replaced by a psychoanalytically trained psychiatrist, is well enough known in its broad outlines (see Wallerstein, 1974, 1980). What is critical here is one seemingly inevitable concomitant of that effort—and the one central to the theme of this book. It was as if to strengthen its claim to psychological hegemony within psychiatry that American psychoanalysis felt it had to divest itself of its nonmedical cohorts, so prominently in place in Europe, no matter how glorious the contributions from these rich and diverse nonmedical sources may have been. Was this sacrifice necessary to the waging of what turned out to be so successful a campaign? In the sense I have described, psychoanalysis *did* succeed in establishing itself centrally within the main intellectual strongholds of American academic psychiatry, a position we are all painfully aware is now sadly lost (but that is another story). Would this campaign have been less successful if this sacrifice had not been made? It is hard to determine this categorically in hindsight; but certainly the American analysts of the time felt it to be necessary.

---

[2] The psychobiology of Adolf Meyer was essentially an effort to encompass the wholeness of interrelated biological and psychological development and functioning, trying to place symptom formations, both somatic and psychological, meaningfully into this "life-bullet" developmental context, but without concepts of the transference and of the dynamic unconscious. This should not be confused with modern-day biological psychiatry built on a neural science substrate and expressed clinically therapeutically in clinical psychopharmacology.

And I have not mentioned to this point any of the so-called baser economic motives that may have played some role in the adamant opposition of the American analysts to allowing nonmedical practitioners to share the psychoanalytic marketplace, motives that have always been in the forefront of the charges by the American opponents of this position. It is not that such economic motives are ever nonexistent. With the tidal wave of Hitler-refugee analysts transplanting mainly to America as the spreading Nazi hegemony in Europe depopulated the major analytic centers in Germany, in Austria, and in Hungary during the decade of the 1930s, and this occurring during the Great Depression, when doctors everywhere were increasingly fearful for their livelihoods, concerned medical voices were being raised about the economic threat that would be posed by an additional pool of nonmedical providers crowding an already difficult economic arena. But my principal point here is that far more powerful currents fueled the contending positions; these were deeply principled convictions about what psychoanalysis should be and do, what place it should occupy in our professional worldview, and what it should mean to be a psychoanalyst. Certainly, from the accounting to this point, one should see the clash of apparent irreconcilables that was building up on the two sides of the Atlantic.

The clash came over the organization and purview of the International Training Commission (ITC) established by the IPA at its 9th International Congress in Bad Homburg, Germany, in 1925, with Max Eitingon installed as its first chairman. At a preliminary meeting, Eitingon had called "a conference on the whole problem of analytical training and especially on the plan of forming an international training organization, in order that there might be a uniform system of psycho-analytical instruction in different countries" (Bulletin IPA, Int. J. 7: 130, 1926). Eitingon laid out the purposes of this proposed training commission, among them. "The International Psycho-Analytical Association should *as far as possible* work out a standard of uniform principles and should exact the same qualifications for the training candidates, though *at the same time local peculiarities must be taken into consideration*" (p. 131; italics added). The italicized phrases represent a willingness to try to work out a mutually acceptable accommodation with the American position. The next day at the Business Meeting, with Ferenczi in the chair, Sandor Rado proposed as a resolution: "That the Training Committees of the Branch Societies shall combine to form an International Training Board. That the International Training Board be the central organ of the International Psycho-Analytical Association for all questions connected with psycho-analytical training" (p. 141). This resolution was adopted unanimously and Eitingon was acclaimed the first chairman of the new Board.

The intent was laudable, and supported by all, to establish and monitor internationally agreed standards for training in analysis, modeled primarily upon the first organized psychoanalytic training institute, established only five years earlier in 1920 in Berlin. This was also intended to ensure the portability of psychoanalytic credentials as trained analysts emigrated from their countries of origin, which at the time meant mostly to the United States. What this raised for the Americans was the specter of the immigration into the United States of trained nonmedical (i.e., lay) analysts with credentials from the various European training centers, all of which accepted nonmedical applicants for full psychoanalytic training on the same basis that they accepted psychiatric physicians. This possibility led Oberndorf, the leader of the American contingent, to declare the contrary American position.

> Dr. Oberndorf explained the point of view of the American Societies. The strictness of the American law against quack treatment, as well as certain unfortunate experiences in connection with American candidates for membership, who wished in this way to set up an illegitimate practice, made it necessary to exclude persons other than physicians. . . . This decision of the American Society gave rise to a long debate. Dr. Stern and Dr. Glueck [both Americans] held that the American rule was necessary, but most of the other speakers pointed out the importance of non-medical psychoanalysis . . . and regarded the American restriction to physicians as a scientific retrogression. Dr. Ferenczi was even of opinion that this decision was contrary to the statutes. . . . In general, the meeting was of opinion that the work of the newly created International Board would automatically bring about an increasing similarity in the conditions of membership in the societies, but that, until this happened, the societies should take each other's points of view into consideration [p. 142].

This last optimistic projection was a pious hope that was not to be realized. In fact, in the month following this Bad Homburg Congress, it was recorded in the October 27 Minutes of the New York Psychoanalytic Society that "after considerable debating the house arrived at the unanimous decision that it is opposed to laymen practising therapeutic psychoanalytic therapy" (Gay, 1988, p. 499). A year later, in November 1926, this was embodied in a formal resolution: "The practice of psycho-analysis for therapeutic purposes shall be restricted to physicians (doctors of medicine) who are graduates of recognized medical schools, have had special training in psychiatry and psycho-analysis and who conform to the requirements of the medical practice acts to which they are subject" (Gay, 1988, p. 499). At the time, the New York Society had 32 members and the whole American only numbered forty (though not all New York members also belonged to the American). "In the autumn of that year [1926] the New York Legislature passed a bill, on Brill's instigation according to Ferenczi, declaring lay analysis to be illegal, and the American Medical Association also issued a warning to its members against any cooperation with such practitioners" (Jones, 1957, Vol. 3, p. 293).

Strenuous efforts continued to be made over the next six international congresses, through to the 15th in Paris in 1938, to somehow accommodate these seemingly unbridgeable differences so that a viable ITC could function across the whole psychoanalytic world, but these efforts were each time unsuccessful or created just temporary patch-works that promptly broke down. For example, at the 10th Congress in Innsbruck in 1927, Eitingon proposed a two-part resolution at the ITC meeting:

> (1) That Congress instruct the Training Committees of the Branch Societies to lay stress upon the importance of possessing or acquiring a full medical training to candidates who present themselves for training in psycho-analytic therapy. But that no candidate shall be rejected solely on the ground of lack of medical qualifications, provided that he is personally specially well fitted to become a practising analyst and that he possesses an equivalent preliminary scientific training. (2) Apart from this fundamental principle, it shall be open for each Branch Society to lay down independently its conditions for admission to training. In the case of foreign candidates [meaning, it was understood, American lay applicants seeking training in European institutes] the Training Committee shall take into account not only their own regulations but those of the Training Committee of the particular candidate's native country. When a foreign candidate has been accepted for training, the Training Committee in his own country shall be notified. Objections to any candidate shall be laid before the International Training Commission [Bulletin IPA, Int. J. 9: 140, 1928].

As anticipated, there was vigorous discussion and the Americans objected strongly to even this effort at strained accommodation. "Dr. Oberndorf took the view that the American Societies could not in any circumstances admit lay candidates to training as therapeutic analysts, on account of the conditions in America" (p. 140). When the vote came, the first paragraph was passed as a nonbinding recommendation, and the decision on the second paragraph was postponed. At the full Business Meeting two days later a resolution proposed by Sandor Rado of the Berlin Institute was passed, calling for the creation of a committee to formulate "a scheme of conditions of admission to training for the profession of therapeutic analysts and of the whole course of psycho-analytical training in general, and in particular of the regulations to be enforced having regard to the conditions in the individual countries concerned, and, finally, of the lines on which the separate Training Committees may co-operate in the technique of training. And that, until such a scheme be drawn up, no decision on these matters be taken" (p. 153). Rado was named chairman of this three-person committee.

That the committee's task was not an easy one was expressed at length in a January 16, 1929, letter (in German)[3] from Eitingon to Jones (Archives, Brit. Psychoanal. Soc.)[4] which is cited in extenso for its detailed dissection of the growing controversy and its expressed alarm that positions might well harden on both sides of it.

> I do not at all consider the first draft [of the new committee report] as a "dictatorial act" and the commission had every right to hope that the Americans would not "get mad," but that they would see in the cautions with which the draft of a lay analysis proposal is fenced about, a challenge to begin, in place of their simplistic *non placet*, to consider at long last under what conditions, no matter how stringent, they could try to come closer to the position of the majority in the IPA. After all, I myself stood behind the draft, and I do believe to have earned that much confidence. I am of course ready for any personal negotiations with the Americans, and will gladly be as many days in Oxford ahead of the Congress as you may deem necessary. I do not consider the changes in the numerical representation of the various groups to be particularly decisive. The essential is the existence of a true will to unification, and to date I do not despair of it. I do not know whether anyone wants to chase the Americans away; I do not believe so, and shall myself make every effort, with all means at our disposal, to maintain them in our circle.
>
> But we must be quite clear about one thing, and I am not issuing it as a warning to you if I beg you to keep the following clearly in mind, but it is merely the naked formulation of a simple circumstance: what you call autonomy for the Americans,

---

[3] Translation of this and other material from the original German text by Wolfgang Lederer.
[4] Throughout this book the reference to Archives will in all cases mean the Archives of the British Psychoanalytical Society.

that, as things stand now, we cannot give them. If that were the only way to hold them in our midst, then I too would begin to doubt whether it could succeed. Hence our efforts must be directed towards finding other means to hold them, and to give them time to come closer to the Continent. The autonomy of which you speak could be given them only under one condition, namely: the prior establishment, in principle, of a unitary platform with the IPA. Without that any autonomy proposal, in other words the Jones proposal in Innsbruck, would signify merely a declaration of war against the Continental majority. . . .

The maintenance, for some time to come, of the status quo would comparatively be the lesser evil, and it would by no means be as passive as it seems to you. I am doing my best to urge the groups favoring lay-membership to ever increasing strictness and ever more vigilant caution in the admission of laymen. If this should not seem like much, then one thing is even more certain: that meanwhile no more can be achieved. Quite apart from the numbers the old groups still weigh considerably more. I can also not share your fear, at least for the foreseeable future, that this passive status quo would soon produce a consequence that would cause us much trouble, namely the recognition of a lay group. Back in Innsbruck one already whispered of a lay group that asked to be admitted, and one was tactless enough to claim even more. There actually was something to those rumours; a group of American laymen actually had the effrontery to beg for admission. But they seemed so insignificant that I did not bother our public awareness with this request, but said No so energetically that the group dispersed utterly and will not so easily come back together.

So we do have a number of means to prevent what may be unpleasant and improper, for the case that the other side finally should decide to be more accommodating and to reflect whether they could not somehow adjust to the Continental position. And I can truly do no more than to await "que ces monsieurs commencent." Just plain demands on the part of the American won't do it. In that awareness we shall have to try and foreclose such a discussion altogether. Hence my request in my last letter for your assistance. Perhaps it would be well if you started right now to exert your influence over the Americans, and even took this second draft which we are mailing as a pretext to talk to them, even though necessarily the content of this second draft has to be based entirely on the first one. . . . This commission could not do any better.

We can clearly see in this letter the increasing strain within the European psychoanalytic world between those led by Eitingon, who were working toward an accommodation by the Americans to the European position, and those led by Jones (primarily the British),[5] who were working toward an accommodation by the Europeans to the American position, albeit Eitingon and Jones were strongly united in their overriding concern for the unity of the IPA. Freud was actually much more in despair that this gulf between Europe and America on this issue could ever be bridged. Gay (1988) notes that "By early 1929 as the controversy did not die down, Freud wondered whether it might not make sense to separate from the American analysts peacefully and remain firm on the matter of lay analysis" (p. 500). Jones (1957) quotes a letter from Freud to Eitingon (March 1929) proposing "a friendly separation with the Americans. I have no desire to give way in the lay question, and there is no means of bridging the gulf" (pp. 297–298).

Actually, what became clear at the 11th IPA Congress in Oxford, 1929, was that the impasse continued with Rado ruefully confessing that his committee had "failed to discover a common platform" (Bulletin IPA, Int. J. 10: 509, 1929). The committee therefore resigned and a new committee of 11 members (including two Americans) was appointed, along with a request to the Congress, "to defer all resolutions of a general or a special technical nature connected with the question at issue until the newly appointed sub-committee has arrived at positive results" (p. 509). At least this statement could be passed unanimously. In October of that year, Jones made a trip to New York to personally negotiate with the Americans and received an encouraging letter from Freud (dated October 19) on the coming journey, wishing him well in the endeavor (Archives).

And a year later, on November 7, 1930, Jones responded positively to a letter he had just received from Brill (Archives), which must have seemed like a possible basis for acceptable mutual accommodation.

> Your letter came to-day and I hasten to congratulate you on accomplishing what probably was not an easy feat. In my opinion

---

[5] Though Jones and the other British were more sympathetic to the American position that at least in America, nonphysicians should be denied access to psychoanalytic training and practice, the British Medical Association (BMA) was expressing itself at that same time as quite broadly tolerant of lay analysis. In a supplementary Report of the Council of the BMA published in the *British Medical Journal* on June 29, 1929, the following was approvingly stated: "It is to be noted that all these workers, including Freud, consider that psycho-pathology, even in its therapeutic aspects, is not limited by its contact with general medicine. The problems they work at are far more social than medical, and they receive at least as much assistance from several other sciences, e.g., anthropology, as they do from medicine itself" (p. 265) (Archives).

the resolution you have passed is entirely satisfactory and I hope it will be to Eitingon as well. . . . As a matter of fact I should like to insert into our [proposed IPA] draft even stricter words than those of your resolution. It does not seem to me that a mere baccalaureate degree is suitable for our purposes if it is only in Latin and Greek. It ought definitely to be one in science and preferably in biology or physiology, for what we want is some preliminary education in scientific *method*. In London we do not rigidly adhere to this standard and are willing to waive it in selected cases, but it is very useful to have to give one an excuse for rejecting unsuitable people. My experience here shows me, and I am sure you would confirm it from America, that if we did not have this standard we should be absolutely flooded by a host of uneducated and unsuitable lay people who would before long change the whole character of the psycho-analytical profession.

What emerged for consideration at the 12th IPA Congress in Wiesbaden, in 1932, was an elaborate document prepared by the committee of 11 appointed in 1929, influenced no doubt by all the draft documents that had been passing between Europe and America in the three-year interval between the two congresses. The heart of it was in the paragraph titled, Special Considerations on the Selection of Lay Candidates: "The Sub-committee is of opinion that it would be wiser, for some time at least, to lay down no general recommendations but to leave the rules to be established by each Training Committee. We would only suggest that any set of rules drawn up by a Training Committee should not be regarded as invariably binding, so that room be left to permit exceptions of specially suitable applicants who may fail to conform to particular rules" (Bulletin IPA, Int. J. 14: 157–158, 1933). In the next paragraph, on conditions governing the acceptance of candidates in general, a special stipulation was added.

Lay candidates should in addition subscribe to the promise that they will never engage in independent consultative practice, i.e. that they will receive for treatment only patients who have first consulted a physician and not attempt to share his sole responsibility for the diagnosis and therapeutic indications. It should be explained to them further that this physician remains legally responsible for the whole treatment of the case, so that it is desirable for the therapeutist to consult him in the event of any untoward complication, e.g. of organic or psychotic nature [p. 158].

It is reported in the minutes of the full Business Meeting that "the regulations worked out by the sub-committee were received with applause and adopted unanimously" (p. 176).

Jones continued on in his role as the most active mediator between the Americans and the Europeans. This of course reflected not only his personal involvement in this issue on behalf of himself and his British colleagues, who were eager to broker the relations between the Americans and the Europeans, but also his official position as president of the IPA from 1920 to 1924, and now, newly elected president again, from 1932, to be continued in that office up through the 16th IPA Congress in Zurich, in 1949, not quite president for life. In a letter to Anna Freud on September 19, 1933 (Archives), Jones proposed an additional perspective upon the American situation: "As you know, an active discussion is still going on with the New York authorities about the question of lay analysts, so I do not see that anything can be done there until that is settled. On the other hand, I wish we could find out particulars about other states in the Union where the law is not so strict. This seems to me the only possible solution of the American lay question, because obviously we have to keep within the law. I am writing to Brill again about this matter." And then, in a reprimand to an extreme advocate on the other side, Jones wrote curtly to Theodor Reik on December 20, 1933 (Archives).

> The contradiction you do not seem to observe is this: When I point out that lay analysts here can only receive patients from British medical analysts, you answer that you are quite prepared to abide by this rule. But then you proceed to say that there would be no need for you to receive such patients from us, since you have other sources of your own. Can you not see how the one statement contradicts the other? I have no doubt you could provide a few patients of your own to begin with, but this does not solve the problem of how to earn a *permanent* livelihood if you settled in England. And this is the question the Home Office would expect me to answer. Unfortunately I see no way of answering it, nor have you suggested any. It is therefore beside the point to say that I could help you if I would; the truth is the exact reverse.

It is also clear that nothing was settled either at the 13th IPA Congress in Lucerne, 1934. What is noted in the Minutes there is that Anna Freud complained that the New York Society was not abiding by what she called the "Oxford agreement":

> Anna Freud raised the question of lay analysts in connection with the co-operation between the New York and the Vienna

Societies. At the Oxford Congress the European Branch Societies undertook not to admit to training any American candidates who had not previously been accepted by the Training Committee of his local Branch society. The New York Society, on its part, recognized the principle of the admission of lay candidates to training. The Vienna Society had kept its undertaking, but the hostility of the authorities to lay analysts had made it impossible for the New York Society to observe the principle agreed upon. Anna Freud asked what, in these circumstances, was the attitude of the American Societies to the Oxford agreement.[6] Dr. Lewin, President of the New York Training Committee, pointed out that in New York they had to contend not with any mere obsolete legal enactments which would not be enforced, but with most severe and vigorous action on the part of the authorities. If lay candidates were admitted, the result would be the closing of the Institute and the prosecution of those members of the medical profession who had encouraged them. . . . Dr. Lewin, representing the New York Society, asked that the Oxford agreement should be cancelled as far as the American Societies were concerned. He requested, however, that the European Institutes, if they admitted lay candidates on their own responsibility, should make it perfectly plain to them, before they began their training, that it would not entitle them to pursue their studies at the New York Institute or to become members of the New York Society. The proposal was carried [Bulletin IPA, Int. J. 16: 244–245, 1935].

And as by now would be expected, yet another committee was appointed, this to consider the position of training analysts who had left their own countries. This was in 1934, with the Nazis in power in Germany and forcing the emigration of at least the Jewish analysts from Berlin; most of these would want to come to the United States, and among them would be lay analysts.

This last consideration would of course make the issue of the portability of credentials, that separated trained lay analysts from individuals

---

[6] I found no record in the Minutes of the 1929 Oxford Congress of any such definite "agreement" and certainly nothing of the Americans in any way recognizing the principle of the admission of lay candidates to training. What might be being referred to is the much vaguer proposal worked out by the committee appointed at that congress and "adopted unanimously" in Wiesbaden in 1932. That, of course, was only a "suggestion" that any set of rules drawn up by a component Training Committee not be regarded as "invariably binding" and leave room for "exceptions of specially suitable applicants."

not analytically trained, into an acute problem in the psychoanalytic world, and this no doubt powered the escalation of the conflict over this issue, manifest both in the intensifying of the recorded correspondence crossing the Atlantic, and in an American proposal brought to the 14th IPA Congress in Marienbad, 1936. On January 28, 1935 (Archives), Oberndorf wrote a letter to Jones asking for European acknowledgment of the legitimacy of the American position: "I am quite sure that the International has no desire nor would it have the power to attempt to force regulations on individual societies or to decide questions with which its members can necessarily have no intimate knowledge."

The complexity of the situation in America as well as efforts at accommodation being made from America are reflected in two letters written by Ernst Simmel, a former leading figure in the Berlin group and the first medical analyst to come to Los Angeles, as described previously. Both these letters were written on September 2, 1935 (Archives), after Simmel's first year in Los Angeles. One was to Jones in Europe.

In founding this organization [the Psychoanalytic Study Group of Los Angeles], we have had to take into consideration the fact that the psychoanalytic movement in California is going through its primary state of development. This means that we have encountered the same situation here which has existed in other countries, namely, that physicists, psychologists, pedagogues and other scientists rather than physicians, have a real understanding and interest for psychoanalysis.

In a somewhat different tenor, the letter to A. A. Brill in New York states:

As I had expected, I found a large number of quacks here. I also found a situation which exists in other cities: psychoanalysis being practised by physicians in a manner little different from that employed by the quacks. On the other hand there are seven lay analysts in Los Angeles who have been trained in the psychoanalytic institutions of Berlin and of Vienna. These analysts have done good analytic work here, real pioneer work, the proof of which lies in the fact that several reputable physicians, who have both an interest in and understanding of psychoanalysis, consult with them and regularly send patients to them.

Jones, in his reply to Simmel dated September 25 (Archives), said, "One naturally regrets the predominance of the lay analysts and, as you remark, this would seem to exclude—at all events for the present—a participation in the American Psychoanalytic Association."

On October 10, 1935 (Archives), Jones undertook to write a detailed and lengthy critique to the members of the committee that had in the meanwhile been created to draft definitive statutes for the American Psychoanalytic Association. He was responding to a proposed draft that had been sent to him.

> . . . the most fundamental matter concerned. I would naturally assume, and Dr. Oberndorf also gives me assurance on this point, that the intention of your committee is that the re-constituted Association should function within the framework of the International Psycho-Analytical Association. Yet one cannot help observing that your draft ignores both the relevant resolutions of the International Association and its functioning organs in the matter of training; nor does it ever specify the relationship of the American Association to the International.

Here Jones, the European leader, who all along had assumed the role of interpreter of the American position to the European analytic community, was raising his own cry of alarm at the first clear hints of an actual secessionist threat arising in America.

Jones went on to make his concern completely explicit.

> Naturally if American psycho-analysts wished to organise themselves and their Societies in a separate Association which would be on terms of friendly affiliation with the body of psycho-analytical Societies in the rest of the world, they would of course be free to do so, and then any comments from me on the proposed draft would be impertinent. Assuming, however, that they wish to continue to function within the framework of the International Association I would have the following comments to make on the draft. At the Lucerne [1934] Congress, which sanctioned the re-organisation of the American Association, the resolution passed asked your Committee to "agree upon a final draft in accord with the statutes and traditions of the I.P.A. and submit it to the Central Executive of the I.P.A. The Central Executive will then consider this constitution for temporary ratification, awaiting its final acceptance by the next Congress." . . .
>
> [But] In your preamble you forthwith "establish this Constitution" and the only reference in the draft to any ratification . . . is by the individual societies in America. An independent action such as that proposed would ignore all

reference to the parent body from which your powers derive so long as you remain members of it. . . . It was anticipated at the [last] Congress that one of the clauses of your proposed constitution would refer to the task of investigating new psycho-analytical groups in the United States and so assist the International Association in its decision about accepting such groups as constituent branch Societies. Your draft goes beyond this and proposes to assume the right of accepting a new Society without reference to the International Association. In that event we should have the anomaly of a psycho-analytical Society being a member of the American Association but not of the International Association. . . .

[And responding to an implied American imperialist claim] I notice that in the draft the "United States of America" has been replaced by the words "North America." . . . [And] If, for example, as we hope will soon happen, a psycho-analytical group is formed in Canada (or Mexico), it itself should be asked to decide whether it preferred to be in any special way affiliated with an America Society, the British Society, or simply to become straightaway an independent branch Society of the International Association. It is not permissible for one particular country to dictate in advance the future action of an unborn Society in any other countries. . . . [And finally, the American draft proposes a "Council on Professional Training" and] ignores the existence . . . of the International Training Commission with its Executive. It would obviously be impracticable to have two separate bodies legislating, or making recommendations, for the problems of psycho-analytical training, probably the most important with which our whole organisation is concerned.

Jones ended this heartfelt plea with the sentence: "I shall look forward with interest and sympathy to any decisions you reach."

Further to this long effort at intervention by Jones, Oberndorf wrote to Jones on January 14, 1936 (Archives), indicating that he was sending Jones a copy of the new constitution of the American, which had been just adopted in Boston "subject to ratification by the International" because everything should be fully in accord with the IPA. There had been opposition by New Yorkers who favored only "friendly cooperation," but they had been outvoted. What Oberndorf did not make clear in his letter was how much the draft constitution had been altered in response to Jones' representations. But the change must have been substantial enough, for Jones in his February 18 (Archives) reply to Oberndorf stated: "Many thanks for the further draft. . . . My main impression was one of gratification, since there is no doubt that it has been much more thoroughly thought out and better brought into relation with the International than the first draft was. I was especially glad to see the stress laid on the importance of the training aspects." Then after a series of detailed comments, Jones ended with, "As you see, these are mostly very minor points and I wish to say again how very pleased I am with the principles on which the draft has been drawn up and the care which has been given to it."

It was all this that led up to the 14th IPA Congress in Marienbad, 1936, where to everyone's apparent surprise, Sandor Rado, formerly in Berlin but now in New York, offered a motion that was said to be sponsored by the Training Institute of the New York Society:

> We are opposed to an I.T.C. in its present form, as well as to any reorganization which would retain it as a legislative or administrative body. We suggest that the I.T.C. should be replaced by an *entirely informal* International Training Conference, to be open for instructors and various officers and committee members of our Institutes and Societies, convening on the occasion of Congresses under the Chairmanship and Secretaryship of the President and General Secretary of the International Psycho-Analytical Association; that is, without special officers of its own. There should be no voting, no representation, nothing of that kind [Bulletin IPA, Int. J. 18: 346, 1937].

This was a radical call for the abolition of the ITC in all its monitoring and standard-setting functions, to be replaced by an informal information-exchanging conference of component organizations, each fully autonomous in its control over its own admission, training, and qualification standards.

The discussion of this proposal was stormy and the alarm raised by Rado's radical call was intense. Even the delegates from the New York Institute felt constrained to disavow it, claiming it to be Rado's own private opinion that did not represent the officially formulated views of the New York Training Commission.

> In the course of the discussion several speakers expressed their surprise that these proposals, the aim of which was practically to abolish the I.T.C., should emanate from precisely that quarter in which, as recently as two years ago, at the Lucerne Congress, there was such a strong insistence on a rigid central organization and authority in the I.T.C. that the Council raised objections. . . . [In the end] Rado's resolution was put to the vote and unanimously rejected [p. 347].

Nonetheless, Rado's effort presaged accurately the events played out at the next, the climactic and fateful, 15th IPA Congress in Paris, 1938. Again, there was intense activity on this score in the interim prior to that congress. Bernhard Berliner, another immigrant medical analyst from Europe, wrote to Jones after his first seven months in San Francisco, on October 12, 1936 (Archives). He complained that "there is a strong resistance against psychoanalysis among the people of San Francisco and particularly amongst the medical profession. Bad experiences given by pseudoanalysts and 'quacks' are said to be the cause." After indicating that "I for my part have never discriminated between medical and lay analysts, provided they are trained according to the rules of the International Psychoanalytical Association," he expressed the hope that psychoanalytic development might be much enhanced with the expected arrival in San Francisco of Siegfried Bernfeld, a prominent Viennese lay analyst.

To this Jones responded with a cautionary letter, dated October 26 (Archives), outlining his concerns about the situation of psychoanalysis in America.

> As regards the views you express, we are only partly in agreement. I sympathise very much with your insistence on good training, and with your sympathy with lay-analysts who have been well trained, though I should not myself go so far as to make no discrimination whatever between them and physicians. I cannot but think that any physician, who has fully absorbed the background and implications of his training, must feel that they represent something of value which the others are deprived of. And in your actual situation in America I incline to go further still. I know enough of America and American history to appreciate the significance of the strong feeling that has been aroused through the intense and never ending fight that scientific workers, and particularly those in the medical profession, have to put up against all the forces of charlatanry and low standards of intellectual integrity which are so peculiarly rife in the United States. I am therefore very inclined to agree with those analysts in America who think that it would be very undesirable to burden such unpopular work as psycho-analysis with the additional prejudice of lay-status.

Closer to the 1938 Paris Congress, Anna Freud was writing actively to Ernest Jones on this issue (her letters in German). On February 20, 1938 (Archives), she raised the question of a possible rupture of the IPA: "Eitingon has sent me the letter of Oberndorf. These new elections now leave no doubts about the intentions of the American side. I am still in favor of our anticipating them at the Congress with a proposal to place the American Association and the IPA on an equal footing, meaning: a separation with maintenance of friendly relations. Otherwise we have a togetherness with active enmity, leading shortly to the destruction of the IPA itself." On May 15 (Archives), very shortly before the Paris Congress, Anna Freud had reason to write to Jones even more pessimistically. The Anschluss of Austria with Hitler's Third Reich had taken place two months earlier. She began by reviewing the already exceedingly grim situation in Vienna under the Nazis.

> Since my last letter a lot that was stuck here has now started to move. This morning Kris and Bibrings have left, tomorrow the Waelders depart. Hoffers and Hartmanns have their passports in order and are only awaiting their final tax clearance. Jekel's application has also been processed and in a few days he will go to America. . . . Federn already has no more money, Steiner and Hitschmann will be penniless the moment they depart; they evidently do not trust themselves to begin a so-called new life. And while I do not find it hard to help the younger people out of their moods, it is of no avail with the others. At most they envy me because I am not yet so old and have more prospects than they. What can one do? It is very sad to be here and to watch it.

Then, after discussing the complex individual plights of a number of individuals, Anna Freud turned to psychoanalysis and the situation with the Americans.

> In the matter of Kubie [one of the leading American analysts], I agree with you fully. The right to full membership with us in the IPA is gained hard enough, through study and work. One should not be able to lose it—as is the case with some citizenships—except by relinquishing the work or by scientific deviation. Years ago, before we had to deal with the lay-difficulties, it was in fact that way with us: we either remained a member where one was, or one would automatically be accepted in another society. But behind Kubie's proposal there has been the whole difficulty of the relationship between the American and the European Association which, I hope, will be clarified at this Congress. I believe that even now there already exists a parallel organization in America, and that—even without the present immigration—this parallel organization is steadily growing. The resignation of Sachs from the Teaching-Committee in Boston and the exclusion of Simmel from the

Chicago Society, etc., of course augments that other side. Nor will the case of Waelder diminish these difficulties, except if an association over there should offer him membership, which is not very probable. That, by the way, was also one of the considerations which, in Waelder's case, argued against America."[7]

These were the clouds under which the 15th IPA Congress convened in Paris in 1938, and the opening was indeed worrisome. For the first time the Americans failed to attend the Plenary Session of the ITC. "Dr. Eitingon . . . referred to the absence of the official representatives of American training organizations: this was in accord with a resolution of the American Psycho-Analytic Association. After some discussion it was resolved to leave the adjustment of relations between the American Psycho-Analytic Association and the I.T.C. in the hands of the Committee or of the Business Meeting of the International Psycho-Analytical Association" (Bulletin IPA, Int. J. 20: 212, 1939).

At the Business Meeting it became clear that the Americans who, in the face of the vehemence of the European reaction, had backpedaled from support of Rado's initiative two years earlier in Marienbad, had now solidly regrouped in presenting the same defiant ultimatum to the IPA. This needs quotation at length because it formally initiated a half-century of official cleavage between the Americans and the remainder of the IPA which tormented the organization until its final healing at the 35th IPA Congress in Montreal in 1987. The citation, from Ernest Jones's Presidential Report, recorded in the minutes of that meeting, is as follows.

At the last moment we have received a dossier of some thirty-seven pages from the President and the Secretary of the American Psychoanalytic Association. There has hardly been time to digest it and I am sure that the matter it contains will furnish material for discussion at the next Congress as well as at the present one. I must nevertheless try to present the gist of it to you now and will confine myself to the essentials.

Substantially the communications on the one hand inform us of various activities of the American Association and on the other hand make various suggestions to the International

---

[7] A month after this letter from Anna Freud in Vienna, in June 1938, the entire Freud family was able to leave Vienna for England. This was accomplished through the strong intervention of Princess Marie Bonaparte, who was at once a leading psychoanalyst, a citizen of France, and a member of the royal family of Greece, and of William C. Bullitt, the American ambassador to France. Both Bonaparte and Bullitt accompanied the Freud family on this flight from the Nazis.

Association concerning the conduct of its organization. The latter are to the effect that the International Association should cease to exist as an administrative and executive body and resolve itself entirely into a Congress for scientific purposes only. Even stronger are the terms in which the suggestion is made that the International Training Commission "as an administrative organization endowed with executive power is not only very undesirable but also a paper institution." The American Association has resolved that from henceforth it shall not be represented on the Executive Committee of the International Association, nor is any member of any American Training Committee to participate in the International Training Commission. We are further notified that the American Societies "no longer recognize Memberships-at-Large in the International Association, or membership in a foreign Psycho-analytic Society, as applicable in the case of any psycho-analyst residing and practising in the United States." They therefore "urge that at the next Congress of the International Association it shall be resolved that the status of Membership-at-Large shall not apply to individuals residing and practising in the United States." . . . They support these decisions with two complaints about the International Association: first that the International Training Commission unwarrantably attempts to exercise its powers in the internal training problems of the United States, and secondly that the International Association encourages and supports those psycho-analysts in the United States who do not conform to the rules of the American Association.

The first part of the communication is a counter-part to the second. Side by side, that is to say, with the advice to reduce our administrative and executive functions comes the information that the centralizing body of the American Association, which originally was to function in a purely advisory capacity, has in practice assumed administrative and executive authority such as has never been imagined in the International Association. The Training Committee of the American Association, for example, have decreed a lengthy statement on the standards for the admission and training of physicians in psycho-analysis (thirteen pages long) which in rigour and binding force far exceed anything that any Psycho-Analytical Society or Association elsewhere had ever contemplated.

In effect these communications if acted on by this Congress would necessitate an alteration in the Statute concerning the constitution of the Central Executive and the Statute on the constitution of the International Training Commission, together with a rescission of the resolution of the last two Congresses concerning the continued membership of political refugees from the German Reich. If these conditions are fulfilled the American Association declares its wish to continue friendly co-operation in the form of an affiliation with the International Association.

It will at once be seen that these are very large problems which cannot be adequately resolved on a single occasion. The complaints from the Americans have caused much astonishment here and do not seem to us to be at all well founded. The American Association had, for the purposes indicated above, instituted a special Committee on the relations of the American Association to the International Association, and I would propose that we form a similar Committee to confer with the Executive of the American Association [Bulletin IPA, Int. J. 20: 121–122].

In his 1957 Freud biography, Jones summarized this report as an announcement that the American would only consider maintaining its affiliation with the International on three conditions: (1) that the ITC be abolished; (2) that "free floating membership" in the IPA be withdrawn from analysts settling in America; and (3) that the IPA meet only for scientific and not for administrative functions (p. 302). This serious American threat of secession from the IPA unless its ultimatum was accepted by the Paris Congress, with a split then of the analytic world into separate American and European hegemonies, was indeed ominous, especially in view of the now vastly altered numerical balance in the IPA over the immediately preceding five years subsequent to Hitler's accession to power in 1933. Where the Americans had been approximately 20% of the total IPA membership at the beginning of the decade, they were now approaching parity, as Hitler's march across Europe systematically depopulated the major psychoanalytic training centers in Central Europe and produced a tide of refugees. These went mainly to the United States, while some, of course, went to Britain, and a scattered handful truly went around the world, to Argentina, Palestine, Ceylon, and elsewhere.[8]

---

[8] It was at this same (Paris) Congress that Jones, in the light of the Anschluss with Hitler Germany four months earlier, announced the "unhappy fate" of the Vienna Society, recommending "the practical dissolution of this, the mother of all psycho-analytical societies" (p. 124). "Of the 102 analysts and candidates in Vienna only some half a dozen still remain in that unfortunate city and we hope that they also will before long be in a position to leave" (p. 117). "Widespread help was at once forthcoming for our dispossessed Viennese colleagues, all of whom, with the exception of four, are settling in English-speaking countries" (p. 124).

The secession threat was therefore very portentous: the IPA would have been split asunder, with the American part growing toward a majority and the European part, such as still existed in 1938, under close threat of the gathering war clouds. Ernest Jones desperately wanted to defer any definitive vote on the American proposal, suggesting "that a special committee be appointed to consider the matter and to enter into negotiations with the American Psychoanalytic Association. Dr. Balint supported this proposal, which was carried. The following were elected as members of the subcommittee: Dr. Edward Bibring, Madame Marie Bonaparte, Miss Anna Freud, Dr. Edward Glover, Dr. Ernest Jones. With regard to the nomination of American members to the Central Executive . . . it was decided to postpone any such nominations for the present" (p. 126). The small hope in all this was that some viable, or at least face-saving, compromise might yet emerge by the time of the next congress, scheduled for 1940.

Toward that end there was a renewed flurry of correspondence in 1939 with plans for a negotiating meeting in America that fall. On May 22 (Archives), Lawrence Kubie, as the newly elected secretary of the American Association, wrote to Jones looking forward to meeting with Jones and Glover that fall in New York: "In view of your visit, all action on the official formulae which govern the relationship of the American Psychoanalytic to the International was deferred until after our joint discussions in the autumn." Kubie did mention the resentment in America at the character of Jones's report to the Paris Congress and expressed his satisfaction that Jones intended to "correct" the report. Kubie did not specify what the "erroneous implications" of the report, that had roused such resentment, consisted of. Four days later, on May 26 (Archives), Franz Alexander, as immediate past-president of the American, also wrote to Jones, naming the seven members of the Executive Council and the 12 members of the Council on Professional Training with whom Jones and Glover would meet and reiterating that it had been unanimously decided that all "necessary changes in our constitution should be postponed until after we have discussed the matter with you in September."

Ernest Jones in a letter to Alexander on June 13 (Archives), responding to those from both Kubie and Alexander, expressed his "surprise at the course events have taken. An astonishing edifice seems to have got built on my very tentative enquiry of you last winter about whether any good might be served by my coming to America." What astonished Jones was that no ground seemed to have been prepared on the American side for the forthcoming meeting.

> We had stated our point of view very comprehensively and, of course, expected a similarly comprehensive reply to our statement, probably to be accompanied by counter-proposals from

your side which we could discuss together here before arranging any such meeting. We waited eagerly but patiently . . . as the months passed by. . . . To our great surprise . . . we learn that no reply is forthcoming and that it was announced at the Chicago meeting [of the American's Council in May]—on whose authority I do not know, but certainly not on mine—that there was no need to consider the matter any further at that time since I had arranged to meet the Council in New York in September. This news has taken us all aback and we have nothing to go on in the way of material to discuss.

Jones then went on to renew his earlier request:

I am asking you therefore to be good enough to communicate, by return mail if possible, some statement of how your Council regarded our memorandum, i.e. Dr. Glover's letter,[9] and what counter-proposals or resolutions they would be likely to wish put forward to meet the situation. There have been hints enough that your Council, representing American psycho-analysts, are dissatisfied with their present relationship with the International Association and would therefore wish for various changes to be made. But we should naturally like to have some idea of what these changes would be and would therefore ask you to give us an approximate summary, even if an unofficial one, of their scope.

Alexander did respond to this request by Jones in his letter of reply on June 30 (Archives). The Americans had chosen "not to send you any rigid formulations" because they had wanted the free give and take of open, uncommitted discussion. Alexander, however, certainly could state "the general principles along which we feel certain changes in the constitution have become necessary." There then followed a long statement in which he made the following points: (1) the IPA was still working by a constitution that was by now outgrown; (2) in America, psychoanalysis was becoming more and more coordinated with the rest of medicine and that training for it would best be handled locally in cooperation with the other medical organizations in the country; (3) the IPA should transform itself into a

---

[9] This prior letter of Edward Glover's could not be located in the Archives of the British Psychoanalytical Society where Jones deposited all his files relating to his official positions within the British Society over his lifetime, as well as those covering his years of presidency of the IPA. At that time, all IPA official records were housed in the British Society.

merely scientific body arranging international congresses but should devolve all administrative and educational responsibilities to its component organizations; and (4) that the American should be represented in the IPA as a whole, not through its local groups, and in fact the IPA "could be transformed into an International Association of the (1) European, (2) American and (3) Asiatic (Japanese) Psychoanalytic Associations, giving each of the three an equal status and full responsibility and independence in dealing with its own administrative affairs concerning training and practice."

Alexander then ended his letter with the expressed hope that the forthcoming meeting with Jones and Glover would have "constructive results" for both sides.

> No matter how much I and most of my colleagues are convinced of the validity of these principles, I must say that we are most eager to hear your arguments. I wish to reassure you that the members of the American Association are not only desirous to continue the friendly cooperation with the psychoanalytic groups abroad but also to understand fully your point of view. The majority looks upon the question of our relation to the International in a calm, sympathetic and understanding spirit. This more than anything else justifies the expectation that the personal conference with you will have constructive results. . . . The constitutional amendments we shall have to work out together during our discussions and not one-sidedly in advance.[10]

On September 1, 1939, Germany invaded Poland and World War II was launched. The planned September visit by Jones and Glover to meet with the Americans never took place. Though Jones remained as president, the IPA practically ceased to function as an international organization during the war years, and the 16th Congress, originally scheduled for 1940, did

---

[10] This was the same Franz Alexander, now in America and a major spokesman for the American position in this struggle, who in 1927, when he was in Berlin, joined Freud in strongly advocating the great importance, for the work of psychoanalysis, of proper psychoanalytic training within a training center of the International over the medical qualification (see chapter 1). I have noted this same reversal of posture on the part of Sandor Rado, indicating his proposal (when he also was in Berlin), at the 1927 IPA Congress in Innsbruck, on behalf of the European viewpoint, and his completely opposite proposal at the 1936 IPA Congress in Marienbad, when he had located in New York. He then proposed to split all administrative and educational functions from the IPA, devolving them completely unto the national component organizations, and proposed the ultimatum on this issue that the entire American contingent pressed two years later.

not take place until 1949 in Zurich, 11 years after the preceding 15th Congress in Paris, 1938. During that period the American went ahead with its proposed reorganization as if IPA approval, or at least acquiescence, had been achieved. The American asserted full autonomy concerning training standards and requisite professional credentials for psychoanalytic recognition in the United States. As part of this, the American promulgated what came to be known as the "1938 rule," that psychoanalytic training in American institutes would be limited to psychiatric physicians, and that membership in the American Psychoanalytic Association would be barred to all nonphysicians, except for a grandfathered handful of acknowledged and prominent psychoanalytic leaders like Peter Blos, Erik Erikson, Ernst Kris, and Robert Waelder, all of them fully trained in Europe before 1938.

Freud, for his part, to the end of his life, on September 23, 1939, in London, never wavered over his own convictions—decisively rejected in America—on this issue. On November 16, 1953 (Archives), Jacques Schnier, a sculptor and a lay analyst, analyzed and practicing in San Francisco, wrote to Ernest Jones congratulating him on the Freud biography (the first volume had just appeared) and sending him copies of an exchange of correspondence that Schnier had had with Freud on the subject of lay analysis in the summer of 1938, after Freud's arrival in England. Schnier, in his letter to Freud of June 20 (Archives), stated: "European analysts who are arriving to settle in our land are bringing with them the report that you told them you have radically and completely altered your viewpoint regarding the lay-analyst as contained in your volume *The Problem of Lay-Analysis* [1926b]. The report states that you are demanding that the future practitioners in the field of psycho-analysis be confined solely to members of the medical profession." Schnier was worried and "earnestly requested that you favor me with a reply as to whether or not the above report is true." Freud's reply, in English, dated July 5 (Archives), was quite brief and very blunt: "I cannot imagine how that silly rumour of my having changed my views about the problem of Lay-Analysis may have originated. The fact is, I have never repudiated these views and I insist on them even more intensely than before, in the face of the obvious American tendency to turn psycho-analysis into a mere housemaid of Psychiatry." Jones later included this response by Freud in his discussion of this issue in the third volume (1957) of his Freud biography. It should be noted, too, that this exchange of letters between Schnier and Freud took place on the eve of the 1938 Paris Congress, which was so riven by the American ultimatum.

The last citation in this regard is from a very short article by an American analyst, Martin Peck (1940), describing a brief visit with Freud in the summer of 1937, at Freud's country place in Grinzing. Peck stated that Freud spoke (in excellent English) on the subject of lay analysis.

The essence of his comment was that in America medical application of psychoanalysis was the rule, and contributions to its structure were the exception: He used the term "medical fixation" for the American scene, and regretted the alliance between psychiatry and psychoanalysis. He made frequent reference to the "core of psychoanalysis" and expressed his belief that this core should be kept separate from other disciplines for a long time to come. He stated with deep conviction that "psychoanalysis is a part of psychology and for its proper development, it should be kept free from biology, philosophy—and also psychiatry" [p. 205].

This statement in 1937 is hardly the picture of a man whose views on this subject had changed one iota, and so it is hard to see how the rumors of a change of mind that so agitated Jacques Schnier in 1938 could have come into circulation. What is clear is that Freud's personal influence within organized psychoanalysis on this matter had indeed dwindled, as witness the denouement of the 1938 Paris Congress which led to the American Association's setting the "1938 rule" just as the war was extinguishing ongoing psychoanalytic activity on the European continent.

The Post–World War II
Resolution of the Crisis

T hough psychoanalytic activity continued throughout the World War II years in America, and even in England under the wartime conditions of the London Blitz,[1] it was either extinguished or was carried on clandestinely in occupied Europe under the Nazis, or became a corrupted and co-opted activity within Nazi Germany and Austria, organized there by an Aryan and pro-Nazi remnant of the original Berlin Psychoanalytical Society as part of the newly created German Institute for Psychological Research and Psychotherapy (totally outside the IPA).[2] The IPA itself practically ceased to function during these years, though Ernest Jones continued on as president. It was not until after the war that plans were made to reinitiate international IPA activities, including resuming the congresses. This would of course again raise the issue of the American relationship to the International, and Ernest Jones, as IPA president, together with Anna Freud and other colleagues from the British

---

[1] For example, the remarkably productive, though also very contentious "Controversial Discussions" of the British Psychoanalytical Society, which have shaped the educational and scientific life of the British Society ever since, with reverberating impact on much of the British-influenced part of the psychoanalytic world, took place in wartime London. This fascinating story is exhaustively chronicled in the book edited by Pearl King and Riccardo Steiner (1991).

[2] For a thorough exposé of this long story, almost unknown to the English-speaking world, see the book by Geoffrey Cocks (1985), *Psychotherapy in the Third Reich: The Göring Institute.* The designation Göring Institute stems from the central role in this organization played by Matthias Heinrich Göring, a psychotherapist and a cousin of the Nazi leader, Hermann Göring, Commander of the Luftwaffe. It was under the protection of the Göring name that the German psychotherapists, including the rump group of psychoanalysts, functioned and prospered until the war ended in 1945.

Society, took the lead in exploring this issue prior to the setting of a firm date for the first postwar congress.

In the February 2, 1948, Minutes of the Council of the British Society, with John Rickman presiding, there is record of a discussion of an American draft of proposed new bylaws for the IPA.[3] Anna Freud felt that it would be more appropriate that the American draft first be considered by the IPA Executive. The decision was made to invite Ernest Jones to a meeting of the British Society Council, and for Rickman to write Lawrence Kubie in America, informing him that it would be impossible to schedule an IPA congress in 1948. In the March 10, 1948, Minutes of the Council, John Rickman again presiding and with Ernest Jones present, there was further discussion of the American draft with various emendations suggested. Rickman was charged to draft a reply.[4] Of the American proposal to organize the IPA by Continental groupings, the Minutes state, "This was felt to be impracticable at this juncture, though it was agreed that the American Societies should have special recognition and authority. Moreover it was suggested that a new isolated Society [referring to potential psychoanalytic development in Canada] should have freedom to choose to which existing regional group [the American or European] it should become affiliated." Again on March 15, 1948, with Rickman presiding, Rickman's draft of a reply to the American memorandum was discussed, after which it was agreed that Rickman would write a still further draft, with copies of that document to go to Jones and also to all the reestablished European Societies. Last in this sequence of meetings to this topic, on May 31, 1948, at the British Society Council meeting, with Rickman in the chair, Clifford Scott suggested that the British and all the Continental Societies should mutually inform each other of their replies sent to the American in response to the American's draft of proposed bylaw revisions.

Later in that same year,

> a number of leading American analysts came to London and had meetings with Ernest Jones, Anna Freud and other members of the British Society. The topic was the relationship between the Americans and the International Association. In 1938 at the Paris Congress the Americans had announced that they had set up their own Association with its own very stringent rules; this amounted almost to a declaration of independence. Owing to the war there was no further Congress till 1949. Meantime, partly due to immigration from Europe, the American Associa-

---

[3] This American document could not be located in the Archives of the British Society.
[4] Also not located in the Archives.

tion had become a very large and powerful body. The 1948 meetings in London were in the nature of a free discussion between equals. An amicable "gentleman's agreement" was reached which promised a high degree of autonomy to the American Association, and it became understood that the Presidency [heretofore always in Europe] would alternate between Europe and America. Later on, the Constitution of the International Association was completely re-drafted in this sense; this task was carried out mainly by certain members of the British Society which, in this sphere as well as in its own domestic affairs, can take credit for successful efforts to promote concord whilst respecting independence [undated note by Pearl King, Hon. Archivist of the British Psychoanalytical Society].

With all this preparation (and prepared agreements), the 16th IPA Congress could now convene in Zurich in August, 1949. Jones was still president and his report to the Business Meeting started with a description of the new postwar climate in the IPA with its altered balance of power and then went on to discuss the unsettled issues between the Americans and the International Association. About the former he referred to "the unprecedented exodus of analysts from the Continent to England and especially to America" (Bulletin IPA, Int. J. 30: 181, 1949), so that the membership "is now preponderatingly concentrated in the West" (p. 181), and "Even the language of psycho-analysis has changed; twenty years ago nine-tenths of it was German, while now more than nine-tenths is English" (p. 181). About the relationship with America, he began by stating that "For some years before the war there had existed certain administrative difficulties and disagreements between the European and American divisions of our Association" (p. 181), and after some indication of what these were, he went on to state: "One result was some uncertainty about the precise relation of the American to the International Association, and at the last Congress, in 1938, I proposed the formation of an *ad hoc* American committee to consider all such matters and to make recommendations" (p. 181).

Due to the war, the committee never met, and in 1946, after the war, Jones asked the then president of the American to reconstitute a similar committee.

[A]fter some discussion had taken place a delegation met us in London last summer [1948, the meetings referred to in the note from Pearl King cited above] and we went thoroughly into all the points with extremely satisfactory results. There were present Drs. Bibring, Binger, Dunn, Lorand, Millet, Murray and Parker on the American side and Drs. Gillespie, Payne, Rickman and

Usher, with Miss Freud and myself, on the European. We agreed on the desirability of various alterations being made in our Statutes, and the amendments suggested were accepted, but for minor details, at the meeting of the American Association last May. These will presently be laid before you for discussion [p. 181].

What these new agreements, prepared ahead of time by the British (speaking for the Europeans) and the Americans, consisted of was not made precisely clear during the balance of Jones's report as recorded in the IPA Bulletin—perhaps a deliberate glossing over. Adam Limentani, IPA President from 1981 to 1985, and after that, Hon. Archivist of the IPA, in a Brief History of the International Psychoanalytical Association (1996) reported it as follows.

> Tensions between the IPA and the APA had lessened[5] as the President reported how representatives of the two organizations had met in London in 1948 in Anna Freud's house, where an agreement had been reached. From now on, the admission of new American groups was left to the APA. However, the APA was forced to concede that the category of direct membership, with no other affiliation than the IPA, would remain in force. This concession did much to avert an open conflict between the APA and the IPA because, as a result of it, some lay analysts could continue to work. At the end of the meeting, Anna Freud paid a handsome tribute to Jones who was retiring after seventeen years as President, mentioning how, "with his actions

---

[5] In a preceding paragraph Limentani had summarized these prewar tensions at the 15th IPA Congress in Paris in 1938:

> The Business meeting, however, was dominated by a dossier from the APA [the American Association], mainly suggesting that the IPA should in future resolve itself entirely into a Congress for scientific purposes. The document also showed how undesirable the ITC was felt to be in the USA, underscoring the feeling with the announcement that henceforth the APA would not be represented on the Executive of the IPA or on the ITC. Even more startling was the refusal to accept the category of Direct Membership of the IPA—which was widely used by members who had been forced to emigrate—especially if they were not medically qualified. In a brief reply, the Chairman of the ITC, Eitingon, insisted that his Committee did not have any powers at all over the constituent branches. In spite of this, to all intents and purposes, the Commission's work had been extinguished by the American intervention. To understand the difficult position of the IPA, it must be realized that out of 560 members, one third were members of the APA [p. 152].

and advice, he had saved a great many lives and careers and existence" [p. 153].

The reference here is to Jones's tireless prewar and wartime activities on behalf of the resettlement of émigré European analysts in the English-speaking world (America and Britain) and even a few elsewhere.

From all this, the form of the 1948 American-British agreement can be made out. The ITC was defunct and was not to be resurrected. The American had, in effect, asserted full control over training standards in the United States, including the limitation of training in American institutes to the medically qualified, and barring the admission of all nonphysicians to its ranks except for the handful grandfathered under the "1938 rule," and the IPA acquiesced to this assumption of total American autonomy in training matters. From Limentani's document it is also clear that the American would control all future access to the IPA of psychoanalytic groups formed in America, in effect granting an "exclusive franchise" within the United States to the American, outside the monitoring and oversight authority of the IPA. This agreement keeping the Americans within the IPA fold thus had two main components: (1) the American would have total autonomy in regard to training standards in the United States with no IPA oversight (such as did exist in relation to all the other component Societies in other nations); (2) the American would have this "exclusive franchise" in its geographic area, meaning that the IPA would recognize no training bodies in the U.S. other than those under the auspices of the American. In addition, as a sign of the new equality, the alternation of the IPA presidency across the two sides of the Atlantic was agreed upon. The major concession made by the Americans was the agreement to allow the category of Direct Membership in the IPA to continue, so that nonmedical analysts who had immigrated to America, though barred from the American, could still maintain Direct Membership in the IPA, even without a component society base. Put all together, it was an agreement to proceed, as of 1949, as if the American proposals of 1938, which had actually never come to a vote, had been formally accepted.

The formal codification of this new and special status for the American within the IPA was not finally accomplished, however, until the 23rd IPA Congress in Stockholm in 1963, another 14 years and seven congresses after Zurich in 1949. A number of relevant events marked that period. One was the unclarity introduced by the Americans (see Jones's October 10, 1935, letter to the members of the committee formed to draft the statutes for the American, chapter 2) over whether the jurisdiction of the American extended over the entire North American continent. In November 1951, a Canadian psychoanalytic group in Montreal applied to the American for Study Group status within it, but in February 1952, when informed of the

American barrier against nonmedical training, the Canadians withdrew their application from the American and accepted sponsorship by the British Society. In September of the same year, however, via a letter to Heinz Hartmann, then President of the IPA, the Canadians, for whatever reason, withdrew from the British sponsorship and in November reapplied to the American, stipulating that they would observe all the American requirements in the psychoanalytic training program they wanted to set up around McGill University in Montreal.

The British Society had not been formally notified of this change, however, and still considered itself the official sponsors of the Canadian group, which led finally to a letter of November 23, 1953, from Ives Hendrick, president of the American, to Clifford Scott, president of the British Society, asserting the American's hegemonic intentions over North America.

> The views of the American, expressed in former President Robert Knight's letter to Dr. Gillespie concerning our traditional belief that Canada does come properly within the American (or North American) professional sphere represents our basic policy for at least fifteen years [meaning ever since the Paris confrontation of 1938] and the results of our efforts to insure maintenance of standards most suitable in North America for the development of the Montreal group, and its future professional relations and that of its members, in the U.S. [Archives, British Society].

It was some time before this issue was resolved, the American relinquishing its claimed jurisdiction over Canada and the Canadian Society constituting itself independently as a component Society of the IPA, adopting the European policy of nondiscrimination toward nonphysicians in training issues.

The codification by the IPA of the American-British détente on the issues of control of training within the United States worked out prior to the 1949 Zurich Congress, and accepted there as if formally agreed upon, began at the very next, 17th Congress in Amsterdam in 1951. There, the first American president of the IPA, Leo H. Bartemeier, took up the thorny issue of Direct Membership in the IPA.

> The Congress will remember that there are still *lay members* who have no affiliation with any Branch Society of the International Psychoanalytical Association. The American Psychoanalytic Association suggests that they should receive the status of Members-at-Large after careful evaluation of their qualifications. The American Society offers the assistance of a

Screening Committee consisting of the President of the American Society, the Chairman of its Board on Professional Standards, and a member of the Executive Council of the International Psychoanalytical Association who at the same time is a member of the American Psychoanalytic Association [i.e., *all* to be members of the American Association]. Dr. Grete Bibring[6] has set up a list of these lay members who have no affiliation with any Branch Society and could give you any information she has gathered about them [Bulletin IPA, Int. J. 33: 256, 1952].

Grete Bibring, in her capacity as the first American secretary of the IPA, explained further that according to the IPA Constitution, membership in the international organization could only be granted to members of a component society, but: "the component society of the I.P.A. in the United States is the American Psychoanalytic Association. Its constitution excludes from membership any lay analyst who was not a member of one of its affiliated societies in 1938" (p. 256). Therefore: "In order to straighten out this anomalous situation the question of establishing a membership at large for these analysts has been considered under the conditions which Dr. Bartemeier suggested" (p. 256). Anna Freud immediately rose to state the full European acquiescence to this proposal.

I should like to support this proposal very warmly, and I think we in Europe should be grateful for it. I well remember the time when we hesitated to make these lay analysts Members-at-Large because we felt that thereby we might offend our American colleagues by sending them members of our own making before asking them to acknowledge this status. It is very fine indeed that the proposal to make them Members-at-Large now comes from our American colleagues. I think it is a great step forward in the collaboration between the American and European societies, and I think it very fair that the situation will be eased by an initiative from the American side where these colleagues live and work [p. 256].

Following this statement, the American proposal was carried unanimously.

---

[6] Now of Boston, but a former Viennese trained by the circle around Freud, Bibring had nonetheless, after coming to America, identified with the American position on this issue, as I have previously noted with Franz Alexander in Chicago and Sandor Rado in New York, both of them originally from the Berlin Institute and the circle around Eitingon.

At the 18th IPA Congress in London in 1953, with Heinz Hartmann as president and Ruth Eissler as secretary, a report was given on the functioning of this Joint Screening Committee of the IPA and the American that had been set up in 1951. At that Congress it was stated that the IPA had close to 1,000 members, half of them in the American. The Joint Screening Committee, chaired by Ruth Eissler, announced that nine lay analysts had been successfully screened and were now Members-at-Large of the IPA. Alphabetically they were Berta Bornstein of New York, Edith Buxbaum of Seattle, Frances Deri of Los Angeles, Hanna Fenichel of Los Angeles, Jakob Hoffman of New York, Anna Maenchen of San Francisco, Lili E. Peller of New York, David Rapaport of Stockbridge, Massachusetts, and Bertha Tumarin of New York (Bulletin IPA, Int. J. 35: 280–281, 1954).

The issue of where the Canadians fitted into the IPA structure surfaced at the 19th IPA Congress in Geneva in 1955. Hartmann was still president, and in his report to the Business Meeting he described the Canadian situation.

A case in which we have come up against difficulties is *Canada*. I have talked to you about the history of these difficulties at the Congress in London. The Committee on Sponsorship, formed in the meantime, now recommends the following: If the Canadian group wishes to be recognized as a Study Group under the sponsorship of the British Society and if the British Society wants to give this sponsorship, the Central Executive should consent to it.

However, thinking ahead to the time when the Canadian group could be provisionally recognized as a Component Society, the Committee on Sponsorship considers it of the utmost importance that the Canadian group formally pledges itself to observe strictly the generally accepted agreements; i.e. if United States citizens apply for training there, the application should not be accepted without prior authorization of the American Psychoanalytic Association or one of its affiliate Societies. All of you know that such an agreement exists between the American Association and the other Component Societies. This means that if an American student applies for training in Canada, the Canadian group shall first ask the permission of the American Psychoanalytic Association or of an Affiliate Society of the American. The same rule, incidentally, will apply in Mexico. Furthermore, the Committee on Sponsorship considers that the Canadian group will have to continue to co-operate with the American Psychoanalytic Association on such questions as the free exchange of instructors and students, in order to arrive at training standards which should be as nearly comparable as possible. However, these recommendations concerning the Canadian group are, according to an agreement we reached at the last Congress, subject to the approval of the American Psychoanalytic Association [Bulletin IPA, Int. J. 37: 124–125, 1956].

This proposal, including the veto power accorded the American Association, carried unanimously. Thus the long wrangle between the Americans and the Canadians and British over how psychoanalytic development would take place in Canada was finally resolved with the Canadians being granted formal independence of the Americans, subject to their adherence to the American standards and American oversight concerning the psychoanalytic training of American citizens who might opt to be trained in Canada (clearly meaning nonphysicians who might seek to circumvent their exclusion from training within the Institutes of the American). At the 20th IPA Congress in Paris in 1957, the American Association having in the meanwhile resolved to take no action on the IPA plan for the Canadians, the Canadian group was accepted as a full IPA Component Society (Bulletin IPA, Int. J. 39: 281–282, 1958).

The next, the 21st IPA Congress, in Copenhagen in 1959, turned seriously to the issue of codifying the various special circumstances and privileges assumed by and accorded to the American Association over the span between the two congresses of 1938 and 1949. A European, William H. Gillespie of the British Society, was now the president, and Pearl King of the same Society, the secretary. First, in his opening address, Gillespie, somewhat nostalgically, looked back to the prewar days and the effort then to maintain uniform international training and qualification standards through the now long defunct ITC. He said:

> An examination of the activities of the Association in the past, that is, before the Second World War, makes it clear that it attempted to exercise a considerable degree of control over training in the various Component Societies. Here again we find Ernest Jones playing a leading role [and Gillespie then detailed Ernest Jones's activities in this regard over a span of years]. . . . However, at the Paris Congress in 1938 our United States colleagues informed the International Association that they wished to set up their own organization for the supervision of training in North America, independently of the International. The onset of war prevented the international discussion of this project; the Americans went ahead and, as we all know, they have developed a highly organized system of

training standards and machinery for their enforcement, certainly a great deal more elaborate and strict than anything the International Association ever attempted. Since then analysis has spread rapidly in the western hemisphere, leaving only a handful of fully active societies on this side of the Atlantic; the effect has been a tacit abandonment on the part of the International of the work formerly undertaken by the International Training Commission, except insofar as in the United States this has been delegated to the American Association who have continued this work [Bulletin IPA, Int. J. 41: 170, 1960].

From there, Gillespie went on to describe the obstacles in the way of any effort to revive an ITC mechanism to promulgate and monitor uniform training standards in Europe; the wide discrepancies between the older, established Societies and the newer, struggling ones; the lack of a common language, albeit English was widely understood; lack of money in view of the very nominal IPA dues (just recently raised to five dollars per year), and so forth. The only practical leverage that the IPA could exert over analytic training standards at the time was "by the scrutiny of the fitness to train of new groups which are aspiring to the status of Component Societies" (p. 171).

Later at the Business Meeting of the same Congress, Gillespie announced that he was setting up a working party or a committee to consider all the standing statutes of the IPA and to propose revisions that would bring them fully into accord with all the decisions and practices instituted since the 1949 Congress. He noted that the statutes had not been extensively revised since Ernest Jones had drafted their present form in 1949 (p. 175). In an interview with Pearl King in London on November 3, 1993, she informed me that Gillespie had actually set her to work on this task of properly revising the IPA Statutes two years earlier (in 1957) just after his election as president and his designation of her as secretary. At the Business Meeting of the 22nd IPA Congress, in Edinburgh in 1961, Gillespie reported on the Proposed Revision of Statutes.

Dr. Gillespie reported that, as agreed at the last Congress, a committee had been appointed to consider the Statutes and the possibilities for changing them. The committee consisted of Dr. Sylvia Payne, Dr. Elliott Jaques, Miss Pearl King, and himself. A great deal of preliminary work was done by Miss King and Dr. Jaques, who presented first a provisional draft of the revised Statutes. After discussion of this draft, Miss Anna Freud and

Dr. Willi Hoffer were invited to join the committee.[7] Further changes were then made and a revised draft was sent to the members of the Central Executive, several of whom made valuable suggestions leading to further revisions. The sixth, most recent version of the proposed Statutes was considered by the Central Executive during this Congress. It was then agreed that this last revision should be referred to the new President and Central Executive for final study prior to circulation to the Component Societies for consideration [Bulletin, IPA, Int. J. 43: 365, 1962].

It was given to the next, the 23rd, IPA Congress, in Stockholm in 1963, to bring to closure the task of revising the IPA Statutes to make them conform to the functioning reality. The president was again an American, Maxwell Gitelson, and his secretary was Elizabeth Zetzel. At the Business Meeting, Gitelson declared the revised Constitution and Bylaws to be the most important item on the agenda, the product now of six years of labor on the subject and many revisions. He called on Pearl King as the principal architect of this multiply revised document to introduce the discussion. King first reviewed the history of the process, reminding the assembly that a sixth draft had been discussed at the Edinburgh Congress two years earlier. She expressed the philosophy of the task as "not to write rules for the Association, but rather to help create a phase adequate social structure, and they realized that this was as important to an Institution as ego structure was to an individual. They therefore felt that the new Statutes should be syntonic with the preferred modes of functioning which had been developed by the Association" (Bulletin IPA, Int. J. 45: 461, 1964).

The committee next examined the functions of the IPA, which they felt to be threefold: (1) scientific interchange among colleagues; (2) the promotion of psychoanalysis; and (3) authorization of training and qualification of analysts by component societies. All the various international scientific organizations whose structures the committee had studied shared

---

[7] It should be noted that there was no objection from the assembly to the fact that all six members of this committee, charged with the task of promulgating the codification of the relationship of the American to the IPA, were from the British Society. This speaks not only to the skillful and respected leadership of Gillespie and King, but to the general appreciation of the crucial brokering role played by the British Society and especially, of course, historically by Ernest Jones, in mediating between the contending American and European positions—a role played from the very beginning (in the mid-20s, three and a half decades earlier) of the open controversy within the IPA over the issue of lay analysis and the associated training issues.

the first two of these functions, but in regard to the third, the training function, "the Association appeared to be unique" (p. 461), and it is this, of course, that led to its special organizational complexity. In addition, the International seemed to have another unique feature, that it was "ruled by the principle of group responsibility for the selection, control of training, and qualification of psycho-analysts" (p. 461), and "these two primary factors have represented central considerations in the design of the constitution now presented" (p. 461).

"Miss King then noted that the constitution did not in fact include many real innovations. In general, it represented a verbalization of the existing practices of the Central Executive previously passed as resolutions, but never brought together in one document" (p. 461). On the central issue of the relationship between the American and the IPA, the new Statutes created the designation, Regional Association, and gave explicit recognition to the status of the American as a Regional Association different from all the others, the Component Societies. The rationale for this was stated as follows:

> The position of the American Psychoanalytic Association as a Component Society had for some time differed considerably from the position of other Component Societies. This Association had achieved a degree of organization and responsibility in respect to standards that no other Component Society had yet reached. In the hope that other regions may in the future reach this standard, the Statutes had included the recognition of the status of "Regional Associations" in its new Constitution [p. 461].[8]

After presenting a range of other proposed alterations in the IPA Statutes not germane to this particular issue, King proposed the following

---

[8] The American has continued as a distinctive Regional Association ever since, although the terms of the Regional Association status were modified at the 35th IPA Congress in Montreal, in 1987, during my presidency of the IPA. This was one of the aspects of the alteration in the administrative organization of the IPA, as well as of the fundamental transformation of our identity as a discipline, consequent to the process of resolution of the lawsuit against the American and the IPA, chronicled in detail later in this book. The hope expressed by Pearl King that other, comparable Regional Associations might come into being, has not come to pass, nor is it likely to. The whole trend of the IPA over the 16 years that I served on its Executive Council, from 1977 to 1993, has been toward diminishing the distinctness of the Regional Association status, and currently there is neither any movement within the European Psychoanalytic Federation (EPF) nor the Latin American Psychoanalytic Federation (FEPAL) toward seeking the prerogatives of Regional Association status, nor would the Executive Council or the membership at large likely countenance such a movement, should it arise.

action: "She would like to see the Statutes now proposed adopted for an experimental period, say four years, giving the Central Executive and President power, at their discretion, to make modifications if, in special cases, undue hardship would result. The membership as a whole could all take part in this experiment, both as individuals and societies, informing the Honorary secretary of suggestions and proposed amendments which could be considered at the next meeting" (p. 462). Following this, Zetzel, as IPA Secretary, reminded the assembly that there was a commitment to a definitive vote at this Congress. After a long and vigorous discussion, reported verbatim in the Minutes (pp. 462–466), which ranged over many aspects of the proposed new Statutes, and was not limited at all to the Regional Association issue, Gitelson called for a vote, adding that, "Acceptance under the conditions stated included our recognition that this is not a finished document. The next two years would present an opportunity for important and essential corrections" (p. 466). A vote was taken, and there was only one negative vote: "The Constitution and Bylaws were therefore approved in accordance with the stipulations formulated with respect to its acceptance" (p. 466).

Appended to the Minutes of that 1963 Congress was the complete text of the new IPA Constitution and Bylaws. That dealing with the Regional Association status was Article VI (a)(i) under Component Organizations:

> A Regional Association comprises a number of Societies in a Continental, Subcontinental or National Region in which *ultimate responsibility* for matters related to the *training and qualification* of psycho-analysts is assigned to the Regional Association. The Regional Association is also *responsible* for the *development and recognition* of new Societies and training facilities *within its geographic area.* Societies belonging to a Regional Association are defined as Affiliate Societies of that Regional Association. The Regional Association is recognized accordingly by the Association. The Affiliate Societies of a Regional Association derive recognition through the Regional Association and are not directly recognized by the International Association [p. 475].

The phrases I have italicized underscore the two crucial prerogatives of a Regional Association that have been indicated already and now fully legitimated in this new Constitution: the complete autonomy of the Regional Association in training matters, and the exclusive jurisdiction of the Regional Association in its geographic area, so that no other psychoanalytic group, with possibly different training standards, could seek IPA affiliation in the domain covered by the Regional Association.

Thus was resolved, in Stockholm in 1963, the process within the IPA of accommodation, now in a spirit of friendly reconciliation, to the ultimatum set forth by the American Association in Paris in 1938, to settle the issue of access to official psychoanalytic training—at least in America—on the American terms, barring the training there of nonphysicians. This achieved the two major intentions that had powered this struggle from the American side. One was to demarcate psychoanalysis sharply from all imputation of charlatanism, allowing it to take its place alongside the purified medical training and practice that resulted from the implementation of the Flexner report. The other was to free psychoanalysis in America of the burden of its nonmedical cohorts in order to better campaign for the psychoanalytic idea in the strongholds of psychiatry in the nation's medical schools and teaching hospitals, and thus to become an integral part of academic medicine and the university establishment and to avoid the exclusion from organized medicine and the university that was still the fate of psychoanalysis in Europe.[9]

This, however, did not end the American story. Nonphysicians were excluded officially from training within the American Psychoanalytic Association, but in the wake of World War II, clinical psychology, and slightly later, psychiatric social work, emerged as vibrant, rapidly growing mental health professions, which soon burst institutional bonds and began to enter the private-practice market. The growth of clinical psychology as an independent discipline was given enormous impetus in the immediate post–World War II period by the United States Veterans Administration. Ten million men and women had been in the military services during the war, and with the rapid postwar demobilization, large numbers of neuropsychiatric casualties flooded the many new Veterans Administration (VA) Hospitals, most of which had been converted from wartime Army hospitals. The VA, whenever possible in collaboration with nearby medical school departments of psychiatry, instituted a great number of training programs for psychiatric residents, and also pre- and postdoctoral clinical placements

---

[9] At the 24th IPA Congress in Amsterdam in 1965, the IPA first renewed its efforts to bring some order and uniformity in training standards, which had ceased with its forced dissolution of the ITC in 1938, caused by the American withdrawal and declaration of independence, and by Hitler's march across Europe, which had dismantled the main Continental analytic training centers. This was now on a totally voluntary, collegial basis, through the instituting of Precongress Conferences for Training Analysts. These two-and-a-half-day intensive meetings have served ever since as vehicles for exchanging information, comparing experiences, and considering varying solutions to shared training problems. In more recent years, starting in my administration in 1987, a standing Committee on Psychoanalytic Education (COMPSED) was created to create guidelines for psychoanalytic education to which all component Societies of the IPA would be urged to adhere.

linked to university doctoral programs for clinical psychology, in order to meet the treatment needs of the large numbers of veterans who crowded its hospitals and mental hygiene clinics. Because most of the psychiatrists in these residency programs opted for the private practice of psychotherapy rather than VA staff jobs after they had finished their residency training, the VA focussed increasing resources in its psychology programs; at least in those early years, clinical psychology was relatively new in the private market and psychologists were more willing to take VA staff positions.

Over the years, however, more and more psychologists did enter the private market. As they did so, they spent more time in the practice of psychotherapy than in diagnostic testing, personality assessment, or in the research activities that were the hallmarks of university positions, and jobs in departments of psychiatry. Not too long after, psychiatric social workers, who had also been employed largely in psychiatric hospitals, clinics, and social agencies, and had dealt primarily with the social and psychological ills of the indigent and the disadvantaged, also began to enter the more lucrative private-practice market. Many among these various mental health practitioners were inspired by the challenge as well as the prestige of psychoanalysis, and like their psychiatric confreres, turned to whatever possibilities for a more intensive and psychoanalytic training might be available to them.

The greatest concentration of such aspirants in those early days was in New York City, where there was also the greatest number of immigrant analysts, both medical and lay; only the former had access to membership and official training status, through the New York Psychoanalytic Institute. Among that immigrant group, the most charismatic figure was Theodor Reik, the individual on whose behalf Freud had written *The Question of Lay Analysis,* and who had come as a Hitler refugee to New York, carrying the imprimatur of his closeness to Freud and his self-designation as the carrier of Freud's authority in the New World. Sherman (1988), said that: "Reik's famous feud with the New York Psychoanalytic Society, to which he continually referred in his books, started at this time. When Reik arrived in New York, he expected to be treated as Freud's intimate colleague, someone who would be admired and looked up to by ordinary New York Society members who had never had the opportunity to be close to Freud" (p. 385). This did not happen. The New York Society did make some overtures, offering Reik the opportunity to teach and a small salaried position. But this was far from the central honored position Reik insisted on. Though Paul Federn and Herman Nunberg tried to get Reik to accommodate to the New York Society, he would not do so. Sherman said that "Reik was far too proud and contentious a man to make even the slightest concession. In fact, in view of Reik's own emotional needs, the situation was just the opportunity he needed to view himself as a worthy, talented man met with unwarranted hostility and neglect" (p. 385). Sherman also called Reik an antiestablishment rebel and a provocateur.[10]

Though Reik did teach a course at the New York Institute, he neglected the substance, which was supposed to be applied psychoanalysis, and instead turned it into a diatribe against the Institute, a detailed recounting of his grievances; he charged that the Institute authorities had even tried to bribe him not to practise psychoanalysis. The course was soon withdrawn, and Reik promptly, in 1941, founded his own Society for Psychoanalytic Psychology. In 1948 he founded his own rival training center outside the American, the National Psychological Association for Psychoanalysis (NPAP). This was the first institute devoted to training nonphysicians, and clinical psychologists and psychiatric social workers flocked to it. Its prestige was greatly enhanced by the enormous popularity of Reik's most acclaimed book, *Listening with the Third Ear*, published in that same year. In 1952, NPAP started its own journal, *Psychoanalysis*, and in 1956, that journal absorbed *The Psychoanalytic Review*, founded in 1913 by Smith Ely Jelliffe and William Alanson White; it continues to this day as *The Psychoanalytic Review*, the official journal of NPAP (Lerner, 1988, recounts the history of this journal). It can indeed be said that Reik's quarrel with the New York Society was the critical impetus to the development of nonmedical institutes in the United States.

From these beginnings with NPAP, gradually other groups spun off from it in New York, most notably the Institute for Psychoanalytic Training and Research (IPTAR) and the New York Freudian Society (NYFS), the latter of which now has a branch program in Washington, D.C. These two groups, IPTAR and NYFS, have grown to far exceed the original NPAP in scope and impressiveness of program, and they were among the very first of the nonmedical psychoanalytic training groups that grew up in the United States after World War II, to be taken as Provisional Societies into the International Psychoanalytical Association, outside the framework of the American, when that became possible in the wake of the settlement of the lawsuit. Depending on how one counted them, at the time of the lawsuit there were anywhere from a dozen to some 30 independent psychoanalytic training groups, composed essentially of psychologists and social workers, existing in the New York area alone. These had varying academic affiliations, track records, and reputations. By the time of the lawsuit, there was another, smaller cluster in Los Angeles, of which two, the Psychoanalytic Center of California (PCC) and the Los Angeles Institute and Society for Psychoanalytic Studies (LAISPS), have also sought and attained

---

[10] Sherman's account, written from his position as former editor of the *Psychoanalytic Review*, the official journal of the psychoanalytic training center later founded by Reik, is based on interviews with Reik and with a number of Reik's family members.

independent affiliation status with the International. Beyond this, there were others scattered through Massachusetts, Michigan, Illinois, Colorado, Florida, and elsewhere, most of these sponsored now by Division 39, the Division of Psychoanalysis, of the American Psychological Association, actually the fastest growing division, now numbering 3000 to 4000 members, within that organization.

The problem that all these independent, nonmedical, psychoanalytic training centers had, however, from the beginning, excluded as they were from the American Association and from official access to its training cadres, was that of ensuring the quality of the training experience. There were of course prominent and eminently qualified individuals like Reik who kept themselves out of, or were excluded from, the training institutes of the American, while they taught in these independent and "unofficial" groups. More, just as there were prominent European analytic leaders—Alexander, Rado, and Grete Bibring have already been noted—who, when they became part of the American psychoanalytic world, identified with the American's position on the issue of lay analysis, so there were others, equally prominent, among both the European refugees and even among the American born and trained who were always more sympathetic with the European (and Freud's) position on this issue. While these officially went along with the posture of the American, unofficially they were quite willing both to analyze and supervise nonmedical aspirants who used these analyses and supervisions as credentials in their outside training programs, usually with the stipulation adhered to on both sides that these analyses and supervisions not be publicly known, that is, not outside their own training institution.

Because there were large numbers of such willing psychoanalytic mentors—as analysts and as supervisors—in the New York area, and the largest concentration of psychologist and social worker aspirants was there, a whole network of these outside, unofficial, and in some instances clandestine training organizations first took root and grew up in New York City. Of course there also were numerous other individuals who sought out personal analyses and private supervisions and put together their own seminar sequence of solo analytic readings and attendance at such analytic courses as were available to interested mental health professionals. These became autodidacts in psychoanalysis, without affiliation even with such organized groups as NPAP, IPTAR, or the NYFS. In this whole early period, covering the first 15 or so postwar years, the American officially ignored these activities completely, though they were known to, and participated in, by many of the members of the New York Psychoanalytic Society, even by some who became presidents of the American Psychoanalytic Association during that period.

Of this period, Reuben Fine (1982) in his historical survey of nonmedical psychoanalysis in the United States, said in summary, "Nonmedical psychoanalysis in the U.S. developed after World War II in spite of the determined opposition of all the medical groups. 'Unauthorized' training proceeded, sometimes in a cloak-and-dagger hush-hush atmosphere, but it proceeded, and eventually succeeded. Today, it has the same kind of legal protection that medical analysis has, i.e., through the groups with degrees, primarily Ph.D. psychologists and M.S.W. social workers" (pp. 518–519). This last statement refers to the fact that all psychoanalysts are licensed in the United States through their disciplines of origin, medicine, clinical psychology, or clinical social work; almost nowhere is psychoanalysis recognized as a separate clinical discipline and licensed as such.

In an effort to capture the nature of that period and the flavor of that activity, I interviewed Drs. Martin and Maria Bergmann, two among the best known pioneering nonmedical psychoanalytic students who succeeded in being analytically "trained" in these independent and somewhat surreptitious channels, and who then went on to establish influential psychoanalytic careers that have become increasingly "accepted" within the official American channels. These interviews took place on April 10, 1994, in New York, first with Martin Bergmann, and then with Maria (Ridi) Bergmann.[11]

As I put it together, here is Martin Bergmann's story. He was born in Prague in 1913, in a strongly Zionist and Hebrew-speaking family. In 1920,

---

[11] An account of the still earlier training of William and Esther Menaker is given in detail in an article by Esther Menaker (1988). Briefly, it was as follows: She and her husband went to Vienna for training in the 1930s, encouraged to do so by Fritz Wittels, who was then teaching at the New School for Social Research in New York. At the time, there was as yet no formal training in New York, and all Americans seeking psychoanalytic training had to go to Europe. But the understanding was already in place that Americans had to be approved for such training by the admissions committee of the New York Psychoanalytic Society, which required that they have medical or medically related training. Bill Menaker had been a dentist for 10 years, and this, together with the fact that three visitors from Europe—Franz Alexander, Helene Deutsch, and Rene Spitz—who had been attending an international congress in America, happened to be guests at the admissions committee meeting in New York where the matter was discussed, "forced" the Americans (according to Esther Menaker) to honor the agreement and sanction Bill Menaker's training in Vienna. There he went to Helene Deutsch for analysis, and she arranged for his wife to go to Anna Freud.

"As might have been expected, the New York Psychoanalytic Society did not welcome us upon our return" (p. 377). Practice grew slowly, with few referrals from the New York analysts. Some of their patients were the spouses of medical analysts who did not trust the discretion of the medical colleagues. Mostly the Menakers were isolated professionally, though this diminished with the marked influx of Hitler refugees at the end of the 1930s, and small unofficial study groups emerged amongst these individuals. World War II became a real professional opportunity when so many of the American analysts served in the armed forces, and with the great enthusiasm for psychodynamic therapy generated by the wartime military experience, psychoanalytic treatment became increasingly popular. By the 1950s there was a big change, and by then the independent nonmedical psychoanalytic institutes were springing up in New York.

the family immigrated to Palestine where Martin's father was Rector of the Hebrew University and Martin participated in the Zionist youth movement. While in Jerusalem he had a period of therapy with an Adlerian therapist because of the onset in adolescence of a speech symptom, a stammer. As an adolescent he read Freud's "The Future of an Illusion," which impressed him greatly. Martin then lived for a period on a kibbutz where he contracted typhoid and nearly died of it. At 20 (1933), he left the kibbutz and Palestine and went to California to study agriculture at U.C. Davis, a leading agriculture college in America.

From Davis, Martin went to nearby U.C. Berkeley, where he became a psychology student under the famed Edward C. Tolman, and from that base he gravitated to Siegfried Bernfeld, also a strong Zionist and a Socialist, as well as a very charismatic and influential lay analyst, who had recently arrived as a Hitler refugee in San Francisco. Martin and Bernfeld were planning to write a book on Hitler's psychopathology, but the wartime mobilization ended that project, with Martin's being drafted into the Army. He was by then a psychologist and became an expert in Rorschach administration to soldiers with various neuropsychiatric syndromes. In the army he worked with two psychiatrist psychoanalysts from New York, Arnold Eisendorfer and George Goldman, and wrote his first professional papers, published in *Psychosomatic Medicine,* the *Bulletin of the Menninger Clinic,* and elsewhere, including one on inducing regressions in soldiers under hypnosis and administering Rorschachs in these regressed states.

After the war, Martin stopped in Topeka, where he was offered a position at the Menninger Foundation, and then went on to New York, where Lewis Wolberg also offered him a position, as the chief psychologist in his clinic, at $5000 per year, which Martin accepted with alacrity and held for several years. In New York he met and married Ridi. When his friend Rudi Ekstein left New York for The Menninger Foundation, Martin inherited Rudi's patients, around whom he established his private practice. He then undertook personal analysis, first with Gustav Bychowski and then with Edith Jacobson, both well-known, distinguished pillars of the New York Psychoanalytic Society. He took Fenichel as his ideal, to emulate and to compete with, and he also aspired, grandly, to write Fenichel's book.[12] At the same time he became intensely interested in the history of psychoanalysis. Martin studied with Paul Federn and with Theodor Reik, though

---

[12] Of this Martin wrote in his letter of comment on my account: "Since Edith Jacobson had no husband I selected her analyst, Otto Fenichel, as my rival. I was determined to know psychoanalysis as well as he did, and if possible, exceed him. This fact, and also the fact that my father was a renowned teacher, made me go into teaching in a big way. There was such a hunger for psychoanalytic teachers in the 1950s and 1960s outside of the Psychoanalytic Institute that I made it a habit to give a seminar every day. This I still continue today."

he never enrolled in Reik's NPAP nor in any other organized training program. He arranged for supervisions privately from Moses Barenbaum and Franz Cohn, and he joined every study group that he could, one group run by William and Esther Menaker, another led by Joel Shor along with Moses and Geesa Barenbaum, and another with a group of candidates in the New York Psychoanalytic Institute, Zel Aarons, Merl Jackel, William Niederland, and David Rubinfine—though this last group was forced to drop him.

It was from ingredients such as these that Martin Bergmann put together his own analytic training program, and both the involvement in it of different figures in the New York Psychoanalytic Institute as well as obstacles put in its way by the same Institute are clear. When Paul Federn died, Martin and Ernst Federn created a Federn Study Group, and along with Peter Glauber and Eduardo Weiss, Martin organized a series of lectures commemorating Federn's life work. His first paper, published in the *Journal of the American Psychoanalytic Association,* was on Federn and ego psychology, trying to reconcile Federn's outlook with Hartmann's. He also organized meetings in which he got prominent members of the New York Society like Herman Nunberg and Hartmann to speak on their work; for a period the group had Robert Waelder on alternate weeks. He began to attend meetings as a guest at the New York Psychoanalytic Society—where guests had to sit in a roped off rear section at the time—and at the American and the International. Actually, psychoanalysis seemed all of life, and Martin Bergmann imbibed all he could and profited richly. He said, "We met everybody," speaking of himself and Ridi, "particularly among the European refugee groups."[13]

During all that time Martin did not formally join any organized psychoanalytic groups, though as he gained in experience and reputation he would teach wherever he was asked, and he was one of the central teachers of the faculty at the New York Freudian Society in its early formative years. When it became possible to acquire IPA membership after the 35th IPA Congress in Montreal in 1987, which altered the Regional Association agreement with the American, Martin (and Ridi) joined the New York

[13] In his letter of comment, Martin wanted to make clear that though the exclusion of nonphysicians from official psychoanalytic training was firmly enforced, he nonetheless felt the climate within which he grew psychoanalytically was personally receptive. He regularly attended meetings of the International, was permitted to read a paper at the 1965 Amsterdam Congress, participated in a symposium at the American in 1971, and gave an invited paper to the New York Psychoanalytic Society in 1974. He ended his comment with, "What is important here, beyond the personal, is the fact that, while the avenues for training were closed during this era, if you had something to say, the American Psychoanalytic and the journals gradually opened to you, and I believe this is worth stressing." This was offered as a corrective to the tone of my text.

Freudian Society as their component organizational membership in the IPA. He stated, reflecting back on the overview he had presented to me of his psychoanalytic development and career, that personally he had profited enormously from his position as an excluded outsider to the American's psychoanalytic world. There were so many younger people like himself coming after, who he was free to teach openly, and he enjoyed over the years conducting psychoanalytic seminars on a whole range of analytic topics. When asked why he felt so many analyst members of the New York Society were willing to foster his own analytic development and help promote his career, some of them openly and others much more discreetly, he saw it as an expression by these (mostly European émigré) analysts of loyalty to Freud and resentment at the implacable oppositional role of the American to Freud's position on this issue. He singled out Max Schur, who had been Freud's personal physician during his long siege with cancer, as well as a distinguished analyst in his own right, as most vociferous in this regard.

By contrast with Martin Bergmann's stepwise and almost serendipitous turn to psychoanalysis, Maria Bergmann was born into the Vienna psychoanalytic world in the immediate wake of World War I. Her father was a distinguished scholar, a mathematician, a chess master, and a logical-positivist member of the Vienna Circle, but as a Jew his academic teaching opportunities were very limited in Vienna. He was a major intellectual influence in her life. Her mother was trained as a pedagogue by Anna Freud and worked with difficult children—a grandson of Trotsky, children of the Reichs and of the Bernfelds—all of whom were in child analysis and were being cared for by Maria Bergman's mother in her home. Ridi was herself an only child, but she was also mother's helper with all the children under mother's care.

Like Martin, Ridi also grew up in the Socialist youth movement, but was also heavily psychoanalytic, with the effort always to link Marxism and psychoanalysis. The readings of this adolescent period included "Beyond the Pleasure Principle," "The Future of an Illusion," "Civilization and Its Discontents," and also Wilhelm Reich's *Sexual Struggle of Youth*. Along with all of this went intensive piano study and involvement in a children's and then an adolescents' chorus. It was this idyllic world carved out in psychoanalytic Vienna, that was shattered in March 1938 by the Austrian Anschluss with Germany. The immediate problem became getting passports to leave, which was very difficult despite not living in a Jewish district and despite having an uncle who was Chief of Police. The family applied everywhere and did get an affidavit from an American family whose children had been under Ridi's mother's care. Even so, she had to leave illegally and very dangerously on a train for Switzerland in October 1938; from there she made it to England, where she was able in turn to get her parents out of Austria. Her first job in England was taking care of children, and in 1940, with the war on, the family came in a boat convoyed to America.

Once in America, Ridi went to the University of Louisville on a scholarship and then to Bryn Mawr. She had been engaged to a Viennese boyfriend who was interned and sent to Australia. In 1947 she met Martin; they were married after six months, and from there on they shared their lives of analytic study and work.

The Bergmanns attended the first postwar IPA Congress together, the 16th, in Zurich in 1949, and were the only nonmembers present. Ridi had grown up in Vienna with mathematics and music and psychoanalysis, but now she devoted herself fully (along with Martin) to psychoanalysis. She too mentioned three analytic study groups in which they simultaneously participated as students. She describes herself as an "analytic purist" at that time and felt quite alien in one of the groups, which was quite Sullivanian. She and Martin never joined Reik and his NPAP, but they did participate in the formation of the New York Freudian Society where she helped to build the curriculum and taught development seminars. Her personal analysis was first with Gustav Bychowski and then with Lillian Malcove. Her supervisions were with Marcel Heiman, Joachim Flescher, and Marianne Kris. She helped Martin and Ernst Federn organize the Federn Study Group for psychologists and social workers. She took a course with William Menaker on female psychology, with Ernst Kris at the New School on Piaget and on ego psychology, and with Robert Bak on schizophrenia and on perversions. She mentioned an array of others she had contact with, Phyllis Greenacre, Edith Jacobson, Herman Nunberg, Lili Peller, Rene Spitz, and Robert Waelder.[14]

Much more than Martin, Ridi emphasized how black-market and secret this all was. You were not supposed to talk about it and no one did. Socially, she and Martin felt quite isolated at the beginning, having only a small circle of friends; Rudi Ekstein was one of the closest. She emphasized, too, the red rope at the meetings of the New York Psychoanalytic Society behind which guests like themselves had to sit. But it was through this process that she too became an analyst. She felt that she was "very orthodox"; she affiliated with the Menaker group, who referred her first patients to her. She worked for a while in a clinic, then in private practice, first in psychotherapy, then in psychoanalysis. She felt very much that she and Martin were much ignored in the early days, though she singled out Bert Lewin and Leo Stone as being helpful with referrals. These cases often

---

[14] In her letter of comment, Ridi Bergmann emphasized more strongly the role of Robert Waelder (a nonmedical, grandfathered member of the American) in her training process. "I want to stress that Robert Waelder, who took over the Federn Group after Federn's death, was our first very clear and very systematic teacher. He guided us through, at that time, new and difficult psychoanalytic ideas with the utmost clarity. He came regularly for many years and we shall always be grateful to him."

turned out to be individuals who had to be analyzed outside the membership of the New York Society, wives of analysts, for example. The first paper she published was in the *International Journal*, and she remembers clearly her first lecture given at the New York Psychoanalytic Institute in 1978.[15]

Clearly, with both Drs. Martin and Maria Bergmann psychoanalytic study and training was very much a bootstrap operation, teaching and learning with and from each other and like colleagues, simultaneously students and teachers. But it was from prototypical beginnings like this that cadres of analytically trained and qualified individuals gradually grew to professional maturity, first in New York, but after a while in other cities as well, as the number of willing teachers and eager potential students came to a critical mass in each locale. Some, like the Bergmanns, stayed outside of organized training structures, from which Martin felt they had personally profited. Most, however, clustered in these independent nonmedical institutes that were forming, and as these organizations evolved over the years they gradually developed their own teaching faculties and training-analyst groups from their own graduated student bodies, and had to rely less on the happenstance of analysts from the Institutes of the American willing, overtly or covertly, to participate in their training.

It remains in this chapter only to mention briefly the official doings of the American Psychoanalytic Association in relation to these training issues of nonphysicians, during the first postwar decade and a half. At this time, the IPA was preoccupied with legally clarifying and codifying the détente between Europe and America which held the IPA together, essentially on the American terms of barring the training of nonmedical applicants in the Institutes of the American; in response, those excluded in this way from "official" training in America were so busily engaged in fashioning their own "unofficial" or "independent" psychoanalytic training institutions, abetted so much by members of the American who were out of sympathy with its official stance.

This whole issue of lay analysis was also being formally debated during that period in the councils of the American. The principal argument on the side of those opposed to the exclusionary rule was the deprivation in psychoanalysis of the talents of those with various disciplinary backgrounds other than medicine, in contrast to the long history of enrichment of the analytic culture in Europe through the contributions of a long and distinguished roster of lay members. The special emphasis was the loss to

---

[15] Like her husband, Ridi Bergmann in her letter also wanted to stress the gradually changing climate in which they lived and worked: "So, it is true that our attitude concomitantly changed as we moved from being excluded to being accepted and even were asked to make contributions. It is only fair to stress this change."

psychoanalytic scholarship in a range of interface and applied fields and the loss to creative research in analysis itself. The opposition to change in the statutes of the American was no longer centered around arguments over quackery and charlatanism, as in the earlier part of the century, but around the position psychoanalysis had achieved within psychiatry, and therefore within medicine, and its declared essential nature as a special treatment method for the ills of psychiatric patients. Under the pressure of this ongoing debate, the first alteration in the "1938 rule" occurred almost 20 years later, in 1956, when the Board on Professional Standards and the Executive Council of the American agreed to create a new Committee of the Board—the Committee on Training for Research (CTR). This would be the national committee through which the affiliated Institutes of the American could seek waivers of the usual (medical) requirement for training, on behalf of distinguished nonmedical academic scholars and accomplished researchers whose contributions in their own disciplines would be enhanced by psychoanalytic training and knowledge. Those who could satisfy this requirement could be granted waivers for partial psychoanalytic training (personal analysis by a training analyst plus the sequence of theoretical and clinical seminars) or full training (the personal analysis, the seminars, and conducting analyses under supervision), with the stipulation that those individuals so trained would continue their academic, scholarly, and research careers, supplemented only by that amount and kind of ongoing psychoanalytic clinical work required by or warranted by their academic scholarship and research.

These were stringent waiver requirements indeed, and the intent was that the numbers would be very small and the individuals very prominent and established as academic scholars and researchers. It is at the point of the formation of CTR that my personal scientific life story first intersected with the issue of lay analysis, and it is to my own scientific and professional life story to this point that I next turn.

My Life into Psychoanalysis

Iwas born in Berlin on January 28, 1921. My father, the descendent of a line of rabbinic scholars in Prague, came to Germany from Vienna at the beginning of World War I, leaving behind an unhappy, arranged first marriage and the beginning of a rabbinical career in order to seek out a new life as a student of medicine at the prestigious Kaiser Wilhelm Universitat in Berlin. My mother came to Berlin from Galicia, part of Russian-occupied Poland, fleeing before the advancing Tsarist Russian army into the welcoming safety of Germany, also in the earliest days of the first world war. They met and were married in 1919 when my father was in his medical residency training at the Charite Krankenhaus in Berlin, within the defeated, war-ravaged, inflation-ridden, postwar Weimar Republic.

The postwar inflation destroyed the value of money and my father's carefully guarded savings, and this ended his residency training and drove my family from Germany. According to the story I was told, my father had two choices. One was to follow up on the favorable answer he had received to a letter he had written in response to a newspaper ad, to come to America, to New York City, and enter as an assistant into the medical practice of a Manhattan gastroenterologist. The other, by far more glamorous, was to follow the blandishments of a wealthy patient in his hospital, a foreign potentate, member of the Persian royal family, and the governor of one of that nation's provinces. The position would be that of court physician in the provincial capital. What apparently dissuaded my father, and led him to opt for the more conventional life of a New York doctor, was that the journey to the new home in Persia would have involved a train ride of several days from Berlin to Teheran, and then several more days by camel over wilderness roads to the provincial capital. This he felt to be too difficult and risky for my mother and me, and so when I was one year old, he left for New York, his money totally depleted, and left my mother and me to subsist on the remittances he sent each month from the New World. A year later, in 1923, when I was two, he sent for us; this was our lucky escape, ten years before Hitler came to power, and the beginning of my American life.

I have no memories from that period, but when I was in analysis, some 30 years later, I had a recurrent dream, sharply and clearly etched, of being in the street looking up at a woman in an apartment window, seeing a house that seemed so real, yet a building unlike any that I knew, but one I felt that I would instantly recognize should I see it. When I was willing to return to Germany for the first time, in 1985, 40 years after the fall of Hitler, in order to attend the 34th IPA Congress in Hamburg, my wife and I visited Berlin before the Congress. This included a day with a German colleague in East Berlin where, along with the splendid museums, we went to see the Kaiser Wilhelm Universitat (now the Humboldt Universitat) and the Charite Krankenhaus, and Schumannstrasse where I was born and had lived, all in a cluster just over the Berlin Wall. Schumannstrasse is a short street of just a few blocks, and all the apartment houses on those blocks looked like the house in the dream.

In New York we lived on the Grand Concourse, a then elegantly middle-class street in the Bronx. German was my first language and I taught rudiments of it to my playmates. In those days, before the growth of nursery and preschools, one could go to kindergarten at any time after age three, but had to stay there until one was by age ready for the first grade. I entered kindergarten at three-and-a-half, and at that point announced that I would henceforth only speak English. Though my knowledge of spoken German persisted for some years, so that I could understand a fair amount of the conversation when family friends, also German-Jewish emigres, would come to our home for cake and coffee on Saturday evenings, that knowledge gradually faded. In high school, when I took both French and German as foreign languages, I felt no especial advantage in my German studies over my American friends.

I grew up, or was brought up, with the image of preparing for a career in medicine as a solo family practitioner, as my father had by then become. Though I had conduct difficulties at times, which brought my mother to school periodically during my elementary school years for conferences with the teacher, I was always a sterling student and took this naturally. At one point in my early high school years I expressed an interest in a career in architecture or engineering—I had engaged in very elaborate and imaginative constructions with building blocks during my childhood years— but my father gently dissuaded me. A genteel anti-Semitism was pervasive in the academic and business worlds of the 30s, and my father pointed to the reality of the solo practitioner physician as the one professional path that did not make one dependent on seeking employment in a firm or an institution. (Somehow the life of a lawyer never seemed a consideration; perhaps it seemed too closely linked to the world of business.) I was reading voraciously all through elementary school and high school, with sports involvement, mostly basketball, with handball and running a distant second. As with so many of my generation in those Depression years of the thirties, I was fired up with visions of Sinclair Lewis's *Arrowsmith* and Paul de Kruif's *Microbe Hunters*. That was the beginning of my preoccupation with the research ideal, its excitement and allure.

I graduated from DeWitt Clinton High School at 15-1/2 in 1936, having been skipped a grade—which was the custom then with bright students—a total of five times. At that point, my mother intervened in my life course more decisively than ever before. She and my father had always had a difficult and distant marriage. He was a very respected and even revered family doctor, also a politically conscious intellectual with a Socialist ideology, a dedicated Zionist, and a secular Hebrew scholar, at home in the medieval texts of Maimonides and Judah Halevi and Ibn-Gabirol. On the High Holy Days he would assert his early religious upbringing and attend orthodox services, asking me to go along with him. A passion my father and I shared was for chess, and through my early high-school years we had a ritual chess game at the start of each evening. We stopped, through mutual loss of interest, at the point that I began to beat him fairly regularly. We didn't talk about this stopping and at the time I didn't understand it. But with all that, my father was a poor businessman who had difficulty providing adequately for a middle-class family during the Depression years, and this was the bane of my mother's existence, because she felt the full burden of stretching the household finances and ensuring that his patients' bills were being adequately attended to.

My mother had been a textile designer during my earliest years, and I have memories of being taken as a child to the shop while she worked, sketching the design on the stretched silk fabric which other women then filled in with the indicated colors. My mother left this work when my brother was born, when I was ten, and my persisting memories of that period are of the chore of wheeling and watching the baby carriage while my schoolmates were playing street games, tag, and ringelevio, and roller-skate hockey. After a time my mother again took up a multimedia art career, which she pursued for the rest of her life, painting in a variety of successive styles, making enamel tiles, and wood constructions, and cut-outs in the fashion of Matisse. In her later years she was represented by a gallery and sold modestly. She was one Jewish mother who did not aspire to a medical career for her son, but encouraged me into art lessons, charcoal and pastel figure drawings of nude models in a Saturday class run by a teacher from the Art Students League.

When I was graduating high school, she was the one who declared me too young to go to college and arranged for me to be out of school for a year and live with her bachelor brother, a restless and romantic adventurer who seemed to live just seven years in each locale. At that time he was a very successful pediatrician in Mexico City with affiliations at multiple hospitals serving the foreign colony, the American, the British, the French, and the German Hospitals. I was, at 15-1/2, barely into adolescence, having graduated in a class of 1250, graduating that many each semester from the then largest high school in the city (10,000 students), with me the third highest in the class of 1250 academically, but also the third shortest when we marched across the stage in size places to receive our diplomas.

My mother's intention for me in Mexico was that I would grow up (and I did return six inches taller), learn Spanish, and absorb an exotic culture, study art, and perhaps be deflected from medicine. I did take art lessons, painting still lifes and landscapes in water colors and oils, with an elderly art teacher, Solares, who was reputed to have been one of Diego Rivera's teachers, at the National Academy of San Carlos. I did enough to appreciate that my artistic talent was limited, and the winter in Mexico City was the end of my art career. My mother was faced with this disappointment upon my return home in the spring, but she had by that time turned her energies to my younger brother Immanuel, and enrolled him in a special school for professional actors. His dramatic career was also short-lived, but he did attain some professional roles, the most important being the child in Lillian Hellman's *Watch on the Rhine*, in which he toured with the professional road company on its circuit outside New York City. My mother accompanied him, and his schoolwork was done on the road and sent back regularly to the school, which had been set up for children in the performing arts, the Professional Children's School. After a time, he got out from under these performing art pressures to pursue a more usual college and academic career, and is now a very distinguished professor of sociology, currently president of the International Sociological Association.

My other activities in Mexico City were more successful. I learned enough Spanish to get along, partly under the pressure of Maria, my uncle's Indian housekeeper who knew no English, and partly under the tutelage of my uncle's mistress Alicia, a divorced woman with two small children. Her aristocratic lineage went back to the Conquistadors who came with Cortez, and her political connections were powerful, a cousin having been one of Mexico's recent presidents. She gave me regular Spanish lessons and introduced me to the heady world of the Mexican artistic luminaries, Orozco and Siqueiros and Covarrubias, as well as the exciting radical leftist and anti-American circles of LEAR (*Liga de Escritores y Artistas Revolucionarios*), the League of Revolutionary Writers and Artists. At one of their gatherings I heard a frenzied speech by Waldo Frank at which the packed audience burst into repeated thunderous applause with the repetition, in what seemed every other sentence, of the phrase *Yanqui imperialismo*. I also saw an enormous part of the country on trips with my uncle and Alicia, often shopping trips for handicrafts in distant cities for a Mexican handicraft shop they were planning to open the following year in New York—which they never did. I also learned to smoke in Mexico, at first surreptitiously.

Upon my return to New York after a year away, I did then enter college, firmly enrolled as a premedical student. I had applied to four or five colleges and my first choice was Harvard, which accepted me; but the scholarship I was offered was insufficient to cover the considerable extra expense of living away from home, so I went to my next choice, Columbia, where I could be a commuter student. This was now the height of the Depression, 1937, and my father's practice, like that of a goodly number of physicians in New York, was in real trouble, with many patients reduced to paying him with services or goods rather than money. It was my mother's tight management of the household budget and finances, together with some small student loans and the $100-a-year New York Regents' Scholarship that I obtained, that enabled my family to afford my college tuition—then $400 per year— and my other incidental expenses, books, and lunches, and subway fare.

Through my college years (1937–1941), my future professional career in medicine seemed well set in its preordained course. I took more than the proper sequence of premedical courses, going on in mathematics into differential and integral calculus, and chemistry into quantitative as well as qualitative analysis, and then colloidal chemistry and physical chemistry. The first two more general college years included, of course, forays into history and English literature and even philosophy, where I impressed several distinguished professors but resisted the lure of those discursive paths in favor of the life of the sciences, physics and chemistry and zoology. College is also where academic achievement—and the goal of access into medical school against the then existing tight quotas for Jewish students—became a consuming passion. I studied hard and compulsively and developed a cluster of neurotic compulsive symptoms, consisting of reading each college assignment twice, the first time rapidly to comprehend the overall picture, and the second time more deliberately in order to fasten it into memory for future exam-taking, all accompanied by quite exhaustive note taking. I became the center of a small circle of friends, all also premeds, who would gather in my home to study together prior to all important examinations, with me the driving, organizing force of the study group. My college grades were uniformly A's and in my sophomore year were mostly A-plus; I was clearly establishing myself at the top of my college class.

By the time I graduated from college my study compulsions had dwindled away, and when I entered my analysis years later they had long since disappeared from my life. In my last year in college, I met my wife Judy, through our memberships in our separate college chapters (mine at Columbia, hers at Hunter, both in New York City) of Avukah, the American Student Zionist Federation. This was sponsored by the mainstream Zionist

Organization of America and committed to the Zionist ideal, but in its politics it was radically left-wing Trotskyite and bitterly anti-Stalinist, and in its vision for the Palestine mandate under the British authority, it was dedicated to the conception of a binational Jewish-Arab state.

Coming to college graduation in the summer of 1941, I was the head of my class with an all-A average. My premed advisor, a laconic and acerbic chemistry professor, forbade my applying to more than three medical schools because "You can go wherever you want." Again Harvard (Medical School) and Columbia (College of Physicians and Surgeons) headed my list, and again, though I was selected by Harvard, the scholarship offer, though substantial, was not sufficient to cover all living expenses, and so I once again settled with Columbia, where I could continue as a commuter student. I was my college class valedictorian in June 1941, in the shadow of the World War then raging in Europe and but six months before the United States was itself precipitated into active belligerency by the Japanese attack on Pearl Harbor. My talk was sober, focussed on the onrush of the totalitarian idea and our endangered visions of democracy, social justice, and scientific progress. My premed advisor and mentor berated me for the talk because I had failed to call us immediately to arms.

I was in the midst of my freshman year in medical school, my eyes fastened on a future career in internal medicine, hopefully academically and research focussed, when Pearl Harbor was struck. In the first flush of military fervor that swept the nation, numbers of medical students around the country dropped out of school to enlist in the armed services. The military, dismayed by this threatened depletion of needed medical manpower, promptly responded by creating the Army Specialized Training Program (ASTP), and similarly for the navy, and then drafted all the medical students, except the physically unfit, into military service, with the assignment first to complete medical school, albeit on a shortened timetable. What had been four nine-month years with summer vacations became four consecutive nine-month years without vacation, so that our class that had entered in September 1941 would graduate in September 1944. This was to be followed by a nine-month internship and perhaps a nine-month residency period, and then active service as an army doctor. Being in uniform had the material advantage that the Army took over the tuition expense, relieving my family finally of this burden, while I could continue to live at home and commute to school.

During that whole time in medical school, the conviction that my future lay in internal medicine strengthened. The major excitement was the advent of penicillin, and then of subsequent antibiotics, which were replacing the sulfa drugs as far more effective—and safer—agents in the struggle against infectious diseases at home and infected war wounds on the battlefields abroad. Our psychiatric teaching in medical school was in the Kraepelinian tradition and uninspiring. Only one classmate, Kenneth Calder, was fixed at the time on a psychiatric (and psychoanalytic) career, though a number of us came to psychiatry and psychoanalysis by a more circuitous route later.

Upon graduation from medical school, I had a rotating nine-month internship at Mount Sinai Hospital in New York, then the most prestigious, and also the most competitive, of the network of Jewish community hospitals around the country. This was followed by a second nine-month residency period in internal medicine, also at Mount Sinai, before being called to active military service. Actually, in my last year in medical school, I had moved to Mount Sinai where, in exchange for room, board, and laundry, I had a night-time job doing emergency lab work (blood counts, urinalyses, pneumococcal typings for treatment of pneumonia with antiserum, electrocardiograms, and fluoroscopies) while going to school by day.

I was caught up during that whole period at Mount Sinai—my year doing lab work, the internship, the medical residency—by the frenetic intensity of its medical culture and the charisma of its Chief of Medicine, I. Snapper, a world-famed Dutch physician. He had been captured by the Japanese when they invaded Beijing, where he had been Chairman of the Department of Medicine at Peking Union Medical College, and was exchanged for some Japanese prisoners at the beginning of World War II, after which he had come to New York and Mount Sinai. He upheld a high ideal of clinical bedside medicine, and clinical research in medicine, and a do-it-yourself credo for his house staff who were not to call on hematology or radiology or electrocardiography for diagnostic help, or for help with procedures like sternal marrow aspirations, liver biopsies, fluoroscopies, electrocardiograms. It was demanding and exhausting, but was also formative of high morale and a confident arrogance that we residents were an elite at the very cutting edge of modern internal medicine and competent in all its diverse areas. Psychiatry simply did not exist as a separate hospital service at that time (1944 to 1946); psychiatrists were barely visible, either as attending physicians attached to the neurology service or as consultants on call to the medical and surgical services.

My active military service began in April 1946 with the war recently over. After a month as a medical officer at Edgewood Arsenal, Maryland, the Army's major research chemical warfare center, and then another month at Brooke Army Medical Center in San Antonio, Texas, the Army's special training arena for medical officers, I was assigned to Madigan General Hospital at Fort Lewis, Washington (near Tacoma and Seattle), an encampment that had been a major jumping-off point for troops headed for the Pacific Theatre and still holding, in this immediate postwar period, 100,000 soldiers. At Madigan I ran an infectious disease ward that was always busy and an electrocardiography lab; one of my friends there, a fellow medical officer, Harvey Powelson, was assigned to the dermatology and venereal disease service, where he became intrigued by the constant recidivism of soldiers infected by gonorrhea over and over despite the barrage of propaganda films they were repeatedly exposed to, pointing out readily available—but clearly not used—preventive measures. This prompted Harvey into psychiatry and psychoanalysis after his release from the Army, but at the time he and I only shared the insights about behaviors and motivations that he gathered in his amateurish psychiatric interviewing.

I was released by the Army in January 1948 and returned to the chief medical residency that Snapper had promised would be held for me, whenever I came back from the Army. That year was the culmination of my career in internal medicine. The work again was extremely demanding but again just as rewarding, with the same constant twin ideals of clinical medicine and clinical research. The chief residency year was structured to be 11 months of ward service with the last month off to write up, for publication, the papers based on the unusual clinical cases or events that had been designated by Snapper for that purpose over the year. Actually, even earlier (1946) I had been chief author of a publication in the *Journal of Infectious Diseases*, from a laboratory investigation during my internship year of the relationship of pleuropneumonia-like organisms (between bacteria and viruses in size) to Reiter's disease, rheumatoid arthritis, and ulcerative colitis, an investigation carried out in the evenings with two fellow rotating interns at Mount Sinai. That had been my first piece of laboratory investigation. The hectic library work and writing of my final residency month yielded six further papers published in clinical medical journals, and this helped instill a lifelong commitment to scholarly writing as an obligation of a proper professional and scientific career.

That final residency year in internal medicine was also, of course, the period of lasting career choice beyond the residency education. What I saw among the staff physicians at Mount Sinai was not encouraging. Except for the full-time department chiefs, like Snapper in medicine, they were all earning livelihoods in private practice, which seemed not very exciting or challenging from my vantage point, while striving to carve out enough hours to devote to their hospital commitments, to clinical service and clinical research, where all the cutting-edge action seemed to be. Since Mount Sinai was not then a primary teaching hospital for a medical school, I saw no direct route to a full-time academic medical career. I wrote to one of my two co-authors on my first laboratory-based paper, who had not had to serve in the military and was now a research assistant in Edwin Cohn's physical chemistry laboratory at Harvard Medical School, the laboratory which had pioneered all the blood and plasma fractionation work that had been so important to military medicine during the war years. My friend proposed me to Dr. Cohn, who offered to sponsor me for a two-year Fellowship from the recently established National Institutes of Health, to be spent in his laboratory. I secured the Fellowship offer and was uneasily planning for the two following years of laboratory study in Boston—uneasily because it would also remove me totally from clinical contact and from my clinical knowledge base in medicine.

At the same time I was looking questioningly at my wife Judy's arena of activity. We had been married in 1947 during my army service, and she was then a graduate of the New York School of Social Work (later the Columbia University School of Social Work). She had a position as caseworker with Emergency Jewish Children's Aid, aiding the resettlement of Jewish war orphans from the Displaced Persons camps of postwar Europe. Her small collection of books included Fenichel's recently published (1945) *The Psychoanalytic Theory of Neurosis.* Its pages offered exciting glimpses of a completely different range of clinical phenomena, the disorders of mental life. I began to think of psychiatry, meaning for me psychoanalysis, as that branch of medicine where, oppositely from internal medicine, the life of clinical work and experience and the life of scholarly investigation and "research" could be combined in the selfsame activity. At the time I was not explicitly aware of Freud's dictum that in psychoanalysis the road to (research) understanding and the road to (clinical) cure were one and the same, but something like that notion served for me as the adequate rationale for my rather abrupt decision to withdraw from the pending NIH Fellowship at Harvard, and a biomedical future, and to opt instead for full residency training in psychiatry. I figured that whatever the "deeper" or "truer" meanings of my career change might be, I would discover those in my future analysis. This decision would of course extend my student days still further, perhaps an additional three years, but I was then not yet 28 years old, though with almost four and a half years of internal medical training and experience after medical school.[1]

At that point, therefore, I cast about for the best psychiatric residency training I could find. I was attracted by a brochure I read of the new program created at The Austen Riggs Center in Stockbridge, Massachusetts, by

---

[1] I of course took for granted in all this that psychiatric residency training would lead directly into psychoanalytic training, that psychoanalysis and psychoanalytic psychotherapy comprised almost the totality of psychiatry at the time, except for the care of the chronically and severely mentally ill, segregated away in large state hospitals, ministered to by a handful of hospital psychiatrists (old-fashioned alienists), to be avoided by the psychoanalytically interested and trained. That indeed was both the perception and the reality of psychiatry in those days, before the growth of modern-day neurobiology and its applications in clinical psychopharmacology, and before also the advent of the community mental health movement, or the systematic growth of alternative treatment models, the behavior modification techniques, systems theory approaches, group and family therapies, brief therapy and crisis intervention, self-help movements, or the development of such subspecialty areas as addiction and drug abuse, forensic psychiatry, geriatric psychiatry, and consultation-liaison services, all of which have made for the diversity and complexity of present-day psychiatry.

Robert Knight and those who had come with him just a year earlier from The Menninger Foundation. I received a response to my inquiry that Riggs was only accepting applicants for a fourth and fifth year psychotherapy fellowship, for those beyond the basic three-year psychiatric residency. I wrote to the one person I knew in psychiatric residency training, my best friend from internship days and the co-leader with me and a third colleague of a successful house staff strike against the hospital, which had secured us improved working conditions plus basic internship and residency stipends of $25 a month for interns and $50 for residents. My co-ringleader was David Rubinfine, who was then in Topeka, Kansas, at the Veterans Administration Hospital and The Menninger School of Psychiatry. I wrote and asked, "How is it, Dave?" And he wrote back, "Great. Come."

Snapper was quite dismayed by my decision for a career turn, which he felt to be such a betrayal of medicine, and when he granted me permission to take the several days to go to Topeka for interviews, he admonished me: "You may be very lucky; they may turn you down." They accepted me, however, and during the balance of the year, completing my medical residency, Snapper would at intervals interject into discussions at medical rounds, "Next year, when you are in Toledo." I would at first correct him, stating, "Topeka, not Toledo." It didn't help. By that time I had also heard that my friend and psychiatric guide, David Rubinfine, who had so enthusiastically drawn me to Topeka, would himself be back in New York when I arrived there.

There was one other complication: My medical residency in New York was ending December 30, 1948, and my psychiatric residency was to start in Topeka on July 1, 1949, leaving a six-month unfilled hiatus. I therefore went to visit M. Ralph Kaufman, a senior psychoanalyst recruited from Boston to head the department of psychiatry with both an inpatient and outpatient service, which had been established at Mount Sinai Hospital while I had been away for military service. There were four residents on the 20-bed psychiatric inpatient unit, but Kaufman willingly accepted my offer to be a fifth, on an unsalaried basis, for the six-month interim.

At the time the psychiatric service was dedicated exclusively to so-called psychosomatic patients; there were no direct admissions from the outside, but rather all the patients had to come on referral from the medical and surgical wards where they had been hospitalized because of the severity of their medical or surgical condition. They were transferred to psychiatry after psychiatric consultation because of the role emotional components were felt to play in the aggravation or maintenance of their somatic illness. While on the psychiatric ward, they were monitored daily by their own internist or surgeon, while at the same time participating in psychotherapy five times a week with a psychiatric resident, intensively supervised by the senior psychiatric attending staff. The patients had such illnesses as intractable peptic ulcers requiring continuous intragastric drip, ulcerative colitis with daily spiking fevers and multiple daily bloody stools, status asthmaticus, uncontrolled thyrotoxicosis with thyroid storms, brittle diabetics in crisis, and so forth. This was altogether an extremely somatically ill and difficult patient population. Snapper had been wont, uncharitably and cruelly, to call the psychiatric ward the sewer of the hospital, where unwanted patients could be flushed down.

From my first day in psychiatry I had four inpatients, each of whom I was to see an hour each day, with three hours of intensive supervision to help manage my 20-hour psychotherapy case load. When I expressed my bewilderment the first day to the chief resident, George Naumburg, he grabbed my list and pointed to one of the names and said, "See that one first. She's a real chatterbox and you won't have to say anything!" But somehow this sink-or-swim atmosphere worked. My case supervisor was Sydney Margolin, a very charismatic and idealized mentor, whose decisive supervision held me up and enabled me to do much better psychotherapy than I was actually capable of doing. When the patients' medical conditions stabilized to the point where their managing physician felt they could be discharged from the hospital, the psychiatric resident in most instances continued with them as outpatients who came to the clinic usually for only a once-weekly session on one of the two afternoons of outpatient work that each resident did. One thus had the interesting experience of comparing and contrasting the psychic material of the five-times-weekly inpatient therapy, so often focussed on dream, fantasy, and otherwise very regressive material in these very ill and usually bed-ridden patients, with the subsequent life-event-oriented material when the patient made the abrupt transition to once-weekly outpatient therapy.

In addition to this intensive supervised psychotherapy, life on the ward also included working up new patients and managing their hospital life under the general supervision of Harry Weinstock, a very kindly and urbane senior analyst, the epitome of our vision of the Park Avenue psychoanalyst, and also a weekly case conference in the "Chief's" office, where Moe Kaufman presided and the entire attending staff on the ward, as well as the whole resident body, gathered. After presentation of the case by the assigned resident, everyone in the room was called on in turn by Kaufman in the exact order of increasing seniority. Each person felt impelled to have something to contribute to the discourse that had not yet been said by any of the more junior ones who had spoken before. It seemed an ordeal by fire.

The Psychosomatic Ward was also my first contact with psychiatric and psychoanalytic research. Charles Fisher was one of the "young Attendings" embarked upon his innovative experimental investigations of suggestion, subliminal perception, the Poetzl phenomenon, and the sleep-dream studies involving combined REM-state observations and dream inquiries after waking. Chuck delighted to talk of this and opened exciting vistas of brain-mind correlative studies. Sydney Margolin, my supervisor, was conducting an ongoing psychoanalysis with a gastric fistula patient undergoing concomitant studies of gastric physiology, thus enabling the correlation of the ongoing unconscious mental processes with the varying responses of the several gastric functions (acidity, vascularity, motility) to varieties of physiologic stimuli. I knew this patient, who was periodically briefly hospitalized, and I assisted then in her hospital management.

Besides these first excitements about what psychoanalytic research (or at least, psychoanalytic psychosomatic research) could be, the psychiatric service at Mount Sinai also brought me my first awareness of the heated issue of nonmedical therapy. Kaufman was among those high in the councils of the American Psychoanalytic Association most committed to the conception that psychoanalysis was entirely a therapeutic specialty within medicine, and most adamant against psychologists or other nonphysicians assuming therapeutic roles. His very gifted chief psychologist on the service, Fred Brown, seemed committed to the same position, and Fred's much-sought-after teaching comprised the roles of the psychologist as diagnostician (the projective psychological test battery), as investigator, and as teacher, but never as therapist. From him the psychiatric residents learned the elements of psychological diagnostic testing, especially Rorschach and TAT interpretation.

The six months on the Mount Sinai Psychosomatic Service gradually reshaped my career expectations. I only needed to go to the Menninger School of Psychiatry in Topeka for the one year of obligatory psychiatric closed ward service that was unavailable at Mount Sinai. I could then return to Mount Sinai to complete the balance of my required psychiatric residency time on the psychiatric service there and simultaneously enter psychoanalytic training at the New York Psychoanalytic Institute. Kaufman, Weinstock, and Margolin all offered to write strong letters in support of my application. The vistas for psychoanalytic research opened up by Fisher and Margolin beckoned invitingly, and Margolin offered me a part-time training position as a psychiatric evaluator and psychophysiological experimenter in his fistula research program. This would carry some fellowship stipend. Weinstock offered me a monthly subvention, as a long-term interest-free loan, to be repaid as I was able, once established in private practice, plus, as long as I needed it, the use of his Park Avenue office, rent-free, when he was not using it himself. Kaufman would use his good offices to help secure for me a non-interest-bearing loan from the Blanche and Frank Wolf Foundation to cover the cost of my ongoing psychoanalysis, again to be repaid when I felt able. This Foundation was managed by a New York attorney, Edward Greenbaum, who, I gathered, was both a friend of Moe Kaufman's and a member of the Board of Trustees of the Mount Sinai Hospital.

As it turned out, during this period of excited future planning, there was one near deflection that could have altered my life completely. The new State of Israel was in the midst of its desperate war of independence. A high-ranking Israeli medical officer was visiting in New York, recruiting needed medical personnel for the new nation and its fighting forces. He came to Mount Sinai and I made an appointment to see him and, pulled by old yearnings, talked of going to Israel to throw in my lot with the new nation. I said that I thought I could go quite shortly. He asked where I stood in my psychiatric specialty training. I indicated that I was at the start of a training process that would take me to Topeka for a year and then, most likely, back to New York. He said that it was far better than the residency training that could be offered to me in Israel in the foreseeable future, and that I could serve the new country better if I remained the several years of residency in America and could come then as a fully trained psychiatrist. I acquiesced in his logic, and the moment had passed; I returned to my immediate career planning in the heady Mount Sinai atmosphere, with a glowing present and future.

It was with these high anticipations that Judy and I set out for Topeka in the last week of June 1949, all our worldly possession, our clothes, some books, some records, packed in our car. We arrived just before July 1, in the full heat of a Kansas summer, staring at a billboard on the outskirts of town which proudly proclaimed: "Welcome to Topeka, Kansas, the Psychiatric Capital of the World." Topeka and The Menninger School of Psychiatry were indeed a new and different world. I arrived as one of 100 psychiatric residents when only 800 were being trained in the entire nation, one in eight in that small unlikely midwestern town on the prairie. Topeka, with its quiet residential streets arched by elm trees, its open backyards and doors where children roamed freely in and out of neighbors' houses, and its friendly shop clerks who knew all their customers by name and face, was a far cry from the big city urban America of New York. On one of my first days, jaywalking across the wide and expansive downtown main street, Kansas Avenue, a policeman took me gently by the arm, stating, "Sir, in Topeka, we walk *with* the lights." And he escorted me safely across the street. Yet, though the capital of what was in pre–Civil War days the free state known as "bloody Kansas," it was in 1949 still a Southern Jim Crow town, with all the racially segregated restrictions that that connoted, and the centerpiece later of Thurgood Marshall's strategy in the landmark *Brown v. Topeka Board of Education* case that overthrew the doctrine of "separate but equal" as discriminatory and unconstitutional. A member of the Brown family was a Menninger Foundation employee and she carried the sustained support of the entire Menninger community.

Established in this middle-American setting, and by 1949 the third largest industry in town—after a Goodyear Tire plant and the main yards and repair shops of the Atchison, Topeka, and Santa Fe Railway system—

The Menninger Foundation was the center of a linked psychiatric empire, the sprawling Veterans Administration (VA) Hospital, with 1100 of its 1200 beds designated as psychiatric (and the heart of the Menninger School of Psychiatry), plus the soon-to-be-taken-over 1000 bed Topeka State Hospital, plus lesser psychiatric outpatient facilities. Central was the huge and enormously prestigious psychiatric residency program, which had sprung full-blown just three years earlier from a residency of only four a year, under the combined manicky visions of Karl Menninger, an irrepressible impresario, and Arthur Marshall, one of the demobilized army doctors seeking a psychiatric training and career for himself. Marshall had come to the Menninger brothers as an army colonel, the aide de camp to General Hawley, who had been Chief Medical Officer in the European Theatre of Operations, and was now the civilian Chief Medical Officer of the VA medical system. The offer was that the Topeka army hospital would be turned into a neuropsychiatric VA hospital if the Menningers would agree to take responsibility for its intended psychiatric residency training program for up to 100. Thus the Menninger School of Psychiatry had been brought to instant birth. Prior to resigning his position with General Hawley and coming to Topeka to take his slot as a resident and staff member within this newly created School of Psychiatry, Arthur Marshall had spent a busy last month in the central VA Medical Office in Washington, commandeering all the equipment and supplies that this new Menninger-run VA psychiatric hospital could possibly need to be a state-of-the-art training center for this largest and most ambitious of psychiatric training programs.

Alongside the Menninger School of Psychiatry was the also just recently established Menninger School of Clinical Psychology, considerably smaller but at least equally high-flying and with high morale, that had been brought into being through a collaboration between David Rapaport, as the Menninger Foundation's chief psychologist and Director of Research, and the Department of Psychology at nearby Kansas University (in Lawrence). The academic course work (and the doctorate degree) were given in Lawrence, and all the clinical internship work was under Menninger auspices, and Rapaport's tutelage, in Topeka. Thrown into the mix also were a clinical training program for psychiatric social workers and another for pastoral counselors, psychologically interested clergy who came to Topeka for a year of intensive, supervised experience with counseling issues.

The equally swiftly put-together faculty that was to manage this array of training programs consisted mainly of demobilized military medical officers, who like Marshall had been co-opted into military psychiatric service on the basis of 90-day crash courses. Now, with this intense experience of military psychiatric first-aid behind them, they sought proper training and diversified clinical experience, in the combined quasi-residency, full-staff positions that marked them as learners who were at the same time most enthusiastic teachers. They in turn were presided over by the small cadre of training analysts, the majority of them European refugee analysts recruited by Karl Menninger to the improbable (for them) Kansas locale, a town that both welcomed them and puzzled over them. The overall atmosphere within this setting was one of egalitarian ferment, and in seminar and clinical contexts, in which members of different disciplines were thrown together around shared theoretical and clinical concerns, it was the cogency of ideas rather than of disciplines that prevailed. This was a far cry from the rigidly hierarchical Mount Sinai setting in New York, with its exclusive reservation of the therapeutic activity for the medically qualified. Over the whole, the ebullient Karl Menninger presided, alternately genial and irascible, but always challenging and provocative, imbued simultaneously with an old-fashioned conservative morality, and a free-wheeling and radical search for new ideas and new twists to old ideas. He was Dr. Karl to everyone, and the not-always-benevolent presiding tyrant over his vast psychiatric domain.

In this setting I was a new psychiatric resident and Judy obtained an excellent job as a social worker and child therapist at the Menninger Clinic children's division, the Southard School, with intensive supervision by two of the training analysts, Rudi Ekstein and Nelly Tibout, and the beginning of her own training in child analytic work. It was there that her own first professional papers were written in collaboration with Ekstein. These centered on the clinical and countertransference issues of working with very disturbed borderline and over-the-border children, and were published in *The Psychoanalytic Study of the Child*. Arthur Marshall, to whom I had been sent by David Rubinfine, took me in as a pater familias (he was close to a decade older) and undertook to co-opt me into his vision of the Topeka of socially responsible psychoanalysis, spreading this healing mental-health doctrine to the beleaguered veteran population in the VA Hospital and VA Mental Hygiene Clinic, and to the unfortunate, long-neglected patients in the Topeka State Hospital. (He had a fine disdain for what he considered the rich neurotics who were private patients in the Menninger Clinic itself.) Arthur urged unremittingly that I apply for psychoanalytic training at the Topeka Institute and throw in my lot with the ever-enlarging prospects of our Menninger Camelot. This picture seemed increasingly attractive, both in terms of Judy's unfolding training and career opportunities and the vistas of psychiatric and psychoanalytic combined clinical-educational-research activity that seemed to be opening in front of me.

I bit this bullet by applying for psychoanalytic training at *both* the New York and the Topeka Institutes, with no clear vision of which I preferred. So fate decided for me. Despite strong letters of recommendation to New York from Kaufman, Weinstock, and Margolin (all senior figures there), and what I thought were good interviews, the New York Institute turned me down. When my disappointed mentors in New York inquired into this on my behalf, it was made clear that the Admissions Committee had felt that I was "a young man too much in a hurry," that I had had a life of unbroken educational and career successes, and that the chastening effect of being rejected on a first application and having to reapply could be helpful to my emotional maturation.[2] The Topeka Institute had meanwhile accepted me forthwith, and so the die was cast for a Topeka career, earlier planned to be for one year, that was to last seventeen years (1949–1966). Of course my New York sponsors accepted my decision to enter psychoanalytic training in Topeka rather than waiting to reapply to New York a year later, only expressing the hope that I would still return to New York for the planned career there when I had graduated from the Topeka Institute. In the meantime, Moe Kaufman assured me that the grant from the Blanche and Frank Wolf Foundation of a long-term interest-free loan to underwrite my training analysis expenses would follow me to Topeka. This grant, which I eventually repaid together with an additional gift to the Foundation to enlarge its coffers a little, made possible a more economically comfortable training period in Topeka, while living on the then very low Menninger salaries—no comparison with the remuneration of a private practice in New York.

My research career began while this analytic training decision was crystallizing, during my residency period at the Topeka VA Hospital when I, together with psychologist John Chotlos, created a comparative treatment study of hospitalized alcoholic patients. This consisted of three specific intervention modalities: antabuse (then a new experimental drug, available only on protocols for clinical trials research), conditioned-reflex aversion therapy (then a standard therapeutic approach to alcoholism in psychiatric sanatoria), and group hypnotherapy (an interest in the Menninger School of Psychiatry), with a fourth "control group" that had only the same general hospital management and psychotherapeutic help that was common to all the groups. The project was actually born out of despair at the treatment courses and outcomes in the then "routine" hospital and psychotherapeutic

---

[2] Since then I have been honored several times by the New York Psychoanalytic. I received the Heinz Hartmann Award of the New York Psychoanalytic Institute for 1968 for Outstanding Contribution to Psychoanalysis, for the paper "The Psychotherapy Research Project of The Menninger Foundation." David Kairys, the chair of the Award Committee, informed me that this was the last occasion, shortly prior to his death, that Heinz Hartmann had personally participated in the award decision. In 1985 I gave the Freud Anniversary Lecture at the New York Psychoanalytic Institute, titled "Psychoanalysis as a Science: A Response to the New Challenges" (Wallerstein, 1986b). In 1994 I gave the Charles Fisher Memorial Lecture at the New York Psychoanalytic Society, titled "Psychotherapy Research and Its Implications for a Theory of Therapeutic Change: A Forty-Year Overview" (Wallerstein, 1994).

management regimen of these patients. The patients were randomly assigned to the four groups, and with a reasonable spread of the different kinds of alcoholic patients in terms of their overall character organization and level of functioning into each of the four treatment modalities, we could see which, if any, of the four modalities did better with the patients, including into a planned substantial follow-up period. We could also see which did differentially better with which *kinds* of alcoholic patients, and then draw what conclusions we could about the psychological fit between the meaning of the treatment modality to the patient (for example, the very unpleasant aversive conditioned-reflex treatment being regularly conceptualized as a punishment) and the character propensities of the patient (for example, the self-punitive and self-defeating masochistic patient). The aversion treatment was in fact more successful with strongly masochistic alcoholic patients than it was with any other character organization! This project was published (with collaborators) in book form, my first book, *Hospital Treatment of Alcoholism: A Comparative, Experimental Study* (Wallerstein et al., 1957).

It was because of this study of alcoholism, in which I had been the principal investigator, that my friend George Klein,[3] an experimentally-minded psychoanalytic psychologist and a leading proponent of the New Look perception and cognition research during the 1950s and himself a core figure in the Research Department of The Menninger Foundation, called me to the attention of Gardner Murphy, the recently arrived Director of Research. Gardner was seeking a research-minded psychiatrist to come into his Department with a central commitment to the development of a clinical research program that would link the Department more closely to the professional concerns of the large clinical community (the majority psychiatrists) treating the Menninger Clinic patients. The Research Department's chief strengths to that point had been experimental (perception, cognition), personality (projective psychological testing in the Rapaport tradition), evaluation (selection for psychiatry and other mental health professions), and developmental (chiefly infancy, in the tradition started by Sybille Escalona and Mary Leitch, and now with new ventures into the childhood and grade-school years initiated by Lois Murphy).

Gardner met with me and offered me a position at The Menninger Foundation, half-time in the Research Department and half in Outpatient

---

[3] I had a circle of close friends within the Menninger psychologist group, all former Rapaport students (though Rapaport himself had left to go with Robert Knight to the Austen Riggs Center in 1947, before I came to Topeka). Besides Klein, these included, in those early days, Herbert Schlesinger, Philip Holzman, Gerald Ehrenreich, Martin Mayman, Robert Holt, and Lester Luborsky. On the basis of these friendship and professional ties, I shared, with Merton Gill before me, the distinction of being accorded honorary membership in the Topeka Psychological Society.

Clinical Services. It was 1953, and I was a staff psychiatrist on the Psychosomatic Service (actually with the title of Chief) at the Topeka VA Hospital—a position I had been offered on the basis of my combined residency training in both internal medicine and psychiatry—and barely two years beyond my psychiatric residency period itself, having just recently started my psychoanalytic training. I had started analysis with Robert H. Jokl, an elderly Viennese refugee from the circle around Freud and himself analyzed by Freud. Parenthetically, my status as a "grandson" was brought to me on occasion when Jokl would respond to my associations with the statement, "At a time like this the Professor would say to me . . ." and I would receive one of Freud's interpretations, which I was not always sure fitted me. When Jokl left Topeka to go to Los Angeles, I was at another choice-point, but in view of the very gratifying work situations that both Judy and I had in Topeka, I chose not to move with him and pursue my career in Los Angeles (as any number of analysands did in Topeka when their analysts left). I decided to remain and to complete my analysis with Nelly Tibout, an immigrant analyst from Holland. I was in analysis with her when I received Gardner's offer. I had realistic misgivings and my own considerable trepidation about accepting a position as a designated researcher with no formal research training or knowledge, but Gardner felt that my work in the alcoholism project had established my research credentials to his satisfaction. My new job would start January 1, 1954.

When I started at The Menninger Foundation, I discovered that Gardner had given me a title (Assistant Director of Research), along with the charge to foster and carry out research on and within the Clinical Services, which were, after all, the chief raison d'etre of the entire institution. In the first capacity, as Assistant Director to him, I had regular meetings with Gardner, at least once a week and often more, during which he earnestly solicited my views on a great range of research issues, both scientific and political; these, to my surprise, he most often acted on directly. I quickly learned to temper my off-the-top-of-the-head responses into more carefully reasoned and modulated statements.

In relation to my charge to initiate a clinical research program, I met with Lewis Robbins, the Director of Clinical Services, and we forged a partnership to build a research study of the enterprise that was the heart of the clinical activity of The Menninger Foundation, long-term psychoanalytic therapy. We started with the intent to investigate two simple, though not simple-minded questions: What changes take place in (analytic) therapy? (the traditional research outcome question). And how do those changes come about, or how are they brought about, through the interaction of what factors in the patient, in the therapy and the therapist, and in the patient's evolving life situation? (the traditional research process question). There had been for the several prior years a clinical research study group, spearheaded by Paul Bergman, that had gradually evolved one instrument, the 100-point, anchored, seven-dimensional, Health-Sickness Rating Scale (HSRS) to assess overall cross-sectional level of psychological functioning, the progenitor from which the GAS, probably the most widely used psychotherapy outcome measure, was subsequently adapted. Lester Luborsky, the principal architect of the HSRS within that group, joined with Robbins and me, and we had the good fortune to recruit Helen Sargent from the Topeka VA Hospital as the fourth member of our planning and steering group. Helen, a Carl Rogers-trained academic psychologist, though not psychoanalytically grounded, had a fine feel for the psychodynamic clinical enterprise, and also an extraordinary sense for the philosophy of science issues involved in providing the conceptual framework and the operational conditions that would allow a fruitful melding of the rigors of proper research method with the suppleness of clinical problems. With her began my own education in the philosophy and the methodology of clinical research, though not at all in the specifics of experimental or statistical method.

The story of the research program we created, the Psychotherapy Research Project (PRP) of The Menninger Foundation, which evolved into a 30-year-long project following the treatment careers and the subsequent life careers of a total of 42 patients, half treated with psychoanalysis and half with the range of expressive and supportive psychoanalytically based psychotherapies, has been told by me and by others in a variety of contexts and will not be repeated here. My own overall accounting of the full 30-year span of the research program has been written from a clinical perspective in my book *Forty-Two Lives in Treatment: A Study of Psychoanalysis and Psychotherapy* (1986a) and has been summarized from various angles in several publications (Wallerstein, 1977, 1988, 1989). Altogether, six books and some 70 articles have appeared from the project, involving some 20 different authors. The project marked my own somewhat serendipitous evolution into a recognized psychotherapy researcher, through on-the-job training in my role as principal investigator of this 20-person enterprise. Over a dozen-year span of active following and data gathering on these treatment courses and outcomes, I managed a budget I had garnered of about one million dollars of research support (in 1950s dollars). This was all combined with the good fortune of the collective talents of the group and the clinical-research wisdom of our several consultants. Through all of this I absorbed a reasonable state-of-the-art grasp of the then nascent field of psychodynamic therapy research. The project published regularly and frequently, starting in 1956,[4] and quickly became the most prominent—and ambitious—psychoanalytic therapy research program in the nation.

---

[4] The 68-item PRP bibliography through 1986 is listed in Appendix IV of *Forty-Two Lives in Treatment* (1986a, pp. 756–760).

From there my research credentials grew. Our project was invited to participate in all three major conferences on Research in Psychotherapy sponsored by the American Psychological Association, in Washington, D.C., in 1958 (Rubinstein and Parloff, 1959), in Chapel Hill in 1961 (Strupp and Luborsky, 1962), and in Chicago in 1966 (Shlien, 1968), conferences that significantly shaped the defining parameters of this crystallizing field of research activity. I presented papers at two of those conferences, the first and the third, and others of our group at the first and second. I was also invited, in 1958, to join the very influential Group for the Advancement of Psychiatry (GAP), the young Turks' organization started by William Menninger just after the war, to infuse progressive and psychoanalytic ideas into psychiatry, and to join its Committee on Research, of which I became Chairman two years later. I continued this through the publication, under my chairmanship, of its Report No. 63, *Psychiatric Research and the Assessment of Change* (1966a), at which point other national commitments I had in the meanwhile assumed, mostly with the American Psychoanalytic Association, led to my going on inactive status with GAP.

All this seemed to make logical, upon my graduation from the Topeka Institute for Psychoanalysis in 1958 and my being elected to membership in the American Psychoanalytic Association in 1960, after the then-stipulated two-year wait, that I would be immediately invited to membership on one of the Board on Professional Standards' committees, the Committee on Training for Research, which is where my life story first intersected actively with the then half-century (1910–1960) scientific and political issue of lay analysis. The Committee was established by the American in 1956 as the first breach in the then almost 20-year-old exclusionary rule (1938–1956) barring nonphysicians from psychoanalytic training within the Institutes of the American; it was to be the national gateway to the approval for clinical training in psychoanalysis of a very limited number of gifted academic researchers whose scholarly and research activity was relevant to psychoanalysis and would be enhanced by full psychoanalytic training and knowledge. I came to this task out of my own lifetime of formative influences that molded me into a medical career, first in internal medicine and then psychiatry, as the gateway to psychoanalysis; out of the exclusively medical psychoanalytic world of Mount Sinai Hospital where, however, I first glimpsed the possibility of an intellectually challenging and gratifying career line bringing clinical and research interests into the same compass; and out of the far more egalitarian psychoanalytic world of The Menninger Foundation, where my own clinical and research activities were fostered and grew and had become, by 1960, nationally recognized.

Training for Research
The First Crack in the Door

The 1938 American ban on any training of nonmedical analysts was never as absolute as it was generally understood to be. Frederic Levine (1989), in citing the three statements published in the *Bulletin of the American Psychoanalytic Association* in 1938, quoted from the third one, "Resolution Against the Future Training of Laymen for the Therapeutic Use of Psychoanalysis": "henceforth they will not admit into training for the therapeutic practice of psychoanalysis anyone who is not a physician"; but he followed this immediately, quoting from the same brief document, that nonetheless, "each institute remains free to train laymen for the use of psychoanalysis not for therapeutic purposes, but for research and investigation in such non-medical fields as anthropology, sociology, criminology, psychology, education, etc." (Levine, 1989, p. 7). This was quite in keeping with the way that Martin Bergmann (1988), in an historical account of this controversy, described the American's attitude during these early years toward those distinguished lay analyst refugees from Europe, trained before 1938, who were admitted to the American's ranks, like Ernst Kris or Hanns Sachs; that their analytic work in America should be strictly limited to conducting the training analyses of candidates and to teaching Institute courses. (This was, of course, the kind of offer also made at the time to Theodor Reik, which was spurned.)

The overall American attitude toward the training of lay analysts was, however, so hostile in the first two decades after the passage of the 1938 resolution that this "window of possibility" for some kind of nonmedical training was for the most part ignored by the affiliated Institutes of the American. There were two notable exceptions, however. The Boston Institute, with so many links into the Harvard University community, undertook the partial psychoanalytic training—meaning the personal analysis with a training analyst and the sequence of theoretical and even clinical seminars, but no supervised analytic treatments—of a significant number of distinguished Harvard scholars, mostly under the influence of Talcott Parsons and Robert W. White and mostly from the then recently established Department of Social Relations (an amalgam of anthropology, sociology, and social psychology). None of these individuals, however, became analytic practitioners, and their partial training, though quite open, was uncontested, and mostly unremarked.

The other institute that undertook to train nonmedical candidates, Topeka, was much more counter to the spirit of the 1938 Resolution, though it strained to stay legalistically within the parameters laid down by the American. This early Topeka history was detailed in a report prepared many years later by Herbert Schlesinger (1961) for presentation to the then recently established Committee on Training for Research of the American's Board on Professional Standards. The first of these nonmedical candidates was Margaret Brenman, who started in analytic training in 1943, just five years after the laying down of the 1938 exclusionary rule, ostensibly for research purposes—to facilitate her psychoanalytic research on hypnosis—but with the intention to make it full clinical psychoanalytic training. Brenman informed me (personal communication) that it was David Rapaport, whose research assistant she was at the time, who persuaded Karl Menninger to get the Topeka Institute for Psychoanalysis to admit her as a candidate for full training without undertaking to clear this in any way with the American.

Schlesinger, in his 1961 report, indicated that between 1947 and 1949, four other nonphysicians (he, Gerald Ehrenreich, Philip Holzman, and Lester Luborsky), all clinical psychologists, were taken into full analytic training. In order to keep within the letter of the American's exclusionary rule, it was understood (stipulated?) that all training, including the supervised psychoanalytic work, would have to be done within The Menninger Foundation clinical setting, that is, a medical clinic that undertook overall medical responsibility for all the patients treated by its staff. The training analysts for these nonmedical candidates were Rudolf Ekstein from Vienna, with a patchwork of unofficial training himself, assigned to the first cluster, and later Ishak Ramzy, an Egyptian trained at the London Institute, assigned to subsequently accepted nonmedical candidates. Both were psychologists trained after the 1938 cut-off date, and were therefore not recognized officially by the American. But since they were staff members of The Menninger Foundation, they were exempt from the official state licensure requirements that would have applied if they had been self-employed private practitioners. (The Menninger Foundation was reluctant to have the regular medical candidates analyzed by Ekstein and Ramzy in those early years, lest that create difficulties when those medical candidates later applied for certification of their training and admission to the American. This would not, of course, be an issue with the nonmedical candidates because at that time they were simply not eligible for membership in the American, no matter what status they were accorded locally by the Topeka Psychoanalytic Society.) In 1954, this arrangement in Topeka was actually formalized as the Special Student Training Program.

Lester Luborsky has furnished me with the full documentation of how he became one of those who obtained clinical psychoanalytic training in this way at the Topeka Institute. Luborsky received his doctorate in clinical psychology from Duke in 1943 and then went for his first academic position to the University of Illinois in Champaign-Urbana. In 1945 he started seriously seeking psychoanalytic training. An exchange of letters at that time with John Dollard at the Yale Institute of Human Relations was not very encouraging about possibilities in New England. In 1947 there was a further exchange of letters, this with J. C. Flugel in London, who had analyzed Luborsky's mentor at Duke and Illinois, Raymond Cattell. Cattell recommended Luborsky to Flugel, who accepted him for analysis in London, but John Bowlby, the Secretary of the Training Committee at the London Institute, wrote to Flugel on July 31, 1947, rejecting the training application. The letter, which dealt with a number of matters, said, "re Lester Luborsky, I brought this matter up at Council last week because it would raise great difficulties were we to undertake to train non-medicals from the States, since, as you know, they are not recognized there. The Council reached the decision that we cannot accept any of them."

At that point, Luborsky turned his efforts to Topeka. He moved there in August 1947, recruited by David Rapaport to work in the Research Department of The Menninger Foundation on a Selection Research project, with a promise that Rapaport would try to facilitate his acceptance for analytic training in the Topeka Institute. The application process, however, dragged on, and in 1949, Luborsky was accepted for analysis by Theodor Reik in New York (on the recommendation of a Topeka colleague, Milton Wexler, originally a lawyer, and himself analyzed by Reik), subject to a personal interview to assess his suitability. On April 13, 1949, Luborsky wrote back thanking Reik for the offer but stating that "the Topeka Institute is going to act finally on my application within the next month or two. . . . Since I want to feel free when I see you to make commitments, I would like to delay for a month or two and then write you again to arrange a date of appointment." Shortly after this the Topeka Institute did act favorably on Luborsky's application, and he became one of the cadre of four nonmedical analytic candidates in that early wave of accepted lay applicants. Afterwards there were many others, but the subsequent ones went through the channel later established in 1956, with the organization by the American of the Committee on Training for Research.

Other Institutes that offered some degree of psychoanalytic training to nonmedical candidates during those first decades after the establishment of the 1938 exclusionary rule did so in less systematic and less open ways than did Boston and Topeka, and I know of no comprehensive accounting of these activities. Roy Schafer was trained by the newly formed Western New England Institute during that period, and there were, no doubt, a sprinkling of others around the country—all of these, of course, ostensibly for research purposes. This is to say, however, that the establishment of the Committee on Training for Research by the American in 1956 did not take place within a vacuum as an absolute change in policy and practice, but was rather an effort to accede to the rising tide of dissident voices within the American, through the creation of an official, formalized channel for the recognized psychoanalytic training for "research" purposes of a limited number of closely monitored and controlled nonmedical candidates. The compelling argument that brought this formal policy change about was that of the dearth of psychoanalytic research, an increasing embarrassment to a discipline portraying itself as a *science* of the mind, as well as a healing art. The assumption (actually only partially warranted) was that an infusion of nonmedical candidates, especially psychologists who had had formal research training as an essential component of their doctoral studies, would greatly strengthen the all-too-small cadre of psychoanalytic researchers.

The opposing argument was that any such nationally established avenue for "research training," however safeguarded, would become a back door for full nonmedical clinical training and access to the private practitioner market, in contravention of the longstanding American policy declaring psychoanalysis a subspeciality of psychiatry, its clinical practice reserved for the medically qualified. The adherents of both sides were closely enough balanced in numbers and in influence that the Committee on Training for Research, when established, was charged with a very restrictive mandate. Institutes affiliated with the American would be authorized to accept nonmedical candidates for partial analytic training (personal analysis with a training analyst and whatever sequence of seminars was deemed appropriate) and graduate them as such, but without recognition as clinical analysts or the right to conduct analysis. Full clinical training, meaning conducting analyses under supervision, with preparation then for going on to do analytic work after graduation, would be subject to the following stipulations: (1) a waiver of the usual medical requirement for clinical analytic training would have to be recommended in each instance by the national Committee on Training for Research and then granted by the Board on Professional Standards, and further ratified by the Executive Council of the American; (2) those granted the waiver would be fully established and widely recognized research and academic scholars, whose specific research activities were relevant to psychoanalysis and would be significantly enhanced by the knowledge of analytic concepts and activity accruing from immersion in clinical analytic work; and (3) that there would be an understanding that the individuals so trained would continue in their academic and research careers, do psychoanalytic or psychoanalytically informed research, and do only that amount of clinical psychoanalytic work necessary to or supportive of their research activity. This last stipulation was translated by a number of Institutes (New York was most widely known in this regard) as a requirement that the nonmedical candidates sign a pledge not to shift into careers of independent psychoanalytic clinical practice. This "yellow-dog contract" was deeply resented and strongly attacked by those required to submit to it and the New York Institute had a galaxy of distinguished nonmedical candidates through the decade of the 1960s— George Klein, Fred Pine, Don Spence, Leo Goldberger, and David Wolitzky among them—who were all subjected to this demeaning condition.

It was this Committee on which I was invited to membership by Sara Bonnett, then Chairman of the Board on Professional Standards, when I became a member of the American in 1960. The invitation was based on my established career in psychoanalytic research (The Psychotherapy Research Project of The Menninger Foundation) and was proposed by a committee member, Robert Cohen, then the chief of the Intramural Psychosocial Research Program (largely psychoanalytically oriented) at the National Institute of Mental Health (NIMH), and strongly supported by the committee chair, Alfred Stanton, known for his own pioneering research with Morris Schwartz (1954) on the psychoanalytic understanding of the impact of the hospital milieu on the hospital course and treatment of the psychotically ill. At the time of my joining, the Committee (CTR) was still very much in the process of working out its procedures and its guidelines for sponsoring institutes. In a report that I wrote (1961) on the operation of this national program for the information of the Topeka Institute for Psychoanalysis, I noted that in its first four years of official operation, CTR had only been called upon to process seven waiver applications from sponsoring Institutes around the country (only two per year), and that of these, six had been granted; the one denied was on behalf of an individual who clearly had shown no promise as a researcher to that point or in his plans for his future activity.

What the opponents of the research training program in the American had feared as an opening of the floodgates to backdoor clinical training by large numbers of eager nonmedical applicants simply had not taken place. In May 1966, at the 10-year mark for this program, I gave a report (1966b) to the Board on Professional Standards in my capacity as Secretary of CTR, a report that included an historical accounting to that date and a summary of a sequence of meetings with a series of distinguished psychologist consultants to the committee, wherein we discussed the reasons for the failure of this research training program in the American to thrive as much as had been anticipated and expected. The numbers were as follows: in 10 years there had only been 28 waiver applications for full training (three per year). These had come from only nine institutes, and 23 of them from five institutes. Twenty-three applications had been approved, three rejected, one deferred, and one withdrawn. Only six of these candidates had graduated over that decade, three of those in that tenth year. Clearly where too many had been feared, too few had actually come forward.

The consultants with whom the committee had discussed this state of affairs were Robert Sears, Dean of Graduate Studies at Stanford (himself a graduate in the pre-CTR days of the partial training program of the Boston Institute; David Shakow, Chief of the Psychology Laboratory at the National Institute of Mental Health (and known in general psychoanalytic ranks for his theoretical collaboration with David Rapaport); and Robert Holt, Co-Director, with George Klein, of the Research Center for Mental Health at New York University, and a former research colleague of David Rapaport's in Topeka. The reasons adduced in these conversations for the sluggish response by the field to the psychoanalytic research training opportunities within the American were many: (1) the program was inadequately publicized in academia; where it was known it was often inadequately understood and represented by psychoanalytically not well-informed faculty in university graduate schools; (2) the need for the academic scholar seeking psychoanalytic training to take on the time and intellectual burdens of becoming a multidisciplinarian; (3) the feeling of many psychoanalytically-interested academics that they had already acquired a knowledge of analytic thinking sufficient for their purposes from their own often-intensive psychoanalytic reading and available university course work, especially if they had come through clinical psychology doctoral programs; (4) the aura of dogma, closed-mindedness, and poor teaching that seemed to permeate many observers' views of psychoanalytic training in the American's institutes; (5) the greater attractiveness to many psychoanalytically interested scholars of the interpersonal and culturalist schools (the followers of Karen Horney, Erich Fromm, and others) existing outside the framework of the American, that seemed to be more congenial in spirit, more "liberal" in outlook, and with surer promise of acceptance; and (6) the common fear that immersion in psychoanalytic training with its self-directed preoccupations could interfere (at least temporarily) with the continuing research productivity required by the exigencies of an academic career.

This is not to speak of the time commitment, the length and cost of the analytic training for a group who would not have the future compensating rewards of a lucrative full-time private clinical practice. And at this point there was a lessening interest by previously available funding agencies—primarily the National Institute of Mental Health, and to a lesser extent, some of the larger private foundations interested in the field of mental health—in subsidizing the high cost of psychoanalytic training. This was also a time of waning interest in psychoanalysis and psychoanalytic research within academic psychiatry and the medical schools. Suggestions also were made of two additional obstacles to the success of this research training program generated by the American's own requirements. The first was that only the already well-established academic and prominent scholar and researcher was eligible for this program. This guaranteed the research commitment and capacity, of course, but such individuals would also be older, more fixed in particular research channels, and less willing and able to seek out new and more promising directions opened by their psycho-analytic immersion. The recommendation was to alter the requirement, allowing for the acceptance of younger researchers of promise rather than only those of fully established reputation. The second was the aura of second-class citizenship that hung over the entire program. This began with what was felt to be suspicious initial scrutiny (the search for those really motivated to become clinical practitioners), the feeling that their sense of dignity was compromised by being in the program (accentuated among those required to sign the pledge to eschew the private practice clinical career), and ended with the graduates, though usually eligible for membership in their local psychoanalytic society, not having any formal membership category open to them in the American, where they could only participate as "guests" at the scientific meetings. Many had consequently dropped away from scientific participation in the American altogether, so that the organization had failed to garner the fruits of even this small program. It was strongly recommended that this failure of membership recognition in the American be rectified in some appropriate way.

I became chairman of CTR after this May, 1966, meeting, and for the following four years (until I left the committee when I was President-Elect of the American in 1970) I reported regularly to the Board, twice annually. Along with recommending specific waiver applications for approval, averaging, as in prior years, about one per meeting, I pressed a series of proposals in line with the recommendations that derived from the original meetings with the committee consultants. In the December, 1966, report I prefaced these proposals with the statement that: "In the competition for research talent, the conditions are such that we are unhappily not faring well. Under existing conditions, we cannot hope to do much better." And then three specific recommendations from the committee were formally put to the Board. The first was that the selection criteria for research training be broadened to include younger individuals of promise, with research and clinical interest and aptitude, not necessarily accomplishment; the greater risk in this would be compensated by the larger pool and the greater potential reward. The second was that analysts more aggressively pursue academic teaching assignments beyond their customary involvements as clinical faculty in departments of psychiatry, that is, in graduate psychology programs particularly (here the American's own research graduates might be expected to play a critical role). The third was that a suitable membership category be created in the American for our research graduates.

At the May 1967 meeting, the Board did agree to take up the proposal to widen the selection criteria for research training from "especially qualified research fellows," to those "qualified in their own field of primary scientific or professional endeavor, and with demonstrated research aptitude." Both the Board and Council also approved in principle the creation of a membership category in the American for research graduates and an ad hoc committee was appointed to bring in an appropriate new bylaw recommendation to accomplish this. It was also agreed to appeal to the entire membership to widen their university teaching involvements beyond the medical school departments of psychiatry, more broadly into all the psychoanalytically related graduate disciplines.

At the December 1967 meeting the widened selection criteria were formally approved and the ad hoc committee on the membership category was reported working on the bylaw change. The following May (1968), the widened selection criteria were in place and CTR reported that it was turning its attention to the broader concern with the issue of research and research education for all psychoanalytic candidates, with the intent at least to make every analyst a sophisticated consumer of research. Meetings were being set up by CTR with representatives of all interested psychoanalytic institutes to explore this domain and to inventory the kinds and degrees of institute research teaching in place across the country at the time. These meetings with institute representatives continued over a sequence of several successive meetings of the American, with the presentation of both outstanding and discouraging experiences in this regard. A central question seemed to be the extent to which different institutes found research and clinical training to be complementary or, oppositely, antithetic. Another question concerned the extent to which the goals of research education in psychoanalytic institutes should go beyond the creation of sophisticated consumers of research to that of creating knowledgeable producers of research. All this was leading in the direction of devising a proposed ideal research training curriculum for those institutes with both the will and the resources to implement such a plan.

Meanwhile the proposal to amend the American's bylaws to create an appropriate membership category seemed to be unaccountably languishing in the ad hoc committee, or was being stalled somewhere in the Board or Council. Clearly making our research graduates *members* of the American, under whatever designation, was creating a problem for those members of the American (presumably still the substantial majority) who saw it as a medical organization of psychoanalytic practitioners, limited to those first medically, and then psychoanalytically, qualified. It was this imprimatur that it was so strongly felt should not be encroached upon by anyone lacking proper medical credentials. From the point of view of both our nonmedical research candidates and graduates and of those of us in the American concerned with the broader issue of widened disciplinary avenues of access to psychoanalytic work, this whole process of accommodation to the small cadre of new nonmedical "research" psychoanalysts, and according them proper recognition for their contributions, was painfully slow. Waiver approvals, even with the widened selection criteria, were still only averaging two per year, though with a somewhat widened array of sponsoring institutes. In 1965, Kurt Eissler, a strongly influential European-refugee member of the New York Psychoanalytic Society, and very openly a close adherent of Freud's position on the issue of lay analysis, published his *cri de coeur*, a large book entitled *Medical Orthodoxy and the Future of Psychoanalysis*, in which he spoke of the "final defeat that lay analysis suffered." He stated in the preface that he hoped this would not be seen as just an angry book and that he had tried to temper his language accordingly; he stated that he would "have preferred to give this book an accusatory title such as 'Futile Remarks on Lay Analysis' . . . [but that] since this was considered too chilling as a title," he had decided to drop it (p. viii).

At the December 1970 meeting of the American, Bernard Bandler, a former president of the Association, who had recently assumed the position of Director of the Psychiatric Training Branch of NIMH, suggested to Albert Solnit, the President of the Association, and Francis McLaughlin, Chairman of the Board, that NIMH could be interested in funding a Conference on Psychoanalytic Education and Research (COPER), updating the survey and report made to the American over a decade earlier in the comprehensive report and book by Bertram Lewin and Helen Ross (1960). After careful consideration, the American did decide to sponsor such a Conference and appointed a joint Board and Council Planning Committee, cochaired by me, as President-Elect of the Association, and Herbert Gaskill, perhaps the leading psychoanalyst chairman of the Department of Psychiatry at a medical school (the University of Colorado School of Medicine in Denver). Gaskill and I, together with our other Planning Committee members, conceived this as a prime opportunity to assess the present state, and to promote the future development, of psychoanalytic education and research, under the guiding conviction that both were equally essential to our vitality as a profession and a science, and within that overall umbrella, to assess thoughtfully the present and potential future place of our research candidates and of nonmedical training in psychoanalysis.

The conference involved complex detailed planning. Position papers and critical discussions were prepared in nine domains of inquiry laid out by the Planning Committee, and the conference finally took place over the week of September 30–October 4, 1974, at The Homestead resort in Hot

Springs, Virginia, an ideal setting for sustained and unhurried intellectual and social interchange. There were about 180 invited participants, mostly the leaders in the scientific and organizational activities of the American and its affiliated institutes and societies, but with some effort to reach out to younger, less well-known colleagues and even some invited analytic candidates. Of the nine commissions, two of them, on The Ideal Institute and on Psychoanalytic Education and the Allied Disciplines, bore directly on the issues raised by the question of lay analysis.

The Commission on The Ideal Institute was chaired by Stanley Goodman, and the summary of its proceedings prepared for the book of the conference proceedings (Goodman, 1977), under the heading "Who Will be Taught?" offered a description of the potential advantages of a medical-nonmedical mix in the candidate body and came to the following statement:

> Do we still, or did we ever, have sufficient reason to believe that a complete medical school curriculum and degree is so important for the development of a psychoanalyst that it would continue as an absolute prerequisite for regular admission to the psychoanalytic professional school? There is now an increasing conviction that the present policy may have unnecessarily restricted the choice of suitable applicants, and may have excluded many who would have been admitted if the primary consideration had been psychoanalytic aptitude, judged by the applicant's personal qualities, intellectual capacity and motivation [p. 144].

Coming from a group of 16 leaders of American analysis, only three of them nonphysicians (Ishak Ramzy, Helen Ross, and Herbert Schlesinger), this temperate but firm statement could clearly be seen as a reflection of some significant shift in the overall climate on the issue of nonmedical training by the early 1970s.

The other Commission concerned with this issue, Psychoanalytic Education and the Allied Disciplines, chaired by David Kairys and deliberately loaded with candidates and graduates from the research training program, devoted essentially its entire report to the history of that program (the activities of the Committee on Training for Research) and its current and future problems. That history was stated in essentially the same form as already depicted in this chapter. The update was reported that in May 1974 the membership of the American had finally approved the bylaw change according active membership in the Association to the graduates of the research training program. It was quite clear, however, that the entire program still comprised only a very limited number. In a 1971 count, there were 774 medical candidates and only 34 nonmedical, or but 4.5% of the total student body. Of the 34, 20 were psychologists. The Commission ended by recommending three distinct tracks for nonmedical research training: (1) the clinical track for those in full training via the national waiver mechanism; (2) an academic track, equivalent to what was called partial training, but without the insistence in all instances on the personal analysis as a necessary component; and (3) a "general studies" program in psychoanalysis, analogous to the extension division activities in many institutes, but with a more scholarly and research rather than clinical orientation.

A further note on the history of the Committee on Training for Research: When I was elected President-Elect of the American in 1970 and relinquished my position on the committee, I was succeeded as Chairman by Morton Reiser; during his stewardship the selection criteria were again broadened to include not only researchers but other strategically placed academic scholars whose teaching or administrative activities could be important to the spread of psychoanalytic interest and knowledge in the general university community. In accord with this broadened selection mandate, the Committee name was then officially changed to the Committee on Research and Special Training (CORST) and it has continued under this name unto the present. But at that time the main action on the struggle over the issue of nonmedical analysis had shifted into the broader question raised in the 1974 COPER Commission on the Ideal Institute: Who should we train, or what would be the proper or ideal candidate mix in our educational programs?

During the days of my representing the Committee on Training for Research in its semiannual reports to the Board (Wallerstein, 1966–1969), I could be seen to be engaged in what would today be called "consciousness raising" about the issues of research training and nonmedical analysis. I was identified by many as the spokesman for a historically minority position, one open to consideration of the place of diverse disciplinary routes to training within American psychoanalysis. At the same time, as chairman of a Board Committee and thereby a member of the powerful Coordinating Committee of the Board (which basically set and directed the agenda for Board consideration), I was also seen as a rising member of the central "establishment" within the American, and therefore in a position to articulate views that could have been more readily dismissed had they come from an outsider to the central workings of the organization. My election in 1969 as a Councilor-at-Large of the Executive Council of the American, and the following year as President-Elect of the organization, reflected, I think, the greater willingness of the Association to at least bring the entire body of views that I was seen to champion to the table for open discussion and review. The COPER Conference, the planning and direction of which I cochaired, then could serve as a forum in which this whole complex of issues could be made central to the deliberations of the total organization, and in a sympathetic way embodied in the official COPER Commission reports in their role as a hopeful blueprint for the organization's future.

I have already indicated that by 1974 the American took the step of conferring active membership upon the graduates (then, of course, only a handful of individuals) of the research training program. This had been actually preceded by another opening of the membership door to a special (and also very small) group of lay analysts, a total of fourteen individuals scattered around the country, all European refugee analysts who either could not or did not obtain membership in the American under the 1938 grandfather clause, but were serving as training analysts in the American's affiliated institutes, and as senior leading members in the American's Societies. I became involved in the movement to grant this special group membership in the American when I left The Menninger Foundation (where I had become Director of Research) in September 1966, in order to embark on a new career in San Francisco as Chief of Psychiatry at Mt. Zion Hospital, then a leading psychoanalytically run training center in the mental health professional disciplines—adult and child psychiatry, clinical psychology, and psychiatric social work—and also as a training and supervising analyst in the San Francisco Psychoanalytic Institute.

The recently elected Chairman of the Education Committee of the San Francisco Institute at that time was Stanley Goodman, and in his capacity as Director of the Institute, he was a Fellow of the Board on Professional Standards of the American. Goodman was then a rising influence within the organizational affairs of the American: he was elected Secretary of the American in 1970, serving in that capacity during my period as President; in 1975, he was elected to a three-year term as Chairman of the Board on Professional Standards. Back in 1966, as a new Fellow of the Board representing the San Francisco Institute, Goodman was the eloquent and tireless spokesman for what came to be called "the San Francisco resolution." It was to accord membership in the American to the nonmedical training analysts in our various member institutes, who it was said, "analyzed our candidates and treated our wives and our children." More than half of the 14 were child analysts, usually the central figures in the child analysis programs of their respective institutes. By 1966, the ban that the American had tried to enforce in the 1940s, that those European-refugee analysts, like Blos, Erikson, Kris, and Waelder, grandfathered into membership in the American under the 1938 agreement, or those who were never granted membership by the American but obtained membership and training analyst status in their local institutes and societies, like Ekstein and Ramzy, with the stipulation that they only teach and do training analyses, had long since been quietly buried.

The anomaly in all this, that senior training analysts who we entrusted to analyze our candidates and our family members were not eligible to join our national Association, which was open to their students and analysands, was what the San Francisco resolution was designed to redress. The particular San Francisco investment in this issue stemmed from its own history as a society and institute. Three of the six founding members (in 1942) were lay analysts: Siegfried Bernfeld, Erik Erikson, and Anna Maenchen. Goodman was a member of the first postwar candidate group in 1946, and among these three were his analyst and his most important teachers. It was this sense of gratitude toward, and respect for, their own esteemed founding members and mentors that impelled the united San Francisco Institute and Goodman, as its articulate and eager spokesman, to persuasively advocate the cause of this group of "unfairly" disenfranchised senior training analysts at the American's Board on Professional Standards.[1] There was by that time sufficient support around the country for the rectification of this "injustice" to this group of colleagues (the 14 at issue were scattered around, and had comparable centrally esteemed positions, at almost as many institutes) for the bylaw change to accomplishing this purpose to be passed in the early 1970s. I had the privilege, as President of the American, to sign the membership certificates of the group, including Anna Maenchen, my senior colleague in San Francisco, and Rudolf Ekstein, my teacher and mentor in Topeka, with whom I had coauthored a book, *The Teaching and Learning of Psychotherapy* (1958), the first book-length effort to study the supervisory process in psychoanalytic therapies. It was shortly after this (in 1974) that the second nonmedical membership category, that for the research training graduates—likewise a very small number indeed—was voted by the membership of the American, as already described.

It was these events, followed by statements so sympathetic to the cause of nonmedical analysis that appeared in the book of proceedings of the prestigious COPER Conference, that together reflected an altered climate in the American. It seemed like a logical next step that the Chairman of the Board, who in 1975 was Edward Weinshel, appointed an ad hoc Committee on Prerequisites for Training (CPT) with Homer Curtis as Chair. The charge to the committee was to explore the proper prerequisites for learning to be an analyst in order to improve the psychoanalytic educational system for everyone. The committee of nine members was almost evenly balanced

---

[1] At the time, the late 1960s, only Anna Maenchen was still active in the affairs of the San Francisco Institute. Bernfeld had died in 1953, and Erikson had left in 1951 to pursue his career first at the Austen Riggs Center in Stockbridge, Massachusetts, and subsequently as a professor at Harvard University.

between medical and nonmedical members (the latter group from the research candidate and graduate pool) and also reflected, deliberately, a range of varying perspectives on the issue of lay analysis.

To a significant extent, CPT was a balancing effort that grew out of the American's voting down an abortive attempt by the Chicago Institute (also among those friendlier to the cause of research and nonmedical analysis) to create an independent Ph.D. program under the Institute's own auspices, specifically in psychoanalysis, that would be directly open to college graduates and thereby bypass *both* doctoral-level graduate studies and medical school study—that is, an effort to create a truly independent graduate discipline of psychoanalysis. Though this led to spirited debate within the councils of the American, it was deemed too radical a step and was voted down by the Board and Council, with CPT being created instead, to make a fresh start at reconsideration of the whole issue of the proper prerequisites for psychoanalytic training, including, of course, the necessity and/or the sufficiency of the medical credential for that purpose.

I played a particular lobbying role in the deliberations that led to the creation of the CPT, beyond my general concern with the whole breadth of involved issues, and that was on behalf of the graduates of a program that my colleagues and I had by then started in San Francisco. This program was similar in spirit, but very distinct in structure to the abortive Chicago Ph.D. in psychoanalysis. In 1971–1972, at Mt. Zion Hospital in collaboration with the University of California, Berkeley, and in 1975, when I left Mt. Zion to become Chairman of the Department of Psychiatry at the University of California, San Francisco School of Medicine, in collaboration with the Medical School in San Francisco, we created, under those joint auspices, a new professional mental health discipline, a Doctorate in Mental Health (DMH), not a doctorate in psychoanalysis.

The story of the organization and operation of that program from 1973 to 1986 is long and complex and has been written up in detail elsewhere (Wallerstein, 1978b, 1992). Relevant here is that it was a 13-year effort to create a new and autonomous mental health profession, drawing upon aspects of medical-psychiatric, clinical psychology, and social-work education germane to the clinical functioning of the mental health professional. It combined the functions of psychotherapy, deployment of psychoactive drugs, and management of psychiatric hospitalization, drawing upon the relevant ingredients from the traditional educational pathways of these established mental health disciplines into a new five-year program of graduate studies. This comprised two preclinical years of biological, psychological, and social science course work, followed by three clinical years alongside the trainees in the traditional mental health disciplines, the psychiatric residents, and the clinical psychology and social work interns, and working in the whole range of psychiatric settings, inpatient and outpatient, adult and child, as well as on the panoply of specialty services, substance abuse, consultation-liaison, forensic, geriatric. All of this was required for a Doctorate of Mental Health, a new degree pioneered over the life of the program by the University of California.[2]

As with so much else in our field, clear roots for this development can be found in the writings of Sigmund Freud, though Freud actually wrote very little directly in relation to training issues *per se*. Two statements, however, from the brief number devoted to this issue, set the framework within which the DMH concept arose. The first is from a relatively little known source, the collection of letters to his minister colleague Oskar Pfister. In 1928, Freud wrote: "I do not know if you have detected the secret link between [*The Question of*] *Lay Analysis* and [*The Future of an*] *Illusion*. In the former, I wish to protect analysis from the doctors and in the latter from the priests. I should like to hand it over to a profession which *does not yet exist*, a profession of *lay* curers of souls who need not be doctors and should not be priests" (Freud and Pfister, 1963, p. 126; italics added). The second is the more detailed statement, already cited in chapter 1, from Freud's best-known writing on training issues, *The Question of Lay Analysis* (1926b) in which Freud gave his description of the ideal curriculum for the "college of psycho-analysts" (p. 246). In that passage, Freud insisted on the necessity of teaching all the sciences familiar to medicine, but also disciplines remote from medicine, like the history of civilization, the psychology of religion, mythology, and literature. He concluded, "Unless he is well at home in these subjects, an analyst can make nothing of a large amount of his material" (p. 246). A few pages further on Freud restated all this even more tersely than in the "college of psycho-analysts" passage: "A scheme of training for analysts has still to be created. It must include elements from the mental sciences, from psychology, the history of civilization and sociology, as well as from anatomy, biology and the study of evolution" (p. 252).

The more modern restatement of this call for a new mental health profession was made by Lawrence Kubie in America in a series of papers in the 1950s, most comprehensively articulated in "The Pros and Cons of a New Profession: A Doctorate in Medical Psychology" (1954). Kubie's vision was in a sense breathtakingly simple. Three major mental health disciplines, psychiatry, clinical psychology, and psychiatric social work, shared the psychotherapeutic marketplace. In terms of their education for this activity, the practitioners of each came trained very relevantly and appropriately in

---

[2] This was a very bold attempt to create by planning and fiat a new profession, which is of course counter to the manner in which new professional groupings have characteristically arisen. Witness in this connection how many hundreds of years it took barbers to evolve into surgeons.

some respects, grossly overtrained in others (like the totality of biomedical knowledge that equally equips the physician graduate to go into a medical or surgical career) and with developed capacities, attitudes, and ways of working that often have to be *un*learned in order to work effectively in the mental health arena, though at the same time lacking in some vital areas of knowledge and skill that have been acquired in the other disciplinary routes to mental health therapeutic work.

In the face of this situation, Kubie's bold proposal was simply to start wholly afresh, to fashion a completely new postcollege graduate *professional* curriculum built on a new amalgam, a more appropriate (and more equal) mixture of studies in the three main relevant knowledge areas, biological science, psychological science, and social science, to be welded together into that preclinical curriculum that would be the most appropriate knowledge base for the succeeding clinical years of training in mental health professional work, that is, application of the relevant knowledge from within these three realms of basic science to the clinical problems of patients with mental and emotional disorders. It was this minimum five-year program—Kubie's concern was not for shorter, but for better training—that would eventuate in the new professional degree for which Kubie proposed the name Doctorate in Medical Psychology.

Kubie foresaw, realistically enough, that however simple and logical this conceptualization might be, that such a proposal would not be easily adopted. In some circles concerned with mental health educational philosophy the idea gained some currency. People compared the simple clarity of Kubie's vision with the existing confusions in the amorphous and unregulated psychotherapy marketplace, where all ideologies, all degrees of professionalism, all kinds and levels of training, and all degrees of seriousness and commitment vied clamorously for attention—and for their share of the public purse. In 1963, a conference, sparked by Kubie, was called by a group of supporters of the Kubie idea, bringing together some 32 educators from the fields of psychiatry, psychoanalysis, psychiatric social work, and clinical psychology, to discuss over several days "An Ideal Training Program for Psychotherapists." I was an invited participant, asked to present a position paper on the place of research training in the proposed ideal training curriculum for the psychotherapist: whether, how much, when, where. The conference outcome was a strong endorsement given to the idea by this group of practitioners and educators, all reaching for common ground, for ways in which they could complement each other's skills in working in the same arena, and ways in which they would like to have added to and subtracted from their own training development, in order to come to their practices more relevantly equipped, rather than having to, in so many instances, engage in supplemental and on-the-job training, often far less adequately than was desirable. The book of the conference proceedings, entitled *New Horizon for Psychotherapy: Autonomy as a Profession*, was published under the editorship of Robert Holt (1971), the conference organizer.

This brings us to the same year, 1971, that marked my own active entry, together with a like-minded group of colleagues drawn from the staff of the Mt. Zion Hospital Department of Psychiatry, into the process of planning and implementing the first functioning program for the training of a version, our version, of this new kind of mental health professional whom we called Doctor of Mental Health (DMH), a modified version of Kubie's dream, and, less distinctly perhaps, of Freud's dream before him. The nature of our conceptualization (reconceptualization)[3] of the Kubie-descended-from-Freud vision, and the manner of construction of the program designed to implement it, has been described in detail (Wallerstein, 1978b, pp. 382–386) under three thematic lines. First, the multidisciplinary nature of the Mt. Zion Hospital Department of Psychiatry at that time made it a very receptive home to such an undertaking. Second, the particular happenstance of timing made 1971 a propitious year to essay this undertaking. The diminishing availability, in those years of the Nixon administration, of funding support for training in the "traditional" mental health disciplines, and the shifting NIMH and private foundation priorities created a seeming "window of opportunity" for new and innovative training proposals. Third, the evolving history of psychiatry and psychiatric practice between 1954 and 1971 made the group of Mt. Zion planners believe that our reconceptualization of the assumptions and conditions of the training program would necessarily have to differ in many significant (even, depending on one's point of view, fundamental) ways from Kubie's original, clear conceptualization of 1954. (This despite the fact that the Kubie proposal still persisted in close to unaltered form during that same year in two landmark books devoted to this subject [Holt, 1971; Henry, Sims, and Spray, 1971].)

What is germane here is that the DMH program did get underway (in 1973), that I was able to persuade the University of California to embark

---

[3] Kubie's plan was basically to create a better and more directly trained psychodynamic *psychotherapist* through an amalgam of the most relevant educational and training experiences from within each of the traditional mental health disciplinary routes, dropping the unessential and irrelevant, and filling in the hiatuses in the educations of each of the traditional disciplines. Our intent was broader, to create *mental health professionals* competent in the entire array of practices and interventions needed for comprehensive mental health care, meaning not just psychotherapy and its form variants, but also the administration of psychoactive drugs and the management of psychiatric hospitalization. This would require, of course, a deeper biological and biomedical knowledge. It would also, as we later painfully learned, arouse more intense official medical and psychiatric opposition.

on a professional graduate degree granting program for a degree never before given in human history, and that it would last 13 years, graduating nine successive cadres of six to twelve students each year through nine consecutive five-year classes, before it was closed down in 1986, out of a combination of the increasingly stringent fiscal exigencies of the University, and the implacable opposition of the organized medical and psychiatric professions in California, who saw the DMH program as an unwanted (and, to them, an unqualified) competitor in the mental health marketplace, and who succeeded in the mid-1980s in blocking the necessary enabling licensure legislation in the California legislature, vital both to independent practice, and to qualification for the third party reimbursement from insurance carriers that was beginning to cover so much of the available mental health care arena.

For our purposes here, when the American was forming the Committee on Prerequisites for Training (CPT) in 1975, the DMH program and its degree were just in the process of being definitively approved by the University of California, and its future looked bright indeed. My vigorous lobbying around the charge with which CPT was being set up had to do with my efforts to ensure that as the CPT surveyed the various potential disciplinary routes to psychoanalytic training, the DMH graduates should be deemed to warrant equal consideration among that number. In fact, from my perspective, they would be better equipped than their confreres from the traditional mental health disciplines to qualify for a psychoanalytic career, just because of the specific focus in the graduate level training for the DMH degree on that knowledge and those skills and attributes designed to produce the best prepared specific mental health professional. This would be a psychodynamic therapist able to treat the whole array of the mentally ill, not just those whose treatment needs could be met by psychotherapy alone. In this lobbying effort I succeeded. In the initial charge to CPT, the DMH training program was designated as one that should be considered as a possibly appropriate disciplinary route into full psychoanalytic training, along with the traditional mental health disciplines. With the creation of CPT in 1975, the American embarked on the path that led inexorably— but not for another decade and more—to the revision in 1987, almost exactly a half-century after its institution in 1938, of the 1938 rule, and the opening of the doors to full clinical psychoanalytic training in the United States for medical and nonmedical candidates alike.

The Four Committees of the American
and the Precipitation of the Lawsuit

T he Committee on Prerequisites
for Training (CPT) deliberated carefully over a six-year span, from 1975 to
1981. It was appointed by Edward Weinshel, then Chairman of the Board
on Professional Standards, and consisted of nine members,[1] with Homer
Curtis as chair and Paula Bernstein (one of its nonmedical members) as the
very conscientious secretary who created minutes of its discussions in
assiduous detail. The nine committee members were selected to represent
the spectrum of views within the American on the issue of the place of lay
analysis within the discipline; four of the nine were nonmedical, all products
of the research training program under CORST auspices.

At the first, December 1975, meeting, the committee set its overall
agenda, to explore the valid prerequisites for learning to become an analyst,
in order, ostensibly, to improve psychoanalytic education for everyone. The
question was set as, What does training to be an analyst require? The tone
was framed by Charles Kligerman, a medical analyst from Chicago and an
earlier promoter of the aborted Chicago Plan to train in an independent
doctoral-level discipline of psychoanalysis, as the query, How can we justify
not taking nonphysicians into training? The assertion was advanced that
we (psychoanalysts) have for a long time felt that there has been an
intellectual drying up in psychoanalytic advance and that this could
significantly reflect the narrow medical-psychiatric track from which our
candidates have been drawn. This was declared to have eventuated in a
state of scientific stultification, educational dogmatism, and increasing

---

[1] The nine members were Paula Bernstein, Ph.D. (Secretary), Homer C. Curtis, M.D.
(Chair), Leo Goldberger, Ph.D., Seymour Handler, M.D., Edward D. Joseph, M.D., Charles
Kligerman, M.D., Robert Michels, M.D., Arnold Rogow, Ph.D., and Abraham Zaleznik,
D.C.S.

isolation from cognate disciplines of intelligence of the human mind (Bernstein, CPT Minutes, December 19, 1975).[2]

At the second committee meeting (May 1976) the discussion circled around the question of malaise and stultification within the research and educational body of psychoanalysis. Was there really a consensus on a declining creativity within psychoanalytic ranks? Reference was made to Anna Freud's call for a wider recruitment net with, however, the maintenance of stringent acceptance criteria. Arnold Rogow, another of the nonmedical members, offered the conception that the idea of high "minimum standards" had been oversold and accepted too unthinkingly. After all, in the early days of analysis, many of the first analysts were rather wild, crazy people. Did they really do a lot of harm? In that so-called Golden Age, the organized institutional aspects of training were minimal and individual latitude and initiative was great. Perhaps the nonmedical exclusionary policies were simply a covert expression of a veiled intellectual and economic competitive bias. Certainly the prime requirement in those early days (an argument advanced by both Bernstein and Abraham Zaleznik, also a nonmedical committee member) was of psychoanalysis as a calling, something one fell in love with. In that Golden Age, this was all that it took to enter into the discipline. Of course, it was cautioned, there would be no magic answer to all the problems of psychoanalysis if nonphysicians were to be admitted for full clinical training—"that's just our version of the myth of the Noble Savage"—but the focus should nonetheless be on delineating the kind of prepsychoanalytic education that would give an individual the best preparation and psychological capacity for a psychoanalytic career (Bernstein, CPT Minutes, May 7, 1976).

By the third committee meeting (December 1976) positions began to crystallize within the group. Curtis, as chairman, began by reminding the committee that he had resisted the proposal that CPT be created as a Study Group under COPE (the Committee on Psychoanalytic Education of the Board on Professional Standards); he wanted it established as an ad hoc committee of the Board, which would be an action group charged to bring specific recommendations to the Board. Kligerman, who since 1969 had been chairing a conceptually related committee of the International, an IPA Committee on Evaluation, began by saying, "It appears that if the

---

[2] Throughout the six years of deliberations by CPT, the officers of the American, including both the President of the Association and the Chairman of the Board on Professional Standards, attended meetings of this Committee (and participated actively in its discussions) far more than they did in most of the committees of Board and Council that they were equally responsible to oversee. This reflected the high importance and great sensitivity felt to surround the work of CPT. It also reflected (and helped shape) the sympathetic involvement of the officers in the discussions that led ultimately to a positive proposal to widen the avenues of access to clinical psychoanalytic training, albeit to only a limited extent, surrounded by cautions and "safeguards" and clearly to be labeled "experimental."

person wants very much to become an analyst, seems to be analyzable, and has a track record that shows he can carry out what he makes up his mind to do, there is no reason to turn him down." In the discussion engendered by this proposal, Robert Michels outlined the arguments for and against the proposed broadening of the American's selection policies. In favor were (1) the declining numbers of regular candidates; (2) the "justice" argument, that it simply wasn't fair to allow categorical restrictions on access to training, if the specific restrictions were not relevant to the ultimate psychoanalytic tasks; (3) that the current restrictive policy was counter to the inherent ideals and values of the professions; and (4) that present policy diminished the potential intellectual vigor of the field. Opposed were (1) the trade union argument; (2) the bottom-line caution about quality control of "people like us" by "people like us"; (3) the putative importance of the medical identity of psychoanalysis; and (4) the analogical metaphor of Gresham's Law, that the accession of nonphysicians would tend to drive out physician applicants. The whole committee then agreed on broad governing attributes to be required of all candidates of whatever discipline; a broad "humanistic" education, a prior clinical training and "feel," experience as a responsible caretaker of suffering people, role socialization into a caring profession, and adequate knowledge of "clinical psychiatry."

For its afternoon session of that day, CPT invited me to present an overview of our Mt. Zion Hospital–University of California Doctor of Mental Health program so that its relation to the committee charge could be clearly delineated. During that presentation I made explicit our intention that the DMH graduates should be fully equipped to undertake psychoanalytic training along with recruits from any other disciplinary avenue, and I stated that our San Francisco Psychoanalytic Institute had already voted to accept this contention in principle. There was much discussion of the inculcation of the "physicianly attitude" (Stone, 1961), that is concern, responsibility, and so forth. Michels paraphrased this particular discussion of the DMH program as the argument that, "You don't have to be a physician but you do have to be a psychiatrist to become an analyst, so let's make psychiatrists who are not physicians," and he called that one plausible answer to the committee's question (Bernstein, CPT Minutes, December 14, 1976).

At that same meeting of the American, Curtis, as the CPT chair, presented his first report to the Board on Professional Standards (BOPS). There he reviewed the various sources out of which CPT had been brought into being: (1) the concept of "enhancing our ranks" through the research training program, CORST; (2) the reports of the various (COPER) commissions from the 1974 Homestead Conference; and (3) the debate over the Chicago proposal for an independent Doctorate of Psychoanalysis. Curtis then stated that, "One important and recurrent theme in ... [CPT's] discussions was the question of the pre-existing personal and educational qualifications which were most important in helping the candidate utilize analytic training to become a competent analyst." To this, Curtis cautiously made CPT's opening gambit, in order to elicit maximal support for the direction its deliberations were taking.

> Thus we have been led to consider the aspects of the long, arduous pathway through medical school, internship and residency which affect the capacity to understand and be concerned with suffering and personal problems without being drawn into them, to combine empathic responses with objective judgment, to develop detached concern and the physicianly attitude, to acquire therapeutic intent without therapeutic zeal. It is obvious that the medical pathway can lead some to less favorable attitudes such as isolation from human feeling, reaction formation and even callousness, but a process of self-selection plus careful selection procedures can screen out most of these. . . . On this foundation we are now beginning to explore the possibility that there might be other pathways to psychoanalytic education that can encourage the development of such attitudes and skills—the clearly intended thrust of the report [Curtis, Report from CPT to BOPS, December 15, 1976].

I was invited back for the morning session of the fourth CPT meeting in April 1977. I was able to report at that time that the decision of the Education Committee of the San Francisco Psychoanalytic Institute to consider DMH graduates eligible for psychoanalytic training on the same basis as psychiatrists had been strongly endorsed by a membership vote of the San Francisco Society. It was argued in the discussion about this program that the DMH program afforded important insights into what supplemental clinical experiences would be valuable for psychoanalytic candidates coming through disciplinary routes other than the medical-psychiatric. There was question whether the Board (BOPS) would ultimately broadly approve the DMH concept or limit its approval for candidacy purposes specifically to the graduates of this one (California) program, with all others that might arise like it having to seek acceptance, one by one, on an individual basis. As usual, the discussion hovered around the issue of "lowering" or of "broadening" standards. It was clear that there was unease about making general recommendations; it would be more acceptable to individualize programs just as applicants for training are scrutinized individually in terms of their personal qualities and their suitability for training. In this regard, everyone agreed on the search for "excellence," meaning qualities of intelligence, integrity, empathic capacity, tolerance for delay and anxiety, "analyzability" (however construed), and psychological-mindedness (Bernstein, CPT Minutes, April 26, 1977).

At the fifth CPT meeting, in December 1977, the committee advanced the distinction between the coarse filter of general educational prerequisites and the fine sieve of the assessment of individual personal qualities. There was growing agreement on the high value of appropriate clinical experience prior to psychoanalytic training, whatever one's disciplinary background, as well as on a broad humanistic educational background, and what were called the psychological aspects (including role socialization) of medical education. The operative selection mechanism would be via a CORST-like committee to grant waivers on a national basis for the clinical training of nonmedical candidates. But what should be the selection criteria? Should such a committee insist on adequate *prior* clinical experience or not? Should there have been supervised psychotherapy experience? Should this be supervised by the psychoanalytic institute faculty? Should the whole array of social sciences (and even the humanities) be considered part of the eligible recruitment grounds, or should candidacy be limited to the mental health caretaker professions, like clinical psychology and psychiatric social work (and DMH)? In this regard, should the institutes require the same amount (three to four years) of intensive clinical experience as the psychiatric resident applicant characteristically has had? It was agreed that most Ph.D. programs in clinical psychology do provide significant caretaking experiences and considerable supervision of (usually psychoanalytically oriented) psychotherapy (Bernstein, CPT Minutes, December 13, 1977).

At this same meeting of the American (December 1977), Curtis presented his second report to the Board. In this report the shape of the specific recommendations that would be finally brought to the Board could begin to be discerned. The distinction was set forth between the fine sieve of the individual personal qualities to be used in the *selection* process, and the coarse filter of the more general qualifications of educational and experiential background that should serve as the basis for the *eligibility to apply* for analytic training. Curtis quoted from Freud's *The Question of Lay Analysis:* "So long as schools such as we desire for the training of analysts are not yet in existence, people who have had a preliminary education in medicine are the best material for future analysts" (1926b, Postscript, 1927, p. 257). Curtis went on to declare, however, that "with this as our basic position we have been trying to tease out those experiences in the medical-psychiatric track which are most significant in enhancing the qualities which are fundamental to the development of a psychoanalyst." From medicine he singled out the role of human caretaker and the focus (to whatever degree it was emphasized in medical school) on the psychological aspects of physical illness. From psychiatry he singled out the clinical training and experience, with its emphasis on psychotherapy supervision. In terms of mechanisms to be proposed, Curtis outlined the concept of local institute screening for initial acceptance, but a national committee under the Board to process waivers to undertake supervised psychoanalytic work. To reassure those uneasy about this whole trend of thinking, Curtis added, "It is the feeling of our Committee that if the Board wishes to consider such a plan the guidelines should be sufficiently rigorous to select out a relatively small number who can be followed carefully in a controlled experiment in analytic education" (Curtis, Report from CPT to BOPS, December 14, 1977).

In May 1978, CPT did not meet, but Curtis did make his third report to the Board from the Committee. He indicated that CPT had carefully studied three major categories of educational prerequisites for psychoanalytic training: (1) education in science and the scientific method, (2) social and humanistic studies, and (3) clinical theory and practice, with experience and responsibility in the role of human caretaker. In this psychiatrists, clinical psychologists, and DMH graduates would all clearly qualify; no mention was made of psychiatric social workers at this time. "At this point in our thinking we believe that individuals from these types of programs should represent the limit of any proposed extension of our admission standards in our efforts to attract additional superior applicants." All of this, of course, should be subject to careful monitoring with some form of national waiver procedure. In a final policy statement, Curtis added that "We should not be in favor of accepting applicants with minimal clinical experience with the hope of providing them with supplemental clinical experience after admission since this would not only compromise the experimental value of such a project but would also burden the local institutes, most of whom would be hard-pressed to supply such additional training" (Curtis, Report from CPT to BOPS, May 3, 1978).

At the sixth CPT meeting in December 1978, Curtis announced that the Board on Professional Standards, now clearly anticipating the shape of the coming final report from CPT, had just set up another ad hoc Committee on the *Feasibility* of Non-Medical Training, to hammer out the guidelines and the monitoring procedures for the expected proposed plan to undertake a limited amount of full clinical psychoanalytic training of nonmedical candidates. The new committee had six members, all but one of them physicians, with Kenneth Calder as chair; it included Homer Curtis (chair of CPT) and Herbert Schlesinger, the psychologist member (chair of CORST).[3] Curtis read to CPT from the letter of charge to the Feasibility Committee written by Stanley Goodman, the then chairman of the Board.

> The achievement of a sufficiently broad consensus as to *whether*
> an experimental program to offer clinical psychoanalytic training

---

[3] The other three members were Paul A. Dewald, M.D., Otto F. Kernberg, M.D., and Morton F. Reiser, M.D.

to other than Medical Doctors will depend to a great extent on *how* it would be implemented. It is hoped that the Committee [on Feasibility] will be able to offer a broad perspective on the possible short and long term consequences for psychoanalysis of non-medical training and to recommend specific guidelines for the selection by the Institutes of non-medical applicants, appropriate waiver procedures, monitoring methods, and periodic program reviews.

Curtis stated that the intention was now clearly that CPT delineate the governing principles and that the new committee fashion the implementing machinery. It was evident to some at least on the Committee that the fundamental issue at stake, though not explicitly formulated as such, was that of psychoanalysis (in America) reconstituting its identity as an independent or a primary profession, no longer a derivative profession, a subspeciality within psychiatry. That is, "medicine is not the only prerequisite educational track, but beyond saying a person has to have demonstrated excellence in some advanced field of study and perhaps have had some minimal experience doing psychotherapy, we can't say anything. It remains a matter of personal evaluation of that individual." But one thing *was* clear; prior psychotherapy experience under supervision was deemed essential. (Bernstein, CPT Minutes, December 12, 1978).

One brief statement from Curtis's fourth Report to the Board from CPT in December, 1978, delineates the demarcation line now drawn between the tasks of these two committees dealing with the issue of nonmedical training.

The Board's approval of the new ad hoc Feasibility Committee last May now delegates the job of suggesting guidelines for selection, waiver procedures and periodic review programs to that Committee. The Committee on Prerequisites for Training will now proceed on its preferred course of further study and refinement of the type and nature of those optimal educational experiences which prepare individuals for the unique experience of analytic training [Curtis, Report from CPT to BOPS, December 13, 1978].

After this, little additional transpired in the further meetings of CPT or in the reports by Curtis from it to the Board. At the seventh CPT meeting in May 1979, Curtis gave an accounting of the first meeting of the Feasibility Committee, which he had attended the preceding December. All the minutes of the CPT meetings had been sent to the new Committee in the hope that they would not have to traverse territory already covered by CPT in formulating their own recommendations. The Feasibility Committee had talked about how to implement the recommendation that the American carefully widen the group eligible to apply for analytic training to include, first of all, Ph.D.s in clinical psychology. About the DMH program, the sense was to consider it a special case, consideration to be limited just to those graduated from our San Francisco program; it didn't seem likely that there would be other such programs, certainly not in the near future, conceived as ours was under a very particular combination of circumstances, and with our level of assurance of high training quality (Bernstein, CPT Minutes, May 12, 1979).

At the eighth meeting of CPT in December 1979, the only noteworthy discussion centered around the question; would the proposed restriction of widened access to analytic training only to mental health professionals be too confining and not truly in keeping with the spirit of the original charge to the Committee? No consensus emerged on this issue. It was also noted that Curtis had written a letter to the Board, "expressing his understanding that we are to function as a study committee concerned with examining general principles regarding the prerequisites for training while the Feasibility Committee is to bring back to the Board proposals for implementing recommendations we have made." From this discussion it was unclear how much Curtis and his committee regarded this as an explicit alteration—and restriction—of the original charge at the time of their formation (Bernstein, CPT Minutes, December 14, 1979).

In May 1980, CPT met for the ninth time, and now it was explicit within the group that ever since the Feasibility Committee had been established, CPT had become just a study group, leaving all action recommendations to the new Committee. The Committee discussion centered around general issues of professional roles and socialization and the concept of psychoanalysis as a separate profession, distinct from all the professions of origin of its members. Michels seemed most active in articulating the issues under discussion. For example, "If something in the socialization of physicians tends to work against their humanistic interests and talent, the solution is not to add three humanists to the group. The solution is to reflect upon the medical socialization process." At more length, on the relationship of medical education to psychological and social concerns: "To examine the medical school curriculum in terms of what we might say that might be useful in thinking about its adequacy as a prerequisite of psychoanalytic training: The critical issues might not be around the introduction of psychology, but rather the modification of more basic structural aspects of medical education. Medical students are worked too hard, required to put in too many hours. They have no time to talk to a patient or to read a novel" (Bernstein, CPT Minutes, May 2, 1980). Curtis's fifth report to the Board at that same spring meeting of the American covered no new ground (Curtis, Report from CPT to BOPS, April 30, 1980).

At the tenth meeting of CPT, December 1980, the entire stress was on review of the socialization process in all the professions under discussion, with special focus, of course, for applicability to the problems of socialization into a firm psychoanalytic identity. There was mention at the end of one further committee meeting, tentatively scheduled for May 1981, but there are no minutes to indicate that that meeting actually took place (Bernstein, CPT Minutes, December 19, 1980). At that same meeting of the American, Curtis's sixth report to the Board likewise emphasized the issue of the values involved in proper socialization to a profession and the attainment of a firm professional, in this instance, a psychoanalytic, identity (Curtis, Report from CPT to BOPS, December 17, 1980).

In December 1981, Curtis presented his seventh, and final, report to the Board. He reviewed the history of the Committee, the appointment by Edward Weinshel in May 1975, the prehistory going back through the establishment of the Committee on Training for Research in 1956, the recommendations of the Homestead Conference on Psychoanalytic Education and Research (COPER) in 1974, and the contentious discussions around the rejected Chicago proposal for a separate doctorate degree in psychoanalysis. The Committee had met for 10 full days over the 6-year span. It had worked out to its satisfaction the "coarse filter" of the proper educational and experiential background for eligibility to apply for psychoanalytic training. It rested on the Freud quotation that medicine has been to this point the best pathway, but declared clinical psychology (and the San Francisco DMH program) the next closest. The educational criteria that should constitute this coarse filter were now stated in fourfold fashion: (1) education in science and the scientific method; (2) social and humanistic studies; (3) immersion and experience in the role of human caretaker; and now (4) socialization into a professional identity which reinforces standards of responsibility and ethics (which was expanded to include the need to subordinate individual styles of expression and behavior to overarching professional standards, declared to be essential when the welfare of human beings is at stake). Beyond the acceptance and establishment of these general prerequisite criteria, the fine filter of the individual selection process should then operate.

In summation the Committee declared: "On these grounds, we have come to the conclusion that a modest expansion of our eligibility requirements to include doctors of clinical psychology and mental health allows us access to an additional source of highly qualified applicants without changing the essentially medical nature of our organization. . . . To be able to take the cream of this crop and train them in our institutes would be a service to our organization, the community and psychoanalysis." Curtis's report ended thus:

> As a result of our Committee's conclusions, the Committee on Feasibility of Non-Medical Training has been established and has already presented the Board with its recommendations which are now being discussed. Our Committee feels that while we have obviously not exhausted the many possible lines of investigation, we have essentially fulfilled our charge. It has been a most rewarding assignment which has provided us with new insights and perspectives which we hope will be of value to you in your discussion. But now, we respectfully request our discharge [Curtis, Report from CPT to BOPS, December 16, 1981].

Modest and even somewhat condescending as this final report and summary of recommendations now sounds, its acceptance by the American's Board on Professional Standards did mark a truly signal shift for that body, the first acceptance ever by this central educational arm of the American of the concept that full clinical psychoanalytic training need not be limited to medical-psychiatric applicants, that other routes to analytic training could be acknowledged and agreed upon. Obviously this reflected the gradually shifting Zeitgeist within the American on this issue, but on the other hand we should not fail to acknowledge the incisive role in this process of Homer Curtis, who so masterfully shepherded the deliberations of his Committee over its years of operation, and the quietly persuasive manner in which he defined its consensus thinking in his reports to the Board and prevailed upon that body to coalesce in support of the Committee recommendations. That it would come to this conclusion had already been foreshadowed, of course, in the 1978 appointment of the Feasibility Committee, while the Committee on Prerequisites was still midstream in its own deliberations.

As already stated, the Feasibility Committee, chaired by Kenneth Calder, had been appointed in June 1978 by Stanley Goodman, the then chairman of the Board. The charge, most succinctly, was "to recommend specific guidelines for selection by the Institutes of non-medical applicants, appropriate waiver procedures, monitoring methods and periodic program reviews." There seemed to be a general consensus within this new group on the desirable prerequisites for such training, within the frame already laid down by CPT, as follows: (1) a doctoral degree, Ph.D. or DMH; (2) a license to practice psychotherapy; and (3) sufficient clinical experience with a range of psychopathology and a variety of psychotherapeutic approaches. There also seemed to be agreement that this would be an experimental program for a limited number of highly qualified individuals, and would operate via a national waiver mechanism comparable to that of CORST (Committee on Research and Special Training) (Amer. Psychoanal. Assn. *Newsletter*, 14:2, June 1980).

This committee brought its final report to the Board three and a half years later, in December 1981. The conclusions that Calder reported were clear. It was indeed feasible to offer clinical psychoanalytic training to nonphysicians. There were no legal problems. The committee had consulted counsel and were advised that the American could legally limit the number of nonphysician candidates to some preestablished fraction of the student body, with a figure of one-third being most frequently proposed. And there were clear-cut guidelines in the CORST committee experience, using a comparable national waiver mechanism, with different operative criteria, to be focused now on clinical rather than research capacities. The Committee on Feasibility did not, however, make a recommendation to the Board on the *desirability* of such nonmedical training from the standpoint of all the interests of the American, but, limited itself to a listing of what it called the pros and cons in this regard.

In favor of such training the following considerations were listed: (1) Deserving nonmedical therapists would have a better training for the practice of analysis than it was felt could be secured outside the framework of the American; (2) As a consequence, a certain number of patients would receive better analytic treatment; (3) A broader talent base would be tapped, with consequent improvement in the learning and teaching in the psychoanalytic institute theoretical and clinical seminars; (4) Classes would, of course, also be larger, overcoming the problem of their being too small in some of the institutes of the American; (5) More broadly, this enhanced talent base could better preserve the quality of psychoanalytic service in the face of possible adverse pressures on the field in times to come, and; (6) With reference to the rationale for the work of CORST, the participation of nonphysicians could enhance the institute psychoanalytic classes as a result of their greater familiarity with scientific and experimental models.

Arrayed on the other side, the following considerations were advanced: (1) Nonphysicians as clinical practitioners of psychoanalysis could become economic competitors of their physician confreres; (2) Medical analysts might have their ties to the American Psychiatric Association, the American Medical Association, and biomedical science in general weakened as a result of the training of nonphysicians in the psychoanalytic institutes; (3) Potential physician candidates might be less attracted if the field were equally open to nonphysicians, thus, over time, fundamentally altering the nature of the discipline; (4) A long-range consequence might actually be a loss of control of the American Psychoanalytic Association by its physician members; (5) The dilution of institute classes might lessen the quality of the classroom

experience (the other side of numbers three and six on the pro side); and
(6) Nonphysicians, not having been socialized into medicine as a responsible
and caring profession, might not have the same sense of clinical
responsibility and concern, to the detriment of their patients.

This is the essence of the Calder report that was then subjected to
intense discussion at the December 1981 meeting of the Board. Finally
there was a motion by Robert Michels.

> The BOPS accepts and approves with gratitude the reports of
> the Calder and Curtis Committees, and affirms its approval of
> the goal of developing a program for the psychoanalytic training
> of clinical psychologists and certain mental health professionals
> consistent with the general guidelines outlined in those reports.
> It directs the Officers of the Board to communicate this view
> to the other components of the Association [meaning the
> Executive Council, and then the Business Meeting of Members,
> as the ultimate authority] and to report back proposals for the
> implementation of this program.

This was passed by a vote of 28 to 20 (Minutes, of Board of
Professional Standards, Dec. 16, 1981).

At the meeting of the Executive Council of the American the next
day, Arnold Cooper, President of the American, brought the two reports,
from the Curtis and the Calder Committees, to the Council as New
Business. The Council minutes reported Cooper's statement as follows: "If
implemented, this proposal [Calder] has wide reaching and profound
consequences for the American Psychoanalytic Association, for the practice
of psychoanalysis, and for psychoanalytic education. . . . Clearly, Dr. Cooper
stated, this is an issue to be addressed by the entire organization and one
that required careful and deliberate study in connection with its implications
for the future of psychoanalysis as we know it." In the discussion that
followed it was stated that such a plan, if approved and activated, could be
set up under the auspices of CORST, but most felt it should not; the research
and the clinical training objectives should not be confounded. It was felt by
many that full implementation of the plan would require a bylaw change by
the American, since the current Constitution and Bylaws limited full clinical
training in psychoanalysis to psychiatric physicians.

A point emphasized by Morton Reiser was "that this proposal could
potentially change the basically medical character of the Association.
[However,] If this proposal is approved by the membership, he felt that the
institutes were capable of selecting the very best amongst those who apply
to them without a new committee of the Board being established to oversee
these selections"—a reference to the use of CORST, of which Reiser had

once been chairman, as the possible vehicle for this new program. Finally, Cooper "asked the approval of the Council to appoint an ad hoc committee [this one to be a committee of the Council, felt overall to be less sympathetic to this concept of nonmedical training, and no longer a committee of the Board] on *Desirability* of Non-Medical Training which would study all the issues and problems now and for the future if the Association should decide to embark in this new direction." This now third committee, the Committee on Desirability, was appointed with Richard Isay named as chairman and a total of six members,[4] one of them a psychologist research graduate (Minutes of Executive Council, Dec. 17, 1981). The charge to the Isay Committee was as follows: "Granted the feasibility, is it organizationally, scientifically, and educationally desirable for the Association to embark on a program of clinical training of nonmedical candidates beyond that currently pursued for research and special candidates? If it is desirable, is this the right time, with regard to our relationship with medicine and psychiatry? If so, what is the most prudent way to proceed?" (Amer. Psychoanal. Assn. *Newsletter*, 16:1, May 1982).

Clearly, the tenor of the Board had been more sympathetic to the proposals to inaugurate some degree of nonmedical training, but the Board had been concerned enough and was clearly unwilling to proceed on its own. Its new chairman, Laurence Hall, had said to the Board at its meeting the day before: "The Board might express its inclinations, but it has no intention of going forward on a program which might have wide and long-lasting implications for the Association as a whole, without collaboration with the Council and without action ultimately coming from the membership at large" (Minutes of BOPS, December 16, 1981). The move in Council, initiated by Cooper, to appoint this new Isay Committee, was widely interpreted by the strong advocates of the directions of the earlier Curtis and Calder Committees as simply a delaying tactic; after all, hadn't all the involved issues been thoroughly ventilated in the meetings of the Curtis and Calder Committees and then, at each step, comprehensively reviewed by the Board? This perception was reflected in the headline in the Association's next Newsletter: "Board Approves Non-Medical Training— Council Votes Further Study."

The Isay Committee did not report at the May 1982 meeting of the American, but the matter was nonetheless discussed at both Board and Council. The Board, with Hall in the chair, was clearly more sympathetic to the positive momentum that had been generated over the years in the

---

[4] The six members were Alan J. Eisnitz, M.D., Leo Goldberger, Ph.D., William M. Granatir, M.D., Richard A. Isay, M.D. (Chair), Edward D. Joseph, M.D., and Robert Michels, M.D.

discussions of the Curtis and Calder Committee reports, but was equally clearly unwilling to set up such a training program on its own, despite its clear purview and autonomy in educational matters (for the reasons outlined in Hall's statement to the Board at the just prior meeting in December 1981). There also was a consensus that even if ultimately ratified by both Council and membership vote, nonmedical training for clinical psychoanalysis under the auspices of the American would be a voluntary option of the member institutes for those that desired to proceed with it, but not an obligatory requirement (Minutes BOPS, May 12, 1982). At the Executive Council, Reiser, now the President of the American, assured the Council that all points of view were reflected on the Isay Committee and that it would not be expected to make a single recommendation, but rather to present a range of views with the positive and negative features of each spelled out for the Council's consideration. He said that he expected the final committee report by the December meeting (Minutes of Executive Council, May 13, 1982).

As anticipated by many, at the December meetings of the Board and Council, Isay declared his Committee had been unable to reach consensus on whether or not nonmedical training for clinical psychoanalysis was desirable, and that his report would rather limit itself, without recommendation, to a restatement and perhaps an elaboration of the final Calder Committee report, listing the various pros and cons advanced over the years of discussion and leaving the decision, entirely unguided, in the hands of Council. The difference, however, was that this was now a Committee of Council, not of the Board. What was listed on the pro side was: (1) that the scientific base of analysis could improve; (2) that more analysts would increase the visibility of the profession; (3) that in turn this could lead to more patients; (4) that there is little professional interaction anyway between psychoanalysts and other physicians; and (5) that physicians might already be starting to gravitate toward more remunerative specialties. Of this last point it was said that "the economic penalty for becoming an analyst is becoming greater every year, and this is one reason fewer and fewer medical people may choose to enter the profession. Unless there is a non-medical route, the profession may disappear." Going ahead with the proposed training would consequently increase the size of the applicant pool leading to higher quality of those selected, to better classes, to broadened classes, to better overall training inside the American, and to less dependence upon medical school departments of psychiatry, which were becoming increasingly antipsychoanalytic in their teaching (in the 1970s and 1980s).

Even more arguments, however, were lined up on the con side: there would be (1) a falling off of medical candidates (a kind of Gresham's Law); (2) sanction would be given to less rigorous training, or at least, less rigorous prerequisites; (3) public perception of the viability of psychoanalysis would be diminished; (4) the distinction from the independent institutes outside the framework of the American would be blurred; (5) the "physicianly" qualities of the analyst would be attenuated; (6) psychoanalysis would be "desomatized," its links to the body weakened; (7) the interface with neuroscience would be lost; (8) all of psychotherapy would be demedicalized, and (9) medical and psychiatric referral sources would dry up. If implemented, the proposed training program would result in fewer psychiatrist candidates, fewer medical analysts to teach in medical schools and departments of psychiatry, the institutes having increasing burdens of preparatory preanalytic training, and a drop in public esteem as the medical orientation shifted to one embracing more psychologists.

In terms of the impact on the American as an organization, the Committee noted only one positive: an increase in membership. On the negative side, however, the catalogue included, the loss of medical orientation, alienation from the American Psychiatric Association, the tensions between "first" and "second" class candidates, the pressure of doctoral psychologists now (who later?) and the increased intellectual and economic rivalry between the disciplines. It was clear enough from the nature of the Isay Committee report, and the overall cast it seemed to have, that the tide had shifted back and no firm action on the part of Council would (or could) come from it. The resolution of this bogging down of momentum was the appointment of yet another (a fourth) committee, this one chaired by Vann Spruiell, consisting of seven members,[5] including two nonmedical and two chairs of the earlier committees (Calder and Isay). This was the first to be a joint Committee of Board and Council, appointed together by Reiser as President of the American, and Curtis as now Chairman of the Board. In the letter of appointment by the two, written to Spruiell and dated February 3, 1983, the charge given was "the *development of a proposal* for a mechanism that would enable outstanding nonmedical candidates to obtain full clinical training in our institutes." The far more positive direction of this letter could surely be a function of one of its two guiding signatories, Homer Curtis, chairman of the first committee on prerequisites, and now Chairman of the Board.

In a planning memo written for the new committee on April 23, 1983, Spruiell laid out the following issues: (1) that the Board and Council wanted *recommendations about mechanisms* for nonmedical training and guidelines on how best to put this to the membership for vote; (2) that a mechanism

---

[5] The seven members were Kenneth T. Calder, M.D., Philip S. Holzman, Ph.D., Richard A. Isay, M.D., Charles Kligerman, M.D., Robert Michels, M.D., Herbert J. Schlesinger, Ph.D., and Vann Spruiell, M.D. (chair).

like CORST, if not CORST itself, could be created, based on individual waivers, which *might not* require a bylaw change; (3) that an alternative could be to create a new Board committee on the model of the Child and Adolescent Analysis Committee, which would accredit and monitor institute programs and not individuals, though this would more likely require a bylaw change; or (4) that a combination of the CORST and Child Analysis models could be used, that is, both individual waivers *and* monitoring of programs. Again the setting of a ceiling of one-third nonmedical candidates was floated. Incidentally, Helen Fischer, Administrative Director of the American, in a memo to Spruiell a month earlier (March 28) had stated that legal counsel for the American had indicated that a bylaw change *would* be in order. The issue of a bylaw change was quite crucial, because this would require a two-thirds rather than a simple majority affirmative vote by the membership, and this looked at the time nearly impossible to achieve.

The Spruiell Committee, under some pressure to act expeditiously, met over two days, April 26 and 27, 1983. It agreed to propose several models to the Board and Council, each an alternative way to implement the intention to establish some form of nonmedical clinical training. All of these models would adhere to the following guidelines: (1) they would maintain the fundamental medical character of the American; (2) there would be a ceiling on the percentage of nonmedical candidates (which they had been assured by the American's attorneys would be legal); (3) there would be no distinctions, however, between candidates based on primary discipline, no "second class" candidates; (4) that however this was to be done, it be kept apart from CORST; (5) that a bylaw change would only become necessary to establish a membership class for the nonmedical graduates of our institute training programs. Three models were proposed: (1) admission by the local institutes on the same basis as medical-psychiatric applicants, the only monitoring being that of the overall institute training program by the Committee on Institutes; (2) new committee of the Board, akin to the Child and Adolescent Analysis Committee, which would accredit and monitor the Non-Medical Training Programs of the institutes but not the individual candidates; (3) new committee of the Board, which would accredit and monitor the programs and also grant waivers nationally for each individual candidate accepted locally (Report of Joint Committee on Non-Medical Training, April 26–27, 1983). This report was brought to the Board and Council in May 1983, with an explanation of the three primary models that might be followed if the Association elected to proceed with its intent to train qualified nonmedical mental health professionals.

Following this meeting, Spruiell sent a questionnaire survey out to all the member Institutes of the American. (Through some parliamentary maneuvering within the Council—which had not officially asked for the survey—the President of the American did not authorize sending the questionnaire to the Societies.) The intent of the questionnaire was to ascertain how strongly individual institutes (and societies) were in favor, or not in favor, of making the bylaw changes that would be required if psychoanalytic training for clinical practice within the American were expanded to include nonphysicians. It also was an attempt to get estimates on how strongly these bodies supported or opposed each of the three possible models that were set forth for such training. It quickly became clear that the questionnaire was poorly devised and phrased. Several institutes felt that it was inadequate to the task of obtaining reliable responses; several others felt that they simply did not understand its intent or its method. Spruiell, frustrated, tried to clarify the questions and answers by a follow-up telephone survey of the respondents.

What did emerge when the results were tabulated in terms of the responses of large, medium, and small institutes was that the same wide range of opinions existed within each of these groupings. There was no consensus on whether the American should change its bylaws at that time to allow the extension in the direction of nonmedical training, or if the American voted to make these required bylaw changes, which of the three mechanisms, if any, was preferable. To Spruiell, a stalemate existed in the American on these issues, at least as reflected in the reports from the institutes surveyed. To some extent he felt this reflected the "stalemate" on these issues within his committee, which had formulated the questionnaire. To a significant extent he felt it reflected the "paralysis" within the Association caused by its "fearful uncertainty" concerning this proposed direction (personal communication, May 28, 1994). One generalization seemed to emerge from the survey: those institutes that were usually identified as "conservative" tended to oppose any changes at this time, while those usually identified as discontented with the current structure of the Board tended to protest that the range of choices was unsatisfactory or poorly framed. At best estimate, 11 institutes expressed themselves as strongly opposed to any changes in the current operations of the American, 15 favored some changes; but there was simply no consensus in favor of any of the proposed models.

This whole issue then came to a head at the spring meeting of the American in San Diego in May 1984. Presented with the confused outcome of the survey report, the Board came to no vote and the Executive Council voted 32 to 7 "not to take any action." In effect, after a 10-year span from the appointment of the first (Curtis) Committee in 1975 to the vote on the report from this fourth (Spruiell) Committee in 1984, the American was back where it had started on this issue, with no immediate plan for any action other than the expressed intent to go "back to the drawing boards." This was put by Arnold Schneider and Helen Desmond (two of the watching psychologists who were later to be among the four plaintiffs in the lawsuit):

"It was clear that the American Psychoanalytic Association had arrived at a state of paralysis on this issue. The forces in support of non-medical training, and there appear to have been many, were neutralized by those who feared change—change in the market place and change in the medical identity of the American Psychoanalytic Association" (Schneider and Desmond, 1994, p. 318).

But by this time the American was no longer the sole actor on this stage. Reuben Fine (1982) had spearheaded the organization of Division 39, the Division on Psychoanalysis of the American Psychological Association, in 1979, and had become its first President. In the first year, 845 members were enrolled, and by the fall of 1980 they numbered 1400.[6] The Division was a broad interest group, but it included, of course, the greater number of those psychoanalytically trained in the various analytic training centers that had sprung up over the years (mostly beginning in New York) outside of the American, and very many of those who were not psychoanalytically trained wanted this training. Many of them would prefer it within the well-established institutes of the American.[7] At the time of publication of his article (1982), Fine could point to a whole group of nonmedical psychoanalytic training programs just in New York: Reik's National Psychological Association for Psychoanalysis (NPAP); the New York Postgraduate Center (known as the Lewis Wolberg Center), the William Alanson White Institute; the New York Freudian Society (NYFS); The Institute for Psychoanalytic Training and Research (IPTAR); The New York Center for Psychoanalytic Training (NYCPT); The Modern Center for Psychoanalytic Studies (with Hyman Spotnitz the central figure), as well as three university-based programs at Adelphi, NYU, and City University, and an estimate of 1000 varyingly trained nonmedical analysts. There were also smaller clusters in Los Angeles and in other cities around the country.

All these psychologists—psychologist psychoanalysts and psychoanalytically interested and oriented psychologists—had been watching the 10-year-long succession of the four Committees of the American with a growing impatience. Many were very anxious to have the American's doors

---

[6] As of May 1992, Division 39 had 3433 members, making it at that time "the largest psychoanalytic organization in the United States" (Lane and Meisels, 1994, p. 1).

[7] Probably the majority of the psychologists trained in the institutes of the American under the CORST program were also active members of Division 39. Some, like Fred Pine and Herbert J. Schlesinger, became prominent in its councils (Pine became President at one point), and during the difficult negotiations over the course of the lawsuit, these individuals played an invaluable role in interpreting perspectives between the contending parties, the American Psychoanalytic Association and the four plaintiffs backed by Division 39 of the American Psychological.

opened to them so that they could apply for what they felt was superior training in the American's institutes; in most of the cities in America, except some of the very largest, it was the only available training. They were clearly deeply frustrated and disappointed as the progression toward this goal began to founder in the American. Reuben Fine, as President of Division 39, had met with the officers of the IPA in New York but had simply been referred back to the American, which under the Regional Association agreement had exclusive jurisdiction over training under the IPA umbrella in the United States. Contacts were established with the officers of the American, but any commitments were deferred, pending the progression and outcome of the American's successive committee proceedings.

As definitive action began to seem less likely within the American, talk of legal action (on antitrust, restraint of trade grounds) began to surface in various cities. Schneider and Desmond (1994) mentioned Florida, Seattle, Los Angeles, and Baltimore (p. 320) as possible sites, though none of these eventuated. There was serious talk of a lawsuit by a disaffected psychologist and social worker group in the San Francisco Bay Area; funds were being actively solicited, and the wholehearted moral and financial backing of several key members of the Education Committee of the San Francisco Psychoanalytic Institute—all strongly out of sympathy with the established policies of the American in this matter—was secured. Within Division 39, which in 1984 numbered at least 2000 members, there was a swelling sentiment, led by Bryant Welch, to institute a nationwide class-action suit to force the opening of the American to psychologist training. When the American tabled the whole issue in San Diego in May 1984 it seemed clear to many (myself included), both within and outside the American, that a lawsuit was now all but inevitable. I thought that there would be at least two, the national effort via Division 39 and a local one in the San Francisco Bay Area.

The perceptions—and frustrations—governing the psychologist complainants at that time can be captured in two quotations from the account of these events published by Schneider and Desmond (1994).

> After 10 years of discussion and despite favorable reports from committees about the prerequisites for, feasibility of, and desirability for non-medical training, the issue was placed on the back burner during the May 1984 meeting of APsaA. The headline of their Fall, 1984, Newsletter [18(3)] read: "Issue Appears Dead for Now: Board Recommendation to Poll Members is Defeated in Council (p. 1)." The new President of APsaA, Edward Joseph, confirmed the demise of the issue. In the APsaA Newsletter [18(3), 1984], Papernik's report stated: "The new President is relieved that the recent polarization of

the membership over the issue of non-medical training is, for the time being, no longer in the forefront. Having determined at the recent annual meeting that we have done all that we can for now, our institutional energy can now be diverted into other channels (p. 6)" [p. 319].

The other quotation Schneider and Desmond drew from a report of a scientific panel I had chaired at the December 1980 meeting of the American Psychoanalytic Association[8] titled "Beyond Lay Analysis: Pathways to a Psychoanalytic Career" (Fischer, Panel Reporter, 1982). The panel, held when the Curtis and Calder Committees were still meeting and had not yet presented their final reports, was intended as a scientific—not a political-administrative—discussion of the issues involved in this controversy. In the panel report, Michels was reported as having summed up the issues as follows:

> Michels underscored the fact that our group [the American] is involved in a situation of considerable role conflict. As a *science* we aim to enrich the quality of our participants and want to be sure not to screen out any who might enrich our dialogue. As a *profession* we have to be cautious about the people we present to the public as psychoanalysts, and here the issue of the caliber and qualifications of other institutes must be considered. As a *trade*, like other trades, we traditionally try to restrict competition, limit membership, and train no more practitioners than the market will support. So from a scientific point of view we want to increase the number of participants, as professionals we want to be careful, and from a trade position we want to lower the number of participants. How to resolve this conflict is not clear [Fischer, 1982, pp. 714–715].

This passage is cited by Schneider and Desmond as evidence of the "anti-competitive nature of the non-medical issue" (p. 323) and as buttressing the argument of the lawsuit on antitrust, restraint of trade, grounds.

The atmosphere heated up rapidly after the American's unfortunate tabling of 10 years of work by four committees at the May 1984 meeting in San Diego. There was active talk, to which I was regularly privy, in the San

---

[8] The other panel participants were Homer C. Curtis, Newell Fischer, Robert Michels, Albert J. Solnit, and Herbert J. Schlesinger, the last named a nonmedical member of the American.

Francisco Bay Area, concerning the ongoing preparations with legal counsel for a lawsuit against my own institute (and the American). I was also hearing about the energetic preparation, spearheaded by Bryant Welch, by members of Division 39 of the American Psychological for a lawsuit against the American (and probably also the International) and I undertook a last effort to ward off this eventuality through appealing to the officers of the American to reopen the whole issue with a renewed positive initiative. At the time, I had long been out of executive office in the American—my presidency had been in the year 1971–72, a dozen years earlier—but I was still very active in its committee structure (serving at the time on eight of its committees), and counted all the current officers as personal friends. I readily persuaded my close friend and colleague in San Francisco, Edward Weinshel, himself a former chief officer of the American (Chairman of the Board, 1973 to 1976), also still very active in the American's committee structure, and also a personal friend of all the officers, and equally concerned about the potentially dangerous consequences of the unfortunate San Diego decision, to join me in a request to meet with the Executive Committee (the half-dozen chief officers) of the American at the December meetings in New York to see what leeway there might be to reverse the directions seemingly set in San Diego in May. This request was agreed to and the December meeting was scheduled.

Meanwhile, the officers of Division 39 and of the parent American Psychological Association, undertook a last effort to break through the impasse that the San Diego action had caused. Before committing themselves to the lawsuit, with all the tremendous cost it would entail in time, energy and money, they asked to meet with the officers of the American Psychoanalytic to explore the possibilities for a mutual accommodation that could render litigation superfluous. The invitation came from the psychologists and the meeting was agreed upon for October 12, 1984 in Washington, D.C. The psychologists were represented by Janet Spence, then President of the American Psychological, as well as Nathan Stockhamer and Bryant Welch, two of the central planners of the pending lawsuit within Division 39. The American Psychoanalytic Association was represented by Edward Joseph, the President, Richard Simons, the President-Elect, and Homer Curtis, Chairman of the Board.

There are divergent accounts of that meeting. From the point of view of the psychologists, the meeting was an attempt to forestall the need for the legal action that was being considered "because the nonmedical training issue had been declared dead by APsaA" (Schneider and Desmond, p. 321)—a reference to the San Diego action. The conclusion that the psychologists reached at the October 1984 meeting was that the representatives of the American were "obdurate" (p. 321), for which they held Joseph, President of the American and its chief spokesman in the meeting, primarily responsible. The psychologists also stated that they were told that the training matter was a "pocketbook issue" (p. 322) for the members of the American Psychoanalytic. From psychoanalytic sources there were well-substantiated accounts[9] that were, as would be expected, at some variance with this perspective. One of these stated:

> In spite of our efforts to convince them that the evolution of our work toward non-medical training was not derailed, and was ongoing, Welch had the bit in his teeth by that time and may have only needed a spur to start running. This spur was provided by Ed Joseph's two gaffes: one, his statement that the conflict was basically a 'pocket-book issue,' and two, his submitting a claim to the American Psychological Association for his expenses for the trip to Washington [personal communication].

The second account (also a personal communication) was to the effect that Joseph had actually submitted a bill to cover expenses for himself and his wife for the Washington trip and that "that story, right or wrong, was used to inflame members of Division 39." The story was certainly used as a reflection of the arrogant and overbearing nature of the leadership of the American in its dealings with the psychologist complainants, attitudes that would make any equitable accommodation to the interests of both contending parties almost impossible to achieve. My understanding is that Joseph's account was that his secretary had sent the bill by mistake, and that it was, of course, withdrawn when it elicited such an angry response from the Psychological Association. According to the Schneider and Desmond account there were, after this fiasco, several other futile efforts at meetings with the officers of the American, but essentially the lawsuit was now taking form. Also during that fall of 1984, the officers of the American met with Lewis Kaplan of the well-known New York law firm of Paul, Weiss, Rifkind, Wharton, and Garrison, presumably to discuss the conditions for engaging his services if a lawsuit should eventuate.

As yet, however, nothing had been heard officially on that front when Weinshel and I met with the officers of the American in December. Though three of them had participated in that fateful October meeting with the psychologist representatives, they seemed as a group not yet convinced that the lawsuit was certain to come. Our plea was that the situation was indeed extremely serious and dangerous, and that from all our understandings, a lawsuit was indeed pending and all but certain to be filed. The only real

---

[9] I have two such accounts in writing.

chance to head it off would be a dramatic new initiative by the American along the lines that had been set in motion by the Curtis Committee report of several years earlier, stated now as an ironclad commitment to some positive action that might regain, to some extent, the American's vanished credibility in the psychologist world.

Toward this end, Weinshel and I felt that we had succeeded. The officers agreed to revive this presumably moribund issue immediately by creating a Special Advisory Committee to the Executive Committee, in order to reopen full consideration of these issues of nonmedical training for clinical psychoanalysis which had been initiated with the creation of the Curtis Committee on Prerequisites for Training almost a decade earlier, in 1975, then successively refined by the three successor Committees—the Calder, the Isay, and the Spruiell. This had been temporarily set aside in San Diego in order to regroup and come up with a plan that would meet the legitimate aspirations of the potential psychologist (and possibly other) nonmedical applicant groups, and yet do so in a manner that could enlist the consensus support of the American. Put this way (in a memorandum to the members of the American by Edward Joseph, President, and Shelley Orgel, the new Chairman of the Board, a year later, in October 1985), that in 1975 "the Association began a process which has continued to the present day," the American could claim, and did on occasion over the years, that all the developments that subsequently took place, leading to the opening of the American's doors to full clinical training for nonmedical applicants, as part of an overall package of changes within the American and in its relation to the International, were already in process and not at all direct responses to the lawsuit (which was subsequently filed). This, of course, has been roundly disputed by the psychologist complainants as a gross distortion of the actual causative sequence of events.

In the discussions in December that led to the creation of the Special Advisory Committee, Weinshel and I were asked for suggestions for the chairmanship. I proposed Herbert Gaskill, with whom I had worked closely as the cochair of the 1974 Conference on Psychoanalytic Education and Research (COPER) at Homestead—one of the major milestones along this particular path. He was a distinguished member of the American who had been President in 1976–77 and was quite universally esteemed as a thoroughly fair-minded, even-handed, and thoughtful individual, with no personal axe to grind, and temperamentally disposed to give every side of a controversial issue a full and open hearing. He also had a long career as Chairman of the Department of Psychiatry at the University of Colorado School of Medicine, a major psychoanalyst within academic medicine and psychiatry, and a major psychiatric statesman and educator within psychoanalysis. Edward Joseph willingly designated Gaskill the chair of the new committee, and to increase its efficiency appointed but two other members, Robert Gilliland and Justin Krent.

Within the American, the announcement, in the December 1984 meeting of the appointment of the Gaskill Committee was hailed as reopening the seemingly derailed dialogue over the possible manner of including nonmedical candidates within the training orbit of the organization, and thus possibly (or even probably) forestalling the perceived psychologist pressures for a lawsuit. The psychologist complainants, now led officially by Welch, saw this only as another Committee—now the fifth—without any perceived assurance that the outcome of its deliberations, whenever that might be, would lead to anything different than the labors of the preceding four committees. Their preparations were therefore neither slowed nor altered, and on March 1, 1985, four psychologist plaintiffs, Bryant Welch, Toni Bernay, Arnold Schneider, and Helen Desmond, brought a civil action suit, on their own behalf and on behalf of a class of several thousand psychoanalytic psychologists, which was filed in the United States District Court for the Southern District of New York.

The suit was primarily against the American Psychoanalytic Association on Sherman antitrust grounds, alleging that the American had illegally conspired to restrain and monopolize the training of psychoanalysts and the delivery of psychoanalytic services to the public, and that this had deprived qualified psychologists of proper access to this way of earning a livelihood. The International Psychoanalytical Association was secondarily named for allowing its American component to engage in these alleged improper and illegal practices. In addition, two of the three accredited training Institutes of the American in New York were also named as defendants: the New York Psychoanalytic Institute and the Columbia University Center for Training and Research. It was never clear to the defendants why these two member institutes were singled out nor why the third institute in New York, the Psychoanalytic Institute of the New York University Medical Center, was spared, despite its reputation as one of those most adamantly opposed of all the member institutes of the American to opening the doors to nonmedical training.

7

My Career in the IPA and
the Filing of the Lawsuit

The lawsuit was filed on March 1, 1985, by the four psychologists acting on behalf of a declared class of several thousand, and under the official auspices of a newly created entity, the Group for the Advancement of Psychotherapy and Psychoanalysis in Psychology (GAPPP), which had been established for that purpose in 1984 under the umbrella of Division 39. It had a war chest of several hundred thousand dollars. The suit claimed that the American unfairly monopolized the quality psychoanalytic training market across the nation and thereby barred psychologists from proper access to this training and practice, which deprived them of this lucrative and prestigious means of earning a livelihood. As stated previously, the International Psychoanalytical Association (IPA) was named as a codefendant for allowing its American component to engage in these practices, contrary to the practice of the IPA's other component organizations around the world.

At the time that the lawsuit was filed, I was a Vice-President and member of the Executive Council of the IPA and a nominee for the presidency; the election was to take place at the 34th IPA Congress to be held in Hamburg at the end of July, five months later. Because it was expected at the time that I would probably run unopposed, which in fact turned out to be the case, I could look forward to the lawsuit being a major, or rather, *the* major concern of my coming presidency, which is indeed what happened. The signing of the settlement agreement did not take place until October 1988, more than three-and-a-half years after the initial filing, and after more than three years into my four-year presidency (1985–1989).

To explain how I came to be in this critical position in organized international psychoanalysis at this critical time, when it would become my task to lead the IPA effort to resolve the contending positions vis-à-vis all the issues, scientific, educational, and professional issues surrounding

137

the question of lay analysis which had festered within the discipline over three-quarters of a century, I will resume the threads of my own scientific biography begun in chapter 4.

Though I had been active in the organizational affairs of the American, joining its committee structure (as a member of the Committee on Training for Research, CTR) and participating in its semiannual meetings from 1960, the year I became a member, I did not involve myself in the International until 1967, though my membership in it had begun, concurrently with my membership in the American. We lived in Topeka, Kansas, and I had worked at The Menninger Foundation (ultimately as Director of Research) up to 1966. We then left for San Francisco, where I was recruited to be Chief of Psychiatry at the Mt. Zion Hospital. While in Topeka, and while our children were young, we took our summer vacations as a family, driving vacations, in alternate years we would go east to visit family—my mother, Judy's mother, and others in New York—then west to visit and camp in different clusters of national parks. After coming to San Francisco in 1966, our three children were old enough (ranging from 15 down to 9) that their summer vacation wishes and plans began to diverge, usually involving differing camp experiences, and Judy and I could begin to vacation by ourselves, and in Europe.

Because the biannual IPA Congresses rotated at the time among major European cities (usually capital cities), we began to attend the Congresses, beginning with the 25th in Copenhagen in 1967, and planned our European vacations around our Congress attendance. At the 26th Congress, in Rome in 1969, the International, for the first time, held a plenary panel on what had up until then seemed to be a peculiarly American preoccupation: the relationship of psychoanalysis to psychotherapy. This provided the opportunity to consider this relationship from the vantage point of the experiences of psychoanalysts in the national and regional centers of psychoanalytic activity around the world, in all their diverse historical developments and ecological settings. On the basis of my intensive study and research in this area, as the principal investigator of the Psychotherapy Research Project of The Menninger Foundation, which by then had been in operation for more than 15 years and had already resulted in nearly 50 publications, I was invited by the Program Committee of the IPA Congress to chair this panel and to present its opening paper. It was titled "The Relationship of Psychoanalysis to Psychotherapy: Current Issues" (Wallerstein, 1969). This presentation to a large plenary session first brought me to the attention of an international psychoanalytic audience.

In 1973, Serge Lebovici of Paris, the newly elected President of the IPA, invited me to cochair with Evelyne Kestemberg of Paris as chair, the coming sixth Pre-Congress on Training—an invitational meeting of training analysts from the worldwide component IPA organizations regularly held just prior to the official week of the IPA Congresses—to be held in London in 1975. This was my entry into the administrative organization of the IPA. The topic of that Pre-Congress was The Contribution of Child Analysis to the Training in Adult Analysis. As it turned out, illness in her family prevented Kestemberg from attending, so at the Pre-Congress I had to assume sole responsibility. My final summarizing address to the Pre-Congress was published in the International Journal (Wallerstein, 1976). Counter to the usual custom of rotating, in 1975, Lebovici invited me again, this time to chair, with Kestemberg as cochair, the coming seventh Pre-Congress to be held in Jerusalem in 1977. At that Pre-Congress the topic was The Principles, the Aims, and the Procedures of Psychoanalytic Training as Represented in our Member Institutes. I gave the opening address, entitled "Perspectives on Psychoanalytic Training Around the World," based on a detailed questionnaire survey of the philosophy and practices of training in our responding member institutes (also published in the *International Journal*, Wallerstein, 1978a). In 1977, the new IPA President, Edward Joseph of New York, invited me to chair—this I stated would be the last occasion—this time by myself, the coming eighth Pre-Congress to be held in New York in 1979. The topic this time was The Impact of the Theory and Practice of Psychotherapy on Training in Psychoanalysis. My own contribution was entitled "Education for Psychotherapy and Psychoanalysis: The Questions," given at the opening plenary session. This was intended to compare and contrast the views expressed in three precirculated papers to the Pre-Congress participants (by Otto Kernberg, Joseph Sandler, and David Zimmerman) in order, on the basis of those three papers, to set up the questions for discussion in the following two days of small group discussions (Wallerstein, 1982).

Meanwhile, as a major figure in the scientific planning for the IPA Pre-Congresses in 1975, 1977, and 1979, I had been invited to the IPA Symposia initiated by President Serge Lebovici, which took place in the years between Congresses, starting in 1976. These had come about as follows: The venue of the 28th IPA Congress in 1973 was the UNESCO building in Paris. The rental fee was nominal, with the stipulation by the UNESCO management that any profits accrued by the Congress not be folded into the general IPA Treasury but be sequestered for specific purposes of scientific and educational advancement. Lebovici, who had been party to this original agreement with UNESCO, conceived the idea that the profits, which were considerable because of that nominal rental, be used to support a sequence of week-long scientific Symposia, on topics of central importance to the IPA, to be held in the years between Congresses. The Symposium would have 40 to 50 invited participants, representing the IPA's administrative and scientific leadership. The scientific Symposium proceedings would take place every morning for the week, and the afternoons would be devoted to meetings of the IPA Executive Council and of the major Committees, Program, Pre-Congress, Arrangements, and others involved in the central planning for the Congress in the following year. In my capacity as chair or cochair of the three successive Pre-Congresses, I was part of this IPA "leadership" group within which I developed intimate working relationships.

This brings us to the 1977 Jerusalem Congress (the 30th). It was the American turn to succeed the European presidency (that of Lebovici). There were two declared contenders, Edward Joseph of New York, whom I had known since we were residents together at my entry into psychiatric training at Mount Sinai Hospital in New York in 1949, and Edward Weinshel, my immediate predecessor as Chief of Psychiatry at Mount Zion Hospital in San Francisco and my close working colleague in my career there. I had promised my full support to Weinshel in this election. At almost the last minute Weinshel withdrew from the race (which was to be decided by vote at the Business Meeting during the Congress) because of his wife's suddenly diagnosed, serious illness. A group of Weinshel's key supporters asked me to allow them to put my name in contention in his place, assuring me that my involvement in the IPA had by then been intense and conspicuous enough for my candidacy to have a good chance of succeeding.

I declined to run. My reason was that two years before (in 1975) I had left my position as Chief of Psychiatry at Mount Zion Hospital to assume the chairmanship of the Department of Psychiatry at the University of California San Francisco School of Medicine, and that I could not compromise my attention to the organizational and building tasks of the Department by taking on another time-consuming role. To try to do both, I felt, would be unfair to each. I agreed, though, to be nominated for one of the eight IPA vice-presidencies (of which three would be from North America), which would make me a member of the IPA Executive Council, its governing body, responsible to the biannual Business Meeting of members. Joseph then ran unopposed, and I was one of the three elected North American vice-presidents from a field of five North Americans who were running. Two years later, at the 31st Congress in New York in 1979, I was reelected for another term as a Vice-President and member of the Executive Council.

When the 32nd Congress, set for Helsinki in 1981, was approaching, I intended to follow the usual custom and not run for reelection, and I let this be known. About six months before that Congress, however, I was urged by Irene Auletta, then the full-time Administrative Director of the IPA at its London headquarters, who spoke, she said, on behalf of many of the IPA leaders, to run again for a vice-presidency and thus remain on the Executive Council. The IPA President had always come from among sitting members of the Executive Council, and I was being looked at by many as the "logical" candidate for the next American turn at the presidency, starting in 1985 (i.e., eight years after the Jerusalem election of an American, Joseph, in 1977, and four years after the coming election of a European as President, to take place in Helsinki in 1981). To make her plea more persuasive, Auletta divulged that in the elections for the vice-presidency, in which those elected from each region are voted on by the entire worldwide membership in attendance at the biannual Business Meeting, I had garnered the highest vote of any of the eight elected. This was news (and a surprise) to me, because the procedure at the time had been to withhold the exact vote count (only seen by the tellers and the sitting President) and only declare the winners. By 1985 I would have been the Chairman of the Medical School Department of Psychiatry for 10 years and could see my commitments and their time demands in a different light.

I then decided to keep my options open, and I was reelected a Vice-President for a third time in Helsinki in 1981 and a fourth time in Madrid in 1983. By that time I was indeed interested in running for President at the coming 34th IPA Congress to be held in Hamburg in 1985. The other individual who could have been a very logical contender in terms of his activity and prominence in the IPA at the time, and also then one of the North American vice-presidents, was my close friend and colleague, and a leading child analyst, Albert J. Solnit, the Director of the Child Study Center and Sterling Professor of Pediatrics and Psychiatry at Yale University. Solnit and I had worked very closely together over the years, both in the International and in the American, especially so during the year in which he was President of the American (1970-71) and I was President-Elect. As it turned out, Solnit chose not to run and I ran unopposed—the last such IPA election without a contest. The election was scheduled for the Business Meeting in Hamburg in the summer of 1985 and turned out, of course, to come just five months after the filing of the lawsuit. As it happened, I left the chairmanship of the Department of Psychiatry at the Medical School on July 1, 1985, after filling 10 difficult years in that post, becoming then a Senior Professor in the Department, free to pursue whatever teaching and scholarly activities I elected. I would now have adequate time for what I perceived to be the more than usually arduous responsibilities of the IPA presidency, given the extraordinary challenge posed by the lawsuit.

Two other aspects of this coming election and presidency starting in Hamburg should be stated here. One had to do with the Congress venue in Hamburg, in what was then West Germany. Between 1949, when the IPA Congresses resumed in Zurich after the eleven-year hiatus caused by World War II, and 1985, the biannual Congresses took place in one or another major European city, except for the 1977 Congress in Jerusalem and the 1979 Congress in New York. Congress venues were chosen at the Business Meetings two or three ahead, after consideration of competing invitations from different applicant host Societies and the recommendations then from the Executive Council. In all the years up to 1985 (40 years after the end of World War II), the IPA had been steadfastly unwilling to consider returning to Germany, though that nation had hosted several Congresses in the pre-Hitler days.[1] At the 1977 Jerusalem Congress one of the invitations was for the 1981 Congress (which did go to Helsinki) to come to (West) Berlin. I was among the several who spoke passionately at the Business Meeting against accepting this invitation. The argument was that it was an invitation tendered in the wrong city (at the first meeting ever in the capital of Israel) to come to the wrong city (Berlin, Hitler's capital), and at the wrong time, when the IPA still contained in its active ranks so many Hitler refugees who had not yet been able to bring themselves to return as visitors to the German world. To the great disappointment of the German analysts, almost all of whom had grown to adulthood in post-Hitler Germany, the invitation was rejected.

At the 1981 Congress in Helsinki, the German Psychoanalytical Association tendered the invitation again, for 1985, and this time to Hamburg, the only major German city that had not given the Nazi party a majority in the last free election, in 1933, that had led to Hitler's accession to power. This time the whole climate surrounding this issue was different, and the invitation was accepted. The IPA was committed to its first return to Germany since the 12th Congress in Wiesbaden in 1932, at a point, 1985, forty years after the fall of Hitler's Germany. For me and for many other IPA members it would be our first return to Germany—I had left as a two-year-old in 1923, but many others had left as adolescents or adults under great difficulty, and at great risk, after Hitler's coming to power—and the Congress was a powerfully moving experience for visitors and Germans alike. When I was installed as IPA President in Hamburg, the German hosts made special mention that this honor was being bestowed upon me in the country of my birth and on my first return to it after 62 years. Some of the spirit of the meeting was conveyed in the poignant statement to me by a German colleague and friend: "We've lived with our shame for forty years wondering if you [meaning the IPA] would ever come back."

The other aspect of the preparations for the Hamburg Congress had to do with the heavy reality of the lawsuit brought against the IPA on March first that year. It was then widely anticipated, but not yet certain, that I would be the next president, in keeping with the agreement worked out in the immediate post–World War II years, when the IPA was being reconstituted as a functioning organization, of the alternation every four

---

[1] Six of the 12 Congresses prior to Hitler's rise to power in 1933 had taken place in Germany, in a different city each time.

years of the presidency between Europe and North America.[2] Some questions were raised—detailed later in this chapter—about the awkwardness that could be created for the IPA with an American president (who was also a member of the American Psychoanalytic Association) during the time of a lawsuit against the American and the IPA. It was already clear that the American and the IPA might have differing interests and differing responses in their preferred defense, creating a potential conflict of interest for the American president. The custom of alternation of the presidency, however, was so compelling that this question was not seriously pursued, and I assured those who expressed concern that if elected President of the IPA, I would for the four-year duration of that office represent only the interests of the IPA and would resign all official committee posts in the American where I would be only an ordinary member.

A somewhat more insistent question was raised about the post of Secretary. In the IPA this has not been an elective office, but an appointment by the President. The reasoning has been that these two highest ranking officers in the International should be individuals who could work very closely together on the basis of their own intimate personal and professional relationship; it was customary that on election, the new President would announce his Secretary, typically a colleague from the same city, though not always from the same component Society. I had decided to adhere to this custom and designate Edward Weinshel as Secretary, rather than accede to the requests that I "balance" my administration with a European choice for Secretary. My reasoning here was identical with that for my own assumption of the presidency. There were also additional considerations. The convenience and congeniality of our working together had already been established in our years together in San Francisco (1966–1985), both at the Mount Zion Hospital Department of Psychiatry and on the Education Committee of the San Francisco Psychoanalytic Institute. I also felt, contrary to the representations being made by some on this issue, that only an American President and an American administration of the IPA could be willing to represent the IPA unflinchingly in the face of potential conflicts between the IPA and the American positions vis-à-vis the defense of the lawsuit (and the forms that these conflicts could take were already in the air).

All this reflected aspects of the climate within the IPA during the period leading to the Hamburg Congress with my unopposed election there as IPA President. The IPA's encounter with the lawsuit had already begun

---

[2] Since then, in fact during my administration, it was worked out to include Latin America in a three-way rotation of the presidency, and to equalize the number of vice-presidency positions to three from each of the three major regions, in acknowledgment of the recent tremendous growth and spread of psychoanalysis in Latin America, which brought that region within respectable distance of parity in numbers with Europe and North America.

for me earlier, with a "Private and Confidential" memorandum from Adam Limentani of London, President, to the Executive Council dated April 19, 1985. It began with a statement that he had been informed by Kenneth Calder, an Associate Secretary of the IPA who resided in New York, that he (Calder) had been served with a summons notifying him that the IPA had been named as one of the four codefendants in a civil action, as a class action complaint asking for a "declaratory judgment, an injunction, and treble damages" for "violation of the antitrust laws." The suit had been brought by the four psychologists as representatives of Division 39 of the American Psychological Association. Limentani had met immediately with Lista Cannon of Boodle, Hatfield & Co., the IPA's attorneys in London. Their determination was first to free Calder from the burden of appearing in court, because he was only an Associate Secretary of the IPA, an appointive office, and a nonvoting member of the Executive Council. Second, that an American attorney, Charles (Trip) Dorkey of Richards, O'Neill, and Allegaert, the New York firm affiliated with Boodle, Hatfield & Co., would be appointed to represent the IPA and to appear in due course in court in response to the suit. The third determination was that

> the IPA should in no way join the American Psychoanalytic Association or any other parties being sued—this in support of our contention that: (a) the IPA does not come under the jurisdiction of the courts in the United States, being incorporated in Switzerland, and with a President and a permanent office in the United Kingdom; and (b) that the IPA does *not* restrict training in psychoanalysis to medically-qualified applicants only, which forms the basis for the Complaint now lodged [Limentani memorandum, April 19, 1985].

The initial court hearing had been set for April 22. (Later an extension to June 1 was granted for the response to the suit, with time for additional documents until June 15.)

On May 15 there was a planning meeting in London. Present were Limentani, IPA President, Moses Laufer, also of London, IPA Secretary, Irene Auletta, IPA Administrative Director, and Lista Cannon and Trip Dorkey, the attorneys from London and New York. In a second private and confidential memorandum to the Executive Council, dated May 29, Limentani said of this meeting:

> The Attorneys had considered the question of a plea by the IPA against the jurisdiction of the American courts as outlined to you previously. Following further discussions between us, the professional and considered advice of the Attorneys was not to

pursue this line. Quite apart from the notorious ability of the U.S. courts to extend jurisdiction as they see fit, it was felt that the existence of our Treasury in the United States, and our recognition as a not-for-profit organization by the Internal Revenue Service of the U.S.A., gave little hope of our proving non-jurisdiction. It was, in addition, felt that the IPA should stand by its stated principles and be seen to be, and to have been throughout, behaving in an entirely open and ethical manner. Our "defence" was, in fact, that there was no need for us to defend ourselves, since there was no case to answer by the IPA. This reinforced our decision to be represented by Attorneys quite separate from those representing the other defendants [Limentani memorandum, May 29, 1985].

Limentani went on to indicate that:

Early in May it became clear from discussion between Mr. Dorkey and the Attorneys acting for the Plaintiffs that the latter might consider ending the case against the IPA if the IPA were willing to agree to promulgate a policy . . . to have our Institutes consider qualified psychologists for admission to training on the same terms as M.D.s. In accordance with the advice of our Attorneys, we instructed them to receive *on a totally without prejudice basis* the draft form of settlement terms proposed [Limentani, May 29, 1985].

In a May 23 draft of the proposed settlement between the plaintiffs and the IPA, the key items 2 and 3 declared that (2) the IPA would adopt and support to the full extent of its powers that each IPA-affiliated institute would admit doctoral-level psychologists from the United States to its training programs on the same nondiscriminatory basis as medical doctors; and that (3) the IPA would admit psychologist-analysts from the United States to full membership, again on the same nondiscriminatory basis as medical graduates, even if such psychologist-analysts were barred by the American Psychoanalytic Association; and further that the IPA would recognize and accredit all psychoanalytic institutes in the United States which met its standards, even if they had not been recognized and accredited by the American—in contravention, of course, of the terms of the Regional Association agreement between the IPA and the American.

This settlement proposal had been "found to be unacceptable as drafted," and the IPA attorneys had been directed to continue negotiating on the basis of a reworded draft that would indicate that "the IPA shall continue its policy to admit non-medical applicants to full training and full membership privileges in the IPA," but also indicating that in regard to the American, the IPA could only promise and propose, "within its power and authority"—a clear reference to the restraints embodied in the Regional Association status of the American. At the same time, Limentani reported that:

> During the second week of May, the Annual Meeting of the American Association took place in Denver. At that time—we have since been informed—there were rumours repeated that the IPA was settling with the Plaintiffs without prior consultation with the American, without considering its position, and against its interests, and that the IPA was acting entirely independently without any consultations with the Attorneys of the American [Limentani, May 29, 1985].

Limentani then indicated that he had been in touch with a number of American colleagues, making clear (1) that the IPA attorneys *had* been in touch with the attorneys of the American; (2) that the proposed draft settlement was only an initial exploratory document, and no agreement would be entered into without the consent of the entire IPA Executive Council and full consultation with the American; (3) that in fact the American had taken actions of which the IPA had not been informed; (4) that it was obviously to the interest of the plaintiffs to sow discord between the IPA and the American; (5) that, in his opinion, the plaintiffs had been "very badly advised" to include the IPA as a defendant in the suit, since it would have been more to their advantage to reserve the IPA officers as potential (subpoenaed) witnesses called to testify to the IPA's own open policy in regard to training nonphysicians; and (6) that the IPA would like very much to play the role of concerned mediator between the positions of the plaintiffs and of the American. Limentani went on to declare that "our Attorneys have pointed out that in fact if the IPA settles separately, it will do damage to the defence of the American Association. Our Attorneys were instructed to make it clear to all concerned with the case that the IPA was trying to reach a settlement purely in the spirit of compromise, in the sincere hope that the IPA could act as mediators, and in no way to exacerbate the adversarial aspects of the case" (Limentani, May 29, 1985).

In light of all of this, Limentani went on to notify the Executive Council that he had instructed the IPA attorneys to notify the attorneys for the plaintiffs: (1) that the proposed settlement terms were "entirely unacceptable"; (2) that the IPA had no alternative but to defend the case in court; (3) that he felt the plaintiffs had been ill-advised to sue the IPA because, "The general policy of the IPA has always been totally liberal towards the training of non-medical people and remains so"; (4) that "the

IPA feels that the American was working appropriately to resolve the situation" [a reference no doubt to the deliberations of the Gaskill Committee], though there was no expectation of an early solution"; (5) that "the American has chosen to this point not to train non-medical people while others of the Component Organizations have chosen to do so"; in each instance "That has been their prerogative"; (6) that "The hope and aim of the IPA throughout, since before the lawsuit was filed, has been to find a way in which the IPA could play a role as mediator. This hope and aim has continued through these present negotiations and will do so in the future"; and (7) that "The inclusion of the IPA as a defendant in this case would seem to suggest that the Plaintiffs feel that the IPA has no role to play in such mediation, and indeed that they have relinquished any hope of any kind of future relationship with the American and the IPA. The IPA suggests that Plaintiffs should seriously reconsider this matter" (Limentani, May 29, 1985).

Thus Limentani comprehensively laid out his overall assessment of the situation created by the lawsuit and the stance and policy line that he trusted the IPA would pursue. It was a framework that was completely congenial with my own, whatever concerns Limentani may have had on this score. As he went on to say, "We can only sympathise with our American colleagues in Council, but must add that it is not only they who may feel a division of loyalties in this matter." He ended his long memorandum with three points, one reiterating the aims of the IPA in the matter, the second pointing to the potential expense of the lawsuit and the fracture lines that this could open in the IPA, and the third stating the special difficulties he felt his successor (American) president could face.

On the first score he said, "Our aim and purpose has throughout been to protect the interests of the IPA and its members, and of course its Component Organizations, which include the American Association, but also 36 other Societies around the world. If there had been, or indeed proves to be, any honourable way in which the IPA could be removed from the litigation, and hopefully act as mediators in any degree in this matter, that would, we felt, have been the best answer." On the second score, the expense of the pending litigation and its impact on the solvency of the IPA treasury, he said, "We are then faced with the question as to whether it could be *ethical* for our funds to be entirely taken up with fighting this case when those funds are subscribed by over 60% of our members who do not belong to the American Association, many of whom are themselves non-medical and nearly all of whom belong to Component Organizations who freely admit non-medical applicants to training and membership?" (italics added). Here Limentani accurately foreshadowed what later became a major threat of actual fracture of the IPA—the fall 1986 resolution to be proposed by ten highly prestigious members of his own British Society.

In reference to his successor, who would bear the brunt of dealing with the lawsuit both vis-à-vis the plaintiffs and the fellow defendants, he said that "during these past weeks we in London have also been very much aware that an American President of the IPA might indeed find this situation a more 'delicate' one to deal with, and our aim was to look for a possibility to avoid such a confrontation for him" (Limentani, May 29, 1985). Here Limentani's hope was clearly in vain; it seemed highly unlikely that the plaintiffs would accede to the IPA's wish to be released from the role of defendant and shifted to that of (impartial) mediator, and even less likely, if not impossible, that any negotiated settlement could be reached between the plaintiffs and the four defendant groups in the two months that yet remained of Limentani's four-year presidency.

Limentani had invited responses from the Executive Council members to both his April 19 and May 29 memoranda. Written responses were received from seven, about half the members, five of them physicians and two nonmedical. From the North American members of Council, Francis McLaughlin of Baltimore, Treasurer of the IPA,[3] pledged full support to Limentani's efforts and indicated that our treasury could stand the burden of defending the lawsuit if need be—which turned out to be a serious underestimation of what the legal costs of such a defense would be. Kenneth Calder of New York, an Associate Secretary of the IPA who had been served the original summons, expressed apprehension that the IPA and the American could get pitted against each other, that the lawsuit could be bitter and protracted, with Bryant Welch (the leader among the plaintiffs) reputedly driven by the ambition to bring the American to its knees, and that a best estimate of the cost of defending the lawsuit was one-and-a-half million dollars. He also drew a gloomy scenario of the outcome of the lawsuit, win or lose. In either case he saw

> disaster. In the best outcome we would win everything in a court of law, seriously damage psychoanalysis . . . alienate all parties concerned, decimate our treasuries, bankrupt the N.Y. Psychoanalytic (Columbia would survive),[4] lose large quantities of time and energy in pursuing our case and make us defensive

---

[3] Because the IPA had not been able to that point to secure tax-exempt status as a "charitable organization" in the United Kingdom (where the IPA had its permanent office) and dues would have been subject to taxation as income if collected in pounds, the Treasurer was always an American; dues were collected worldwide in dollars, the treasury held in American banks, with regular disbursements to the London office for operating expenses. During the presidency of Joseph Sandler (1989–1993), tax-exempt status was secured in the U.K. so that dues can now also be collected in pounds or ECUs, and the Treasurer no longer need be an American.

[4] Its legal defense would have been provided by the attorneys of Columbia University, with which it was officially affiliated.

even with each other. And that is the *best* outcome. In the worst outcome we would lose in a court of law, be forced to restructure the American, the IPA, and our individual Institutes, be forced to pay millions of dollars in damages ("treble damages") and we'd all lose confidence and trust in the world around us [Calder to Limentani, June 9, 1985].

Two council members responded from Latin America; both expressed concern about the "delicate" issue that would be posed by an American president succeeding Limentani, and inheriting the burden of the lawsuit. Inga Villarreal of Colombia, an Associate Secretary of the IPA, expressed first her sentiment that, "the whole idea of the IPA and its Component Organizations being forced by an American Court into anything regarding training or admission of members is not acceptable and would provoke indignation on the part of many colleagues world-wide, even from the ones who fully accept the idea of admission of psychologists." She then went on to talk of the "possible 'delicate' situation for the future North American President. I realize that you have been working very hard to get this settled or well on the way before the next presidential term. Perhaps the new President could appoint a Secretary from another continent and delegate this issue to him." Agustin Palacios of Mexico, a Vice-President of the IPA, raised the same problem this way: "One final point is the great concern which you express over the delicate position in which an American IPA president might find himself . . . I feel that this matter requires careful consideration and merits lengthy discussion at the Council meetings in Hamburg."[5] Palacios then went on to offer the most insightful and accurate assessment of what would prove to be the plaintiffs' strategy:

As I see it, the plaintiffs do not seem to have been quite as misled as would seem in their having included the IPA in their lawsuit. Rather it would appear to have been a shrewd maneuver whereby the plaintiffs hope to profit from the tensions created by pitting one organization against the other . . . they hope (I believe) to use us as leverage and as a weapon in the subordination of the APA [American Psychoanalytic Association] stance . . . rather than being naive it would seem that the plaintiffs have an inordinate awareness of the IPA's intimate internal political structure which allows for the APA to retain a

---

[5] Actually these cautions proved to be a complete misreading of the IPA internal political situation. As it turned out, only an American President of the IPA, and one willing to use the full weight of his office personally, could confront the American Association to the extent necessary to help broker an ultimate negotiated settlement acceptable to the American, to the IPA, and to the plaintiffs.

unique position in terms of status and autonomy. . . . Should, however, the IPA, for whatever reason, decide to accept and accede to the plaintiffs' demand for independent recognition, we would be infringing upon the privileged jurisdiction of the APA which, as I see it, would call for a direct confrontation between the IPA and the APA. . . . When seen in this light it does not seem likely that the plaintiffs will show much interest in dropping the lawsuit against the IPA.

All in all, this was the most prescient foretelling of the future unfolding events.

There were three responses from Europe, two of them from nonmedical members of Council. Of these, Janine Chasseguet-Smirgel of Paris, a Vice-President of the IPA, took a position that harked back to Freud and to the International Training Commission (ITC) created by Eitingon in 1925.

It is in the interest of both parties, I mean the Plaintiffs and the American Psychoanalytic Association, at least in my opinion, to accept that the IPA play the mediator as you stress in your letter. . . . An agreement should be found in their own interest. If the American accept to recognize the authority of the IPA in matters of training (i.e. *who* is to be trained and *how*). . . . This of course would require a preliminary agreement between the American and the IPA.

This proved, in fact, to be the exact strategy that the IPA would pursue, though with no effort to re-create the long defunct ITC. The other nonmedical Council member, Janice de Saussure of Switzerland, also a Vice-President of the IPA, took a line more accommodating to the position of the American: "If we are to be accused of violating the antitrust laws because of establishing training standards in regard to basic requirements for admission to the program, then we, as well as all professional groups are in serious trouble." And further, "As you know I personally do not agree with the limitations of training to medical doctors but I think it of prime importance to recognize the right of a group to do so." The third European, Harald Leupold-Lowenthal, a medical analyst from Vienna and an Associate Secretary of the IPA, took a historical overview of the issue: "Perhaps this unpleasant legal proceedings, well handled so far by the IPA, will in the end bring something positive: a final answer to the 'Question of Lay Analysis,' satisfying for all parties concerned since 1927. Since the Paris IPA Congress in 1938 this question was rather more negated and denied than satisfactorily discussed and solved."

After this initial charting by Limentani of the IPA's stance regarding the lawsuit and his gathering of advice and support from the Executive Council membership in advance of the full Executive Council meetings in connection with the coming Hamburg Congress, a number of further events took place during the two-month balance of Limentani's presidency. First, he received a response to his May 29 memorandum from Edward Joseph, President of the American, dated June 7, 1985: "You eased my mind. . . . I had of course heard the rumors that circulated in the corridors of the meeting of the American [in Denver in mid-May] that the IPA was planning to settle the suit on its own." Joseph then went on to inform Limentani of the activities of the American in regard to the lawsuit. Formal action had been entered at the beginning of March in the Federal District Court of Southern New York. "The formal charges claim that by restricting admission to training to medically qualified individuals only, the American and the Institutes were acting in restraint of trade serving thereby to restrict training opportunities, increasing cost of psychoanalytic services to the public, and acting in violation of the anti-trust provisions of federal law" (Joseph to Limentani, June 7, 1985).

The American had hired as its attorney Lewis Kaplan, with whom the officers had had preliminary discussions in the fall of 1984, four or five months before the lawsuit was definitely filed; the New York Institute had now retained the same attorney. The Columbia Institute was being defended by Columbia University, which had hired an outside firm that worked closely with Mr. Kaplan and his associates. The American felt that it "seemed reasonable" that the IPA would engage the same firm, "but obviously you preferred to work through your London attorney and their New York associate law firm." But there were ongoing consultations between the attorneys for the IPA and the American.

The preliminary step already taken by the American was to enter a blanket denial of the various items charged and to request dismissal of the suit on a variety of grounds. The motion for dismissal had yet to be heard in court. The "discovery" phase was now being entered upon, meaning the defendants' meeting the request for various documents required by the plaintiffs. Meanwhile, the four plaintiffs had moved formally to have this certified as a class-action suit on behalf of all Ph.D. psychologists who desired psychoanalytic training under the auspices of the American and the IPA. A preliminary hearing on this class-action motion was set for June 5. The American would not be opposed to a class action, but would want it extended to all nonphysicians, not limited only to doctoral-level psychologists, so that however the lawsuit would eventually be decided, the decision would cover all potential nonmedical applicants.

Joseph then briefly reviewed the recent history of the American on the issue of nonmedical training (the research training program [CTR and then CORST], the decade of study by four committees, the deadlock in San Diego in May 1984, and the December 1984 decision to appoint the Gaskill Committee), "to see if it could come up with a single proposal that would be reasonable and clearly stated [and] could be ultimately submitted to the membership of the American for its approval or disapproval." This Committee had already submitted a report to the Executive Committee, the Board, and the Executive Council at the just concluded Denver meeting. "All three bodies approved the principle of the report which provided for some training of non-medical people for clinical practice through the utilization of a separate waiver procedure and concluded with a statement that could be answered by the membership in a yes or no manner so that a clear sense of the wishes of the membership could be obtained." This proposal would now be further refined and considered again in December 1985. "If it once again passes the administrative bodies of the organization it will then be sent to the membership for its opinion as to whether this step should be undertaken" (Joseph, letter to Limentani, June 7, 1985).

Joseph then tried to underscore the continuity of these events within the American, pointing out that "the Gaskill Committee was well underway before the lawsuit entered the picture," which was technically true if one considers just the date of filing of the suit. "Thus these are not considerations that have been brought about by virtue of the lawsuit." Joseph then indicated that the attorneys for the American believed the organization had a strong defense based upon the principle of academic freedom, and he indicated that he also was not clear why the IPA was included in the suit, but also felt it to be ill-advised. He ended by expressing his appreciation of the IPA's wish to act as a mediator, and added that personally he "was sure that the rumors were false and that the IPA would not in any way do anything that might possibly undermine the position of one of its component organizations" (Joseph, June 7, 1985). In this detailed response to Limentani, Joseph laid out what the American's intended strategy in defending the lawsuit would be, and, like Limentani, he foresaw the tension lines that could develop between the two organizations in attempting to coordinate a common defense.

A week later, in a June 13 letter to Irene Auletta, Lista Cannon, the attorney in London, brought the IPA up to date on legal proceedings to that time. The plaintiffs had requested that the IPA produce a large range of official documents for discovery by June 17. Cannon's advice was that the IPA should not open its entire files to this request; the American's attorneys were trying to limit the plaintiffs' requests only to those documents directly relevant to the litigation, and for these purposes an index or catalogue of all IPA files would be useful. Was this available or could it be readily prepared? Our attorneys would then produce all "relevant" documents for "mutually convenient inspection," either at IPA headquarters or the

London attorneys' offices, except those that are "protected by attorney/client, work product or other privilege." For these purposes the attorneys would wish to review all "relevant" documents before the inspection, which wouldn't be until some time in July.

Meanwhile there had been a pretrial hearing before Judge John F. Keenan. Six attorneys attended; the three principal ones were Cliff Stromberg on behalf of the plaintiffs, Lewis Kaplan on behalf of the American, and Trip Dorkey on behalf of the IPA. The purpose of the hearing was to consider the class-certification motion made by the plaintiffs. The American was forcefully opposed to this motion as framed by the plaintiffs, "on the ground . . . that there was no logic to limiting the class to Psychologists with Ph.D.s." The American wanted to take specific discovery, by documents and depositions, of the class issue, including first the deposition of all the named plaintiffs. The Judge allowed 60 days to complete discovery on the class-action motion with another conference on this issue set for August 7. If the defendants, particularly the American, still opposed class certification as proposed by the plaintiffs, at that time, the Judge would set a schedule to allow written objections to be put to the Court, after which he would rule on whether class certification as proposed was appropriate to this litigation.

The attorneys for the American also indicated that they might move to dismiss the complaint altogether, prior to completion of discovery on the class issue. The judge said that such a motion could be submitted at any time. Because the judge also indicated that discovery at this point would be limited to the question of class certification, and should not address the overall merits of the action until the certification issue was settled, Cannon advised that it was unlikely that any depositions could be taken of IPA witnesses until after the judge ruled on the class issue. At the earliest this would be August 7, and if the American continued to oppose the class certification, then it might not be until months later, that is, well into the successor IPA administration, with its new IPA officers.

Cannon's letter ended with a description of the discussion between Dorkey and Kaplan after the hearing, which already presaged the range of problems that could—and actually later did—arise in reconciling the differing perspectives of the IPA and the American concerning a common defense of the lawsuit.

> After the hearing, Mr. Dorkey met briefly with Mr. Kaplan. . . . Mr. Kaplan is going to take the depositions of the named plaintiffs on the class issue and he said that he thought this could be useful to gather information relevant to a motion to dismiss the entire action. He has invited the IPA to join such a motion. Mr. Dorkey has told the American's lawyer that we

would like to see the American's motion papers in advance and that we would consider joining such a motion or serving a slightly different version if it was in the best interests of all concerned. . . . Mr. Dorkey has stressed to Mr. Kaplan that the IPA wishes to cooperate and be an honest broker between the parties. Mr. Dorkey believes that the American appears to have taken the offensive in the case by aggressively opposing class certification . . . the initiative now appears to lie with the American [Cannon, letter to Auletta, June 13, 1985].

In response to this letter, Auletta had a phone conversation with Cannon and wrote her two letters, all on June 18. In sum, the production of an index or catalog of the IPA's sprawling records was a "horrifying" prospect, something that could not be undertaken with the time and resources available. Also conveyed was a description of the heavy work schedule in the IPA headquarters during this very busy period just prior to the pending Hamburg Congress, to be followed directly by the planned August staff vacations. Further conveyed was a general description of the state of the IPA records. Until 1959, all papers had been passed from one president to his successor and all six presidents before 1957 were now dead. Of them all, only Ernest Jones's papers would be still available through the Archives of the British Psychoanalytical Society. Under the presidency of William Gillespie (1959–1963), a separate office had been established for the IPA, housed in a room at the British Society, with all its files to remain henceforth in IPA custody. Between 1971 and 1985 the IPA office consisted of a single room in Auletta's home, and until 1977 she was the sole employed staff member. At this point—1985—the IPA was in the process of moving into its own headquarters building; "we have always just muddled along."

The next events took place in July. On July 15 and 16, Kaplan deposed Bryant Welch, with Stromberg present on behalf of Welch, and Clint Fisher, Dorkey's associate, on behalf of the IPA. Of moment to the issues of the suit, Welch was trained both as a lawyer and then as a clinical psychologist. He was currently the Chair of the American Psychological Association's Board of Professional Affairs, organizer and member of the Board of Trustees of GAPPP, the Group for the Advancement of Psychotherapy and Psychoanalysis in Psychology (the actual sponsors of the lawsuit), and the Chair-elect of the Coalition of Applied and Professional Psychology. He had been in personal analysis, had applied for analytic training under the CORST program of the American in 1981, but had not been accepted because of insufficient research credentials, and then had reapplied and been accepted in 1984. Welch also revealed the financial arrangements between the plaintiffs and the attorney they had hired, Clifford Stromberg of the Washington law firm of Hogan and Hartson, an expert in the interface between healthcare and antitrust litigation. The plaintiffs would pay hourly rates through the completion of the discovery process. At that time, a "modified contingency" arrangement would become effective. Under this arrangement the plaintiffs would only pay one third of the hourly rates, but if they were to win the case, Hogan and Hartson would recover double what their fee would have been. By this early stage, plaintiff costs already had totaled approximately $50,000. The financial commitment in support of the lawsuit had been undertaken by GAPPP, an organization incorporated in 1984 with a three-member Board of Directors, Welch, Nathan Stockhamer, and Ernest Lawrence. Thus far $250,000 had been received, and all of this had been committed to the costs of the legal action. In a May 7 circular letter sent out over the signatures of the three officers of GAPPP, additional funds had been solicited with the statement, "We need money. The lawsuit is expensive, and it is imperative that we have a large war chest so that the merits of the case need not be compromised by financial considerations. If we prevail on the merits and receive attorney fees from the court, large contributors will be offered reimbursement." It was indicated that "many leading psychologists" had contributed or pledged up to $3,000 a person. A further appeal for funds was made in another informational letter of July 16. These were the essential discoveries of six hours of depositions over two days.

On July 18, three days after the deposition of Welch, the attorneys for the American (who also represented the New York Institute) and the attorneys for the Columbia Institute filed a motion requesting the Court to render a summary judgment dismissing the lawsuit on the ground that there was no genuine issue as to any material facts. The basic argument presented was that the issues at stake—the propriety of nonmedical or lay analysis—had been matters of professional and scientific discourse and controversy for 60 years (dating to Freud's *The Question of Lay Analysis*, in 1926) and that no court could have competence to adjudicate this longstanding professional and scientific dispute.

This brief by the defendants' attorneys had begun with a comprehensive and very fair summary of the long and complex history of the controversy around lay analysis. Then, in regard to the restriction of clinical psychoanalytic training in the Institutes of the American to the medically qualified, the brief went on to argue that academic admissions criteria, however much in dispute, are solely issues for decision by the academic scientific community, that they are a noncommercial aspect of the learned professions and therefore not subject to review under the antitrust laws: "these admissions decisions do not implicate the antitrust laws; the Sherman Act never was intended to turn antitrust courts into super-admissions committees for colleges, universities or psychoanalytic institutes (p. 27). . . . [A]dmissions criteria, while they may have economic effects, simply are not the sort of commercial restraints to which the Sherman Act was directed" (p. 28).

Any effort to apply the Sherman Act to such issues, it was argued, would be a clear violation of the First Amendment rights to free speech (academic freedom).

> Plaintiffs ask this Court first to sit in judgment on the lay analysis controversy and to resolve this "theoretical dispute" by pronouncing that there is "no reasonable basis" . . . for the M.D. requirement and that those who believe otherwise are wrong [p. 33]. . . . [T]he notion that the Court should sit in judgment as to who is right and who is wrong about lay analysis is, we submit, misguided both as a constitutional and as a practical matter [p. 34]. . . . That the Sherman Act stops where First Amendment concerns begin is well established [p. 37]. . . . The antitrust laws provide no objective standards by which this Court can resolve a doctrinal controversy that has divided the professional community for sixty years. . . . [P]sychoanalysts and others in the mental health field are not in agreement on the best qualifications for future analysts. . . . Currently, these disputes are pursued in the marketplace of ideas [p. 39]. . . . Plaintiffs' claims ultimately come down to a difference of opinion and belief. They do not believe medical training should be an admissions criterion for psychoanalytic training and defendants believe it should. This is not a dispute that belongs in the courts. It is not an issue of antitrust law. The complaint should be dismissed [p. 4].

Here was laid out the essential litigation argument fashioned by the attorneys for the American in an uncompromising defense in the lawsuit and a flat rejection of the plaintiffs' legal claims. It was a stance away from a continued search for a negotiated settlement, that is, away from the IPA's preferred posture, in which the IPA would act in the role of "honest broker" (cf. the Limentani memoranda).

On July 30, in the midst of the 34th IPA Congress in Hamburg, Lista Cannon sent a letter to Irene Auletta transmitting all the materials in connection with the motion of the American, which asked for a summary judgment dismissing the complaint, plus the verbatim text of the motion itself, all its supporting documents, and a memorandum from Clint Fisher (July 18) summarizing the Welch deposition. Cannon added that at a very late point, the American had asked whether the IPA would be willing to sign the motion as a party in support. In view of the very short time permitted by the American, the IPA attorneys felt unable to make a decision to sign the memorandum. Cannon stated that, "We had not been able to do any independent research to support the legal and factual conclusions in the American's memorandum, and we had not had the benefit of asking the IPA for its views of the facts as set out in the American's memorandum." Additionally, "We think that the motion of the American may be premature in that it would have been more strongly based if the American had waited until the conclusion of discovery." The letter ended with the briefing schedule on the American's motion. The plaintiffs' response was due August 19. The American's reply, if any, was due September 17. Judge Keenan might agree to hear oral arguments on September 29 and would be free thereafter to reserve his decision; there was therefore no indication at this time when judgment might be made on this first major move of the lawsuit. Meanwhile, Judge Keenan had stayed all discovery except the deposition of Bryant Welch, which had taken place on July 15 and 16. This stay of discovery ensured that no demands would be made on the IPA to produce documents in London until after the ruling on the American's motion.

This was the state of affairs as the IPA Executive Council met in Hamburg at the end of July and the beginning of August 1985 at the IPA Congress, when the European administration of the IPA with Limentani as president would be succeeded by an American administration (for the next four years) with Edward Weinshel of San Francisco as the designated Secretary and Howard Schlossman of New Jersey as the newly elected Treasurer. The lawsuit had been filed five months earlier; the discovery process had begun with the Bryant Welch deposition; and the American had already filed the motion to dismiss the lawsuit, with the participation of the New York and Columbia Institutes, but with the IPA abstaining. Within the American, the Gaskill Committee, only created in December 1984, had already, by May 1985, brought a preliminary report geared to proposing a mechanism for the inauguration of a limited program for training nonphysicians in clinical psychoanalysis, with the expectation that this would be brought to definitive membership vote within a year. It was already evident, at this early stage in the course of the lawsuit, that the American and the IPA saw their interests, or at least their strategies, somewhat differently, and that their respective attorneys, Lew Kaplan and his associates for the American, and Lista Cannon (of London) and Trip Dorkey and Clint Fisher (both of New York) for the IPA, were pursuing different tactics in the implementation of their partly divergent interests. It would become my task, and that of my (American) administration of the IPA, to somehow reconcile our position with that of the officers of the American, so as to fashion a common defense in a very serious and difficult lawsuit.

The First Year of the Lawsuit

I was elected President of the Inter-
national Psychoanalytical Association on July 31, 1985, and the next day, as
my first official act, I presided over a joint meeting of the outgoing and
incoming IPA Executive Councils. Customarily, this is a ceremonial and
social meeting marking the biannual "changing of the guard." On this
occasion it was, however, a serious discussion about the lawsuit and the
IPA's position in relation to it. Moses Laufer voiced the common European
view that the IPA was in a lawsuit only because of the actions of the
American, with which most Europeans were totally out of sympathy, and
expressed concern for the potential divisiveness of these perceptions within
the IPA. Several people, in a variation on this theme, felt it important that
there be significant European input into the IPA decision-making process,
in order to keep the matter from being seen as a wholly American issue, or
one in which the American's position would be perceived as having primacy
within the counsels of the IPA. In line with this, it was decided that the
main direction of the legal representation on behalf of the IPA would be
centered in the London attorneys, with their American legal associates guided
and constrained by this European oversight. It was also decided, however,
not to attempt to move the Treasury out of the United States; this would be
"morally indefensible." One weakness in the defendants' position was pointed
out. There was a clause in the IPA Bylaws that if an American sought
psychoanalytic training in an IPA Institute outside the United States,
clearance should be requested from the American (part of the price of the
post–World War II reconciliation of the American with the IPA), and this
could be seized upon by the plaintiffs as evidence of the restraint of trade
intentions of the American. Though it was stated that such permission was
always granted when requested, the requirement was nonetheless there, and
I have already presented the documentation of Luborsky's experience in the
late 1940s when Flugel tried to obtain permission to analyze him under the
auspices of the London Institute, and Bowlby, then Secretary of the Training

Committee, wrote back rejecting the application on the ground that "it would raise great difficulties were we to undertake to train non-medicals from the States."

At the urging primarily of American members of Council it was agreed to send a letter of explanation of all the issues in the lawsuit from the point of view of the IPA to the entire membership (Arnold Cooper), and that all minutes of our official meetings, memoranda, and other documents pertaining to the lawsuit should be vetted first by our attorneys before being released (Ed Joseph, a member of the outgoing Council in his role as the then immediate past-President of the IPA). Toward the end of the meeting, Agustin Palacios, a Latin American member, expressed strong support of the Europeans' concerns about the potential for divisiveness within the IPA: "Inevitably, many members outside the States will get angry and see it as a fact that the IPA's limited resources will be used up simply to rescue the American from a situation into which it has got itself." It was finally agreed that a meeting would be held in December (1985) in New York between the officers of the American (the six-member Executive Committee) and all the IPA Executive Council members who would be in New York then, with the stipulation that I make sure there would always be at least one European and one Latin American present (Minutes, Executive Council IPA, Hamburg, August 1, 1985).

Four weeks later, Limentani, immediate past-President of the IPA, wrote to Richard Simons, President-Elect of the American, that he had uncovered several letters in the Archives of the British Psychoanalytical Society that demonstrated that the American had never interfered with the enrollment for training in London of nonmedical applicants from the United States—documents that could be a critical component of the American's defense against antitrust charges. For example, one of the letters, dated July 2, 1969, was from Jacob Arlow, as Chairman of the Board on Professional Standards of the American, to Enid Balint, Hon. Secretary of the Training Committee of the London Institute. It stated: "Our policy in the matter has been that the institute abroad must determine for itself whether or not it should accept the applicant as a student. You must appreciate that for our Association to act otherwise would put us in the position of setting standards for institutes outside of the United States as to who is and who is not qualified to study psychoanalysis. This is a position which we are most loathe to assume" (Letter, Limentani to Simons, August 29, 1985). This was followed by an information letter a week later from Lista Cannon to Irene Auletta, notifying the IPA that the August 7 pretrial conference with the judge had been cancelled and that therefore the determination of the class-action certification would be further delayed. Cannon also reiterated that the IPA attorneys still felt the time not right for the IPA to join the American's motion to dismiss the suit. The IPA's attorneys felt the motion to have been premature and would have been stronger if filed after completion of the discovery process, but of course it still could be filed again then. Cannon also warned that after the decision on the class-action motion, the schedule of depositions and the requirement to produce documents for discovery would be on in earnest (Letter, Cannon to Auletta, September 6, 1985).

On September 27, Lewis Kaplan, on behalf of the American and with associated separate attorneys representing the New York[1] and the Columbia Institutes, respectively, filed a reply memorandum to the plaintiffs' brief on the issue of the defendants' motion to dismiss the lawsuit. The crux of Kaplan's argument was that the case simply did not fall under the antitrust laws.

> The antitrust laws do not apply to academic admissions criteria, even if those criteria are alleged to have adverse economic effects or purposes, at least where the criteria in question reflect a controversy of the kind at issue here [p. 2]. . . . It is one thing to say that professionals may not fix prices when they go to the marketplace to sell their services. It is quite another thing to say that the antitrust laws require courts to second-guess institutions of higher learning on the kind of background that is necessary or desirable for the study or practice of a profession. In seeking to apply the antitrust laws to such matters, plaintiffs' reach far exceeds their grasp [pp. 4–5]. . . . Plaintiffs do not dispute the long-standing existence of the lay analysis controversy—a controversy that lies at the heart of this case and that cannot be resolved by antitrust litigation [p. 6]. . . . Defendants' requirement that candidates for admission to full psychoanalytic training in the American's accredited institutes have completed a psychiatric residency reflects their adherence to one of a spectrum of views on the lay analysis question—a view that, the literature shows, is bound up with considerations of the nature of psychoanalysis, the proper care of patients, and the advancement of knowledge. In short, the psychiatric residency requirement is a manifestation of a view on a controversial and inherently professional and scientific question. And such disputes are not the stuff of antitrust litigation, both because they involve non-commercial aspects of professional life and because there simply is no appropriate way for courts to resolve them [pp. 7–8]. . . . If the controversy concerns the substance of professional views, as does this one, it is beyond the court's competence. If it concerns only

---

[1] The New York Institute had by this time hired separate attorneys.

the manner in which professionals market their services to the
public, that is another matter [p. 31].

Kaplan advanced an additional argument: even if the Sherman Anti-
Trust Act were to be construed to be applicable to this case, First Amendment
protection would still shield the American's psychiatric residency requirement
because it is a professional judgment resting on considered opinion.

Kaplan concluded his memorandum: "there is no basis in law for this
complaint. The antitrust laws simply do not apply to the psychiatric residency
admissions requirement, at least on the facts of this case. . . . There are no
factual issues that are material to resolution of the dispute. In consequence,
dismissal is warranted as a matter of law." In support of this memorandum,
Kaplan submitted excerpts from previous cases on similar issues, which the
American Psychological Association had used to argue the opposite side
from what it was taking now on this selfsame issue. These prior decisions
stated that the courts had long held the learned professions to be totally
exempt from antitrust scrutiny, but that in a series of decisions from 1975
to 1982 the Supreme Court had reconsidered this total exemption, deciding
that such commercial aspects of the learned professions, as fee-setting, but
only those aspects, were not exempt from antitrust examination. In one
such case, involving admissions to Harvard Medical School,

> the Court found that the establishment of admission criteria by
> medical schools was "distinctly non-commercial" and therefore
> outside the ambit of the antitrust laws. The Court explained:
> "Academic admissions criteria may well have a purely incidental
> effect on the commercial aspects of the medical profession. They
> are, however, non-commercial in nature. The Sherman Act was
> certainly not intended to provide a forum wherein disgruntled
> applicants to medical school could challenge their rejections"
> [p. 66]. . . . [T]he learned professions have a strong public service
> aspect, as well, which is motivated not by business concerns but
> by the desire to serve and safeguard the public. Standard-setting
> . . . is perhaps the purest example of this type of professional,
> non-commercial activity. Congress cannot have intended to
> prohibit such conduct when it passed the Sherman Act [p. 67;
> Reply Memorandum, Lewis Kaplan et al., U.S. District Court,
> Southern District of New York, Bryant Welch et al. against
> American Psychoanalytic Association et al., September 27,
> 1985].

On October 15, 1985, Edward Joseph, as President of the American,
and Shelley Orgel, as Chairman of the Board, sent a joint cover letter to all

members of the American, together with the final report of the Ad Hoc Committee (the Gaskill Committee) to the Executive Committee and a detailed summary of the discussions on the earlier draft of the report at the Board and Council meetings in May. The cover letter traced the 10-year history of the four successive committees (Curtis, Calder, Isay, and Spruiell) that had dealt with the issue of nonmedical training, culminating in the May 1984 San Diego decision not to take any action in order to "allow time for further study, reflection, and for further efforts to formulate a clear, understandable, thoughtful proposal," which was followed immediately by the statement that the Gaskill Committee was appointed in December 1984 "to develop such a proposal which Board and Council could agree was suitable for submission to the membership."

This letter was followed by the Gaskill Committee report. In view of its importance to the American—and to the meaning and resolution of the issue of nonmedical or lay analysis, the central theme of this book—it is quoted here in full.

> The Ad Hoc Committee believes that the current educational program in psychoanalysis carried out under the auspices of the American Psychoanalytic Association through its Board on Professional Standards with a primary emphasis on the requirement of medical-psychiatric education as a prerequisite has demonstrated its effectiveness and success. It has been of fundamental importance in the evolution and achievement of the standards which have given the Association national recognition. The prerequisite of medical-psychiatric education has also been a vital factor in effecting our professional identity in the role of human caretakers. We recognize, however, that standards are never achieved with uniformity and that they are in constant need of revision and upgrading in the light of new and validated knowledge both from within and from without our science broadly defined. The Association should continue to emphasize these principles and standards as it continues to seek for more effective education and higher standards in implementing its tripartite educational program. The Association's search for excellence has been significantly enhanced over the years by those non-medical psychoanalysts who through outstanding clinical practice, teaching and research have made preeminent contributions to our field.
>
> With the above statement clearly in mind we would suggest that it is appropriate for our institutes to accept candidates with exceptional qualifications coming from other educational backgrounds. Such broadening of the prerequisites should place

emphasis on identifying to the degree possible those individuals who have the potential for excellence as analytic practitioners. The selection criteria for non-medical applicants will continue to be based on excellence with the goal of maintaining the ambience of the current educational programs and the medical identity of the Association. Further it would permit this new group of candidates to be fully integrated as colleagues.

To accomplish this goal the institutes would have the responsibility for the selection of these candidates, subject to a waiver procedure at the national level similar to that of CORST but with different criteria. The Board on Professional Standards would create a waiver committee to review these applicants and the selection process by which they are chosen with the goal of insuring that all accepted candidates, medical and non-medical, meet equivalent standards. The waiver to the Institute on behalf of the individual applicant would be obtained prior to beginning the educational experience to avoid placing these candidates in an ambiguous status. Both the national waiver committee and the individual institute selection committees should carefully consider the issue of a balance of medical and non-medical candidates so as to maintain the current perspective of the Association.

As part of the usual selection criteria we expect in general that such individuals will have achieved a professional identity as human caretakers through therapeutic clinical activities of demonstrable excellence. Consonant with the goal of excellence such applicants should very likely have gained recognition as teachers and/or supervisors and/or have demonstrated competence through scholarly publications, among other professional achievements.

To foster and maintain dialogue between the national waiver committee and the institute a representative of each institute should be available for consultation at the time a waiver is sought.

In conclusion we emphasize the need to approach such change gradually. The Association's standards and principles have evolved over time, too slowly in the minds of some, but they have contributed significantly to the current esteem in which the Association is held. While the modification being proposed may appear radical to some, restrictive to others, we believe it reflects our organizational heritage of gradual evolution, not abrupt change.

The Committee believes it has fulfilled its original charge and requests that it be discharged.

> Respectfully submitted,
> Robert M. Gilliland, M.D.
> Justin M. Krent, M.D.
> Herbert S. Gaskill, M.D., Chairman

With this report was appended the detailed summary, written by Austin Silber, Secretary of the American, of the discussions by Board and Council on the earlier draft of the report in Denver in May. Many familiar points and some new ones were raised in those discussions: the concern that there should not be a double-standard or two-tiered admissions process for medical and nonmedical applicants; that a doctorate in clinical psychology should not be the sole available nonmedical pathway to psychoanalytic training; that the overall medical ambience and character of the American not be lost; that rigid quotas should be eschewed but that overall balance be maintained in the admissions process so that nonmedical applicants not swamp the medical; that the traditional ties with the American Psychiatric Association be safeguarded; that an appropriate waiver mechanism be securely built into place and not compromised; and of course, that "quality" and "excellence" be maintained throughout. Interestingly, in all three documents there was only one possible allusion to the ongoing lawsuit. One Councilor had said "It seemed to him that it [this report] was extremely timely in terms of the political realities" (Silber summary, p. 5). It was almost as if the stresses of the lawsuit and the risks in it to the organization, and the very considerable sums already spent on its legal defense in this first half-year of the suit, had no relation at all to the content or progression of the Gaskill Committee report, or, indeed, that it hardly existed.

On October 30, 1985, eight months after filing the lawsuit on March first, the first courtroom battle was joined in the hearing of oral arguments before Judge Keenan on the motion to dismiss the complaint. Lewis Kaplan spoke first, for the defendants who had brought the motion. His statements recapitulated his written brief and his reply memorandum on the matter. He stated that the essence of the plaintiffs' position was that there was no reasonable basis for the American's admission requirement of medical-psychiatric training, but that this was a matter of opinion of subjective people, with no objective empirical way to decide this question, and there was a whole professional literature conveying the spectrum of views on the matter. The antitrust laws were not designed for a controversy of this sort, and to bring it under antitrust law would be a perversion and a tremendous legal extension; the question of qualifications for admission to an educational institution is simply a different kettle of fish than direct restraints on competition in the marketing of goods and services. The court was simply not competent to second-guess professionals on what constitutes reasonable admissions criteria for professional training, and, within this frame, the issue of economic motives was declared "fundamentally immaterial."

Clifford Stromberg then spoke on behalf of the plaintiffs and against the motion for dismissal. He argued that the defendants wanted the judge to decide, "before there has been any substantial discovery, that the essential conduct of the defendants is in its essence non-commercial and academic." The plaintiffs asserted, to the contrary, that the defendants' behaviors *were* economically motivated to exclude a class of competitors, and that such monopolization of a segment of the health services market is not an ivory tower or academic issue. To quote Thurman Arnold, "most times when people say it's a matter of principle, it's a matter of money, and that applies to this case." Though the American did train a certain number of nonmedical people under the CORST waiver system, Stromberg contended that they allowed this precisely because those research and academic scholars would not be economic competitors in the clinical marketplace.

Stromberg then outlined the various additional methods the American allegedly used to stifle competition in the marketplace, beyond excluding nonphysicians from its own training programs: (1) it declared it unethical for its members to teach in psychoanalytic training programs outside its ranks, thus depriving aspiring psychologist institutes of experienced faculty; (2) it prevailed on IPA training institutes in other countries not to accept American applicants who would not be eligible for admission to the American's institutes, even though these institutes were fully open to nonmedical applicants; and (3) it established referral patterns, restricted to people trained under its auspices. Stromberg declared that the court could and should decide whether this exclusionary policy toward nonphysicians was indeed reasonable, despite the welter of conflicting expert claims. Besides, the issue in antitrust cases is not only whether the constraints are reasonable, but also whether or not they are intended to be anticompetitive, and whether, if the goals are appropriate, there are less restrictive ways of accomplishing them. All these are clearly matters of fact, to be decided by the court. In regard to the First Amendment, "it doesn't protect organizing the marketplace. It may only protect expressing a view." Stromberg ended by calling this a relatively unique case, not to be compared with the seemingly similar cases cited by Kaplan. "Very few people have been able, through control of academic admissions criteria and these other practices, to block a market."

At the end of the oral arguments the judge stated that he would further study all written materials that had been submitted and would reserve decision on the motion, "and if the matter survives, there will be a future conference date set." He also indicated that he found the arguments on both sides very well put, and very helpful to him. As it turned out, the judge did not give his ruling on this motion to dismiss the lawsuit until April 4, 1986, five months later. The IPA did not participate in this October 30, 1985, hearing before the judge; its attorneys were not present.

After that hearing on the motion to dismiss, the courtroom struggle went into temporary abeyance. The IPA's main attention shifted to its interface with the American, the concern over the uncertain fate of the Gaskill Committee proposals, which were to be debated at the American's Board and Council in December (and if agreed to in final form in those two bodies, sent out to the membership for vote) and to a (partial) meeting of the IPA Executive Council in New York, also in December, for the first comprehensive review by Council of the matters of the lawsuit—and all the other more "ordinary" IPA administrative business—since the August 1 meeting of the old and new Executive Councils in Hamburg. A major issue was being argued in the American at the time around the Gaskill Committee recommendations. Would their implementation entail a bylaw change by the American? This would require a two-thirds vote, and with the American as strongly divided as everyone felt, this seemed almost impossible to attain. Or would a bylaw change be unnecessary? In that case a simple majority vote to adopt, which did seem in reach, would suffice. It was felt that the strategy of those opposed to opening the doors of the American to nonmedical training would be to push the view at Board and Council in December that the fundamental alteration in longstanding and time-honored admissions standards of the institutes of the American proposed by the Gaskill Committee would indeed require a bylaw change, and if this view carried the day, the Gaskill Committee proposals would face all but certain defeat.

I was not sure at the time what the precise attitude of the several American members of the IPA Executive Council was on this issue. They were all influential in the councils of the American and could of course have an added weight if they spoke up at the December debate in the Board and Council of the American because of their official positions within the IPA executive body. They were all good friends, but I felt that, with at least one of them, Joseph Sandler (of London), then an IPA Vice-President (and four years later my successor as President), had an even closer relationship and so I wrote to Sandler on November 25, 1985, asking his help in sounding that individual out and using his own persuasive power to urge adherence to the position that the IPA hoped the American would adopt; that the Gaskill Committee proposals did not necessarily represent fundamental and irrevocable change in the structure and character of the American, but rather a controlled extension of admission criteria, just as the CORST program had been, and no more revolutionary in its consequences. In retrospect, I believe that the proposed change was indeed more fundamental in its implications for the nature of psychoanalysis as a discipline than I let myself realize at the time, and in this sense the vigorous opponents of the change were more accurate in their assessment of its ultimate meaning.

In a return message, Sandler agreed to talk with at least the one person about how we saw the consequences for the American and for the IPA should the Gaskill initiative fail. In a follow-up letter to Sandler of December 2, I took the occasion to spell out more fully the scenario I foresaw in that eventuality. I indicated that I felt that the lawsuit would be pressed more vigorously by the plaintiffs, with a far lesser chance of a negotiated settlement, and that other lawsuits might be mounted, including one in our own San Francisco Bay Area, with all the prohibitive costs and increased divisiveness in analytic ranks that would ensue. In my own, perhaps over-gloomy scenario I stated, "There would be major pressures toward fracturing the American since some Societies and Institutes like our own in San Francisco might actually be tempted to talk about seceding from the American and opening the doors unilaterally to some form of non-medical training. At least several of our training analysts are talking that way." Plus there would be increased pressures from nonmedical psychoanalytic training programs in the United States to ask for direct affiliation with the IPA outside the framework of the American, leading, if events took this course, to the specter of two rival psychoanalytic training associations in America. And from the standpoint of the IPA's component organizations in Europe and Latin America, many might be unwilling to codefend an expensive lawsuit on behalf of training restrictions that were anathema to them, which could, in turn, create a serious rift between the American and the rest of the IPA world, fully comparable in effect to the crisis of 1938. I quote from these letters to mark out the full flavor of the grave climate that I experienced at the time, even wondering—in the extreme extension of this thinking—whether I might be destined to preside over the formal dismemberment of the IPA.

It was in this atmosphere that 10 of the 16 members of the IPA Executive Council, who were all attending the December 1985 meeting of the American, met in all-day session on December 20. In addition to all six American members,[2] four others were in attendance, Roger Dufresne (Vice-President, from Canada), Albrecht Kuchenbuch (Vice-President, from Germany), Adam Limentani (past President, from the UK), and Joseph Sandler (Vice-President, from the UK). A wide range of agenda items were discussed, but the most detailed and time-consuming discussion was on the status of the litigation. I reported on a variety of developments. First, a formal letter had been received from the New York Freudian Society (NYFS) asking if they could make application for IPA affiliation; the letter stated

---

[2] Arnold Cooper (Vice-President), Otto Kernberg (Vice-President), Leonard Shengold (Associate Secretary), Howard Schlossman (Treasurer), Robert Wallerstein (President), and Edward Weinshel (Secretary).

that in their membership they numbered several, like Peter Blos and Fred Pine, who were also members of the American and therefore of the IPA. Similar letters were expected momentarily from the Institute for Psychoanalytic Training and Research (IPTAR), and from the National Psychological Association for Psychoanalysis (NPAP), both of them also New York groups. I had written back to the Freudian Society that the current situation was still that all IPA-approved training in the United States was through the Institutes of the American and that I would advise them if that situation changed.

Concerning the status of the litigation itself, I reported on a two-hour meeting that Weinshel and I had had with our New York attorneys three days before. The lawsuit was now in stage one, consideration of the motion for summary dismissal. The next, stage two, would be on the issue of class-action certification, with the plaintiffs seeking to keep the class narrow (just doctoral-level clinical psychologists), and the defendants wanting to broaden it as much as possible, so that the decision on one suit would get things settled for all comers. After that would be stage three, with discovery and resumed depositions. Because each of these matters had to get onto the court calendar and be argued before a very busy judge (at this time he was dealing with the Bhopal disaster among other matters), the timetable for all of this could stretch forward for several years. To this point, the IPA had largely piggy-backed on the American; our attorneys were regularly in touch with the American's attorneys, who had carried the vast bulk of the legal maneuvering up to now. The American to date (in less than a year, with everything still in very early stages) had spent $105,000[3] and the plaintiffs were estimated to have spent somewhat more. IPA costs to this point had only been $11,000, which no doubt accounted for the lack of more membership agitation on the issue up to now.

I then presented the various contingencies that had been discussed with the IPA attorneys. The attorneys wanted to know at what point IPA interests would diverge seriously from those of the American and whether splits could be avoided and harmony still be maintained at that juncture. The American was already buzzing with rumors that the IPA might pull out and opt for a separate settlement, leaving the American in a much weakened defensive position; similarly, voices were being raised in Europe and Latin America of serious reluctance to codefend the lawsuit and use financial resources on this contentious issue. Within the American, some

---

[3] At the Executive Council meeting of the American on the previous day the question had been raised of the possible need for a special assessment of $150 per member (which could raise over $300,000 from the more than 2000 members) in order to defray the current and projected legal expenses.

would seriously prefer to quit the IPA and go it alone organizationally and in defense of the lawsuit; others would prefer that there be a second, nonmedical, psychoanalytic association in the United States, so that the American could remain more securely medical. And if there were such a second association, would some of the affiliated institutes and societies of the American choose to secede and join forces with the second association? The IPA lawyers advised us to be as prepared as possible for each and every one of these possibilities.

The 35th IPA Congress in Montreal in the summer of 1987 was a year and a half away, and would be the first under my presidency. Would the special Regional Association status of the American, established during the immediate post–World War II compromise negotiations and designed to keep the IPA intact and to prevent the threatened secession of the Americans, now be seriously questioned? Would it be viewed as the codification of special privileges that were no longer warranted and, in fact, had become seriously divisive organizationally. A letter had already been received from the Secretary of the British Society. It stated that the members of the Society might propose an amendment to the IPA constitution at the Business Meeting in Montreal, whereby each component organization would be responsible to hold the IPA harmless, and to fully defray all expenses incurred by the IPA, in the case of litigation brought against the IPA by virtue of its association with that component.

All this was followed by vigorous discussion involving every one of the participants in the meeting. Cooper took an especially active role. He stated that for the American, the major question vis-à-vis the IPA was its "contract" with the IPA, its special Regional Association status. For the nonmedical groups in the United States, the big issue was access to the IPA through or outside of the American; mostly they wanted it outside the framework of the American, because basically they didn't care that much about the American (or care *for* it either). As for the prospects of the lawsuit itself, Cooper indicated that at least the attorneys for the Columbia Institute were confident that it would be won on academic freedom grounds, so long as the established standards could be defended as reasonable, not capricious, and not counter to public policy (e.g., racist, sexist). Up to now, he pointed out, the IPA had stood by the American's right, through its Regional Association status, to establish and control its own training standards.

My own view was that if the Gaskill proposal passed, an acceptable accommodation could be worked out both with the plaintiffs and with the nonmedical psychoanalytic training groups in the United States seeking IPA affiliation. But what if it were defeated? Cooper asserted that even if it passed, opening the doors of the American to nonmedical training, this would still not resolve the core issue for the nonmedical training groups that wanted direct access to the IPA, bypassing the American; this was precluded by the existing Regional Association agreement. The question was also raised as to whether the letter from the British Society constituted formal notice that such a bylaw amendment would be proposed to be voted on at the 1987 Business Meeting in Montreal. If so, what about the possibility that further motions might be offered to alter the Regional Association agreement, revoking the special prerogatives of the American, either wholly or partially? Any of these potential motions could instantly reignite the bitter pre–World War II struggles, with the same risk of splitting the IPA asunder.

It was agreed that the three IPA main officers should meet with the officers of the American (the six members of its Executive Committee) to explore these issues. "Whether the Gaskill report passes or fails, there will still remain the question of two Associations or one in the United States; and if it passes there will still be the issue of whether people will be satisfied with training and membership in the American." As for the Gaskill proposal, it had been decided by the Board and Council of the American that it would go out for mail ballot in February 1986 without specifying whether it necessarily entailed a bylaw change. The full IPA Executive Council (all 16 members) was to meet next during the IPA Symposium week in March 1986 in Taunton, England, but the results of the American's balloting would not likely be known at that time (Minutes, Executive Council IPA, partial meeting, December 20, 1985).

On December 31, Nathan Stockhamer, President of Division 39, wrote to Ed Joseph, President of the American, thanking Joseph for a December 18 phone call suggesting a meeting to discuss possible settlement of the lawsuit. Stockhamer proposed that such a meeting should include all four defendant parties as well as any attorneys any of the parties wished to bring along. He also proposed a six-item agenda: (1) the admission of psychologists to full training; (2) future career tracks for psychologists within organized psychoanalysis; (3) access to the IPA; (4) monetary damages; (5) attorneys' fees; and (6) terms of settlement of the lawsuit. In a January 8, 1986 letter of response, Joseph expressed surprise at the content of Stockhamer's letter on several counts. He had thought that the plaintiffs were seeking a meeting to discuss a settlement on the basis of the American rendering assistance to psychologist-run programs established independently, and he had wanted to ascertain if this were true. He was surprised at most of the agenda items advanced by Stockhamer. There was then a further exchange of letters, Stockhamer to Joseph on January 17 and a response, Joseph to Stockhamer, February 5. Again there was a failure to agree on the proper scope of potentially productive settlement discussions. Joseph made two points strongly: any settlement agreed upon would have to include dismissal of the lawsuit with prejudice, and the American would not entertain any monetary payment. He proposed that rather than pushing this correspondence, they should meet, and he suggested March 9.

In preparation for such a meeting with the plaintiffs there was a first joint strategy meeting of the defendants held Friday evening, February 3, at the office of the American in New York. The American was represented by Ed Joseph (President), Richard Simons (President-Elect), Bernard Pacella (Treasurer), Shelley Orgel (Chairman of the Board), Helen Fischer (Administrative Director), and two attorneys, Lewis Kaplan and Janet Hoffman. The IPA was represented by me, our treasurer Howard Schlossman, and our attorney Trip Dorkey. The New York Institute was represented by Leo Loomie, its President, and by its separate attorney group, Mark Bunin and Christopher Hitchcock. The Columbia Institute declined to attend. They indicated that they were not prepared to negotiate anything at this time: they had a principled position on the issue of nonmedical training and were prepared to take a legal stand on behalf of their institutional autonomy and academic freedom. (It was pointed out that they had insurance against such litigation, and also had access to the full-time staff of the legal counsel for Columbia University.) At this meeting, Joseph reviewed his several exchanges with Stockhamer and their failure as yet to agree on an agenda for the proposed meeting. Stockhamer insisted that however the defendants would try to circumscribe the agenda, the plaintiffs would raise the issue of monetary damages. It was agreed nonetheless to go ahead with the March 9 meeting date and that Kaplan would draft a formal letter of response for Joseph; it would be a meeting to discuss settlement of the lawsuit, it must be confidential, and the defendants would in no instance consider monetary damages. In the general discussion that evening it was considered that the American might be willing to allow access to the IPA by qualified nonmedical training organizations in the United States; that it might be willing to allow its members to teach in these outside institutes; but that it would be adamant on maintaining its freedom of action and its full control in regard to its own admission and training standards. This potential compromise offer would entail the American's surrender of one of the two pillars of the Regional Association agreement, the "exclusive franchise" within the continental United States, while holding on to the other, total autonomy and control over its standards. It was also clear, however, that there was another position among the defendants, indicated forcefully by the Columbia Institute; to fight the lawsuit to the end (with the professed expectation of success) (Memorandum, Dorkey to Cannon, February 7, 1986).

On February 5, 1986, Dorkey sent me a letter detailing the chronology of his memorandum exchanges with Cannon over the span of almost a year, with the covering stipulation that he felt "there is no benefit from sharing this material with the American at this point." This history went back to a first contact in April 1985 with Ira Greenberg, the New York colleague of Stromberg's, representative of the plaintiffs. These were preliminary soundings, that the plaintiffs might let the IPA out of the case if it made some unspecified "self-imposed limitations." Dorkey had expressed that the IPA would be interested to see what these would be. This was followed by a May letter from Stromberg indicating the plaintiffs' desire to compromise and terminate the action against the IPA, if the IPA would publicly declare and implement as policy that all Institutes and Associations affiliated with it should admit psychologists to training, "on the same basis as physician-analysts and without discrimination," and that since the IPA was held less culpable than the American, it would only need to pay the plaintiffs $10,000, but should also make all its books and records available for purposes of this litigation, and agree to allow the court to retain jurisdiction to enforce this agreement. Dorkey felt that this offer might be promising and that the IPA should formulate a counterproposal.

In a return memo from Cannon on May 20, 1985, Auletta conveyed concern about rumors reported out of Denver—where the American was then having its spring meeting—that the IPA was negotiating a separate settlement, and that the Americans on the IPA Executive Council might try to block any such settlement agreement (it was still Limentani's European administration) because they might not understand or be concerned about the honest-broker role of the IPA. She asked that Dorkey impress upon Stromberg the need for the utmost confidentiality of these talks with him. She also stated that the attorneys for the American had been telling their clients that the IPA lawyers were secretive with them, and this, of course, didn't help matters. Everyone needed to be assured about the IPA's good will. Dorkey in his reply memorandum said that Stromberg agreed about the need for the utmost confidentiality, but in this "very political climate" he could not guarantee that none of his clients had leaked the information that there was a settlement proposal circulating—though he agreed that it would not have been in their interest to do so. Stromberg also indicated that the plaintiffs might drop the monetary request, but that no settlement would be possible with the IPA if any part of it involved going through the American.

These possible settlement talks had, of course, come to naught over this issue of excluding or overriding the American and its established Regional Association status, but they could well have been leaked by one of the plaintiffs and become the basis for the rumors circulating at the American's May meeting that the IPA was considering opting out at the expense of the American, rumors that had so exercised Ed Joseph, President of the American. This certainly indicated the incomplete trust at the time between attorneys for the American and those for the IPA, if not between their respective clients. Of this, Dorkey said, "It seems to me that hawks within the American are trying to sabotage any settlement. It also seems that the American's lawyers may be trying to have the IPA represented by lawyers within their control." As we know, Limentani, who was still IPA

President at the time, had closed off these settlement talks with the statement that the proposed terms were "entirely unacceptable," that the IPA was working *with* the American, and that "the IPA feels that the American was working appropriately to resolve the situation" (a reference to the deliberations of the Gaskill Committee). That is, the IPA felt that it had to stand with its American component. This is, of course, what Limentani conveyed to Joseph, to which the latter had responded, "You eased my mind." The full details of all the 1985 exchanges between the attorneys for the plaintiffs and those for the IPA had, however, not been made known to me until this February 5, 1986, letter to me from Dorkey.

This was followed a week later (February 13, 1986) by an explanatory memorandum from Joseph and Orgel to all the voting members of the American, sending them the Gaskill Committee proposal for vote, and conveying with it the endorsement of the Board on a 32 to 10 vote of approval (with two abstentions) and by the Executive Council on a 38 to 5 vote of approval. This support by Board and Council of the final draft of the report was overwhelming, and there was no stipulation that a two-thirds membership majority was required. Also, the vote was called a "referendum," a request for the members' "opinion." The clear implication was that this vote would be only advisory to the executive bodies, the Board and Council, and not necessarily binding upon them. At that same time I received a letter from Norbert Freedman, then President of the Institute for Psychoanalytic Training and Research (IPTAR) also dated February 13 (the second such letter from one of the nonmedical psychoanalytic institutes in New York), asking to explore the possible affiliation of their group with the IPA, though they were aware that historically this had not been possible. The letter requested "a review and possible reconsideration of this long-standing policy" and presented the following plea: "I wish to add that the IPA is home for us both historically and intellectually. Many of us contribute regularly to the International Journal or the International Review; we attend the meetings of the IPA and, indeed, a forthcoming scientific conference in 1986 is devoted entirely to the review of the 1985 Hamburg Congress. It is painful to many of us to remain guests at a place which we consider to be home." As with the New York Freudian Society (NYFS), I wrote back that we were still operating by the same rules as always, and that we would indeed notify them should those rules be changed.

A third item, also dated February 13, was a letter from Auletta to Cannon responding to one from Cannon of February 11, indicating that Cannon's letter would only go at this point to me and to Weinshel (as current President and Secretary), but that the whole situation would be discussed with the entire IPA Executive Council when it would meet in Taunton, England, on March 23. The February 11 letter had conveyed Trip Dorkey's summary of the February 3 meeting of the defendants and their attorneys, at which they tried to prepare jointly for the pending meeting with the plaintiffs initiated by the Stockhamer-Joseph exchange of correspondence, the meeting at which the IPA had been represented by Schlossman, Dorkey, and me. Cannon had then stated that

> Mr. Dorkey and I agree and suggest to the IPA that it is not in the long term interests of the IPA to be involved in depth in the early stages of settlement discussions. This is because it is clear that the door to settlement has been opened by the American and the plaintiffs. There are strong professional reasons for the IPA to be seen as the "honest broker" in this difficult dispute. It is not yet clear how far the American and the plaintiffs will go to reach a negotiated settlement and if the IPA is seen to be involved in depth in the early stages and the settlement discussions fail the IPA would perhaps lose the leverage it has to force a negotiated settlement.

Implicit here was the club that the IPA always had available, the threat to move to opt out of the lawsuit by negotiating a separate settlement with the plaintiffs. Cannon also expressed concern that the Columbia Institute was not prepared to negotiate on any substantive issue, though it was by no means clear how serious an impediment to an ultimate overall settlement that position would be. Finally, a cautionary note: "It is ultimately a question of balance and certainly no impression should be given that the IPA is seeking to distance itself from settlement."

In the next month, on March 7, 1986, Dorkey sent a memorandum to Cannon reviewing the procedural history and current status of the case. It had been filed a year earlier on March 1, 1985. On May 6 the three American defendants had responded in court, rejecting the allegations of antitrust law violation. At that time, the IPA was considering a motion to declare itself outside the jurisdiction of the American court, but had rejected that approach as not effective; in April and May the plaintiffs and the IPA had exchanged tentative proposals for a separate settlement, but the IPA had found the terms unacceptable, and on June 7 the IPA had responded in court to the complaint. On June 5 a hearing had been held before the judge on the motion for class certification to which the defendants indicated their opposition. The judge ruled that there would be 60 days for discovery on this issue and the defendants then advised the judge that they were considering filing a motion to dismiss the complaint. On July 18 the American filed this motion, and all discovery was then stayed except for the Welch deposition, which had occurred on July 15 and 16. The plaintiffs responded to the American's motion in September, and the American replied in turn in early October. The judge heard the oral arguments on this issue on October 30 and reserved judgment, which was still pending. If the judge granted this motion by the American, the plaintiffs would have the right of appeal to the U.S. Court of Appeals. If the judge denied the motion, the case would proceed to discovery, discovery on the class-action motion, and then on the merits of the case, though the judge could allow discovery on both issues to proceed concurrently. The lawyers' comment on Judge Keenan was that he was highly regarded, considered first rate, tough but always fair. All this—after one year—with the first legal issue, the motion for summary dismissal, not yet decided.

On the advice of the IPA attorneys, the Sunday March 9 meeting between the American (represented by Joseph, Simons, Orgel, and Kaplan) and the plaintiffs (represented by Welch, Stockhamer, and Stromberg) took place with the IPA absent. Its substance was conveyed in a telephone report from Kaplan to Dorkey, which the latter in turn passed on via a March 13 memorandum to Cannon. The plaintiffs' demands were for full rights of admission to the American and to the IPA, plus reimbursement of all their legal fees. The response was that the issue of fees was out of the question, that the American was a medical organization, but that the American was prepared to discuss mechanisms for training of nonmedical people in the United States outside the auspices of the American, with right of access then directly to the IPA. Kaplan pointed out in this discussion that settling on the plaintiffs' stated terms would be no different in outcome than what would happen if the case proceeded to full trial and the American lost. Dorkey stated that, "No one from the American said anything to bind the IPA," and that the American certainly had in mind that the IPA supported the goal of settlement, and that the American also seemed open to the idea that qualified nonmedical analysts in the United States be given membership access, in some appropriate manner, to the IPA. For their part, the plaintiffs had expressed no interest whatsoever in the still-unknown outcome of the vote on the Gaskill Committee proposals.

Dorkey reported Kaplan's overall analysis as follows: (1) that Stockhamer was difficult but genuinely interested in improving training; (2) that Stromberg had spent a great deal of time and effort being a mental health lawyer and must now decide between rolling dice and being a hero by winning the motion, or losing years of effort by being knocked out of court; (3) that Welch was a fanatic who was prepared to destroy the American if he could; but that (4) "the case will probably settle if reason and cooler heads prevail."

Cannon, in a March 14 covering letter to Auletta, sending on the Dorkey memorandum about the meeting between the plaintiffs and the officers of the American, added her own similar perspective on the role the IPA should take at this time.

We remain of the view that the IPA should act as "honest broker" in any settlement discussions but that it is extremely difficult at this stage to assess whether the Plaintiffs are serious in their desire to settle. The most recent meeting between representatives of the American and of Plaintiffs on March 9 did not encourage us to believe that the IPA should become more deeply involved in discussions at this stage. . . . If the discussions between the American and the Plaintiffs are serious, there will be a moment for the IPA to make a significant contribution to the spirit of settlement. Until the discussions produce serious proposals, however, we do not believe that the IPA should take the lead in attempting to reconcile differences.

It was in this climate that the IPA Executive Council met during three days (March 23, 26, 27, 1986) in Taunton, England, and the status of the lawsuit was the most urgent and most time-consuming agenda item. I spent a considerable period reviewing the entire history of the matter, starting with the IPA's International Training Commission, which was finally dissolved with the American's institution of the 1938 rule, and bringing the story up to date with the meeting between the officers of the American and the plaintiffs just two weeks previously, which, on the advice of legal counsel, the IPA officers had not attended. A few items were highlighted: (1) the vote on the Gaskill Committee proposals would be counted in just a few days, but it should be remembered that it was set up as a nonbinding opinion poll, and that it still remained a question as to whether a bylaw change requiring a two-thirds vote would yet be mandated; (2) the American had already spent $150,000, and the IPA, because of its piggybacking, only $20,000, but we were still in the very first phase of the case, the pending decision on the motion for summary dismissal; and (3) Judge Keenan had a strong reputation as a settling, not a litigating, judge; one of his favorite tactics was to lean heavily on each of the parties, pushing each toward settlement by pointing out what he saw as weaknesses in each argument that could lead to an adverse judgment should the case proceed to trial.

In regard to the meeting between the American and the plaintiffs two weeks earlier, it was reiterated that the plaintiffs felt the pending outcome of the vote on the Gaskill Committee proposal to be totally irrelevant, that what they seemed to want most was for the American to relinquish its exclusive franchise so that nonmedical psychoanalytic institutes in the United States could have direct access to the IPA, and that in turn the plaintiffs might then be willing for the American to remain internally restrictive or not, as it wished. I added that Ed Joseph in a call to me had indicated, "that the American might be willing, in order to preserve its own medical hegemony, to allow, outside of the American, another group, or series of groups perhaps, directly affiliated with the IPA."

Several hours of discussion followed my presentation, occupying 12 single-spaced, legal-size pages in the official minutes of the Executive Council. Sandler talked of the moral dilemma in which the IPA found itself. The American, as our largest component organization, was asking us to stand by them, not to leave them in the lurch. But if not for the American, the IPA path would be clear, to recognize these nonmedical institutes and societies directly. But of course, if we did that, the American in turn could sue the IPA for violating the Regional Association agreement. A number of people indicated that the American was finally taking the lawsuit very seriously, that its coffers were almost empty, and that it would probably very shortly be asking a special assessment of $150 over its regular dues of each of its more than 2,000 members in order to gather the resources needed to continue the defense of the lawsuit. Moses Laufer added to this discussion that when he was the IPA Secretary under Limentani, the American had really not taken the lawsuit threat seriously. It was also added that the Columbia Institute had unlimited resources available and seemed intent to fight the suit to the end, on the academic freedom grounds that were so very vital to the University and its attorneys.

During this discussion I asked for a mandate from the Executive Council to guide the IPA officers in our pending negotiations with the officers of the American in May in Washington. Harald Leupold-Lowenthal warned of the rising tide of anti-American feeling around the world over the involvement of the IPA in this litigation. I projected some complicated possible scenarios. If the existing nonmedical training groups in the United States should gain IPA affiliation, they might become attractive to medical-psychiatric candidates as well, and begin themselves to train physicians. Pari passu, some of the institutes of the American disaffected over this issue— San Francisco, Denver, Topeka, possibly Western New England were named—might break away from the American and also seek direct affiliation with the IPA. The potential consequences of all of this for the American could be extremely damaging. And at this point, the need for the total confidentiality of these discussions was reiterated; if the current "delicate" negotiations were to break down, we didn't want the IPA blamed for having upset things by leaking information, or for working at cross purposes.

At this point, Weinshel raised the issue of the letter from the British Society about a possible amendment to the bylaws designed to protect the IPA from the financial consequences of litigation against one of its component organizations. Laufer (a nonmedical member of the British Society) said that the letter reflected the feelings of many members, "who found themselves fighting an issue that they did not believe in, and underwriting something they had nothing to do with." Roger Dufresne, a Canadian, added that the medical members in his country, and in many around the world, would be in solidarity with their nonmedical confreres, not with their fellow physicians in America. And Janine Chasseguet-Smirgel, from Paris, added further that in Europe, "the idea of a psychoanalytic identity was not connected with a medical background, and this will be taken as an ideological issue in fact." Then someone interpolated the irony that when the IPA congress had taken place in America for the first time ever (in New York, in 1979), the American, which refused to train nonphysicians, had as three of their main "stars" on the scientific program, three nonphysicians: Peter Blos, Erik Erikson, and Roy Schafer.

Otto Kernberg here proposed that the Executive Council give me a mandate to negotiate with the American over relinquishing their "exclusive franchise" in the United States—in the utmost secrecy, of course, because any leak of this could strengthen the plaintiffs' bargaining position in the coming settlement discussions. And Leonard Shengold, of New York, warned the group of an opposite danger to consider—a rising tide of anti-IPA feeling in the (beleaguered) American. I reminded the group that two of the nonmedical psychoanalytic training institutions in New York had already pressed inquiries concerning possible affiliation with the IPA, and that proportionately, more of their number had attended the Hamburg Congress than from the three institutes of the American in the New York area. I spoke of two interrelated dangers if some accommodation, satisfying to all the contending parties, were not arrived at—a possible fracturing of the American, and equally, a possible fracturing of the IPA. There was some speculation about the attitude of the main protagonists in this matter in the American: Curtis, the immediate past Chairman of the Board, was felt to be most favorable to the IPA position; Joseph, President of the American, even though a former IPA President, was felt to be most reluctant; and Simons, President-Elect, was felt to be in between. Finally, Weinshel raised the question of what the attitude might be worldwide about the American officers of the IPA negotiating secretly with the officers of the American. Both Limentani and Dufresne felt that it would be far better if any actual compromise proposals that emerged would seem to come from the officers of the American, and not be seen by the American membership as being imposed upon them by the IPA, even with its American administration.

Almost directly after this meeting of the IPA Executive Council, a memorandum, dated March 28, 1986, was sent out by the official tellers, Stephen Levitan and Mervin Hurwitz, announcing that with 1585 eligible voting members of the American, 1130 legal ballots had been received, and that the tally was 768 (68%) in favor of the Gaskill Committee proposals, and 363 (32%) opposed. My own prediction had been for a very close vote, with, guardedly, a small majority in favor. The size of the positive margin stunned me, and of course, made me much more hopeful of an ultimately positive outcome to the current turmoil. Some settlement might be agreed upon, close enough to the lines that seemed to be emerging in the IPA dialogue with the American, to which the plaintiffs could agree. After all, with this vote, and the great sea change in the climate of the American on this issue that it signified, it seemed that two avenues of access to training and membership in the IPA could at last become open to nonphysicians. One was outside the American, through the American giving up its exclusive franchise and allowing direct affiliation of qualifying nonmedical institutes and societies in the United States with the IPA, and the other was through the American, using the channels to be established in the implementation of the Gaskill Committee proposals, approved now so decisively by the American's membership—by more than two-thirds, be it noted.

Very close upon this news came a letter, dated April 8, 1986, from Cannon to Auletta, enclosing a copy of the April 4 opinion and order of Judge Keenan dismissing the American's motion for a summary judgment in the case. In his opinion, Judge Keenan cited a number of statements from the minutes of several of the committees of the American and from various minutes of the Board on Professional Standards, in which there was mention of potential economic competition, of jeopardy to the psychiatric and medical alliances of the American. One section prominently quoted was from the Report of the Secretary of the American at the December 1981 Executive Council meeting.

> There was never any question during the discussion about the feasibility of non-medical training. We know that it is feasible. Non-medical analysts have made important contributions to psychoanalysis from the very beginning.... So it is not feasibility, but rather desirability, that is the issue. Granted that it is feasible, is it organizationally, scientifically and educationally desirable for the Association to embark on training beyond the very restricted training [of nonmedical people] that has taken place up to this time.

As for the applicability of the antitrust laws to this case, "the Court determines that additional facts are needed for it to ascertain whether the American had sufficiently commercial motive such as to bring its activities within the antitrust laws or whether its activities were only 'incidentally' commercial." Just before that passage, the Judge had cited various rulings that in antitrust cases dismissal prior to discovery should be granted very sparingly, based on the concept that in antitrust cases, "the proof is largely in the hands of the alleged conspirators." On this basis, the judge declared that, "The summary judgment motion is premature, and is denied at this time, without prejudice." As for First Amendment and academic freedom issues, "the First Amendment will not protect acts found to be illegal under the Sherman Act."

In overall conclusion the judge stated: "The motion for summary judgment . . . is denied at this time. Additional facts are required before the Court can determine whether defendants are entitled to an exemption from the antitrust laws on the grounds that their challenged policies are non-commercial in nature. As a matter of law, moreover, it is determined that the First Amendment does not protect the defendants' activities, so that summary judgment on this ground is also inappropriate." With this issue settled, the judge directed that the discovery process go forward, and the parties were ordered to appear for a status conference on April 16, 1986 (later postponed to April 21) to set a precise discovery schedule. The IPA Executive Council was now reminded by a memorandum from Auletta that the discovery process (and the concomitant depositions) would now get seriously underway and that we would be required to produce all the records and documents requested by the plaintiffs, except those that could be proved to be privileged.

Thus ended the first phase of the lawsuit, the judge's decision denying the defense motion for a summary dismissal, after a little more than the first year. This was the motion in which, on our attorneys' advice, the IPA did not participate; they had considered it "premature," that it could possibly have been better grounded if made after some period of discovery. Meanwhile the Gaskill Committee recommendations had been approved decisively by the members of the American, with more than a two-thirds majority, which no one had dared predict. This, of course, signaled the opening of the doors of the American to some (still unspecified) amount of training of nonphysicians (not necessarily just Ph.D. psychologists) for clinical psychoanalytic careers. At the same time, in the first very tentative overtures between the plaintiffs and the officers of the American exploring possibilities for settling the lawsuit, there seemed some movement toward a willingness of the American to relinquish the "exclusive franchise" aspect of the Regional Association agreement, so long as it could retain its other major prerogative under that agreement, its complete autonomy and internal control over its training standards. If an agreement along these lines could be worked out with the plaintiffs, one that would make it possible for nonmedical psychoanalytic training groups formed outside the framework of the American to qualify for IPA affiliation—and if private exchanges between the IPA and American officers and attorneys indicated they could agree to such a solution of the lawsuit crisis—a settlement of the lawsuit indeed seemed in reach. Thus, despite the defeat of the American in its motion for summary dismissal of the suit, the overall atmosphere for the American resolution of the issues of lay analysis—with two channels opened for nonmedical training leading to IPA membership in the United States, one inside the American and one outside—was somewhat optimistic in early April 1986.

The Settlement Negotiations that Failed
April to October 1986

T he second year of the litigation began in this reasonably optimistic climate; a settlement of this lawsuit, so contentious and divisive for both the American and the IPA, seemed within reach. On April 16, 1986,[1] Lewis Kaplan wrote a formal letter to Clifford Stromberg offering, confidentially, the terms of a proposed settlement: (1) that the American would not oppose an IPA bylaw change relinquishing its "exclusive franchise" in the United States, thus allowing individuals trained outside the American an avenue of access to IPA affiliation provided they met the usual IPA standards; (2) the American would declare affirmatively that its members should feel free to teach in psychoanalytic training programs outside the auspices of the American, without conceding that the American ever interdicted such "unauthorized training"; and (3) the American would actively promote training of nonmedical psychoanalysts in an institute under the authority of the American Psychological Association through an Advisory Committee of five training analysts (one of them a child analyst and one a nonmedical member of the American) which would function for five years by way of full site visits at least once a year and periodic meetings and contacts in the interim between visits as mutually determined. In return, the American asked that settlement "be conditioned upon certification of a class for settlement purposes, including all non-medical mental health professionals who have sought or might seek psychoanalytic training at American-affiliated institutes," that the entire lawsuit be dismissed on the merits and with

---

[1] By this time, fax machines had become commonplace, and it should be assumed that almost all the letters, memoranda, and similar documents cited from this point forward were sent by fax and could be responded to almost immediately. This is certainly true of communications among the attorneys, between the attorneys and the London IPA office, and between the attorneys, the London IPA office, and me as well.

prejudice, and that there be no payment by defendants of any damages, attorneys' fees, or costs in connection with this litigation. Kaplan ended by calling this "a fair basis for a negotiated settlement" and hoped that the plaintiffs would give it serious consideration. In a cover letter to me, however, dated April 17 and accompanying a copy of Kaplan's letter, Dorkey stated that in a general discussion with Stromberg about the discovery process, Stromberg had described Kaplan's letter as "not promising."

On April 18, 1986, Irene Auletta sent a memorandum to all the members of the IPA Executive Council with a number of enclosures, received along with a letter of April 16 from Lista Cannon, all relating to the discovery process that was now to get underway. For the IPA this would take place in London, and at the plaintiffs' expense, though it was not yet clear how much the IPA would be focused on altogether, because the American was the primary target of the plaintiffs. If any IPA documents were to be restricted as confidential, we would need to go through those documents line by line with our attorneys so that they could prepare a legal basis for the withholding. In Cannon's letter to Auletta, she indicated that she would meet with Dorkey in London the following week to discuss proposed objections by the IPA to the scope of discovery, and a schedule for him to propose at the Status Conference before Judge Keenan on April 21. Included with the letter from Cannon was an eight-page, single-spaced letter of complaint from Stromberg to Kaplan from the previous year (June 27, 1985) alleging that many requests by the plaintiffs for the production of documents, including their willing granting of three separate extensions of time, had nonetheless been met by unfair and unacceptable efforts to limit discovery and by unconscionable delays in the process. Stromberg specifically charged that many legitimately requested documents had been withheld by the American because it was planning to file a motion to dismiss and hoped thereby to avoid discovery altogether. Another letter from Stromberg to Kaplan, dated almost a year later, on April 10, 1986, was also included, this one proposing a "consolidated" discovery process now that the judge had rejected the motion for summary dismissal and had reactivated the discovery phase. Stromberg here said that because of "the considerable overlap between class and merit issues, bifurcated discovery of class action and merit issues would be highly inefficient and duplicative. . . . Therefore if counsel for defendants agree, we would propose to conduct consolidated discovery." And, "If the parties do not so agree prior to the status conference, then we will at that time request the Court to authorize consolidated discovery."

Thus, efforts to negotiate a settlement and the prosecution of the discovery process preparatory to courtroom litigation were being pursued simultaneously on parallel tracks. Further to the accelerating discovery process, a May 2, 1986, letter from Cannon to Auletta outlined the plan for attorneys from both the IPA's New York and London firms to come together to the IPA London headquarters, to review and then photocopy all IPA documents to be disclosed, then to carry them back to New York for the planned production on May 23. In another letter from Cannon to Auletta on May 6, 1986, the timetable was stated for the deposition of the three other plaintiffs in the suit than Bryant Welch (Toni Bernay, Arnold Schneider, and Helen Desmond), all to be made later in the same month, as well as the decision to produce on, May 23, all those documents relevant to the class certification issue, but to withhold at that time those adjudged to relate to the merits of the case.

On May 6, 1986, in Washington, D.C., the IPA officers (myself, Adam Limentani, the past-President; Ed Weinshel, the Secretary; Howard Schlossman, the Treasurer; and Irene Auletta and Dorothy Unwin, both of the IPA Central Office staff) met with the officers of the American. On May 8, 1986, three meetings dealing with the lawsuit took place: a partial meeting of the IPA Executive Council (with all American members in attendance, plus Limentani, Auletta, and Unwin), the parallel all-day meeting of the full Executive Council of the American, and during the luncheon break that day, another two-hour meeting between the IPA officers and the officers of the American. I began the meeting of the IPA Executive Council members with a full report on the meeting two days earlier with the officers of the American, where it had become clear that the IPA officers and the American's officers envisaged somewhat different strategies in the effort to resolve the lawsuit. First I outlined the IPA position, which rested on a number of considerations: (1) the Regional Association agreement, which had seemed necessary at the time it was granted in order to avert the threatened IPA rupture in 1938, was now being increasingly viewed around the world as granting the American an unwarranted special status accorded to no other component organization; (2) outside of the United States, every other IPA component in the world (except in Colombia in South America, where the laws of the country forbade it) admitted medical and nonmedical applicants on an equal basis (with the medical usually the majority); (3) that the European and Latin American members were becoming increasingly vocal about their opposition to having their IPA dues used to defend a lawsuit around a practice that was anathema to the entire non-American membership; and (4) the IPA had far fewer financial resources than the American, and would be unable, even if it were willing, to levy a special assessment on its members for this purpose, as the American was preparing to do.

It was obvious that the IPA wanted out of the lawsuit on the most favorable terms possible, and I indicated further the feeling of the IPA officers that the plaintiffs' legal case had been strengthened by the judge's ruling: to wit, it was possible that antitrust laws had been violated, and in order to ascertain whether this was so, the full discovery process would be necessary. Lew Kaplan, the attorney for the American, had put a different spin on this, claiming that the judge had made it more difficult for the plaintiffs, because the burden of proof would be on them to establish that the admissions policies of the American were actuated in a major way by economic motives, and that this constituted a conspiracy in restraint of trade under the antitrust laws. As for the passage of the Gaskill Committee proposals, it seemed clear that the plaintiffs saw this as irrelevant to their pursuit of the litigation; what was offered under these recommendations was simply perceived as too little and too late, a restricted amount of training offered to especially qualified nonmedical people with special (discriminatory) admissions procedures (the waiver process) attached. From the IPA standpoint, the best possible outcome would be to have one unified, totally open organization in the United States as existed everywhere else in the world. This clearly could not come to pass at this juncture. The next best would be if the IPA could negotiate with the American a revision of the Regional Association agreement, allowing the American to keep this special status with continued total internal control over its own admissions and training standards, but relinquishing its "exclusive franchise" so that other psychoanalytic training groups in the United States could seek IPA affiliation through the usual procedures operative in the rest of the world.

If the American would agree to this, we felt that it should be widely publicized at this time, in order to lessen the financial support in psychologist ranks for continuing the lawsuit. The officers of the American had not agreed with this position; it was important to them "not to give away any one of their bargaining chips" for their own negotiations with the plaintiffs. Contrariwise, the IPA officers felt that time was of the essence, that the IPA had already spent $40,000 in these very preliminary phases of the litigation, and that this could easily escalate to $200,000 over the next year or so; if this proved to be the case, there would be enormous trouble at the 1987 Montreal Congress, now only a year away. The main difference in strategy at this point was that I (and the IPA officers) wanted to proceed rapidly and to make a major concession to the plaintiffs openly and immediately, simply to try to cut the ground out from under their feet, and thereby accelerate their willingness to accommodate to a compromise, whereas the officers of the American felt under much less pressure to hasten negotiations and wanted to preserve their full bargaining strength. Of course, the American could afford to continue to spend money and the IPA could not. It also seemed that the attorneys for the IPA and the American were advising their respective clients differently. All of this was preparatory to the lunchtime meeting with the officers of the American, for which the IPA officers were now asking for advice and guidance from the IPA Executive Council members. In this connection, I also mentioned a private meeting I had just had with Richard Simons, the new President of the American (as of this May meeting), who had stressed the need for better communication between our two organizations and, hopefully, closer agreement on common strategy and tactics.

In the intense discussion that followed this presentation, a variety of viewpoints and issues were raised. Clearly the IPA had been piggybacking expenses on the American, and had strained to coordinate its policies as much as possible with those of the American. Our attorneys were close to advising us that our interests might be diverging sufficiently to begin openly espousing different positions. The group was reminded that the British Society proposal was still pending, and that if this came to the floor in Montreal in the summer of 1987, it would openly mobilize the full depth of the anti-American sentiment in the IPA. There was a warning advanced at this point that, simultaneously, anti-IPA sentiment within the American would equally be mobilized. My own sense of urgency, of course, was to resolve all this *before* any such fracturing floor fight at the coming Montreal Congress.

Several people emphasized repeatedly the importance of the negotiations between the officers of the IPA and of the American as evidence of the IPA's wanting to help us all out of an extremely difficult situation, not as an effort to coerce the American into unwanted and injurious policy changes. Germane to all of this was the view expressed by Arnold Cooper that the attorneys for the Columbia Institute believed the weakest link in the defense was the issue of the geographic franchise, and that this might be sacrificed in the interest of settlement, or equally, of enhanced legal defense. After this discussion, the IPA officers (together with their attorney, Trip Dorkey) were to meet at lunch with the officers of the American, and following that, all of them were invited to attend the afternoon discussion of the lawsuit issues at the Executive Council of the American, where Lew Kaplan, the attorney for the American, would also be in attendance. It was not clear to the IPA officers how much of the previously secret exchanges between the American's officers and the plaintiffs would now be revealed to the members of the Executive Council of the American.

During the entire month of May 1986 I recorded a chronology of intensive meetings and conversations among a variety of principal parties, all to culminate in a planned effort at a settlement meeting between the plaintiffs and the defendants to be scheduled at my initiative on May 31 in New York—the first such meeting in which the IPA would officially participate, Unfortunately I did not record the detailed substance of these discussions. On May 10, I met with Herbert Schlesinger, a close friend, a nonmedical member of the American, and an individual strongly identified with the IPA perspective on the optimal strategy to negotiate a settlement, who undertook to utilize, unofficially and on the IPA's behalf, his strong personal influence with the officers of the American, especially with the American's new President, Richard Simons, a close colleague of his from their work together over years in the Denver Institute for Psychoanalysis. On May 16, I talked with Trip Dorkey, our attorney, who reviewed his discussions of that date with Bryant Welch and Cliff Stromberg on their view of the negotiations that they had had to that date with the officers of the American. On May 17 I talked with Simons, and we agreed to propose a May 28 meeting in New York with the plaintiffs, to be called by me under my chairmanship. On May 18, after a round of calls to Simons, Bryant Welch, Herbert Schlesinger, and to Ed Weinshel, the proposed meeting was agreed to, but at Welch's urging and with the agreement of the others, it was moved to a later date, May 31. The day after that, on May 19, in further talks with Trip Dorkey, Irene Auletta, Ed Weinshel, and Dick Simons, the meeting was scheduled at a suite I would take at the Waldorf-Astoria Hotel in New York. It was reported to me that day that Lew Kaplan was upset that Simons (and therefore the American) had acceded to this meeting under IPA auspices. Then again, on May 20, I had further talks with Trip Dorkey, Irene Auletta, Ed Weinshel, Dick Simons, Herbert Schlesinger, and Bryant Welch, nailing down the arrangements and agenda items for the coming meeting. At almost the last minute before the May 31 meeting in New York, I had further clarifying and preparatory talks with Bryant Welch (May 28) and Dick Simons (May 29). This would be my second trip to the East Coast from California in a month.

Meanwhile, alongside this frantic planning for a possible settlement agreement, the schedule for the mandated discovery process had been proceeding. This was documented in letters from Cannon to Auletta on May 21 and May 27, detailing which kinds of documents were to be disclosed, which redacted, which names were to be removed from documents (not to include removal of any names of IPA officers), and which disclosures to be resisted. Quotation from the letter of May 27 makes this clear.

> We confirm that other than public documents available generally, all documents will be made subject to the protective order which we expect to be agreed between the parties in the next few days. . . . To the extent that general correspondence is disclosed, the names in that correspondence of those individuals other than IPA executives or heads or regionals, will be redacted or removed from documents. . . . . Our overview of all the documents made available by the IPA in London under your guidance is that the IPA's position is consistent and well thought out. We have not found any "smoking guns" or documents which could arguably embarrass the IPA not only in the litigation but generally as the IPA makes efforts to resolve the dispute.

This was followed by a report the next day, May 28, from Auletta to me and another to the IPA Executive Council. She expressed herself and the IPA attorneys as troubled by a report from Cannon that Dorkey had ascertained that the American's attorneys would be making a motion in court the next day (May 29) to limit disclosure to the attorneys and "experts" only, that is, specifically to deny the plaintiffs themselves access to these materials. Cannon advised that it would be a difficult and uphill struggle for the American's attorneys to get the court to agree to this. But it could certainly further alienate the plaintiffs and might endanger the settlement negotiation meeting scheduled for two days later in New York (May 31). The IPA would be willing to make all the relevant documents appropriately available in stages and without such a restriction, but again we did not wish to antagonize the American. In this dilemma, "The IPA's Attorney's advice . . . was that the IPA should *not* submit a position on this matter but should declare that we are happy to be in the Judge's hands in this matter. . . . This would seem to be most consistent with the IPA's position from the beginning that we would wish to be seen as mediators in this matter."

On May 29, 1986, (the next day) Stromberg sent a friendly letter to Kaplan and Dorkey, reminding them that the plaintiffs had met with representatives of the American on March 9 in New York, and that on the basis of this meeting, and of Kaplan's April 16 letter of proposal to the plaintiffs on behalf of the American, and of further useful discussions with Dorkey on behalf of the International, "a good number of points have been raised. On some, substantial progress has been made and there do not seem to be major disagreements between us. On others, there appear to be significant differences of view which remain to be bridged, but we remain open to the possibility that this can be achieved." On this most hopeful note in negotiations to this point, Stromberg announced the plaintiffs' formal acceptance of the invitation to meet two days later, May 31, in New York.

But on May 30, just before the May 31 meeting, Kaplan wrote to Judge Keenan concerning the American's proposed Stipulation and Protective Order in regard to the defendants' documents sought by discovery. Kaplan expressed what he called the legitimate concerns of the defendants about giving the plaintiffs blanket access to confidential documents. Because of the highly personal and confidential nature of many of these internal documents (such as minutes of various committee meetings) Kaplan stated, "we believe that the legitimate needs of both sides are best accommodated by precluding the individual plaintiffs from having access in the first instance to Confidential Matter, subject to their right to seek access to particular documents once their counsel has had an opportunity to review them and make an informed judgment as to whether there really is a need for the individual plaintiffs to see them." Kaplan indicated that the American would be willing to abide by the same rules in regard to plaintiffs' documents that the American sought, and he acknowledged "Mr. Stromberg's concern as to his possible inability to use the Confidential Matter effectively without the plaintiffs' assistance." Nonetheless, the concerns for the confidentiality of sensitive matter should have primacy and the burden of seeking judicial relief as to particular documents designated as confidential should fall on the party seeking to challenge the confidential designation. Kaplan ended his letter with a request that the court resolve this dispute in favor of his proposed order, and then appended to the letter the proposed "Stipulation and Protective Order for Confidential Information" together with two previously issued Stipulation and Protective Orders in what Kaplan felt to be completely analogous cases.

It is within this overall ambiguous ambience that this first meeting of the plaintiffs and the principal defendants—the American and the IPA—was held on Saturday, May 31, 1986, in a suite at the Waldorf-Astoria Hotel in New York under my chairmanship. From 10 A.M. to noon, five of us, who represented the IPA, met together: Ed Weinshel, the Secretary; Howard Schlossman, the Treasurer; Irene Auletta; our Administrative Director; Trip Dorkey, our New York attorney; and I. (Auletta had come from London for this meeting, Weinshel and I from San Francisco.) At noon we were joined for a luncheon meeting by the five representatives of the American, their principal officers and Lew Kaplan. At 2 P.M. we were joined by the four representatives of the plaintiffs: Bryant Welch and Arnold Schneider (two of the plaintiffs), Nathan Stockhamer, the President of Division 39, and their attorney, Clifford Stromberg; this meeting went on until 7 P.M. No minutes were kept of that meeting, and it subsequently became clear that there were differing perceptions about what had actually been accomplished and agreed upon. At the conclusion of the meeting there was, as I remember, a general agreement that we had reached the overall framework of an agreed settlement of the lawsuit. In my own telegraphic notes I had marked down four features of this agreement: (1) the American would agree to an alteration of its Regional Association status in the IPA, giving up its "exclusive franchise" in the United States, while retaining control over its own admission and training standards; (2) the existing and some new nonmedical institutes in the United States outside the aegis of the American would be free to achieve IPA recognition and affiliation, if they met its training and professional standards; (3) members of the American would be completely free to teach and train in these settings outside the American without any prejudice to their rights and prerogatives within the American; and (4) a good faith effort would be made to reconcile two contradictory demands of the plaintiffs, "color-blind" admissions and some guaranteed minimum percentage of nonmedical candidates in the admissions procedures of the American's institutes under the soon-to-be-implemented Gaskill Committee recommendations. Nothing was stipulated about monetary awards, or attorneys' fees, or other expenses of the contending parties. Before adjourning, the group agreed that Cliff Stromberg would formulate the proposed settlement agreement embodying these agreed-upon terms, to be written and distributed to the meeting participants by the end of June, that is, before people dispersed for the summer vacation period.

As I remember my own feeling at the end of the day, I was exhausted but quite euphoric. We had been meeting for a total of nine hours under my chairmanship and the outcome seemed quite precisely what I had hoped for: a proposed settlement agreement that seemed acceptable to all, that was very much along the lines proposed in talks between the IPA and the American, and all of this reached in the first intensive face-to-face meeting of the principal parties to the lawsuit and their attorneys. From the point of view of my concern for the integrity of the IPA as the institutional embodiment of the psychoanalytic world, this seemed to me the best possible resolution for all the concerned parties, and to the extent that I let myself think in grander terms, for the health of psychoanalysis as a discipline. Certainly the issue of the *question* of lay analysis finally could be laid to rest, and the fracture lines of 1938 could be healed, not quite a half-century later.

In a June 2, 1986, letter to the members of the Executive Council, Dick Simons, President of the American, informed them that discussions had taken place at the meeting of May 31, attended by the chief officers of the American and IPA, and the plaintiffs' chief representatives, where "Possibilities for settlement of the legal action were discussed with legal counsels present." Nothing, however, was said of the substance of the discussions; "I intend to advise you of developments to the extent appropriate." On June 3, 1986, in a memo to Dorkey, Auletta advised him of the IPA's constitutional time constraints in relation to the possible settlement of the suit. If there were to be an agreed-on alteration of the Regional Association status of the American, the required amendments to the IPA Bylaws would need to be in the IPA Central Office by December 1, mailed out to all the IPA-affiliated Societies by January 1, 1987, and published in the first issue of the IPA Bulletin in 1987. Only then could the bylaw changes be voted on at the IPA Congress in Montreal in July, where a two-thirds vote would be required for approval, and which in turn would need to be ratified by a two-thirds vote in a subsequent mail ballot of the total membership. This could bring the proposed changes into effect then by January 1, 1988. If the December 1 deadline were missed, the entire proceedings would be put off for two years, that is, to the next, 1989, IPA Congress. From the point of view of the lawsuit pressures, this would be an unacceptable delay, so time was becoming very much of the essence.

On June 4, 1986, Cannon sent an upbeat letter to Auletta. The discovery process was going on, and Dorkey was talking with Stromberg about that, but Dorkey had reported "that Stromberg is quite pleased with the IPA's position and general willingness to resolve the suit. Indeed, Mr. Dorkey told me that Stromberg was 'impressed' with Wallerstein and his sincerity. This can only be constructive. The visit to New York has obviously

moved us further than we were some weeks ago and that has to be positive."
On June 9, 1986, Cannon sent three separate letters to Auletta. One of
them simply advised Auletta of the scope of the IPA documents that had
been produced for review by the plaintiffs' attorneys three days earlier.
Another advised Auletta that she, Cannon, was coming to New York the
next day; she would there devote 11 days to reviewing with Dorkey all the
documents being produced for discovery, as well as the draft settlement
proposal from Stromberg, which she apparently expected could be available
that quickly. The third letter dealt, more substantively, with her understandings on how the draft of the settlement proposals was shaping up.
There had been a June 6 conference telephone call between Stromberg,
Kaplan, and Dorkey to discuss this document. According to Dorkey, Kaplan
continued to maintain "an extremely adversarial tone with Stromberg."
Nonetheless, it was agreed that Stromberg would prepare and send to Dorkey
a draft containing six points: (1) that the defendants would not object to
their member analysts teaching outside the American's Institutes; (2) that
the defendants would not object to their member analysts referring patients
to nonmedical analysts; (3) that the defendants would implement procedures
for nonmedical analysts to have access to IPA membership; (4) that the IPA
would commit itself to establish institutes for the training of nonphysicians
in the United States; (5) that the defendants would commit a to-be-agreed-
upon sum of money to underwrite this training [the first projected
consideration of financial outlay]; and (6) that a stipulation of class
certification defining the class in the broadest terms be allowed by the court,
and a dismissal of the suit to then be sought.

In deference to this apparent progress in the settlement talks, Ira
Greenberg, representing the plaintiffs and with the full concurrence of the
attorneys for all four defendant groups, on June 9, 1986, asked the court for
a stay of all proceedings until July 11, "with full recognition of the consequent
brief delay in the resolution of the matter should further discussions fail."
In the June, 1986, Quarterly Memorandum to the Presidents of all the IPA
Component Organizations, Weinshel and I limited ourselves to a general
progress report on the status of the litigation, that the cost to the IPA to the
end of 1985 was $21,786, that the defendants' motion to dismiss the suit
had been denied by the judge in March, that the discovery process was now
going on and documents were being produced, and that the class-action
hearing would soon be scheduled, after which the trial itself could come. In
an even more guarded stance than the officers of the American took with
their constituency, we said nothing at this time of the progression of the
settlement agreement talks.

By the end of the month, however, Stromberg and the plaintiffs had
not yet produced a draft of the proposed settlement agreement, which had
been expected, and which we thought had been specifically promised in

June. Shortly after, in July, Weinshel and I were to embark on a several-week-long tour of all the Latin American Psychoanalytic Societies and would be out of daily touch with our attorneys and our London Office. All that essentially transpired within the balance of June was embodied in a June 24, 1986, letter from Cannon to Auletta. This letter discussed the progress of the discovery process and the several categories of IPA response concerning requested documents; those the IPA would produce forthwith, those to be produced upon entry of a Stipulation and Protective Order, those to be produced "if they exist," and those to be defended against disclosure. Cannon enclosed a copy of the brief filed with the court indicating the nature of the proposed IPA response to each of 23 separate requests for different kinds of documents.

Pressures were raised another notch by the receipt of a memorandum dated July 8, 1986, signed by 10 members of the British Psychoanalytical Society,[2] giving formal notice of their intention to bring a bylaw amendment before the Business Meeting of the coming 1987 IPA Congress in Montreal, specifying the following: "Should any component Society find itself in a situation of litigation into which the IPA is drawn, the IPA will accept no legal or financial responsibility for the failure of that component Society to take adequate steps which would have protected itself against such litigation, e.g., by making itself fully conversant with the legal implications of any action which would attract such litigation." Appended to this memorandum were two prior letters, one written more than seven months earlier (November 29, 1985) from Ronald Baker, as Secretary of the British Society, to Adam Limentani (a fellow member of the British Society), as the immediate past-President of the IPA and still a member of its Executive Council. This had been sent to Limentani so that he could bring it to the coming December 1985 IPA Executive Council meeting as a preliminary notification of the British members' intent. At that time the wording was still imprecise, with acknowledgment "that this leaves room for maneuver." The second appended letter, also from Ron Baker, was addressed to Ed Weinshel, as IPA Secretary, and was dated February 19, 1986. That letter stated:

> As you will have noted, there was considerable disquiet voiced at Hamburg regarding the law suit and its potential implications financially for member societies of the IPA who feel that they are in no way implicated by the actions of a single defaulting component society. This is the reason why we at the British

---

[2] Ronald Baker, Eric Brenman, Nina Coltart, William Gillespie (a past President of the IPA), Thomas Hayley, Ilse Hellman, Pearl King (a past Secretary of the IPA), Hanna Segal, Raymond Shepherd, and Harold Stewart.

Psychoanalytical Society wish to put forward a proposal which would make it binding on component societies of the IPA to adopt a posture of responsibility when it comes to indulging in unilateral activities which may be a breach of the law in their country.

Baker expressed a wish for some guidance in drafting a proper proposal since, "you will immediately see that there is some difficulty in formulating a concise proposal but the gist of what we are aiming at is . . . contained in the above." He then added: "Furthermore, there is a good deal of strong feeling about the whole matter, as you will no doubt pick up from this letter."

Irene Auletta acknowledged receipt of this memorandum and the appended letters in a letter of response to Nina Coltart dated July 16, 1986, and indicating that, as required, this Resolution would be published in the January 1987 Bulletin of the IPA and circulated as required to all the Component Organizations. This exchange of correspondence was studied by the legal counsel for the IPA, and in a letter of July 30 from Cannon to Auletta it was stated categorically, and then backed up by considerable legal citation, that "the IPA has power to pass a new regulation which seeks to prevent the IPA from being financially penalised as a result of the activities referred to," and that "the IPA (a) has power to pass the British Resolution and (b) the British Resolution will have effect." Cannon cautioned, however, that any such new regulation should state exactly how and when it becomes operational and how it is to be enforced against any component organization that is unwilling to meet this obligation. Clear procedures would need to be in place, including the right of appeal within the IPA against an adverse decision. Finally in this matter, Weinshel wrote to Coltart on September 19, officially acknowledging the receipt of the British Resolution, indicating that it had been studied by both the IPA legal counsel and also its Constitution and Bylaws Committee, chaired by Jerome Beigler of Chicago, and reiterating that the IPA did have the power to pass the Resolution, that it would be properly published and circulated in adequate time, and giving full assurance that "our membership should be familiar with the British Society Resolution by the time of the IPA Congress in Montreal next summer."

The grave threat of fracture of the IPA should this resolution ever come to vote—pitting, as it would, the British and their allies in this matter in the rest of the world against the embattled Americans—has already been indicated. And meanwhile, on July 15, 1986, Dick Simons sent an informational letter to the entire membership of the American indicating that settlement talks were proceeding and that the discovery process was therefore temporarily in abeyance. He thanked all those who had responded so promptly to the assessment that had been voted to help pay the mounting legal costs of defending the lawsuit, and then he made a plea: "As we engage in negotiations toward a possible settlement of the suit, we must do so from a united position. Whatever the wide range of differences in our Association in regard to the issue of non-medical training, it is important that we all work together to preserve the organizational structure in which these differences can be openly discussed, studied and eventually resolved." This plea for organizational unity was ostensibly addressed to the American's own divided house on this issue, but Simons was also cognizant of the British Society's proposed Resolution, and implicitly there was also a plea that the international house of psychoanalysis likewise maintain its organizational unity.

Finally, at the end of July, a full month after it had been promised, came Stromberg's draft of the proposed settlement agreement, ostensibly based on the marathon talks held on May 31 at the Waldorf in New York. This document was accompanied by a letter from Stromberg to the four principal attorneys representing the four defendant groups, dated July 28, 1986. The letter stated that this proposal was "being submitted on a confidential basis, for settlement discussions only, and without prejudice to any position taken should litigation continue." The tone of the letter was optimistic: "We believe this proposal is a realistic and fair one which merits your clients' full consideration." He said that it would preserve the freedom of the American to admit or not admit psychologists to its ranks as it saw fit, but that, "On the other hand, it assures some meaningful opportunities for training of psychologists and others in psychoanalysis, both in individual institutes of the American and in new institutes which the International would sponsor." The proposal also addressed "other issues and elements of relief which we believe, in fairness, are warranted in light of the history of the matter." Stromberg then went on to say that there was now an opportunity to settle disputes and to work together on behalf of psychoanalysis, "after decades of acrimony . . . we have an opportunity to achieve the culmination of the hopes of many that the best minds in this field, from varying backgrounds, can sit side by side and together foster the growth of psychoanalysis." He ended with a cautionary note, "that your clients may not like or agree with every provision of our proposal," but, "Likewise, in order to limit disputes and develop a realistic settlement proposal, we have not included all the elements of relief we will seek if we are forced to litigate the matter to a conclusion and we prevail."

Then followed the 17-page settlement proposal, drafted as a brief to the court, asking that, based on "arms length negotiations," all claims in the lawsuit "shall be compromised and settled and dismissed with prejudice, upon and subject to the terms and conditions set forth below": (1) agreement on a class to include (only) all licensed psychologists with a doctoral degree;

(2) declaration of a policy by the American within 120 days that it is appropriate and desirable for members of the American to teach and supervise in psychoanalytic training programs outside the American, and to refer patients to those trained in those settings; (3) within 180 days, notification to each of its members by mail of these policies and placement of at least one-half-page ads in a group of listed professional journals stating these policies; (4) agreement not to make any changes in these policies for 10 years; (5) within 60 days, notification to the IPA by the American that it would pose no objection to the training of qualified Americans in the component Institutes of the IPA, and notification of this in turn by the IPA to all its component institutes and societies around the world; (6) agreement that all nonphysicians currently in partial analytic training (under the CORST program) in the institutes of the American be allowed to proceed to full training, and when particular individuals are deemed unsuitable for full training, they would have the right of appeal to an "independent decision maker" whose judgment would be final; (7) immediate permission by the American to its institutes to train nonphysicians, either in their existing programs or in separate administrative structures outside the American, but of equal quality; (8) agreement that 10 institutes of the American admit and begin training nonphysicians by September 1, 1987 (a year off) on an equal basis with psychiatrists and in equal numbers; (9) agreement that nonphysicians could advance to any position or status within the institutes of the American; (10) provision within 120 days of a completed canvas of the membership of the American indicating which of its members were willing to teach in outside groups; (11) agreement that the IPA would provide certification of all graduates of such outside training programs; (12) creation by the IPA of 10 new institutes in the United States, as provided in what follows; (13) provision by the American within 120 days of the list of its institutes that would be conducting nondiscriminatory training of nonphysicians and the selection by representatives of the IPA and of the plaintiffs of 10 additional sites for the new IPA institutes to be picked from among the 22 cities in which institutes of the American currently functioned; (14) agreement that by July 1, 1987, (a year off) the IPA provide the plaintiffs' lawyers with the names and curriculum vitae of at least 10 faculty members (at least five of them training analysts) who would be the initial faculty in each of these 10 new institutes; (15) appointment by the IPA, by April 1, 1987, of three members of a New Institute Development Committee (NIDC) to serve together with three members to be appointed by the plaintiffs; (16) agreement that the NIDC work with and advise all new institutes established under this settlement agreement; (17) agreement that the number of new Institutes actively functioning be no fewer than five by September 1988 (in two years) and 10 by September 1989 (three years), each with classes of at least 10 members; (18) agreement that all the new institutes be "Provisionally

Accredited" by the IPA when they began training candidates, with final accreditation to be conducted by a New Institute Accreditation Committee (NIAC) comprised of three members designated by the IPA and three designated by the plaintiffs, with all new Institutes to be fully accredited within four years of their beginning training; (19) agreement that it would take a vote of five of the six members of either the NIDC or the NIAC to decide that a particular new institute would not progress towards successful operation, in which case the NIDC and/or the NIAC could cease to work with that entity and begin to work with another (replacement) entity; (20) declaration that all existing nonmedical psychoanalytic training programs in the United States be eligible for IPA affiliation and be evaluated by the regular IPA criteria, with the William Alanson White Institute (Stockhamer's Institute) to be approved for IPA affiliation by September 1, 1987 (within a year); (21) stipulation that the NIDC and the NIAC consult regularly with the American Psychological Association and Division 39; (22) $150,000 to be paid by defendants to defray the plaintiffs' legal costs; (23) $125,000 to be paid by the other defendants to the IPA within 60 days to defray the cost of IPA participation in the NIDC and the NIAC; (24) $125,000 to be paid by the defendants to the plaintiffs within 60 days to defray the cost of their participation in the NIDC and the NIAC; (25) $500,000 to be placed by the defendants in escrow in an Education Fund within 60 days, to be used by new institutes for development purposes, under the supervision of an Education Fund Committee composed of three members appointed by the IPA and four by the plaintiffs; and (26) agreement that the Court maintain jurisdiction over this settlement agreement for ten years.

The most startling aspect of this clearly preposterous document was that Stromberg in his cover letter implied that it was in fulfillment of the consensus arrived at in the May 31 meeting of all the concerned parties. Clearly it laid out a scope of work and a timetable for it that would be impossible of attainment even if the defendant parties would be agreeable to all the propositions in the document and had the human and fiscal resources to carry them all out. It would also have ceded control over the IPA's accreditation and governance structures to outside bodies—"an independent decision maker," an NIDC and NIAC in which IPA representation was but half, and an Education Fund Committee in which it would even be a minority. Of course, it was absurdly far beyond anything that had been agreed upon at the May 31 meeting. This is not to speak of the $900,000 monetary assessment to be delivered within 60 days. What became clear, of course, given the detailed plan formulated in the plaintiffs' proposal, was why it had taken all of June and July to prepare. At the time that this settlement proposal came (the end of July, 1986), Weinshel and I were in the midst of our four-week-long tour of all the Latin American psychoanalytic societies, though it was of course sent to us immediately by mail and fax.

Irene Auletta did, however, respond in a preliminary way on our behalf in a letter of August 1, 1986 to Lista Cannon. She began, "To say that I was dismayed would be to react a little too spontaneously, because on further reflection the points contained in the settlement were all to be expected, to some degree." She went on to say that those of us in the IPA had "been inclined to be naive, ever-hopeful, occasionally floundering," characteristics which Stromberg clearly did not share. She could now "foresee months of attempted negotiation, but in all honesty cannot now see anything at the end of it but the continuance of the litigation. I shall try to explain why." She then went on to state that in regard to the American, this proposal went far beyond anything that would possibly be considered. The IPA had gotten the American to consider training nonmedical people under their aegis, "but as part of their very controlled procedures, slowly, carefully, and gradually," and would also consider an organization of training for nonmedical people in the United States under the IPA aegis, but separate from the American. Clearly, however, the whole proposed settlement agreement went far beyond this, and far beyond what the American would or could agree to. In regard to the IPA there was also totally insufficient attention to the extant IPA procedures, including, centrally, the impossibility of ceding control over training progression to bodies that included equal numbers or even a majority of nonmembers of the IPA. This is not to mention the financial considerations to which she expected none of the defendant bodies would agree.

Auletta then offered her opinion about likely pressures in the IPA: "In the light of the British Resolution, and what will happen in Montreal if no equitable settlement can be reached meantime [still a year away], we can envisage that even if the IPA cannot negotiate a separate settlement with the Plaintiffs, a move towards forcing us to do so will be made; but, on the other hand, what the Plaintiffs were demanding of the IPA would in fact be unacceptable to the non-American membership as outlined in these present proposals." She ended her letter with the statement: "I suspect that Mr. Kaplan will be delighted by these proposals; his initial stand and wish for an aggressive defense will be strengthened by them. I feel it is very important that the IPA is *not* utterly dismayed by them to the extent that it joins in, even now, that aggressive stance. We are somewhat caught in the middle, but have to bear in mind both our dual responsibilities and our dual sympathies."

Upon my return from the Latin American tour (August 21), I wrote a Response to Proposed "Settlement Agreement" Drafted by Plaintiffs, dated August 30, 1986, and sent it to the IPA attorney (Trip Dorkey), the IPA officers, and the officers of the American, with a cover note dated September 4. The cover letter stated that my document of Response was, "of course not written in proper legal language which will come after we have agreed on the substance of this or some modification of it." It was indicated that my Response would be made available to all those who would participate from the four defendant groups in a meeting being called on September 19, 1986, at the central office of the American in New York[3] to endeavor to formulate a collective formal response to the plaintiffs' proposed settlement agreement.

In my lengthy Response of August 30, I began with a review of the May 31, 1986, all-day meeting of the American, the IPA, and the plaintiffs, at which, "A general agreement was reached that the lawsuit could be settled if the American and its affiliated Societies and Institutes were to give up their exclusive representation of the International within the United States and agree to the establishment of other psychoanalytic training institutions in the United States that could freely train doctoral level clinical psychologists (and other qualified non-medical mental health professionals) under the direct auspices of the International." This concept was agreed to as the basis for a draft of a settlement agreement that would be "on terms as favorable as possible to the plaintiff class, consistent with defendants' interests—and would thus be far preferable (to both parties) to extended, and very costly, litigation, with uncertain outcome." The principles that were to govern the draft agreement had been articulated by me at the May 31 meeting as follows: (1) the Regional Association agreement between the American and the IPA would be altered by agreement between both parties; (2) under the altered agreement the American would renounce its "exclusive franchise" within the United States, but would retain complete control over its own admission and training standards; (3) the American would place no barrier in the way of its members teaching and training in other IPA sponsored training groups to be developed within the United States outside the American; and (4) all training under this agreement would be in full conformity with the standards and procedures of the IPA.

It had been agreed that in the interest of efficiency, the counsel for the plaintiffs would draft a settlement proposal that would embody this general understanding, and this document had taken two months to prepare, arriving in the midst of my Latin American tour. I then stated:

> This settlement agreement proposal does indeed intend to accomplish all that was agreed to at the May 31 meeting. However it is not possible to do so on the proposed basis. Many

---

[3] On behalf of the American, they would be George Allison, Homer Curtis, Shelley Orgel, Bernard Pacella, Austin Silber, and Richard Simons, and their attorneys, Lewis Kaplan and Janet Hoffman. On behalf of the IPA, they would be me, Howard Schlossman, and Edward Weinshel, and our attorney Charles Dorkey III. Ethel Person would represent the Columbia Institute along with an attorney, and Bernard Brodsky, the New York Institute, along with an attorney. Actually, a total of 21 people participated.

of the proposed timetables are simply not feasible within the allotted time, the procedural frameworks, and the available resources of the American and the International. Even more serious, many of the proposed procedures would drastically alter the operating framework of the International and would be totally unacceptable to its membership including the majority membership in Europe and Latin America, where there is so much sympathy and support for the plaintiffs' position and where psychoanalytic training is already available to non-MDs and MDs on the same basis. To attempt to provide psychoanalytic training within the International on the proposed basis could effectively destroy the International's capacity to ensure the very quality training that is desired.

I then indicated concretely in a point-by-point response where proposed timetables were simply not possible within the constitutional constraints of the American and the IPA. I pointed out where proposed procedures would be totally unacceptable, like the requirement that the American allow an outside expert ("an independent decision maker") the right to reverse individual training decisions made by the responsible training bodies within its institutes, or like the American guaranteeing that its member institutes would admit and train nonphysicians on the timetable and in the numbers proposed (including rigid ratios and quotas on admission rates), where the Gaskill Committee proposal as passed only gave permission to the American's institutes to do so on the basis that they individually felt feasible and desirable; or like the IPA guaranteeing that it could develop 10 new institutes in the United States of the proposed scope and on the proposed timetable at a time when a considerable share of its available budgetary resources were consumed in the development of but three new training centers around the world; or like allowing outsiders to the IPA the right of participation in its training decisions. Of this last, I said; "It is not acceptable to the International that there be outsiders (non-members and non-training analysts) on these committees [the proposed NIDC, NIAC, Education Fund Committee]. To do so in the way proposed would destroy the International's control over its own training standards and thus vitiate the very quality training that it is the object of the lawsuit to make possible." In connection with this last, I pointed out that "the average time of progression from Study Group status through Provisional Institute and then to full component Society and Institute is at least a decade." After such a point-by-point response to almost every one of the 26 proposals advanced by the plaintiffs, I added that all the defendants would reject the claim of monetary damages or of attorneys' fees. The costs of developing new psychoanalytic centers is of course very high, usually borne, at that time, 50% by the local group in development, and 50% by the IPA from its dues. How the vastly expanded costs that would be incurred in undertaking new IPA-sponsored institutes in the United States could be met would clearly require consultation among all the concerned parties.

I ended this document by reproposing a Settlement Agreement that would embody the following: (1) the American would at its December 1986 meeting in New York bring a proposal (a) to alter its Regional Association agreement with the International and give up its exclusive franchise in the United States, (b) express a clear policy that its members would be free to participate and teach in organized training programs outside its aegis, and (c) remove any barriers to free referral of patients to those trained outside its ranks; (2) the American would concurrently expeditiously implement the mechanisms for training nonphysicians in accord with the Gaskill Committee recommendations; (3) the IPA would agree to begin to sponsor new training centers in the United States as soon as the Regional Association agreement was altered, hopefully at the July 1987 Montreal Congress, and this would proceed as rapidly as circumstance, resources, and finances allowed; (4) the IPA would concurrently establish mechanisms for evaluating the qualifications of existing nonmedical psychoanalytic Institutes in the United States, so as to facilitate their applications for IPA affiliation; and (5) all concerned parties would discuss together how the expenses incurred in this process of developing new IPA Societies and Institutes in the United States outside the framework of the American could best be covered. This was essentially a restatement of exactly what I felt we had all agreed upon at the May 31 meeting.

At the same time, Dick Simons, as President of the American, and Shelley Orgel, as Chairman of its Board, sent a letter to all the members, dated September 8, 1986, reviewing the history of the legal action against the American and indicating the present uncertain status of the settlement negotiations. The letter emphasized that "the history of the American Psychoanalytic Association has been built on the foundation of monitored training standards in the interest of competent and responsible patient care, not on anti-competitive, economic motives," but that in response to the lawsuit, "We want to continue to make every effort to bring about a negotiated settlement that is fair and honorable, and which preserves the maintenance of standards for psychoanalytic practice and psychoanalytic education in this country and throughout the world." With then a historical harking back to the Flexner Report of 1910, which led to the closing of 92 substandard "diploma mill" medical schools, and then the founding of the American Psychoanalytic Association just a year later, it became readily understandable that "the medical-psychiatric prerequisite for training, and that is also the basis for the attack in the legal action against us, was rooted in the medical identities of the Founders of the Association, and nourished by the call for excellence in medical education as championed by the Flexner Report." Now, "if there are to be any changes in the fundamental medical and psychiatric identity of the Association, those changes must be gradual and not abrupt. They must also be consistent with our heritage of developing and maintaining the highest standards for psychoanalytic education and psychoanalytic practice."

The letter then reviewed the story of the Gaskill Committee from its appointment on December 22, 1984, through to its very impressive ratification by the membership in the referendum counted on March 28, 1986. Because the Committee was appointed in December 1984, more than two months before the lawsuit was filed on March 1, 1985, the letter could state that "the report of the Gaskill Committee was not a response to the legal action. It represents an independent initiative to offer analytic training to selected individuals of clinical excellence without a change in the By-Laws. For this reason, the Gaskill proposal cannot be viewed as a step in a possible solution to a settlement of the legal action." The letter ended with a statement presaging the alteration in the Regional Association status of the American that was on the negotiating table with the plaintiffs:

> If we ... and our colleagues in the International Psychoanalytical Association are now to consider a change in the Regional Association status of the American, we must recognize the consequences of such a change for both organizations. ... If this were done in accordance with the By-Laws of the International, and in accordance with the standards for training and practice as established over many decades by those By-Laws, it is possible that psychoanalysis in this country and throughout the world would benefit.

At the September 19, 1986, meeting in New York of the leaders of all the defendant groups and their attorneys (a total of 21 people), Kaplan brought to the court a draft of a brief titled "Stipulation of Settlement and Dismissal," the response he had drafted (with the cooperation of Dorkey, the IPA attorney) to the settlement proposal of the plaintiffs, and one that presented, in proper legal language, stipulations very much in accord with what I had proposed in my own August 30 letter of response to the plaintiffs' proposal. In his brief, Kaplan stated that while denying all culpability and liability, the defendants considered it desirable to settle and dismiss this legal action in order to avoid further expense, to dispose of protracted and burdensome litigation, and to get on with their essential work. He proposed the following terms and conditions: (1) the American would immediately adopt as formal policy that (a) its members could teach in outside training programs without sanction or disfavor, (b) its members could make patient referrals to any practitioner they deemed qualified, again without sanction or disfavor, and (c) it would in no way impede the admission of Americans to training in IPA Institutes outside the United States; (2) the IPA would evaluate and, where appropriate, recognize for membership *existing psychoanalytic training institutions* in the United States outside the framework of the American; (3) for ten years the IPA would bend its "best efforts" to sponsor, establish, and have operational new institutes in the United States for nonphysicians, at least two by (date to be inserted) and five by (date to be inserted) with priority given to (insert cities); (4) for 10 years the American would cooperate with the IPA in this endeavor, through encouraging the participation of its members in the faculties of these new groups and through participating in the work of the IPA Sponsoring Committees; (5) the IPA would undertake these endeavors in accord with its regular operating procedures and they would be on behalf of all nonmedical mental health professionals, that is, not limited to clinical psychologists; (6) for ten years there would be a three-member Mediation Committee, one appointed by the American, one by the IPA, and one by either the American Psychological Association or the plaintiff group, but none of the three would be an officer of the American, or of the IPA, or one of the plaintiffs, and all disputes about the implementation of the settlement agreement would go first to this committee, which would have up to 90 days to try to resolve the dispute before legal recourse could be sought; (7) concomitantly the American and the IPA would have renegotiated the Regional Association agreement in order to make all the foregoing possible; and (8) with all of the above the parties to the lawsuit would apply to the court (a) for an order declaring a class of all nonmedical mental health professionals, (b) for the establishment of a four-person (two from each camp) Settlement Committee authorized to carry out all notice procedures, (c) for an order directing the publication of the terms of the agreement in the official newsletters of all the organizations party to the dispute, (d) for the scheduling of a court hearing to ensure that all the terms of this agreement were being fulfilled, (e) for an order requiring that any member of the designated class who objected to the settlement and wished to be excluded from it would have adequate time to file notice to that effect, and (f) for the establishment of a post office box in New York City to receive completed requests for exclusion. December 31, 1987 (somewhat over a year later) was suggested as the settlement date for dismissal of the case with prejudice on the basis of action toward compliance with all the settlement stipulations in the interim. Class members who wished to be excluded from the settlement agreement would have up to 60 days after publication of the Notice to file their requests for exclusion, and both plaintiffs and defendants would have the right to withdraw from this agreement if too many class members opted out and reserved the right to bring individual suits. Costs of proper notice would be borne equally by the plaintiffs and the defendants, and there was no mention of any other monetary exchange.

At the September 19, 1986, meeting, general agreement was expressed with the tenor and content of this counterproposal, and on the basis of the detailed discussion at that meeting three modifications were worked out that were incorporated by Kaplan into a revised Stipulation of Settlement and Dismissal dated three days later, September 22, 1986. These were (1) the IPA could only commit itself to developing three new training facilities (not five) in the United States within the framework and timetable of the proposed agreement, which was equal to the number at the time under sponsorship by it throughout the rest of the world; (2) the number of allowable exclusions of individual class members from the settlement agreement be limited to ten, and any more than that would accord the American and the IPA the option to withdraw from the agreement; and (3) the class of mental health professionals to be defined to consist of psychiatrists, psychologists, psychotherapists, psychiatric nurses, social workers, psychoanalysts, "and others performing similar services."

A number of further cautions and suggested modifications of the proposal Kaplan formulated emerged in the two following weeks. Auletta, in a letter of September 24 to Cannon, offered a number of procedural, though not substantive, cautions. To meet the constitutional requirements of the IPA, any proposed changes in its operating procedures would need to be published no later than January 1, 1987, in order to be voted on and made operational at the Montreal Congress in the summer of that year. Other procedural cautions had to do with the mechanisms whereby the IPA could elect direct members and meet its own requirements for sponsoring and establishing new training groups. A letter of September 26 from Ethel Person, not in her capacity as Director of the Columbia Psychoanalytic Center (one of the parties to the lawsuit), but as a member of the Executive Council of the American, addressed to Dick Simons as President of the American, was an urgent plea that he call an emergency meeting of the entire Executive Council, some 40 members around the country, in order to fully inform them and enlist the support of all the affiliated Societies behind the American's thrust towards a negotiated settlement of the lawsuit. She ended with a heartfelt entreaty that she no doubt felt was absolutely warranted: "I do not believe that the membership of the American yet realizes the seriousness of the litigation, nor the inherent risks. Therefore, in all friendship, respect, and admiration, let me implore you to call a meeting while there is still time to gather support behind you."

This letter certainly touched a sensitive chord in the negotiations, both within the American and the IPA. The leadership of both organizations was trying to work toward a negotiated settlement of the lawsuit within what had to be a confidential context, and yet whatever agreements were worked out would need to be understood and ratified by a membership that was incompletely informed about the vicissitudes of the negotiating and decision-making process. In this sense, Person's appeal, though clearly understandable and appropriate—the 40-plus membership of the Executive Council of the American was the official governing body, to whom the officers were accountable—nonetheless posed a difficult dilemma for Simons. This was all part of the heightening tension of this period in the lawsuit proceedings. A letter from Clint Fisher (one of the attorneys for the IPA) to Kaplan, dated September 29, 1986, and another from Jack Auspitz (attorney for the Columbia Institute) to Kaplan, Bunim, and Dorkey (attorneys for the American, the New York Institute, and the IPA), dated October 2, 1986, also suggested necessary procedural, but not significant content, modifications of the counterproposal draft. The several defendant groups were clearly coalescing behind the revised Kaplan draft of the renewed settlement offer in response to the plaintiffs' proposal. Auspitz in his letter included the tactical advice: "This draft does not impose specific 'affirmative action' on the defendants, on the ground that the best response to an absurdly high demand by plaintiffs is a small offer."

At the beginning of October, 1986, Weinshel and I sent out our quarterly reports to the members of the IPA Executive Council and to the presidents of all the component organizations. Our presentation of the litigation proceedings was as terse and cryptic as the communications by the American's officers to their Executive Council, about which Person had complained so vigorously.

> In regard to the Litigation, we can report that a meeting was held between representatives of the IPA, of the American Association, and of the Plaintiffs, together with their Attorneys, in New York at the end of May. At this meeting it was agreed that there might be the possibility of a Settlement being negotiated, and draft proposals in this regard were submitted by the Plaintiffs to the Defendants recently. This, as drafted, proved to be unacceptable, but there remains the basis for further negotiation, and as a result all Discovery and court action were stayed by mutual agreement. Further meetings are scheduled later this month. We hope to be able to report to you more fully in the coming weeks.

In a special memorandum to those members of the IPA Executive Council who would attend a partial meeting of the Council to be held at the IPA headquarters in London on November 4,[4] the several critical documents

---

[4] Leonard Shengold, Robert Wallerstein, and Edward Weinshel from the United States, Moses Laufer, Adam Limentani, and Joseph Sandler from the UK, and from continental Europe, Janine Chasseguet-Smirgel of France, Albrecht Kuchenbuch of West Germany, and Harald Leupold-Lowenthal of Austria.

were sent; the plaintiffs' draft of the proposed settlement agreement of July 28, my long letter of response of August 30, and the revised counterproposal by Kaplan of September 22, based on my letter of response and on the discussions at the September 19 meeting in New York. At least among the nine members attending the partial meeting of the IPA Executive Council in London on November 4, 1986, there would be a full airing of all the details of the ongoing negotiations.

By this time it was almost half a year since the letter of April 16, 1986, cited at the start of this chapter. In what seemed at the time an optimistic climate for a negotiated settlement, Kaplan wrote to Stromberg outlining the nature of a settlement agreement that the defendants could accept and requested a meeting of all concerned parties to see if an accord could be achieved. This meeting was subsequently called under my chairmanship, and the plaintiffs and the representatives of the IPA and the American reached what I thought was a general agreement, more or less along the lines originally proposed by the defendants. What followed was the two-month hiatus until the end of July, when Stromberg produced a draft, ostensibly embodying the May 31 "agreement," that was so unrealistic *in its reach that the whole* momentum toward a negotiated settlement seemed lost. This was followed by my letter of response at the end of August and the formal counterproposal to the plaintiffs by Kaplan toward the end of September, essentially embodying my August response, itself a restatement of the settlement proposal that the defendants were working out at the start of this six-month period. As Auspitz put it, the plaintiffs had asked for far too much, and our counteroffer almost certainly would be perceived by them as too little. This first round of settlement negotiations had so far failed to advance us towards our goal.

Meanwhile, the clock was running out on the possibilities for timely action. The major changes in the IPA structure that any settlement agreement would call for, involving certainly some alteration of the Regional Association status of the American, would have to be worked out in final form and posted to the IPA membership by January 1, 1987—now less than three months away—in order to be voted upon at the Business Meeting at the coming IPA Congress in Montreal at the end of July 1987. If this January 1 deadline were missed, the next IPA Business Meeting of members would not be until the following Congress in Rome in the summer of 1989. The plaintiffs would certainly find a two-year delay intolerable. What had started out so hopefully in April appeared quite gloomy in October.

10

Averting a Split
Agreement Between the American
and the IPA, December 1986

In the wake of the counterproposal of September 22, 1986, that Kaplan had drafted, it became clear that the defendant groups were not united in wholehearted support of this offer to settle. Some thought that we were offering too much in this early hard negotiating stage, and there was talk of another meeting of all the defendant parties and their attorneys to review matters, again in New York, on October 12, 1986, this time in Lew Kaplan's office. On October 3, 1986, after consulting with Weinshel and Dorkey, I wrote to Helen Fischer questioning the need for the October 12 meeting. I quoted Dorkey's advice, which I endorsed: "We agreed at our September 19 meeting on a proposal that we do not want to change and we cannot allow to be made any weaker since then the plaintiffs will no longer think that we are serious about negotiating a settlement. His feeling is to go ahead and if Columbia won't sign to go ahead without them." Dorkey was intending to call Kaplan to discuss this matter; but I added that if there was to be a meeting, Weinshel and I would fly to New York for it. On the same date, however, Fischer sent a memo to all the invited participants confirming the daylong Sunday, October 12 meeting at Lew Kaplan's office. And on October 6, 1986, Austin Silber, as Secretary of the American, sent a notice to the entire Executive Council (more than 40 people) calling an "extraordinary meeting" a week after the October 12 meeting, on October 19, also in New York, "to discuss the legal action against the Association," to which I and the other principal officers of the IPA were invited as guests (as the officers of the parent organization, and as partners in co-defending the lawsuit). For Weinshel and me it would be two successive weekend trips to New York from San Francisco.

Again, no formal minutes were kept of the October 12 meeting of the representatives of the four defendant groups and their attorneys, but I recorded that 21 people were present. According to my very cryptic notes the meeting involved various proposals that the Columbia Institute offered to be considered as alternatives to what had been formulated by Kaplan, which the Columbia group was loathe to support. These alternatives seemed to be (1) an offer by the American to give up its "exclusive franchise" on IPA membership within the United States, plus an "affirmative action" statement reiterating that its members were free to participate in psychoanalytic training programs outside its auspices, but without the offer to specifically help sponsor new IPA-affiliated training programs outside the American; *or* (2) the American ceding complete local autonomy to its affiliated institutes and societies, letting them each set their admission and training standards however they wished, in effect abolishing the main functions of the American's Board on Professional Standards; *or* (3) most radically, dissolving the American's agreement as a regional association of the IPA, allowing each affiliated institute and society to affiliate directly with the IPA as it wished. I have no record other than that these suggestions were all discussed; clearly none were agreed upon by either the officers of the American or of the IPA.

On October 15, 1986, in the middle of the week between the October 12 and October 19 meetings of the principal parties in New York, Kaplan sent to all the codefendants a further revision of the proposed Stipulation of Settlement and Dismissal agreement, this one prepared for the October 19 meeting of the American's Executive Council. There were few, but significant, changes from the September 19 and 22 drafts. One was that "The International will seek in good faith to sponsor and develop in the United States such new psychoanalytic training facilities as can be undertaken in accordance with demonstrated need and as are within its capabilities and standards." Gone was any reference to specific numbers and timetables, whether the two, leading to five, as in the September 19 document, or the reduced number of three in the September 22 document. To me, it was a clear weakening of the settlement offer, from some clearly targeted numerical commitment to a general "good faith effort" statement that the plaintiffs were hardly likely to trust. Also eliminated from the new document was an important waiver safeguard that the IPA could depart from its usual procedures in recognizing new groups, and do so in the case of nonmedical groups that had grown up in the United States, without regard to the number of already certified IPA members customarily required as members of the organizing cadre in new groups seeking formal IPA sponsorship and affiliation. What was substituted was another weaker provision that the IPA could use its procedures for according direct membership to suitably qualified individuals who had met an equivalent of its training and competency standards, and could then constitute the required core of IPA members around which the new group could be formed.

Procedurally, this would constitute a more difficult hurdle and would again be seen as a weakening of the IPA commitment and offer.

The October 19, 1986, meeting took the entire day and was at times stormily contentious, but again I have no official minutes. Since it was a special meeting of the entire Executive Council of the American, and not a joint meeting of the defendant groups, Weinshel, Schlossman, and I were present only as guests of the American, and our attorney, Dorkey, was not with us. Kaplan, of course, was very much present, as the American's principal attorney, and he played a major role in the day's discussions, beyond just explaining the legal meanings and ramifications of contemplated courses of action. He and I were clearly trying to move the Council in opposed directions. One interchange between us has remained in my memory. At one time, after I had made a particular point in the day's debate, Kaplan took the podium immediately following me and began with the statement; "If Dr. Wallerstein will stop practising law, I'll stop practising psychoanalysis." What I do have a record of is the letter I wrote to Dick Simons, president of the American, when I was back home in San Francisco the next day, October 20, 1986. In that letter, I congratulated Simons on his skillful, statesmanlike handling of the meeting, including his even-handed historical recounting of the events of the lawsuit and the details of the negotiations thus far. The meeting had ended with a ringing and unequivocal endorsement of his and the Executive Committee's conduct of the negotiations to this point, and a mandate to continue on course on behalf of the American.

At the same time, I put into the letter misgivings that Weinshel and I had about possible troublesome repercussions down the line. I indicated that up to now there were two proposals in the hopper that were indeed far apart. The plaintiffs were asking for more than was feasible and in ways that were not possible. I expected that our counterproposal would be regarded as too little and too nonspecific. Somehow the differences would have to be compromised and bridged "in a way that satisfies *their* proper aspirations while conserving *our* vital interests." I continued:

> At that point it will all be translated into commitments of resources, of money and time and energy and people, to foster these new psychoanalytic developments in the United States outside the American. As we have been saying all along, this will mean that the IPA would be taking the American off the hook, but not having adequate resources for this, would need a specific agreement with the American on what resources of money, people and time will be officially committed by the American to the IPA for these purposes. We all hope, of course, that in the negotiating process with the plaintiffs that they can

be pressed to put up comparable resources from their side to help defray the 50% of the cost of developing new institutes that under the IPA by-laws the local groups must carry.

At that point, the American's Executive Committee would have to inform the Executive Council and the entire membership of this sizeable commitment, "which of course will be justified as a saving over the certain very high cost of litigating, with all the uncertainty of outcome of litigation." I reminded Simons that this issue of financial involvement and commitment was one that Weinshel and I had brought up repeatedly, at the September 19 meeting at the central office of the American, at the October 12 meeting in Kaplan's office, and again the previous morning at a breakfast gathering of the American's and IPA's officers just prior to the daylong meeting of the American's Executive Council on October 19. We had felt strongly that it should be discussed at that meeting but, as guests, had deferred to Simons's request that we not do so, "since you felt that it might complicate matters and might jeopardize the whole desired outcome of the meeting." I had thought that had the money matters been fully discussed, Simons would have won everything he was asking for anyway, and in retrospect I felt so now even more strongly. And I then advised Simons that "in terms of my responsibilities as president of the IPA I have to say that I will not be able to sign any possible negotiated settlement unless we have a clear and binding arrangement at that time between the American and the IPA as to how these development and sponsorship costs for new institutes are going to be shared between us."

I then expressed my fear of two possible reactions when such an agreement was brought to the American's Executive Council, both of them unhappy.

On the one hand, they could turn on the IPA as the "heavy" in the piece, extorting money from the American under the coercion of the need to settle the lawsuit, something the IPA is now suddenly springing on them. We would have to say at that point that the money consideration was part of our talk at every one of the meetings, prior to the October 19 meeting of the American's Executive Council, and that we did not bring it up then only because as guests we were asked not to. The other unhappy reaction could be that members of the Executive Council would then turn on the Executive Committee as having been only half candid with them at a time when they were given the impression that the Executive Committee was finally fully candid. That again could lead to a damaging crisis of credibility.

I expressed the hope that of course neither of these would eventuate and that somehow the whole matter could be solved harmoniously and uneventfully, but clearly I was worried.

On October 28, 1986, I had a round of telephone conversations with Dorkey, the IPA attorney, with Simons, and with two representatives of the plaintiffs, and on October 29 another long talk with Dorkey, all in preparation for a partial meeting of the IPA Executive Council to be held in London the following week on November 4. The settlement counterproposal had been sent to the plaintiffs on that same date, October 29, and in its weakest version, that of October 15, which had been discussed and approved at the special meeting of the Executive Council of the American on October 19. As Dorkey and I expected, the plaintiffs' immediate response—on that same date—was that the litigation would go on. Dorkey raised a number of possible next steps for the IPA that I could bring for consideration to the London meeting the following week. I could try to negotiate only with Bryant Welch, together with our respective attorneys, Dorkey and Stromberg. Or we could include Weinshel and Stockhamer. When I raised the question of including in the American, Simons, the president, and Kaplan, the attorney, Dorkey asked whether I wanted to get a settlement or not. But of course there could be a political price to pay if we went to the American with a negotiated deal and put the American in the position of having to take it or leave it. The pressure would be, of course, that the IPA could negotiate a separate deal if the American refused to come along. These were clearly all very consequential decisions to be considered by the IPA. And then there was the issue of the proposed bylaw changes by the IPA, altering the Regional Association agreement with the American, to relinquish its exclusive franchise in the United States. The American had wanted to hold this back as bargaining leverage. Should we go ahead and press to propose these changes immediately, so they could be voted and become effective at the IPA Congress in Montreal in the coming summer of 1987?

Within this framework, eight members of the IPA Executive Council participated in a daylong meeting the following week in London, on November 4, at which the litigation was of course the most important agenda item.[1] In preparation for the meeting, three documents had been precirculated to all the participants: the plaintiffs' settlement offer of July 28, 1986; my letter of response of August 30, 1986; and Kaplan's first

---

[1] Wallerstein and Weinshel from the United States, Sandler, Laufer, and Limentani from the United Kingdom, Chasseguet-Smirgel (France), Kuchenbuch (Germany), and Leupold-Lowenthal (Austria) from the European continent.

counterproposal draft of September 19, 1986. The entire lawsuit was then comprehensively reviewed that day with the strong feeling that some definite tactical and strategic choices might soon have to be made by the IPA. The three most recent big meetings were reported in detail. First there was the September 19, 1986, meeting of the four defendant parties with their attorneys, at which the American and the IPA agreed to the document with the minor changes incorporated into the September 22, 1986, revision, but where representatives of the Columbia and New York institutes had each insisted that they had to first report back to their respective Executive Committees (and Dorkey had reported that he had meanwhile gotten the plaintiffs to agree to an extension of the Stay of Discovery into October). Second there was the October 12, 1986 meeting in Kaplan's office, at which the representatives of the Columbia and New York institutes were persuaded, reluctantly, to endorse the September 22 revised settlement counterproposal that Kaplan had drafted. I had therein presented detailed financial implications for all the defendants of the offer embodied in the settlement counterproposal—to foster the development under IPA auspices of at least three new psychoanalytic training centers in the United States—when the IPA was already financially strained in its current support of three psychoanalytic Study Groups around the world. The IPA would have needed to require that these new costs be borne by the American, and hopefully by the plaintiffs, on a 50-50 basis, drawing on the money that would be saved in ongoing litigation costs if a settlement could be reached quickly. (Ethel Person, of Columbia, had made an impassioned plea at that meeting that the entire Executive Council of the American be fully informed, at this time, of all details and implications of these ongoing negotiation discussions.) Third was the October 19 meeting of the Executive Council of the American, with Weinshel, Schlossman, and me as "guest participants." At that time, the officers of the American (the Executive Committee) asked for and finally received the vote of support of their Council to proceed with the negotiations with the plaintiffs as revealed to that point—a presentation and request for informed endorsement that had not been made at the prior regular meeting of the Council in Washington in May, where also the officers of the American had refused to accede to the request by the IPA officers to present all the financial implications of the settlement counterproposal. The American's officers had felt this would be too contentious an issue, one that could possibly derail their need for a vote of confidence to proceed, but which we considered an unwise decision that could lead to subsequent trouble between the organizations. At this point I read to the IPA Executive Council members present the full text of my letter of October 20 to Simons.

I then reported that the counterproposal offer had gone to the plaintiffs on October 29, and that in my subsequent phone conversations with Stockhamer, Welch, and Dorkey I was given to understand that though the plaintiffs acknowledged that they had indeed asked for far too much, and clearly much more than they had expected to gain, they also felt that the third, weakened version of the counterproposal that Kaplan had sent offered far too little and could hardly be taken as a serious negotiating offer. They were willing, however, to continue negotiating, but not with 20 people in the room. They wanted further meetings kept much smaller, which was the basis for the telephone conversation that Dorkey and I had had, considering the various possible negotiating strategies, including these between only the plaintiffs and the IPA. This was clearly our attorneys' advice that I presented to the IPA Executive Council members, if the IPA seriously wanted to settle the suit, the best chance would be if Weinshel, Dorkey, and I were to negotiate separately with the plaintiffs and return with the best deal possible, granted that this could seriously strain the IPA's relationship with the American.

Weinshel emphasized in this context what he saw as a change in direction of the discussions over the recent period; since the spring, it had been the IPA proposing—as in the May 31 meeting between the plaintiffs and the defendants—with the American reacting, and I had very much taken over the momentum of the negotiations. Though the IPA and the American were together in most regards, there was also conflicting pull as well as mutual need. On a purely practical level, the IPA was dependent on the full support of the American if it was to take on the sponsoring and monitoring of new psychoanalytic training groups in the United States. In the ensuing group discussion it became clear that the participants favored continued discussions with the Executive Committee of the American to try to obtain its understanding and agreement about the advantage of a separate negotiation between the IPA and the plaintiffs, with the understanding, of course, that any agreement would have to be conditional on the IPA being able, in turn, to win the concurrence of the American. The hope would be that along with the willingness of the American to relinquish its exclusive franchise in the United States, together with the other "affirmative action" commitments already agreed to in principle, that the IPA could secure an agreement with the plaintiffs on the scope, procedures, and timetables for organizing new psychoanalytic training groups in the United States under IPA auspices, which would rest on commitments of support and resource from the plaintiffs, the IPA, and the American acceptable to all parties. Whatever evolved over these succeeding months would be up for review at the Business Meeting of the coming IPA Congress in Montreal in the next summer, 1987. Sandler therefore suggested that a memorandum be prepared ahead of time, setting out the historical perspective and a resumé of the entire litigation and negotiation process as concisely and comprehensively as I had done for this partial meeting of the

IPA Council, and that this be circulated just prior to the Congress with a note that it would be "taken as read" before the Business Meeting. This was agreed to.

It was finally agreed that I would make a strong effort to obtain the assent of the American's Executive Committee to these suggestions of separate IPA negotiations with the plaintiffs on the basis here stated, but with the clear recognition that if the American refused to agree and the IPA officers decided to go ahead anyway, they were authorized to do so, with full knowledge that this could have very serious repercussions for relations between the American and the IPA. The discussion was ended with the group formally adopting a motion drafted by Sandler.

> Resolved that the members of the IPA Executive Council meeting at Broomhills on November 4, 1986, approves of and endorses the actions taken to this point by the President and Secretary of the IPA in regard to the ongoing litigation in which the IPA is one of the defendant parties. It is further recommended that the President and the Secretary continue to negotiate along these lines on behalf of the IPA and that as part of this they approach the officers of the American Psychoanalytic Association as soon as possible in order to try to obtain agreement of the officers of the American to the IPA negotiating a separate agreement with the plaintiffs, pointing out the advantages to the American of this proposed course of action. The President and Secretary are authorized to make such a separately negotiated agreement, subject to a (separately negotiated) satisfactory settlement agreement between the Plaintiffs and the American. Failing an agreement between the IPA and the American to this effect, the President and Secretary are further empowered to proceed separately with negotiations toward settlement subject to consultation with the IPA Executive Council as felt indicated and to the extent feasible.

The next day, November 5, 1986, a memorandum came from Karen Burrows who, along with Dorkey, had just met with the attorneys for the other defendants. In that meeting, Kaplan had begun by stating that he had two points to make concerning the IPA: (1) that the IPA consider changing its bylaws to decrease the time it takes to amend them (two years); and (2) that "Dr. Wallerstein should be advised that when he speaks to Welch he is speaking only for himself and not for the other defendants," and that Dr. Wallerstein is "only bidding against himself," and, by implication, the other defendants, in his endeavors. The attorneys representing the three defendant groups other than the IPA all agreed, "that the plaintiffs, as represented by Welch, presently have no real interest to settle." Jack Auspitz, for the Columbia Institute, proposed showing our settlement offer to the judge to demonstrate the defendants' good faith, but Kaplan objected to this because he felt it might give the judge leverage to push the defendants to conceding even more, and more than they were willing. Kaplan felt that the case would be won by the defendants on the basis of the lack of requisite market share, "since we are only a tiny piece of a huge industry"; he believed "that the case is simply another attempt to harass the medical community in general." Meanwhile, discovery would be getting underway, and Kaplan estimated that this could take up to six months, first on the class certification motion, and then on the merits. There was agreement also on procedures to be used to fight full disclosure of documents to the plaintiffs. An open breach seemed to be developing between the IPA and the American at this meeting of their lawyers.

On November 6, 1986, on a parallel front, Carl Davis, as the recently appointed first chair of the Committee on Non-Medical Clinical Training (CNMCT) of the American, the committee established to implement the approved recommendations of the Gaskill Committee, issued its first report to the directors of all of the American's affiliated institutes. CNMCT had met on September 28 and 29, 1986, in New York, and their recommended guidelines had been discussed by the Coordinating Committee of the American (a committee of all the officers of the American plus the chairs of all the Board committees) on October 25. What had been agreed to was that nonmedical applicants should possess the highest clinical degree in their respective fields and should have gained recognition for the excellence of their therapeutic activity. Institutes asking for waivers of the usual medical requirement for admission to full clinical training on behalf of these applicants were advised, at the start, to "submit only the most clear and uncomplicated applications for waiver for the most obviously qualified individuals with unquestionable credentials." Then followed the specifications for an exhaustive investigation of the past educational experiences and clinical training of the applicant, clearly requiring much more documentation than with medical-psychiatric applicants on the grounds that our institutes have simply been more familiar with medical-psychiatric backgrounds and could more readily evaluate them. In all the materials submitted, the applicant institute was asked for the fullest data, not just conclusions, so that "how the Institute's selection committee has evaluated the applicant's clinical work, clinical talent and ability will be demonstrated in sufficient detail and with sufficient specific information that outside reviewers who do not know the applicant can feel confident about the evidence." The institutes were also advised not to submit too many waiver applications at a time because this could lead to a radical change in the institute ambience.

The overall intent of the memorandum was clear: to reassure uneasy members of the American that the changes wrought by the new liberalized admissions policies would be "evolutionary," gradual, and modest. Had the plaintiffs seen this memorandum it would have confirmed their beliefs that the American's change of heart on the psychoanalytic training of nonphysicians was grudging and minimal, far less than they felt justly entitled to. The gulf in perceptions was plainly very wide, and this throws light on why the plaintiffs never attached much importance to the very decisive vote by which the Gaskill Committee recommendations had been passed by the members of the American.

On November 12, 1986, Burrows sent another memorandum to the IPA on a status conference on the litigation before Judge Keenan at which the discovery process was restarted. The judge ruled in favor of Kaplan's argument that it would be premature to grant Stromberg permission to disclose to his clients all the documents to be turned over to him in discovery before he had even become aware of their contents. Kaplan had also opposed this move because it "might chill the candor of the on-going discussions between the parties." Sixty days were set (until January 12, 1987) in which to complete the production of documents, their inspection, and any negotiations over the Protective Order, and the next, pretrial, conference was set for January 14, 1987, at which time any outstanding discovery issues would be resolved and the schedule set for the hearing on the class-certification motion. On November 17, 1986, Cannon sent a letter to Auletta, reporting a discussion she had had with Dorkey about the November 5 meeting of the defendants' attorneys which he had attended. She underlined what Burrows had stated in her memorandum of November 5: "The principal area of concern was the negative approach taken by Lewis Kaplan to the efforts which the IPA, and, of course, Dr. Wallerstein, have been making to settle the litigation. It is Mr. Kaplan's view that the plaintiffs have no real intent to settle at this time. As matters now stand it appears that the litigation will proceed unless the IPA can find a way of settling on its own."

The memorandum then went on to discuss the November 12 status conference before the judge and Stromberg's pressure to disclose to his clients the confidential documents being produced for discovery but currently protected by the Protective Order and Stipulation. Though now declared premature by the judge, Burrows (and Dorkey) felt that it would become increasingly difficult to restrain disclosure to the plaintiffs. As for the IPA: "We have always taken the view that although none of our documents are harmful to the merits of the claim against the IPA, the settlement discussions would stand a better chance of success before extensive discovery was disclosed." Lastly, about money: "The escalating legal fees are of primary concern. Consideration should be given to asking the APA [the American] to contribute all, or a portion, of the IPA's legal costs if the APA is going to stand in the way of a satisfactory settlement." This was the first occasion on which the issue of the American reimbursing at least a share of the IPA's legal costs—which would become a significant negotiating issue in the following month—was directly raised.

Meanwhile, however, events had taken a major (and to the IPA, an unexpected) turn. On November 15, 1986, there had been a conference telephone call involving the principal officers of the IPA and the American, in which, pursuant to the mandate from the partial IPA Executive Council meeting in London, November 4, I had made the case for the officers of the American to permit me (and the IPA) to negotiate directly with the plaintiffs on behalf of both our organizations. Simons called me back the next day with two pieces of information: (1) the American would not agree to solo negotiations by the IPA; (2) the American had dropped Lew Kaplan's New York law firm and in its place had hired Joel Klein of the Washington law firm of Onek, Klein, and Farr. The stated reason had been that Kaplan's firm had been unwilling to put any cap on the potential litigation expenses. It turned out that Simons had been exploring this change over a period of several months—Simons had become president of the American at its May meeting in 1986—and at first without even the knowledge of his Executive Committee. Klein was known as a "negotiating attorney" in contrast to Kaplan's reputation as a "litigating attorney." Costs with Klein's firm would be considerably less.

One potential obstacle to hiring Klein had been the fact that his firm had long represented the American Psychiatric Association, and that the American Psychiatric and the American Psychoanalytic could have occasions for a divergence of interests, although the American Psychiatric Association was in no way involved in the current lawsuit against the Psychoanalytic. Agreement had been worked out between Simons and Klein that Klein's firm was only being hired to represent the American Psychoanalytic in this one action, and it was understood that in the event of future controversy between the Psychiatric and the Psychoanalytic, the firm would represent only the American Psychiatric and Joel Klein himself would not be involved in such action. The next day, November 17, I talked by phone with Joel Klein, whom I knew personally from earlier contacts involving the relations of the Psychoanalytic and the Psychiatric going back to my own days (1971–72) as President of the American Psychoanalytic Association. I also spoke with Trip Dorkey, and gathered that they, Dorkey and Klein, had already conferred together on the IPA's and the American's postures in the lawsuit.

Also, on November 17, Herbert Schlesinger circulated a memorandum, "Paradoxical Scenarios," to the main officers of the American and of the IPA in which he tried to make the case that whichever side won the lawsuit, should it come to actual trial, the final outcome would not be substantially different. His argument could be summarized as follows: If the American were to win the suit, it would maintain control over its admission and training practices, and in accord with the approved Gaskill Committee proposals, would be admitting qualified clinical psychologists to training probably up to 25% of its classes—and the overall character of the American would not be substantially altered. The American would have surrendered its exclusive franchise—the momentum for which was already underway—and psychologist institutes would be allowed to form and be recognized by the IPA. Members of the American would feel free to teach in these institutes outside the American, though given the high level of training within the American's own institutes and their new openness to nonmedical applicants, the impetus towards the formation of such new independent institutes would probably lessen. Division 39 would become an "interest group" for psychologist psychoanalysts, and though psychology would have suffered a setback in its turf battles with organized psychiatry, psychology would have won the major points that impelled the lawsuit in the first place. In Schlesinger's summation, "The filing of the suit will have been seen to speed up developments that would probably have occurred in time without the suit"—though the plaintiffs would no doubt staunchly dispute this contention—and though at least a million dollars would have been spent by the two sides to the litigation, there was the small possibility that the American could recover its legal fees from the plaintiffs.

On the other side, should the plaintiffs win the suit, the American would have to admit psychologists on a fully equal basis (without its special waiver mechanism), and Schlesinger feared that "since the admissions process will be under the scrutiny of the court, the American will be inhibited from refusing admission to marginal or even poorly qualified psychologists"; that is, there would be more, but perhaps of overall lesser quality. At the same time there would probably be more new Institutes outside the American, but again, he felt that over time this impetus would falter because of the pull of the established superior training within the American. Of course, the costs of all this would now fall more heavily on the American, but in the end a "victory" by the plaintiffs would probably lead to essentially the same ends as a "victory" by the American.

So why continue the suit from either side? Schlesinger stated his feeling that most members of the American probably felt that "the psychologists had a strong moral position in regard to being kept out of the International and being deprived of good teachers and opportunities for psychoanalytic training"; how else, he asked, could one interpret the more than two-thirds vote in favor of the Gaskill Committee recommendations? In effect, Schlesinger stated that the American and the IPA had already yielded on all the essential points. They were ready to sacrifice the exclusive franchise and had stopped trying to prevent "unauthorized training." In effect, "the American has slowly backed into official recognition that it means to undertake the training of qualified non-medical as well as medical candidates," and "all the issues that could be won by the suit have already been conceded." Couldn't all sides recognize this and sit down to an amicable agreement? All of this memorandum resonated well, of course, with the IPA position. It was not immediately clear, however, how much the leadership of the American concurred, though the shift of attorneys to Joel Klein probably portended some move in that direction.

At the same time, in the fall *Newsletter* of Division 39, Fred Pine, the president, and like Schlesinger, a psychologist member of the American, trying to effect bridges between the American and Division 39, in his presidential column made a plea on behalf of high standards of psycho-analytic training, implicitly those of the American, and affirmed (non-defensively) that education is inherently elitist but that he didn't hold it to be rigid, only properly functional. He also acknowledged that this issue of what should constitute proper training standards bitterly divided his own Division 39 membership, and simply made a plea for mutual tolerance and continuing dialogue—again, implicitly, an appeal to his psychologist confreres not to demonize the American's concern for the maintenance of standards as simply exclusionary and elitist.

On November 26, 1986, Bryant Welch, the principal protagonist in the lawsuit in his capacity as President of GAPPP (Group for the Advancement of Psychotherapy and Psychoanalysis in Psychology), sent a memorandum to all the members of the American Psychoanalytic Association, outlining the plaintiffs' position in the lawsuit. He began with the historical context, indicating that the plaintiff group had been trying to negotiate all the issues of the suit with the officers of the American since 1981, for four years prior to the actual filing on March 1, 1985. Of this he said:

> While it would be impossible to elaborate fully on these meetings in this letter, despite protestations to the contrary, they have consistently demonstrated the unlikelihood that the matter would ever be settled cooperatively by the American. In a final negotiation session which we requested in an attempt to forestall the lawsuit, we were told that the training matter was a "pocketbook issue" for the American's membership, and did not feel encouraged about the possibility for resolving the matter amicably.

Here he was referring to the October 12, 1984, meeting in Washington, D.C., at which this statement, called a "gaffe" by one of his colleagues, had been made by Ed Joseph, then the President of the American.

In the light of these perceptions, Welch then stated that "while a lawsuit we knew would be arduous, expensive, and upsetting, after years of failure to achieve training opportunities for psychologists through professional discussions, litigation remained the only viable avenue."

Welch then went on to cite the plaintiffs' objectives in the lawsuit; to obtain "quality psychoanalytic training in well-organized and responsibly run settings," and to secure membership in the IPA, "so that psychologists responsibly trained in psychoanalysis can participate in scientific dialogue with their colleagues around the world" (and also, he added, "a request for attorneys' fees and damages for loss of income suffered by the plaintiffs and the class they represent"). He stated that

> while the settlement proposal we submitted to the American gave detailed specifics for training opportunities [referring to Stromberg's draft of July 28, 1986], the American's proposal to us [Kaplan's counterproposal draft of October 15, 1986] contained only generalities. It proposed only that the International would sponsor in some unspecified way some new opportunities for psychologists and that the American would in some unspecified way cooperate in the effort. We have been seeking a tangible commitment for training but none has been offered.

The Gaskill Amendment was dismissed as helping only a very small number, which in fact turned out to be a drastic underestimation of the powerful changes that the implementation of the Gaskill Amendment would bring about within the following decade, though the perception was certainly in keeping with the expressed thrust of the first, November 6, 1986, report from the Davis Committee.

Welch then offered what he proposed as a reasonable compromise settlement.

> While it is our belief that full integration of training is the optimal arrangement, there are a number of compromises which we feel could possibly bring the matter to resolution. For example, it is our understanding that many institutes of the American would like to be free to train psychologists and other qualified mental health professionals. Others apparently do not wish to do so. One resolution might be to permit those institutes who wish to train psychologists and other qualified mental health professionals to set up companion programs for training these individuals *under auspices other than the auspices of the American Psychoanalytic Association*. Such individuals would not need to be certified by the American nor admitted to membership in the American.

It was by now approaching December 1986 and the pending meeting of the American in New York, at which the IPA officers would be meeting again with the officers of the American, with two major agenda items to be settled: (1) the effort at accord upon an alteration of the Regional Association agreement between the IPA and the American that could induce the British Society to withdraw its proposed amendment to the IPA Constitution and Bylaws; (2) the effort to achieve a better common front between the IPA and the American in the continuing defense of the lawsuit, which might be easier to attain with Klein and Dorkey as principal attorneys advising the American and the IPA. For that period I have little documented correspondence, but do have notes on numerous telephone conversations. There is one letter of November 26, 1986, from Cannon to Auletta, clarifying the way the IPA could enforce the requirement in the British Society resolution, should it be voted upon and passed the following summer, that component organizations bringing legal expenses on the IPA would have to indemnify the IPA for those expenses; this, of course, could not be enforced retroactively.

And on December, 8, 9, and 10, 1986, there were three successive drafts of a letter from Morris Peltz, as Chairman of the Education Committee of the San Francisco Psychoanalytic Institute, to Richard Simons and Shelley Orgel, which is quoted here to indicate the temper of one of the Institutes of the American that wished to move the American more in the direction of the IPA's position. He stated flatly that the San Francisco Institute simply did not agree with the stated policy of the Davis Committee—the CNMCT or the Committee on Non-Medical Clinical Training, established under the chairmanship of Carl Davis, to implement the Gaskill Committee recommendations—to operate in such a way as to "assure the preservation of the medical milieu of the American Psychoanalytic Association." Rather, Peltz stated, "We believe the future health and vitality of our Institute is best assured by an admissions policy which is, in effect, color-blind with respect to the medical degree. Moreover, we believe such a policy is also ultimately best for the future health and vitality of the American Psychoanalytic Association" (draft of December 8, 1986). The draft of the next day added the further point that rather than fostering new institutes outside the American, which could be duplicative, competitive, and divisive: "To us the preferred resolution of the litigation would consist of an adequate opening the doors of the American to properly qualified non-medical mental health professionals." In implicit agreement with the complaint of the plaintiffs, Peltz declared that the charge under which the Davis Committee was operating was too restrictive. In the final December 10 draft, which was the one sent, Peltz called for a reassessment of the Davis Committee position, "that a primary consideration for the American is the preservation of its medical identity. Should not the more urgent mandate be the maintenance of our high professional standards?"

The sentiments here expressed were indeed shared by a significant number of the American's Institutes, giving more hope to those of us guiding the IPA for a fuller accommodation between the IPA and the American.

The phone calls were indeed very numerous in this period, leading up to the December meetings in New York. On November 25 there was a conference call involving Weinshel, Clint Fisher, and me for the IPA with the officers of the American and Joel Klein. The general feeling among the officers of the American seemed to be that settlement negotiations were now stalemated and that it would be best to let the litigation process unroll. The figure of two more years like this was bruited about, with the expectation (hope?) that after all the intervening depositions and discovery, we might be in a stronger position then to bring the plaintiffs to a more reasonable negotiating posture. Meanwhile, the American was asking of the IPA that we close ranks with them and "sit tight"; that if we did feel impelled to explore separately with the plaintiffs, we do it as confidentially and quietly as possible; and that in the meantime we state nothing publicly about the status of the litigation, in order not to further raise anxieties within and between the IPA and the American.

Over the next three days I had several telephone discussions with Weinshel and Auletta extensively reviewing these considerations, and then on November 28, 1986, I had a long conference call with Trip Dorkey and Clint Fisher. They sensed some hardening of the line in the American, and that perhaps the change in attorneys meant more a change of style than of substance. They felt that the "hawks" in the American were in no mood to compromise with the IPA and certainly not to help the IPA in any way with its now escalating legal fees. They felt that Stromberg, on the other hand, was offering concessions, to no longer talk of monetary damages and to offer to defray half the costs that would arise in the creation of new institutes under IPA aegis. They opined that Stromberg was also having to deal with a split in the plaintiffs' ranks, between those who wanted to fight for full equality and integration into the American and those who wanted to push for "separate but equal" training institutions outside the American. Of course it would be to the American's advantage to bring that division out into the open during the deposition process.

In any case, Dorkey and Fisher felt that the IPA could no longer just piggyback on the American in the negotiating process. Certainly the IPA attorneys would need to be present at most of the depositions, and all of this would entail a very sharp escalation of our legal expenses. In regard to a letter that I was considering, appealing to the plaintiffs over everyone's head for us professionals to again sit down and negotiate in good will the settlement that conceptually seemed so near, the IPA attorneys advised holding it back until after the New York meetings with the officers of the American. They, however, urged that I consider setting up an "exploratory meeting" between the IPA and the plaintiffs while in New York, but of course notifying the officers of the American (by way of a conference telephone call) that I was considering doing so.

All of this represented another crisis point for the IPA in its relations with the American. To jump ahead to the meetings of the IPA Executive Council in New York three weeks later, on December 17, 18, and 20, attended by 14 of the 16 members (all but two of the Associate Secretaries) plus Dorkey, I cull from those minutes the following main points: The IPA Executive Council discussion was prefaced by a full review of the events of the lawsuit, going back to the May 1984 action by the American at its San Diego meeting, tabling all consideration of opening its doors to the training of nonphysicians, after what then appeared as ten years of fruitless consideration of the issue, which was the initiating event that precipitated the lawsuit officially filed the following March 1, 1985. It turned out that the IPA officers learned for the first time, at a painful meeting with the Executive Committee of the American the day before this IPA Executive Council meeting (that is, on December 16, 1986), that on April 16—*before* the May meeting under my chairmanship at which I felt an agreement in principal on a negotiated settlement of the lawsuit had been arrived at by the attending representatives of the plaintiffs, the IPA, and the American— Kaplan, the American's attorney, had communicated to Stromberg, the plaintiffs' attorney, that a settlement could be reached on the basis of the American's willingness to sacrifice the "exclusive franchise" aspect of the Regional Association agreement, to remove any perceived obstacles in the way of its members teaching in outside institutes, and to help set up at least one such institute outside the American. This tentative conciliatory initiative by the American had been kept secret, not only from the membership of the American and from its Executive Council, but also (for whatever reasons) from the IPA officers who had been collaborating in good faith with the officers of the American in trying jointly to negotiate with the plaintiffs, and had always advised the American immediately of any action that we contemplated taking.

Kaplan had apparently felt from whatever response he had received from Stromberg that the plaintiffs were not in a mood to negotiate seriously. Apparently it was this that had powered the reluctance of the American's officers to press actively for settlement discussions with the plaintiffs, and had impelled me and the other IPA officers—puzzled by the American's holding back—to seize the initiative and call the daylong meeting on May 31, 1986, in New York of the three principal parties to the suit (attended by 17 or 18 people). The Columbia and New York institutes had not been invited to that meeting because they were not direct affiliates of the IPA (but rather affiliated through the American), and this was an IPA-sponsored meeting. This May 31 meeting had turned into the ill-starred effort wherein

I wrongly felt that we had reached enough accord in principal that a settlement agreement could be fashioned by the attorneys that all parties would find acceptable. This is the document that had come back two months later from Stromberg, but on a scale and in a form that would be impossible for the IPA (let alone the American) to live with. Yet the counterproposal that had finally gone back from Kaplan to Stromberg after the October meetings in New York, which I knew was less than the IPA would have offered, yet as much as the American would offer—again reflective of the continuing unresolved differences in the defendants' camp—was one that predictably would lead only to the growing impasse in the settlement negotiations.

In a flurry of telephone calls on October 28 and 29, 1986, the plaintiffs made clear that they felt the American was not serious about negotiating a settlement at this time, and Welch put out feelers asking if I would be willing to meet for discussions with him alone: if the two of us could not come to an agreement, then no agreement would be possible. Welch said he felt that nothing could be negotiated with too many people in the room. I indicated that even should I agree that we meet, each accompanied by some colleagues (albeit not necessarily our attorneys), any agreement reached between the IPA and the plaintiffs could only be partial, because the American, as the principal target of the suit, would necessarily have to be involved and delaying this could only make the process more suspect and more difficult. Welch finally agreed, but indicated that he felt there would be no point to any meeting that involved Kaplan, whom he saw as the center of the American's resistance strategy.

It was at this point that I first proposed directly to the American that they concur in the IPA officers' and attorney' undertaking to explore with the plaintiffs the possibility for bridging the differences between the Stromberg-proposed settlement and the Kaplan counterproposal, and it was on this that "all the members of the IPA (partial) Executive Council meeting in London in November had agreed that Dr. Wallerstein should go ahead and negotiate with the Plaintiffs letting the American know he was doing so but not allowing the American to veto these further efforts" (Minutes, IPA Executive Council, December 17, 18, 20, 1986). I advised the officers of the American to this effect in a further conference call in November, and it was to this that Dick Simons, president of the American, said in response that the American would not agree to such separate negotiations, but then also informed me of the switch of counsel from Lew Kaplan of the New York firm to Joel Klein of the Washington firm. It turned out subsequently that Simons had been discussing this possible shift with Klein over a considerable period of time, but had not even hinted at such a possibility in a telephone talk with me just the day before this announcement to me, when we were discussing together the roles of our respective attorneys in our negotiating postures.

Dorkey had initially felt that this change from a "litigating attorney" to a "negotiating attorney" augured well for the possibility of favorable renewed settlement talks, but a little later, of course, he had indicated that this shift of attorneys might result more in a change of style than a change of substance. This may have been in part, a reflection of his perception of Klein's response to contacts with Stromberg, reported in a conference call on November 25 of the IPA and American officers and our respective attorneys. In that discussion, Klein reported that Stromberg had taken a very hard line with him in a meeting between the two of them; Stromberg seemed to indicate that because the plaintiffs had won the first round in court, they would rather let the discovery and deposition process now unroll, and were at this point less inclined to negotiate. This was the discussion in which the American stated strongly that we should all sit tight, that they were against separate negotiations, that if the IPA insisted on going ahead on its own, at least it should be done totally confidentially, and that if any word of it leaked out, the American would publicly disavow any link to it.

At this point, I contacted Bryant Welch and set up a meeting between the IPA and the plaintiffs in New York, at a time that would work out to our mutual convenience, which was December 15, before the meeting between the officers of the IPA and of the American (set for December 16), and before the full IPA Executive Council meetings, starting on December 17. In a conference call on December 9, involving the principal officers of the IPA and of the American with the respective attorneys (Fisher and Klein), we informed the American of the planned "exploratory meeting" with plaintiffs set for December 15. The officers of the American did not approve, and Simons informed the IPA not to count on any commitment of money from the American to the IPA—"it is wrong in principle"—to aid in establishing new IPA institutes in the United States outside the framework of the American, as a component of a possible settlement agreement. To Weinshel and myself this represented an unhappy backtracking from what we thought had previously been agreed upon (again, "in principle") between the American and the IPA. It was indeed part of a worsening climate in the relations between our two organizations, within a group that had heretofore been longtime close friends and working colleagues—after all, this was an "American administration" of the IPA.

The next day, December 10, I had phoned Helen Fischer, Administrative Director of the American, to inform her of the exact date, December 15, for the IPA meeting with the plaintiffs, and she in turn informed me that on that same date the officers of the American and of the codefendant New York and Columbia Institutes and their respective attorneys would be meeting together. They would try to work out some way to make things politically and monetarily easier for the IPA, so that the IPA might be more willing to go along with the other defendants in a hardening attitude to continue the legal battle of the lawsuit, rather than trying to negotiate a settlement. The officers of the other three defendant groups all seemed convinced that we could either win the suit ultimately or could negotiate a settlement further down the road that would involve less accommodation to the plaintiffs' demands. It came out that this meeting of the other three defendant groups had been planned over some time, but this again was the first that I was informed about it. Fischer also informed me that the officers of the American planned to have their attorney present when they met with the IPA officers on December 16. I indicated that we would then want the IPA attorney present and I arranged this in a phone call with Clint Fisher that same day. He underlined his strong feeling that at the moment, the officers of the American were not in a serious negotiating mood.

On our arrival in New York on Saturday, December 13, Weinshel and I were invited to a Sunday morning, December 14, meeting with the officers of the American to bring us up to date on all these fast-moving events. At that meeting, Simons reported that Arnold Schneider, one of the four plaintiffs, had talked with him on the telephone, and that it had been a useful talk; they had understood each other.

> Schneider had implied that Stromberg and Welch would not let the others negotiate, that Stromberg and Welch were an embarrassment to the other plaintiffs. Dr. Simons said that in these circumstances the IPA by negotiating separately would strengthen Welch and Stromberg. After further telephone calls following this meeting Dr. Wallerstein had himself talked with Schneider, in Topeka, and he had asked him about this, and Schneider had said that Dr. Simons' impression was 180 degrees off course; Welch and Stromberg fully represented all the Plaintiffs in all matters [Minutes, IPA Executive Council, December 17, 18, 20, 1986].

On Monday, December 15, the IPA officers (Weinshel, Dorkey, and I) met for four and a half hours with Welch, Stockhamer, and Stromberg to discuss the possible basis for a settlement. Welch emphasized that they were only talking about a settlement with the IPA; he insisted that they had quite separate issues in regard to the American and the other defendants. Welch brought up points for discussion under several headings. By his count there were seven currently existing nonmedical institutes that would seek

IPA affiliation (six in New York and one in Los Angeles);[2] he indicated that there were many fly-by-night groups in various places that he was not concerned with. When asked how many of the seven might prove to meet IPA standards, he replied at least three or four. It was clarified that each of these applicant groups would have to be separately evaluated, that those that met IPA standards and already contained at least four IPA members could be recognized under existing procedures, and that those without sufficient IPA members already in their ranks would need as well to go through a process of recognition of individuals for Direct Membership if they individually met IPA criteria. It was also clarified that the IPA adhered to frequency criteria of at least four times a week for training and supervised analyses, and in response to the issue of older, respected senior members who had been analyzed years before at a lesser frequency, it was indicated that these cases would be assessed individually, and that there would be no blanket grandfathering.

In regard to possible pathways for training nonmedical candidates, Welch offered four possibilities in descending order: (1) Most desirable for the plaintiffs would be a completely "open-door" policy in the American, though the plaintiffs realized that the American did not then seem willing to accept that; (2) that the American allow its institutes a local option on training nonphysicians which would be acceptable to the plaintiffs; (3) that the American allow access to the training courses in its own Institutes for candidates in outside parallel institutes; and (4) the least that the plaintiffs would accept is that the American permit its members to participate in the organization and the training programs of these outside institutes. The plaintiffs' aim was to have 21 cities, other than New York, in which training would be available to nonmedical candidates; they realized that we would need to jointly arrive at a realistic timetable. (How different from the tenor and content of Stromberg's draft of the settlement proposal at the end of July, not quite a half-year earlier.) In regard to money, the plaintiffs made clear that they would have no monetary claims upon the IPA; this would be an issue between them and the American and its institutes. However, they would not wish to allow the IPA a clear-cut financial bonanza from the dues that so many new members would be bringing in. For that reason, they felt that the expenses of sponsoring new institutes, ordinarily split 50-

---

[2] Welch named, in New York, the New York Freudian Society (NYFS), the Institute for Psychoanalytic Training and Research (IPTAR), the William Alanson White Institute, the Postgraduate Center for Mental Health (the "Wolberg" Institute), and the postgraduate psychoanalytic training programs at Adelphi University and New York University, and in Los Angeles, the Los Angeles Institute and Society for Psychoanalytic Studies (LAISPS).

50 between the IPA and the group in formation, should be shifted to the IPA bearing perhaps 60%; but they also indicated that this issue was not a major concern.

There was some discussion of the necessity of IPA bylaw changes should these various points under discussion be agreed to in a settlement accord. Stromberg felt that this might not be necessary, depending on how one read the Regional Association agreement. Clearly the plaintiffs were anxious that a bylaw change, which would require a two-thirds affirmative vote, could be blocked by a determined minority. In the end, it was my feeling that though this was not an easy meeting, it was a cordial one, with a sense of mutual goodwill and a feeling that it should be possible to find a reasonable basis for settlement between the plaintiffs and the IPA—which was, of course, exactly the feeling that I had had at the end of the May 31 meeting involving the three main protagonists, the American, the IPA and the Plaintiffs.

On Tuesday, December 16, there was a four-hour meeting between the IPA Executive (this time represented more fully by Weinshel, Schlossman, Limentani, Auletta, Unwin, Dorkey, Fisher, and I) and the full Executive Committee of the American (Simons, Orgel, Curtis, Allison, Silber, Pacella, Fischer, and special guest Jay Katz), and including their new attorney, Joel Klein. This meeting began with my report to the officers of the American on the meeting with the representatives of the plaintiffs on the previous day. Klein reported briefly on the meeting the American's officers had had with representatives of the New York and Columbia institutes, from which actually very little had come. I then offered our view (Weinshel's and mine) that our meeting with the plaintiffs had convinced us that there was a basis for a settlement with the plaintiffs on terms compatible with the interests of the American. I also reported to them the telephone conversation that I had had with Arnold Schneider, which was absolutely contrary to what Simons had reported about Schneider at our meeting three days before. There was an intense to-and-fro discussion in which Weinshel and I faced the officers of the American—all long-time close friends of ours—with their lack of candor in their dealings with us, which they denied, but which we countered with examples, which made a sad and painful meeting. On behalf of the IPA we had insisted that the IPA needed some definitive change at the coming Montreal meeting the next summer (1987), which would need to be set into motion in the form of proposed resolutions before the first of the year, within two weeks. We strongly preferred that it be on the initiative of the American that the Regional Association agreement be altered, but that the issue would come to the floor of the Business Meeting in Montreal in any case. There was to be a closed meeting of the Executive Council of the American two days later (Thursday, December 18), and I strongly urged the absolute necessity of obtaining the Council's assent to the ending of the exclusive franchise in the United States through modification of the 1938 action as later codified in the Regional Association agreement.

That evening (December 16, 1986), I called Bryant Welch and advised him that I did not feel that a further meeting with the plaintiffs this week would be useful. I did ask him directly, If the IPA and the plaintiffs could manage to settle on the basis of the previous day's meeting, what more would the plaintiffs want from the American? Welch was willing to talk about that; he said that if the IPA settled with them on that basis, it would give them 80% of what they wanted, and that they would then have to discuss further whether it was even worth going on with the lawsuit, given all its uncertainties and expense.

On the next day (Wednesday, December 17), there was the almost full meeting of the IPA Executive Council (14 of the 16 members, all but two of the Associate Secretaries), which lasted four hours. I gave a brief chronology at this meeting of all the events since the precipitation of the lawsuit by the American's tabling all consideration of clinical psychoanalytic training for nonphysicians at the 1984 San Diego meeting and then reported in detail the events of the past month, with special elaboration on the meetings that week in New York: the Saturday, December 13 meeting with the Executive Committee of the American; the follow-up phone call to Arnold Schneider; the Monday, December 15 meeting with the plaintiffs; the Tuesday, December 16 meeting again with the Executive Committee of the American; and the follow-up phone conversation with Bryant Welch. What had not yet come up in any of these meetings was the question of financial help from the American in regard to the IPA's legal costs should the IPA continue in the suit. The most urgent pressure at the moment was that of the bylaw amendment altering the Regional Association agreement, because this would need to be published within two weeks (by January 1) in order to be discussed and voted on in Montreal in July. I also indicated that I had come to the conclusion that it was essential that I give an up-to-date report on the current status of the lawsuit to the entire IPA membership as the central item in my Presidential Message in the coming January 1987 IPA *Newsletter*.

At this point the floor was opened for general discussion. The feeling was expressed (by American members of the IPA Executive Council) that many members of the American had been unhappy at the way the litigation was being pursued by the American's previous attorney. The Columbia Institute had specifically felt that the American's membership was insufficiently informed all along and it had been only at their insistence that the full meeting of even the American's Executive Council (technically, the governing Board of Directors of the American) had been held in October. On the other hand, considerable faith was expressed in the new attorney of the American (personally known by several of the American members of the IPA Executive Council), and I was advised against publication of the IPA *Newsletter* article I was planning, on the grounds that it could be construed as an invitation to an open confrontative ballot on the IPA position vis-à-vis the American's position. I responded that this was a delicate tightrope, both internally within our executives and openly with our memberships. The IPA officers certainly felt that "the IPA could no longer live with the American's way of doing things as the price of unity" (Minutes, IPA Executive Council, December 17, 18, 20, 1986). Certainly, however, the aggrieved feelings and contentions between us would not be made public; the proposed *Newsletter* article would not be inflammatory in any sense, but simply a recital of facts and a review of the issues over the past years. Personally, I hoped very much that the American would decide (at this New York meeting) to itself propose the alteration of the Regional Association agreement, for its own sake as well as for that of the IPA. In response, Arnold Cooper made the point that the officers of the American would be willing—in a lawsuit settlement—to alter the Regional Association agreement, but that they had been holding this offer back as part of their negotiating package.

Weinshel, in support of my position, added his strong view that the IPA officers had done everything they could to avoid a fight with the officers of the American, but had reached the point where they had had to confront them with their withholding and lack of trust. There had even been statements that the American could muster all its votes to defeat the peaceful passage of the necessary IPA bylaw changes if the IPA did not fall in line with the position of the American's Executive Committee. Dorkey pointed out that, in his view, the American had used the IPA as its currency to settle the lawsuit, and that the IPA's earlier efforts toward settlement had been blocked by the American. Dorkey added that we had to face the fact that the interests of the IPA were distinct and different from the interests of the American and that one side or the other would have to compromise. There was discussion of the wisdom of giving the American a deadline to come to an agreement, which, if not met, would free the IPA to actively pursue a separate settlement of the suit. There was also discussion of the absolute legal requirement that altering the Regional Association agreement would necessitate a bylaw change, and that if the American insisted on the IPA's remaining in the lawsuit with them, at least they should assume the burden of the IPA's legal expenses. The meeting ended with the IPA Council asking Weinshel and me to approach Simons for permission for me to address the closed meeting of the American's Executive Council the following day, in order to convey the dilemma of the IPA, caught between its American and its non-American membership and asking the American's help in order to maintain the IPA as an intact functioning organization.

The December 17 meeting of the IPA Executive Council then adjourned until the next day.

When it reconvened on Thursday morning, December 18, I informed the IPA Council that Simons was not in favor of my addressing the closed session of the Council of the American, but that he would discuss this with his attorney and get back to me during the luncheon break. I had also heard from other people that some members of the American's Executive Council had expressed concern that IPA officers might be present during their discussion of the lawsuit issues at the afternoon closed meeting. I felt it quite possible that my request to address the meeting would be refused. Such a refusal could easily intensify the aggrieved feelings on both sides. It was even asked (by Sandler) whether it was in fact possible that the American's Executive Council might be discussing an actual secession from the IPA. Most of us (myself included) did not believe that this was so; we rather believed that the officers of the American feared that they might lose control of their meeting if I presented the IPA position persuasively enough. It was finally agreed that Weinshel, Dorkey, and I would go to the American's meeting room just prior to their afternoon session to make our request of Simons and Klein once again. At that point, the IPA Executive Council turned to its other agenda business for the balance of that morning session.

It turned out that Weinshel and I were allowed to attend briefly the closed afternoon meeting of the American's Executive Council, at which I was permitted to address the Council. My talk was a plea to those present, both as members of the American and as members of the IPA. I covered the history of the entire problem, with focus on the recent events, including the meeting with the plaintiffs' representatives three days previously. I covered the terms of a possible settlement, which I felt to be in reach for the IPA, and possibly even for the American. The specification of the precise terms of a possible agreement was in response to a specific question from a member of the Council, and with Joel Klein's agreement that I could do so. I had then said that, "Psychoanalysis is not at stake; it will thrive and is bigger than us. But our organized institutional structure and the organizations through which we work are at stake, and we face a shared crisis" (Minutes, IPA Executive Council, December 17, 18, 20, 1986). I then frankly stated that the IPA's back was against the wall, that any proposed bylaw changes had to be published in January, that I had great anxieties concerning the coming Montreal Congress, and that I would certainly need to communicate fully with the entire IPA membership (including, of course, the Americans) well in advance of the Congress. At the end of my talk, the Council of the American wished to discuss these issues further, and Weinshel and I were excused. We came back then to the IPA Executive Council, which had been discussing its agenda business other than the lawsuit, and

I reported on my talk to the Executive Council of the American and its reception by them. Weinshel then added, when I finished, that my report there had been comprehensive and to the point, that it had not attempted to attribute blame to the American, but had clearly pointed out differences in viewpoint. He said that he had found it hard to read the overall mood of the audience; some appeared tired and distracted, but others had been paying close attention and taking notes.

On the following day, Friday December 19, the officers of the IPA (this time, Weinshel, Schlossman, Limentani, Auletta, Unwin, and I, with our attorneys, Dorkey and Fisher) met with the full Executive Committee of the American (Simons, Orgel, Curtis, Allison, Silber, Pacella, Katz, Fischer, and two of their attorneys, Klein and a younger associate) in what turned out to be a fateful four-and-a-half-hour meeting ending with a new accord and, for all of us, renewed hope. What emerged from that meeting was a firm agreement that the IPA rejoin the American in a unified defense of the lawsuit as part of an agreed-upon three-part package between our two groups.

The first part was an agreement, reached with some hesitation, that the American would unilaterally offer to alter the (1938) Regional Association agreement, relinquishing its exclusive franchise on IPA membership within the United States, while maintaining its title as Regional Association and its autonomy over training standards within its member Institutes. This would come to the Business Meeting of the 1987 IPA Congress in Montreal as a motion for a bylaw amendment, signed by the requisite ten members of the American, including all six officers,[3] with the text to be submitted to the IPA officers within a day, for publication on time in the January issue of the *IPA Bulletin*, as constitutionally required. This could be voted as a binding resolution, effective immediately, at the Business Meeting in Montreal, subject to subsequent ratification by mail ballot of the entire membership. This would enable the IPA to immediately notify the Institute for Psychoanalytic Training and Research (IPTAR) and the New York Freudian Society (NYFS)—both of which groups had previously inquired about the possibility of IPA affiliation—that the possibility for evaluating established, nonmedical psychoanalytic groups would be coming into effect and that this evaluation process could get underway immediately after the Montreal Congress. In addition, in localities where there were ready pools

---

[3] The ten signatories on the document prepared that same day were Richard Simons, President; Homer Curtis, President-Elect; Austin Silber, Secretary; Bernard Pacella, Treasurer; Shelley Orgel, Chairman of the Board; George Allison, Secretary of the Board; and four Executive Councilors, Jay Katz of Western New England (also Chair, Committee on Psychoanalysis, Legal Issues and Legal Review), Philip Mechanick of Philadelphia, Edith Sabshin of Washington, D.C., and Rafael Padro-Yumet of Puerto Rico.

of potential candidates and willing, qualified teachers, the process of developing new groups could get underway simultaneously.

The second part of the package agreement concerned the financial relations between the American and the IPA. Joel Klein's law firm had agreed to put an annual cap on expenses at a level that was bearable to the American. The American had proposed that the IPA relinquish its separate legal representation and that Klein represent both organizations. This the IPA could not agree to, in view of the heretofore often divergent interests of the two organizations. The IPA did agree to intensified, continuous, and open discussions between Dorkey and Klein on all pending legal issues, and that wherever possible, where there was agreement between them, Klein would represent both organizations and then inform Dorkey on the happening (deposition, interview, and so forth). Besides cutting the IPA legal expenses by not maintaining separate representation, except where we deemed it indicated, we agreed on the formula that as of January 1, 1987 (within two weeks), the American would, in addition to its own legal costs, pick up 60% of all IPA legal expenses. This formula had been arrived at on the basis that 60% of the IPA dues-paying membership was outside the United States[4] and that those members' dues would not be used to help defray legal expenses of a suit to which the IPA membership outside America overwhelmingly took exception. The 40% to be covered by the IPA was deemed to represent the proportion of the dues paid by its American members, who presumably would not object to the continuing defense of the lawsuit. Certainly this division of legal costs did much to diminish otherwise expectable major objections, at the 1987 Montreal Congress, to the IPA continuing alongside the American in the lawsuit.

The third component of the package agreement was the quid pro quo, the commitment that I made on behalf of the IPA to desist from any further unilateral settlement agreement talks with the plaintiffs. This would not preclude us from talking with the plaintiffs' representatives, but there would be no further negotiations aimed at a possible separate settlement. The American, for its part, would not object to the IPA informing the Plaintiffs of the bylaw change to be proposed by the American at the forthcoming Montreal Congress—now but six months off—which would open the doors immediately for psychoanalytic training leading to IPA membership outside the aegis of the American. And the American would not object if the plaintiffs then decided on this basis to drop the suit against the IPA.

---

[4] Actually, when we later checked the office records, this number turned out to be more like 70%, but once agreed, the IPA did not ask that the formula be revised.

All in all, it was a hard-bargained agreement, but one that, on the basis of major concessions made by the American to the IPA, and toward lowering the barriers to nonmedical psychoanalytic training in the United States, now firmly locked the IPA and the American into full partnership in the further joint defense of the lawsuit. The Executive Committee of the American had even agreed that the American would not mount any opposition in Montreal against the British Society proposal, should that not be withdrawn. At a one-hour meeting of the IPA Executive Council the next morning, Saturday, December 20, where the agreement worked out the previous day between the officers of the American and the officers of the IPA was presented in detail, the general feeling was that this agreement was the most that the IPA could have hoped for, given all the circumstances, and that it would, at least in the short run, avoid an otherwise threatening fracture of the IPA. Not everyone was equally sanguine about the long-term prospects should the lawsuit drag on and consume mounting energies and monies. I also stated that I would be modifying the presidential message for the IPA *Newsletter* in the light of these new developments, would notify IPTAR and NYFS about them as previously discussed, and would ask the plaintiffs to survey the various cities in which they hoped to identify pools of potential applicants for training (along with our own survey of pools of potential qualified teachers). Lastly, the IPA Executive Council agreed that it was now timely to create a Commission on Psychoanalytic Education (COMPSED), to be chaired by Weinshel, to consider needed new procedures and mechanisms for the evaluation of the existing nonmedical institutes that would be applying for IPA affiliation, and for the evaluation, as well, of individuals trained outside the IPA for qualification for direct IPA membership. It was felt particularly appropriate to bring this new Commission into being now, since the original International Training Commission had become defunct with the 1938 American refusal to recognize its authority any longer—almost a half-century earlier. Mostly, the calendar year could close with the vastly relieved feeling of a major step forward in the safeguarding of the internal integrity of the IPA, if not yet in the settlement of the lawsuit itself.

As an addendum to this chapter, to convey the very personalized flavor of the emotionally intense confrontations between (and within) the IPA and the American during the events here described, I quote from an exchange of letters immediately thereafter between Shelley Orgel, Chairman of the Board of the American, and me; the two of us were long-time friends, who had become the respective central contesting protagonists in the struggles between the two organizations. Another equally unexpected letter came from another close friend, David Sachs, who was torn, as so many American members of the IPA were, by the tensions between the sister organizations. Orgel's letter (in toto), is dated December 22, 1986:

Dear Bob, This note is just to say that I feel very good about where we ended up last week. I guess we all fought hard, but it seems in retrospect to have been a necessary struggle and I believe we can now look to a more harmonious future in which *Psychoanalysis* rather than our separate positions will benefit. I also want to say that our friendship is very valuable to me and I feel it is on firmer ground than it was a week ago. Whatever holidays we believe in or celebrate will be happier ones. As ever, Shelley.

My response (also in toto) is dated December 30, 1986:

Dear Shelley: Your welcome letter came and I want to answer it immediately and in kind. I trust just as much as you do that the friendship among Doris, you, Judy, and myself will not be marred in any way by the fact that we have represented different points of view about the realities of the lawsuit and about the best means toward our shared goal, the benefitting of psychoanalysis. I hope that as between our two organizations that we can both continue together and work together toward the earliest "good enough" resolution of our current turmoils. Let's, of course, talk more together in Chicago in May. Best season's greetings from us to you. Warmly, Bob.

And a long excerpt from a letter by David Sachs, dated December 23, 1986:

In view of your presidency of the IPA, your attachment to your American colleagues, and the pressures of the current lawsuit, it seems to me that you are in an awfully difficult spot. And I want to say that in addition to my feelings of sympathy for you, you also have my support for trying to work out some reasonable solution. . . . my concerns are based on my personal experiences in the American. It seems possible to me that an exaggerated attitude about our uniqueness might make some members of the American unable to grasp the position of the plaintiffs and thereby set up an even more destructive fight than is necessary. As you may know I have long advocated a more open admissions policy toward non-medical candidates as a way to improve our standards through a more merit-based selection process. I have never been able to comprehend the idea that psychoanalysis belongs to medicine although I do not believe that it is not a legitimate pathway to becoming an analyst. Since my Institute

is probably 90% against non-MD training, I can—perhaps—
empathize as well as sympathize with you. . . . Mainly, I wanted
to tell you that some of your friends appreciate what you're going
through and realize that you're doing it for the sake of a most
valuable science—psychoanalysis. As in most political fights the
dangers from the conservatives are hardly less frightening than
the dangers from the radicals. My guess is that you want to
salvage the middle ground and preserve psychoanalysis from its
too good "friends" and too bad "enemies." If you can do that
you have my gratitude in advance.

Clearly, this conveyed exactly the position that I felt I was trying to
represent—a viewpoint that I always felt was held by a very significant
number of colleagues within the American. It was a very heartening letter
to receive in the wake of a period when I was not always sure that my own
morale would persist or that my will for the maintained integrity of the
IPA and our collective vision for the future of psychoanalysis would indeed
prevail.

Revisions of the "1938 Agreement," July 1987
The End of a Half-Century of Controversy

The agreement fashioned in New York in December 1986 between the officers of the IPA and of the American did not, of course, immediately erase all the escalated tensions within the American or between the American and the IPA over the question of lay analysis. An example was the distressed letter to Simons, as President of the American, and Orgel, as Chairman of the Board, from Morris Peltz, Chair of the Education Committee of the San Francisco Psychoanalytic Institute on December 27. On behalf of the Education Committee of one of the American's institutes that was in full sympathy with the IPA's position on the issues in contention, Peltz wrote:

> The San Francisco Institute felt that the best course for psycho-analysis in America scientifically and professionally would consist of a fully adequate opening the doors of the existing approved Institutes in the American to properly qualified non-medical mental health professionals. [In my prior letter of December 10] I expressed our collective concern that the guidelines being proposed for its operation by the Davis Committee would inevitably reflect a spirit of tokenism and second-class citizenship that would be contrary to the very thing we were trying to foster, to offer the best training possible to the best applicants, whatever their mental health disciplinary background, and for the best good of the discipline of psychoanalysis.

The prior letter had been a request that this whole matter be brought to the Board and Executive Council meetings to be held in the following week in New York to have the "opportunity to have the full discussion in those bodies that would have revealed the degree of agreement with our position among other Institutes and Societies in the American." The officers of the American had not placed the letter from San Francisco on the agendas of the Board and Council, and the angry letter by Peltz in the wake of the New York meetings served notice that if this second letter were not on the Board and Council agendas at the next meetings, in May 1987, the San Francisco representatives would bring the matter up from the floor. What San Francisco proposed was that the American should at least immediately grant its component societies and institutes a true "local option" to train nonmedical mental health professionals on a fully equal basis with psychiatrists if they should wish to do so, and that San Francisco in turn would be willing for those of its nonmedical candidates who would bypass the American's strict "waiver" gateway to seek direct access to IPA membership outside the American. The letter ended with the statement that. "Certainly the proposed alteration of the 1938 Regional Association agreement between the American and the IPA which will be voted on in Montreal this July would allow the possibility of various roads to IPA membership for individuals properly trained in America, whether through the American which we in San Francisco would prefer, or outside the American if that had to be."

On another front of this multisided institutional struggle I wrote on January 7, 1987, to Nathan Stockhamer, who was a central figure in all the negotiating sessions with the plaintiffs and was a member of the William Alanson White Institute (in New York), one of the independent psychoanalytic groups that was considering whether to pursue application for IPA affiliation *if* (now becoming *when*) that should become possible. In that letter I indicated that a good deal of progress had been made between the American and the IPA in the week of meetings in New York in December, but not yet enough to call a meeting with the plaintiffs that could fashion a mutually agreed-upon settlement agreement at this time. I did inform him, however, of the intent of the officers of the American to move a bylaw change at the coming IPA Congress in Montreal in July, which would surrender the "exclusive franchise" of the American with the IPA for the United States, and that we expected this would pass at the Business Meeting in Montreal by a wide margin with subsequent equally decisive ratification in the mail ballot of the full membership. This action would be taken unilaterally, "without respect to the progression of the suit around the other issues that divide the plaintiffs and the defendants." I then notified Stockhamer that both the New York Freudian Society and IPTAR had already inquired officially about applying for IPA affiliation and indicated that the IPA "would be equally receptive to an official inquiry from the William Alanson White Institute."

This was followed by a January 15, 1987 letter from Dick Simons to the members of the American apprising them of all these latest developments. The letter made the following points: (1) on October 22, 1986, the American had proposed what it felt to be a fair settlement agreement of the lawsuit, but in early November that had been rejected by the plaintiffs; (2) on November 12, Judge Keenan had ordered that the discovery phase of the lawsuit now proceed; (3) on November 17, the American had hired Joel Klein's law firm to represent it in the further defense of the suit, replacing Lewis Kaplan's law firm; and (4) on December 18, the Executive Council of the American had voted unanimously to empower the Executive Committee to assist the IPA with its continuing legal costs, and had also endorsed the proposal that the American take the initiative at the IPA Congress in Montreal the following July in proposing the modification of its Regional Association status, renouncing its exclusive IPA franchise in the United States. He ended with a plea to the American's membership to come to the Montreal Congress and to participate in the Business Meeting on July 29, 1987. This letter was the notice to the membership of the American of the new accord with the IPA.

In May, however, I was sent a copy of a January 29, 1987 letter from Murray Meisels, a member of Division 39 in Ann Arbor, Michigan (and, I discovered later, president-elect of Division 39) in which he angrily denounced the "appalling" willingness of GAPPP to consider the kind of settlement proposals that were being exchanged between the defendants and the plaintiffs. He had contacted two of the plaintiffs (Bryant Welch and Arnold Schneider), and with their knowledge proposed: (1) that GAPPP meet immediately with the Board of Division 39 in order to fully describe all developments to date; (2) that Division 39 appoint an oversight committee that would be apprised of and review all lawsuit developments, and the Division secure an attorney to provide an independent appraisal of these developments; (3) that the Division be formally represented at all future negotiations; and (4) that any proposed out-of-court resolution of the lawsuit be reviewed and discussed to the satisfaction of the Division 39 Board "and other American Psychological Association bodies." Otherwise, he warned, the Division's support of GAPPP's negotiating postures could not be "unambivalent" and "divisiveness and rumor might undermine GAPPP's efforts." So the plaintiffs also clearly had their differences between those seeking a negotiated settlement and "hard-liners" eager to push towards a fought-out maximal "victory."

This letter was followed temporally by two juxtaposed *Newsletter* documents. The Winter 1987 *Newsletter* of the American carried an announcement by Dick Simons of the proposed alteration in the American's Regional Association status with the IPA and also of the appointment of Joel Klein as the American's new legal counsel in the defense of the lawsuit.

It also carried a long interview with Joel Klein by Elise Snyder, reviewing the whole history of the lawsuit and talking to its likely future. Klein discussed his understanding of the events leading up to the lawsuit, the specific allegations of the defendants adding up, in their view, to a clear violation of the antitrust laws, as well as the specific defenses that the American (and its codefendants) had pursued to this point, declaring the issues in contention to be noncommercial in essence, thus rendering the antitrust laws inapplicable, and additionally that the academic freedom protections of the First Amendment also precluded any antitrust basis for the suit. The defendants' motion for summary dismissal of the suit made in late 1985, however, had been denied by Judge Keenan on April 4, 1986. The judge had "concluded that, at such an early stage, the facts were insufficiently developed to enable him to rule on whether the Antitrust Acts even applied in this particular context," and that therefore the discovery phase of the lawsuit should proceed. Klein also reviewed the several meetings between the defendant groups and the plaintiffs both before and since the filing of the lawsuit, but felt that at present the protagonist parties were still too far apart to justify further settlement discussions. He did reiterate what Simons had announced, that the American would help underwrite the continuing IPA legal expenses in connection with the lawsuit and that the American would be proposing the alteration of its Regional Association status to the coming July 1987 Montreal IPA Congress.

Almost simultaneously, Sy Coopersmith, in his presidential message in the *Council News* of the Council of Psychoanalytic Psychotherapists (CPP) (February 1987), reviewed the efforts made decades earlier by the National Psychological Association for Psychoanalysis (NPAP) in New York to explore the idea of direct affiliation with the IPA. Five leading members had met in New York in December 1975 with then president of the IPA, Serge Lebovici, and then secretary, Daniel Widlocher, both of Paris. The meeting had been cordial and both Lebovici and Widlocher had "agreed, in principle, that 'non-medical' analysts should be recognized and admitted, in accordance with its by-laws, to the IPA. But they said, their 'hands were tied,' the IPA was bound by contract to the American. The empathy of the IPA for the inequity of 'medical' and 'non-medical' analysis seemed, at the time, to be a moral victory without tangible benefits." This whole dynamic was of course now profoundly altered by the existence of the lawsuit, and Coopersmith called for renewed and intensified efforts by all psychoanalytic psychologists and their organizations to join in advocacy by writing (and pressuring) the American and the IPA on behalf of full admissions of psychologists, with parity, to all American and IPA training bodies. What was not clear (to me, anyway) was the relationship of CPP to GAPPP (the organization prosecuting the lawsuit) or to Division 39 of the American Psychological.

During the same month (February 1987), a column on the lawsuit, written by Bryant Welch, appeared in the American Psychological Association's newsletter, the *Monitor*. This column pointed to the possible influence of the American Psychiatric Association in stiffening the resistances within the American Psychoanalytic to any accommodation to the demands of organized psychology for access to psychoanalytic training within the Psychoanalytic. Welch said:

> The extent to which organized psychiatry has a role in the defense of the lawsuit is somewhat unclear. However, the American Psychoanalytic Association is now represented by the attorney for the American Psychiatric Association.[1] The suit was precipitated to a large extent by a speech by a prominent member of the psychiatric association to the American Psychoanalytic Association. That speech warned the psychoanalytic group not to have anything to do with training psychologists and to stick close to their 'medical roots.' Up to the time of that speech, psychologists had been involved in negotiations with members of both associations [American Psychiatric and American Psychoanalytic] in hopes of resolving the training issues amicably. But because the speech was delivered by a member of that negotiating team,[2] it greatly eroded hope that the matter would be negotiated in a mutually satisfactory manner.

This column by Welch seemed clearly to herald some stiffening in the plaintiffs' negotiating posture vis-à-vis the defendants.

The individual referred to in Welch's column was Melvin Sabshin, Medical Director of the American Psychiatric Association and a trained

---

[1] I never knew whether Welch was aware that Joel Klein, the attorney in question, would be more interested in negotiating a settlement of the suit than Lewis Kaplan, the replaced attorney, seemed to have been, and that far from this change representing a hardening of the American's defensive posture, it actually portended greater flexibility. It is possible that he did not know this and took the change of attorney to represent the negative development— for the plaintiffs' interests—that he implied it to be. In this case, it would have been an unfortunate misreading of the actual situation that could render subsequent negotiating meetings more difficult. If Welch did know the true state of affairs, one could only assume his description to be a deliberate tactic designed to rally his own troops for continued battle. In either case, it would add to rising tensions between the plaintiffs and the defendants.

[2] I have found no evidence that the American Psychiatric Association had ever participated alongside the American Psychoanalytic in any negotiations with the plaintiffs, either before or after the filing of the lawsuit, or that the individual referred to, Melvin Sabshin, had ever been present at any of the negotiating sessions that did take place.

psychoanalyst, though never with any official position in the American Psychoanalytic. The talk referred to was an invited plenary address delivered by Sabshin at the December, 1983 meeting of the American Psychoanalytic Association in New York. Under the title "Psychoanalysis and Psychiatry: Models for Potential Future Relations," Sabshin had discussed various indications of a lessening togetherness in the aims and directions of organized psychiatry and organized psychoanalysis. He said of the ongoing discussions within the American Psychoanalytic about opening its admissions procedures to nonmedical candidates[3] that such a decision would have "irrevocable consequences" (Sabshin, 1985, p. 480):

> Even-handed admissions (to use a euphemism common in other areas of conflict) would end the fundamental tie between organized psychiatry and the American Psychoanalytic Association. I believe that the number of M.D.s entering training would dwindle and become a trickle at the end of the decade. . . . the broad institutionalization of nonmedical candidates would convey the message that psychoanalysis is not a medical field per se [p. 480].

Sabshin counterposed to this development his own vision of a "new beginning" (p. 482) in the relations between the two organizations, the psychiatric and the psychoanalytic. He stated, "The combination of holding the line on nonmedical candidates by the American Psychoanalytic Association and a commitment to a new beginning with psychiatry could strengthen our institutes and our academic departments, help recruitment into psychiatry and psychoanalysis, and raise the scientific status of both psychoanalysis and psychiatry" (p. 490). Despite this strong tone and powerful advocacy, this plenary address by Sabshin was not received happily by the audience, as I sensed it at the time; it was in no way taken up as a rallying cry in any of the ongoing discussions over the lay analysis issue, and it played little if any role in influencing the internal discussions of the early, prelawsuit dialogues with the later plaintiffs. Yet from Welch's point of view, this invited plenary presentation was clearly seen in a very different light (and recalled and given this weight in a column written more than three years after that address), or at the very least, it was now being used, tactically deliberately, in a grossly exaggerated form.

On February 3, 1987, at the beginning of that same month in which these various newsletter columns appeared, I received a memorandum from

---

[3] The specific references by Sabshin were to the ongoing discussions within the Curtis Committee (Committee on Prerequisites for Training, 1975–81) and its successor committees.

Clint Fisher who had participated in a discovery conference (attended by attorneys for the plaintiffs and all four of the defendant groups) before Judge Keenan. At that conference the judge had set the discovery schedule on the class action issue, including the following timetable: (1) by March 20, Stromberg would distribute a letter to all the defendant parties defining the proposed class; (2) the plaintiffs' motion for class action certification would be due on July 1; (3) the defendants' response would be due on September 18; (4) the plaintiffs' reply would be due on October 23; and (5) the evidentiary hearing before the judge to determine the issue of class action certification would be on November 3, that is, nine months from this date (February 2, 1987). Judge Keenan, "indicated that he believes this case is extremely complicated and will be both difficult and time consuming to try. (There were repeated jocular references to passing this case on to our grandchildren, trying it in the 1990s, etc.) Defense counsel believe that Judge Keenan may urge the parties to settle after the class issue is decided."

In the same memorandum, Fisher also reported on a meeting among the defense attorneys the day before (February 2) at which Mark Bunim, the attorney for the New York Psychoanalytic Institute, had displayed a letter from Zenia Fliegel, a member of Division 39, written to its board to urge it to drop the lawsuit. "She says that the suit has achieved its aims by virtue of the recent agreement between the IPA and the American and she claims that efforts to open the American's institutes to psychologists are actually counter to the best interests of psychologists. Bunim said that he understood there was a 'ground swell' of support for the position expressed by Ms. Fliegel." Actually, it was this letter from Fliegel that had so aroused Murray Meisels' ire (as president-elect of Division 39) and had been a strong prompt to his January 29, 1987 "Dear Colleague" letter. Among the attorneys at the February 2 meeting there was agreement that uncovering such dissension within Division 39 over the wisdom of continuing to pursue the lawsuit would be very useful in demonstrating to Judge Keenan the difficulty in certifying an appropriate plaintiff class for class action purposes.

On February 18, 1987, Morris Peltz of San Francisco again wrote to Dick Simons and Shelley Orgel as President and Chairman of the Board of the American, in response this time to a January 30 announcement of a coming May 12 special meeting of the Board to discuss, "The Impact of Non-Medical Clinical Training on Institutes Today and Tomorrow." Peltz applauded the decision to have this meeting for the opportunity it would present "to discuss this topic which may become so vital for the health and vitality of American psychoanalysis." Peltz took this opportunity to reiterate even more strongly the plea he had made in his December 27 letter that the American would be served best by "an admissions policy which would equally evaluate, without prejudice, all qualified applicants, medical and non-medical alike," and that this should take precedence over any effort to ensure the preservation of the "medical milieu" of the American. He further proposed that if the American was not prepared at this time to swiftly adopt such a totally merit-based admissions policy, it allow its constituent institutes a true "local option" in this regard. "Those Institutes that wish to train non-medical mental health professionals on an equal basis with psychiatrists would be free to do so, while those that did not wish to would not feel in any way obliged to follow this option." Again he reiterated his confidence that it would be possible to work out direct access to IPA membership outside the American for the graduates of such "local option" programs, "if the American wanted to preserve its basic membership categories and overall 'medical' character intact."

A month later, in March 1987, there was another unhappy exchange of letters between Shelley Orgel and me that reflected the continuing strain in the relations between the American and the IPA, stoked by continued, separately pursued, and only partially shared, agendas driving the two organizations. This occurred despite the resolution of differences and the fashioning of an agreed approach to our joint problems that we seemed to have arrived at in the December détente described in the last chapter, and despite the assertion of a repaired friendship between the two of us in our exchange of letters immediately after those December meetings. For over a month I had been hearing of the special meeting of the American's Board of Professional Standards, together with "a few invited guests," to be held in Chicago on May 12 in order to have a comprehensive (and leisurely) discussion prior to, and apart from, the administrative pressures of the Board's regularly scheduled meeting—a discussion of the issues to be posed for psychoanalytic education by all the changes coming about consequent to the lawsuit pressures and the reverberations of these in the altering relations of the American to the IPA.[4] I had not been invited to this meeting, and it turned out that Edward Weinshel, IPA Secretary and my close colleague in all of our negotiating meetings, was invited. We together could only surmise that this represented an effort to stir some divergence between us over our own already conflicted identifications with our two organizations, the American and the IPA, in both of which we had each risen to high policy-making office. Ed urged me strongly to write to Shelley about this matter, which I had been reluctant to do.

I did, however, follow his advice. On March 10 I wrote a long letter to Orgel, stating that I was "puzzled and troubled" that I had not been invited to this important meeting as one of the "few invited guests." I put this on two grounds. First, on the grounds of my presidency of the IPA, the American's parent organization: "literally there is nothing more important

---

[4] This meeting was the same one that Peltz referred to in his February 18 letter to Simons and Orgel.

to the relationship between the American and the IPA than the way the American now handles this issue of nonmedical training. Since you are a component organization and this concerns us and our relationship (between the two organizations), I would have thought it unthinkable that you would have a meeting on this subject with 50 or 60 people in the room and me not be invited to it." Second, I pointed to my particular history in the American, as a past president and as someone with endless committee involvements, especially around the issue of nonmedical training.

> I was ten years on the Committee on Training for Research, five years as its chairman, and was the spokesman in the Coordinating Committee and to the Board for the whole program under which nonmedical training was being carried out. I was also . . . one of the prime pushers in getting the first of the many committees, the Curtis Committee, underway. If there is anyone in the American who gets some of the credit and a lot of the blame for always keeping this issue alive with our membership, it has been me.

I ended the letter with a personal plea.

> The reason I didn't want to write this letter in the first place and didn't until urged is that I felt I couldn't write it honestly to a good friend without indicating the extent of my distress about this and what I was afraid it portended for the relationship between our organizations, let alone I feared for our personal relationship. I trust that you will read it in the spirit that I have intended it, of looking for ways to overcome the difficulties that divide us so that we can concentrate on our common goal of doing what is best for psychoanalysis even though we seem to be interpreting that quite differently these days.

Orgel responded very promptly with an even longer, and an equally pained, letter, on March 18. He put the strained feelings between us in the very first paragraph:

> Just as you write as a friend and also as President of the IPA, I am mindful that in writing back as Chairman of the Board I may be appearing personally unfriendly. I trust we are both aware that our official responsibilities may sometimes place us in different positions on issues and at odds over procedures. I also believe that our basic good feelings for each other and our conviction that we are both honorably carrying out our charges

as best we can will insure that our relationship will outlast these stressful days. I want us to remain warm friends.

Orgel then outlined his reasons for structuring this coming special meeting of the Board as he had. Basically it was to be an open-ended exploratory discussion of all the potential issues for psychoanalytic education posed by the fast-moving developments that would inevitably result in an enhanced number of nonmedical candidates in clinical psychoanalytic training, no matter how the Davis Committee undertook to implement procedurally the Gaskill Committee recommendations, and no matter how the lawsuit played out. He wanted this meeting to be free of administrative or political action pressures and felt that my presence at the meeting would necessarily be perceived as such a *pressure*—a word repeated several times in the letter—in the direction of actions I deemed essential to secure a settlement of the lawsuit, or to have some positive impact upon the eventual outcome of the suit. Weinshel had been invited along with the other past chairmen of the Board, "but he will obviously also be perceived as an officer of the IPA, and he will be able to express his views in whatever way he wishes"; but other than the past chairmen of the Board, the members of the Davis Committee, and the current Executive Committee of the American, there were to be no invited guests. Clearly I had different feelings about how this special meeting could be structured most productively, but also of course this was not my meeting. Orgel did address what was a clearly understood difference of perspective between us: "I do believe the implementation of the Gaskill proposal through the Davis Committee marks a very significant moment in the Board's history. I am also aware that you have questioned whether this effort is a genuine attempt to move the development of non-medical training forward, or whether it is a bureaucratic roadblock to slow progress in this direction. I certainly respect your skepticism."

In this manner, events seemed to lurch forward from the December 1986 agreement between the IPA and the American that the latter would propose a major alteration of its Regional Association status in the IPA, relinquishing one of its twin pillars—its "exclusive franchise" on IPA membership within the United States—as a major step on the road to a negotiated settlement of the lawsuit, at the coming July 1987 IPA Congress in Montreal, where this alteration would be effectuated. I next received a letter dated the same day as Orgel's, March 18, this one from Reuben Fine, the leader of one of the independent psychologist psychoanalytic institutes, the New York Center for Psychoanalytic Training (NYCPT), expressing support from within that community for the IPA positions in the lawsuit negotiating process: "I admire greatly the revolutionary ideas which you are planning to put into effect and which will undeniably mark an enormous step forward in the history of psychoanalysis." Even more heartening was a letter dated March 19 from Moses Laufer, President of the British Society, to Weinshel as IPA Secretary: "On Monday evening at the Council meeting it was decided that the motion by some members of the British Society be deferred/withdrawn and will not be presented at the Business Meeting in Montreal. I wanted to let you know of this straight away." Here my (our) relief was enormous. The threat of a major confrontation in Montreal between the Americans and the British (and all their European and Latin American supporters), with the renewed specter—as in 1938 in Paris, almost a half-century earlier—of a fatal rupture of the IPA, was at last removed. At least the house of international psychoanalysis could now be more united in facing the shared pressures of the continuing lawsuit.

On March 30, 1987, Richard Simons sent another informational update letter to all the members of the American. He detailed the schedule for the current class-action discovery phase of the lawsuit, starting with the February 2 conference in Judge Keenan's office, at which the timetable had been set through November 3, when the judge would hear the oral arguments on both sides on this issue. Simons indicated that following upon the judge's ruling on that issue there would be an additional phase of pretrial discovery on the substantive merits of the plaintiffs' claims before an actual trial date could be set—obviously not until some time in 1988, with all the continuing legal costs. Simons also reviewed the internal actions in the American in 1986, the 68% approval by the membership of the Gaskill Committee proposals, the establishment of the Committee on Non-Medical Clinical Training (the Davis Committee), and the December agreement that the American would propose a change in the IPA bylaws in Montreal, altering one aspect of the Regional Association status. This change, if approved by the required two-thirds majority at the Business Meeting in Montreal, followed by ratification by a two-thirds majority in a mail ballot of the whole IPA membership, could become operative by January 1, 1988. Simons ended by again thanking the membership for its support and reminding them that, "The legal action is now focused on the fundamental principle of academic freedom, and I feel truly hopeful that on that issue we will be able to bring the suit to a just and honorable conclusion."

In tandem with Simons's letter, Weinshel and I sent out our quarterly memoranda to the Presidents of all the IPA Component Societies and to the members of its Executive Council. In the memorandum to the Presidents, we called attention to the publication in the 151st (January 1987) *Bulletin of the IPA* of the bylaw changes being proposed for vote in Montreal by the American, and then said, "This, as you will all appreciate, is a historic change in the organization of the IPA, and one which will, we are sure, be very much welcomed by all our members and component Societies around the world." In the memorandum to Executive Council members we added; "There is no further news at present about the actual litigation, but Plaintiffs have been made aware of this forthcoming change that will allow the IPA to recognize new groups/Institutes within the United States in due course. Those groups outside the American which had already expressed an interest in such direct recognition have already been informed." In keeping with this now more optimistic climate for the acceptance by organized psychoanalysis in America of the training of nonmedical candidates for clinical psychoanalytic practice, the National Psychological Association for Psychoanalysis (NPAP), another of the nonmedical psychoanalytic training centers in New York, announced an all-day scientific conference on April 18, 1987, marking the 60th anniversary of the publication of Freud's *The Question of Lay Analysis*. The conference title was *The Question of Lay Analysis—60 Years After: Who Should Be a Psychoanalyst?* Among the array of speakers were Martin Bergmann and Esther Menaker, whose remarks on that occasion are referred to in chapter 3.

On April 23, 1987, Shelley Orgel sent a memorandum to all the Fellows of the Board on Professional Standards, formally calling the special May 5 meeting of the Board a day prior to the semiannual regular meeting, the meeting that had been the subject of the unhappy exchange of letters between us a month earlier. The general topic would be "the impact of nonmedical training on Institutes today and tomorrow." With a careful eye to his divided constituency, between those eagerly and those reluctantly moving in this direction, Orgel stated that "the central idea [is] that the core of what is valuable in a medical-psychiatric identity, so important in the growth of the American, will not [should not] be lost as we progress in this new direction." He talked of training "selected individuals from other educational backgrounds" and of the need to "consolidate through further education the component of a professional identity most crucial for psychoanalysts. This quality is a profound, unwavering commitment to the physicianly care of patients." Orgel spoke pointedly to the marked differences across and within institutes on this issue.

> Occasionally, an Institute may believe it can best solve its own current problems by acting independently. But the task of maintaining an ongoing, viable educational program may limit an individual Institute's ability to pay appropriate attention to future educational and professional consequences locally and especially nationally. The Board, at some distance from local situations, serves to maintain national standards in part by setting collectively agreed-upon restraints on some local actions.

This cautious statement can of course be read as Orgel's measured response—one for which he hoped to secure the Board's backing—to the thrust of Peltz's call from San Francisco (and from how many other institutes?) for a "local option" that would enable a more thorough and immediate openness to nonmedical training on the egalitarian basis of merit, rather than of particular credentials. At that special May 5 Board meeting, Weinshel, in his dual capacity as a former Chairman of the Board and a present officer of the IPA, read a brief statement, explicitly on behalf of the two of us, which included this sentence: "It is evident that we are not all of one mind in respect to the goals and the approaches to these vexing problems; and we recognize that the positions of the American and the IPA are not necessarily always congruent." I do not at this writing have available any minutes or other account of what actually transpired at that meeting of the Board.

Meanwhile, action was picking up on the class-action discovery phase of the lawsuit. I received a May 15, 1987 memorandum from Trip Dorkey concerning Stromberg's request to set up my deposition of at least a day in either San Francisco or New York to explore ten questions, all of them facets of IPA policy in regard to nonmedical training and its relationships with its component organizations on these questions. Stromberg also reserved the right to depose Edward Weinshel if he felt my deposition responses to be insufficiently comprehensive or clarifying. This I responded to on May 20, indicating that I felt perfectly comfortable in being the chief respondent for the IPA on all the issues addressed in Stromberg's listing, and that, after myself, I felt that of all the current members of the IPA Executive Council, only Weinshel would be additionally conversant enough with both the current IPA positions and its past history. As for venue, I expressed willingness to have this deposition almost any time in San Francisco, but my already committed travel schedule was such that, if it had to be in New York, it would need to be put off until September (i.e., after the IPA Montreal Congress in midsummer). As it turned out my deposition was set for August 10 in San Francisco.

During that same time, in mid May, I was first sent a copy of Murray Meisels's "Dear Colleague" letter of January 29—the one in which he called for an oversight committee from Division 39 to monitor what he felt to be the plaintiff negotiators' willingness to compromise the lawsuit issues with the defendants. Because I felt his letter to be based on serious errors of information about inside happenings, I undertook to write to him on May 18, 1987, though his letter had, of course, not been addressed to me. I stated that as a vitally concerned party to the lawsuit, I wanted to try to correct "the gross misinformation and factual distortions in what seems to have been conveyed to you." I then reviewed the four-hour settlement discussion in my suite at the Waldorf on May 31, 1986, at which "at least some of us felt that we had come to some consensus on the general principles of a possible settlement," a presumed consensus that the plaintiffs' attorney, Cliff Stromberg, undertook to put into writing. This is the document that had arrived after a considerable delay—and had been found unacceptable by the IPA and by the American, because it went far beyond what had been discussed and, we thought, agreed to, at the May 31 meeting. The figure of ten Institutes to be established in ten American cities by the IPA, within 120 days of the effective date of the settlement, had been a plaintiff demand, never an IPA offer, on which the IPA was said by Meisels in his letter to have reneged. From the IPA standpoint, there had never been agreement on such a number or such a timetable, both clearly far beyond the bounds of what could be possible even if quality or standards were no consideration. The second item in contention in Meisels's letter was the statement that the IPA needed to be blocked in its intention to discriminate against the William Alanson White Institute in its evaluation procedures for IPA affiliation. The facts were that the Stromberg-proposed settlement document called for the White Institute to be directly approved for IPA affiliation, presumably without evaluation and not later than September 1, 1987. The IPA response had been that there would be no such grandfathering and that the White Institute would have to make application (which it had not done) in order to be evaluated and processed alongside the New York Freudian Society and IPTAR, which had already formally requested this of the IPA as soon as the changed bylaws (to be voted in Montreal) would permit.

After documenting this whole sequence of events in great detail (in a three-page single-spaced letter), I ended with the following paragraph:

> What led the members of the plaintiff group to misinform you so completely about a historical sequence that has been so fully documented I don't know. . . . Like yourself, I would like nothing more than that this whole lawsuit should be settled as promptly as possible on the basis stated earlier in this letter, "on terms as favorable as possible to the plaintiff class, consistent with defendants' interests." The misinformation that you were given and the subsequent conclusions that you were led to draw have obviously not helped in that process. I would, of course, welcome your response to this letter since clearly the more lines of dialogue that are open among us the sooner we will all get to the point that we desire, the settlement of the suit and the fullest carrying out of our collective psychoanalytic enterprise.

However naively quixotic or perhaps even ill-advised my letter, I was quite unprepared for the full blast of Dr. Meisels's response, dated June 2, 1987. He declared it remarkable that I had replied to a letter that had not been addressed to me, and indicated that I had entirely missed the point of his letter and of the lawsuit as well, for that matter. His letter had not been intended to be about the July 28, 1986 settlement proposal by the plaintiffs, but that "no terms should be proposed without the prior involvement of the diverse constituencies of psychologists who are interested in the issue and that Division 39 should hold an emergency meeting to discuss and rectify that very point." They had held such a meeting (on March 7, 1987) and had pronounced that particular settlement proposal by Stromberg "a dead issue." Meisels's reading of that settlement proposal had been "vastly different" from mine. He stated:

> My reaction was that the plaintiffs were settling for half-a-loaf instead of the whole loaf. For me, a satisfactory settlement would include provisions which allow all qualified American psychologist-psychoanalysts to be forthwith admitted to the IPA; would designate all senior psychologist-psychoanalysts so admitted as training, supervising and teaching analysts; and would provide that this now-enfranchised group of psychologists immediately constitute a regional society of IPA.

Now, of course, the lawsuit was ongoing:

> Psychologists have been greatly inspired by this, feel a sense of pride, feel empowered, and feel new self-respect. . . . Psychologists will not withdraw. The significant point of the lawsuit, as I understand it—and the point that you seem to miss—is that unilateral actions of the IPA or the American are no longer final decisions because those actions are now subject to judicial review. It may be that the IPA views its proposed by-law changes as momentous, and it may be that the Gaskill Amendment is revolutionary for the American, but be advised that for psychologists these are tokens—doors that open when the wind blows but then could be closed again when the wind shifts—and the lawyers will argue, and the judge will decide. The judge will decide, not the IPA.

Following Dr. Meisels's signature was the title, "President-Elect, Division 39," which certainly did not bode well for the prospects for future negotiations, which would now involve this important player in the litigation process.

In view of the tenor of Meisels's letter, my reply, dated July 9, 1987, was guided by the IPA attorney, Clint Fisher, and kept very brief: "My efforts to clarify the IPA's position with respect to issues related to the lawsuit and to open a line of dialogue with you were clearly misplaced. I'm sorry that I took up your time in that endeavor. Needless to say I will not attempt again. . . . Unfortunately, as you say, it appears that such issues are now out of our hands and in the hands of attorneys." And Meisels's response, dated July 17, 1987, was not much longer:

> I am pleased that we agree that the issue is now in the hands of attorneys. As I understand it, this means that: if the IPA wins, it can act autonomously, so that the policies you describe can be effected; if the IPA loses, the court will decide IPA policy and procedure; and if there is a negotiated settlement, it must be approved by the judge and thereby become legally binding, i.e., a violation of the agreement would be in contempt of court, and be subject to legal penalty. At this point, the only way that the issue will not be resolved through the legal process is if the plaintiffs withdraw, which they will not do.

This interchange between Meisels and me clearly was given wide currency within the ranks of the plaintiff group and their sympathizers. Some five months later I received a letter, dated December 10, 1987, from an old friend and colleague, Roy Schafer, sharply dissociating himself and his wife, also a psychologist analyst, from the tone and thrust of Meisels's letter:

> My wife (Rita Frankiel) and I are writing to say that we hope you will be able to keep in mind that there are those, like us, in Division 39 of the American Psychological Association who, though they do not question the basic merits and aims of the lawsuit, are unhappy with the provocative tone of the letter to you by Dr. Murray Meisels, our current president. For that letter we apologize, as we deeply appreciate your fair-minded leadership in trying to arrive at a solution to the problem and a settlement. We expect that our next president, Dr. Zanvil Liff, will continue the negotiations next year with a more constructive sense of decorum and respect, having this expectation simply from knowing him and not by way of any indirect assurances.

This letter was signed by both of them and appended to it was a draft of a proposed letter from the two of them, and also from Donald Kaplan, to all members of Section 1, Division 39 (the Section of actual practitioner psychologist-psychoanalysts). Though this letter opposed as premature the view of those psychologists in the plaintiff class who were urging acceptance of the settlement terms that had been offered by the defendants—premature because the memberships of neither the American nor of the IPA had yet ratified the terms of the settlement offer—it also drew back even more sharply from the position that had been embodied in the plaintiffs' settlement demands, but had not been presented and discussed within Division 39 when it had agreed to support the suit:

These demands include complex and costly machinery for setting up a number of Institutes for mental health professionals (not just psychologists!); these Institutes are to be set up by the IPA with the collaboration of the American; also, established Institutes of the American are to maintain arbitrarily a roughly 1:1 ratio of medical and nonmedical candidates; additionally . . . exceptionally favorable treatment is provided for one free-standing Institute (the William Alanson White); further, considerable authority is lodged with the plaintiffs, or those they designate, to work out differences, handle appeals, and review procedures, etc., when not all the plaintiffs are even fully trained analysts! And finally, crushing sums in costs and alleged damages are to be paid by the defendants. Proposals of such vast and possibly lasting significance and destructive expense should not be rationalized, as they have been, as improvisations that became necessary for the sake of negotiation, as ways to put teeth into the suit, and in order to insure diversity of points of view within the IPA. (Is this suit to allow us to rule the psychoanalytic world?)

The letter then went on to offer proposals that I felt, as I read it, to be fully consonant with the sort of settlement agreement that the IPA had been working for so doggedly.

For a number of tactical reasons put in a P.S. to the letter, it seems not to have been sent. This draft, however, together with the letter from Schafer and Frankiel and similar letters that I received over the same time period from Sydney Smith, an old psychologist colleague from my Menninger Foundations days,[5] and Mary Libbey, the editor of *Round Robin,* the newsletter of Section 1 of Division 39, provided me a much appreciated—and much needed—bolstering of my feeling that the IPA could yet chart a path that would draw support from both sides of the divide and become the basis for a viable and worthwhile resolution of these difficulties in a way that could be (to quote the phrase from my letters), "on terms as favorable as possible to the plaintiff class, consistent with the defendants' interests."

---

[5] The letter from Smith, dated January 6, 1988, came a month after that by Schafer and Frankiel: "Just a short note to indicate to you how embarrassed most of us connected with Division 39 are over the behavior of our leader, Murray Meisels. . . . Several of us have been attempting to cool him off and allow him to recognize that your efforts could go a long way toward bettering the fortunes of psychologists who want to learn how to become good analysts. Also, as president of Section 1, I wanted you to know that we are aware of your good efforts and hope you do not allow Meisels' vituperations to become too upsetting."

In June 1987, in the run-up period to the summer IPA Congress in Montreal, the newsletter *Behavior Today* (June 8), under the title "IPA Likely to Admit Psychoanalytic Training Institutes," carried a news item calling attention to the proposal to alter the American's Regional Association status in the IPA that was to be voted on at the coming Montreal Congress: "While the voting process has not taken place yet, Robert S. Wallerstein, M.D., president of the IPA, expects these changes will be approved. If they are, any established psychoanalytic training institution will be able to seek affiliation by submitting its credentials and asking for a site visit to ascertain if the institution meets the IPA requirements." Thus a climate of opinion and expectation was clearly building in this direction within both the defendant and the plaintiff organizations. In a letter to all members of the American dated the following day, June 9, 1987, Simons added to this growing positive climate with a conciliatory clarifying statement that "the American has never taken disciplinary or punitive action against any member who has been involved in training candidates in non-affiliated institutes or programs." On the contrary, the letter pointed out, many prominent members of the American had been doing just that over many years and in 1956—the only time the membership was asked to vote on the matter—it had rejected a bylaw that would have prohibited its members from conducting such training at unaffiliated institutes.

Simons did acknowledge, however, that there had been occasions when individuals in leadership positions in the American had asserted that such participation in outside training programs was "not in the public interest and, consequently, that it would violate established principles for our members to engage in such training." However sincere or principled such statements, they had not represented official policy of the American, and in order to avoid any possible confusion in the matter, Simons wished to stress two main points: first, members, of course, should conduct training only in institutes and programs that observe high-quality standards; second, there was no requirement to treat the standards promulgated by the Board of the American "as the only educational and training standards that are appropriately high." Therefore, Simons declared unequivocally that there were no restraints whatsoever on members of the American teaching in whatever setting they wished, so long as they were satisfied by the training standards adhered to in that setting. And he ended, "We are also of the view that each of our accredited Institutes and affiliate Societies should be guided unequivocally by this position."

This growing harmony between the postures of the American and the IPA with some comparable sentiments being articulated by some very visible figures in the plaintiff class did not translate, however, into any lessening of the concomitant vigorous adversarial pursuit of the legal action. On June 18, 1987, Karen Burrows (from the IPA's law firm) wrote a memorandum summarizing her attendance three days earlier at the deposition of Homer Curtis conducted by Cliff Stromberg at the latter's law offices in Washington. The deposition apparently went very smoothly, and Stromberg asked few irrelevant or poorly formed questions. Burrows felt Curtis to be an excellent witness, thoughtful and intelligent, with a rather gentle demeanor. He responded carefully and obviously had been well-prepared by Joel Klein, who had spent the entire preceding day with him. Curtis had stated pointedly that qualified nonphysicians should be admitted for training in the American because they would make excellent analysts and would help "stimulate psychoanalytic practice." Klein had chosen Curtis for this lead position among those being deposed from the American's leadership because he had been known all along to hold just these moderate views and this strategy seemed to have worked very well as the day progressed. Stromberg, for his part, had seemed eager to depose Curtis because he had been chair of the Committee on Prerequisites for Training (CPT) of the American, the first of the sequence of four committees wrestling with these issues over the decade 1975 to 1984, and had been a member as well of the first three of the four committees. Much of the deposition centered around the CPT proceedings, which had been so well-documented in the very detailed minutes taken by Paula Bernstein.[6]

According to a memorandum of June 30, 1987, from Clint Fisher to me, the deposition of Richard Simons took place on June 19, four days after that of Curtis. Ed Joseph and Bryant Welch were scheduled for deposition in the week of July 11; Edward Weinshel would be deposed in San Francisco on August 6 and I in San Francisco on August 10, both of us after our return from the IPA Congress in Montreal at the end of July. Further, we were informed that on June 15 our case had been transferred from Judge Keenan to Judge Richard J. Daronco of the same court. The reason seemed to have been the severe overload on Judge Keenan's docket; among his other cases was the litigation over the Bhopal disaster. This change was experienced as a real blow, probably by both sides of this legal dispute; Judge Keenan had been seen as so eminently thorough, careful, and fair-minded. And for the new judge, at the very least he would have to inform himself thoroughly about the case, which by then had been in process for more than two years (March 1985 to June 1987). This would cause some inevitable stretching out of the proceedings. In his memo, Fisher informed me that "we will let you know when we learn more about how Judge Daronco might view this case."

---

[6] For a detailed description of the deliberations of CPT as chronicled in Paula Bernstein's minutes, see chapter 6, pp. 113–122.

On July 21, 1987, Joel Klein and Cliff Stromberg, representing the defendants and the plaintiffs respectively, jointly petitioned Judge Daronco to set back the filing dates for the class certification motion essentially one month each, because of the intensive discovery schedule underway and the difficulty of scheduling certain witnesses during the summer. The new dates would be: (1) plaintiffs' brief, October 14, 1987; (2) defendants' responsive briefs, December 21, 1987; (3) plaintiffs' reply brief, January 29, 1988, with the date of oral hearing before the judge to be then decided. This would bring that hearing date to approximately the three-year mark from the initiation of the lawsuit. And not until that issue had been decided by the judge could the actual trial be set.

The next fateful event was the long-awaited IPA Congress in Montreal at the end of July 1987. The Executive Council met on July 22, 23, 24, and 25, and the status of the litigation in the United States was the dominant issue over those days. At the July 22 session, I reviewed the series of meetings with the officers of the American in New York in December and the accommodations then arrived at; the agreement that the officers of the American would sponsor the IPA bylaw change modifying the Regional Association status of the American; that the IPA would retain its separate attorney, but when the two attorneys agreed it was apropos, the IPA would forego representation at legal proceedings at which its interests would be equally served by the attorney for the American; that the American would reimburse the IPA 60% of its legal expenses (a figure that could have been set more accurately at 70%); and that for its part the IPA would not pursue a separate settlement with the plaintiffs, however much this might be available. It was reiterated at this IPA Council meeting that maintaining legal representation for the IPA, separate from that of the American, was deemed very important by the non-American membership of the IPA around the world, no matter how congruent the positions of the American and the IPA might be or become.

That wariness still existed on both sides of these interorganizational discussions was underlined by the report to the Executive Council of the three further meetings between the officers of the two organizations held in Chicago in May. The American was concerned for assurances that IPA groups in the United States not have lower training standards than the institutes of the American, and additionally was concerned about the possibility that disaffected societies and institutes within the American might be tempted to break away and escape the oversights of the American through direct affiliation with the IPA. Though there had been unhappy and tense periods during these May discussions, the officers of both organizations had come out reassured that their anxieties would be appropriately addressed by the other, that the IPA *would* ensure proper training standards in any new groups it allowed to affiliate, that it *would not* provide a ready escape hatch for temporarily disaffected affiliates of the American, and so on.

Less happy was my "report that the impression was now that Attorneys for both sides—the Plaintiffs and the other three Defendants—were digging in":

> Mr. Dorkey had felt all along that a settlement was possible; the Attorney for the Plaintiffs and for the American both feel that they can get a better settlement in the months, or years, ahead. In the meantime, the judge hearing the case had of course changed and is no longer Keenan, but a new judge. Keenan had said the case was a very complicated one and would probably "not be settled before I retire" [Minutes, IPA Executive Council, July 22, 1987].

Adding to this somewhat gloomy assessment was the notification that the presidency of Division 39 had just passed from Fred Pine, who was at the same time a psychologist member of the American and had striven resolutely to play an honest broker mediating role between the plaintiffs and the defendants, to Murray Meisels, whose hard-line attitudes and maximalist settlement demands have already been portrayed in the correspondence with me.

On the other side of the ledger, however, the proposed British Society resolution had been formally withdrawn. The expected bylaw change at this meeting, modifying (and limiting) the Regional Association status of the American, might well take some of the steam out of the pursuit of the lawsuit. The main officers of the American (Simons, Orgel, and Curtis as president-elect) were coming to meet with the IPA Executive Council at the Friday afternoon session in order to help iron out any divergences in outlook and to strengthen our common front in defense of the lawsuit. In addition, the American's Davis Committee had, in May, processed 27 waiver applications for full clinical psychoanalytic training for psychologist candidates and had approved 18 of them. (I could report that our San Francisco Institute had proposed three and all three had been accepted, and that the mental health professional group that had been positioning itself to file a lawsuit locally had now abandoned that intent.)

I then reported that a total of 14 organized psychoanalytic groups in the United States had already inquired about evaluation procedures for direct affiliation with the IPA, eight of these in New York, three in Los Angeles, and one each in Denver, Chicago, and Boston. Some of these were well-organized psychoanalytic groups (societies and institutes); some were just clusters of people meeting informally and studying together; some would be asking for Study Group status, some for admittance as Provisional Societies. Discussion then turned to the nature of the evaluation processes that could be set up after the proposed bylaw change became operative (by January 1, 1988) and direct IPA affiliation became possible for these groups. There were issues to be decided of evaluation procedures for functioning groups, societies and institutes, and also for their individual members. For example, how could the qualifications and experience of individuals originally trained by lesser standards than those of the IPA be fairly evaluated? Would there be any "grandfathering," and if so, by what criteria? It was clear that even with the groups felt to be most ready for IPA membership, the New York Freudian Society and IPTAR, which had already declared their willingness to adhere to all IPA standards, there was still the question of what the IPA would do for their older members trained at a time when lesser standards had been acceptable. Other difficulties became apparent in this long discussion in the Executive Council as well. Within the new applicant groups within the United States there was the potential great divisiveness, with real danger of rupture, that could be engendered within well-functioning groups if it should turn out that the group as a whole, and most but not all of its members, would be deemed acceptable to the IPA. Would such a group fragment, or better put, how could it be held together on behalf of all of its members?

From outside the United States, the concern was raised by a vice-president from Latin America, Carlos Aslan (a concern shared no doubt by many from outside the United States), that through the lawsuit and the detailing of all its aspects, including the close review of the special Regional Association status of the American, it had become clear to IPA members around the world that while American members had all along been members of sponsoring committees and site visit committees, and thus had participated in the IPA's monitoring functions in all other parts of the world, the reverse had never been allowed. The American had had total control over its own training functions, and this was now being widely perceived as undemocratic and unbalanced. It was pointed out that this imbalance would no longer be so in regard to the new groups that would be directly affiliated with the IPA outside the framework of the American, and it was agreed to make this partial correction of the imbalance completely clear at the IPA Business Meeting to be held a few days later. Everyone agreed that many bad feelings could be expressed on all sides at the Business Meeting. And everyone also agreed upon the enormity and complexity of the tasks ahead. Would there even be the material and personnel resources within the IPA to knowledgeably and comprehensively evaluate 14 applicant groups? It was finally agreed that although Weinshel and I would meet with representatives of IPTAR and the New York Freudian Society for preliminary discussions, as per their request, during the following week of the Congress, and although formal applications for evaluation for IPA affiliation could be received after January 1, 1988 (assuming no hitch in the approval of the proposed bylaw change at the Business Meeting the next week and its subsequent mail ratification by the membership in the fall) no action would be taken on any of these applications until the IPA Executive Council had time for full consideration, at the week-long symposium to be held in England in March 1988, of all the issues that would have arisen in the application process.

After these exhaustive and exhausting deliberations within the Executive Council, the actual IPA Congress (July 27–31) and Business Meeting (July 29) were—politically—anticlimactic. The proposed bylaw change passed unanimously. The American would relinquish its "exclusive franchise" on access to IPA affiliation in the United States, so that the independently organized existing psychoanalytic societies and institutes within the United States could apply directly for IPA membership. It would still retain the other pillar of its special status, total autonomy in regard to its training standards and practices. The mail ballot ratification process was set up with a December 11 deadline and implementation after ratification set for January 1, 1988. Fourteen inquiries for evaluation and possible IPA affiliation were on record at IPA headquarters in London, and productive and pleasant exploratory meetings did take place with representatives of IPTAR and the New York Freudian Society during the Congress week. In a letter from Irene Auletta to Lista Cannon, the IPA's attorney in London, dated after the Congress (August 7, 1987), the only disquieting note in the description of the Montreal Congress events was a statement about the earlier, "distasteful exchange between Dr. Wallerstein and Murray Meisels, which quite frankly made us all feel that no settlement would ever be possible!"

This was now two-and-a-half years from the start of the lawsuit. What all this augured for the continuing course and duration of that suit was quite unclear. Would it be seen by the plaintiffs and the preponderance of their supporters as substantial progress towards an agreed settlement, or only as tokenism and disingenuous posturing? What was clear was that in the first week after our return from Montreal to San Francisco, Weinshel and I were to face our own depositions, ostensibly to be limited to discovery on just the class certification motion by the plaintiffs, and that, formally, the lawsuit was proceeding unaltered.

The Clash over Class Certification
October 1987–February 1988

T he litigation process resumed in earnest after the July 1987 IPA Congress in Montreal. Weinshel and I were both deposed in San Francisco in early August as scheduled. Our depositions "went very well," according to Clint Fisher, our attorney, who had come from New York in order to attend them. Mine occupied only four hours instead of the entire day that had been set aside for it. This, of course, was Stromberg's decision; there was nothing more of significance that he felt he could usefully find out from me. From my standpoint, the whole exercise was more boring than otherwise, endlessly repetitive questions covering ground very familiar to both of us, and with no real surprises or new perspectives emerging from either Stromberg's questions or my answers. The most difficult part for me was to contain my natural impulse, in a dialogue, to expand on and develop lines of inquiry that were opened up; I had been carefully schooled by Fisher on the previous day to confine my responses to the simplest, most direct, and most literal (of course, always truthful) responses to the question asked—just a yes or no, if possible—and never to voluntarily amplify my statements. Fisher, who was keenly monitoring my performance, felt that I had succeeded admirably in this, though for me it was a strain.

Following our two depositions there was, in August, a series of interlocutories between Stromberg, on the one side, and on our side, Fisher, Weinshel, Auletta, and me. Stromberg was asking for complete copies of various documents that had been referred to in the depositions; published articles by Weinshel or by me, unpublished talks we had given in scientific or administrative contexts, minutes of meetings. All of these contained passages relevant to the issues of the lawsuit; in almost all cases they were either sent to Stromberg, or if they were not immediately available, he was referred to the appropriate source. In a few instances, as in an introductory statement I had made at a scientific panel on the question of lay analysis that I had chaired at a meeting of the American, the material was no longer available—I had not retained the manuscript of my remarks in my files— and Stromberg could only be referred back to the summary report of the whole panel, including my remarks, that had been published by Newell Fisher.[1]

On August 21, 1987, Dorkey and Fisher, in consultation with Weinshel, Auletta, and me, filed Responses of Defendant International Psychoanalytical Association to Plaintiffs' Request for Admissions, a series of responses to 85 specific "Requests for Admissions" that had been put by Stromberg. In many cases these were simple acknowledgments or denials of statements of fact concerning the existence or correctness of certain IPA documents or statements about IPA policies, procedures, and the like. But a good many of the statements were responded to with the declaration that the IPA was unable to either admit or deny the statement because it was unclear or ambiguous, or that the IPA lacked sufficient knowledge to either admit or deny it.

This relatively quiescent period in the lawsuit trajectory was brought to an end on October 14, 1987, when Cliff Stromberg and Ira Greenberg, as counsel for the plaintiffs, filed a 108-page brief, entitled "Memorandum in Support of Plaintiffs' Motion for Class Certification" (with copies delivered on the same date to the attorneys for all the defendant groups). This lengthy document consisted of several sections. First it comprised assertions about the thrust and intent of the lawsuit, that the American (and its affiliated institutes) had long pursued an exclusionary policy in regard to the clinical psychoanalytic training of nonphysicians because of concerns about "unwanted professional competition," that it was a "pocketbook issue," that the members of the American feared "economic competition," that there were "too few patients now," and that "non-physicians might charge lower fees," and thus undercut the market. To remedy this alleged unfair and monopolistic position, the excluded psychologists had established GAPPP (The Group for the Advancement of Psychotherapy and Psychoanalysis in Psychology) as a "non-profit corporation organized to enhance professional opportunities for psychologists in psychoanalysis. Its principal activity has been to raise funds and pay legal fees and other expenses to support this litigation on behalf of the proposed class." Bryant Welch was president of GAPPP, and the organization had raised "more than several hundred thousand dollars." But GAPPP did not determine the lawsuit strategy and tactics: "GAPPP raises funds; it has played no decision-making role in the action." Presumably

---

[1] The substance of this panel has been briefly described in chapter 6, p. 132.

this was entirely in the hands of the four individual plaintiffs and their legal counsel.

The history of the lawsuit to that point was then recounted, starting with the filing on March 1, 1985. There was discussion of the Motion for Summary Judgment that had been filed by the American (and the Columbia Institute) on July 18, 1985. The argument stated there was summarized in this brief as threefold: (1) the admissions policies of the American and all its affiliated institutes were "academic" matters and thus inherently non-commercial; (2) a court of law was not competent to decide such academic and professional controversies; and (3) the plaintiffs lacked standing to pursue such a lawsuit. Judge Keenan had denied the defendants' motion, and then settlement negotiations had been undertaken, which the plaintiffs labelled "unavailing." Intensive discovery had therefore been resumed in 1987, and "Thus far, the parties have exchanged large amounts of documents, and more than 20 depositions have been taken."

From there the brief went on to discuss the nature of psychoanalysis and the history of the lay analysis controversy going back to Freud's landmark 1926 book *The Question of Lay Analysis*. This was followed by an intensive documentation of the defendant groups' declared longtime anticompetitive conduct; the exclusion of psychologist candidates from the institutes of the American; the American's preventing its members from teaching outside the American's own institutes (the so-called ban on unauthorized training); the anticompetitive intent and use by the American of the central waiver system it had created via the Committee on Training for Research (as far back as 1960), which monitored the limited psychoanalytic training of selected nonpsychiatrists for careers in psychoanalytic research; and the denial of access to IPA affiliation of psychologists trained in independent institutes outside the American. The brief then declared that the cumulative economic impact of this ensemble of exclusionary tactics had been to create a monopoly by the American on good psychoanalytic training almost everywhere in the United States, and the dominance of the American as the only national network of "official" or "recognized" psychoanalytic institutes, with a closed referral system for prospective patients amongst its membership. The plaintiffs' brief then stated that there was a lack of any principled defense against these charges concerning their anticompetitive economic motives because there simply is no principled defense. After all, voices within the defendant groups had themselves conceded many times that psychologists can indeed be trained as competent psychoanalysts.

After these statements, the brief went on to recount the story of the four successive committees of the American (those chaired sequentially by Homer Curtis, Kenneth Calder, Richard Isay, and Vann Spruiell) that had considered these issues of nonmedical training over a decade (1975–1984), culminating, after what had seemed significant progress toward a reversal of the American's exclusionary policies, in the 32 to 7 vote by the Executive Council of the American in May, 1984, in San Diego "not to take any action on this issue." Among the statements highlighted from the reports of these committees was one from the Calder Committee (December 15, 1982) that: "(1) non-medical training is feasible; (2) it is legally valid to set percentage limits on the number of non-medical candidates in a class or Institute; (3) if the concept is accepted, the first group admitted should be individuals with a doctorate in clinical psychology or mental health." This section of the brief ended with the futile October 1984 meeting in Washington between the officers of the American and representatives of the American Psychological Association at which Edward Joseph, then president of the American Psychoanalytic, had referred to the entire matter as a "pocketbook issue." The Gaskill Committee recommendations, and the Davis Committee established to implement those recommendations following their adoption, were dismissed as constituting "a very limited experimental expansion of training." In the first round of implementation (May 1987) only 18 psychologist candidates had been approved for training, among the 26 institutes of the American—and of course the American could curtail this process at any time it chose.

Finally, on page 81, the brief took up its declared central substantive argument, that the plaintiffs did satisfy the four prerequisites for maintaining a class action as embodied in the Federal Rule of Civil Procedure 23(a): (1) the numerosity requirement to establish a class was met; (2) substantial questions of law and fact were common to members of the class; (3) the claims of the representative plaintiffs are typical of the claims of the class; and (4) the representative plaintiffs will fairly and adequately protect the "interests of the class." The brief documented this in each instance with citations both from legal precedents and from the unquestioned facts of this case.

Further, the brief stated that the requirements of Rules 23(b)(1), (2), and (3) were also met: Rule 23(b)(1), the class should be certified because prosecution of individual actions in different jurisdictions would risk "inconsistent or varying adjudications," which could "establish incompatible standards of conduct"; Rule 23(b)(2), the defendants have acted on grounds generally applicable to the entire class; and Rule 23(b)(3), common questions of law and fact predominate, and a class action is a superior method for resolving the dispute. Again, in each instance legal precedents and matters of fact were cited. This was all summarized in the statement that:

> Defendants apparently believe that variations in the situations of individual psychologists should defeat class certification. However, these variations are all variations on a dominant, common theme: restrictions of every aspect of the psychoanalytic

market by defendants. Likewise, any differences in the type of training particular class members might ultimately desire are secondary to the common desire to end the American's monopoly—which stifles virtually all training opportunities for them. [Plaintiffs' class action brief, October 14, 1987, p. 100].

Attached to the brief were a variety of documents, the first of which listed alphabetically all the deponents with a "biographical index" identifying each. There were 23 all told, eight among the plaintiff class and 15 among the defendant groups.[2] This was the first time that I had seen the entire list of those who had been deposed during these very busy (for the attorneys) few months prior to the filing of the class action brief on behalf of the plaintiffs. This listing was followed by the other appended documents: an organizational chart of the American and its relationship to its affiliated institutes; an affidavit by Leonard Goodstein, Executive Vice-President and CEO of the American Psychological Association, indicating that organization's wholehearted support of the lawsuit; an affidavit from Murray Meisels, President of Division 39 of the Psychological, indicating that organization's equally wholehearted support; a professional listing of the plaintiffs' counsel; and a roster of the 26 institutes of the American. And finally a stipulation was added that up until the date that the lawsuit was filed, the Columbia Institute had never admitted a nonphysician for full psychoanalytic training and had never applied to the American for a waiver to that effect on behalf of any nonmedical candidate.

---

[2] The eight from the plaintiff group were (alphabetically), Tony Bernay, a plaintiff; Helen Desmond, a plaintiff; Zenia Fliegel, a psychologist-analyst member of IPTAR (whose feeling that the lawsuit had already achieved its major objectives has been cited in chapter 11, p. 243); Murray Meisels, President of Division 39; Fred Pine, immediate past-President of Division 39, but also a member of the American; Arnold Schneider, a plaintiff; Charles Spezzano, the central figure in an independent Institute constituted outside the American, the Colorado Center for Psychoanalytic Studies; and Bryant Welch, a plaintiff. The 15 from the defendant groups were (alphabetically), Bernard Brodsky, President, defendant New York Psychoanalytic Institute; Kenneth Calder, Chairman of American's Committee on the Feasibility of Non-Medical Training; Homer Curtis, President-Elect of the American and Chairman of its Committee on Prerequisites for Training; Carl Davis, Chairman of Committee on Non-Medical Clinical Training; Alan Eisnitz, Chairman of Ethics Committee of the American; Herbert Gaskill, chairman of Advisory Committee to the Executive Council of the American, which produced the "Gaskill Committee" recommendations in 1985; George Gross, immediate past-President of defendant New York Psychoanalytic Institute; Edward Joseph, immediate past-President of the American; Robert Michels, member of three of the four successive committees of the American that considered these issues over the decade 1975–1984; Shelley Orgel, Chairman, Board on Professional Standards of the American; Ethel Person, Director, defendant Columbia Institute; Richard Simons, President of the American, Vann Spruiell, Chairman of Joint Committee on Non-Medical Training; Robert Wallerstein, President, IPA; and Edward Weinshel, Secretary, IPA.

In a memorandum to Weinshel, Auletta, Lista Cannon, and me, dated October 26, 1987, Clint Fisher sent us an 11-page summary of the plaintiffs' brief plus its Table of Contents with his own summary statement: "There do not appear to be any surprises in this memorandum. It is a long, well-written statement of what we know the plaintiffs' position to be. Defendants' opposition to plaintiffs' motion is due December 21, 1987 and, in the meantime depositions of the parties and of third-parties are continuing." Further to this process, the IPA received another memorandum, this one from Michael Morrissey (an associate of Trip Dorkey and Clint Fisher), dated November 4, 1987, stating that he had attended a hearing on November 2 in Judge Daronco's chambers concerning a request by the William Alanson White Institute to quash a third-party subpoena served on it by Columbia, and a request by the New York Institute to compel Fred Pine to answer certain questions that he had refused to answer at his deposition on the grounds of attorney-client privilege. (Pine had claimed that because he was involved in the case on the plaintiffs' behalf, he did not have to answer questions about a meeting of Division 39 addressed by Stromberg.) Judge Daronco's clerk read a statement from the judge ordering that (1) all pretrial discovery disputes, including the deposition subpoena of the White, be referred to Magistrate Michael Dollinger; the class certification issue would remain with Judge Daronco; and (2) Fred Pine would have to answer the questions regarding the Division 39 meeting.

This was the situation when a (partial) IPA Executive Council meeting was held in London on November 5, 1987. Seven Council members were present. Besides Weinshel and me, they were the past-President, Adam Limentani, two vice-Presidents, Joseph Sandler and Janine Chasseguet-Smirgel, and two Associate Secretaries, Albrecht Kuchenbuch and Leonard Shengold. In view of the events of the Montreal Congress, the atmosphere was much less fraught with apprehension, certainly with respect to the relationship with the American. In the interim I had appointed a task force, chaired by Charles Hanly of Toronto, to examine all the issues involved in the anticipated evaluation of applicant independent psychoanalytic groups seeking affiliation with the IPA and to come up with recommended guidelines and procedures for that process.[3] Of all the many appointments to various IPA tasks that I made during the course of my four-year presidency, I have always regarded the appointment of Charles Hanly to the leadership of this group as one of the most felicitous. He took on what turned out to be a most complicated and time-consuming undertaking, and

---

[3] The other original members of this Ad Hoc Committee on New Groups were Moses Laufer of London, David Sachs of Philadelphia, Janice de Saussure of Geneva, and Inga Villarreal of Bogotá.

from the start he carried it through with a rare combination of tact, fairness, and thoughtfulness, coupled with a dogged determination. At the same time, he showed a diplomatic ability to dodge endless bureaucratic and narcissistic potholes and to maneuver often sharply divergent and contending viewpoints toward an effective, workable compromise that preserved intact the IPA's commitment toward a fair, respectful, and helpful process, without in any way weakening the integrity of the IPA's training standards.

At this IPA Executive Council meeting I was able to report on initial interchanges between the Hanly committee and me. We had decided that applications by psychoanalytic groups for consideration for IPA affiliation could begin to be accepted and reviewed after the deadline on the ratification mail ballot of the IPA membership. By the time of the IPA Symposium in March 1988 in England, the Executive Council would be able to examine and discuss the application material received to that point and to consider the suggested guidelines for the site visits and evaluation procedures. There were clearly many different situations in the potential applicant groups. Some were well-organized and longstanding, with a proportion of well-known members, including some who were IPA members. Some groups had members trained by IPA members in accord with IPA standards, others by IPA members *not* in accord with IPA standards, and still others by non-IPA members who nevertheless worked in accord with our standards. Inevitably, the application and evaluation process, to be focused both on group functioning *and* on assessment of individual capacities, could risk seriously splitting an ongoing functioning group, or give rise to serious pressures for widespread "grandfathering." The task force was already grappling with all of these complex issues.

As for the litigation itself, there had been no word from the plaintiffs acknowledging anything that had happened in Montreal, and thus far, at least, the litigation was unaffected by the proposed changes in the IPA. Almost all the planned depositions had by now been taken on both sides and the plaintiffs had filed their class action certification motion. The class they claimed to represent consisted of all "Ph.D. psychologists" interested in analytic training. That had many implications for us. Even if we prevailed and that particular "class" did not secure that right of representation, other "classes" could still sue us; it might have been to our interest to have the claimed class enlarged to include all mental health professionals, and then fight out the class certification issue on that broader basis. With Clint Fisher present on the IPA's behalf at the sequence of depositions, an additional bill of $20,000 for legal expenses had accrued to the IPA, but the American would reimburse 60% of that. Meanwhile, a good working relationship was being cemented between the attorneys for the IPA and the American, which was indeed helpful in keeping the IPA's costs down.

I was also able to advise the IPA Council that Division 39 would be holding an executive meeting of its Board in San Francisco in February 1988 to argue their strategy in regard to the continuing litigation. One group held the position that the suit continue aggressively, so that the defendants would "be kept running." Another group seemed to feel that they had obtained the substance of what they sought from the IPA and wondered whether the suit should be carried further, or if so, whether the IPA should be dropped from it. Joel Klein had made it clear that the American would not object if the plaintiffs dropped the IPA from the suit, but would object strenuously if the IPA actively sought this. Relations at this point with the officers of the American were very harmonious, and there would be another meeting between the officers of the two associations in New York the following month, in December.

Meanwhile, the IPA had received inquiries from 17 groups, ten in New York, four in Los Angeles, and one each in Boston, Chicago, and Denver. Four had already made formal application and provided all the requested documentation: the New York Freudian Society (NYFS), the Institute for Psychoanalytic Training and Research (IPTAR), the New York Center for Psychoanalytic Training (NYCPT), and the Los Angeles Institute and Society for Psychoanalytic Studies (LAISPS). Site visits to these would begin in the spring of 1988; to delay beyond that could be widely perceived as stalling. But this would be after the agreement on guidelines and procedures that was expected to emerge at the IPA Symposium in England in March. It was also agreed that the composition of the Site Visit Committees should be truly international, with at least one representative each from North America, Latin America, and Europe. Lastly, Irene Auletta was able to report happily that of 898 mail ballots already received, 770 were in favor of the proposed bylaw alteration, 74 were opposed, and 54 had abstained—an overwhelming 86% approval.

On November 18, 1987, Michael Morrissey (from the firm of IPA attorneys) sent a memorandum to the IPA files reporting on the depositions of Nathan Stockhamer and Bryant Welch, which he had attended. On November 6, Stockhamer had been deposed, with the deposition conducted by Chris Cerf (of Joel Klein's firm). Stockhamer's official capacity was Director of Clinical Services at the William Alanson White Institute. The questions centered around the plaintiffs' general claim of having been injured in their professional entitlements by the policies of the American. Stockhamer was hard put to document any instance in which he had been personally injured or deprived of a referral, though he claimed that he had "lost patients because they preferred 'a real psychoanalyst.'" Stockhamer testified that Division 39 was in full support of the lawsuit and that GAPPP had raised between $300,000 and $400,000 to fund it. One day was insufficient, and it was agreed that the deposition would be completed at a later date.

Joel Klein conducted the deposition of Bryant Welch, which took place over three full days, November 9, 10, 11. Klein explored Welch's knowledge of the workings of the American and the IPA and of the recent events in those organizations. Welch was very familiar with the new Gaskill-Davis waiver process, but he dismissed it as the American's holding out the possibility of obtaining a waiver in order to avoid having to grant full and unencumbered training for nonphysicians. Welch was also pressed on the issue of defining the class for class action purposes, and whether he, as someone who had decided to discontinue his own psychoanalytic training within an institute of the American (for which he had been accepted) in order to accept fulltime employment with the American Psychological Association—a "fulltime lobbyist," Klein called it—could be a valid representative of the class litigating on behalf of that larger number. After three full days (literally 24 hours), Welch's deposition was still not completed and was adjourned to a later date. At the same time, the lawyers for both sides entered another stipulation. This put the court timetable still further back; the defendants would now have until January 15, 1988, to serve papers in response to the plaintiffs' motion for class certification, and the plaintiffs' time to serve reply papers was extended to March 4, 1988.

Much of the December 1987 issue of *Round Robin*, the newsletter of Section 1 of Division 39 (the Section of psychologist-psychoanalytic practitioners) was devoted to the events of the lawsuit and commentaries on it. There was an article on the July 1987 IPA Congress in Montreal that reported the bylaw change altering the Regional Association agreement by a unanimous vote of 195 to 0 (with 24 abstentions), to be followed by a mail ballot of the IPA membership, with the final results to be reported on December 17, 1987, at the IPA Executive Council meeting in New York. It was stated that: "The Proposal is expected to pass by an overwhelming majority." The article also announced that 18 independent institutes had already made formal inquiry of the IPA concerning membership affiliation and that "four of these institutes are already at various stages of the formal application process" (IPTAR, NYFS, NYCPT, all in New York, and LAISPS in Los Angeles). Last was the announcement of the IPA task force appointed to recommend guidelines and procedures for the evaluation process of these applicant institutes, which would be discussed at the IPA Symposium in March 1988 and submitted for formal approval to the IPA Executive Council Meeting in London in July 1988. All in all, this was a straightforward and positive account of the steady progression on these issues of nonmedical training and practice in the United States under IPA auspices.

Another article in the same issue of *Round Robin* updated the progression of the GAPPP lawsuit against the American and the IPA. This article (by Stockhamer) reported on the class certification motion and its timetable. After the plaintiffs' reply (now extended still further to March 15, 1988) to the defendants' response to the motion, this would be argued in oral hearing before the judge, at a still undetermined date. When the judge finally ruled on that issue, the case would itself come to trial (unless settled in the interim), presumably some time in 1988, which would be more than three years after its initial filing on March 1, 1985.

Most arresting in connection with the evolving perceptions concerning the lawsuit within the plaintiff class was a long letter of commentary by two distinguished psychologist-psychoanalysts, Steven Ellman and Irving Steingart, both in New York. Of signal interest are the following excerpts: "We are in favor of the lawsuit. . . . We are not uneasy with the lawsuit, but with where we may unwittingly be going with it" (p. 17). They wanted recognition of nonmedical institutes by the IPA, but were against pressure to require medical institutes to admit them or medical analysts to train them.

> We think that at this time it is particularly important to continue to establish a professional identity as psychologist-psychoanalysts. . . . [We] argue for the necessity of a psychologist-psychoanalyst identity which can make its own unique contribution to psychoanalysis. In our view, this can only occur in psychoanalytic Institutes organized and administered by psychologist-psychoanalysts. Therefore, we believe that insisting that we need medical Institutes to give us this training is both incorrect and damaging to our identity as psychologist-psychoanalysts, as well as to the special contribution we can make to psychoanalysis [p. 18]. . . . Nothing in this proposal is intended to affect the opportunity of an individual psychologist to decide which type of Institute—psychologist-run or American Psychoanalytic-run—he or she wishes to attend for psychoanalytic training. But it is our contention that a lawsuit that represents us all as a profession should not envision a solution which could give over psychologists' psychoanalytic training to the American Psychoanalytic [p. 18]. . . . It is our position that we wish to help our colleagues in underrepresented areas, and we maintain that there are ways we can accomplish this task with the help of Division 39 and by using medical analysts as teachers and supervisors under our auspices. Requiring medical Institutes to take psychologists would be a blow to our professional identity and a burden to those psychologists trained under these conditions. This may be one of the few times where separate but equal might be the better alternative [p. 39].

Quite aside from the intellectual arguments over educational philosophy and the conditions for the development of a psychoanalytical identity, or even what such an identity comprises and how it is circumscribed, the Ellman-Steingart letter, from a political point of view certainly spoke to the softening, or even the potential fracturing of the plaintiffs' united continuing pursuit of the lawsuit. Certainly the arguments advanced by Ellman and Steingart could be read as implying that the plaintiffs could be well advised to settle on a basis that embodied mutual agreement on all the steps taken to this point by the American, and in the altering of the relationship between the American and the IPA (the revised Regional Association agreement). Certainly the plea by Ellman and Steingart could be fully realized within such a settlement agreement.

But the very next event chronicled here jarred matters in the very opposite direction, away from any possibility of settlement in the near future. Murray Meisels, writing for the Board of Directors of Division 39 and as President of the Division, sent an open letter, dated December 4, 1987, to all members of the New York Psychoanalytic Institute.[4] This letter charged that at the November 9 deposition of Bryant Welch, Joel Klein, as attorney for the American, and Mark Bunim, as attorney for the New York Institute, had asserted the following:

> The lawsuit is based on the assumption that the plaintiffs are or were analyzable; that, by virtue of filing the lawsuit, the plaintiffs, therefore, have "put their mental condition into dispute" and have waived their rights to confidentiality and privacy; and that the defendants reserve the right to gain access to the information divulged during the personal psychoanalyses of the plaintiffs, such information to be used in the legal proceeding to determine whether the plaintiffs are "analyzable" or for other purposes.

Meisels then declared that in a subsequent telephone conference call among the Board of Directors of Division 39 held on November 22, 1987, the Board members "were shocked and appalled that psychoanalytic organizations would attack the confidentiality, privacy, and integrity of the psychoanalytic situation." Other words and phrases that were used were "unethical," "an intimidation tactic," "using the psychoanalytic situation to intimidate plaintiffs and to silence dissent," "The Board considered that the 50 years of injustices that had been heaped on psychologists are now being compounded by harassment and intimidation, even at the cost of

---

[4] Though the copy of Meisels's letter I received was addressed as "An open letter to the New York Psychoanalytic Institute," the reply by Dick Simons to all members of the American, dated December 21, 1987, indicated that it seemed to have been sent to a larger number of psychoanalyst members of the American.

harming the integrity of psychoanalytic confidentiality." All this was declared a threat, not only to the plaintiffs, "but also [to] all past, present, and future analysands." After condemning this threat by the IPA's attorneys, Meisels's letter went on to call it "particularly reprehensible because its impetus derives from psychoanalytic organizations that should know better," and "called on the world psychoanalytic community to condemn this policy," and on the American and the New York Institute to "cease and desist" from any legal effort to gain access to this confidential material.

I had no direct knowledge at that time of the events referred to in this letter nor of the validity of the charge. It was responded to in a letter sent to all members of the American by Dick Simons, dated December 21, 1987. Simons flatly rejected the charge that the American would seek to use the litigation to "attack the confidentiality, privacy, and integrity of the psychoanalytic situation" by seeking access to "information divulged during the personal psychoanalyses of the plaintiffs." He explained that the charges in Meisels's letter were based solely on a single episode that had occurred during the deposition.

> We believe that the characterization contained in the letter about what occurred at the deposition is seriously distorted. . . . We wish to make it clear that this Association has not pursued and will not pursue any confidential information disclosed by any analysand during psychoanalytic treatment. At the same time, however, it may become necessary to elicit certain information if a party, in pursuing a claim in this litigation, discusses statements by his or her analyst that have a direct bearing on the issues of the lawsuit. For example, the following occurred during the deposition in question. The plaintiff had produced a letter from his training analyst to the Director of his Institute, and then disputed the accuracy of what the analyst said in the letter. It was necessary at the time, and would remain necessary under similar circumstances in the future, to preserve the legal right to discuss the specific matter at issue with the analyst.

Clearly this interchange between the plaintiffs and the American, between Meisels and Simons, represented a renewed heating up of the lawsuit antagonisms, and served to dampen what had seemed like a growing willingness—on both sides?—to again seek an agreed settlement.

The (partial) meeting of the IPA Executive Council took place in New York on December 16 and 17, 1987, that is, between the receipt of the letter by Meisels and the response by Simons, and it was one of the major items for discussion in connection with the status of the lawsuit. I was able to report what I had heard from Simons of the actual interchanges during

Welch's deposition. One of the questions raised had to do with the conditions under which Welch's psychoanalytic training as a research candidate in an institute of the American had stopped. I had known that he had given up his training and clinical practice in order to take up his fulltime position with the American Psychological Association. A letter from his former training analyst stated that Welch had left the area to take this full-time position elsewhere, and therefore his analysis had stopped, but that the analyst would be glad to resume work with him should Welch move back to the area. On the stand, Welch disputed this, stating that his analysis had been completed. Because there was such a difference of viewpoint, Joel Klein had asked if he could get a letter from the training analyst to help clarify the situation. Welch had asked what other information would be requested, and he was assured that no other information would be sought, but Klein had added the usual legal stipulation that he would not waive his right to make inquiry about other matters in the future. It was this usual legal caveat that had become the basis for Meisels's inflammatory letter directed at the defendants and their attorneys. I was able at this time to indicate how Simons was intending to respond to Meisels's letter.

This discussion widened into consideration of what it might portend for the future of the lawsuit and some speculation about how many members of Division 39 who had contributed to the plaintiffs' war chest were still in full support of the continuing suit (as represented by Meisels) as against how many would be seeking to now drop it, or to alter the conditions under which it was being pursued. The latter could be inferred, perhaps, from the several outspoken dissenting or critical voices I have been quoting, people like Zenia Fliegel, Roy Schafer, Rita Frankiel, Steven Ellman, and Irving Steingart. All agreed that the current contretemps between Meisels and the defendants not only hardened the climate, but in the battle of current psychoanalytic opinion, cast the American and the other defendants in an odious light, as potential unscrupulous blackmailers. The other news reported at this meeting was that there now seemed to be six serious letters of application for evaluation for membership in the IPA: IPTAR, NYFS, NYCPT, and NPAP, all from New York, and LAISPS and PCC (Psychoanalytic Center of California), both from Los Angeles.

The last event of the calendar year 1987 was a letter of report, dated December 30, from Clint Fisher to me. He enclosed a copy of the plaintiffs' memorandum in support of their motion for class certification and stated that Joel Klein expected to have a draft of the defendants' memorandum in opposition to the motion available for circulation and comment early in January. He also sent a copy of an affidavit that Bryant Welch had submitted to the court on December 22, 1987, which reported on fund-raising and expenditures by GAPPP on behalf of the lawsuit. More that $450,000 was reported raised (through December 2, 1987) and almost every penny of it spent, of which almost $400,0000 was for legal fees. Fisher added, cautiously, that "the affidavit does not address what, if any, funds have been raised through or spent by other organizations or individuals on behalf of the plaintiffs." This was indeed a sobering year-end appraisal of just the financial costs of the lawsuit to this point, and for only the plaintiffs.

It was in 1988 that the lawsuit settlement was at last reached. From the IPA's standpoint, the year began with a Draft Report of the IPA Ad Hoc Committee[5] on the Admission of Groups, dated January 1988. This report began with a statement of the final official count in the IPA mail ballot that altered the Regional Association agreement between the American and the IPA and made this whole process of evaluation for IPA membership possible. The vote was 853 to 84, more than 90% approval. There was then discussion of the special circumstances in the United States that led to the growth of independent institutes outside the auspices of the American, and the reiterated caution that however the coming evaluation process would be carried out, the training standards of the IPA would be maintained, and that in consequence, some individuals in those groups that did qualify might be found not qualified. There was an additional caveat. Although the half-century ban on the recognition of nonmedical psychoanalytic training in the United States had now been reversed by the action voted at the IPA Congress in Montreal, and procedures were being worked out to process applications for IPA membership of independent (nonmedical) psychoanalytic institutes heretofore denied that opportunity, somewhat similar circumstances existed in parts of Latin America where IPA institutes had only recently begun to accept nonmedical candidates. Thus, whatever the Hanly Committee worked out procedurally for United States groups could be seized upon as a precedent by similarly placed groups in other regions of the world.

Given these constraints and these potentially complex issues, the Hanly Committee report devoted itself to the issues of guidelines and procedures. The central problem would be how to assess and classify individuals trained over a period of many years, often (or usually) by standards that differed from those of the IPA in one or another particular, and (again, usually) by individuals, analysts, and supervisors outside the IPA. An important issue was how all this could be accomplished, how given the very costly and time-consuming nature of the usual site visit process and in the face of the IPA's own limited resources in money and manpower. Groups, psychoanalytic societies, and institutes would pose fewer problems in this regard than would the training, experience, and qualifications of

---

[5] The Committee chaired by Charles Hanly with the members as listed in footnote 3, this chapter.

individual members. Organized groups could provide ready documentation; constitution and bylaws; code of ethics; curriculum; procedures and requirements for admission, progression, and graduation; requirements for membership and training and supervising analyst status; minutes of committee meetings; records of scientific meetings; CVs and bibliographies of members. All these functions could readily be observed during the course of the usual kinds of site visits carried out by committees of the American or of the IPA.

With individuals, the assessment task would be more complicated and time-consuming. Certainly there would be the issue of "grandfathering," especially in the case of the most senior, prestigious, or distinguished members. Five possible bases for "grandfathering" were elaborated: (1) the standards now required were not in effect at the time that the individuals in question were trained; (2) the training received was "functionally equivalent" to the IPA training standards; (3) the professional functioning and experience demonstrated adequate psychoanalytic competence; (4) it would be patently unfair and unnecessarily disruptive to require further training and study; and (5) such a demand would be particularly unfair in view of the fact that the individuals in question had met the requirements of their own day and circumstances and thus had every expectation of pursuing a lifetime career on that basis. Discussion of each of these issues and the attendant circumstances was indeed complicated. For example, concerning criterion five, the Committee report stated:

> Circumstances at the time the individuals in question took their training were such (however unfair some of us may consider this to have been) that they would not have expected to become members of the IPA; nor would non-membership in the IPA— then or now—have deprived them of any right they then had, or now have, to practice psychoanalysis and to advance their careers. They chose to become psychoanalysts outside the IPA because they believed that they could still successfully practice psychoanalysis. This circumstance would not be altered by their continuing in their present status outside the IPA, even though they may have preferred to be trained by an IPA-accredited institute.

Given this kind of reasoning, the Committee stated that "there are no *prima facie* compelling reasons for the use of standard, universal, and automatic grandfathering." Rather, the assessment process would be individualized—however laborious and manpower-intensive this might have to be—and therefore, "The justification for grandfathering will have to depend on whether, and under what circumstances, it can be made compatible with the maintenance of IPA minimum standards." The relevant questions were declared to be: "1. Did the training actually received meet the minimum IPA standards? 2. In the absence of (1), can the individual provide sufficient evidence of his/her psychoanalytic knowledge and clinical ability to warrant his/her acceptability—clinical experience and skill, teaching and research activities, publications, etc.? Affirmative answers to these questions would seem to be adequate grounds for grandfathering." Here was laid the basis for what came to be called the establishment of "functional equivalence" in the training and experience of these individuals.

The rest was a matter of detailed specification. For example, those who had been analyzed and supervised by IPA-accredited training analysts, as a goodly number in the New York and Los Angeles areas had been (see chapter 3), and had taken seminars in independent institutes that maintained acceptable standards and procedures, could be accorded immediate IPA membership through their component (acceptable) society or in the absence of the formal seminar experience, those who could demonstrate an adequate standard of professional performance on the basis of publications, examination of clinical ability through case presentation, informal education, additional supervision, and so forth. If some such individuals could be accredited as IPA members with training analyst status in their own institutes, then the membership net could be widened by also accepting those *they* had trained. "This concept of grandfathering could make it possible for a large number of otherwise ineligible members of the applicant group to become qualified retroactively by virtue of the status granted to the group's training analysts."

Beyond this would be those with gaps in training or experience that could not be covered this way and would have to be otherwise evaluated or made up. For example, if some but not all of an applicant group's training analysts met the above-elaborated IPA criteria for that status, then the group members would divide into five categories: (1) training analysts whose credentials and work led to IPA accreditation as such; (2) training analysts whose credentials and work led only to IPA membership and that same status in the local group; (3) ordinary members eligible for IPA membership by virtue of having been trained by members of subgroup (1); (4) ordinary members partially eligible for IPA membership (ranging from "all but" to "scarcely at all") because they had been trained partly by members of group (1) and partly by members of group (2); and (5) ordinary members not eligible for IPA membership because they were trained wholly by members of group (2). Of course, for all those not eligible for immediate IPA membership on these bases there would have to be opportunities to become eligible through additional appropriate training experiences. As a "procedure of last resort," those not immediately eligible could be offered, as an alternative to these various forms of grandfathering, a program of examination, the opportunity to present their credentials and samples of their clinical work to an IPA evaluation committee (as part of the site visit process). Here the costs in time and energy (and money) could mount very steeply, especially with the large memberships—well over 100—in some of the applicant groups.

This material from the Hanly Committee draft report has been recounted in such detail to illustrate the thoroughness, conscientiousness, and care with which the IPA was undertaking its new tasks in the wake of the Montreal action that undid the American's exclusive franchise on IPA membership in the United States and made independently established psychoanalytic societies and institutes, some of which had functioned for several decades, eligible for IPA affiliation. All of this was quite apart from the vicissitudes of the continuing lawsuit. The last I will quote from this draft committee report is from the final section, entitled "The Cost of Admission," a sober appraisal of potential unhappy and hurtful fallout. Under cost to groups, the report stated, "Clearly, no matter what procedures we adopt, it will create in some groups, conceivably in all, two or more types of membership. Some of the applicant groups have already expressed their acceptance of this consequence. The responsibility of seeking membership, and the responsibility for any consequences that may follow from that decision, can only be borne by the groups themselves." Under cost to individuals, the report stated,

> Inevitably the application of these or any other possible policies will involve some disruption and hardship. Anyone who has gained part of his livelihood by his work as a training analyst but fails to receive IPA accreditation as such, for instance, will almost certainly feel it in his/her pocketbook. And what about the candidates already in analysis or in supervision with him/her who wish to upgrade their own training in order to be eligible for membership in the IPA? This kind of disruption, and even temporary injustice, cannot be avoided in any process of reclassification; nor can such consequences really be mitigated." All that could be recommended in this regard was that, "For the sake of fairness it is important that these possibilities should be pointed out to applicant groups, and that they in turn should make sure that their members are aware of them. . . . The IPA should make it clear to applicant groups that they have a responsibility to keep their members and candidates adequately informed about any pending or actual changes in status due to the work of the Site Visit or other IPA committees, or arising from the operation of any procedure we adopt.

Accompanying the draft report (a 24-page document) was another, half the length, actually written by Charles Hanly in November 1987, entitled "Some Initial Reflections," which outlined the background thinking that undergirded the report. It began with a five-fold classification of the members of existing independent psychoanalytic societies and institutes in the United States: (1) those who were already IPA members; (2) those trained unofficially by IPA training analysts in accord with IPA standards; (3) those trained unofficially by IPA training analysts, but not fully in accord with IPA standards; (4) those trained by non-IPA training analysts of their own institute but in accord with IPA standards; and (5) those trained by non-IPA training analysts of their own institutes and not in accord with IPA standards. This document then went on to develop the various possible combinations and permutations of guidelines and procedures, a Radical Position, Intermediate Position, Conservative Position, and so on. This was to become systematized in the January 1988 committee report.

On January 12, 1988, came a slightly revised version of the Committee report, tightening and clarifying some of the language, with a handwritten note: "Dear Bob, Here is my first draft of a first draft of the report. I will be doing the final first draft, hopefully with David Sachs, on January 23–24. If you wish to make any input at this stage that weekend will be your last opportunity. We are still more or less on schedule. Best wishes, Charles." The reference to schedule was to the coming IPA Symposium (at Linden Hall in Northumberland, outside of Newcastle, England, set for March 1988) where the entire report would be taken up by the IPA Executive Council and, if approved there, become the basis for the impending evaluation process of the applicant psychoanalytic societies and institutes. By now, preliminary IPA questionnaires, asking for a great deal of information about the organization and functioning of the groups and about the training and professional experience of the individual group members, were in the hands of 15 potential applicant groups, eight in New York, four in California, and one each in Boston, Chicago, and Denver.

In connection with that same pending IPA Executive Council meeting, I received a letter from Murray Meisels, as President of Division 39, dated January 11, 1988. The letter began, "I have received information to the effect that the IPA will be meeting in England in March 1988, to devise procedures for implementing the IPA By-Law changes which are supposed to enable USA psychologist societies to join. I am hereby requesting that Division 39 be allowed two or three representatives to participate in this meeting, or to be present as observers." After some intervening text, the letter ended with the sentence, "Division 39 participation in such a meeting would not be related to the lawsuit." I responded to this letter on January 25, 1988. I explained that these would be week-long IPA executive meetings at which the full range of IPA organizational business would be discussed, including the planning for the coming IPA Congress in Rome in July 1989, combined with a scientific program for the 40 or so invited participants (all with major executive or administrative responsibilities in the IPA). I then added, "Among the many items on our agenda, you are correct to note that we do plan to formulate our guidelines for implementing our bylaw changes which do enable psychoanalytic groups in the United States to affiliate with the IPA outside the framework of the American. Our meetings are not just for that purpose as your letter seems to suggest, but that issue is certainly one among our many agenda items and certainly a very important one."

Though I pointed out that as executive meetings, the coming Symposium week was not open to outsiders to the organization, I did solicit input:

> We do recognize the strong interest that many members of Division 39 have in the way in which the IPA will be implementing the recently enacted bylaw changes and we would welcome any written input from you or other interested parties . . . that would give us your perspective on issues that we will be dealing with in the evaluation process and suggestions for procedures that could best respond to these issues in ways that are best for psychoanalysis and psychoanalytic training.

I ended the letter with the statement that decisions worked out and voted by the IPA Executive Council would be published in the *IPA Newsletter,* which would be available to Dr. Meisels on request. There was no response to this letter.

Meanwhile, in connection with the ongoing litigation process, I received a letter from Clint Fisher, dated January 25, 1988, enclosing a (140-page) draft of the defendants' brief in opposition to the plaintiffs' class certification motion. Fisher informed me that at a discussion among the attorneys for the four defendant groups a few days earlier, it was agreed that the brief was too long but did contain all the arguments the defendants should make. Joel Klein and his colleague Chris Cerf would now be revising the brief, and my input would be welcomed at this point. Another letter from Clint Fisher to me, dated a day later, enclosed a draft of my affidavit to be submitted with the defendants' opposition to the class certification motion. This was for my review and signature. Two days later on January 28, 1988, I wrote back to Fisher indicating that I had read the entire 140-page draft. I felt that it was well-researched, well-written, and very persuasive indeed, but also that it was indeed far too long, unduly repetitive, and I could easily see 50 pages knocked off. I did correct one error of fact in the recounting of some of the IPA organizational history. Along with this letter I sent back the signed affidavit, which merely stated that I was the IPA President and that over the preceding year the IPA had been contacted by some 18 psychoanalytic training centers or groups in the United States seeking information about the possibilities for affiliation with the IPA. These groups were located in New York, California, Michigan, Massachusetts, Colorado, and Illinois; visits to the first two of them were already in the planning stage.

The contents of the defendants' 140-page draft brief can be summarized as follows: There was first a statement of the psychoanalytic training status of the four plaintiffs in the lawsuit. Three of them had been accepted for training by institutes of the American and two of them were at various stages in that process, while one, Bryant Welch, had voluntarily withdrawn when he assumed his position with the American Psychological Association and GAPPP. One of the four had been rejected for candidacy by two institutes of the American. This was followed by a detailed recapitulation of the events of the lawsuit since its inception, including the judge's denial of the defendants' motion for the summary judgment of dismissal followed by the setting up of arguments on the class action certification issue and the concomitant discovery and deposition process. By now, the plaintiffs had taken about 15 depositions and the defendants about a dozen. From all of this, it was stated that the plaintiffs' brief "relies on a few isolated quotes out of a 10-year period of deliberations to make it appear as if economics were the driving force in defendants' decision making concerning non-psychiatrist training." To counter this, the defendants' brief then went back to the Flexner report of 1910 and its decisive impact on medical education in the United States—the same Flexner report to which I dated the American concern with the issue of the proper qualifications for psychoanalytic training. The brief then pointed to the founding of the American Psychoanalytic Association by eight physician-analysts in the following year. "In this climate [the great outcry over the Flexner report], when the American was chartered in 1911, its founders decided that this new and controversial undertaking would be best served in this country if it were allied with medical training and its new commitment [i.e., the reforms underway in response to the Flexner report] to high standards."

The brief then recounted the story of the Gaskill Committee report, which had passed by a 68% vote of the membership of the American, under which nonmedical candidates were now being processed for full clinical psychoanalytic training in the institutes of the American, together with the most recent (May 1987) statement of the Executive Council of the American, reaffirming unequivocally that members of the American were free to teach at independent (psychologist-run) institutes outside the American, subject to only two conditions: (1) that there be no representation that this was a program sponsored by the American, and (2) that the teacher be satisfied about the "reasonable ethical standards" of the program where the teaching took place, this latter in order to safeguard the interests of both the patients and the profession.

After that, the document turned specifically to the class action issue. A sequence of points were made to try to demonstrate that the plaintiffs were unable to satisfy the basic prerequisites for class certification. First, competitive foreclosure antitrust cases were stated to be inherently ill-suited for classwide treatment; it was not a violation of the antitrust laws in the abstract that was at issue, but whether a particular individual was damaged, and if so, how much. Second, the class definition designed to cover 50,000 licensed clinical psychologists with diverse training and experience was stated to be "impermissibly vague and imprecise." Third, each plaintiff's claim raises individualized issues that were stated to predominate over common issues. For example, "Each individual must affirmatively show that, among the world of possible reasons for not entering the market, it was, in fact, the restraint that kept him or her out," and the individual, "must also show that if he had been able to enter the market, he would have been successful, i.e., that as a result of the alleged restraint, he actually suffered economic harm." Fourth, the plaintiffs cannot "fairly and adequately" represent the proposed class, because that class is riddled with conflicts and inconsistencies; a suit brought by competitors for access to a limited market inevitably creates conflict among the class members. Fifth, the plaintiffs cannot satisfy the "typicality" requirement of class action certification.

These were stated to be the kinds of reasons why no court had ever certified a nationwide class for either damages or injunctive relief in an antitrust suit alleging competitive foreclosure, and it was declared that the plaintiffs had not offered any reason why this should be the first such instance. Antitrust injury on a classwide basis simply could not be proven in a competitive foreclosure case. In fact, it was stated, even the standing to sue would have to be shown on an individualized basis for most potential class members; certainly, establishing antitrust injury would also require highly individualized proof for every class member.

Further, it was stated that the predominance of individual issues was compounded by the necessity of examining both injury and damages in more than 20 highly individualized geographical markets across the United States. Still further, the American now admitted psychologists to full clinical psychoanalytic training under the Gaskill Committee plan, the American had recently reaffirmed that its members were free to teach in programs outside the American without fear of sanction or reprisal, and the IPA had amended its constitution and bylaws in Montreal in 1987, so that properly qualified psychoanalytic training groups in the United States outside the American could now obtain direct affiliation with the IPA. And the fourth plaintiff had now been accepted for training in an institute of the American under the Gaskill Committee plan as implemented by the Davis Committee.

The inherent conflicts in the proposed plaintiff class were highlighted as follows. The proposed class consisted of at least three separate broad groups, each of which was pursuing different and mutually exclusive goals via this lawsuit: those who wanted training in the institutes of the American; those who rejected the American and wanted training in their own psychologist-run institutes, which would be recognized by the IPA; and those already trained, whether in the institutes of the American or outside it, who were currently in practice. The remedial objectives sought by each of these subsets of the class were clearly antagonistic or mutually exclusive. For example:

> For precisely these reasons, those psychologists who have nothing to gain from the present suit but monetary damages—because they are philosophically opposed or practically indifferent to gaining access to the American—cannot be fairly represented by those whose overriding objective is to be trained at an American-accredited Institute. Moreover, even beyond this basic conflict over the appropriateness of inflicting a mortal thrust on the American, plaintiffs' insistence on using the lawsuit to gain access to the American embodies a vision of the profession and of psychoanalysis itself that has been explicitly rejected by much of the class they seek to represent. In light of the radically different—and inherently antagonistic—objectives of significant portions of the class, it is abundantly clear that plaintiffs cannot satisfy the "fair representation" requirement.

On the basis of all of this, the draft brief ended with a one-sentence Conclusion: "The motion for class certification should be denied."

Two weeks later, on February 12, 1988, the defendants filed with the court the now shortened 68-page (though mostly now single spaced) Memorandum of Law in Opposition to the Motion for Class Certification. The argument was now both tightened and, at the same time, amplified. Among the new arguments advanced was the assertion that the plaintiffs had created a "fictionalized account" of the merits of their motion for class certification. They had repeatedly attempted to portray this as a classic discrimination case, akin to one based on race or gender under Title VII of the Civil Rights Act, where it is much easier to satisfy the requirements for class definition. The defendants' brief, however, contended that Title VII was simply not applicable, because it is perfectly appropriate to treat people with different professional backgrounds differently. This is not a Civil Rights case, but an antitrust case in which a different order of proof is required, because "each individual plaintiff must show impermissible economic foreclosure in a distinct product and geographic market that has caused real and provable antitrust injury (as well as monetary damages) to him or her."

In regard to the several statements culled by the plaintiffs from all the defendants' documents they had studied in the discovery process which referred to economic or trade issues, the brief now stated: "almost always, however, these references were made by *proponents* of non-medical training [within the American] who were purporting to describe the motives of those who disagreed with their position. It may be that reducing one's opposition to a position of self-interest, while seeking the high ground for oneself, is an effective debating tactic. But such rhetorical flourishes are hardly an accurate place to search for true organizational motive." The brief then went on to state more compactly all the arguments advanced in the initial longer draft that have already been stated in summary form. Again the court was reminded that "plaintiffs have failed to cite even a single case in which a court has certified a nationwide class for either damages or injunctive relief in an antitrust suit alleging competitive foreclosure." Further, "these plaintiffs, through artful pleading, are improperly attempting to sweep a multitude of separate economic (and even political) grievances into a single antitrust class action." The brief ended with the same plea as in the earlier draft, that the class action motion be denied. Thus the issue over class action certification was joined and would now be on the judge's calendar for response by the plaintiffs and then for oral argument before the judge and his subsequent decision. All of this was still preliminary to the trial itself, which could be many months further off. By this time, February 12, 1988, almost exactly three years had passed since the original filing of the lawsuit on March 1, 1985.

On March 7, 1988, Simons sent all members of the American a copy of the defendants' legal memorandum that had just been filed with the court. The covering memorandum by Simons encouraged all members to read the entire document, but it called special attention to an outline of the contents of this brief, prepared by Joel Klein, indicating that the Introduction, the Statement of the Case, and the Statement of Facts provided an excellent summary of the class action issues and of the basic position of the defendants in regard to them. Simons's memorandum pointed out that because the plaintiffs were seeking triple damages and injunctive relief under the antitrust laws, the success of the plaintiffs' motion for class certification would mean that all Ph.D. psychologists who might claim that they would have sought training at an institute accredited by the American would become party to the case—a tremendous escalation of the risks to the American (and the other defendants) should the plaintiffs ultimately prevail in the trial itself.

As a coda to the events of this chapter, there was another exchange of letters between Murray Meisels and me in these last days just before the filing of the defendants' brief. As I have indicated earlier, the Board of Division 39 was meeting in Executive Session in San Francisco in February 1988 to consider its further strategy in pursuit of the lawsuit. Apropos of this meeting, I received a letter from Meisels dated January 26, 1988, proposing a meeting on the evening of February 26 between three representatives of Division 39 (Meisels as President, Zanvel Liff as President-Elect, and Bryant Welch as the central figure among the plaintiffs) and two representatives of the IPA (me as President and Ed Weinshel as Secretary). The meeting topic would be "An informal discussion of the lawsuit, its impact on psychoanalysis, and the possibility of resolving the issues it raises."

I considered this request in consultation with the IPA attorneys, and wrote back on February 3, 1988, regretfully declining because we felt "that the particular meeting as proposed and at this particular time wouldn't give promise to be as fruitful as we would hope and that, therefore, I would suggest it be deferred." The reasons I gave for this were several. The IPA officers represented only one of the four defendant parties, and any meaningful and useful discussion would necessarily have to involve at least the representatives of the American, the principal target of the suit, as well. In the absence of the attorneys, the conversations would not be privileged, and I had been distressed by the way an earlier exchange of correspondence between us had been used (Meisels had unilaterally, and without consulting me, made public one half of that earlier correspondence). The timing would not be the best, because at that very time the class action certification issue was moving toward a hearing in the judge's chambers and the judge's decision on this matter would importantly influence the further possibilities in the lawsuit.

I ended my letter,

> For these reasons, I do have to regretfully decline your invitation at this point. I say regretfully because I am committed to the idea that when things of this kind are at issue, we do better increasing rather than diminishing our dialogue so as to see what common ground we can arrive at. Also, as you know, I myself have taken a leading role in the past in initiating discussions between the plaintiffs and the defendants (and their attorneys) to this suit. Despite our not meeting at this time, I trust that we continue to share the hope that the suit will be settled in ways most satisfactory to both sides as soon as possible.

The Settlement Agreement
October 1988

On March 31, 1988, the full Executive Council of the IPA met at Linden Hall in Longhorsley, in the north of England, in connection with the week-long IPA Symposium. As expected, the progress of the lawsuit and the planning and procedural recommendations of the Hanly Committee on Admission of New Groups were central agenda items. The completed report (dated March 1988) of the New Groups Committee was available ahead of time to all Executive Council members. This report was substantially the same as the earlier drafts discussed in detail in the preceding chapter, but now with consensus on the precise recommendations to be brought to the Executive Council on the evaluation procedures for both the training groups (the independent Societies and Institutes) and their individual members. As outlined in detail in the preceding chapter, the intent was to develop a fair and *workable* assessment process that would nonetheless ensure the maintenance of the IPA's minimum training standards. This eliminated automatic grandfathering based only on achieved status within the applicant groups, and substituted grandfathering based on the conception of demonstrated "functional equivalence" of training and competence, yet devised to be feasible in terms of IPA resources of manpower and money available to the task.

First, of course, the quality of the group functioning would have to be assured: "There can be no question of grandfathering [individuals] or upgrading [remedial activities by those who fell short of meeting the grandfathering criteria] unless the academic quality of the Society or Institute itself, and of its training program, is acceptable." But as indicated in the earlier discussion of this issue, assessment procedures for group functioning had been well established over years of activity by Site Visit Committees of the IPA (and also of the American) and would pose no special problem or undue drain on resources when being applied directly to these new applicant groups. At this point (on the basis of already submitted application materials)

285

only four groups were adjudged to be in a position to warrant immediate site visits.

Therefore, given a favorable decision on the institutional educational functioning of an applicant society or institute, it was proposed that the evaluation of individuals be along three procedural channels. Procedure A would be for those eligible for immediate "grandfathering" into the appropriate category of IPA membership. This would apply first to designated training analysts in an applicant group that met proper standards of institutional functioning, whose own training analysis and supervisions had been by IPA-accredited training analysts, and who, in addition, had either taken seminar and training sequences adjudged to have met proper IPA standards or, in the absence of this seminar training, could nonetheless demonstrate an adequate standard of professional performance. This could be done on the basis of publications (especially clinical papers), examination of clinical ability through case presentations, or other additional educational or supervision experiences. Similarly, nontraining analyst members of these same groups who met the same criteria would likewise be accorded comparable status within the IPA. The basis for this "Immediate IPA Membership" was stated as follows:

> Meeting the criteria for functional equivalence outlined above should provide at least *prima facie* evidence of training equivalent to IPA minimum standards. We should remember that no formal criteria can be infallible. However, since IPA training analysts have been appointed through a process of selection which is intended to vouch for the quality of their performance, and we have constructed our criteria on the assumption that they have maintained the same standards outside the formal structure of the IPA Institutes, we believe it is safe to recommend that individuals meeting these criteria be accepted directly as members of the IPA.

Procedure B would then apply to those who had been trained within the applicant group by its training and supervising analysts who were to be accorded that same status within the IPA on the basis of Procedure A.

> This would allow many more of Group X's members to qualify under our criteria for functional equivalence if the IPA status granted to the group's training analysts is allowed to qualify *retroactively* those people trained by them *before* this status was granted. In this way a form of grandfathering (retroactive qualification) consistent with IPA minimum standards could occur, and would extend the possibility of qualification to otherwise ineligible members of the applicant group.

Procedures A and B could then leave five categories of members in a qualifying applicant group: (a) training analysts accorded IPA training analyst status; (b) training analysts not qualified for IPA recognition as such; (c) regular members eligible for IPA membership by virtue of having been trained by a member of subgroup (a); (d) regular members who are partially eligible (ranging from "all but" to "scarcely at all") because they were trained in part by training analysts in subgroup (a) and in part by those in subgroup (b); and (e) regular members not at all directly eligible because they were trained wholly by members of subgroup (b). That is, those in subgroups (a) and (c) could be accorded direct membership and status within the IPA on the basis of a (readily feasible) review of credentials. All the others would then fall under Procedure C, with varieties of individual evaluation (i.e., no grandfathering possibility). This could comprise some combination of individual review and evaluation via the Site Visit Committee mechanism and/or agreement on remediation or filling of training gaps, such as additional supervision or even more analysis with a now IPA-approved training and supervising analyst. The Hanly Committee report suggested that these individual evaluations could be made by a special evaluation committee: "Our committee suggests that this committee be made up of IPA members sufficiently remote to avoid local bias but sufficiently proximate to avoid heavy travel costs." Hopefully, within each qualifying group, enough members would be directly qualified for appropriate IPA membership and status through Procedures A and B that the individual evaluations required by Procedure C would be brought into manageable compass in terms of the resources needed to be mobilized for the task.

The report ended with the same statement of cautions about the potential costs of this application and admission process, both to the applicant groups and to the individuals in them, that were expressed in the earlier drafts of the report.

> Anyone who has gained part of his livelihood by his work as a training analyst but fails to receive IPA accreditation as such, for instance, will almost certainly feel it in his pocketbook. And what about the candidates already in analysis or in supervision with him who wish to upgrade their own training in order to be eligible for membership in the IPA? This kind of disruption, and even temporary injustice, cannot be avoided in any process of reclassification; nor can such consequences really be mitigated.

The only recommendation regarding this problem was to call for the utmost openness and honesty on the part of the applicant groups to make certain that their members were fully informed in advance about these various possibilities and (by majority vote?) could declare themselves willing to take the risks entailed.

The meeting of the IPA Executive Council took place on the Thursday of the Symposium week. I introduced the discussion of the New Groups issue with a report that Hanly's five-member Committee, which had been meeting daily during the Symposium week, now had some internal disagreements over the recommended procedures, and that David Sachs, one of its members, had asked Inga Villarreal, another member, who was also an Executive Council member, to bring a somewhat different alternative proposal—newly fashioned at the last minute—for consideration by Council as well. Hanly was objecting to this on the grounds that the entire Committee should review the alternate proposal internally before it came to Council. Although there was some support in Council for seeing both proposals directly, I ruled procedurally in Hanly's favor, indicating that Council should at this time only consider the full Committee recommendation, subject to reconsideration should the Committee majority itself propose an alternative or decide to submit a minority report. I also indicated to Council that the current plan was to go ahead (on the basis of the procedures to be agreed upon at this meeting) with the first two site visits—to IPTAR and NYFS—before the July meeting of Council in London.[1] This would give us some sense of what proposal for action on these applications that it might be possible to bring to the next IPA Congress, July 1989, in Rome. This would already be two years after the bylaw changes voted in Montreal in 1987; any delay beyond that could readily be construed as IPA stalling on the promised changes, and could lend added fuel to the continuing lawsuit. There were, in addition, at least two other applicant groups that warranted site visits, and these could be scheduled in the fall of 1988. At this point, Charles Hanly joined the Executive Council meeting for discussion of his committee report.

The long discussion revolved around the many problems and pitfalls that could emerge or be created if the Site Visit Committees were to proceed in accord with the Hanly Committee recommendations. If we visited an applicant group, didn't that already imply a recognition of the group? Shouldn't we rather visit (and evaluate) individuals in the group who, if found to be acceptable, would then coalesce into a new applicant group (for IPA Study Group status) without the burden of group members who could not meet IPA standards? If we evaluated a group and declared it acceptable,

---

[1] The Site Visit Committees for these had already been appointed by me as follows: For IPTAR, Charles Hanly, Toronto (chair), Leon Grinberg, Madrid, Max Hernandez, Lima, and Anton Kris, Boston; for NYFS, David Sachs, Philadelphia (chair), Luis Feder, Mexico City, Moses Laufer, London, and Eva Lester, Montreal. The principle was that all major IPA regions should be represented on each committee, with one from Europe, one from Latin America, and two from North America (one from the United States and one from Canada).

but then only a percentage (even if a high percentage) met IPA criteria for individual membership, how could we have an IPA component organization with a subset of its members declared unacceptable by the IPA? In response to this it was pointed out that many of the American's affiliate societies had significant numbers of members who had not qualified for membership in the American, and that this system worked without confusion about who was certified by the American and who not. Mainly the point was made that we were anticipating problems that might or might not arise in the course of the actual fact-finding site visits, and if they did arise, would represent problems for the applicant group to resolve on its own. They would not be IPA problems and the IPA would have no prior commitments.

For example, an applicant group, two-thirds of which would be acceptable to the IPA and a third not, would itself have a range of possible choices. It could withdraw its IPA application and remain intact in its independent status and prior functioning. It could proceed with IPA affiliation, with the understanding that only two thirds of its members would be IPA members (carrying IPA responsibilities and functions), with remediation plans to be worked out between the group and the IPA in order, over time, to qualify as many of those currently unqualified for IPA membership as possible. It could even divide into two groups. One would include those becoming IPA members and thereby constituting an IPA-affiliated group; the other would include those not coming into the IPA, who would constitute an independent analytic group (as before), with as many of those coming into the IPA as would wish, also maintaining their membership in the outside group (i.e., having dual membership). The overall point was that it was not the prerogative or desire of the IPA to dictate which choice should be made; that would be up to the concerned group to decide, if and when matters came to that point.

The main point of this long discussion was to help work through the many anxieties within the IPA Executive Council about the uncharted waters into which our new circumstances were taking us. Weinshel made it clear that we were confronted with a unique situation in terms of our organizational history, and we were anxious to deal with it in our usual ways. Our emphasis needed to be on how we deal with this totally unique situation rather than on how we fit this new situation into our customary procedures. Our problem should be standards, not procedures, and we shouldn't confuse the two. That we maintain our standards in as reasonable a manner as possible was of course crucial, but if we insisted on constraining our work within our preexisting procedures, there would be no way to accomplish our designated task. Harald Leupold-Lowenthal helped end the discussion by remarking that in discussing all the terrible things that might happen along the way, we were in fact dealing only with our fantasies; what was to be done now was to get on with the task and find out what the reality was. On this note, the discussion ended, to Hanly's and my considerable relief, with an endorsement to his committee to proceed along the lines charted in the draft report. Incidentally, at no time during this discussion or the discussion of all other agenda items with which the Executive Council had to deal during this meeting, was there any consideration of the current status or future uncertainties of the lawsuit itself. The arguments had been made on both sides over the class action certification motion, and the next important event would be the oral arguments before the judge on that issue.

The next development was a memorandum, dated April 6, 1988, from Clint Fisher to me (also to Irene Auletta and Lista Cannon) which represented the beginning break in the three-year-long impasse in the lawsuit struggle. Fisher reported that Joel Klein had just received a "very serious" settlement offer from the plaintiffs and was flying to New York for a meeting with the other defense counsel that afternoon. Klein had not revealed any details of this "strictly confidential" offer, except that it involved the defendants paying the plaintiffs $650,000 attorneys' fees. Klein had stated that he knew the IPA would not and could not contribute much to this amount, but asked whether the IPA would consider making a "token contribution" to the settlement, say of $50,000 or even only $25,000. Fisher ended by asking whether I could get back to him that same day before the scheduled 3:00 P.M. meeting of all the attorneys, in order to inform him of my views.

The next day, another memorandum came from Fisher, addressed to the same three of us, reporting on the meeting of the attorneys of all four defendant groups (including himself for the IPA) that had been held the previous afternoon. Joel Klein had received a call the previous week from Allen Snyder (of the same law firm as Cliff Stromberg) presenting a six-point settlement proposal on behalf of the plaintiffs. The points were (1) that the American formalize its statement that its members were free to provide training outside of the American's own institutes and that this would be guaranteed for a minimum of 10 years; (2) that the American would guarantee to implement the Gaskill-Davis procedures, without discrimination, for a minimum of 10 years, and would encourage all its member institutes to participate in this program; (3) that the IPA would implement in good faith, for a minimum of 10 years, its evaluation proceedings for the admission of existing independent institutes; (4) that the four individual plaintiffs in the lawsuit be granted waivers for full clinical training in the institutes of the American if they wished; (5) that the case be dismissed with prejudice as to a certified class of plaintiffs as defined in the plaintiffs' class action certification motion; and (6) that the defendants pay the plaintiffs $650,000 to cover litigation costs, placing whatever balance remained in a fund to help establish new institutes.

In discussion amongst the attorneys, Klein had indicated that he had absolutely no problem with the first three points in the settlement offer; in fact, the plaintiffs had already been accorded those benefits by the actions of the American and of the IPA. As to the fourth point, concerning the four individual plaintiffs, Klein had indicated to Snyder that as a matter of principle, the American would not automatically waive the admissions procedures in any of its institutes; he felt that the American could agree to an expedited review process, but that no more could be promised. Snyder later replied to Klein that the demand for automatic waivers "probably will not be a sticking point"; in actuality, none of the defendants were being held back at the point of waiver consideration. As to point five, Klein favored a stipulation of dismissal rather than a judicial order or consent decree, because he did not want the spectre of a judicial order hanging over the heads of the defendants. Toward this end he was prepared to accept the plaintiffs' definition of the class.

Klein felt that the sixth point, the financial settlement, would be the major hurdle at this time. He had told Snyder that the amount was simply too high, but Snyder had then stressed that the plaintiffs "will not settle for much less." "Snyder told Klein that the plaintiffs believe that the changes in the defendants' positions with respect to the issues raised by the lawsuit have resulted from the lawsuit itself and that therefore they should be compensated for the fees they have paid."

At this point, Klein's recommendation to the American was that it pay $400,000 (which would be covered by its insurance carrier) toward the settlement and that the other three defendants manage the other $250,000. Mark Bunim reported for the New York Institute that he had the authority to settle the case within the financial parameters proposed by Klein (also backed by insurance). Jack Auspitz, representing Columbia, indicated that this would be a problem and that Columbia believed it "should not pay one cent" to settle. He reported that Columbia was "losing patience" with the amount of money already spent in defense of the lawsuit and felt that other institutes of the American who were benefiting from the defense by Columbia should actually reimburse Columbia for the money it had already spent. After a good deal of discussion of this allocation of payments it was suggested that a settlement agreement would be framed with the American taking the burden of the entire amount; New York would then reimburse the American by at least $200,000, and Columbia might effectively pay nothing.

Overall, this new settlement proposal was received very positively by the defendants' attorneys. In fact, "it was [even] noted that defendants would have accepted this proposal a year ago and that it is substantially less broad than any proposal plaintiffs have discussed or made in the past." The opinion was offered by one of the participants that Stromberg was probably anxious to settle the case before there was an adjudication of the class certification motion, because the plaintiffs had confidently expected all along to win that motion and, if they did not, Stromberg would "look like an absolute fool."

At the conclusion of the meeting it was stressed that the terms of this settlement proposal must remain strictly confidential at this time, because the plaintiffs might back away from any agreement if the terms offered became public.

I can add further that it was not only a year earlier that this present settlement offer would have been received positively by the defendants as reported from the meeting of the attorneys for the four defendant groups. Actually, apart from the financial demands now being made, this present settlement proposal by the plaintiffs was, in substance and also in spirit, substantially identical with the one that had been worked out at the all-day meeting that I had called and chaired in New York on May 31, 1986, almost two years earlier (see chapter 9). I quote from that earlier account: "In my own telegraphic notes I had marked down four features of this agreement: (1) the American would agree to an alteration of its Regional Association status in the IPA, giving up its 'exclusive franchise' in the United States, while retaining control over its own admission and training standards; (2) the existing and some new non-medical Institutes in the United States outside the aegis of the American would be free to achieve IPA recognition and affiliation if they met its training and professional standards; (3) members of the American would be completely free to teach and train in these settings outside the American without any prejudice to their rights and prerogatives within the American; and (4) a good faith effort would be made to reconcile two contradictory demands of the plaintiffs, 'color-blind' admissions but also some guaranteed minimum percentage of non-medical candidates in the admissions procedures of the American's Institutes under the soon-to-be-implemented Gaskill Committee recommendations. . . . As I remember my own feeling at the end of the day, I was exhausted but quite euphoric."

This was the agreement, strongly promoted by the IPA, which I thought had been worked out then, on May 31, 1986, but which clearly the plaintiffs did not accept, as evidenced by the much more far-reaching and totally unacceptable proposals embodied in Stromberg's written formulation of that "agreement" that arrived some two months later, and which Lewis Kaplan, representing the American, seemed also very willing to back away from, in favor of resuming the confrontational battle of depositions and discovery. It was as if the attorneys for both the plaintiffs and the American were convinced that their side could do better down the line, after further discovery and after the stipulated depositions if this IPA-promoted settlement were not agreed to as initially formulated. Clearly, both sides could not be correct in this belief (equally clearly, the attorneys on both sides would benefit from the continuation of the lawsuit), but the settlement talks could not be successfully concluded in 1986, and the subsequent two years of discovery and deposition, of motion for class action certification and of motion opposing this, all ensued. Now, two years later, after the interim expenditure of very considerable sums by both sides, the plaintiffs were offering virtually the same settlement proposal that they had earlier rejected, and now to a very different attorney for the American, Joel Klein rather than Lewis Kaplan. What had not been discussed at all at the May 31, 1986 meeting, however, was the issue of monetary compensation for legal fees, which at this point, in April 1988, seemed the main obstacle to a (finally) agreed settlement of the suit.

Just a few weeks after our receipt of the still highly confidential, "very serious" settlement offer, Simons, on April 25, 1988, sent a letter to all members of the American reviewing the major events of his two-year tenure as president, but he did so without reference to the new settlement discussions. He meant this letter as a report to the membership, as he was preparing to leave office in May, and he made sure to say that the events he was reporting were not simply responses to the lawsuit: "While these changes have occurred during the period of litigation against us, they reflect the evolution of our organization and are not temporary or expedient responses to the litigation." The happenings he highlighted were these. The American had established its program for the full clinical psychoanalytic training of nonmedical candidates through the committee chaired by Carl Davis. In the two years since the strong positive vote on adopting the Gaskill Committee proposals, 32 nonmedical clinical candidates had been approved for training (in addition to 12 nonmedical research candidates under the long-standing CORST program). Simons added that the American was already initiating a process to effect a bylaw change that would make these nonmedical candidates eligible for full membership in the American upon their graduation from the clinical training. The American had initiated the alteration in the Regional Association agreement with the IPA so that analytic programs in the United States not affiliated with the American could now be eligible for IPA affiliation, provided they met IPA standards, and he added that the IPA was now developing its evaluation procedures for that task. The American had reaffirmed to all its members that they were free to participate in training programs outside the American without any concern for sanction or disapproval related to that activity.

Simons then went on to state: "We have taken these important actions because we believe them to be the right thing to do. . . . we will [however] oppose any change that is not in the best interests of the discipline of psychoanalysis, our patients, or the American. While we would welcome the opportunity to resolve the litigation, we will not agree to demands that would undermine the American's historic commitment to psychoanalytic training and practice of high quality." Simons added further about the litigation, that the plaintiffs had filed their class certification motion and that the defendants' attorneys had "filed a brief to oppose that motion and we believe our opposition is well founded." This issue was still to be resolved by the court, but in any case, "we are prepared to proceed with our defense regardless of what the ruling on the class action issue may be." This was a clear blanket of silence on the hopeful new turn initiated by the plaintiffs' current overtures.

Events were, however, beginning to move swiftly in the settlement negotiations. A memorandum from Clint Fisher, dated May 3, 1988 (not quite a month after the first in this sequence), to Irene Auletta, Lista Cannon, and me, stated that Joel Klein had phoned him that morning to advise us that the parties are "close to reaching acceptable settlement language." Meanwhile, however, to keep within the prescribed timetable, the plaintiffs had filed their reply to the defendants' opposition to their motion for class certification. That reply brief was 115 pages long, with two appendices, one of several hundred pages. Klein also stated, however, that the two parties (the American and the plaintiffs) planned to ask Judge Daronco to defer ruling on the class action motion pending the resolution—or the collapse—of the current settlement discussions. Fisher had confirmed to Klein that the IPA would join in this request, which would be the first notification to the judge that the contending parties were finally seriously talking settlement.

On May 12, 1988, the lawsuit made the Health page of *The New York Times*, in a column written by Daniel Goleman. The article covered the overall interdisciplinary struggle between organized psychiatry and psychology over issues ranging from hospital privileges to access to psychoanalytic training. The principal protagonists who were quoted at length were Melvin Sabshin, the Medical Director of the American Psychiatric Association, and Bryant Welch, identified as Executive Director of the Office of Professional Practice of the American Psychological Association. The lawsuit against the American Psychoanalytic (and its codefendants) was prominently featured, and it was stated that "Freud himself argued that non-medical specialists should be allowed to practice psychoanalysis." Immediately after that I was quoted as saying, "My personal position is that psychoanalysis is a discipline of its own, not part of psychiatry. There is no reason that you should have to be a physician to be an excellent psychoanalyst." I was identified as a professor of psychiatry at the University of California at San Francisco and as President of the IPA. Further on, Dick Simons, identified as the President of the American until the preceding week, was quoted as maintaining that the American was changing its stance on nonmedical training as part of a gradual process that had begun ten years earlier. Bryant Welch was the last to be quoted, stating that the lawsuit would nonetheless be continuing for now: "The admissions policy could be changed back at any time if we were to withdraw the suit. The question is how extensive and genuine the changes are. But I'm hopeful we can reach an out-of-court-settlement." That same day, I received a faxed memorandum from Clint Fisher enclosing a copy of the proposed settlement agreement together with Joel Klein's cover letter. He also added that he was sending a copy of *The New York Times* article to Irene Auletta and Lista Cannon in London, stating that "the article, and the timing of its appearance, has apparently caused a bit of an uproar among the defendants" (I was not at all clear about this reference).

The covering letter from Joel Klein enclosing the settlement draft was also dated May 12, 1988, and the settlement draft itself was dated three days earlier. Essentially it put the six-part proposal, presented to the defendants' attorneys by Allen Snyder a month earlier, into proper legal language, with, however, some clarifications in the service of precision. The three major policy changes—which were actually all already in place—to which the American and the IPA would commit themselves for at least 10 years were the same as in the initial presentation by Snyder, with the following detailed specifications concerning the operation of the American's waiver process via the Davis Committee: It would be "at least at a level, and with a geographic distribution, generally consistent with the current process, which is based on the availability of qualified applicants," and the information was added that in the first year of implementation of the American's waiver process, 17 of the American's institutes had applied for a total of 38 waivers, of which 32 had been approved, and this had represented 28% of the total candidate body accepted for training by the American's institutes that year (these waivers being in addition to those approved under the research training program). Presumably, this would be the intended benchmark for future performance. Instead of automatic guaranteed waivers for the four individual plaintiffs, there would be a commitment to no discrimination against them because of their involvement in the suit (and some elaborate safeguards including rights of appeal and review were built in to assure this). The $650,000 figure remained, to come from the defendants collectively. The request to the court would be that the settlement class, as defined by the plaintiffs, be certified, that the settlement agreement be approved, and that the lawsuit then be dismissed, with prejudice, as settled. Obviously, if a settlement were agreed upon, it would be to the defendants' advantage that this cover the entire class as claimed by the plaintiffs so as to preclude the possibility of any future suits by dissatisfied individuals within that class.

Just a few days later, I received a letter, dated May 16, 1988, from Mary Libbey, editor of *Round Robin*, the newsletter of Section I of Division 39. I had previously sent her my exchanges of correspondence with Murray Meisels, suggesting that she might want to publish them in the interest of an even-handed explanatory exposition, since Meisels had already presented his side of the correspondence in another psychologist newsletter. This she regretfully declined to do, because "it would draw too much unnecessary attention to conflictual aspects of the process going on (like Dr. Meisels's letter has already done in another newsletter) without necessarily adding news." Instead, she invited me to submit an article to *Round Robin*, sharing my perspectives on the meaning or significance of any of the developments in the litigation process. In view of where the settlement talks now stood, her decision not to use the proffered correspondence turned out to have been the wisest, and I did not pursue the opportunity she offered me.

On the quickening pace of the settlement talks themselves, I next received a memorandum from Clint Fisher, dated May 19, 1988, which covered an enclosed draft of a proposed letter he had drawn up to send to Cliff Stromberg after telephone conversation with me. This was the beginning of the process of clarifying side-letters as support for the terms of the settlement agreement. This letter, in response to anxiety expressed by the plaintiffs and conveyed through Stromberg, read as follows:

> Dear Cliff: This will confirm that I have been authorized by the IPA to convey the following to you: Although the IPA has not yet determined the procedures whereby it will implement in good faith the policy embodied in the Amendments to Articles 5 and 6 of the IPA Constitution and By-laws adopted at the 1987 meeting, it is not the intention of the IPA to require as a condition of membership in the IPA that psychologists and other non-medical persons in the United States have been trained by a member or members of the American.

This statement was based, of course, on the approval by the IPA Executive Council a month earlier in England of the Hanly Committee sequential Procedures A, B, and C, for the evaluation of individual members of the new applicant groups.

This was followed the very next day by another memorandum from Fisher to me, stating that after two more lengthy battles with Stromberg, he had agreed to send for my consideration an altered, now "final version of the side letter" putting the IPA intentions positively rather than negatively, which in Stromberg's accompanying words was "probably the absolute minimum I can get my people to accept." The altered phrase now read, "It is the intention of the IPA to consider for membership in the IPA psychologists and other non-medical persons in the United States regardless of whether they have been trained by a member or members of the American." During this time of near daily back-and-forth contact between our attorneys and me, I was making very consequential day-by-day decisions on behalf of the IPA, with time only for telephone consultation with Ed Weinshel in San Francisco and discussion with Irene Auletta in London. I informed Fisher that I accepted this modification of the side letter.

On May 23, 1988, however, I received a memorandum from Clint Fisher reporting a tragic event. Judge Daronco had been killed over the weekend. For us, the impact was that, "Because a federal judge must approve the dismissal of cases before him, Judge Daronco's death may affect the timing of the settlement of this case." But the settlement talks marched on nonetheless. The next memorandum from Clint Fisher was dated four days later, May 27, 1988, and it came with an enclosed letter and attachments, a reworked draft of the settlement agreement dated May 19, 1988, which Fisher thought should not affect the IPA's position, though he solicited my views after I had a chance to review this new version. The accompanying letter from Snyder stated: "The plaintiffs feel strongly that the proposed agreement is a reasonable settlement for all parties. We are hopeful that all defendants agree with that assessment, and that it will be possible to resolve this litigation without further divisive and expensive court proceedings." Snyder's letter then went on to state that the plaintiffs had agreed to numerous proposed changes in the wording of the successive drafts of the agreement, in order to accommodate concerns raised by the defendants, and had done so without pressing for additional points desired by them. They looked at this present draft as a "bottom-line" product of the negotiation process, having made now a good-faith effort to respond to additional suggestions and proposals recently made by attorneys for the New York and Columbia institutes. They very much hoped that this would now resolve the issues raised by New York and Columbia so that those two groups could join the American and the IPA in agreeing to settle: "In our view, it would be highly unfortunate if any of the defendants refused to join, or withdrew from participation, in the proposed settlement." Basically, the latest alterations were two. One was the stipulation that none of the member institutes of the American would be *required* to participate in the program of training nonmedical candidates through the new waiver proceedings, only that this would be strongly urged. The other was the inserted statement that "nothing in this agreement shall be construed as an admission of liability or wrongdoing on the part of any of the defendants." This was now the new last-minute uncertainty, whether the New York and Columbia institutes would sign onto this settlement, which the other parties, the American, the IPA, and the plaintiffs, were now agreeing to.

Perhaps inevitably in this kind of legal negotiating, last-minute haggling still continued. On June 23, 1988, in the absence of Clint Fisher, Michael Morrissey of the same firm sent me a memorandum enclosing a copy of the proposed final judgment order, settling and dismissing the case, to be proposed to the judge. Apparently, Jack Auspitz, the attorney for the Columbia Institute, had indicated that before Columbia would take an official position concerning the draft settlement agreement (as once again refined in a June 7, 1988, letter), they would need to review the proposed final judgment that would be an attachment to the settlement agreement. That document was attached and seemed to present no difficulties for the

IPA. It defined the agreed-upon class as: "All persons who: (1) possess a doctoral degree in psychology; and (2) are licensed or certified as psychologists; and (3) have engaged in the practice of psychotherapy; and (4) have demonstrated their commitment to the psychoanalytic way of working." The accompanying letter from Snyder addressed to the attorneys for all four defendant groups ended with the plea: "As we have discussed, I believe it is extremely important that we move this process to a conclusion as rapidly as possible. Accordingly, please call me as soon as possible to let me know whether the proposed form of judgment is acceptable."

But on the same day, Christopher Hitchcock, from the firm representing the New York Institute, sent a letter to Allen Snyder offering his "principal comment" on the proposed final judgment. The New York Institute would not agree to pay any share of the cost of notice to the plaintiff class, unless New York were permitted to deduct that cost from the $650,000 payment referred to in the Settlement Agreement. About this, Michael Morrissey commented, in a memorandum to me dated June 30, 1988, that this should not affect the IPA's position and its willingness to sign this accord.

One "final" succeeded another. On July 12, 1988, Clint Fisher sent me a memorandum enclosing what Joel Klein had just described to him as "the final proposed draft agreement" between the plaintiffs, the American, and the IPA. By then it had been worked out that the Columbia and the New York institutes had agreed upon and would enter into a separate agreement with the plaintiffs. This final document contained no changes of substance, only (again) minor modifications, presumably clarifications, of wording. Fisher ended with a short paragraph: "Joel [Klein] says that plaintiffs' counsel would like a letter from us by Friday confirming that the IPA will accept this agreement. Because you have previously signed off on this document, unless I hear from you to the contrary I will send such a letter by telecopier on Thursday night. As I understand it, you will not need to actually sign the agreement until sometime after Friday." On July 14, 1988, Clint Fisher sent a one-sentence letter to Allen Snyder: "Dear Allen: This will confirm that the IPA accepts and will execute the Settlement Agreement in the form of the July 11, 1988 draft. Very truly yours." Thus settlement was finally agreed to and I was committed to sign. It had been nearly three years and five months since the initial filing. The claimed expenditure by the plaintiffs was approximately $650,000, with enough by all the defendant parties to bring the total well past the million-dollar mark, probably in the neighborhood of $1,300,000 (i.e., an amount for the combined defendants roughly equivalent to what the plaintiffs had spent).

This was the situation when the IPA Executive Council convened for a three-day meeting some two weeks later, July 29 to 31, at IPA headquarters in "Broomhills," London. The lawsuit and its consequences was again the most time-consuming item; only this time, the litigation proceedings and the settlement agreement (now wending its way through final legal steps) took up the least of the discussion time, and the planning for its full implementation along the lines charted by the Hanly Committee proposals was what became enormously time consuming. I began the discussion by informing the Council about the recent rush of events to the present, when the lawsuit was "on the verge of being settled completely." I reminded Council that, legally, matters still stood at the point where the plaintiffs had filed their motion for class action certification, the defendants had filed a countermotion, and the plaintiffs in turn had filed their response. The hearing on this matter before the judge was still pending.

In the meantime, there had been all the movement on both sides that I have chronicled to find if the suit could be settled by agreement out of court. In this there had been close cooperation between Joel Klein and Clint Fisher, lead attorneys for the American and the IPA. The plaintiffs apparently had been finding it harder to raise money for the continuation of the suit now that there was the alteration of the Regional Association agreement between the American and the IPA, with new possibilities for nonmedical people to be trained and accepted for membership both in the American and outside the American directly with the IPA. The basic six-point settlement agreement was presented to Council including, of course, the $650,000 monetary payment to reimburse the plaintiffs for their legal expenses. I indicated that Council should be aware that even if the defendants had chosen to continue the litigation, rather than settle, and "won" in the end, it could well cost even more than that reimbursement payment to do so. Out of all the negotiations amongst the defendants on this expense, the IPA was not being asked to contribute anything. Columbia held fast that it would not, and the final division was $450,000 by the American and $200,000 by the New York Institute (both covered by their respective insurance policies).

I also explained that there would be two settlement agreements, one signed by the American and the IPA, the other by the New York and Columbia institutes. The latter was still held up by haggling over details, including the continuing New York insistence that the expense of notifying its members of all the terms of the agreement within 30 days of its ratification by the judge be deducted from the settlement payment. Reviewing expenses, the IPA had overall spent $90,000 on the lawsuit up to the December 1986 agreement with the American, when the latter undertook to pick up 60% of the IPA's continuing legal costs. Since then, because of this agreement, and because of the considerable "piggy-backing" the IPA attorneys were able to do through their close working relationship with Joel Klein and his colleagues, the IPA had only spent an additional $25,000, making a total expense of $115,000 thus far. Significant as this was in relation to the always strained budget of the IPA, including its current near-bankrupt state, it was nevertheless a smaller amount than incurred by the other defendants and far less than the American had spent. And in all this recent time there had been close cooperation between the attorneys for the IPA and the American as well as between the officers of the two organizations. It was, of course, to be understood by Council that all this information was all still confidential; it would not be public until all parties had signed the settlement documents, and they were all ratified by the judge.

In the ensuing discussion, Adam Limentani stated that it could be said that the plaintiffs had won their case after all. Edward Weinshel averred the contrary, that neither the American nor the IPA was being forced into doing anything that they were not already doing. Arnold Cooper added that nothing was being imposed on member societies and institutes by the American, that the opening for the training of nonmedical people was permissive, not compulsory with the individual institutes. Harald Leupold-Lowenthal remarked that the American nonetheless had been pushed to give the IPA the possibility of admitting (nonmedical) groups outside the framework of the American, directly to IPA affiliation. I offered my view that this was not simply a "victory" of the plaintiffs over the defendants, because nothing was being legally imposed upon the IPA that was contrary to its wishes; we had maintained what was most important to us, the right to set and monitor our own standards. In that sense it was also very much a "victory" for the defendants. Limentani stated that all this should be explained and clarified by me in the Presidential column in the next IPA *Newsletter,* which I indicated I would do in the first issue after the settlement was legally finalized.

The greater bulk of the time devoted to lawsuit issues and their organizational consequences at this three-day, full IPA Executive Council meeting was spent on the Hanly Committee draft of principles and procedures for the evaluation of the applicant "New Groups" in the United States, including full discussion of the preliminary information from the initial site visits that had already been conducted with the first two of them, IPTAR and NYFS, both in New York. The detailed minutes of this discussion filled 20 pages, single spaced, of legal sized paper. The central thrust of the lengthy, at times seemingly interminable, to-and-fro had to do with the many apprehensions voiced about the innovative and creative proposed procedures for the evaluation of both the applicant groups and their individual members, as outlined in the several drafts of the Hanly Committee proposals detailed in the preceding chapter and this one. We discussed how evaluations could be conducted in a manner that would be both comprehensive *and* feasible (given the constraints of available resources in time, money, and manpower) and at the same time would properly safeguard the IPA's commitment to the integrity of its training standards.

The many possible pitfalls, worst-case scenarios, political (and public relations) pressures from the applicant groups and from the watchful plaintiffs to the lawsuits were all elaborated. We discussed the concerns of apprehensive members of the American that the IPA would willingly, or reluctantly under pressure, admit groups or individuals whose training qualifications and standards were deemed inferior to those of the American, thus giving credence to the fear that these "coerced" decisions to admit independent psychoanalytic training groups in the United States directly into the IPA (outside the framework of the American) would result in a two-tier standard of psychoanalytic accreditation in the United States, and a downward pressure on the American's own cherished standards of excellence. A number of times I pointed out that we now seemed collectively fearful about implementing something that we all (at least all the Europeans and Latin Americans and many of the North Americans) had been ostensibly wanting and working for over a very long period of time.

In all of this, Weinshel was an invaluable ally, especially from his position of past-Chairman of the Board on Professional Standards of the American and his long identification as one of those most strongly committed to the maintenance of the integrity and quality of the American's training standards. In his presentation to the group he again emphasized that we were not dealing with a routine or ordinary situation, but one that was unique to the organizational history of psychoanalysis in the United States. We were dealing, at this point, with procedures to be applied to well-organized, functioning psychoanalytic groups that had long histories and highly visible track records, both as groups and in the individuals comprising them. Altered or innovative procedures did not necessarily equate with altered or lowered standards. After all, we were in no position to do everything in an ideal way—as if time didn't matter and resources for the task were endless—and given all this, it was indeed necessary to invoke and creatively deploy conceptions such as waivers, functional equivalence, and grandfathering. It was emphasized by both of us, and by some others as well, that "waivers" or their equivalents would only apply to past activities and achievements, in order to rectify historical inequities that it was beyond the control of either the applicants or ourselves to undo, and that each of the applicant groups would be required, as a condition of their acceptance, to immediately alter whatever current operating policies and procedures differed from, or fell short of, IPA requirements and standards, so as to operate henceforth in full compliance with the IPA's standards of functioning.

Considerable time was also spent in detailed review of the reports from the two site visits already carried out, the one to IPTAR, chaired by Hanly, and the one to NYFS, chaired by Sachs. One of these had gone exceedingly well and the other had run into problems, yet the two groups had long been vying with each other for recognition as the leadership or the elite independent nonmedical psychoanalytic training group in the New York area (albeit with some overlap in the memberships of the two groups). With one of the groups, a contentious and adversarial tone had gotten into the site visit proceedings. One side charged that the Site Visit Committee brought preformed biases to the evaluation, for instance, that thrice-weekly analyses were inherently unsatisfactory, and that supervision practices that differed in any way from those current in the American were necessarily inadequate. The other side charged that real and troubling problems in the group functioning were being uncovered, in the largely self-selection process for achieving training analyst status, in the melding, without proper distinction, of psychotherapy and psychoanalytic training procedures, and so forth. None of this seemed really insoluble, and it all would be dealt with on the successor visits, but there was a very aggrieved tone to part of the visited group's reactions: they were being mistreated as well as disappointed; the site visit was not *pro forma;* acceptance for IPA affiliation was not immediate and automatic; and further, it was not an *en bloc* approval process, and all of the group's members might not make it. Beyond this lay the spectre of the unhappy fallout for the IPA and the New York psychoanalytic scene if these differences could not be resolved prior to the IPA Congress in Rome at the end of July 1989, and if only one of the first two site-visited groups were to win IPA acceptance at that Congress while the other had not yet been acted upon or had been deferred.

Other matters brought up in this context were that the IPA had received official inquiries about consideration for affiliation from 23 groups around the country—13 in New York, five in Los Angeles, five in other places—and that six of these had already presented sufficient credentials on paper as to warrant IPA site visits. These additional four were two in New York (NYCPT and NPAP) and two in Los Angeles (LAISPS and PCC). A last, and potentially even more explosive, problem for the integrity of organized psychoanalysis in the United States and for future relations between the IPA and the American, came up for considerable discussion. What if disaffected societies or institutes of the American, unhappy with their relationship with the Executive Council or Board on Professional Standards, were to try to secede from the American and seek direct affiliation with the IPA, as was now possible under the altered Regional Association agreement between the IPA and the American? This would be an enormous (potential) threat to the integrity of the American's functioning. Yet, could it really be blocked within the revised operating rules?

It was agreed that such an eventuality was indeed a political mine field and potentially a constitutional "grey area"; hopefully, a situation putting it to the test would never arise. But it was indeed already a matter of concern to the leadership of the American, and I had already received a letter of inquiry concerning the IPA's attitude in regard to this possibility from Homer Curtis in his status as President of the American. All that I could properly assure him was that this would be, in the first instance, a problem for the American to deal with internally and that the IPA would in no way encourage or invite such a move on the part of any of the American's component groups.

That was clearly IPA policy. Splits had occurred, however, in various IPA component organizations (just as they had occurred in affiliated groups of the American), and in various places around the world (Paris, Buenos Aires, Rio de Janeiro) both groups were now IPA affiliated, the parent group (which had retained its IPA status) and the split-off group (which after a proper site-visit evaluation process had earned IPA-affiliated status). Actually, in the eight years between that discussion and this writing (1988-96), this divisive threat has never been brought up by a single society or institute of the American, despite the many controversial and contentious issues that have come to the fore during this period in the American's history, including episodes of acute tension between the Council and Board of the American over fundamental administrative and training issues in the organization.

On August 9, 1988, Clint Fisher wrote a letter to Charles Hanly in response to the latter's question about the constitutionality of the IPA accepting groups with two classes of members, those who did and those who did not meet the IPA criteria for individual IPA membership. It was Fisher's legal opinion, buttressed by a memorandum, dated the previous day, addressed to Fisher by Michael Morrissey of the same firm, that no constitutional issue would be posed. Morrissey's memorandum, based on his legal research into the matter, opined that (1) actions by private bodies are not state actions and generally private actions do not implicate the equal protection clause, and (2) even if a member of an affiliated society who did not qualify for IPA membership chose to sue, alleging that the IPA discriminated against a class comprised of psychologists who did not meet IPA standards, it was unlikely that such a suit would receive a sympathetic reception in the courts. This was an example of a preemptive action—a request for anticipatory legal opinion—by Hanly in conscientiously building every possible safeguard into the implementation of his committee's recommendations.

On August 10, Clint Fisher sent me a memorandum indicating that Stromberg had called to advise him that the plaintiffs had now approved the draft settlement agreement "subject to the clarification of three points." One of those was relevant to the IPA, and in advance of the letter detailing these, Stromberg "informally" conveyed the substance. Regarding the IPA, there was concern that the plaintiffs desired "a good-faith letter" from the IPA, describing "loosely" what the IPA would be looking for in determining whether an organization is "qualified for membership" within the terms of the settlement agreement. The specific issue was whether the IPA would require every approved individual to have been analyzed more than three times per week or would be willing to give such an individual "fluid treatment." Stromberg had given Fisher the distinct impression that the plaintiffs would be satisfied with a statement that the IPA would not insist on a hard and fast requirement on this point; they would be satisfied with a general (and short) description of the IPA's understanding of the "functional equivalence" concept. Stromberg had also assured Fisher that the three points for clarification "will be the last" and that there are "no more outstanding issues."

On that same date, a letter had been sent by Allen Snyder to Klein, Fisher, Bunim, and Auspitz, lead attorneys for the four defendant groups, outlining the three points of clarifications that the plaintiffs sought in relation to the proposed settlement agreement with the American and the IPA (dated June 9, 1988) and that with the New York and Columbia Institutes (dated July 11, 1988). They were: (1) clarification by the American of the detailed policies and procedures regarding the admissions and training processes under the CORST program (Committee on Research and Special Training, renamed from the earlier Committee on Training for Research) and the CNMCT program (Committee on Non-Medical Clinical Training, the Davis Committee); (2) clarification by the IPA of the concepts *qualified groups* and *functional equivalence*, "so that all parties will have a similar understanding of the meaning of the operative terms of the agreement," and whether the training model would have to be within the prevalent ego psychology paradigm of the American or could subscribe to other psychoanalytic theoretical orientations; and (3) clarification by the American of the mechanisms to be employed to ensure "nondiscrimination" and "nonretaliation" against the four specific plaintiffs in the lawsuit regarding their ongoing and future training within institutes of the American, with evaluation "solely on their merits" and provision "that any negative feelings that may have been generated by the lawsuit do not pose a practical barrier to achieving the objectives of paragraph 4A," which referred to this specific issue concerning the plaintiffs. Stromberg ended his letter with a very positive statement: "The plaintiffs feel that the proposed settlement is a positive and constructive step toward resolving not only this litigation, but also some of the larger issues that have divided us, and toward avoiding a recurrence of problems of this type in the future."

A few days later, on August 15, 1988, Clint Fisher sent me a memorandum with a draft response to Allen Snyder's letter asking for my input and approval. Concerning the evaluation of organized psychoanalytic groups, Fisher indicated that the IPA expected to determine whether the group was cohesive, and in fact functioning adequately, and if so, whether the group's training was functionally equivalent to IPA sanctioned training. A similar assessment of functional equivalence would be applied to individuals. For example, in response to a hypothetical question posed by Snyder, Fisher responded that:

> An individual who has had seven hundred hours of personal analysis on a three times per week basis will not automatically be granted or denied admission to the IPA; it would be expected,

however, that such individuals would be admitted to the IPA if in all other respects their training and qualifications were equivalent to those required by the IPA's minimum standards. Upon admission to the IPA, members must follow the IPA's training standards, including four times per week analysis.

In response to the question of whether the IPA would require a training model or theoretical orientation that is "exclusively or predominantly Freudian," that would depend, in Fisher's proposed statement, "upon the meaning you apply to the term 'Freudian.' The IPA applies a broad definition of the term." He went on to state, as example, that "a Sullivanian orientation such as that of the William Alanson White Institute is not precluded by IPA criteria." This letter was sent off by Fisher to Snyder on August 16, 1988, after receiving my OK. On August 18, 1998, Joel Klein sent in his comparable (in substance and tone) letter of clarification to Allen Snyder.

Meanwhile, the final draft of the Settlement Agreement came back to me for review actually unaltered from the May 12, 1988, draft I have already described. On September 7, 1988, Cliff Stromberg, in a very brief letter, replied to the clarification letters he had received from Fisher (August 16) and Klein (August 18). He said that there were certain points that were still unclear, or about which the two sides might have different views, but nonetheless:

> I am pleased to state that based on this additional information, the plaintiffs have now approved the settlement embodied in the June 9 proposed settlement agreement with the American and IPA, the July 11 proposed settlement agreement with New and Columbia, and the July 19 proposed final judgment applicable to both agreements. Our clients are prepared to execute the settlement documents as quickly as possible. Please let me know when your clients can do so. We can then prepare papers and submit the settlement to the Court forthwith. We appreciate your cooperation in this long, but fruitful, process.

On September 8, 1988, Fisher passed this letter on to me with a very brief covering memo that included: "It looks as though the IPA can finally put this episode behind it. Please let me know your availability for executing the settlement documents." On that same day, Joel Klein sent the final settlement agreement to Homer Curtis, President of the American, asking him to sign it and then express mail it to me for my signature, after which it was to be returned to Klein for forwarding to the plaintiffs for execution.

While these final steps in the settlement were being ratified, the fall 1988 issue of *Psychologist Psychoanalyst,* the official Newsletter of Division

39, appeared, carrying two articles bearing on the lawsuit. One was by Bryant Welch, headed, "Lawsuit: Negotiated Settlement"; the other, also on the settlement, was by Zanvel A. Liff, President of Division 39, headed, "From the President's Desk." Welch's article was overall a very balanced and judicious account of the issues of the lawsuit and the final settlement agreement. It began:

> After nearly three years of litigation and five months of negotiating, I am pleased to report that the respective parties have agreed to a negotiated settlement of the lawsuit. Under the terms of the agreement, the defendants have agreed to resolve and correct the multiple complaints that psychologists have held against them for decades . . . [though] it is expressly understood that the agreement does not constitute an admission of any such wrongdoings by the defendants [p. 1].

Welch then spelled out the substance of the agreement. The IPA would admit all psychoanalytically qualified psychologists under the rubric of "functional equivalency" (a species of grandfathering). Prior training and supervised analyses conducted at a frequency of fewer than four times per week would be acceptable, "if performed over an extended period of time and as part of an overall course of training which would otherwise be satisfactory" (p. 1). One need not have been trained by IPA members, and theoretical diversity would be accepted, "so long as it is broadly construed to be within the 'Freudian' realm which, according to the International, includes the Sullivanian theoretical orientation" (p. 1). Welch further indicated that the American had agreed that its members could teach outside of its own framework without fear of sanction, and that it would "admit significant numbers of psychologists and other qualified mental health professionals to its own Institutes under a non-discriminatory waiver policy" (p. 2). He stated that shortly after being advised of the pending lawsuit, the American had established "the Gaskill-Davis process," and that by the end of the first year of its implementation, 28% of the candidates admitted to its member institutes were CNMCT or "Gaskill-Davis" waiver candidates, with an additional 10% being CORST candidates. This 38% figure was hailed as very substantial, and Welch said that the plaintiffs had stipulated with the American "that if they would maintain the 38% figure as a *minimal* floor under the number of non-medical candidates (and eliminate the procedural difficulties and possibilities for future discrimination), we would accept that as an appropriate minimal level of involvement for non-medical participants in their Institutes" (p. 2). Be it noted, however, that no such numerical quota or floor had been specified in the settlement agreement that Curtis and I had signed.

Welch declared that this overall agreement adequately corrected the injustices to which psychologist analysts had been subjected in the past. He added that the plaintiffs would be reimbursed $650,000 to cover the legal and other costs entailed by the lawsuit, and that, additionally, provision had been made to ensure that the four plaintiffs themselves would not be discriminated against in any way in their future involvement with institutes of the American. All this would, of course, be subject to notification to all members of the psychologist class on whose behalf the lawsuit had been launched, and they would have the right to come to a court hearing to object to, and exclude themselves from, the settlement agreement if they wished to do so. It was also subject to the judge's determination that the settlement agreement is in the interest of the class members and is one that he would approve. Welch stated toward the end that "naturally, we are delighted with these developments and certainly commend the leaders of the American and the International Psycho-Analytical Associations, as well as their attorneys, for their important role in this process" (p. 2).

Liff, in his article, spoke more to the impact of the settlement on Division 39 and on its future, as well as the future of psychoanalytic psychology within organized psychology—the American Psychological Association—as a whole. He began with the statement that "pending court approval, the lawsuit settlement will become a major victory for the entire psychoanalytic community" (p. 3) and he congratulated the four plaintiffs for their "demonstrated heroic courage in fighting the legal battle" (p. 3). He then asked, in effect, where do we, the community of psychoanalytic psychologists, go from here? He stated that the first mandate of the Division 39 constitution was a call for the expansion of psychoanalytic contributions to psychology: "It is my intention to inject more psychoanalytic knowledge into the American psychology corpus, especially the American Psychological Association. With their present state of distress, they could use some psychoanalytic wisdom. As is well known, Freud did consider psychoanalysis to be part of psychology rather than medicine" (p. 3). He went on to state that Division 39 at that point had 18 local chapters, many of them supporting psychoanalytic training programs. He said: "Our ultimate goal is not to be dependent on the Institutes of the American Psychoanalytic Association, but rather to develop our own network of analytic Institute programs. Even with the lawsuit victory, we must remember, it is *their* doors which are opening. We want to build our own house with our own doors" (p. 4). Toward the end, Liff stated, "The lawsuit settlement has elevated our self-esteem and we can now approach our mission with renewed vigor" (p. 4).

On October 6, 1988, Allen Snyder again wrote to the attorneys representing the four defendant groups, attaching the draft of the proposed class notice, the document notifying all the agreed-upon class members that a settlement of the lawsuit had been reached on their behalf, and offering them the opportunity to object and exclude themselves from the settlement agreement if they so desired. Snyder also indicated that he was completing a draft of a proposed joint motion to the court, seeking preliminary approval of the settlement agreement and of the proposed class notice for publication, and would be circulating this soon to all the defendants' attorneys for review and approval. It would be proposed to the court that this settlement notice be published verbatim in the *Monitor*, the newsletter of the American Psychological Association, and be sent by first-class mail to all members of Division 39, with the plaintiffs and the defendants as a group each bearing half the costs of the notice. Snyder further indicated that he was drafting a proposed plaintiffs' memorandum, attempting, in a neutral way, to describe the case background, the nature of the settlement, and the legal standards for court review of a proposed class action settlement such as this. Though he thought it most appropriate that this be a plaintiffs' class representative memorandum, he said he would be happy to share it with all the defendants' attorneys prior to filing, so that everyone could see the entire package before it was put together and submitted to the court.

The attached draft of the Notice of Proposed Class Settlement was addressed to "All Psychologists with Doctoral Degrees who Practice Psychotherapy." It was headed by the statement: "This Notice may affect your rights: Please read carefully." The document began by stating the purposes and conditions of the lawsuit and then specified the class it purportedly represented, doctoral degree psychologists, licensed or certified as psychologists, and engaged or trained in the practice of psychotherapy. After detailing the terms of the proposed settlement, it continued:

> This settlement does not represent a decision in favor of one side or the other. Each party believes its original position was correct. The settlement simply means that all parties decided to end the case before the Court makes a final decision one way or the other. If approved, the settlement will discharge the defendants from any further liability to any and all class members for the conduct alleged by the plaintiffs; there will be no restrictions or limitations on any defendant, or damages paid by them, other than as provided by the settlement agreements.

It was then reiterated that if approved by the court, in return for the benefits and opportunities received by the plaintiff class, no member of that class could have further recourse to injunctive relief and/or monetary damages for any of the alleged conduct of the defendants that had been presented to the court in the plaintiffs' filing of the lawsuit. It was therefore incumbent upon any member of the plaintiff class who took exception to this settlement to appear, together with counsel if desired, before the court on the specified hearing date to voice such objection. Of course, if the court did not approve the proposed settlement, the case would continue to be prepared for trial or for other judicial resolution of the claims and defenses, and of course further discovery would remain to be conducted before such trial.

Less than a week after this letter by Snyder with its attached documents, I received a memorandum from Clint Fisher, dated October 12, 1988, enclosing my copy of the fully executed settlement agreement between the plaintiffs and the American and IPA, signed by the four plaintiffs, by Homer Curtis for the American, and by me for the IPA. This was followed by a letter dated October 13 from Homer Curtis to all members of the American, announcing the settlement of the lawsuit in the same way that Bryant Welch had announced it in the Fall, 1988 issue of *Psychologist Psychoanalyst* published in September. Curtis's letter advised all members of the American that negotiations over the past several months had resulted in a settlement agreement of the lawsuit, which had by now been filed with the court, and was still of course subject to court approval before becoming final. Curtis then indicated that he would review the terms of the agreement and the process to be followed regarding its approval.

First Curtis stated that because of some differences in the interests of the different defendants, there were two settlement agreements, one involving the American and the IPA, the other the New York and Columbia institutes. He then pointed out that though the defendants had opposed the lawsuit being litigated as a class action, they had agreed to settle only on a classwide basis—in order to obviate having to litigate the same issues with other psychologists at some other time—and this had been accomplished. Accordingly, all future claims, monetary or injunctive, regarding the matters covered by the lawsuit would be permanently extinguished. In outlining the terms of the settlement, Curtis began by stating that "in substance, the settlement requires us to adhere to policies that we already have adopted and are implementing." He identified these as (1) the agreement that members of the American, "consistent with their own best judgment," were free to teach in psychoanalytic training programs outside the American; (2) the agreement that the American would continue to implement the program of nonmedical clinical training, "at a level generally consistent with the current process," (but without quotas or numerical requirements); (3) the agreement that there be no discrimination or retaliation against any psychologist plaintiff consequent to this litigation; and (4) the agreement that $650,000 would be paid to the plaintiff class, "by or on behalf of Defendants," to reimburse the legal fees of the plaintiffs, and to be paid by the insurance carriers of the two defendants who had such insurance, the American and the New York Institute (the bulk of it by the American's carrier).

For its part, the IPA had agreed "to implement in good faith and according to existing IPA standards," the recent bylaw changes regarding applications for affiliation by existing independent nonmedical psychoanalytic training programs in the United States outside the American. Curtis then stated that because this litigation was being resolved on a classwide basis, court review and approval was necessary, and that this review process could still take several months before final court approval in order to assure all class members adequate opportunity to object to, and if they wished, to opt out of, the terms of the settlement agreement, which, without such stated voluntary withdrawal, would legally bind all class members to its terms. Curtis ended his letter, "We are confident that the agreement is in the best interests of our Association and that it compromises none of the principles that we stand for and have fought hard to protect. We believe that the litigation had diverted our organizational attention and energies away from the important issues that face our profession at this time. We are hopeful that the agreement will soon be approved by the court and that we can then refocus our full energies on these other issues." My own parenthetical note on this letter: I have always regarded it as a most felicitous happenstance that Homer Curtis, who had played so signal a role as Chairman of the American's Committee on Prerequisites for Training (over the span from 1975 to 1981) in charting the course of the American's opening to the full clinical psychoanalytic training of qualified nonmedical mental health professionals, should be the president of the American during the successful 1988 negotiating process that ended the lawsuit, and thereby became, together with me, signatory to the final agreement that settled this nettlesome issue, hopefully once and for all, on behalf of our two organizations in which we have both participated over so many years.

In a final coda to the events of this chapter, on October 18, I wrote a letter of acknowledgment and thanks to Clint Fisher. In it I said that I wanted, for myself and officially on behalf of the IPA, to thank him and Trip Dorkey, "for all that you have done to bring this about and especially for helping guide me and the other involved IPA officers through these legal thickets in a way that has kept it from being any more burdensome or debilitating than really an absolute minimum. I appreciate all the help and I have appreciated our association, and although I hope that we don't have to be involved with each other over this kind of matter again, that we do have other occasions to be in touch with each other."

Replies came from both Clint Fisher and Trip Dorkey. Fisher's came dated November 2, 1988. It thanked me and stated that "lawsuits are not always interesting and enjoyable, but, to the extent that they can be so, this one certainly has been for me. It has been a pleasure to work with you, Ed, Irene and the other IPA officials and members with whom we have come in contact during the past three and a half years. I share your hope that we have occasion to be in touch again." Dorkey's letter, dated November 8, 1988, came a few days later: "Although a little (very little) work remains to be done on this lawsuit, I think it is sufficiently over that it would be safe to say how much of a pleasure it has been representing you. All of the people from the IPA whom I have met have brought a mature reflective judgment to this lawsuit that I have found both helpful, enjoyable and interesting. I hope our paths cross again in the future without the necessity of a lawsuit being the moving force. If I can ever be of help to you, please let me know." Since then, both Dorkey and Fisher have moved to another law firm, also in New York, and periodically I receive a Christmas greeting card from Dorkey; I also had a friendly exchange of letters with him at the time of his move to the new firm.

The 1989 IPA Congress
Resolution of the Issue

T he November 1988 issue of *The Psychiatric Times*, a monthly newsletter calling itself "The Newspaper of American Psychiatry," and distributed to nearly 40,000 U.S. psychiatrists (a competitor of the official newsletter of the American Psychiatric Association, *The Psychiatric News*), carried as its lead story an account of the lawsuit settlement, under the headline Psychologists Win Over Analysts. The opening sentence began: "American psychologists have achieved a victory as a result of an antitrust lawsuit initiated in March 1985." Bryant Welch was then quoted in the opening paragraph, outlining the terms of the settlement as a sequence of actions that the American and the IPA were now obligated to take and indicating, as well, the monetary compensation to the plaintiffs. It was stated that representatives of the American had declined to comment to the reporter. For my part, I had never been contacted.

Welch then gave a short history of the lawsuit, stressing several sequences: the series of four committees of the American over the decade from the mid-seventies to the mid-eighties which had failed to lead to corrective action by the American; the "turning point" that Welch felt was represented by Melvin Sabshin's warning speech to the American in December 1983, followed by the American's tabling of the issue in May 1984 in San Diego; the abortive meetings with the officers of the American in October 1984, again quoting Ed Joseph that this was a "pocketbook issue" on which the American would not yield; and the initiation of the suit itself, followed by a summary statement of the principal arguments on both sides of the antitrust issue. Welch did concede that after the filing of the lawsuit, the defendants had taken some steps to facilitate the admission of psychologists into full psychoanalytic training programs, but he stated that, "typically, the way antitrust litigation is resolved is that the defendants, once the lawsuit is filed, begin to take corrective steps with regard to their procedures. I certainly commend the American Psychoanalytic Association for doing that."

As for the plaintiffs, Welch indicated that "financial considerations are not irrelevant. But, I think it is fair to say that the plaintiffs and the class we represent are idealistically motivated and that the thing which has really fueled the lawsuit is our concern about quality training. I don't mean to imply that we have not been hurt financially. We certainly have. But it is basically our commitment to psychoanalysis that has motivated us to take the steps that we have taken." This article was the first public account of the lawsuit settlement, and I suppose I should have expected not only the spin that Welch gave it, but also the apparent ready acceptance of this argument within the psychiatric world: The psychologist plaintiffs had been locked in combat with the self-serving psychoanalysts and had been able to force a settlement on the unwilling defendants, that is, had "won" the case.

This, of course, was not my spin on the case and its outcome, and on November 9, 1988, I wrote a corrective letter to John Schwartz, publisher and editor-in-chief of *The Psychiatric Times*.

> Certainly, from the point of view of where the psychologists were when the lawsuit was initiated and where they are now . . . it can be seen as a very substantial victory. At the same time, from my perspective, both personally and as President of the International Psychoanalytical Association, it is also a victory for psychoanalysis. . . . I could add that the specific terms of the settlement (apart from the monetary aspects) have confirmed changes that have come about in the procedures and policies of both the American and the International Psychoanalytical Associations over these several years and are practically identical with a proposal made by the International Psychoanalytical Association through its attorney as a basis for settlement some two years earlier. For various reasons, that was not agreeable to the other involved parties at that time and so the litigation did go on further, though, as you know, it was still not at the stage of coming to actual trial. Certainly, the terms of the settlement represent the embodiment of the position that the majority membership of the International Psychoanalytical Association have taken throughout the course of this affair.

On November 14, 1988, Homer Curtis, as President of the American, added his voice to this dialogue in a long letter to the entire membership. He stated that he had, "received a number of calls from members who have been distressed by the propaganda campaign in the press being carried on by the plaintiffs in the litigation." He expressed his regret that the settlement was being represented as a victory in which the psychologists had "forced us to change our principles and policies to fit their demands." He iterated that the settlement agreement was voluntary, not judicial, "one that accommodated the interests of both parties and had the potential for fostering a conciliatory and amicable relationship in the best interests of the field of psychoanalysis." However, in place of our understanding that a public announcement of the settlement would not be made until it had been delivered to the court—which was only accomplished on November 14—the plaintiffs had called a press conference on October 12, directly after the signing of the settlement agreement, in order to proclaim victory.

Curtis briefly reviewed the history of the Gaskill proposal, from the appointment of the committee in December 1984 (three months before the filing of the lawsuit) to its adoption by a more than two-thirds majority of the American's membership in May 1986. He then asserted that: (1) the American's new policies had been established voluntarily through the organization's natural evolutionary processes; (2) the American had not been forced to renounce the interdiction against its members teaching in training settings outside its framework, because no such formal prohibition had ever existed; (3) that the American had never monopolized the training for and practice of psychoanalysis in the United States, because it had "neither the intent nor the power" to enforce such monopoly; and (4) it was the insurance carriers who decided to pay the $650,000 sum, based on their judgment that this would be more economical than continuing the litigation, especially if it went to trial (and payment of this sum was solely for legal fees, not for "damages"). Finally Curtis stated, "While the plaintiffs offered us this settlement in April 1988, it is essentially the basic proposal we offered to them in October 1986.[1] It is regrettable that this was not accepted at that time, which would have spared both sides the expense and distraction of the past two years."

Of course from my perspective, that of the IPA, it was not only the plaintiffs but the American that were not ready for the achieved settlement agreement in October (or rather, May) 1986, and for me this was therefore a double regret. From the perspective of the plaintiffs, strong exception would

---

[1] Actually, the substance of the settlement proposal that we offered the plaintiffs had been worked out even earlier, at that May 31, 1986, meeting that I had called at the Waldorf-Astoria in New York, at which I had been convinced that we had actually come to agreement on the terms of a mutually satisfactory settlement, to be then put into proper legal language by the plaintiffs' lead attorney, Cliff Stromberg. The October date Curtis referred to was the time of our formal counterproposal (reiterating the substance of what I felt we had all agreed to on May 31) after Stromberg had formalized a totally unacceptable version of that May agreement, delivered to us in midsummer, and which we, the defendants, felt was far beyond what we had all agreed upon, and in ways that were in principle unacceptable, and in practice not possible of fulfillment.

be taken, no doubt, to the minimization in Curtis's letter of the pressure of the litigation, even in advance of the formal filing of the lawsuit, in bringing the about-face in the counsels of the American between April 1984 in San Diego, when the American decided, after ten years of study and deliberation, to table all consideration of opening its doors to the full clinical training of nonphysicians for the practice of psychoanalysis, to the reversal in December 1984 in New York with the appointment of the Gaskill Committee to urgently seek an acceptable resolution of this vexing issue.

Curtis followed this with a letter to *The New York Times*, December, 8, 1986, replying to its inaccurate commentaries, including in letters to the editor, concerning the issues of the lawsuit and its settlement, which could only lead to general confusion among its readership. He particularly referred to a letter printed on November 26, in which a representative of a group of analysts in New York, who wished to preserve psychoanalysis as a medical specialty, attacked what they characterized as the capitulation of the American and the IPA. It stated (inaccurately) that the Columbia Institute had stood properly aloof from the settlement. Curtis's contention in response, after correcting the inaccurate reference to the actions of the Columbia group, was embodied in an overall statement, similar to his letter to the membership of the American.

> The settlement represents a reasonable accommodation of the interests of all parties and does not entail any sacrifice of our principles and procedures. It was not forced upon us by the plaintiffs, who agreed to a settlement substantively the same as the one we proposed in October 1986.[2] It was not "necessitated by legal exhaustion," but rather by a mutual recognition that there was agreement on the basic issues. Nor was it forced on us by our insurance carriers who, in view of that agreement, consented to pay the plaintiffs' legal fees (not damages) as is usual in voluntary settlement

The New York Times, however, did not print Curtis's letter.

This psychoanalytic contretemps was picked up in the December 19, 1988 issue of the weekly newsletter *Behavior Today*. That article quoted the analyst writer of the *New York Times* letter as stating that "The person who walks into the consulting room of a psychoanalyst with the problems we see in daily practice cannot be properly diagnosed or treated by anyone lacking medical and psychiatric training." He had gone on to state that the American and the IPA had agreed to settle the suit only because of financial exhaustion, but that with Columbia the suit had not been settled; it had simply been

---

[2] Again, actually May 1986, as described in footnote 1.

discontinued. *Behavior Today* itself commented that this seemed like "public notice that although the door to the psychoanalytic institutes may now be open, the welcome mat—as far as the letter writer is concerned—is not in front of it."

Behavior Today then quoted Bryant Welch, who dismissed these remarks "as a matter of an individual's personality style," and went on to a lengthy rebuttal as well by Homer Curtis, in part repeating what he had put into his response to *The New York Times*. Curtis said of the letter writer:

> He represents that point of view about which he has been very verbal. It is not a point of view prominent in the American Psychoanalytic. In that letter [to *The New York Times*] he said that Columbia had not joined us in the settlement. That's entirely wrong. They did in fact agree. We all signed the settlement together, Columbia, New York, the International and the American Psychoanalytic. I don't know where he got that information from.

I also entered into this argument, writing clarifying letters, similar to those of Curtis, but from the perspective of the IPA, both to *Behavior Today* (on January 10, 1989) and to *The New York Times*, which the *Times* did publish on December 24, 1988.[3] My letter (printed in abbreviated form by the *Times*) stated that the analyst writer of the original letter to the *Times* had seriously misstated as well as distorted the basis of the lawsuit settlement.; I had been one of the principal parties to the long drawn-out three-and-a-half-year negotiation process and was one of the signatories to the final settlement, and could state that: "The settlement agreement is one that, we have all agreed, is eminently fair to all parties and, in fully maintaining the standards of training, serves the overall best interests of organized psychoanalysis and of the public as well." I made the same disclaimer as Curtis, that the settlement had not come through legal or financial exhaustion, but that rather it was a proper and fair settlement that safeguarded "the highest psychoanalytic trianing standards and quality of care for our patients, while properly accommodating the grievances of the plaintiff class."

Meanwhile, the public relations battle over who "won" the lawsuit continued; another first-page article appeared in *The Psychiatric Times* in the very next monthly issue (December 1988). In this one the headline read "Voluntary Settlement of Suit Called Victory for Psychoanalysis." Here Curtis was quoted, contra Welch, that "the voluntary settlement represented a victory for the entire field of psychoanalysis and a reaffirmation of training

---

[3] See p. 323 for the circumstances under which my letter was published.

policies already in effect as the lawsuit progressed." The long article further on quoted Joel Klein: "Joel Klein, J.D., the attorney for 'the American,' pointed out that the voluntary settlement requires nothing of the Association that wasn't already a policy before the settlement. The $650,000 voluntary settlement to the plaintiffs in the lawsuit for their legal fees will be paid not by any of the four groups who were defendants in the lawsuit, but rather by their liability insurance carriers."

The same issue of *The Psychiatric Times* carried a lengthy interview with Bryant Welch. In this discussion Welch struck a much more conciliatory and accommodating tone than in earlier press conferences (for example, in *The Wall Street Journal*, October 13), perhaps because here he was specifically addressing the psychiatric audience and wanted this time to begin to forge a common cause.

> Both psychology and psychiatry have a great deal to contribute. They each have strengths and weaknesses. The trick is to come up with a system that enables us to take advantage of the strengths of each system but to also safeguard against the potential weaknesses or excesses of one profession or the other. . . . There's a lot that we can learn from each other if we can learn to speak to each other constructively, and if we can preserve the independence of *both* groups.

In an even further explicit accommodation he stated, "Personally, I think it's something where both plaintiffs and defendants basically won. I think that the American can be very pleased that they've protected all of their standards for training and maintained the integrity of their system of training, and certainly psychologists are very happy that they will now have the opportunity to pursue quality psychoanalytic training."

Welch made a comparable bow to the IPA:

> The International as far as I can tell has been dealing with the issue in very good faith. They've established what are called functional equivalents for the standards of the IPA. The International requires that one be trained by a member of the International. Now it would obviously make the settlement agreement meaningless if you take psychologists who haven't been allowed to be trained and then impose that requirement on them. So my understanding is that the IPA is agreeing that they will look to the training the individual has actually received, and if it's functionally equivalent to the membership standards, then those psychologists will be eligible for admission.

Then in a broadly ecumenical statement covering the entire field of mental health care, Welch averred, "I hope the lawsuit will establish psychoanalysis as the crossroads of the mental health delivery system and will enable representatives of a variety of different points of view to study psychoanalysis. This will enrich psychoanalysis and improve the mental health system."

At the same time, the December 1988 issue of *The Round Robin* carried two articles—both actually news reports—on the settlement aftermath. One was by Stanley Grand, President of IPTAR, describing the IPA site visit process that they had undergone and announcing that at its July 1988 meeting, the IPA Executive Council had unanimously voted to recommend IPTAR for Provisional Society status in the IPA at the Business Meeting of the 1989 IPA Congress in Rome. Grand stated proudly that: "By this action, the IPA Council has committed itself, for the first time, to the inclusion of an American nonmedical Society into the IPA, and set in motion an historical event in the development of nonmedical psychoanalysis in the United States." The other article stated the timetable for site visits to three other applicant groups to the IPA, NYFS, NYCPT, and LAISPS.

Unhappily and unexpectedly, a storm was kicked up by these two *Round Robin* articles, and Stanley Grand, on December 21, 1988, sent me an explanatory and clarifying letter informing me about "IPTAR's concerns about the apparent misinterpretation of our intentions in publishing it." Grand stated that IPTAR had been informed of the favorable reaction of the IPA Executive Council to their site visit by the chair of the Site Visit Committee, that they were "proud" and "honored" by this approval, that word of it had spread throughout the nonmedical psychoanalytic community, that they had been besieged by requests to describe the course of events leading to this action, and that after consultation with the IPA Site Visit Committee, IPTAR had agreed to provide a brief factual announcement, but not a fuller historical article, "since such articles would undoubtedly carry politically sensitive overtones."

Nonetheless, NYFS, the other nonmedical psychoanalytic group in New York that was being site visited at the same time was very upset by this early announcement, and one of *their* site visitors had, in response, publicly criticized IPTAR for having "taken unfair political and economic advantage by rushing prematurely to press." This announcement could too easily be construed as a "competitive victory . . . in the struggle to attract new candidates and members." Grand expressed himself as "personally shocked" by such a gross distortion of IPTAR's purpose in making the announcement and added that "we would be very disappointed if our success in being accepted by the IPA were to lead to dissension within the community of nonmedical Societies in this country." All of this clearly reflected the unforeseen interpersonal complexities that beset those hopeful, somewhat tumultuous, and yet unexpectedly anxious and rivalrous days, in the wake of the lawsuit settlement, amongst task-oriented people, all working with consensual good will and common purpose.

The calendar year 1988 closed with a letter from me to Homer Curtis, dated December 22, in follow-up to a long discussion the officers of the IPA had just had with the officers of the American over an issue of growing concern within the American; to wit what kinds of psychoanalytic groups in the United States might be applying under the new procedures for direct affiliation with the IPA outside the framework of the American. Two sorts of situations were envisaged, one of which had already emerged. This had to do with a group in Los Angeles (the Psychoanalytic Center of California, PCC) that consisted of about half psychologists trained outside the American, and about half dissident physician members of the American (from both its Societies in Los Angeles) who wanted to construct a more congenial home for their theoretical views (significantly Kleinian). It had been agreed to handle this application via the site visit process established by the Hanly Committee guidelines. If the application proved successful, it was agreed that the group members could then maintain their IPA membership solely through the PCC if they so wished, or could have dual membership by also maintaining their dues-paying status in their society of the American (the American already had some members with dual membership, one in a society of the American and one in their original society in Europe).

The clearly more difficult situation for all concerned—already the subject of inquiry to me from Curtis a half year earlier—would arise if an entire affiliate society of the American were to be disaffected and try to leave the American and seek direct affiliation with the IPA. That hasn't happened in the eight years now between that letter and the present writing, but it is always a theoretical possibility. Such a move could be a grave threat to the American, and in weakening the American, would of course also be weakening the largest component organization of the IPA. In my letter I said that such a move

> would undoubtedly be looked at just as unhappily by the IPA officers as by the officers of the American. In such an eventuality we would of course try to collectively bend our joint efforts to prevent such a secession and to resolve the problem internally within the American. Only if it were ultimately recognized on both sides that such reconciliation and resolution were truly impossible would we want to consider the alternatives and then how best to do it in a way that would be least detrimental to all concerned.

Clearly this is not an airtight set of guarantees, but it reflected the spirit of goodwill and collaboration which the IPA sought to foster and maintain with all its component organizations, not just the American.

Expectedly, and happily, the pace of activities and correspondence around the lawsuit settlement and its aftermath slackened in 1989. In January there were still the hurt feelings engendered by the flap over presumed priorities with the IPA within the New York nonmedical psychoanalytic community. I had written a letter on December 22, 1988, to William Greenstadt, President of NYFS, and on January 11, 1989, to the editors of *Round Robin*. In both of these I tried to calm these troubled waters, indicating that I felt the *Round Robin* article had indeed been unfortunate, and inadvertently misleading, in the implication that could too readily be read into it, that IPTAR was a good deal further along in its quest for admission to the IPA than any of the other applicants. I assured Greenstadt that both the applications, from IPTAR and NYFS, were being processed simultaneously, that both were on course, and that I expected both would be ready to be acted upon at the coming 1989 IPA Congress in Rome.

This prompted a letter back to me, dated January 19, 1989, from Mary Libbey, editor of *Round Robin*, together with her associate editor, Gil Katz, taking vigorous exception to my letter, feeling that it somehow impugned their integrity and their reputation as a responsible, factually accurate, quality newsletter. They informed me of the care they had taken to present an unbiased factual account, checked for accuracy with Charles Hanly, and stated that "Drs. Grand and Hanly decided together that it was timely and advisable to honor our request for an article that would chronicle these important events." Then, "We believe that we have acted in the interest of the IPA by illustrating how it has so responsibly and expeditiously lived up to its commitment to nonmedical psychoanalysis in America and to its agreement in the lawsuit settlement." I responded to this with a letter on January 24, 1989, that tried to bring this unnecessary tempest in a teapot to closure. I expressed my sorrow that the *Round Robin* editors had misunderstood the intent and the substance of my letter. I felt that no one was at fault, not them nor Grand nor Hanly, when an article published with the best of journalistic intentions had had unexpected unhappy consequences. My only motive in entering into this dialogue was to restore a situation that might have gotten out of hand and could threaten to derail an important continuing site visit process. At my request, this letter from me was not published; I also asked *Round Robin* not to comment further on the progress of the site visits until the presently stirred-up tensions between the applicant groups had subsided, which request they honored.

The issue amongst the involved parties, however, took a considerably longer time to die out. Charles Hanly wrote to me on March 25, 1989, enclosing a copy of a long letter of complaint that Mary Libbey had written to him on February 28, 1989, about this contretemps, in which she made a more detailed indictment of me for having written my original letter to Bill Greenstadt, and through him, to all the members of NYFS. She charged that I was motivated solely by the desire to clear the IPA of responsibility for the many hurt feelings in NYFS by putting the onus onto *Round Robin* and Stanley Grand for publishing articles that were inaccurate and misleading. She further stated that my letter contained erroneous statements that I knew at the time to be untrue. This she felt had seriously damaged her personal relations and that of *Round Robin* with the aggrieved members of NYFS. She and Hanly had telephone exchanges about this matter, and in his letter to me, Hanly expressed his own sorrow about what he felt to be unnecessary and undeserved trouble being brought to me. He felt that he had no best advice as to how to abate this simmering issue.

I then wrote back to Mary Libbey on April 6, 1989, indicating that Hanly had sent her letter on to me and that I had agreed in a telephone conversation with him that I would write to her again in a further effort at clarification of my perspective and in the hope that we could come to some common understanding. I reiterated that I had no intention to impugn her or *Round Robin*, that I felt indeed that some of the statements in the *Round Robin* article had been unfortunate and misleading, but that "this obviously had to do with the fact that your informants either were not fully apprised of all the facts or didn't give them to you, and that the articles, therefore, as written, did carry unfortunate connotations to the members of the New York Freudian Society who did feel put at a serious disadvantage vis à vis IPTAR." My intention in the letter of reassurance I had written to Greenstadt and NYFS was simply to assure them that their own site visit process was equally on course, even though the *Round Robin* article could be construed to indicate that they had been outdistanced. I wanted to "put out fires that could have seriously derailed a process that it was important to carry through in as calm and uncontroversial a way as possible, and this I took to be my primary obligation."

I went on to say directly to Mary Libbey:

> I saw you and *Round Robin* as the innocent conveyors of partial information that then got reacted to very strongly and undoubtedly overstrongly. I don't think that in any of this your professional reputation has been hurt in the slightest nor should it be. I think that there has been a lot of overreaction, in the first instance by the New York Freudian Society members, which is why I suggested [in my earlier letter to her of January 24, 1989] that it is better to let everything quiet down than to get into "a continuing series of justifications and explanations and then counterjustifications and counterexplanations."

Clearly I felt that the overreactions were not just on one side. I felt it necessary to end the letter by rejecting categorically her statement that my original letter to Greenstadt "contained erroneous statements that I knew at the time to be untrue"; this was simply not so. I followed this with the expressed hope that we could all "put all of this into perspective as a minor episode (that could have but did not get out of hand) in a process of great historic importance." This last was indeed my overall assessment, and for me the matter ended there.

In the meantime, there was a happier exchange of letters. The first was from Jonathan Slavin, an officer of Division 39, dated February 23, 1989, expressing his thanks and that of his colleagues for the letter I had written to *The New York Times* (published on December 24, 1988), in response to the aforementioned letter by the analyst in New York who had expressed his anger and concern that the American and the IPA had capitulated to the improper demands of the psychologist plaintiffs. On March 1, 1989, I wrote thanking Slavin, and I took the occasion to elaborate to him the considerable prodding that it took to get *The New York Times* to publish my letter of correction.

> After I wrote it and nothing happened, I found out who to contact, as they have a special editor for letters to the editor. He indicated to me that the *Times* had decided not to publish my letter because they felt that the whole issue wasn't worth it since it was only of parochial interest to a small number of affected individuals. I pointed out that they had, nonetheless, published the letter by Dr. X and that his letter was misinformed and misrepresented the actual facts, that I as a signatory to the lawsuit settlement was in an authoritative position to correct the misinformation, and that the *Times* owed it to its readers to correct clear misinformation and distortions in what it had printed that were brought to its attention. This argument prevailed and my letter was published in a few days.

By this time, it was clear that I had become reasonably adept at maneuvering successfully in murky political and public-relations waters.

In the meantime, back again in February, there was another newsletter article, this one in the *Council News* of the Council of Psychoanalytic Psychotherapists. It was written by the editor, Sy Coopersmith, and was titled "Changing Times and Values in the Psychoanalytic Profession." This article raised openly the issue that had been brought so impressively to the IPA Executive Council by the Hanly Committee report, that of potential conflicts within the applicant groups where some but not all would meet the standards and criteria for IPA membership, given the IPA's rejection of the concept of automatic grandfathering for all. Coopersmith put the issue as follows:

What can we expect in our own psychoanalytic community? Will the Affiliates accepted for membership be creating a problem for those members who do not meet the standards, thus creating a divided membership structure? And what of the Affiliates who choose not to proceed with their applications? Will this create a disaffection of those members, in the minority, who would prefer to become IPA members but must defer to the will of the majority? These are, indeed, monumental questions. Unfortunately, they are moving at such a pace that decisions and conclusions are being reached before all parties concerned have had an opportunity to seek out equitable solutions.[4] Fifty, or more, years of "medical" opportunism cannot be resolved for the many different parties concerned by dispositions which meet the needs of those who would meet the standards of the IPA without concern for those who do not meet those standards.

During these whole first several postsettlement months, contact with our attorneys was minimal. There were occasional phone calls, mostly to touch base about where things stood. Then I received a memorandum from Clint Fisher, dated April 17, 1989, reporting on the hearing that morning before the new judge, the third on the case, Judge Michael Mukasey, on whether the proposed settlement of the lawsuit should be approved by the Court. Counsel for all the parties had been present, along with Bryant Welch and some other members of the plaintiff class. The judge noted that he had received about 15 letters objecting to the settlement and he asked specifically whether those opposing the settlement should be allowed to opt out of the class. Stromberg opposed this, stating that the settlement met the standard for a class action, in being "fair, adequate and reasonable." The negotiations had been protracted, and numerous organizations and individuals had been involved. With a class of several thousand, he called the number of objections minuscule. By definition, neither side gets everything it wants in a settlement. Lastly, Stromberg indicated that on the basis of prior discussions, he felt that the defendants might be unwilling to settle if these individuals could opt out. No one else commented, and the judge stated that in light of all the documents and the argument, he would enter an order that day approving the settlement, with any appeal having to be filed within 30 days. The counsel

---

[4] Compare this perspective with the perception within the IPA Executive Council, already chronicled in my report of those meetings, that any delay in setting up procedures and guidelines for these site visits could be readily construed as the IPA's holding back the implementation of the commitment it had made to process these applications for IPA affiliation and component organization status as expeditiously as possible.

for all the defendants agreed that an appeal would be most unlikely. Fisher ended his memorandum to me, "Thus, in all likelihood, the case is over."

After this came the cleanup work. On June 7, 1989, Curtis sent a short letter to all members of the American notifying them that the lawsuit settlement had become final, with no appeal of the Court's order approving the settlement, and the money to cover the plaintiffs' fees having been paid by the insurance carriers. He expressed his pleasure at this resolution, because "it keeps in place policies and programs that we have previously adopted and to which we fully subscribe," and he then went on to once again reiterate these. On June 19, 1989, Stromberg sent a letter to Dorkey expressing a desire to "establish a routine process by which information on progress under the settlement agreement can be shared with the plaintiffs." This was to be in the service of seeing "a new spirit of trust and cooperation emerge among psychiatrists, psychologists and others involved in the psychoanalytic field." He specifically asked for a copy of the notice to IPA members informing them of the settlement and of its terms, and any policies, procedures or guidelines that the IPA might subsequently adopt in implementing the process of evaluation of applicant nonmedical psychoanalytic institutes and societies, together with an annual progress report on the status of current applications. In a June 30, 1989, letter, Fisher advised me that he and Trip Dorkey had discussed Stromberg's letter and felt it would make more sense (and certainly be cheaper) if the IPA responded directly to the letter (which he forwarded on to me along with his letter) and in fact took up all correspondence with the plaintiffs from now on.

This letter I answered on July 6, 1989. I informed Fisher that the IPA had already posted the notice of the settlement terms in the October 1988 newsletter in the four official languages going out to 7,000 members, and that copies of that (in English) were going to him and to Stromberg; that the IPA Executive Council would be discussing in Rome at the end of the month how most appropriately to keep in touch with the plaintiffs; and that in any case, my own four-year tenure as IPA President was coming to its end at the Rome Congress and responsibility for IPA representation after that would fall on the new (European) president. On July 13, 1989, Fisher wrote to Stromberg notifying him of all this.

All this was leading up to the fateful midsummer 36th IPA Congress in Rome. The Executive Council met on July 27–29 and again on August 1, 1989. The items for discussion stemming from the lawsuit settlement and the New Group applications for IPA affiliation were various. I gave a brief report on the final closure of the litigation and the correspondence with the attorneys and the plaintiffs since that date. The plaintiffs' request for an ongoing information-exchanging relationship with the IPA was discussed, and it was also reported that Homer Curtis had received a comparable request in his capacity as President of the American. There were some concerns raised about this. The point was made that this would create an ongoing relationship with the former plaintiffs and their attorneys, which might not be appropriate. This was not mandated by the settlement agreement and the IPA should get a formal legal opinion from its attorneys as to what kind of contact it would be wise for the IPA to enter into with the plaintiffs. Besides, the "good-faith" requirement on the implementation of the settlement agreement was an obligation to the judge, not to the plaintiffs.

At one point in the several-day meeting of the Executive Council, the officers of the American joined us for a discussion of mutual interests and shared problems concerning the litigation aftermath and the altered relationship between the American and the IPA. A principal concern was the same one that I had tried to address in my December 22, 1988, letter to Curtis, the concern about the IPA's attitudes and actions should an Affiliate Society of the American wish to break away and seek direct IPA component organization status. Again it was emphasized that the IPA would be particularly sensitive to such an issue should it arise and that certainly no precipitous action would be taken. Joseph Sandler put it that as far as the IPA was concerned, institutes of the American were responsible to the American and such a matter would be for the American to deal with. All agreed that there would have to be a real disaster before the IPA would be willing to consider such an application.

A somewhat related issue was raised around inquiries recently received by the IPA concerning possible affiliation by nonmedical analytic or analytic psychotherapy training groups in Europe (where IPA membership had always been possible for nonphysicians through the usual application channels) and in Latin America (where there was a more mixed picture, because in several countries the doors to the psychoanalytic training of nonphysicians in IPA institutes had only recently been opened). This, of course, was the feared issue of precedent being established in the United States, which could then be invoked in relation to various "parallel training" programs, of varying quality, that had been in existence over varying periods of time in other regions of the world. The IPA would have wished to construe narrowly the new procedures, making them applicable only to the particular situation in the United States where longstanding exclusionary policies and historic inequities were now being rectified. Whether this could constitutionally be kept applicable only to the peculiar American history was certainly a grey area. Whatever ultimate path would be charted (or mandated), it was clear that the IPA would insist upon adherence to, and maintenance of, its own training standards, just as was being carried out in the United States.

The most important part of the Executive Council deliberations on all these topics had to do with the recommended actions to be brought to the Business Meeting on August 2, concerning the applications for IPA affiliation in Provisional Society status of six existing psychoanalytic training centers in the United States, four in New York and two in Los Angeles.

Whatever issues there had been along the way in the first two parallel site visit processes in New York, had by this time been resolved, and Hanly obtained full Executive Council concurrence to propose them both to the Business Meeting as new Provisional Societies. In each case there was a listing of those members to be accorded Training Analyst and regular member status in the IPA, in accord with the Procedures (A, B, and C) previously agreed upon by Council and carried out by the Site Visit Committees. There was still the issue of some 20% of the membership in these groups who had not yet qualified for IPA membership, and the question of how the further evaluations and monitoring of remedial activities would be done in order to finally qualify all who could meet IPA standards. Would this be done through the continuing oversight activities of the Site Visit Committees, which would continue functioning until full component Society status was achieved, or through involving the newly designated IPA Training Analysts in these groups in this process?

Two other groups were under consideration in New York. One, NYCPT, was not yet far enough along in the evaluation process to be brought for action at this Congress; the other, the William Alanson White Institute and Society, had decided to withdraw its application after it became clear that a majority of its membership would be unwilling to proceed on the basis required by the IPA, the alteration of its training programs and practices to fully conform with IPA standards and procedures. Concerning the two groups under consideration in Los Angeles, a similar situation had arisen as had occurred in the early days of the parallel visiting process in New York with IPTAR and NYFS. In Los Angeles, one of the two groups (the Psychoanalytic Center of California, PCC), was far smaller, more compact and homogeneous, and literally half its membership already belonged to the two institutes of the American in the Los Angeles area, the Los Angeles and Southern California Institutes and Societies. They had therefore already met the American's (and the IPA's) exacting standards, but wished to affiliate with a new group outside the American, which they felt would be a more congenial home for their (Kleinian) theoretical views. The Site Visit Committee[5] had completed its work satisfactorily, and this group, PCC, was also endorsed by the Executive Council for presentation to the Business Meeting for Provisional Society status in the IPA. With the other group in Los Angeles, a much larger and more heterogeneous one, in which almost none had prior connections with the American or the IPA, the site visit process was necessarily more complex and time-consuming. The inevitable issues that every site visit process had its share of surfaced along the way,

---

[5] This committee, formed along the same lines as the first two for the New York groups, consisted of Owen Renik, San Francisco (chair); Inaura Carneiro Leao, Rio de Janeiro; Pierre Doucet, Montreal; and Alain Gibeault, Paris.

and that group was deemed not yet satisfactorily evaluated to be presented for Provisional Society status at this Congress.

That decision by the IPA Executive Council had been presented at a difficult meeting that Ed Weinshel and I had, during those several days of pre-Congress Executive Council meetings in Rome, with two of the leading (and founding) figures in the group under consideration. The now familiar and expected concerns were strongly expressed about the unfair competitive advantage that our decision would give to PCC in Los Angeles in the struggle for recognition, for candidates. This was to remain a difficult and contentious matter until that group (the Los Angeles Institute and Society for Psychoanalytic Studies, LAISPS) was duly voted into Provisional Society status at the very next IPA Congress in Buenos Aires in 1991.[6]

An unexpectedly contentious issue within the Executive Council meeting in this sequence of discussions had to do with the place on the Business Meeting agenda where the three recommendations for positive action, on IPTAR, NYFS, and PCC, were to be presented by Hanly. The three groups that were to be proposed for favorable action had been notified in advance that this was highly likely. A negative decision, or one to defer, within the Executive Council was not expected, given the very favorable Site Visit Committee reports that had been precirculated to the Council members. Members of these three applicant groups were attending the Rome Congress (in guest status) in even greater numbers than usual, and they were looking forward eagerly to participation in the welcoming ceremony and in their inaugural involvement in the ongoing activities of the IPA Business Meeting. As one of them said to me—in a sentiment echoed by many of them—"We've had to be guests for so many years in what we always felt was our psychoanalytic home; we look forward so much to finally becoming members who belong." The representatives of these groups had petitioned me strongly to have the vote on them as soon as possible in the proceedings of the Wednesday, daylong, Business Meeting at the Congress, so that they could come into the Business Meeting, exchange their guest badges for membership badges, and participate then as members in the balance of the day's proceedings. It was readily agreed within Council to honor this request as much as possible and move this agenda item up from the usual position for action on affiliation status, which was toward the end of the day, to a place as close as possible after the call to order and the acceptance of the minutes of the Business Meeting of the preceding Congress.

---

[6] This Site Visit Committee consisted of first Herbert S. Gaskill, Denver (chair), later replaced when Gaskill became ill, by Charles A. Mangham, Seattle (chair); Victor Aiza, Mexico City; Egle Laufer, London; and Brian Robertson, Montreal.

What became a matter of dispute, however, was whether this should occur even before the usual first substantive agenda item, the election by closed ballot at the Business Meeting of the new (European) IPA President, the Treasurer, and the nine Vice-Presidents, three from each of the IPA's major regions. The new groups very much desired this, because the election of officers had usually been the single most important substantive agenda item at IPA Congresses, and this particular election was a hotly contested one between two outstanding candidates who were, to all intents and purposes, quite evenly matched in the preelection campaigning and mobilization of support.[7] The argument against this was that it could lead to later charges by supporters of failed candidates of loading the vote. It was also pointed out by Howard Schlossman, Treasurer of the IPA, that it was only dues-paying members who had the right to exercise the vote, and these individuals had not paid IPA dues to that point. That argument finally prevailed, and the decision was made to vote on the new group memberships immediately after the completion of the balloting for the new IPA officers.

The politically and organizationally climactic event of the Congress was the Business Meeting itself, Wednesday August 2, reported in almost verbatim detail in the 154th *IPA Bulletin,* issued in the fall of 1989. As promised, the presentation of motions for the according of Provisional Society status in the IPA to the three nonmedical psychoanalytic groups was made directly after the balloting for the new IPA officers (Executive Council) was completed. Hanly made the presentation as chair of the overall New Groups Committee.[8] He began with the statement that the Meeting now had important business of historical significance to transact. He would be placing before the Meeting resolutions that, with the Meeting's support, would make three United States nonmedical psychoanalytic groups Provisional Societies of the IPA. He then reviewed for the Meeting the principles and procedures that had guided the work of the Site Visit Committees. The central principle was the maintenance of IPA training standards, and the main procedures were twofold: the assessment of the functioning of the societies and institutes, and the evaluation of their individual members for training analyst and regular membership status in the IPA. Hanly then presented three successive resolutions, one for each of the recommended groups, including reading the list of the individuals in each group being brought into IPA membership

---

[7] Since then, starting with the 1995 elections, IPA election procedures have been altered. The elections no longer take place by vote of those attending the Business Meeting, but rather by advance mail ballot of the entire worldwide membership.

[8] The committee comprised at this time, Charles Hanly, Toronto (chair); José Infante, Santiago; Moses Laufer, London; David Sachs, Philadelphia; Janice de Saussure, Geneva; and Inga Villarreal, Bogota.

within the group (86 for NYFS, 24 for PCC, and 54 for IPTAR) as well as the list of those being accorded training analyst status within each of these groups. In each instance the vote was unanimously in favor.

Hanly then advised the Meeting that two other United States groups were currently in the process of being site visited. He ended with the statement that it had always been Freud's hope that nonmedical psychoanalysts would take an equal part and be equally accepted in the development and practice of psychoanalysis in the United States. This Meeting had just taken a significant step in that direction, and it seemed particularly fitting that it was on the 50th anniversary of Freud's death. Hanly then left the Meeting to invite the new colleagues to join us for the remainder of the Meeting, and I announced that I intended to invite the representatives of our three new Provisional Societies to briefly address the Meeting.

As the doors swung open and the members of the three new Provisional Societies marched into the meeting hall, the entire audience spontaneously rose, turned toward them, and accorded them a prolonged and moving standing ovation. Standing on the podium watching them come in, I could see clearly that there were tears in many eyes, my own included. It was the single most moving moment I had experienced in 22 years of active involvement in the affairs of the IPA, twelve, to that point, on its Executive Council. This moment brought to my mind another—equally poignant—occasion from the 34th IPA Congress four years earlier, in Hamburg, where I had been elected President, running unopposed. That occasion had been one torn by intense but conflicting emotions. It had been the first occasion on which I (and so many other IPA members worldwide) had been willing to return to Germany, now 40 years after the end of World War II and the collapse of Nazism, within which time an entire post-Hitler generation had come to maturity. For me, it had been 62 years since I had left, as a two-year-old, with my mother, coming to join my father in America. It was also the occasion on which friends among my German colleagues, speaking at the Business Meeting of my election as President, made proud reference that I had come back to be elected President in the land of my (and their) birth, and that this had reflected, and in some sense represented, their own feeling of being at last reintegrated into full acceptance in the worldwide psychoanalytic community.

That Congress had ended, as they all customarily do, with a large Friday evening banquet. My wife and I were doing the customary table-hopping to greet colleagues and friends, some of them very long-time friends from my more than two decades of active involvement in the affairs of the IPA, from the various societies around the world. I remembered clearly stopping at the several tables where the Congress participants from IPTAR and NYFS, many of whom I had by then come to know as colleagues, were sitting, being present at that Congress, of course, in the status of professional "guests." They greeted me and congratulated me very warmly as someone they had come to know as very sympathetic to their intense aspiration to become officially recognized within the organized psychoanalytic world, and more than one of them had taken that occasion—it was July 1985, in the earliest stages of the lawsuit that had been filed some five months earlier— to express the hope that the vexatious issue of the nonstatus of nonmedical psychoanalysis within the United States could finally be resolved within my tenure as IPA President. That had now come to pass.

When this whole sizable contingent of our new members had come into the Meeting and taken their seats among their new colleagues, I invited the presidents of the three groups in turn to address the audience. The first was William Greenstadt, President of the New York Freudian Society. He expressed his great thanks to the IPA in general and singled out the many individuals who had played roles in this process at all levels, including within his own group, the Steering Committee that had shared the long negotiation and meeting process with the IPA Site Visit Committee. Then James Gooch, President of the Psychoanalytic Center of California, elaborated more. He spoke of their long odyssey over the preceding dozen years which had brought them to this point, and went back in his reminiscences to the 1958 visit by Wilfred Bion to Southern California, and the impetus that had given to the ultimate evolution of his group with a broad theoretical base, receptive to a range of psychoanalytic theoretical perspectives. He too thanked the various participants in this final process on the side of the IPA and from within his group. Gooch ended by stating that the group would do all that it could to live up to the new opportunities and challenges presented to it, and to contribute to the IPA.

The last of the three to speak was Stanley Grand, President of the Institute for Psychoanalytic Training and Research (New York). He expressed his pleasure in being at the Meeting in this capacity and spoke to the historic event that was now taking place. On behalf of IPTAR and all its members he expressed the deep pride they all felt at having achieved this goal. They had looked to the IPA for many years as the source of their professional identities, the natural home for their intellectual and emotional commitment to psychoanalysis. Their membership now spoke to a new era for psycho-analysis in the United States which could infuse new energies, talents, and creativity into the institutional structure of psychoanalysis. IPTAR would dedicate itself to meeting the challenges that such a new era would undoubtedly generate and to work toward the increased health and vitality of our mutual enterprise. He ended by thanking all those involved in the process that had brought all this about.

I then expressed particular appreciation of Charles Hanly's work in guiding this whole evaluation process so carefully, conscientiously, and successfully. Then Homer Curtis, President of the American, rose to extend his personal greetings, as well as those of the American, to the new members who fitted so well with the scientific theme of the Congress itself, the search for common ground. He said that only those who had participated in the travail and the creative work of the preceding three years could know the efforts made by the leadership of the IPA and of the American to arrive at this shared platform, in spite of certain differences in perspective and in goal that had been at issue along the way. He ended by stating that the members of the American looked forward to many years of collaboration and work together on the common ground, in furthering the interests of the IPA and of psychoanalysis in the world.

At the finish of a long and exhausting day's business, comprising many important agenda items that were discussed over the balance of the day, I ended the Meeting with the customary expressions of thanks. I was retiring from the presidency, and nine members (over half) of the Executive Council were now leaving it. It had been a very hardworking Executive Council and one that had worked very well together, with four full meeting days in Rome and a fifth day of separate committee meetings. In all this, the Council had worked in a spirit of friendliness and openness and respect for other points of view, even though at times there were differences of opinion, even very sharp ones, about different issues under discussion. We had come to cherish each other as psychoanalytic colleagues and close friends, and it was with sadness that I read the names of the nine departing from the Council, including the past-President, Adam Limentani, and my own closest working comrade, the Secretary, Edward Weinshel. I added that I had always felt as President that I had had the support, the interest, and the involvement of the entire worldwide psychoanalytic community. At that point I received a prolonged and intensely moving standing ovation and stood there tearfully. It is the kind of occasion that does not come often in a lifetime.

As a proper coda to this Business Meeting, I can quote from the final Secretary's Report, also included in the 154th IPA Bulletin. Referring to the admission of the three new nonmedical United States Provisional Societies, Weinshel called it, "a most historic moment in the still relatively brief annals of the IPA and one which will exert a still uncertain impact on the future of psychoanalysis within the United States and the IPA."

In this book I have traced the long saga of the status of nonmedical psychoanalysis in the United States to two critical events in 1910: the Flexner report, which in a surprisingly short period revolutionized medical education in America, and Freud's paper *"Wild" Psychoanalysis*, which first raised the alarm in Europe over what was required to do proper psychoanalytic work. This question reached a state of final substantial resolution with the passage and beginning implementation by the American of the Gaskill Committee recommendations in 1986 and with the alteration of the Regional Association agreement between the American and the IPA at the 35th IPA Congress in Montreal in 1987. It was brought to final resolution with the settlement of the lawsuit in 1988, ratified by the judge in 1989, which was followed, at the 1989 IPA Congress in Rome, by the admission of three nonmedical psychoanalytic groups in the United States as Provisional Societies in the IPA, alongside the American itself, in the company of all the other IPA component societies around the world. What would follow from now on would be the inevitable issues of implementation, of controversies over the "good faith" demonstrated (on either side) over specific problems in the processing of that implementation. Some of these are recounted in the next two chapters, but the fundamental substantive (and ideological) issue of the proper place of "lay analysis" within the house of organized psychoanalysis in America, and therefore around the world, was now finally settled beyond reversal.

Struggles Over Implementation, 1989–1990

T he story of the struggle over "lay analysis" in America did not end with the 1989 IPA Congress in Rome, though the events of that Congress signaled the transformation of the struggle into the ongoing process of the full integration—as yet unfinished at the time of this writing (1996)—of nonmedical colleagues and aspirants in the United States within the organized institutional structures of the American and the IPA. Three important separable aspects of this process have emerged during this time period (1989–96) as the focus of ongoing activity and concern. One has been the continuing negotiations—often intense and at times acrimonious—between the IPA and the American on the one hand, and Cliff Stromberg and his colleagues, as the continuing attorneys for the former plaintiffs and their supporters, on the other hand. These concern the progression of the four independent psychoanalytic training groups identified in the preceding chapter (three of them voted into Provisional Society status in the IPA at the Rome Congress) toward the final acceptance of all four as full component societies in the IPA, plus additional site visits, either initiated or just planned, which have not yet led to any other than the first four groups being admitted to the IPA. The second has been the coalescence of these four new IPA Societies into what was first called the Coalition of Independent IPA Societies, and was then renamed the Confederation of Independent Psychoanalytic Societies (CIPS) in the United States, and the subsequent grouping of this organization (CIPS), together with the American and the Canadian Psychoanalytic Society (CPS) into a loose coalition, the North American IPA Groups (NAIPAG). The latter joined forces around common concerns, including their participation in IPA affairs, and especially their joint involvement in fashioning the North American representation in the IPA's new House of Delegates, an organization designed to accord the component Societies a greater voice in the IPA governance structure, which was brought into being during the IPA presidency of Joseph Sandler (1989–93). The third aspect has been the changing operation over time of the American's Committee on Non-Medical Clinical Training (CNMCT), the original Davis Committee, which had evolved by 1994 into the renamed Committee on Preparedness and Progression (COPAP), with a major shift in monitoring the admission process of nonmedical applicants into psychoanalytic training within the institutes of the American from the centralized oversight of CNMCT to the primarily "local autonomy" of the American's affiliate institutes.

In the first years after the Rome Congress, the major focus within the IPA concerned the ongoing activities of the IPA Site Visit Committees and the difficulties that surfaced during that process; those events especially will be focussed on here. First, however, I want to interpolate a perspective that has been missing—except by inference or by projection—from my account to this point: a view of the lawsuit, its settlement, and the meanings and implications of this sequence of events from the vantage point of the plaintiffs. This became available to me with the publication—five years after the point to which I have just taken this narrative—of *A History of the Division of Psychoanalysis [Division 39] of the American Psychological Association* (Lane and Meisels, 1994). The editors were two former presidents of Division 39, Robert C. Lane and Murray Meisels; the latter had also been one of the protagonists in the litigation process. Of the 59 chapters in that volume, one by Arnold Z. Schneider and Helen Desmond, two of the four actual plaintiffs in the lawsuit, is entitled "The Psychoanalytic Lawsuit Expanding Opportunities for Psychoanalytic Training and Practice."

The chapter begins with a quite straightforward account of the history of the issue of "lay analysis" in America, taking as its starting point, as I have in this book, the Flexner Report of 1910 and the rationale that stemmed from that, namely to limit the training for and practice of psychoanalysis in the United States solely to qualified physicians, in order to avoid the infiltration of charlatanism into this fledgling therapeutic activity. The chapter then cites the usual landmarks, highlighting, of course, Freud's *The Question of Lay Analysis* (which they called, "an unfortunate and antiquated term, erroneously suggestive of differences between analyses with medical and nonmedical analysts"; p. 314). They discuss the declaration of "the 1938 rule" and the subsequent struggle to modify this within the American, with the establishment first of the Committee on Training for Research (1956) and then the four successive committees (from the mid-1970s to the mid-1980s), charged with the consideration of the broader issue, the training of nonphysicians for psychoanalytic clinical practice. Schneider and Desmond then emphasize the quotation in the *Newsletter* of the American in 1984, after the San Diego decision to table this entire issue, that "The new President [of the American, Ed Joseph] is relieved that the recent polarization of the membership over the issue of non-medical training, is, for the time being, no longer in the forefront" (p. 319). Despite assertions by the President of the American later on, during the lawsuit itself, that there was no interdiction of members of the American teaching in psychoanalytic programs outside the American, Schneider and Desmond report that as late as December 1981, the Executive Council of the American unanimously approved the resolution "that all psychoanalytic training by members of the American Psychoanalytic Association be conducted only through authorized training institutes and programs of the American" (p. 319), and that two years later, in 1983, the American's Committee on Ethics prepared an explicit statement forbidding participation in unauthorized training (p. 319).

It is these occurrences—the barring of the American's members from teaching outside its framework and the American's decision in San Diego to table indefinitely the consideration of opening its own doors to the training of nonphysicians for the clinical practice of psychoanalysis—that are declared to be the events that triggered the lawsuit. But first the efforts to negotiate these issues with the American (and with the IPA) are recounted. These went back to the initial efforts by Reuben Fine, the first President of Division 39, who contacted the IPA officers, shortly after Division 39's founding in 1979, to inquire into possible IPA affiliation, only to be referred back to the American, which then enjoyed its "exclusive franchise" in the United States under the 1938 rule. Meetings between representatives of Division 39 and officers of the American were held from 1981 to 1984. Of the last-minute, October 1984 meeting ("an attempt to forestall the need for legal action"; p. 321), Schneider and Desmond state that the American's "obdurate stance during and after that meeting made it abundantly clear that there was no likelihood that the matter would be settled cooperatively" (pp. 321–322). The lawsuit was filed shortly after, on March 1, 1985.

In describing the actual events of the lawsuit, Schneider and Desmond's emphases naturally differ somewhat from those I have presented in this book. For example, they highlight an April 22, 1986 Status Conference before the judge:

> Clifford Stromberg won a significant tactical victory. The previous summer, the Court, in accord with its usual procedure, had ruled that discovery should be conducted on the class action issues initially. Then, only after the class had been established, would discovery on the merits of the case begin. This would have provided the defendants with the opportunity to harass the plaintiffs and expose weaknesses in their case without being subject to like action toward them until the class had been legally

established. After considerable procedural wrangling and over the defendants' strenuous objections, Stromberg persuaded the judge to order consolidated discovery in which both the class issues and the issues of the merits of the case would be examined simultaneously [p. 323].

In connection with this statement, Schneider and Desmond recapitulate the main arguments, pro and con, in relation to both the merits of the case and the appropriateness of the class action motion. For my part, I have no record or memory of this ruling by the judge having been perceived by the defendants as so critical to the course of the lawsuit.

In their description of the complexity of the legal maneuverings over the several-year course of the lawsuit, Schneider and Desmond inserted: "During the course of the lawsuit . . . we as plaintiffs learned that there were limits to what we could expect to garner from such a suit. In short, we learned about litigation as the art of the possible" (p. 324). But on the next page of their narrative, they claimed oppositely that "the course of the suit progressed exceedingly well, with victories achieved at each step on the way, pointing to our ultimate success" (p. 325). They then describe what they call, "the low point, or perhaps the below-the-belt punch" (p. 325), the episode—very oppositely interpreted and described by the two sides (see chapter 12, pp. 271–273)—around Bryant Welch's deposition on November 9, 1987, when the issue arose of contacting Welch's analyst in order to help disentangle conflicting statements that he and Welch had made about the basis on which Welch's analysis had stopped. Schneider and Desmond averred that the vigorous objections of their attorneys and of Division 39 to the outrageous and unethical threats of the defendants' attorneys had led to the defendants backing down and dropping their threat to the integrity and confidentiality of Welch's analysis.

Schneider and Desmond then go on to assert that "clearly, in response to the lawsuit, historic changes were taking place, even before the settlement agreement was reached" (p. 325), and they describe the Gaskill Committee proposal (though not by name) and its adoption by a 68% vote of the American's membership:

While APsaA [the American] staunchly denied that this revolutionary change was motivated in response to the lawsuit, the reality was evident. Even APsaA's own Newsletter began their report about the acceptance of the waiver process with the comment: "In a somewhat unanticipated change from the uncertain and divided attitude expressed in San Diego last spring . . ." [*American Psychoanalytic Association Newsletter*, 18(3), 1985, page 1]. This sudden change, from burying the issue of nonmedical training in May, 1984, to endorsing the clinical waiver process in December 1985, was possibly APsaA's attempt to persuade the Court that legal action was not justified. They hoped to bring the lawsuit to a quick end while denying any culpability. Further, had the lawsuit been dropped at that time, no assurance would have been provided that these changes would continue. The plaintiffs were aware that without a legal resolution this change could quickly be rescinded or altered [pp. 325-26].

From this, Schneider and Desmond go on to state that "a second historic change was completed in July, 1987" (p. 326), referring to the action of the Montreal Congress at which the American's Regional Association agreement (the "1938 rule") with the IPA was altered. They then move directly into stating that a settlement agreement was negotiated and approved by the court on April 17, 1989, after which they state the terms of that agreement. They then give an account of the famous May 31, 1986 meeting[1] and its aftermath, at which I had thought that the general terms of an acceptable settlement agreement had been worked out.

Schneider and Desmond's account is as follows:

At the initiative of Robert Wallerstein, President of IPA, a negotiation meeting was assembled on May 31, 1986. It was, in fact, requested on the heels of Stromberg's tactical victory at the April 22, 1986, Class Action Status Conference. Each defendant was represented by its officers and attorneys. Unlike the tenor of an earlier meeting on March 9, 1986, the tenor now was congenial. The IPA's stance, in particular, was decidedly conciliatory. The discussion was filled with promising ideas and proposals, many of which were suggested by IPA represen- tatives. . . . The meeting was terminated before there were any mutually agreed upon proposals.[2] Rather, the defendants looked to the plaintiffs' attorney in consultation with IPA's attorney, to formalize what had transpired.[3] This summary would then be

---

[1] For my account of that meeting and its aftermath from the perspective of the IPA, see chapter 9, especially pp. 190–204.

[2] In my account I had stated that I felt that we had come to mutually agreed upon proposals which were then to be put into proper legal language, with a first draft by Cliff Stromberg, the plaintiffs' attorney (see chapter 9, pp. 190–191).

[3] This seems, to me, in contradiction to the immediately preceding sentence and more in keeping with my understanding of that meeting, though it was also clear to me that it was Stromberg alone who undertook "to formalize what had transpired."

used as a "single text" point of departure at a later meeting. The
four plaintiffs met in Washington, DC, after the May 31
meeting. . . . The negotiations of the May 31 meeting were
discussed. We had a dual concern. We wished to draw as much
as possible upon the suggestions offered by the defendants,
especially by IPA. At the same time, because the document we
were to submit, in effect, would be the starting point of
negotiations, to begin with our bottom line in effect would be
to give away the store [p. 329].

It is this account that at last made clear to me how the document that
Stromberg sent to us in the summer of 1986 could be so far beyond my
sense of that May 31 meeting, and so totally unacceptable to the defendants
as the basis for a possible settlement of the lawsuit. If one takes Schneider
and Desmond's article as a factual representation of the plaintiffs' thinking
at the time, then what I (and others among the defendants) had felt was an
agreement reached and the end of negotiations was to the plaintiffs only a
set of suggestions and the start of negotiations. This could account for the
nature of the document that Stromberg at last delivered, which was such an
unacceptable surprise to us. The only reading we could give it at that time
was that the plaintiffs were unwilling to settle on the basis discussed at the
May 31 meeting. That is certainly the way we took it at the time, and the
litigation proceeded for more than two more years before the final
agreement.

Schneider and Desmond go on to state that, "Following completion
of the document by our attorneys, it was disseminated to the defendants.
The only response we received from the defendants occurred the following
October [1986]. It was a vague and unenforceable settlement proposal from
APsaA [drafted by Lewis Kaplan, in consultation with the attorneys
representing the other defendants], unresponsive to the issues discussed at
the May 31 meeting" (p. 329). Again, from my perspective, Kaplan's
document restated the proposals made at the May 31 meeting, though not
as forthcomingly as I would have wished. And Schneider and Desmond
went on to add gratuitously about the Kaplan response: "The detailed
elements focused on requirements protecting APsaA from any future
lawsuits by any other mental-health professionals on related matters—even
for future wrongdoings!" (p. 329).

Reflecting overall on the Schneider-Desmond account of the
lawsuit and its settlement, it is clear that there are the different emphases
that I have indicated from the story chronicled in this book. They emphasize
of course that the changes undertaken by the American, namely the
formation of the Gaskill Committee and all its consequences, were, from
the perspectives of the plaintiffs, clearly in response to the pressures of the

lawsuit. I have already given my account of how the Gaskill Committee came into being when Weinshel and I, fearing that the lawsuit was coming, had an audience with the Executive Committee of the American and persuaded them to try to head this off by reopening the issue of nonmedical training and appointing the committee, which I suggested, in response to their inquiry, be chaired by Herbert Gaskill for reasons that were, to me, convincing. I always considered the officers of the American somewhat disingenuous in insisting so stoutly that the appointment of that committee, and all that came in the wake of its recommendations, was simply a "natural evolutionary process" of thoughtful consideration of, and action upon, the issues confronting the organization. Of course this also needed to be put that way as a tactical prop to the defense of the lawsuit.

On the other hand, I disagree with the Schneider-Desmond account of the plaintiffs' perspective on a number of grounds beyond those I have already indicated. They stated that the adoption of the Gaskill Committee proposals and their subsequent implementation would be an ephemeral phenomenon that could "quickly be rescinded or altered" (p. 326), lacking a legal resolution of the case and a legal enforcement of the settlement. This was a natural fear of the plaintiffs, though anyone familiar with the way the American operated (and a number of individuals in the plaintiff camp actually members of the American who were very knowledgeable about its workings and could easily have dispelled this fear) would know that such an eventuality was exceedingly unlikely, close to the vanishing point. And then Schneider and Desmond's statement that I called the ill-starred May 31, 1986 meeting in the wake of Stromberg's "tactical victory" a month earlier in the legal maneuverings as if in defensive response to that event. Perhaps they could not have known that I had no special awareness of, or feeling about, the legal ruling that the plaintiffs had taken to be so important. For my part, I initiated that meeting because the IPA felt that the time was right to see if a settlement proposal could be agreed upon at that early stage of the lawsuit proceedings, and I had absolutely no part in mind of any defensive maneuver to try to counter and defuse a legal tactical advantage that Stromberg had secured for his clients. What mostly I take issue with in the Schneider-Desmond account is that there is no mention of the fact that the "very serious" settlement offer that Stromberg made on the plaintiffs' behalf in the spring of 1988, nearly two years later, and that was agreed upon in the fall of 1988, was substantially identical with the IPA proposals in the May 31, 1986 meeting about which they indeed speak so positively in their own account. Had they grasped the opportunity at the time, and had Stromberg come back with a document embodying those proposals (that I felt we had agreed upon), a settlement of the lawsuit might have come two years earlier, saving a great deal of money, time, and anguish on all sides, and on exactly the same basis as the final settlement—and this despite whatever reservations that the attorney for the American at the time was expressing on behalf of what he took to be his clients' position.

After the discussion of the lawsuit and its settlement, the Schneider-Desmond article has a section titled "Dissenting Voices within Psychology," with a (to me) surprisingly candid account of the various differences that had cropped up along the way in the ranks of the plaintiffs' psychologist supporters. Two main issues are raised, one "that greater access to APsaA Institutes would constitute a threat to the hopes and plans of developing psychologist institutes and to the enrollment of quality psychologists in non-medical institutes currently in existence" (pp. 327–328). This argument is countered with: "The unlikely possibility of developing psychologist institutes in many areas of the country, the importance of freeing APsaA members to teach at existing and developing institutes, and the benefits of membership in the IPA were among the considerations that helped to unify the Division's support" (p. 328).

Of the other issue, Schneider and Desmond write that: "A more significant threat to the unanimity of support arose in 1987" (p. 328). Here they speak of Zenia Fliegel's letter to Fred Pine, then President of Division 39, which had been distributed to the Division 39 Board on March 7, 1987. In that letter she was quoted as saying: "It is our understanding that the suit has been eminently successful in attaining its main objectives [and she cited them]. . . . We respectfully request that the Board make every effort to persuade the plaintiffs to settle the suit, with appropriate safeguards, on the basis of the concessions already offered by the defendants. Failing that, we would urge the Board, with regret, to officially and publicly withdraw its support of continued litigation" (p. 328). Schneider and Desmond make clear that the proposals and concessions referred to by Fliegel were the documents that stemmed from the May 31, 1986, settlement meeting. They then added that, "while the plaintiffs held APsaA's documents in confidence, somehow they ended up in the hands of Zenia Fliegel" (p. 329). One thing I can categorically assert in this connection is that wherever Zenia Fliegel secured access to the documents in question, it was not through the IPA, because I knew absolutely nothing of her involvement in these matters until my attention was brought to her letter to the Board urging it to drop the suit, which had somehow come to Mark Bunim, attorney for the New York Institute (see chapter 11, p. 243). Fliegel's letter, "was signed by 26 psychologists, many of whom were quite distinguished, and indicated considerable dissatisfaction with the lawsuit process to date (especially the secrecy)" (p. 330). Schneider and Desmond then describe the special meeting of the Board of Directors of Division 39, March 7, 1987, at which continuing support of the lawsuit was reaffirmed, but "at which time there was full disclosure of these events as well as a full disclosure of all documents" (p. 330), and GAPPP (the organization specifically created to pursue the lawsuit) "invited the Board [of Division 39] to serve in an oversight and advisory capacity" (p. 330).

The next section of their article, titled from Yogi Berra, "It Ain't Over 'Till It's Over," recounts some of the postsettlement difficulties that arose between the former defendants and the former plaintiffs in the first few years of implementation of the settlement agreement. These are covered in the following chapter. Last, there is a section, Outcome and Benefits of the Lawsuit and an Epilogue. Here Schneider and Desmond state that: "Most objectively, it opened the doors to psychoanalytic training for numerous psychologists (and other mental-health professionals) that would surely have remained closed" (pp. 332–33), and in that vein they claim, "The victory of the settlement agreement for psychology" (p. 333). "Now that we had broken the barriers of APsaA, we would be able to go beyond their doors and build our own homes—'indeed we have matured.' Perhaps the lawsuit was a form of initiation rite, part of a developmental process, expanding our own creativity, resourcefulness, and independence" (p. 333). And, in almost a last sentence, "It is our belief, albeit colored by strong wishes, that it will be the science and art of psychoanalysis that will have benefited" (p. 335). With that last sentence I can agree wholeheartedly, not just personally, but on behalf of the entire stance of the IPA expressed by its Executive Council and supported at every turn by the membership throughout this entire proceedings, before and after the lawsuit. From my perspective, there is sadness that what the plaintiffs feel they forced in the fall of 1988, was willingly offered to them by the IPA, with the concurrence of our codefendants (however internally reluctantly) in the late spring (May 31) of 1986.

I return now to the post-Rome Congress of 1989 events. From that point on I was, of course, no longer President of the IPA, and though I remained on the IPA Executive Council (and the smaller Executive Committee) and, on that basis, received all the mail that was circulated to all Council members, I no longer received every single piece of mail that came to IPA headquarters pertaining to matters of governance, policy, and executive decision. As a close personal friend of my successor as President, Joseph Sandler of the British Society, I was indeed brought into the loop more frequently and with more concern for my viewpoint than would necessarily have been the case in just my official capacity as immediate past-President. On August 23, 1989, I received a letter from Clint Fisher in follow-up to our earlier exchange about how the IPA should maintain postsettlement contact with the former plaintiffs and their attorneys. In his letter, Fisher informed me that Joel Klein had advised Stromberg that he would send the latter a copy of the Annual Report of the American, which contained such general information as the number of applications for training received by the American and the number of accepted admissions. Fisher suggested that the IPA do something comparable, perhaps by sending copies of the *IPA Newsletter* to Stromberg. "In fact, a subscription to the *IPA Newsletter* might be the perfect Christmas gift for Stromberg." I replied to Fisher on August 29, 1989, stating that this sounded eminently sensible to me and that the IPA could do something similar in sending Stromberg, on a yearly basis, general statistical information about the number of groups seeking affiliated status with the IPA and what action was being taken in regard to each one. Fisher suggested that this could be done via the *IPA Newsletter,* which appeared quarterly and brought this kind of information to the membership. I ended by reminding Fisher that Sandler was now the IPA President and that the final decision on this matter would of course rest with him.

I next received a letter from Charles Hanly dated September 6, 1989. He thanked me for my part in our more than two years of participation, dealing with the difficult issues and decisions confronted in working out and implementing the policies and procedures that enabled the application process of the aspirant independent psychoanalytic groups seeking IPA affiliation to proceed as successfully as it did, given the built-in apprehensions and sensitivities inevitably present on all sides in these proceedings. In his letter, Hanly stated:

> I am back in my office for the second day overcome by an intense feeling of sadness as I turned my thoughts and energies to the tasks of the new groups. The sadness is on account of the loss of the close, trusting relationship with you and Ed in the conduct of this work. I was called upon to do it by you. I did it partly for its own sake but very much for the sake of our friendship and out of a wish to help you in the tasks of your administration of the IPA. And so it is that I find that I must write something of this feeling to you before I can enter into the next phase of the work. It can never be quite the same again. Not only because we have broken the back of the problem, but also because I will not be sharing the new problems with you in the way I was able to do before. . . . [The outcome of all of this] is not certain. What is certain is that the IPA could have come apart at the seams over the crises of the lawsuit and that it was you and Ed who kept it together and laid down the foundations for the work that we were eventually able to do through the new groups.

Next came a copy of a letter from Sandler to Stromberg, dated September 14, 1989, in follow-up to my own most recent exchange of letters with Fisher. Sandler wrote that as the new IPA President, he was informing Stromberg that at the recent Rome Congress (a month earlier) three new component organizations in the United States had been recognized as IPA

Provisional Societies, that work with two other applicant groups was continuing, and that "Further inquiries from other groups are, of course, being dealt with as they come in." He added that Stromberg would be regularly receiving the *IPA Newsletter*, in which information cumulating on this issue would be regularly published.

Tensions in regard to this process of integrating the new groups into the IPA organizational structure surfaced dramatically, however, in an October 4, 1989 letter from Stanley Grand, as President of IPTAR, to Hanly, as Chair of the IPA New Groups Committee. This had to do with the issue of analytically trained psychoanalysts (either trained informally or unofficially in the earlier days, as described by Martin Bergmann, or more recently in one of the organized institutes now admitted to, or applying for admission to, the IPA). Some of these individuals were not current members of these groups at the time that the groups were site visited in the IPA evaluation process. There had been talk of a grace period during which such individuals, if they so desired, could be evaluated for membership in these new IPA groups, which could secure the IPA membership for them that had not been previously available through these groups. Grand, in his letter to Hanly, strongly protested a "restrictive policy" in this regard, which Hanly had informed him by telephone was being instituted by the IPA.

There had been a very "intense" discussion of this matter in the IPTAR Board of Administrators, which Grand said could be summed up thus:

> While there was a general appreciation of the broad policy of the IPA concerning the eventual need to limit membership to *graduates* [who are current members] of the new institutes, there was also deep concern that in the immediate situation, such a restrictive policy might adversely affect those "unaffiliated" members of the nonmedical community in the United States who also suffered the same inequities which led to the recent shift in policy on admitting new groups in this country.

IPTAR felt deeply committed "to the necessity for finding a pathway for assimilating those qualified but 'unassimilated' members of the nonmedical community" in its region:

> This group . . . would be adversely affected by the intention of the IPA to restrict membership to graduates of our institute. Throughout our application process, we have always been deeply committed to the idea that for this group, a "grace period" should be instituted lasting from 3–5 years, during which time, such analysts would have the option to become first IPTAR analysts and then IPA analysts. The general feeling of the Board was that unless such a provision were agreed upon, the process of rectifying the past would remain incomplete. The Board also

wanted me to reassure you that we are not, here, dealing with
large numbers of people, but with a relatively small group.

Grand pleaded that "the inequitable situation which has existed here in the
United States for so long, and which the IPA has now taken the first steps
to correct, will require tactful and sensitive handling over the next few years
in order to ensure that these first steps remain on solid ground." This letter
was followed by another, dated November 22, 1989, from Bill Greenstadt,
as President of NYFS, to Hanly, associating his group with IPTAR in this
request to the IPA, and it was reported that PCC, the third of the new
Provisional Societies in the IPA under the "new groups" program, also
strongly endorsed these representations.

Hanly's suggested response came in a seven-page, single-spaced
memorandum, sent on November 22, 1989, to the members of the IPA
Executive Committee (which included me as the immediate past-President),
as well as to the chairs of the five active Site Visit Committees (three of
them to the already accepted Provisional Societies and two of them to other
societies currently in the evaluation process) and also to Arnold Cooper (of
the Columbia Institute in New York), whom Sandler, as the new IPA
President, had designated co-chair, along with Hanly, of the New Groups
Committee. Hanly first outlined the nature of the problem. A total of 30
individuals had been identified as being involved in the issue under
consideration, 15 by NYFS, 14 by IPTAR, and one by PCC. They fell into
at least three categories: individuals who had formally applied for
membership in one or another of these groups prior to or during the site
visit process, but had not yet had their membership evaluations completed;
individuals who had made inquiries during the site visit process, but had
not yet begun to be evaluated; and individuals who were members of groups
that had decided not to apply for IPA affiliation (like the NPAP and the
William Alanson White) and would need then to apply individually to one
of the newly accepted IPA groups in order to secure personal IPA
membership.

Hanly stated that the existence of the first two categories was a direct
consequence of his own administrative decision to require the applicant
groups to declare a moratorium on the processing of new membership
applications during the site visit evaluation process, in order to have an
unchanging membership roster during the period of primary IPA evaluation.
This administrative artifact would have no essential bearing on the
professional qualifications of these individuals. Nor did he feel that
individuals desirous of IPA membership, who were members of groups that
had decided not to make IPA application, should be denied the opportunity
to seek IPA membership through one of the groups that was pursuing that
course.

In substance, Hanly agreed with the thrust of the argument presented by Grand and Greenstadt and proposed in his memorandum the offering of a grace period (later called a "window of opportunity"), during which such applications for IPA membership through one of the new IPA groups could be evaluated, perhaps through the continuation of the site visit evaluation process, or perhaps through delegation to the regular membership processes of the new affiliate in which the IPA had, after all, declared its confidence through the vote at the Rome Congress. All this was to come up for discussion at the (partial) IPA Executive Council meeting scheduled for December 15, 1989, in New York, where in fact Hanly's proposal was accepted, albeit with a variety of concerns raised about the potential open-endedness of what could become a loophole through which some trained less well could slip. There were enough inadvertent ambiguities in the way that this "grace period" was understood that some awkward situations did subsequently arise for the IPA. But to my mind, these were never sufficient to make me question the appropriateness and fairness of the general principle that Hanly was espousing.

Another set of issues concerning the site visit process were brought up in the next long letter from Hanly to me, dated January 3, 1990. The first part of that letter dealt with the same issue, of the operation of the "window of opportunity." IPTAR had suddenly received four applications for membership from four distinguished nonmedical analysts (George Mahl, Werner Muensterberger, Irving Paul, and David Wolitzky) who were not graduates of its program. In fact, they had all graduated from institutes of the American and were members of affiliated societies of the American, but they had never sought membership in the American itself, and were therefore not IPA members. They now sought IPA membership through IPTAR, and Hanly felt—rightly, I thought—that there should be no problem in the IPA's agreeing to have these applications processed through IPTAR, though it turned out that some concerns were voiced within the IPA Executive of the possible awkwardness this might create in the IPA's relationship with the American.

The larger, and new, issue raised in Hanly's letter had to do with the serious structural problems the IPA Site Visit Committee was encountering in its assessment meetings with NYCPT, an applicant group in New York where, among other complexities, their psychoanalytic and psychotherapeutic training tracks, albeit with ostensibly different criteria and goals, were nevertheless inextricably intermingled. This had given rise to serious tensions within the IPA Site Visit Committee. Some of the members (who had the ear, directly, of the IPA Executive Council) felt that the Site Visit Committee chair, Al Solnit, had been insufficiently critical of what was being uncovered, and was implying a greater tolerance of the group's practices than was compatible with proper IPA standards. Apart from the past and present personal tensions amongst the concerned individuals, which are always involved in such matters, the principled issue was over the conception of the site visit task. Should the IPA role be that of actively helping applicant groups to shift into compliance with IPA standards and practices, and thus perhaps risk being drawn into an advocacy stance on the group's behalf? Or should it more neutrally assess and pass judgment on the group's adequacy in relation to IPA requirements and standards, and thus risk being less concerned to help the group (and the IPA) undo the consequences of past inequity? That, after all, had been the whole point of the process we were now collectively committed to and embarked upon. In all this, Hanly was concerned for both the reliability *and* the harmony of the site visit process. His long letter to me was an informational sharing of the problem and the frustration, in elaborate detail, but now I was no longer the IPA President to whom he officially reported.

I responded to this implied plea for support in a letter, dated January 18, 1990, that I wrote to Sandler, the IPA President. I offered my letter as gratuitous advice in regard to the serious contentions around Solnit's handling of the difficult site visit situation, and also in relation to the lesser flap around Hanly's proposal to allow IPTAR to process the four distinguished psychologist-psychoanalyst colleagues, despite their not precisely fitting the category for whom the "New Groups" policies were being elaborated. On the latter issue I felt strongly that if this application process by the four were allowed to proceed quietly and matter-of-factly, with the understanding that it would not be a precedent that could be invoked in other cases, no one would raise any question about it. If the other proposed route were taken, that of proposing the four individuals for direct membership at the next IPA Congress, after which they would be free to join IPTAR, I felt that the whole matter would become more visible and raise awkward questions in other regions of the world as providing a precedent through which other individuals considered to have had "parallel training" could make similar claims on the IPA.

As regards Solnit's committee, I made the strong plea that Hanly had the fullest confidence in Solnit's conduct of the Site Visit Committee proceedings, feeling that no improper promises or commitments had been made, and that Hanly needed and deserved the strongest possible backing in his guidance of the site visit process to all the new applicant groups. I specifically spoke to those other voices within the IPA Executive Council that were more critical of the way the site visits to NYCPT had gone and were in favor of a more peremptory and drastic action in regard to the working difficulties that had been uncovered in that group; I urged that Sandler rather back Solnit's (and Hanly's) approach.

The whole issue around this group boiled rapidly to a head. It seemed that the pressures and requirements of the IPA site visit process had brought out major divisions and differences within the group: between its two geographic centers (one in New York City and one in New Jersey); between those who wanted to maintain the melding of the psychoanalysis and the psychotherapy training tracks and those who wanted to disentangle them into conceptually and technically distinct and separate programs, between those who wanted to comply with IPA training requirements and make whatever changes were necessary, and those who would rather maintain the existing training structure and forego IPA affiliation. Those in the group who were conducting the liaison with the Solnit IPA committee had been trying to gloss over these fracture lines, so as not to impede their progression to IPA acceptance, and this had finally surfaced dramatically with the Site Visit Committee. Solnit, backed by Hanly, now wanted to suspend the site visit process until the group had resolved its own internal issues and could come to a consensus (or not) about resuming its application in accord with IPA specifications. Again, the harder line within the Executive Council was to reject the application outright with the statement that the group simply did not qualify at this time, though they could, of course, reapply in the future if they had achieved consensus around that course and were now in a position to demonstrate that.

Again I entered the lists, with another letter to Sandler, dated January 29, 1990. And again I strongly urged the course proposed by Solnit. Partly, of course, I had an eye on the external situation and the ongoing monitoring of the settlement agreement by the former plaintiffs, as well as by the court.

> There are too many voices in the United States amongst the psychologists who are watching the situation like a hawk, that the IPA was bludgeoned into its By-Law changes under the pressure of the lawsuit, and that its strategy has been to minimize the accession of psychologist groups by letting in the two favorite groups in New York, and then using that as the sign of its goodwill, and then using that as the basis and justification for holding the line and turning down all other groups, like William Alanson White, NYCPT, NPAP, etc. . . . All that could be defused by following Solnit's strategy, which is to suspend the site visit process with the indication that it would be resumed at such point as the deficiencies that led to its suspension could be demonstrated to be corrected, and that such resumption would renew the site visit process without, of course, any commitment to the eventual outcome. There could be three possible outcomes. . . . One could be that the suspension would just go on indefinitely and that they would never be in a position to show that the difficulties have been overcome, and that the issue would finally wear itself out, out of attrition. A second

outcome could be that they could actually work hard to shape up and overcome their problems and come back as a group that might eventually be able to make it as an IPA Provisional Society. The third possibility is that they could convince us that it was warranted to resume the site visit process, but that there could still be enough inadequacies in their functioning from our point of view, that in the end they would be turned down as not yet ready. However, that would be several years off and not something that would arouse big problems at this time. To reject them outright at this time could easily lead to the cry that they had never been given a fair chance, that the IPA was interested only in its minimal strategy of letting in its two favorite groups, and of closing the door against all the rest of us worthy people.

The next document was a calming interlude in these political struggles. In Sandler's Presidential Message in the February 1990 *IPA Newsletter* there was no mention at all of the painful litigation process we had all so recently come through or of any of the troublesome events and issues of this first postsettlement period, except by allusion in Sandler's expression of appreciation to me, with which he began his Presidential Message:

His term of office was marked by the way in which he brought his energy, dedication, experience and capacity for handling complex situations to bear on the difficult problems with which the IPA and international psychoanalysis have been confronted. During his term as President he had to deal with the lengthy litigation over the issue of training non-physicians in the USA. The agreement which he negotiated on behalf of the IPA was a successful conclusion to a serious lawsuit which placed great responsibility on the President. Inevitably the litigation was expensive, but the cost to the IPA was kept to about $16 a member—a remarkable feat.

On February 5, 1990, I again wrote to Sandler regarding the continued battle over the problematic NYCPT site visit. In the interim, Sandler had sent me 16 pages of detailed documentation concerning the problems uncovered in the several visits to that group. I commented in my letter:

There is clearly a lot of trouble between them and their affiliate in New Jersey and there are heated charges on both sides. To what extent this is a scientific and ideological struggle over standards and to what extent it is a personal struggle over administrative prerogatives and control of the finances, simply cannot be ascertained from this correspondence. One would need to investigate carefully and hear both sides. It certainly seems true that Strean [the chief spokesman for the group in its application to the IPA] has been trying to conceal this trouble in his own house from the IPA and one could fault him for that. One can also understand it since he is trying, from his point of view, to get his house in order and be in a position to make the best possible presentation to the IPA. My point is that the only real basis we would have for terminating the site visit process with a negative statement is if we could say and document that they do not meet IPA standards and that they cannot or will not make the changes necessary to ensure that they do. We don't have a basis for that at this time.

I then strongly urged suspension, rather than outright rejection, and called the latter course, "risky morally, as well as potentially legally."

The next contentious event in this postsettlement history centered, however, not around the IPA, but around the American and the process of implementation of the "Gaskill plan" by the CNMCT, the committee chaired by Carl Davis. Disagreements had arisen over the operation of the central waiver process through the Davis Committee. Several of the American's institutes that had had waiver proposals on behalf of some nonmedical applicants deferred or rejected by the CNMCT had protested vehemently, either over the issue of the merits of their waiver application and their dismay at its nonacceptance, or over the issue of the appropriateness of the remote central committee second-guessing the local informed judgment in the first place, or over both. This dispute had become sufficiently noisy and public that it drew a strong letter of protest from Cliff Stromberg, in his continuing capacity as legal counsel for GAPPP, dated February 14, 1990, and addressed to the "Directors and Faculty of Psychoanalytic Institutes." It was the opening salvo of what became a series of interventions by Stromberg on behalf of his clients, directed toward what he stated were violations of the "good faith implementation" called for in the settlement agreement.

In this letter, after restating the main provisions of the settlement agreement, Stromberg went on to say, "When the Settlement Agreement was reached, psychologists were very hopeful—as were many of you—that together we could put litigation and contention behind us and move on in a new spirit of cooperation. And there have been many hopeful signs." He listed several at the local institute level:

[But] Unfortunately, as you know, the American has more often been an obstacle than an aid to this process. There have been endless and unfair demands for more interviews of candidates, more case write-ups, more procedural barriers to hurdle. There have been totally unclear procedures, changed rules, and broken understandings. No clear guidance has been given to Institutes or applicants as to how the process works. It remains shrouded in mystery and apparent illogic. The American seems bent on usurping the functions its own local Institutes know better how to perform, namely, evaluating the personal qualities and preparation of waiver candidates. The American has taken the absurd position that its review of candidates is somehow more objective or insightful than the detailed evaluation over many weekly supervision sessions by several leading senior training analysts at local Institutes. And in the end, the American has simply rejected many candidates that Institutes had carefully assessed and knew were qualified. In doing so, the American is creating legal liability not only for itself but for local Institutes as well.

Stromberg then detailed how several Institutes—Southern California, Topeka, St. Louis, Boston—had begun to fight back, calling the CNMCT process "flawed, capricious, and unfairly enforced" (Southern California), and calling for the dropping of the central waiver procedure (Boston). The Boston Institute was then quoted: "If the American persists in its insistence to make these requirements [for medical and nonmedical applicants] different, it is leaving local Institutes open to being sued and causing there to be grounds for reopening the lawsuit. Our attorney joins us in our concern that the conduct of the American raises a serious question as to whether or not the American has complied with its obligations under the settlement agreement in the Welch case."

This brought Stromberg to what he called the key point of his letter. He stated that the American's institutes had two choices, one toward progress and cooperation, requiring that the waiver process be administered fairly and with an appropriate degree of local autonomy (and with the full support of "GAPPP and the broader psychological community"), or to work hand-in-hand with the American and face renewed widespread litigation. Stromberg warned that the Settlement Agreement extinguished certain claims only against the American, the IPA, and the two institutes in New York, and that all the other Institutes risked lawsuits on antitrust, discrimination, and breach of contract grounds that would put both their assets and their integrity at stake. Stromberg further warned that the American itself could be brought back to court on the allegation that the waiver process was not being administered in good faith. In this letter, in which Stromberg bypassed the American and appealed directly to its affiliated institutes—seeking to widen what he felt was a growing breach between the "controlling" American and the "rebelling" Institutes—he finally urged the institutes to "consider immediate action to dissuade the American" from its misguided course and to prevent it from imperilling "the assets and progressive spirit of local institutes across the country." It was clear that Stromberg was quite ready to capitalize on disputes over procedures within the American to pressure both the American and its institutes toward the more complete and quicker achievement of the original ultimate goals of the now theoretically-settled lawsuit.

Stromberg followed this letter with another, dated February 21, 1990, addressed to Joel Klein as the former (and still current) attorney for the American on lawsuit matters. Here he restated the essence of the Settlement Agreement that the American was to "fully implement in good faith." He added, "Unfortunately, as the chorus of protests from the American's own Institutes proclaims, the American is administering the CNMCT process in a way that is in bad faith, unfair, increasingly burdensome and discriminatory. This violates the clear words and the spirit of the Settlement Agreement." Stromberg called on the American to cease and desist from its "heavy-handed threats" to its rebellious institutes, and warned that "If the American persists in this irresponsible brinkmanship, it will alienate its own Institutes. And if the American forces them to join with it in unprincipled, discriminatory policies, it will subject itself—and its local institutes—to legal liability." This last threat was made still more explicit: "This conduct will result in court proceedings to hold the American in violation of the Settlement Agreement and in separate lawsuits against certain Institutes."

Both of these letters were sent to the IPA by Clint Fisher with a brief cover memorandum dated February 28, 1990. He stated in it, "As you can see, the IPA is not mentioned . . . and all of the vehemence appears to be directed at the leadership of the American." He then wrote, "Please let me know if there is anything you would like me to follow up upon." On March 12, 1990, as one of the recipients of his memorandum, I replied to Fisher:

> From the IPA's point of view, it is good that we are not at all involved in this new quarrel between the plaintiffs to the lawsuit and the American. Actually, although there are exaggerations in it and though the American is being accused of being collectively in bad faith which I think is not true, nonetheless there is enough to the charges to be very troubling—and there are individuals within the American who have been unhappy with the settlement and have been dragging their heels in implementing it. Certainly the quotations that Cliff has from different member institutes of the American are going to look

very bad if they get seen by a judge. . . . I don't see the IPA playing any role but we will surely be interested in knowing how the American hopes to cope with this.

On March 5, 1990, two letters went out on Murray Meisels's stationery. The first was a "Dear Colleague" letter, signed by Karen Rosica for the Conference Planning Committee, announcing a convening by Division 39 of "a conference to discuss the feasibility and desirability of establishing a Federation of Psychoanalytic Educational Organizations. The overall purposes of federating would be to strengthen local organizations and to encourage the development of psychoanalysis throughout the country, in professional and applied settings, and in the general population." It was unclear to me who comprised the target audience of this letter. Was it just the Division 39-sponsored training groups? Did it also include the new nonmedical IPA Provisional Societies? And did it also include those other organized groups outside the IPA who had not applied to it, or even the institutes of the American? And what was its presumed relationship to the American (and to the IPA) intended to be? A parallel and rival organization, or a supraordinate body replacing or subsuming the American's established national organization?

The other letter (also on Meisels's stationery and dated the same) was an open letter to the IPA, signed by Ruth-Jean Eisenbud, President of Division 39. This was the first direct targeting of the IPA over settlement implementation issues—though not coming from Stromberg, as were the demands upon the American. The complaint here was that the IPA's "admission requirements and procedures are having deleterious and even destructive effects on psychologist Institutes." This was because "the IPA had adopted a deliberate policy of admitting only those members of an Institute who meet IPA requirements, and of excluding those members . . . who do not. While the strict maintenance of IPA standards appears to be a worthy goal, it is itself problematic and actually produces dire situations in applicant Institutes and would-be applicant Institutes." The letter then adduced several instances of such (hypothetical or real?) situations. For example: "A number of Institutes that are interested in joining the IPA have hesitated to apply or have decided not to apply, out of the certainty that horrific consequences would ensue should the IPA admit only 50%, or 75%, or less than 100% of its, the applying-Institute's, membership. Such an event could cause a debilitating lawsuit, lead to a split, and/or destroy an existing training program. The IPA policy has actually had the effect of deterring psychologist Institutes from applying to the IPA."

The letter then called on the IPA to cease its current procedures (those devised by the Hanly New Groups Committee) and immediately enter into discussions with Division 39 to devise mutually agreeable policies and procedures that would not be injurious to psychologist institutes. She stated

"That foremost among the admission principles shall be the provision that psychologist Institutes in the USA will be admitted or rejected in their entirety, and that no current Institute member shall be, in any way, disenfranchised by IPA admission. If the Institute is admitted to the IPA, then all members of the Institute shall become IPA members, all training analysts shall become IPA training analysts, and all supervisors shall become IPA supervisors." This would all be implemented by a joint IPA-Division 39 committee which "could evaluate several Institutes in one visit, and which would develop uniform and simplified evaluation procedures." Further, the IPA and Division 39 should establish "a joint committee to consider grievances that might arise in the application process." The letter ended with the statement that it was being sent to the attorneys for both sides and to Judge Michael Mukasey, in whose court the Settlement Agreement had been ratified. This far-reaching proposal would not only undo all the carefully crafted procedures that had been worked out in the New Group Committee deliberations and approved by the IPA Executive Council, but would have involved an outside party—Division 39—playing a coequal determining role in the IPA's administrative and educational structure. It was exactly the kind of proposal that the IPA (and its codefendants) had successfully fought off in the litigation process, and it would, of course, now be equally unacceptable. It was the first broadside in a campaign by some of the supporters of the original lawsuit to try to push the IPA into abandoning the settlement terms and according the plaintiffs the total litigation victory that they had not accomplished during the lawsuit proceedings.

On March 29, 1990, I sent Joe Sandler my own advice as to how the IPA could respond to this Division 39 letter (which I had just received), which I felt was very troubling. My worry was that "there is a high potential for a lot of harassment, spreading of misinformation, and souring the relationship between American psychologists and the IPA. This will pose a particular problem, with a real conflict of loyalties, for those groups we have just taken in. I think that there is a very small potential, if any, that this would lead to an actual reopening of the lawsuit." I then recommended that "we hold to a steady course in following the procedures worked out by Charles Hanly and his committee and defending it all on the basis of IPA standards that we are maintaining, for the good of the whole organization, and also to assure those we are taking in that they are equally well-trained and are not second-class citizens." I cautioned, however, that "we must do all of this with the most correct procedures most deliberately applied." Here I reverted to the issue of the troubled and problematic site visits of the Solnit committee:

That is why I was so strongly opposed to what I felt was the dangerous suggestion to summarily cancel that site visit process.

They may in the end prove to be not good enough, but that is a judgment that we must make only after the fact, and after having gathered all the information we can, and after giving them every chance to make their own best case. Just because we found out that they have internal quarrels, and that they struggle over standards, and that they may have been trying to cover up their internal dissensions has been, to me, a totally insufficient reason to cancel a site visit. Rather, it calls for a more intensive site visit to unearth what is going on.

As if none of these controversies were swirling around the IPA and around the American, the April 1990 issue of *The Round Robin*, carried a President's Column by Robert C. Lane, which was a very detailed, comprehensive, and fair statement of the application procedures for IPA membership of nonmedical psychoanalytic training organizations and also of their individual members. This long account ended with the statement: "I have written this article to share with the membership what an IPA on-site evaluation is like. It is a very careful perusal whose purpose is to see if your Society and its Institute meet IPA standards." At the beginning of the article, Lane had indicated that three of these societies had already been accepted as Provisional Societies by the IPA at its July 1989 Congress in Rome, and that the applications of two others were still pending.

But the ongoing battles were soon resumed. At the spring meeting of the American, New York, May 1990, Hanly and Arnold Cooper, now the co-chairs of the New Groups Committee, met with Sandler and Jacqueline Amati Mehler, the IPA Secretary, and the decision was made to cancel the Solnit Committee site visit process to NYCPT. When I returned to San Francisco, having been informed by Hanly of this decision on my last day at the New York meetings, I sent a long message to Sandler, dated May 14, 1990; the largest item was my strong protest about this decision, which I considered ill-advised for all the reasons I had been presenting all along. I stated that if, as Hanly had informed me, a main purpose for selecting this course was to give himself (Sandler) a totally free hand in reconstituting a new Site Visit Committee afresh, should the group undertake to reapply for evaluation at some future time, that goal could have been accomplished without the rupture of this site visit process, and its potentially unhappy risks, at a particularly delicate juncture, to the relations of the IPA (as well as of the American) with Division 39 and with Stromberg, on behalf of Division 39 or GAPPP or the former plaintiffs.

Sandler's equally detailed response came two days later, dated May 16, 1990. He vigorously defended the appropriateness and correctness of the decision. The primary issue he felt was the cover-up by spokespersons for the group being visited, in an effort to conceal their own severe internal dissensions and lack of consensus about their desire to alter their practices to conform to IPA standards and requirements, and that this had led to a breakdown of confidence in the site visit proceedings under present circumstances. The issue of the constitution of the IPA Site Visit Committee itself Sandler declared to be secondary. He acknowledged that he had become anxious about Solnit's role, "when I felt that he was inadvertently preparing the ground for a possible lawsuit by being over-encouraging about the group's chances of being accepted. Among Al's many qualities . . . is a tendency to be extremely helpful to the underdog—and this has been of great benefit to many people, but it can go wrong."

This officially brought the matter to a close, at least within the IPA. I acknowledged that in my response to Sandler the next day, May 17, 1990. I made one final point:

> I am aware how concerned you are, and properly so, that the American never get the feeling that the IPA is being lax on standards in its scrutiny of these groups. None of us are advocating that and certainly not myself or Charles [Hanly] and I think it is possible to combine a real watchfulness for standards with a total openness to giving them every opportunity to explain everything and to demonstrate everything while not coming to any premature judgment until after all the facts are in. I am sure that my next message to you will be about other things.

The next event—rounding out a full year since the 1989 IPA Congress in Rome, at which the three nonmedical groups were admitted as IPA Provisional Societies—was the 34-page report in July, detailing the activities of the New U.S. Groups Committee over the course of that year. The first item had to do with the cancelled NYCPT site visit. Of the several options confronting the IPA in fashioning a response to the serious difficulties uncovered during that site visit process, which culminated in a concealed rift within the group erupting into an open schism and split, the Hanly Committee's recommendation for formal action by the IPA Executive Council (meeting in July 1990 in London) was that the site visit process be terminated, with an invitation to reapply after a year had elapsed. The reasoning was as follows:

> The failure to inform the Site Visit Committee of the potential schism is a serious failure on their part. The group will need time not only to work out the impact of the split, but also to re-orient themselves to an exclusive commitment to psychoanalysis and carry through all the implications of this change. The group

will benefit most from undertaking to do it on their own, free of a Site Visit Committee looking over their shoulders, and free of the temptation to merely "please the Site Visit Committee," rather than search out the best solutions to their own circumstances whatever the result might be. The invitation to re-apply is a recognition that they have made serious efforts to carry forward the necessary reforms and that they do have strengths.

Some reservation was expressed over the possible political and legal consequences of this move. It was felt that the group itself was unlikely to initiate legal action, "but it is clear that the Division 39 monitoring committee has the will and the means to use any pretext they can to do just that." Nonetheless, this proposal was adopted by the full IPA Executive Council as its official action, and this dropped the number of ongoing site visit evaluations for possible action at the forthcoming 1991 IPA Congress in Buenos Aires to just one, LAISPS.

A second major policy recommendation in this report was to formally authorize the new Provisional Societies to accept individuals into membership who had not graduated from IPA Institutes, but who would be eligible under the criteria applied to the preexisting members in these new groups, individuals who had exceptional merit as clinicians and who committed themselves to participating fully in the life of the society that would admit them. This policy would be discontinued when the 10-year period of legal settlement monitoring would expire, or when the society had become a full component society, whichever came first. This proposal would make provision for the processing of individuals who had applied or were planning to apply for membership in one of the new Provisional Societies when, at Hanly's request, all such membership applications had been frozen for the convenience of the site visit process. This proposal too was adopted by the IPA Executive Council, creating officially the "window of opportunity," which subsequently caused inadvertent grief when a few individuals took advantage of (unforeseen) ambiguities in its operating parameters. The greatest bulk of this July 1990 report was a very detailed informational report from the IPTAR Liaison Committee on how that Provisional Society had operated during the first year of its IPA affiliation.

Thus ended the first year of activity within the IPA (and the American) following the 1989 IPA Congress in Rome at which three of the applicant New Groups had been admitted to the IPA in Provisional Society status. This, we had hoped, marked the final resolution of the half-century-long vexing divisions within the worldwide psychoanalytic community over the issue of nonmedical (or "lay") analysis. The year's events made clear that legal settlement and pledges of mutual goodwill in its implementation process did not automatically translate into fully harmonious working cooperation on all sides. As the year's events unfolded, it became poignantly manifest how much wariness and defensiveness colored the stances of the IPA (and the American) and how much skepticism and suspiciousness continued to actuate the erstwhile plaintiffs. For the most part, the events recorded in this chapter have, by now, faded into the recesses of organizational and personal memories. What importantly remains are the enduring alterations in the structure of American psychoanalysis, ushered in by the changes in the American and the IPA as legally codified in the settlement agreement, with which we continue to live each day, and within which we have redefined our lives as American psychoanalysts. But these events warrant chronicling as part of the historical record; they can help illuminate the expectable, if not always inevitable processes of wrenching sociohistorical change in the structures and functions of organizations and professions as they are lived through and experienced by those protagonists in whose time they occur. These kinds of events are not unique to the discipline of psychoanalysis.

Further Struggles over Implementation, 1990–1991

In the continuing saga of the implementation of the New Groups policy by the IPA, the next event of note was a memorandum, dated August 7, 1990, sent by Charles Hanly to the IPA Executive Committee, titled "New Groups Developments." There were three. The first concerned a letter received from Stanley Grand, President of IPTAR, declaring that his Society had met all of the IPA's requirements and was therefore asking for graduation to full Component Society status at the forthcoming 37th IPA Congress in Buenos Aires in 1991. That would be only two years after admission to Provisional Society status at the Rome Congress in 1989, a progression that customarily is not granted in less than four years. For the working of Hanly's committee, this posed a problem. NYFS, the other nonmedical New Group in New York in parallel progression, wouldn't be ready by the time of the Buenos Aires Congress. It was a larger and more complex organization than IPTAR, and the expectable issues in bringing its procedures and practices fully into line with IPA requirements would certainly take the four years leading to the 1993 Amsterdam Congress. Competitive pressures between the two groups were intense enough that the New Groups Committee dreaded putting one before the other. What to do in such a case? Hanly was recommending reining in the IPTAR enthusiasts, however unfair they might feel that to be, so that both groups could be presented together in Amsterdam.

With LAISPS, the Los Angeles group, still in the midst of its ongoing initial evaluation process, there was another issue. Charles Mangham of Seattle, the chair of the Site Visit Committee, had been approached at a scientific meeting by an individual seeking an interview about the process, representing himself as a reporter for the APA. Mangham had taken this as a representation from the *Newsletter* of the American Psychoanalytic Association; actually it was from the American Psychological Association.

Mangham had given a candid interview in which he had reflected on the expectable kinds of problems that had surfaced in the work needed to bring the LAISPS procedures and practices fully in line with IPA requirements. The article, when it appeared in the APA *Monitor*, was slanted to show how reluctant the IPA had become in its pursuit of its obligations under the settlement agreement, and it gave the impression, as well, that the IPA was gravely concerned, as if the LAISPS training program had already been fully examined and had been found wanting. The LAISPS officers were extremely upset, and Mangham had written a letter of clarification to them, stating that the site visit evaluation was still in process and that final judgments had not been arrived at and were not intended. Of course, it was also the case that the issues that had come up in the site visit process to that point, and had already been discussed with the LAISPS officials, were not to be disregarded, but rather represented the work that still needed to be accomplished between the IPA visitors and LAISPS. It was hoped that a letter of correction that Mangham had sent to the *Monitor* would be published. What was disquieting in all this was the readiness of the *Monitor*, speaking for and to organized psychology in America, to see obstructionism and bad faith in the IPA's careful evaluation processes.

The third issue was one of policy. The New Group's policies and procedures had been created to rectify old inequities, to provide a means for evaluating, for IPA membership, groups and individuals who, prior to the 1987 IPA bylaw changes voted in Montreal, had not been eligible for training within an IPA member institute and had therefore been trained in independent training groups that had sprung up outside the IPA. But how long should this open evaluation process be available, and what exactly constituted eligibility to be considered under this New Groups policy? With his memorandum Hanly enclosed a draft of an IPA policy statement on these matters for consideration. On the first question, he proposed a time limitation of 10 years from the date of the lawsuit settlement. On the second, he proposed that the policy be restricted to groups already in existence for a sufficient time to have graduated candidates prior to the date of the settlement agreement. Groups that came into being subsequent to that would be expected from the beginning to conform to IPA standards, using the same qualifications and route to membership that the IPA constitution makes available to all.

In the next month, issues around the site visiting process were lifted into the realm of major overt controversy by a 13-page, single-spaced letter, dated September 19, 1990, from Cliff Stromberg to Trip Dorkey and Clint Fisher, the IPA attorneys. This was then forwarded on by Clint Fisher to the IPA Executive Committee, with a brief cover note, on the next day. The tone was as aggressively accusatory and threatening as Stromberg's letters to the American and to its affiliated institutes earlier in the same year, in which Stromberg had charged obstructionism and bad faith in the carrying out of the CNMCT evaluation process. This letter also began with the declaration to Dorkey and Fisher that their client—the IPA—was not complying in good faith with the terms of the settlement agreement. Stromberg restated the terms of that agreement and quoted also the content of the August 16, 1988 side-letter, which was specially negotiated as additional consideration for the plaintiffs' willingness to enter the settlement agreement. That was the letter that had spelled out the concept of functional equivalence, as well as what could be encompassed under the rubric of a "Freudian" training model and orientation. And Stromberg added that in its October 1988 *Newsletter* the IPA had touted this agreement with great fanfare.

In fact, Stromberg asserted, the IPA had only judged six of 23 inquiring groups ready for the site visit process, and of those only three had thus far secured IPA approval: IPTAR, NYFS, and PCC. Clearly, according to Stromberg, "these programs, populated by American-affiliated training analysts, seem to have received preferred treatment according to different standards and a different schedule." For the rest, the IPA was charged with having created a review process that, in fact, did not rest fairly on the principle of functional equivalence, and that "the standards demanded of American groups and individuals do not appear consistent with those often applied by the IPA elsewhere in the world."[1] Stromberg ended stating: "Finally, the lack of clear standards, the excessive procedural hurdles, the contradictory instructions and general burdensomeness and delay in the application process for several Institutes, raises a serious question as to whether the IPA is pursuing the process in good faith."

Stromberg then cited in detail two instances of what he called "the totally unfair, unprofessional and incoherent" evaluation processes. One involved the William Alanson White Institute in New York, which in fact had not applied for IPA site visit consideration, and still has not, at the time of this writing. The other concerned LAISPS in Los Angeles, which

---

[1] What Stromberg was referring to was the IPA insistence that the standards for training analyses and supervised analyses be set from now on at a minimum of four sessions weekly in accord with the IPA minimum standards for training (although those who had been trained on a three sessions per week basis could be judged eligible for IPA membership if they met the functional equivalence criteria elaborated originally by the New Groups Committee). Stromberg was also alluding to the fact that a number of IPA Component Societies around the world had deviated from the official IPA standards and were now conducting training in many instances on a three times a week basis. The IPA position was that these were departures from its own standards, and considerable effort was expended both during my administration of the IPA (1985-1989) and Joseph Sandler's (1989-1993) to bring these deviating groups back into line with the officially promulgated standards. This, to us, did not warrant allowing new groups to come in on the basis of a three weekly session training schedule.

had been in the middle of the ongoing evaluation process when the APA *Monitor* article sharply exacerbated tensions that were already present. About the White Institute (WAW), the questions of "functional equivalence" and three- versus four-times per week analysis were declared to have dominated the informal discussions between a WAW Committee, chaired by Anna Antonovsky, and IPA representatives over a two-year period. The IPA representative (Arnold Cooper) had declared the instituting of four-times weekly analysis to be "essential," and that it would not be realistic to proceed with a formal site visit process unless WAW was willing to adopt the four-times weekly standard. This was the sticking point. Of this, Stromberg said, "The IPA representatives seemed totally unconcerned about the divisive effects of their policy on Institutes like the White that had long been functioning on a unified, amicable basis. The IPA representatives suggested it might be advisable for some analysts who met IPA standards to form their own IPA-sanctioned 'Study Group.' In effect, they encouraged divisiveness and defections."[2] Stromberg then went on to quote examples from the current psychoanalytic literature which indicated to him, not the IPA's concern about pressures to erode the official minimum training standards, but rather that, "it is well known that the IPA abides three times per week analysis as a common practice in many IPA affiliated Societies around the world." On this basis, IPA insistence on the four sessions per week standard was declared "particularly indefensible and hypocritical."[3]

In the instance of LAISPS, Stromberg's charged that from the very beginning, LAISPS' willing cooperation had been met with persistent delays, lack of timely reports, and other unconscionable foot-dragging. (For instance, a June 29, 1989 letter from Hanly to Hedda Bolgar of LAISPS had been mis-addressed and was not received until September, 1989.) Problems that needed working out had been declared to exist, but Hanly had been vague and unable to specify details. A meeting that Weinshel and I had had with Bolgar and Norman Oberman of LAISPS in Rome in 1989, at which the two of us were trying to explain to them why our Site Visit

---

[2] However these interchanges were construed, it was never IPA policy to "suggest" any particular course of action to institutes considering making application to the IPA. In fact, the New Groups Committee instructions scrupulously insisted on leaving it to each group, once apprised of the IPA requirements, to make its own best decision on what course to follow in relation to the IPA application process.

[3] Since WAW has not—to this writing—been able to come to a consensus on a willingness to alter its training requirements to conform to IPA minimum training standards, it has not to this point sought IPA site visit evaluation. Individual members of WAW who have wanted IPA membership have been able to do so by applying for membership in other nonmedical groups that had succeeded in this quest (IPTAR, NYFS) through the "window of opportunity" policy.

Committee felt they were not ready to bring the LAISPS application for approval by the Business Meeting in Rome, was reported as my having said: "The error is ours; there is no report; you were screwed." (For my part, I never remembered saying anything like that, nor is it the sort of language I use in that kind of context. In my own September 26, 1990 letter of comment to Sandler on the Stromberg letter, I declared that quotation to be an outright fabrication.) Stromberg added that in his June 29, 1989 letter, Hanly stated he had received and read the report of the first site visit, and so, I, as President of the IPA, was either uninformed or lying.

The catalogue of claimed missteps went on and on. Charles Mangham, who had assumed the chairmanship of the LAISPS Site Visit Committee when Gaskill resigned because of illness, was quoted as saying, in a most unfriendly way, "that it was not his function to help LAISPS get into the IPA, that his function was to evaluate them." This was followed by further charges of delays, of telephone calls and letters being unanswered, and so forth. At one point, LAISPS representatives were ostensibly informed that the IPA leadership wanted to "go slow" in the approval of new institutes. And where individual LAISPS training analysts had seemingly been found unacceptable in that category by the IPA visitors, the promised letters of explanation of the ostensible difficulties had never come. All this time, and despite all these "negative developments," Stromberg averred that the LAISPS representatives kept supplying all the information the IPA requested and continued their unflagging cooperation with the IPA.

After a very long recital of apparent miscommunication after miscommunication, Stromberg concluded that all the substantive issues raised by the IPA Site Visit Committee over the course of its several visits and many exchanges of letters and telephone calls were simply "pretextual at best and unlawful at worst." "In sum, the IPA process as applied to LAISPS has violated any conceivable standards of due process, basic fairness or professional competence." Adding insult to injury, LAISPS was being asked to pay its designated share of the expenses of such a "sham visit." Stromberg stated that Mangham "permitted himself to be interviewed by the press (the APA *Monitor*) concerning the site visits," and he was then quoted in a way to indicate that he had made public statements prejudging the results of the site visit process, before the LAISPS personnel were informed of their supposed deficiencies and before they could respond. As a result this caused "substantial professional harm."[4]

---

[4] Despite the recriminations involved in this recital by Stromberg, the LAISPS site visit process did proceed on schedule and successfully so, and at the very next IPA Congress the following summer (the 37th Congress in Buenos Aires in 1991), LAISPS was voted into Provisional Society status in the IPA.

Stromberg surmised that these unfair procedures that had been applied to other than the IPA's favored nonmedical institutes were perhaps due to the "apparent pressure on the IPA by the American." He quoted a statement made by Homer Curtis, the President of the American, to the American's Executive Council, that the officers of the two organizations were in very close touch with each other on all these matters of common concern: "We are very troubled by this," he said, and by "other indications we have seen that the IPA, the American, and others may be engaging in a *new* unlawful conspiracy to restrain trade. As you know, new actions of this kind can subject the participants to new liability." After calling on the IPA to cease and desist from all these hurtful, obstructionist, and delaying tactics, Stromberg outlined the positive steps the IPA should take and asked for detailed information on how they were being implemented, including detailed reports on the status of each of the ongoing and pending site visits.

He stated that "if the IPA does not in good faith correct this serious situation, the psychology profession has the will and resources to litigate further. . . . The psychologists fervently desire to put these disputes behind us and to work amicably with the IPA. Indeed, many psychologists were hopeful that while the American appeared still obdurate, the IPA seemed to be promising statesmanlike leadership. We still hope that is possible." He then asked for a meeting of the principal parties, if that would be helpful. Thus the gauntlet was thrown down to the IPA, with the partial exculpation that perhaps it was pressure from the American that had led to these serious IPA misbehaviors.

I have copies of two letters of comment and advice to Sandler in his task of fashioning a response by the IPA to Stromberg's challenge: Hanly's, the more restrained, and mine, the more importunate. Hanly's letter is dated September 24, 1990. Concerning the WAW issue, here is the nub of Hanly's response:

> We have been taking the position that until they are willing to change their training standards, we would not consider their application. . . . If it is worth changing inadequate standards upon becoming members, it is worth changing before becoming members. . . . Stromberg continues to hammer at IPA inconsistency. I doubt that their argument is very strong because the IPA has never admitted a Society that did not adhere to its training standards. It has been a question of backsliding afterwards.

On the LAISPS front, Hanly reassured Sandler that despite some confusions and communication failures created by the transition of the Site Visit Committee chairmanship from Gaskill to Mangham, the site visit process was now proceeding on schedule, and in a favorable way. Basically, he was counseling Sandler not to allow himself to be rattled, but to hold a steady course.

My letter to Sandler is dated September 26, 1990. I said that Stromberg's letter was indeed very unpleasant, but not necessarily surprising. There had been awkwardnesses, and inadvertent mixups as well, in two of our site visit processes, the still ongoing one with LAISPS and the one to NYCPT that had been terminated by the Executive Council: "It may be that whatever the IPA did in the handling of these applications, we could not have satisfied all the parties that we were acting in a fair, objective, and honorable way and it might be that in any case something like this would have come." I did feel, however, that the confusions and mishaps in the conduct of these visits left us vulnerable to these charges, and my own choice of Gaskill as the first chair of the LAISPS Site Visit Committee had indeed turned out to be unwise, "perhaps due to his concerns about his own illness, and partly perhaps because of his own unfamiliarity with the whole site visiting process."

Having said that, I stated strongly that the Stromberg letter was full of distortions and outright misstatements. I had never said what he quoted as my interchange with Bolgar and Oberman in Rome. Many other statements Stromberg made I felt were less flagrant but still added up to a skewed and distorted spin on the march of events and on the presumed motivations of the involved parties. I felt strongly that the record needed to be set straight, and would best be done through a letter written by our attorneys. As for the big weakness in the IPA position (Stromberg called it "bad faith"), our insistence that new groups abide by IPA training standards when the plaintiffs knew and could quote documents and professional literature in which we acknowledged that these are not lived up to in all our own component societies: "All we can say about this is that these are our standards that we expect everybody to abide by, and the fact that we have a problem of enforcing compliance with some of our existing groups, does not mean that we should alter our official standards in regard to new groups."

So far, this was on all fours with Hanly's letter to Sandler. But then I added my own plea in regard to a distinction being pushed in the IPA Executive Council, which I felt to be a mistake in tactic and in emotional set:

> This has to do with making clear to those being site visited that the site visitors are only there to evaluate them and not to help them in any way. The distinction can be a subtle one and it is really a matter of attitude that gets conveyed. Clearly, the intent of the By-Law changes voted in Montreal was that there was a major inequity that had existed for 50 years that the IPA was going to try to correct. There were people who for 50 years had

not been eligible for training within the IPA and had had to create their own training institutions the best they could, and to live up to analytic standards the best they understood them. If we could agree that some of these groups and individuals had achieved functionally equivalent IPA standards, then we were committing ourselves to help them in every way that we could to become IPA members, and expecting in return, of course, that as soon as they became members, they would alter all their practices to bring them fully in accord with IPA standards. This doesn't mean that we should take inadequate institutions or individuals into the IPA and it doesn't mean that we have to make positive judgments about every applicant group. It does mean, I think, that we should look at all the applicant groups in the most comprehensive, open-minded way that we can and give them every opportunity to present themselves as fully as possible, and every help we can in working out the things they would need to change to live up to our standards, and then still have for ourselves the right of final judgment as to whether they have succeeded or not.

Here I was referring to my different perspective on the terminated site visit, which, surprisingly, was not mentioned in Stromberg's letter. Even more, I was putting what emphasis I could into the IPA's ongoing posture in continuing to navigate this difficult path, all of it under the suspicious watchful eyes of our erstwhile adversaries.

The IPA's official response to Stromberg was sent in a letter from Clint Fisher, dated October 19, 1990, under the direction of Sandler and the IPA Executive Committee, and was very terse: "The IPA takes issue with a number of the assertions and alleged quotations set forth in your letter. The IPA chooses not to respond to these on a point by point basis at this time, but does want to make clear that by not doing so, it is not necessarily concurring with your characterizations of the matters you describe." Instead, the IPA would send Stromberg the most recently revised (and most precise) statement of its Policies and Procedures for the Evaluation of New U.S. Groups, which spelled out in detail the exact sequence of preconditions, procedures, and expectations in regard to site visit proceedings and evaluations. Further, the IPA officers would indeed be happy to meet with Stromberg and other complainants in December 1990, when they would all be in Miami for the meeting of the American, because "the IPA too would like to put behind it the kinds of disputes that led to the litigation and the kinds of problems that you address in your letter."

This revised policies and procedures statement was being worked on all through October 1990, with one draft dated just a day earlier than Fisher's letter to Stromberg (October 18, 1990). As finally ratified (and then sent to Stromberg) it contained all of the by-now familiar contents, but with specific clarification of existing ambiguities and precise dates, as well as guidelines, for the operation of the new policies and procedures. These major items were clarified and given both procedural and time dimensions: (1) societies and institutes applying for IPA affiliation had to have been established and fully functioning prior to November 1988, the cut-off date that was finally set; (2) training policies and procedures would need to have been altered where necessary to bring them into accord with IPA standards, before a site visit would be scheduled; (3) the "functional equivalence" standard was more precisely spelled out, that is, a demonstrated clinical psychoanalytic competence despite training that did not measure up to IPA requirements in all regards; and (4) in regard to the complicated issue of the acceptance of non-IPA-trained members by the United States New Groups, acceptances of this kind could only take place while the society still retained its Provisional Society status (for outstanding individuals, proposed by the Provisional Society, recommended by the Site Visit Liaison Committee, and then ratified by the IPA Executive Council). Once the New Group was voted a full component Society, however, it could accord membership only to its own graduates or to the graduates of other IPA component organizations. In explanation of the various cut-off dates set, the policies and procedures manual stated that for new groups coming into existence after November 1988, "the functional equivalency criteria and procedures of the New U.S. Groups Policy will not apply. The application of this policy is limited to those groups which did not have at the time of their formation any access to membership in the IPA. That circumstance has not existed since the amendment to the IPA Constitution in 1987."

On October 31, 1990, Anna Antonovsky, a leading member of the White Institute and someone who had been actively promoting efforts within that group to seek IPA affiliation, wrote to Arnold Cooper expressing her dismay at aspects of Stromberg's September 19 letter to Dorkey and Fisher: "I was distressed to see that the letter distorted some of what I had reported to the Council of Fellows of the White Institute regarding the talk we had in September of 1989." She was asking the new White Society Ad Hoc Committee on the IPA to straighten that out with Stromberg, but in the meantime she was sending Cooper a copy of the actual report that her Committee had made to the November 29, 1989 meeting of the White Society's Council of Fellows.

In her report to the Council of Fellows, Antonovsky first stated that a committee of five members of William Alanson White, which she chaired, had met with five IPA officers (headed by me) in December 1988, and we had made clear to them that in order to qualify for IPA membership, they would have to demonstrate the functional equivalence of their present organization and membership, and also that they would have to commit themselves to adherence to all IPA standards from now on, including the four-times-a-week minimal frequency for psychoanalysis. At a January 1989 meeting of their Intra-Society Forum on IPA, there had been four individual presentations and much intense discussion. Strong feelings were expressed both for and against the advisability of trying to join the IPA. Several months later, Antonovsky had had a long talk with Hanly and described to him what had transpired at the January meeting and, "how concerned our colleagues were to preserve the intactness of the entire group."

At the Rome Congress of the IPA, July-August 1989, Antonovsky had asked to meet with Cooper, as the new IPA Associate Secretary for North America, to explore how the new IPA administration might view a possible application by the White Institute. Cooper had made three main points: (1) that the IPA deemed the four-times-a-week requirement to be essential; (2) that the White Institute try out the four-times-a-week standard for at least a year to see how they felt about it, because, "it would not be reasonable for the White Institute to expect that admission to the IPA could precede accepted use of the four-times-a-week standard"; and (3) that the IPA would not wish to be divisive with regard to existing institutes and therefore would not wish to enter an ongoing internal disagreement to strengthen one side or the other. There the matter rested, and the report asked that the Committee on the IPA be discharged: "If an interest in applying to the IPA were to be pursued further, a different kind of discussion would be called for—a fundamental discussion of an Institute consensus and its relation to an IPA consensus." (As already indicated, to the date of this writing—1996—the White Institute has not agreed to make application for IPA membership.)

On November 7, 1990, Fisher wrote to Sandler, enclosing a copy of the October 31, 1990 letter from Stromberg to him in response to Fisher's letter to him of October 19, 1990. In his letter, Stromberg thanked Fisher for his response and said that his clients welcomed the prospect that the IPA would promulgate definitive guidelines and procedures for the consideration of applications from the New Groups in the United States, and looked forward to reviewing them carefully to see whether they were in accord with the Settlement Agreement and the side agreement. They felt however, that such guidelines and procedures could only address some of the "deficiencies" that Stromberg had outlined in his September 19 letter. They would like to know what other steps the IPA was taking to address these matters, and meanwhile his clients would be willing to defer any new legal action. They would be willing to meet with the IPA officers again: "In the past, our meetings with IPA representatives have been cordial in tone and constructive in content. Unfortunately, few of the understandings seemingly reached at these meetings were later implemented by the IPA."

Meanwhile I entered a clarifying letter of background information on this matter, dated November 8, 1990, addressed to Valerie Tufnell who had just recently succeeded Irene Auletta as Administrative Director of the

IPA. First I made clear that although the White Institute had been one of the prime movers in the original litigation against the American, and one of its central figures (Nathan Stockhamer) was one of the chief negotiators in the many meetings between the plaintiffs and the defendants, they had not formally applied for consideration by the IPA when the doors were finally opened in this regard. This was because "the great majority of people in the White have been unwilling to alter their traditional way of carrying out treatment and training, namely analyses three times per week." About Antonovsky, who I stated to be "one of their most distinguished members," she was part of the minority group in White ranks who wanted them to alter their procedures to bring them into conformity with IPA standards. She and I had had several individual talks about this, one at great length at a meeting we had both participated in at the Austen Riggs Center in Stockbridge, Massachusetts, in June 1989. Her group had simply been unable to persuade the majority, and there was talk at the time of a secession of like-minded colleagues from the White to set up a new group that would be formed in accord with IPA standards. This would be a significant number of (very good) people, and Antonovsky wondered how receptive the IPA would be to that. At the time I was still the IPA President, and

> I indicated that we would not get into the position of encouraging or sanctioning her group breaking away and starting a new Institute and that we certainly could make no promises or commitments; however, if they on their own chose to break away and set themselves up as such a new group and applied to the IPA, we would, of course, consider them the same way as we would any other applicant group. The risks, of course, would all be with them since there could be no guarantee that we would find them acceptable.

I had heard no further and thus assumed that the group had decided not to push the secession. In the meantime, Antonovsky had herself sought IPA membership by joining one of the now accepted new Provisional Societies in New York. On November 29, 1990, Fisher wrote to Sandler notifying him that he was sending Stromberg a copy of the IPA's revised Policies and Procedures for the evaluation of new U.S. groups, and that the IPA was also gathering the additional information Stromberg had requested in his September 19 letter.

This dispute initiated by Stromberg's letter became more public when the December 1990 issue of *Round Robin* published a rancorous exchange of letters between Jay Kwawer, representing the William Alanson White Society, and Bill Greenstadt, former President of NYFS and now President of Section I of Division 39. Kwawer, in his letter of complaint about Greenstadt's "President's Column" in the September 1990 *Round Robin*, took strong exception to Greenstadt's description in his column of the IPA "window of opportunity" policy for the acceptance of individual members who were not currently IPA members. He charged that Greenstadt had moved in the direction of operationally defining the "functional equivalence" concept as synonymous with four-times-per-week training. He said that, "In so doing, Dr. Greenstadt is betraying his fidelity obligation as President of the Section to provide leadership and representation of the membership of the entire section, not simply of his own psychoanalytic group and its particular allegiance with respect to what has become a matter of significant controversy surrounding the IPA." Kwawer asserted (correctly) that the IPA had agreed that the concept of "functional equivalence" would not be used to deny admission to the IPA to an individual analyst whose training had been completed on a three-times-a-week basis. He added that it was widely known to IPA officials that departures from this standard existed in many of the IPA component societies around the world.

Kwawer then turned to the White Institute experience with the IPA. Of discussions that took place over a period of two years, he said:

> The IPA's representatives made it increasingly clear during these discussions that the 'four-times-per-week' standard was a non-negotiable entry requirement, and its spokespersons and delegated officers and committee chairs persisted in articulating this view obdurately, despite clear and explicit assurances to the contrary made in connection with the lawsuit settlement agreement by the IPA's own attorneys. Subsequently, when confronted with these extant agreements and promises, the IPA's spokespersons denied knowledge of the existence of these understandings. One is left with the impression that the IPA's current leadership is ignorant of agreements entered into by prior officers."[5]

---

[5] Assuming Kwawer's account to be his true understanding of the situation, here lay the heart of a major misunderstanding and inconclusive struggle between the White Institute and the IPA. In enunciating the concept of "functional equivalence," the IPA had agreed that training and practice conducted in these new applicant groups prior to IPA application might have been inadequate by IPA standards (for example, three-times-per-week training) but might nonetheless have resulted in a level of competence that was "functionally equivalent" to what the IPA required and would therefore not by itself be a barrier to IPA acceptance. From now into the future, however, training practices in these applicant institutes would have to be adjusted to conform to IPA standards. Kwawer seemed to be assuming, and representing the White Institute in doing so, that not only could past training on a three-times-per-week basis be found "functionally equivalent" but that the Settlement Agreement allowed for this different standard to continue as the prevailing training standard, even after successful application for IPA membership. To the IPA, this was never agreed to, and would never have been agreed to, in the Settlement Agreement.

On the basis of this view, Kwawer went on to say that the White Society "voted unanimously at its last annual Business Meeting, in April 1990, to investigate evidence of continued discriminatory, over-restrictive, and exclusionary practices and policies on the part of the IPA." He said that as Chair of the White Society's "Ad Hoc Committee on the IPA," he had been "exploring with my Committee and with GAPPP's Commission on Settlement Enforcement relevant facts concerning existing agreements as well as available options for legal remedies, should such be necessary. We are of course examining the possibility that the IPA may be in violation of agreements entered into with the approval of the federal judiciary, which will continue to monitor compliance with the settlement terms."

Kwawer then mounted his specific indictment of Greenstadt's leadership of Section I.

> It is demeaning to the Section's membership for Dr. Greenstadt to be accepting tacitly the IPA's questionable definitions of who can play the game and how the game is to be played. . . . A more courageous stand, befitting the office of the Presidency, would involve Dr. Greenstadt in enunciating principles for which we stand, and eschewing what Dr. Greenstadt felicitously touts as "the most practical solution," one which (not incidentally) his own Institute stands to profit significantly by. . . . In using the President's chair to establish a forum for interests reflected in his institutional loyalties, Dr. Greenstadt arrogantly betrays the trust of the Section and invites disaffection and alienation from the Section's membership. We are entitled to wiser and more representative counsel from him. We need our President to stand with dignity in pursuing principles, instead of demeaning his office and our Section with deferential pragmatics and strategies of appeasement, even if this means alienating those in whose favor he proudly stands. . . . We are entitled to a higher standard of dignity and probity than his Presidency has thus far reflected.

Greenstadt responded to this vigorous assault with an equally spirited rejoinder in the same issue of *Round Robin*.

> Dr. Kwawer's letter is, in my view, truly regrettable. Anything of value in it is obscured by the crude attempt to blacken me and my motives through the use of innuendo, self-righteous and self-aggrandizing claims of moral superiority, and only thinly disguised threats. Any attempt to defend oneself against false claims is usually taken by others as an implicit confession of culpability; I will therefore let what I have already said and what I say now speak for my integrity. There is, however, a need

to clarify two substantive points: (1) has the IPA officially given sanction to an analytic standard of less than four sessions per week? and (2) has the IPA applied the concept of "functional equivalence" in good faith?

On the first, Greenstadt's answer was an unequivocal no, and on the second, an equally unequivocal yes. Concerning IPA standards, he said he did not know of any formal or informal agreement by the IPA to admit training institutes where the *future* training standards would be specified as three sessions per week, and as for existing full component institutes where these standards were "winked" at, "this is unofficial and frowned upon by the IPA." In this he was stating accurately the IPA position and practice. Concerning the "good faith" issue in the IPA application of the concept of "functional equivalence," Greenstadt stated that in his experience with the IPA application of NYFS, this concept "was indeed employed fairly and successfully in three major areas." The first had to do with the fact that many of the NYFS faculty and members had received their training on a three-times-per-week basis, and yet, of a total membership of about 150, all but 14 of those who applied had been approved at the 1989 Rome Congress. In the second, for the 14 where the training had not led to an assessment of "functional equivalence," a specific plan was devised for each of the 14, which, assuming it would be followed, "almost certainly assures their acceptance at the next Congress in Buenos Aires (August, 1991)." The third area was in the establishment of an IPA-approved cadre of training and supervising analysts within NYFS, which was done by a "clinical group discussion" method in which groups of senior NYFS members met for discussion of case material with the IPA Site Visit Committee members, all of whom were training analysts. Greenstadt viewed all of this as a fair application of the "functional equivalence" concept.

Sandler's presidential message in the January 1991 IPA *Newsletter,* however, made no mention of this controversy stirred up over the William Alanson White situation or that of LAISPS, the other subject of Stromberg's September 19 letter of complaint. Only the final paragraph of the long presidential message said anything of the New Groups process. Mostly it stated the composition of all the component parts of the newly revised organization of the IPA site visit process, with Hanly now the chair of the world-wide Committee and Owen Renik (San Francisco) the chair of the Sub-Committee for New U.S. Groups. He then announced—almost *en passant*—that LAISPS had been approved by the Executive Council for presentation to the coming 1991 Buenos Aires Business Meeting for Provisional Society status.

Very promptly, the NYCPT, whose site visit process had been discontinued (although not brought in as an issue in the September 19, 1990 Stromberg letter) came to the center of attention in a December 26,

1990 letter from its president, threatening the IPA with legal action for its behavior with the group. This caused me to write a very private and personal letter to Sandler, dated January 7, 1991, expressing my concern and offering my advice.

> Obviously, I can't vouch for the truth of the sequence of events as outlined, but if the letter is to be believed—and I don't know that we have real evidence to the contrary—he is saying that he and his colleagues acted in good faith at all times and that they had not failed to make full prior disclosure, because they hadn't known about the planned secession by part of their group beforehand. In fact, what he is saying is that this secession only came to a head when it was clear that the main body was trying to move toward the IPA affiliation and that actually it would have worked out better since the disaffected members would have left and the ones who could have worked with the IPA would remain. If this is truly the sequence of events, then it looks like we acted too hastily and very prematurely in terminating the Site Visit before giving them a full chance to explain the sequence of events that had made us suspicious.

I added that I knew that the original plaintiffs still had a massive war chest and that they and their attorneys were scrutinizing all IPA actions very closely with a readiness to return to court if they could make out a case that we were not living up to all the terms of the Settlement Agreement. I ended with the advice to reopen the dialogue with the group by sending a trusted emissary to meet with them to get a firsthand picture that could then be reported to the Executive Council in Buenos Aires—which in turn, if it went well, could result in a reconstitution of a (new) Site Visit Committee.

Sandler's answer to me, dated January 14, 1991, called this one of the few issues on which we disagreed. He felt that this new letter only confirmed his prior feelings and that the explanations in the letter simply did not address the central issue of the group's failure to disclose their internal tensions until these erupted into the open thrust for a split. Sandler stated, "I don't think we acted too hastily and prematurely in terminating the site visit—perhaps we left it too late. In any case, they will be able to re-apply in six months or so. Hanly is writing to them to point this out." In this heightening contentious environment, with the threat of reinstituted legal action hovering over all the proceedings, Hanly sent a Memo on Equivalency Procedures, dated February 11, 1991, to all the involved IPA officers and chairs of New Groups Site Visit Committees, enjoining everyone to be scrupulous in following the letter and spirit of the New Groups Policies and Procedures statements. If anyone had reason to think that the IPA had not been consistent in its application of these criteria, he should be informed of the details at once, so that he could assess the situation for the Executive Council. He informed the recipients that half of the alleged basis for Stromberg's threat had been removed by the favorable outcome of Mangham's Site Visit Committee report on LAISPS; but the remaining half, the William Alanson White, still remained an issue, and NYCPT "has been rumbling as though it would like to replace LAISPS in making allegations," as the President of the group had already indicated in his December 26, 1990 letter to Sandler.

On February 12, 1991, Sandler responded to a letter that Kwawer had addressed to him directly on January 25, offering a clarification of whatever confusions existed concerning the IPA application process. He stated that in regard to the question of "functional equivalence" in the evaluation of prior training and experience, there were indeed circumstances under which a thrice weekly analysis would be acceptable, but such decision would not be made on the basis of formal criteria alone (such as the number of hours the person had been in analysis or in supervision). It would have to be based on an overall evaluation of the person's performance, knowledge, and understanding. In addition, "prior training and experience apart, we would need to know, before considering an application, that the training requirements for present and future candidates meet the requirements of the IPA, and in this regard thrice weekly analyses for the candidates and control cases would not be acceptable." Sandler ended with an expressed hope: "If there is a real possibility of your making a successful application for admission to the IPA, I would be extremely pleased."

Cliff Stromberg then returned to these wars with a March 4, 1991, letter to Clint Fisher, responding to two letters from Fisher (November 30 and December 11, 1990) which had included a copy of the revised IPA Policies and Procedures for the Evaluation of New U.S. Groups. Stromberg stated that unfortunately, from his point of view, many of the key statements were "so impenetrably vague as to provide no concrete guidance on the very points that you know are in dispute"—such as what constituted IPA standards and how was "functional equivalence" to be demonstrated by an institute. Nor had the IPA furnished the additional information that Fisher's November 30 letter had promised. Stromberg then brought up the two outstanding situations regarding the IPA site visit process, the William Alanson White and NYCPT. (There was, of course, no longer any mention of the resolved LAISPS situation.)

Concerning the situation with White, Stromberg referred to the recent correspondence between Sandler and Kwawer. He called Sandler's letter of February 12, 1991, both cryptic and vague, and then said that:

Putting aside the issue of whether a requirement of four times a week analysis is substantively defensible, it seems indisputable that the IPA cannot expect an Institute to adopt important new policies in advance without even knowing whether the IPA will accept and process, much less approve, an application. It is important to know whether an Institute's commitment that it would abide by four times a week training, *if and when* it is approved by the IPA, would suffice. Otherwise, as a practical matter, the IPA would be requiring a leap into the void, with no promise at all from the IPA.

Concerning the situation with NYCPT, Stromberg cited the several letters to Sandler from the group, "protesting the precipitous and unwarranted aborting of the IPA Site Visit, after the group had committed great energy and resources to fulfill all the Site Visit criteria."

Stromberg then went on to his customary reminder that, "we have the resources, commitment and obligation to enforce the Settlement Agreement and the IPA's obligations thereunder," and giving the IPA until May 15—something over two months—to resolve these issues that had up to then blocked these two applicant groups. Otherwise, "we will assume that you do not wish to avoid a return to court." This letter was sent on to Sandler by Fisher, along with a cover letter dated March 12, 1991. To Fisher, Stromberg's letter (plus its enclosures of a half-dozen letters exchanged between the IPA and the two institutes at issue) was self-explanatory. He would certainly take issue with Stromberg's assertion that the letters from Sandler and Hanly had been "vague" and "cryptic" and did not address the "unfairness issue." He did feel though that Stromberg had a point with his complaint that the information promised on November 30 had not yet been forwarded and that a response to Stromberg, with a list of the organizations that had requested information on applying to the IPA and a list of those who had actually applied, would indeed be in order. He added that, "In some respects, Stromberg's letter looks like another attempt to push the IPA to take action with respect to particular Institutes. Since his September 19 letter, the LAISPS situation has been resolved and he and other representatives of the plaintiffs may believe it is time to exert more pressure with respect to other Institutes." Fisher ended by asking Sandler if and how he should respond to Stromberg.

I again entered the debate with a letter to Sandler, dated March 13, 1991, in regard to the correspondence between Stromberg and Fisher (and also concerning some other IPA matters), concerning the situations of the two institutes.

About the White, although they make a lot of noise, I think that we are in a very good position. We have indicated that we have certain standards and if they want to be admitted to the

IPA, that they would have to make whatever changes it took to meet those standards. Despite what Cliff Stromberg says, I think that our standards are clear enough. Also, I am not impressed by his argument that they shouldn't be required to make any changes unless we would agree to take them in. My position would be that the changes they are being asked to make would bring them into line with accepted psychoanalytic training standards. If they would only do this in order to get into the IPA but without really believing in them, we shouldn't want them anyway. That is, I think that they should want to make these changes for their own sake and not just as a ticket of admission if they were to be properly one of us.

About the NYCPT situation I expressed more misgivings, "just because I still think that we originally made a mistake in canceling the site visit when we did and that they have a legalistic, if not a legal, case." I expressed my hope, however, that the situation would be resolved by the group's going ahead with a new application and putting off thoughts of legal recourse; albeit, if the group were found wanting after the site visit evaluation process, that would be a politically more difficult judgment—coming after the interrupted and then renewed site visit process—than it would have been after an uninterrupted process. But maybe that dilemma would not come to pass; I indicated that I was sorry to keep returning to this issue, but Stromberg wasn't letting us set it aside.

Sandler's response to me came in a letter dated the very next day, March 14, 1991. He agreed with my comments about Stromberg's position and indicated that he personally would be quite pleased if the minority in the White Institute that desired IPA membership chose to secede and pursue that path. As for NYCPT, he indicated that they had asked for a reinstituted site visit starting after a year, as the IPA had indicated they could. He would press, however, for an agreement that the group accept whatever decision the IPA arrived at as final and there be no "raking over of old coals about the previous site visit."

On March 21, 1991, Hanly wrote a memo to the officers of the IPA (and Clint Fisher) asking advice on how to frame yet another letter to Kwawer defining yet again the application of the concept of "functional equivalency." He offered two main options (along with a third that was only a minor variation of one of the two) for how functional equivalency could be evaluated on the basis of clinical evaluations of analytic case material. The one would require the supervisor or the presenter to bring clinical material derived from recent work done on a four-times-per-week basis for some significant stretch of time. Or one could evaluate work done at a lesser frequency, three times a week, with the understanding that the standard of excellence had not changed, but that only the evidence upon which the judgment was to be made had shifted. It was implied in the memorandum that both of these options had operated, in some varying admixture, in the site visit processes that had been successfully concluded with those new applicant groups that had already achieved IPA recognition. Hanly was urging some declaration that the second option could be acceptable, even though it might make the evaluation task more difficult; among other reasons, it would put the IPA in a stronger legal position if the matter went to court.

Four days later, on March 25, 1991, Hanly did write to Kwawer with reference to, and expanding upon, Sandler's most recent letter to Kwawer of February 12. The letter was a long and detailed statement about how the entire site visit process operated, including a description of the various kinds of departures from the IPA training standards that had been found in site visits with other groups, the several kinds of evaluation procedures employed in those instances, and the way that the step-by-step evaluation process, first of the group and then of its individual members, usually unfolded. About the basis for clinical evaluations, there was a statement that evaluation of current work should be made on the basis of clinical reports on patients being seen four times weekly. In justification of this, Hanly prefaced the entire letter with a paragraph dealing with the two counterposed training philosophies.

> As a preliminary matter, it seems to me that a significant difference exists between the groups that have applied to the IPA for site visits and the William Alanson White Psychoanalytic Society. . . . The groups that have applied for site visits generally have adhered to IPA training standards [even when training within IPA component Societies had not been available to them]. I understand from your letter, however, that the White Society has philosophical, theoretical and clinical reasons for a different training requirement. While the IPA has no wish to exclude any group that adheres to the IPA methods of training and practice, neither does it have a missionary zeal to convert others to these methods. At the same time if the White Society now wishes to adopt and adhere to IPA training and other requirements, the IPA would welcome your membership. In any event, you are no doubt thinking about this issue in considering an application to the IPA.

A slight defusing of the tense situation triggered by Stromberg's letter to Fisher (about the White Society and NYCPT) and his earlier letter to Dorkey and Fisher (about the White Society and LAISPS) was reflected in a March 28, 1991, letter from Fisher to Sandler. He had had a "useful telephone conversation" with Stromberg about the various recent exchanges of letters among the principal parties to these controversies. He had conveyed to Stromberg that the fact that IPA responses to his letters were not immediately forthcoming was a result of the IPA's genuine efforts to address the difficult issues raised, and Stromberg had seemed to understand this. Stromberg indicated, however, that the plaintiffs were determined to get answers to their questions, and though they were flexible, the deadlines for a return to court set forth in his letters were real. In discussing the specific issues around the White Society, Stromberg had expressed some empathy with the IPA concerns: "I asked him whether he believes that the White seriously wants to belong to the IPA and he replied 'fair question.' He said that it is his best estimate that some 50 percent of the White's members very much want to belong to the IPA, another 25 percent want to belong but not if to do so means 'being humiliated,' and the final 25 percent do not want to belong. He reiterated that this is an estimate but that these figures are fairly accurate." Stromberg also offered his opinion that lawsuits against individual IPA members carrying out site visits and making decisions on the IPA's behalf would be meritless, and he would advise strongly against them. The two attorneys agreed that dialogue and meetings were useful, not only between the IPA and prospective applicants, but between the lawyers as well.

Further to the diminution of tensions, the April 1991 issue of *Round Robin* carried a column by Charles Hanly, entitled "A Review of the IPA New Groups Policy in the US," which had also appeared in the Winter 1991 issue of *Psychologist Psychoanalyst* (the newsletter of the parent, Division 39). In spelling out how the concept of "functional equivalence" operated, Hanly said:

> The procedures [for evaluating individuals] recognize that the only training available to an individual may have differed from IPA standards either in its frequency, duration or in its training or supervising analysts. The IPA cannot and has not modified its standards of analytic competence. However, it has recognized that individuals may have achieved an acceptable standard of clinical competence despite training gaps. Consequently, the New US Groups procedures provide individuals . . . with an opportunity to demonstrate equivalency of clinical competence in the judgment of an IPA Site Visit Committee.

Hanly emphasized that this evaluation process, carried out so painstakingly, could be arduous and time consuming and that the Site Visit Committees would need the time to become sufficiently familiar with an applicant group and its members so as to make fair and objective evaluations. He also stated that this whole New Groups policy was limited in two ways. It was limited in time to ten years from the lawsuit settlement date, and limited in scope to groups that had been established and were functioning prior to July 1987, when the IPA had altered its Regional Association agreement with the American in order to make this New Groups policy possible.

Not everything was proceeding more smoothly however. NYCPT was officially reapplying for consideration for entry into the IPA. Sandler, very sensitized now to the possibilities for legal action in case of a second rejection, asked, in an April 9, 1991 letter to Fisher whether it would be possible to ask for a (legally valid) waiver in which the group would agree beforehand to accept the IPA's judgment, however that might come out. Sandler ended with, "I am aware that I am probably pursuing a dead end here, but I am sure that you will understand." Fisher responded to this message on April 19, 1991. He advised against seeking such an agreement. The request could generate both practical and political difficulties and, if made to the group, would certainly reach Stromberg and the plaintiffs, who would counsel strongly against making such an agreement and would undoubtedly again raise issues of "good faith." Fisher then added his reassurance that it was extremely unlikely that individuals would be sued or that such a suit would be allowed to proceed, and that in any case, the IPA would take responsibility and indemnify all individuals acting on its behalf. I added, in a letter to Sandler of the same date, that I had just received (by fax) Fisher's letter to him, and his response was just as I had expected; it would be inadvisable to get any kind of preemptive agreement. It would not be a true preventive and would only be grounds for inciting suspicions. In fact, it would give the group a basis, if they were turned down, for saying that the IPA had had that in mind all along, and had tried to protect itself ahead of time against the group's pursuing legal redress. We had an enormously complicated set of considerations with both of these groups at issue, and I trusted that there would be lots of time for discussion of these matters in May, at the (partial) IPA Executive Council meeting in New Orleans (at the time of the meeting of the American), as well as, at the full IPA Executive Council meeting at the Buenos Aires Congress in July.

In the midst of this, Hanly wrote to me on April 10, 1991, with a detailed exposition of how the crystallizing insistence on evaluating current clinical practice on the basis of four-times-a-week work had gradually evolved out of the accumulating experience of the several completed site visit evaluations. There had been a range of views over the appropriateness and feasibility of such a requirement, and practice had indeed varied somewhat among the different Site Visit Committees, some having expected to evaluate current work only on the basis of four times a week, while another allowed more leeway in this regard. One of the Site Visit Committee chairs

(Owen Renik) agreed strongly with my position that we would be on sounder ground in evaluating clinical competence as demonstrated in work as they had been doing it (as, for example, three times a week), without impairing our capacity to judge if an effective psychoanalytic process was being pursued. Wider political considerations in the IPA helped tilt the majority against this view.

> Another factor that weighs with me is the great importance of bringing the ... [component IPA societies that had themselves departed from these IPA requirements] back into line with IPA standards. Both the four times a week and the training analyst issues are crucial to the maintenance of IPA standards and identity. I fully appreciate the historical perspective you bring to bear on the equivalency issue. I agree with it. We are correcting an injustice and a stupidity. The problem is that those within the IPA who wish to be sanctioned in their departure from these standards will not adopt our historical perspective but will seek license for their own departures from standards in anything we do.

The time was now getting closer to the midsummer 37th IPA Congress in Buenos Aires, and the pace of letter writing seemed to be quickening. On May 1, 1991, Fisher wrote to Sandler, trying to set a date for the planned meeting with Stromberg and his clients. Would this be possible in conjunction with Sandler's trip to Buenos Aires, either on the way there or on the way returning to England. If that would not work, how about in September? Fisher and Stromberg had agreed that a firm date should be set to "keep the momentum going" and to avoid the perception, on either side, that the other side was "dilly-dallying." On June 6, 1991, Stromberg wrote to Fisher, complaining about the difficulties encountered to that point in setting a mutually convenient early meeting date. He was now suggesting September 4 or 5, 1991, in his offices in Washington, D.C., though he could certainly make it in New York if that would be better for all the others. Copies of his letter went to three of the four original lawsuit plaintiffs, as well as to Kwawer and Stockhamer of the White Society, and also to "other attendees."

Fisher then wrote to Sandler on June 17, 1991, asking for confirmation of this meeting date and indicating that he expected to ask Stromberg whom he intended to have at this meeting, noting that it had been copied to five named individuals plus "other attendees." Fisher did not feel that such a large meeting would be the most productive format. Sandler's response came the next day. The suggested September dates were suitable, but New York would be preferable for ease in assembling the IPA attendees. He expressed his own concern at meeting such a large contingent of persons accompanying Stromberg, indicating that he thought the IPA should field no more than four or five, including Fisher. On June 19, 1991, I wrote to Sandler in response to his request for my advice on the composition of the IPA contingent at the September meeting with the plaintiffs. I agreed with him that the number of participants should be limited to no more than five or six on either side. I felt that four would be absolute musts: him, Hanly, Fisher, and Jackie Amati (Rome) as the IPA Secretary and its second ranking officer. He probably also should have Peter Fonagy (London) present, as the incoming IPA Treasurer and its third ranking officer (for obviously there would be financial considerations involved), and he would probably want Arnie Cooper (New York) as the IPA Associate Secretary for North America.

Sandler responded thanking me for my advice—"good as usual"—on June 21, 1991. He wanted, however, to clarify a few points. He agreed with all my suggestions about the people (and also thought of adding Owen Renik as the New Chair, under Hanly, for New Groups in the United States) and then went on to add, "I did not invite you because this is one area in which we have differences of approach [referring to the handling of the NYCPT visiting process that had been terminated] and I don't know whether we can resolve them, or resolve them in time for the meeting, even though I don't think that they are differences of principle." He did state, however, that he would want my advice and comments as soon as an agenda was established for the meeting, and said that of course this would all be discussed fully at the IPA Executive Council meeting in Buenos Aires. I responded to this letter on June 24, 1991.

> About the meeting in New York with the plaintiffs in the lawsuit, it had never occurred to me to want to go. I remember as a heavy burden the many, many trips I had to make to New York during my presidency of the IPA just to have meetings around the lawsuit, including October 1986 when there were five weekends and I had to spend three of them in New York. About our disagreements around the way to approach issues, I have felt that in only one instance, the handling of the terminated site visit. By now that, of course, is past history and I hope that the issue of the renewed application gets resolved in the best possible way, though at this point, pending the report, I have no idea what that way would be.

On June 25, 1991, Fisher wrote to Sandler, having confirmed with Stromberg the date (September 4) and place (New York) for the meeting. The attorneys had agreed that an agenda should be established; Stromberg suggested that the IPA begin with a presentation of its activities since the settlement of the lawsuit, including its perception of how things were proceeding, a description of the site visits already made, and expectations for the future. This would be followed by the plaintiffs presenting their views and setting forth "areas for further clarification," including functional equivalence, training requirements, and "certain statements" allegedly made by IPA officials (some of which had presumably been set forth in Stromberg's September 19 letter). Then the specific considerations around the two institutes currently at issue would be taken up. The attorneys had also agreed to keep the attendees down to five to seven on each side. Fisher felt that his talk with Stromberg had been "positive," and though they had agreed that the meeting would necessarily be "somewhat adversarial," they both made clear that their parties were approaching the meeting positively and hoped that it would be useful.

Three days later, on June 28, 1991, Fisher sent another letter to Sandler, thanking him for his memo of response on the proposed agenda order. Sandler had wondered whether the plaintiffs oughtn't to begin with a presentation of their views. Fisher replied that he thought it not a bad thing for the IPA to open with its discussion of recent activities and future expectations: "This could actually give us a chance to set the tone for the meeting, emphasize those achievements that we wish to emphasize and steer the discussion towards issues we want to focus on." He agreed that the IPA should not appear defensive, but "I do think we might be able to make use of setting the stage, as it were, rather than immediately being forced to respond to their gripes." He felt, however, they should wait and talk once more when they received Stromberg's specific agenda proposal.

A month later, the 37th IPA Congress took place in Buenos Aires. Nothing transpired there that in any way altered the activities or the perspectives of the IPA officers and designates in regard to the ongoing negotiations with Stromberg, with the former plaintiffs, and with the two current complainant institutes. The Business Meeting in Buenos Aires was very content to ratify the acceptance of LAISPS as the fourth of the applicant "New US Groups" to secure Provisional Society status within the IPA. From the point of view of the involved IPA officials, the entire year covered in this chapter had been devoted to still unresolved issues around the acceptability of these two institutes for IPA membership from our side, and the willingness and ability to bring their training practices into full conformity with IPA standards in order to win IPA approval, from their side. Stromberg's stance in all this, presumably shared with and on behalf of the former plaintiffs and their supporting constituency organized through GAPPP, was clearly designed to maintain maximum pressure on the IPA to accommodate as much as it could be pushed by threat of legal recourse, to the wishes of the applicant groups.

How the events of the two years since the summer 1989 IPA Congress in Rome were perceived from the perspective of the plaintiffs has been chronicled by Schneider and Desmond (1994). Under the heading "It Ain't Over 'Till It's Over" (pp. 330–332), Schneider and Desmond state that shortly after the Settlement Agreement was signed, they began to hear complaints about its implementation, at first within the CNMCT process in the American. They "heard of lengthy delays of candidates' applications, of overly burdensome demands and of blatant examples in which applicants were rejected or deferred for specious reasons. . . . Several of the American's Institutes objected vehemently to the CNMCT process and, for a period, an insurrectionist atmosphere took hold within the American with threats of disaffiliation and secession"[6] (p. 331).

Then Schneider and Desmond turn to the IPA:

> IPA, too, after rapidly accepting three Institutes for provisional membership—the Freudian Institute in New York, the Institute for Psychoanalytic Training and Research in New York, and the Psychoanalytic Center of California in Los Angeles, suddenly halted its progress . . . the conduct of site visits began to suggest that they were seeking to exclude or limit membership. Procedures were vague and fluctuating and some Institutes' cooperation with one set of demands led only to another and then another set of new demands [p. 331].

Schneider and Desmond also focussed on the controversy around the "functional equivalency" concept, saying that, "despite IPA's explicit statement indicating that analysts whose personal and supervised analyses were conducted three times a week, 'will not automatically be granted or denied admission to the IPA,' many of their later statements and actions contradicted the agreement" (p. 331).

It was this accumulating list of claimed deficiencies in the implementation of the Settlement Agreement, by both the American and the IPA, that led the GAPPP Board of Directors to establish a Commission on Settlement Enforcement (codirected by Schneider and Desmond) in April 1990, "to fulfill a watch dog function regarding compliance and to serve as a central clearinghouse for information regarding settlement issues" (p. 332). They continue that, "At the time of this writing, communication between the respective attorneys has begun in order to rectify these problems

---

[6] These are the perspectives that were central to Stromberg's letters of February 14, 1990, addressed to Directors and Faculty of Psychoanalytic Institutes, and of February 21, 1990, to Joel Klein as the attorney for the American.

[that the Commission on Settlement Enforcement had conveyed to Stromberg] outside the courtroom" (p. 332). Schneider and Desmond felt that the Commission had already proven its value. For example, the site visit process with LAISPS was declared to have "experienced several years of frustrating and apparently obstructionist treatment at the hands of IPA" (p. 332), but appropriate saber rattling by Stromberg, instigated by the Commission, was declared to have been critical to the ultimate expeditious resolution of this issue. What was seen to explain this shift in IPA behavior was the perception by the plaintiffs of a reconciliation between the IPA and the American: "following Joseph Sandler's ascendancy to the IPA presidency, there were indications of a rapprochement between the American and the IPA. Coincidentally, the nature of the [IPA] site visits began to change from a collegial, helpful enterprise to an adversarial process" (p. 332)—though Schneider and Desmond had just been complaining about the site visit process with LAISPS, under my presidency. Certainly it enlarges our overall understanding of these controversies to have this belated perspective on how these events were perceived by the plaintiff side.

Subsidence of the Legal Threat

Following the 1991 IPA Congress
in Buenos Aires, planning resumed for the September meeting in New York
between the IPA officials and those complaining about the claimed
deficiencies in the IPA's implementation of the Settlement Agreement. On
August 6, 1991, Clinton Fisher wrote to Joseph Sandler enclosing the
plaintiffs' proposed agenda for the September 4 meeting that had been sent
to him by Cliff Stromberg. The one proposed alteration in the agenda
sequence was that now the complainants wanted Bryant Welch to lead off
with a "brief summary" of the background of the litigation and the efforts
since. Their six attendees would be Stromberg, Welch and Arnold Schneider
of the original four plaintiffs, Jay Kwawer and Nathan Stockhamer of the
White Institute, and Herbert Strean, representing NYCPT, the group
reapplying after the cancelled site visit. The IPA representatives would
likewise be six: Fisher, Sandler, Charles Hanly, Jackie Amati, the IPA
Secretary, Arnold Cooper, the Associate Secretary for North America, and
Owen Renik, the subchair under Hanly for New Groups in the United States.

Also in August, Hanly wrote several letters dealing with Site Visit
Committee changes. On August 10, he wrote to Charles Mangham (Seattle)
thanking him for having successfully navigated the LAISPS site visiting
process through to the group's acceptance as a new IPA Provisional Society
at the Buenos Aires Congress, and accepting his resignation from the
committee. On the same date, he wrote to Brian Robertson (Montreal)
thanking him for his part in that site visit process and appointing him the
new chair of the LAISPS Site Visit Committee. On August 12, 1991, he
wrote to Herbert Strean, director of NYCPT, the group whose earlier site
visit process had been terminated, notifying him of the appointment of a
fresh Site Visit Committee for the renewed visiting process to be resumed
shortly. The chair would be Ed Weinshel (San Francisco), the other members
Helen Meyers (Columbia) and Anna Wolff (Boston). The committee would
be charged with three responsibilities: (1) to examine the current state of
the society and institute now that its split had taken place; (2) to examine

what steps had been taken relating to the points raised by the Solnit Site Visit Committee; and (3) to evaluate the individual members for eligibility for IPA membership.

Pushing further arrangements for the September meeting in New York, Fisher wrote to Sandler on August 14, 1991, confirming a preparatory meeting of the IPA attendees in his office in New York the day before the meeting with the plaintiff group. Then Fisher wrote again to Sandler on August 28, indicating that he had advised Stromberg that Peter Fonagy (London), the new IPA Treasurer, would be attending, but not Renik, and that Stromberg had in turn advised him that Jonathan H. Slavin (Boston), the new President of Division 39, would be attending, but that maybe Strean would not.

After all the planning and build-up, the September 4 meeting in New York turned out to be frustrating and inconclusive. It could not achieve any level of agreement between the contending parties. Strangely, my only written report of that meeting is in a memorandum, dated September 13, 1991, from Slavin to the Board of Directors and Committee Chairs of Division 39. The key paragraph states:

> I regret to tell you that the results of the meeting were unfortunate. In sum and substance, the IPA officials seem quite prepared to renege on their agreement to implement functional equivalence in the evaluation of either Institutes or individuals. Equally troubling was the fact that their attitude mirrored their position in the discussions. They were condescending, self-importantly moralizing, and incapable of understanding that they were dealing with a group that was trying to address serious issues in a professional way. . . .We may have assumed sometimes that all of the major difficulties with the IPA were over and we could let up on our concern. If this meeting in September is any indication, nothing could be further from the truth.

Slavin promised a full discussion by his Board of "our stance towards both the IPA and the American." From this account, it can be surmised that the IPA representatives at that meeting stuck to their view on how the "functional equivalence" concept was intended, and to their convictions about the fairness and "good faith" with which the site visit processes had been, and would continue to be, conducted.

Site visit plans continued, however, on schedule. On September 27, 1991, Hanly wrote again to Strean, in response to a letter he had received from the latter. It clarified, in response to Strean's inquiry, that the Site Visit Committee reports were internal IPA documents, but after the IPA Executive Council has decided on its formal action, that is conveyed to the applicant group along with an explanation of its basis. He also clarified what information had been gathered during the prior site visit process and what issues had been raised by it. He then stated that Strean should be hearing next from Weinshel, the Chair of the new Site Visit Committee.

A main preoccupation continued to be the unresolved dispute with the erstwhile plaintiffs and the Division 39 Commission on Settlement Enforcement—as witness Slavin's report of the September 4 meeting—and the preparation of as good a legal position as possible in the event of a return to court. Toward that end, Hanly prepared a detailed memorandum, dated October 31, 1991, for the IPA officers and the members of its New Groups Committee. In it he tried to clear up the apparent inconsistencies in past interpretations and past procedures around the "functional equivalency" issue: "Our policies are premised on the view that we will evaluate individuals whose training has been based on three times a week, but that we will base our evaluation of equivalence on the presentation of four times a week cases. . . . In order to establish equivalence notwithstanding departures in training, applicants have to demonstrate an ability as must IPA members generally, to practice analysis at four times a week." In regard to the functioning of the applicant group, the memorandum stated:

> In order to be approved for a site visit, an applicant group that has based its training on three times per week must (1) declare its intent to adopt IPA minimum standards . . . (2) demonstrate progress toward minimum standards. An indication of such progress and the seriousness of its intent would be the number of training analysts in the group who had shifted to four times per week training analysis and supervised cases. This policy makes it clear that we are not willingly going to site visit a group that makes their adoption of IPA standards conditional upon being made a member of the IPA.

Clearly the complainants were sticking to a different interpretation of the "functional equivalence" concept enunciated in the Settlement Agreement and the accompanying side agreement letter that Fisher had addressed to Stromberg. This had come out clearly in the various letters from Stromberg, cited in the preceding chapter, as well as in Slavin's report of the September 4 meeting. Hanly put this succinctly: "the Enforcement Committee takes the view that it means that three times a week analysis is, for these purposes, equivalent to four times a week," and that site visit evaluations should be based on that equivalence. Hanly also indicated that Fisher, as the IPA attorney who had written the original side agreement letter, tended to interpret its meaning more in line with the complainants (and felt also that such an interpretation would be easier to defend in court should the litigation be reopened). This raised questions in Hanly's mind as to whether Fisher could now best legally represent the IPA, and he had begun to make inquiries about alternate legal representation. It also made Hanly raise the point that Weinshel and I had been responsible for the form of the side agreement letter that Fisher had crafted on our behalf, and that those "who were involved in the negotiations, should clarify for us and for him [Fisher] what their intentions were, and whether the meaning they attached to these sentences is the one I have or yet some other different from mine and from the enforcers." At the end of his long document, Hanly gave an update on the two open application processes. The Weinshel committee was preparing for a visit to NYCPT, but with the White Institute, nothing seemed to be happening. There had been no response to Hanly's last letter, and "some of my fairly knowledgeable New York informants are of the opinion that the White will never apply for a site visit, if there is any prospect of their having to adopt IPA standards which there certainly is."

At the same time, efforts were still continuing to find a way for the White Institute to seek IPA affiliation. On November 14, 1996, Hanly sent the IPA officers a draft of yet another letter of clarification and of welcome to Kwawer. He began by thanking Kwawer for the capsule history of the White that Kwawer had included in a letter to him. But he went on to say:

> I have the impression from your letter that you are asking the IPA to alter its procedures and the policies they embody and, as well, to amend our minimum training standards so as to treat the White Institute as an exception [to the standards that all the IPA's component organizations had to subscribe to, including the four non-medical Provisional Societies admitted under the New Groups policy]. If you are suggesting that in order for the IPA to "acknowledge and maintain the clinical excellence, theoretical orientation, integrity and stature of the White Institute's nearly fifty-year-old training program" the IPA would have to accept the White Institute's current training standards concerning frequency, that is something the IPA cannot do.

After detailing the time-consuming but feasible procedures that the site visit process would entail, Hanly went on to say: "I still do not understand why the White Institute has not already requested a site visit unless it is for the reason that your Institute wishes to be able to continue to offer three times a week training as an option which would not be possible if the White Institute were in the IPA." He then suggested a possible early meeting date to further discuss these matters, the IPA representatives to be himself, Arnold Cooper, and David Sachs (Philadelphia), who had replaced Owen Renik as Chair of the North American New Groups Committee. The IPA clearly was making every effort to secure the White Institute's adherence, but not on that group's terms.

I was again drawn directly into these interchanges, including the issue of the original intent of the "functional equivalence" statement in the side agreement, when Hanly sent me a large packet of correspondence, memoranda, and supporting documents dealing with the ambiguities and controversies over this concept. In my very nonspecific letter of reply to him, dated November 11, 1991, I said:

> About all the material having to do with both legal matters and the interpretation of "functional equivalence" and the New Groups Committee, it is all very complex and I expect that I will be involved in discussing it all at the Executive Council in New York next month. I am sorry in all of this that there seems to be some dissatisfactions with Clint Fisher and that there is a possibility of switching attorneys. I also have my differences, as you know, with the way the concept of functional equivalence is being applied, but maybe the differences are more minor than I have thought them to be. Clearly, we will be talking more about all of this.

A shift had been gradually occurring for more than two years now since the 1989 IPA Congress in Rome, when the first three New Groups had been voted into Provisional Society status in the IPA. Throughout the lawsuit, the American was seen by the plaintiffs as the central targeted adversary, with the IPA seen more in the role of honest broker and potential mediator. The main focus now was on the IPA as the obstructionist to "full faith" implementation on terms satisfactory to the former legal plaintiffs and their supporters, and this was made dramatically evident in a November 18, 1991, statement by Slavin, President of Division 39, entitled "What do Psychologists Want?" His opening paragraph stated:

> The recent vote of the membership of the American Psychoanalytic Association to permit its affiliated Institutes to admit psychologists to clinical training, without further recourse to a waiver process,[1] is a landmark event in the history of psychoanalysis. Presumably this change means that in the future

---

[1] After the passage of the Gaskill Committee recommendations by a more than two thirds vote of the membership of the American in February 1986, the implementing committee, CNMCT, first chaired by Carl Davis (New Orleans) met for the first time in May 1986. After three years, Davis was succeeded as chair by John MacLeod (Cincinnati) and by December 1989, after three and a half years of operation, during which time 101 waiver applications had been processed and 77 approved, the Committee and the Board felt that full responsibility for determining personal suitability and clinical aptitude could devolve to the local institutes, with CNMCT only responsible for determining educational eligibility. This was the so-called Ross amendment to the Gaskill proposal, passed by the American's Board on Professional Standards in December 1989. In 1991, this devolution of responsibility was extended still further, with the central waiver requirement dropped entirely for all those with doctoral level degrees in the mental health professions. This was the issue over which Stromberg had called on the American's local institutes to rebel against the parent body.

psychologists will be able to play an equal role with their medical colleagues in all aspects of their participation in their local Societies and within the American. In light of these truly extraordinary and welcome developments the question can be asked, "What more do psychologists want?"[2]

Slavin's answer to this query was multisided. He began by stating that everything that the psychologists as a profession had striven to accomplish over several decades now seemed to be achieved; admission on an equal basis to the institutes of the American, freedom to recruit faculty from the ranks of the American for their own institutes, direct access for their institutes to the IPA, without requiring that this be through the American. All this was attributed to a complex of factors, first and foremost the filing of the lawsuit. But also, "Clearly, the increasing turn of psychiatry back towards 'biology' in the past decade or two, alongside decreasing interest in psychoanalysis among psychiatric residents, were additional factors that made movement towards opening training fully to psychologists likely, if not necessary," that is, the need by psychoanalysis to rethink its pool of potential candidates. But these "coercive" factors aside, Slavin also granted that there had always been voices within the ranks of the American that had advocated these very changes. He doubted, however, that they would have prevailed at this point in time had the "coercive" factors not been operative.

The question then remained: is there anything more that psychologists could want? Some, of course, would feel that they had accomplished exactly what they had wanted. But Slavin felt that "there are some other things that at least some psychologists want. These have to do both with the American itself and with fundamental issues at stake in psychoanalysis today." These would include: (1) some basic assurance that if independent psychologist Institutes applied for accreditation by the American—"a not unlikely event sometime in the next few years, in my estimation"—they would be fairly evaluated on substantive educational grounds, not rebuffed on "arbitrary, ritualized or educationally unsubstantial issues"; (2) "the separation of psychoanalytic scientific societies from practitioner guilds," that is, to welcoming into the ranks, "thinkers from all points of view who may bring very different expertise and sensibility than the practising clinician"; and (3) what may be inevitable, "the eventual evolution of the American from a predominantly 'medical' identity." Of this last he said, "as long as psychoanalysis is thought of as a subspecialty of psychiatry or as a

---

[2] Compare this very friendly and collegial tone with the harshness of Slavin's description two months earlier of the September 4 meeting with the IPA representatives.

part of the field of medicine—which other clinicians may also practice with appropriate training—I believe a bias is introduced into our understanding of what is fundamental to the psychoanalytic process as well as to psychoanalytic education . . . [which I] believe is not to the ultimate benefit of the field."

This is the essence of Slavin's position in this regard:

> The substance of the issue is the degree to which these aspects of a medical model (e.g., the assumption of objectivity, diagnostic acuity, technical precision), and the wish to apply it to the psychoanalytic situation, creates a culture of presumed knowledge, and presumed technical clarity, that neither fits the level to which our field has attained scientifically, nor fits well with what at least some consider to be the most useful stance to take with our patients. Put simply, this sort of model inevitably pushes towards a "one-person" view of the psychoanalytic process in which a presumably neutral, objective, outside observer applies a certain perspective, technical skill and treatment to the individual being observed. In practice, I believe most psychoanalysts, medical and non-medical, work much more implicitly in a "two-person" scheme; very collaboratively with their patients and with a profound sense of the difficulties, ambiguities and uncertainties inherent in this work. Some even welcome the uncertainty and the lack of clarity and objectivity as inherent to what can be productive in the work. . . . But whether one subscribes to some version of the medical model or to some version of the ideas I have briefly alluded to about the nature of the psychoanalytic process, I think at least some psychologists would want the debate kept open and not too quickly resolved.[3]

All of the issues around the application process to the IPA were reviewed at length at a meeting of the North American Subcommittee of the New Groups Committee, held December 17, 1991, in New York in conjunction with the partial meeting of the IPA Executive Council. David Sachs was in the chair.[4] A big issue was the precise intention, if it could be

---

[3] In the final chapter, I develop at length my quite similar version of the argument Slavin makes here, though I do not link the psychiatrist-psychologist juxtaposition so directly to the debate over the "one-person," natural-science perspective upon the nature of the psychoanalytic process as against the "two-person" interpersonal and relational perspective.

[4] The other participants were Charles Hanly, Sydney Pulver (Philadelphia), Owen Renik, Robert Wallerstein, and the IPA Administrative Director, Valerie Tufnell.

ascertained, of the August 16, 1988, side letter from Fisher to Stromberg. In response to pointed inquiry, I affirmed that there had been no private understandings about this letter, neither with any individual nor with any group. Hanly had himself outlined four possible interpretations of the crucial sentence from that side letter: "An individual who has had seven hundred hours of personal analysis on a three times per week basis will not automatically be granted or denied admission to the IPA; it will be expected, however, that such individuals would be admitted to the IPA if the balance of their training and their subsequent experience and work are such as to indicate that overall they have functioned in a way that is equivalent to individuals who have been trained according to IPA standards."

The four meanings were: (1) The sentence allows the IPA to apply its usual standards in assessing the functional equivalence of individual applicants by requiring them to be evaluated on the basis of four times per week cases just as ordinary IPA members have been evaluated; (2) As above, except that, although the analyst must present a case that is currently being seen four times per week, the case may have been a three-times-per-week case prior to the evaluation process; (3) Applicants have the right to present cases seen at a frequency of three times per week, but must demonstrate equivalent skills in conducting the case to those of IPA members who have been trained and work in accord with IPA standards; and (4) "The sentence means only what it says. . . . Nothing is stated, implied, or intended about how that evaluation will be conducted and on the basis of what clinical evidence, specifically with respect to the frequency of analysis. These details, it was assumed, would be worked out on the basis of experience with the site visit process."

The last statement in the Hanly document is that the test of correctness among these four alternative interpretations is not what anyone now considers the right or the best interpretation after the fact, but only what was originally intended in the letter and in the discussions that had led up to it. Unhappily, from the point of view of the inherent ambiguity of the crucial sentence and the understandable subsequent controversies to which this had led—both plaintiffs and defendants later putting their own preferred spins on the intended meanings—I could only affirm at that meeting that it was the fourth meaning, no more nor less, that I, and I assumed the other IPA officers privy to the drafting of the letter, had intended. It was this that had, unintended, brought us into the present controversy and quagmire.

For the rest, all the individual situations were reviewed. There was a problem with LAISPS. One of its original training analysts, to whom the Site Visit Committee had not accorded that status in the IPA, had hired an attorney and now threatened a lawsuit on the grounds of discrimination and lack of proper procedure in the IPA's negative action. There was another, larger problem within NYFS. The evaluation process of its very large number of training analysts for IPA recognition was proceeding laboriously and slowly. A concern was raised that it might not be ready for full component Society status, alongside its New York rival, IPTAR, by the 1993 IPA Congress in Amsterdam. This, of course, could resurrect the unpleasant tension and exchange of charges that had threatened to mar the presentations for Provisional Society status at the 1989 IPA Congress in Rome. There was no new word from the White Society, but in regard to the renewed site visit to NYCPT, the new Committee, now chaired by Sydney Pulver (Philadelphia) after Weinshel proved unable to undertake the task, was clarifying the earlier issues that needed to be reexamined, most specifically the separation of the psychoanalysis from the psychotherapy training programs. They also needed to disabuse the leadership of NYCPT of the notion being circulated in its ranks that it was only "factional politics" within the IPA that had caused so much concern with the original application.

On December 18, 1991, there was a meeting of the International New Groups and Site Visits Committee (to which the North American Subcommittee was responsible) chaired by Hanly, which I was unable to attend.[5] Concerning the litigation issue, Hanly reported

> that the Enforcement Commission of Division 39 would go back to the original judge in the lawsuit to enforce IPA compliance. He said that they were arguing that three times a week training analysis was functionally equivalent to that conducted four times a week. The IPA had taken the view that evaluation must be on the basis of four times a week analysis and had thus far required groups to conform to IPA standards before they were eligible for a site visit. The view of Division 39 was that it was unreasonable to expect groups to change their practice before acceptance, and they argued that in any case IPA procedures were so rigid that many groups were discouraged from making membership applications.

The consensus of the meeting was that acceding to these pressures (under the threat of renewed litigation) would be a grave error. It would be seen as a lowering of training standards and could engender considerable resentment in those applicant groups that had—with varying difficulty—

---

[5] The other attendees were Jackie Amati (Rome), the IPA Secretary, Horacio Etchegoyen (Buenos Aires), the IPA President-Elect; Peter Fonagy (London), the IPA Treasurer, John Kafka (Washington), an IPA vice-President, David Sachs (Philadelphia), chair of the North American Subcommittee, and Valerie Tufnell.

altered their practices to qualify for IPA site visits. It could additionally damage the IPA's now restored relationship with the American: "The consensus of the Committee [therefore] was that if further litigation were threatened the IPA had no option but to fight." On other matters it was reported that NYCPT, the group Pulver's committee was to assess, had agreed to a date for the renewed (second) site visit process to begin. Also, Hanly had again written to Kwawer to arrange a meeting in January; he was still seeking to establish a continuing dialogue that could assist the White Institute to meet IPA requirements if it wished to. Finally, the Committee agreed that the IPA should hire the law firm of Rosenman and Colin in New York to replace Clint Fisher's firm. Joseph Zuckerman, a partner in Colin and Rosenman, would be asked to respond to the aggressive and threatening letter that the IPA had received from Stromberg, on behalf of Division 39, just the day before (December 17).

Stromberg, unaware that the IPA was at that moment in the process of switching attorneys, but aware of the IPA committee meetings taking place in New York, had written that letter to Fisher on December 17, intending it to be passed on immediately (which it was, to Sandler, in his hotel in New York) and considered then by the IPA during its New York meetings. To begin, he stated the feeling among "the representatives of organized psychology" that the September 4 meeting, which they had hoped would be "a watershed in finally resolving long-standing disputes," had turned out to be "a tragic missed opportunity," confirming to the plaintiffs that "the IPA has flat out betrayed and violated the letter and spirit of the Settlement Agreement in a number of important respects." Among these,

> IPA representatives confirmed that the IPA is requiring new groups to show that they meet IPA standards *at the time they apply for affiliation and seek a site visit*, rather than agreeing that they can achieve full compliance prior to actual admission to the IPA . . . surely . . . a deterrent to groups and an unreasonable burden. It would require them to abandon reasonable, long-standing, and well-functioning policies in order to conform to rigid IPA rules—and without any promise by the IPA that it will even admit them after they have done so.

He complained of the IPA insistence on reviewing *every member* of the group, not being content that the group "have a significant number (such as 10) teaching or training analysts who indisputably had IPA approved training or were trained at a level functionally equivalent to the IPA training standards, and of the IPA's rigid position "that only four-times-per-week analysis would be acceptable—not just after IPA affiliation is secured, but even to show eligibility for such affiliation. The process of evaluation, he claimed, was, "slow, redundant, expensive and unfair beyond all reason"; for example, the NYCPT, the re-applying group, had already had six meetings with IPA representatives and was now being told that they were essentially "starting over." The whole procedure, he claimed, was "a travesty of due process and an insult to professional peers"; standards were vague, changed at will or caprice, and inquiries were treated with "patronizing disdain." He cited the "evisceration" of the functional equivalence concept by the insistence on "the same old, rigid four-times-per-week standard and other requirements." "The IPA clearly has shown that it is determined to second-guess local Institutes as to the training of each person—even though the Institutes may have known them for decades."

The result of all this, Stromberg declared, was that highly qualified groups, such as the two currently at issue, have "not achieved affiliation with the IPA despite their best efforts." He stated that, "throughout this sorry process," the IPA had always pleaded that it "needs more time." This was now "the last letter of this kind you will receive. Unless the IPA changes its policies to remedy the problems outlined above, the next papers you receive will be those filed to move for sanctions against the IPA for violating the Settlement Agreement." He gave a January 15, 1992, deadline for the IPA response.

It was, however, not only the IPA that was under fire from the psychologist plaintiffs at this time. The Winter 1992 issue of *Psychologist Psychoanalyst*, the official Newsletter of Division 39, contained two items, a paragraph each, in Jonathan Slavin's presidential column on relations with the IPA and with the American. In the same issue there was a very bitter attack on the American in a letter cosigned by Arnold Schneider, one of the lawsuit plaintiffs and currently codirector of the GAPPP Commission on Settlement Enforcement, and Harriette Kaley, a member of the GAPPP Board of Directors. In his comments on the IPA, Slavin talked of the impasse at the September meeting which "continues an unfortunate process." At that meeting: "I indicated that Division 39 had fully committed its resources to the lawsuit and that, if necessary, we were just as fully prepared to do so again." In his comments on the American, Slavin stated that developments in that relationship "have been more favorable." He cited a letter from George Allison, president of the American, inviting him to a meeting, set for early March 1992, designed to foster a "friendly and cooperative relationship" between the two organizations. Slavin was looking forward to setting an agenda, "which will enable us to begin a process of collegial cooperation that will benefit all of psychoanalysis."

The letter to the editor by Schneider and Kaley, however, published in the same issue and purporting to represent GAPPP, the group established originally by Division 39 in order to prosecute the lawsuit, had a totally different tone. The two writers strenuously objected to a letter by George

Allison, published in the Fall 1991 issue of *Psychologist Psychoanalyst*, which they characterized as a "recruitment letter" soliciting applications from Division 39 members to the American's training institutes. Allison had spoken about "a wish to collaborate" around such issues as "the eventual creation of a [recognized] external credentialing body" for psychoanalysts in the United States, but was arrogantly insisting on "adhering to high standards," meaning the American's standards. Then Schneider and Kaley gave a full blast.

> As with other communications, his letter is replete with omissions, half-truths, and duplicity. He attempts to paint the American as a beneficent and virtuous organization, the guardian of the psychoanalytic mantle. His repetitive use of the term "high standards" deceptively implies a statement regarding quality when the four-times-a-week "standard" is, in fact, a quantitative practice issue. . . . Allison attempts to continue the mythology of the American's omniscience and itself as the sole purveyor of The Truth regarding Psychoanalysis. . . . Allison's seemingly collegial statements should alert all psychoanalysts to the American's intentions to continue its attempts to restrict psychoanalytic treatment in this country to its own ideology and its own favorite brand of psychoanalysis. Allison's letter also betrays a blatantly revisionistic approach to history. His self-serving omissions result in half-truths which further reflect the continuing authoritarian and patronizing attitude of the American's leaders. We could not have believed that, at this late date, we would still need to remind Dr. Allison of how it came about that the American reversed its restrictive policies and practices. . . . This issue's resurrection was instituted only under the pressure of the psychologist's anti-trust lawsuit. . . . From a purely chronological point of view, after 50 years of illegal restrictive practices, it took only nine months from the time that we filed the lawsuit against the American for it to reverse its opposition and endorse the clinical waiver process. . . . Who among us would believe that this sequence was mere coincidence? Who in the American is so gullible as to believe the American's propaganda about what it describes benevolently as an evolutionary process? Allison would have us believe that the recent bylaws change eliminating the waiver process for doctoral-level clinical psychologists is another example of evolutionary change. . . . Clearly, the American has become convinced by experience of the superior quality of psychologist candidates; clearly, the American has been in dire need of a new pool of candidates to prevent the extinction of many of its

Institutes. Still, it seems that it was only a major internal threat to its dominion that led the American to this bylaws change. The threat came in the form of a "palace revolt" when several Institutes adamantly and courageously rebelled against the American's excessive demands upon both the applicant and the local Institute in the waiver process, and against the American's incessant and intrusive second-guessing of the local Institute's selection decisions . . . a move that benefits psychoanalysis, but not one that should be credited to the American's beneficence . . . our perception of the American's leadership as disingenuous. . . . It appears that the latent issues which forced us into the Lawsuit are still alive between us and the American.

Allison's reply, printed directly after this letter, was equally forceful though, overall, much more restrained in tone. He began,

> I'm astonished and dismayed at the bellicose, rabble-rousing tone and content of Arnold Schneider and Harriette Kaley's attack on my earlier letter to the *Psychologist Psychoanalyst*. . . . I infer an ulterior motive on their part: to whip up renewed antagonism toward the American, and to discredit me and the organization I head. My rendition of the chronology of our leadership's attempts to promote psychologists' admission to our training programs is quite accurate, and I don't question that the anti-trust lawsuit promoted the efforts of those of us who were working towards change. . . .[6] Many of the points in Drs. Schneider and Kaley's article are matters of opinion and conjecture. I believe it is they who are revising history and who are distorting my letter and its intent for devious reasons. . . . I can only speak authoritatively for the present and most recent leadership of the American in declaring our wish to join other respected psychoanalytic groups to revive and bolster the training, practice, and scientific achievement of psychoanalysis. I can't see how this smacks of the arrogant or superior attitude alluded to by Drs. Schneider and Kaley.

Clearly, the impassioned interchange of these two letters reflected well the continuing depth of suspicion and wariness that still colored the tenuous

---

[6] From my own privileged position within the IPA and the American, and my close, long-standing friendships with the leaders in both organizations at the time, I can vouch unequivocally for Allison's position as one of the very influential members of the American (and long preceding his presidency of the organization) who had always been vigorously on the side of opening the organization to the full clinical training of nonmedical mental health professionals, something Schneider and Kaley might or might not have known.

relationship between the American (and the IPA, of course) on the one side, and the erstwhile plaintiff group on the other—what Schneider and Kaley referred to as the "latent issues" still between us.

The month of January 1992 saw a greatly intensified stream of letters back and forth, as the IPA, in concert with its new attorney Joseph Zuckerman, sought to deal with Stromberg's ultimatum of December 17. On January 5, 1992, Hanly wrote a long letter to Zuckerman, commenting on the seven points in Stromberg's letter for Zuckerman's consideration in drafting a reply. The first point Hanly found ambiguous because, "if the reference is to Society and Institute, then we do require that the constitution of the Society, its objectives and practices should conform to IPA requirements and that the Institute should train according to IPA standards . . . etc. before a site visit with all its costs is mobilized" but, "If the reference is to individual members, then so long as a reasonable number of members (more than half but not necessarily all) are eligible for IPA membership among whom are a sufficient number of training analysts to sustain the training program of the Institute, the group can be accepted as a Provisional Society. The remainder who are not eligible may or may not establish their eligibility at a later date as they wish." Hanly pointed to the fact that five such groups had actually applied for IPA membership, of whom four had been accepted and one was being currently site visited; a sixth group (NPAP in New York) had applied for a site visit, but then withdrew its application, "because a majority of its members did not wish to proceed as I understand it because the group did not want to give up their training in psychotherapy and because many felt that they would not be able to qualify for membership in the IPA." Second, the IPA Policy for New U.S. Groups had been approved by its Executive Council in March 1988, clearly enunciating the procedures, including the individual evaluation of *all* members who wished IPA affiliation, and these statements had been widely disseminated and clearly known. All of this had been prior to the Settlement Agreement and long before the Enforcement Commission existed. Third, "no such assurances were given outside the side-letter," and "the details of the procedures for evaluating individuals with training departures were worked out in the IPTAR site visit, whether before or after the settlement I am not sure; I think shortly after. The IPTAR site visit was the flagship site visit because it proceeded more rapidly than any other and the Executive Council was satisfied with the methods adopted." The fourth concerned the site visit process being characterized as "slow, redundant, expensive and unfair beyond all reason," and the example of the one that had bogged down and was now being renewed. It was pointed out that there had been unreported difficulties in the group that had surfaced during the course of the initial visits— evidence of "a serious breach of good faith on the part of the group"—and that the process was now being renewed with a promise of "continuity between the first and second site visits although the second Site Visit Committee is obliged to carry out a thorough new site visit." Fifth, "I have spent the great part of my time informing groups about IPA policies and clarifying their applications. I have never felt any particular responsibility to their Enforcement Commission."Sixth, the IPA has given detailed feedback to every individual evaluated and has thus far received only one complaint, from a LAISPS training analyst who was denied that status by the IPA and had been demanding an opportunity for reevaluation, which was indeed being offered. Seventh, about second guessing local institutes, "If'second-guess' means that we evaluate each individual member of a group to determine eligibility for IPA membership, then the assertion is true. As indicated above that is a fundamental ground rule of the process surely known by the plaintiffs and their lawyer before the settlement." (In this connection, Hanly stated that the White Institute had never applied to the IPA nor had it made any effort to conform to IPA requirements, as far as the IPA knew.)

In connection with this letter, Hanly provided Zuckerman a succinct Summary History of the IPA New Groups Policy in the U.S. This statement began with the establishment of the Regional Association status of the American a half-century earlier and mentioned all the major events, from the filing of the lawsuit on March 1, 1985, to the inconclusive and frustrating September 4, 1991 meeting between the IPA representatives and the representatives of the former plaintiffs. The central point of continuing contention was declared to be the still ongoing controversy over the interpretation of the "functional equivalence" concept. The IPA position was that individuals who had been trained by standards that departed significantly from those of the IPA could nonetheless demonstrate their "functional equivalence" by presenting four-times-per-week cases to the site visit evaluators. Oppositely, "the Enforcement Commission wants functional equivalence to mean that three-times-per-week analysis will be considered to be equivalent to four-times-per-week analysis. They claim that the Fisher letter [the famous side-letter] provides a basis for this demand." According to Hanly, at least some within the White Institute "are lending their cause to the Enforcement Commission to see if they can force the IPA to adopt their definition of functional equivalence and to guarantee acceptance of the White Institute before any compliance with IPA standards." Additionally, on January 7, 1992, Hanly sent Zuckerman another document, a detailed elaboration of the entire manner in which IPA societies and institutes were customarily organized and functioned.

On January 7, 1992, Zuckerman sent Sandler a draft of the letter he had prepared in response to Stromberg's letter of December 17, 1991 to Fisher (with a copy to Hanly). In his cover letter to Sandler, Zuckerman said that though he by no means desired to make policy for the IPA, he did need to point out what he felt to be a real discrepancy between Fisher's statement in the original side letter—that the IPA expected to determine "whether the group's training is functionally equivalent to the IPA sanctioned training"—and the IPA Statement of Policies and Procedures requiring that an applicant group had to have current training requirements that fully met IPA standards in order to qualify for a site visit, which Zuckerman felt carried a somewhat different implication. In his draft he said he had tried to cope with this by melding together various portions of the Fisher side letter but, "I must confess that such melding does not square with the IPA's statement of policies and procedures for evaluating new US groups." It is, of course, precisely in this inconsistency that the plaintiffs had found the basis for all of the allegations of bad faith in the implementation of (and from the plaintiffs' point of view, in the redefinition of) the "functional equivalence" concept.

In the draft to Stromberg, Zuckerman introduced himself as the new IPA attorney and then stated, "The IPA categorically disagrees with your accusations that it has 'flat out betrayed and violated the letter and spirit of the Settlement Agreement.' On the contrary, the IPA believes that it has complied with the provisions of the Settlement Agreement that are applicable to it." Since the Settlement Agreement was approved, the IPA had admitted four psychoanalytic groups in the United States to Provisional Society status, including the overwhelming majority of individuals in those groups. Zuckerman then offered his own interpretation of the "functional equivalence" concept as advanced in the Fisher side letter.

> A qualified group thus has to satisfy the IPA that (i) it is a cohesive functioning group in the organizational and/or institutional sense, (ii) that its training '*is*' functionally equivalent to IPA sanctioned training and (iii) that if a group's past training standards, although found to satisfy the functional equivalence test, are not in accordance with IPA training standards, such group would commit itself to follow IPA training standards, including four times per week analysis, after admission.

As for individuals, Zuckerman pointedly reminded Stromberg that the original side letter had said that "the IPA will evaluate *each* member of a group seeking affiliation with the IPA on an individual basis . . . will not automatically be granted or denied admission to the IPA," and that these statements and understandings were embodied in the side letter accepted by the plaintiffs prior to the signing of the Settlement Agreement.

In light of these findings, Zuckerman stated that he had to contradict Stromberg's "seven paragraphs of conclusory allegations." First, at the time of application for a site visit, a new group must indeed be functioning as a group and its training be functionally equivalent to IPA sanctioned training: "Contrary to your assertion, the IPA is not demanding that prospective members fully abandon their existing training policies before becoming members. By like token, however, it seems unreasonable and at variance with the letter and spirit of the provisions dealing with the admission of qualified groups to suggest that a group should be admitted to the IPA if its members have not ascertained whether they *can* or indeed would *want to* comply with IPA training standards, including four times per week analysis." Zuckerman then introduced his ice cream analogy: "Someone who up to now has only eaten chocolate ice cream can make a commitment to only eat strawberry ice cream once he or she is admitted to the Strawberry Ice Cream Association. But before making that commitment and before he or she is accepted into the Association, it seems reasonable to have the prospective member experience eating strawberry ice cream, even if he or she has not yet totally given up chocolate." In reference to the imbroglio over this issue with the White Institute, Zuckerman indicated that he felt it not useful to engage in preliminary arguments over whether individual members had or had not achieved the functional equivalent of IPA standards. Rather, the issue for discussion should be that of the willingness of the White Institute membership as a whole to adhere to IPA standards once admitted to the IPA, and what concrete steps the White Institute membership would undertake prior to admission to ascertain whether it would be willing to follow IPA standards after admission. (Would they try strawberry ice cream—i.e., present case material conducted at four times per week—as part of the IPA evaluation process?) To explore all of this, Zuckerman suggested a direct meeting, without counsel, between the IPA and the White Institute representatives, with the understanding that whatever transpired at that meeting would be off-the-record and not be used in future litigation. The IPA would, however, be willing to have the meeting on the record, with counsel present, if this first recommendation was not acceptable.

The other allegations in the Stromberg letter were answered more tersely. Second, the original side letter had explicitly stated that each member of the applicant group would be individually evaluated and that the majority of its members—not all—would need to be found qualified for the group as an entity to qualify for IPA admission. Third, the IPA had never insisted that each individual must have undergone four-times-per-week analysis in order to show eligibility for IPA membership. Fourth, the IPA did not agree that its process was "slow, redundant, expensive and unfair beyond all reason." In the case of the bogged down site visit process with NYCPT, that evaluation had been thrown asunder when the IPA visitors had discovered that a major segment of that group had broken away to form a separate organization, and that this fissure in the group had not been disclosed to the original Site Visit Committee during its earlier visits. The IPA was being improperly blamed for the consequent disruption and delay in restarting, but a new Site Visit Committee was now in place. It was not "starting over," but would build on the work of the prior committee. Zuckerman declared Stromberg's fifth point too vague and ambiguous to respond to, and asked for specific instances. Sixth and seventh, the overwhelming number of applicant individuals in the four groups already admitted to the IPA under this policy had been found qualified, many of them on the basis of functional equivalence. Again, specification and identification of the individuals referred to was requested: "The fact that a few individuals were found not to have satisfied the criteria is unfortunate, but does not mean that the IPA has breached the provisions of the Settlement Agreement."

Zuckerman ended the letter with the statement that the IPA, too, would like to avoid further litigation over these issues, but it would not disregard a statement from the United States Supreme Court in 1971 that an antitrust consent decree "must be construed as it is written, and not as it might have been written had the plaintiff established his factual claims and legal theories in litigation." He now looked forward to hearing from Stromberg in turn. Zuckerman's draft letter elicited a number of detailed commentaries, most notably by Hanly and by Jackie Amati, the IPA Secretary. Hanly sent a six-page, single-spaced letter of comment on January 9, 1992, followed by another, half the length, three days later. Hanly's commentary was as detailed and as couched in legal considerations as Zuckerman's draft. Hanly also wrestled with a number of different ways to deal with the same inconsistencies in IPA policy and practice that Zuckerman had remarked on in his January 7 cover letter to Sandler, including Hanly's offering a proposal in his first commentary to "unhinge" the concept of the functional equivalence of institutes from that of the functional equivalence of individuals. This proposal, on further consideration, he withdrew in his second commentary. Basically, Hanly was pleased with the Zuckerman letter: "I very much like the tone and force of your draft." He did try to make some points even more explicit. To qualify for a site visit, "current training requirements fully meet IPA standards or, if they do not, the applicant group has submitted a plan of transition to IPA standards that will allow for a valid evaluation of the applicant group's will and ability to train according to IPA standards. . . . As you argue in your letter, promises to conform after admission do not provide the IPA with the opportunity it needs to evaluate the genuineness of the compliance or the ability of the group to actually comply." Hanly here acknowledged that some of the postsettlement difficulties with the continuing complainants had stemmed from the unintended imprecision of the original side-letter, which allowed for such divergent subsequent interpretations. "The Settlement Agreement and the side-letter do require groups to conform to IPA standards even if, for us, the timing of this compliance has been very ill defined in the side-letter, making our site visit process difficult to carry out in the scrupulous way that it should be carried out."

Amati-Mehler's commentary seemed to contain even more reservation than Hanly's. She began, "I think your draft is an interesting approach," and she went on to express her concerns over the "concessions" being made to Stromberg's (and the White Institute's) bargaining position in his (Zuckerman's) efforts to cope with the ambiguities and discrepancies in the various IPA documents and operating procedures. There was this crucial paragraph in her memorandum:

> Certainly, I realize that your observation, again, in your front letter, is very correct. There seems to be a contradiction between the side letter and our demanding that in order to qualify for a site visit, "current training requirements fully meet IPA standards." This is, however, a crucial issue for us because, otherwise, any group (imagine how many around) that declares that its training policy is three times a week (maybe not even using the couch and real analytic ideology or technique) and says that it will change once admitted, could thus become eligible to become an IPA group and site visited.[7] Could we—among other arguments or changes—invoke that precisely this requirement was the result of the field experience that accounts for our having had to build our guidelines and refine them over some period of time? Incidentally, as you know, this was repeatedly told (and written) to the plaintiffs right from the beginning. And the work with the accepted groups at least shows our "good faith."

These and, I presume, other statements of comment were funneled to both Sandler and Zuckerman. Then, with Sandler's full backing, Zuckerman sent a somewhat altered and considerably toughened letter off to Stromberg by fax and fedex on January 15, 1992, Stromberg's deadline date. The changes

---

[7] This concern was here sharply exaggerated. According to the Settlement Agreement and all the understandings surrounding it, the only groups eligible for consideration for IPA membership under this New Groups policy were organized nonmedical psychoanalytic societies and institutes in the United States that had been functioning prior to the 1987 alteration of the IPA's Regional Association agreement with the American, which originally had been created in order to provide psychoanalytic training opportunities in the United States for clinical psychologists and other mental health professionals who had not been eligible for such training in the institutes of the American prior to the passage of the Gaskill Committee proposals in 1986. There were actually only a handful of groups that fully met these criteria, and four of them had already been accorded Provisional Society status within the IPA.

in the original draft included: (1) a footnote stating, "the [applicant] group should prepare a plan of transition to compliance with normal IPA training standards, so as to enable the Site Visit Committee to evaluate the applicant's ability to comply with and train in accordance with IPA standards"; (2) a clear statement that "an individual can establish his or her functional equivalence by presenting four-times-per-week cases to the Site Visit evaluators"; (3) an alteration of a crucial sentence, which originally read, "Contrary to your assertion, the IPA is not demanding that prospective members fully abandon their existing training policies before becoming members" (the last two words were replaced by "applying for membership," a crucial assertion in regard to the much-argued issues of sequence and timing); and (4) in documenting the lack of substance in the allegations of a "slow, redundant, expensive" evaluation process, Zuckerman now included quotations from the several exchanges of correspondence between IPA representatives and Herbert Strean. For example, in a letter from the latter, there was the statement that: "You have instructed us, and we agree with you, that for the (second) IPA Committee, we should (a) Demonstrate how we are doing educationally, as a Society, and financially, since New Jersey left us, (b) Demonstrate how we have implemented all of the Solnit Committee recommendations, etc."

Stromberg never responded to Zuckerman's letter, despite the IPA's having had to gloss over the various discrepancies and inconsistencies that had come to light in its own precepts and practices, as it sought to harmonize, or at least choose between, divergent voices within its own ranks over the proper interpretation of the original Settlement Agreement (most specifically the crucial side-letter), over what was intended by the concept of "functional equivalence," and over how fulfillment of its intended requirements was to be demonstrated—in short, over how much to accede to the construction desired by the applicant groups as against holding fast to a more "conservative" (or "rigid") position on its meaning. Whatever was going on, perhaps one can surmise that despite the ongoing unresolved issues around the White Institute and the NYCPT application processes—which indeed continued to preoccupy the involved parties for some time to come—Stromberg and his clients had concluded there was not a sufficiently strong legal case against the IPA (if there ever was one) to warrant the effort and expense of a return to court. In that sense, the threat of renewed legal action against the IPA was gradually felt to subside, though difficulties over the outstanding application processes continued.

Zuckerman very much confirmed this perception. On June 29, 1992, he wrote a letter to Hanly, who had asked for a report summarizing the status of the psychoanalytic litigation under the 1988 Consent Order, covering the six months since his firm had been hired by the IPA in December 1991. Hanly had asked for the report so that he could bring this update to the IPA executive Council meeting in London in July 1992.

In his letter, Zuckerman first reviewed the Stromberg ultimatum letter of December 17, 1991, the original Settlement Agreement and the attached side-letter, and then his own perception that "the side-letter contained some ambiguities that allowed for uncertainty. The side-letter contained an undefined concept of 'functionally equivalent.'" Zuckerman described how he had tried to deal with these ambiguities, and the differing positions on the meaning of the side-letter that the former plaintiffs and the IPA had subsequently taken, by "recommending certain changes to bring the IPA into conformity with the language of the side-letter while at the same time using the side-letter to support the IPA's fundamental needs." He presented, in very precise language, the position the IPA was now taking about what an applicant group, whose prior training program had not satisfied the IPA's standards, would need to demonstrate before it could be admitted to IPA affiliation, in effect repeating the main points of his January 15, 1992, letter to Stromberg. This seemed to have been a convincing letter, because five and a half months had elapsed and Stromberg had not responded to it nor written any other letters. Zuckerman then stated:

> A few things may be gleaned from that silence. First: Our arguments and positions as set forth in that letter were not only meritorious but were recognized as having merit by our adversaries. Second: If the plaintiff class disagrees with our position, the longer it delays in responding to our position and in seeking to obtain relief from the court, the better off we are. This is due to certain legal doctrines which require a plaintiff to seek relief promptly from a court in equity and not to delay as the plaintiff class has done here. Third: You have advised me through your sources of information that the Division 39 Enforcement Commission has now taken the position that they accept the right of the IPA to maintain its minimum standards . . . [and] they will not support the White Institute if it goes to court to try to force the IPA to accept them on the basis of three times a week training. I have no basis to either confirm or dispute the reliability of your understanding regarding the position of the present leadership of Division 39.[8]

---

[8] If such a shift had taken place in the stance of the leadership of Division 39, it could well have been consequent to the enhanced influence, not only of those who had originally called for settlement of the lawsuit on the grounds that the plaintiffs had already achieved the chief goals of the litigation by virtue of the actions of the American (Gaskill Committee proposal passage in 1986) and of the IPA (altered Regional Association agreement in 1987), but also of those many members in the four applicant groups that had already achieved IPA Provisional Society status, some of whom were also influential in the councils of Division 39.

The clear implication was that the likelihood of renewed legal action by Stromberg on behalf of GAPPP, or Division 39, or both had dwindled, and if it were to be renewed, the passage of time would reduce its persuasive power in court. To this date, it is still unclear to me how much the threatened return to court, expressed in the whole sequence of Stromberg's post-settlement letters to the American and to the IPA, was seriously contemplated and intended, or was simply a scare tactic, designed to exert maximum pressure on the psychoanalytic organizations to bend as far as they could be pushed in the direction of his clients' demands and wishes?

Zuckerman, however, did not altogether rule out legal action in either of the two outstanding unresolved controversies, that with the White Institute and that with NYCPT. Of the White Institute he said:

> In prior communications between representatives of the White Institute and representatives of the IPA, the White Institute had taken the position that the focus of any meeting with the IPA should be on finding a way for it to join the IPA without submitting, as other groups have done, to the New U.S. Groups Policy and to have the IPA make an exception to its requirement that new groups adhere to the four times per week analysis aspect of IPA's training standards. Some softening of the White position may have come about as can be seen from the attached recent exchange of correspondence.

But he stated that it was still possible that the White Institute, with or without Division 39 support, might seek to reopen legal proceedings in order to force the IPA to accept it as a component society on its preferred terms. In regard to NYCPT, after relating the still ongoing controversies (recounted in the next chapter), he indicated that there, too, the group seemed to be in the midst of deciding whether to continue with the site visit evaluation process or to try to engage in litigation.

In connection with both these situations, Zuckerman declared, "I am unable to offer a prediction as to the possible outcome of renewed litigation if they were able to prove that a number of IPA component Societies are not adhering to the four times per week analyzing standard. . . . I would merely point out that it is in the best interest of the IPA to take all appropriate steps to enforce the IPA standards on its component Societies if one or more of them are not currently adhering to said standards." Although it was clear that a half-year after the Zuckerman letter to Stromberg, the legal pressures on the IPA emanating from GAPPP and Division 39 were markedly weakened, if not totally gone, there were still very significant difficulties in the two still-unresolved site visit problems with the White Institute and the NYCPT, and that these carried some continued legal risk to the IPA. Nonetheless, on the eve of the July 1992 Executive Council meeting, the IPA could finally feel that the lawsuit pressures and their long aftermath were significantly alleviated, and that the course the IPA had charted through the lawsuit and the after-struggles was indeed being sustained. Whether the after-struggles, which were still not resolved, needed to be as contentious and as troublesome as they were cannot be easily decided. The chief protagonists within the IPA leadership had had somewhat differing views on this matter, as I have tried to make clear in this narrative.

The Story Brought to Date, 1996

T he ongoing tensions around the applications for IPA affiliation by the White Society and NYCPT continued well into 1992. On January 7, Charles Hanly sent the text of a letter intended for Jay Kwawer of the White Institute to Joseph Zuckerman for legal opinion. He asked again if the White Institute was willing to adhere to IPA training standards as the price of admission: "I know of no instances in which a group that did not subscribe to IPA training standards has been admitted to membership in the IPA. It appears that you are insisting that the IPA must change its admission standards in order to satisfy the requirements of the William Alanson White. Yet it is clear in the agreement that the IPA has no obligation to modify its admission standards." Hanly again offered to set up a meeting to clarify these issues and to exchange information.

On January 15, 1992, Hanly wrote to Joseph Sandler, reviewing all the ongoing activities on the several fronts. Zuckerman's letter of response to Stromberg had just gone off. There was no new news on the situation with the White Institute. Concerning NYCPT, Al Solnit was gathering all his papers on the first site visit sequence to send on to Sydney Pulver, chair of the new (second) Site Visit Committee. Meanwhile, correspondence was proceeding apace between Pulver and Herbert Strean over the stipulations for the new site visit process—"Syd is doing a great job"—and Pulver was making clear that although the new visiting process would build on the earlier one, it would nonetheless still encompass a general overview and evaluation of the society and the institute; nothing would be considered concluded on the basis of the first site visit process.

On February 3, 1992, there was a first reaction back from the plaintiff side concerning the Zuckerman letter to Cliff Stromberg. Stromberg had evidently sent the letter to all concerned parties among his clients, and on February 3, Strean had written back to Stromberg. He was pleased "to have confirmation that the evaluation of the New York Center is not 'starting over' but will build on prior site visits." But he charged that Zuckerman's letter clearly distorted the actual situation regarding the first (Solnit) site visit process.

> We gave every bit of information we had on hand to the Solnit Committee. Our budgetary problems with New Jersey and New Jersey's reluctance to be part of the IPA, for the most part, arose after the Solnit Committee had completed its work. We have reiterated this sequence many times. . . . to this day no one from IPA has sat down with us and explained just what caused the disruption and delay of the evaluation process. . . . We continue to be very disappointed that despite the fact that Dr. Solnit and his Committee visited us five times and examined our Society and Institute thoroughly, we are still being evaluated by the IPA two and a half years later. . . . if the IPA was serious about admitting organizations that adhere to IPA standards, then without New Jersey, we were even more qualified.

Evidently there was still bitter disagreement over the sequence of events of the first site visiting process.

Meanwhile, on February 7, 1992, Hanly wrote to Pulver about the same pending NYCPT visit. Largely, his letter filled Pulver in on the prior history with this group. In flat contradiction to Strean's letter to Stromberg, Hanly wrote to Pulver, "The Solnit Site Visit was discontinued because of the failure of the NYCPT to inform them of the impending split and because of the split itself. The Solnit Site Visit never made any recommendations to approve or disapprove any part or the whole of the NYCPT or any of its members and training analysts. . . . [Nonetheless, the] report identifies areas of difficulty and suggests that despite these difficulties the Site Visit should continue." Hanly also quoted from a letter a year earlier (February 15, 1991) that he had written to Strean:

> If the NYCPT decides to request another Site Visit. . . . a second Site Visit Committee would be instructed to a) satisfy themselves of the viability of the NYCPT after the departure of the New Jersey group, b) satisfy themselves that the four requirements of the Solnit Site Visit Committee had been met, c) undertake individual evaluations according to the established procedures. In this way, there would be a fresh start with a new Site Visit Committee *and* some building on the work you have already done with the Solnit Committee.

Hanly urged Pulver and his committee to canvass all the members of the Solnit Committee to get as much helpful input and insight as possible, and he pointed to the example of LAISPS, where Charles Mangham had taken over a troubled and floundering site visit process and turned it into a reevaluation with a most positive outcome.

In response to Zuckerman's concerns at that time for the legal posture of the IPA, Sandler wrote to him on February 11, 1992, explaining the variations that had developed over time in the training standards of the IPA component institutes.

> [It] is clear that no Society has been admitted to the IPA without the four times weekly analysis being stipulated. The only exception I can trace to this is that for the Hungarian Society, at that time the only Society in (Communist) Eastern Europe, three times a week was permitted in exceptional circumstances. Our minimum requirements were agreed to by the French Association and the Paris Society on entry to the IPA, although it is clear that they, and one or two other Societies (as far as I can tell the Belgian and the Swiss) did later take candidates at three times a week, without the IPA having been notified of the change in the training requirements. It is true that it was generally known that in France training analysis was conducted, since the 1950s, on a three times a week basis, and no action was taken by the IPA to remedy this before the threats of further lawsuits appeared on the horizon in the USA. Nevertheless, the IPA minimum requirements have always involved four times weekly training, although the IPA's control of what went on in its component organizations can be seen to have been—with hindsight—inadequate.

Sandler then went on to describe the overall differences that had evolved in the psychoanalytic training programs in France (and other French-speaking institutes) as compared with those in Great Britain and the United States, as a reflection of the overall structure of university education in France, where the emphasis is not at all on the particulars of the educational process, but on the demonstration of acquired competence and knowledge, however achieved, through rigorous examination at the end.

On February 15, 1992, Hanly followed up his letter of a week earlier to Pulver, concerning the NYCPT site visit, with a letter of report to Sandler.

> I think that I have a letter to Syd Pulver that will provide Zuckerman with a legal position that is consistent with the section of his letter to Stromberg concerning the NYCPT, which provides Syd Pulver with everything that he needs to carry out an acceptable site visit and provides Zuckerman with a basis for defending us in case Strean decides to go to court. Syd found

the consultations with members of the Solnit Committee very helpful. His report will come to us via Zuckerman who wants to see it before it is distributed.

The remainder of the letter dealt with all the other issues confronting the New Groups Committee, but clearly NYCPT was uppermost on the agenda. Hanly agreed with Sandler that it might be useful to put Pulver into direct contact with Zuckerman in case the need for such a consultation developed, and he thanked Sandler for inviting him to the next IPA Executive Council meeting to bring a full report on the activities of the New Groups Committee in person.

On February 21, 1992, a letter came back from Strean to Pulver, dealing with the planning for the site visit of the new committee, now scheduled to begin on March 14. Strean asserted that NYCPT had always

regarded ourselves as a psychoanalytic institute preparing our candidates to conduct psychoanalytic treatment in a disciplined and knowledgeable manner. . . . [However,] the Solnit Committee took the position that those students who were in analysis less than four times a week . . . were in psychoanalytic psychotherapy. The Solnit Committee also took the position that those of our candidates who conducted treatment less than four times a week were conducting psychotherapy. . . . With Dr. Solnit and his Committee's help, we have initiated our present program. Those students who wish to graduate as psychoanalysts must be in four times a week analysis and conduct analyses at the same frequency. For those candidates who wish to remain in three times a week "analysis," we have modified their status and they are now in psychoanalytic psychotherapy. Because of our new arrangement more and more of our candidates are moving into our psychoanalytic program. . . . As you point out in your February 10, 1992 letter "NYCPT has taken many steps to resolve the issues." We all feel that although our distinction between psychoanalysis and psychotherapy is somewhat arbitrary, it helps us move toward satisfying our major objective, i.e. to be an IPA affiliated Institute and Society. . . . If you visit any classroom, you will find that it will be a seminar in psycho-analytic theory and psychoanalytic treatment. You will not be able to differentiate psychotherapy from psychoanalytic students because they are so similar.

At the end of his letter, Strean expressed the agreement of NYCPT that all their training analysts and members be individually evaluated by the new

Site Visit Committee and hoped that after the visit they could all "agree on a lot more."

Pulver's response to Strean, dated March 4, 1992, was a detailed seven-page, single-spaced letter. It reviewed the history between the IPA and NYCPT and interpreted much of it in a manner opposite to the understanding claimed by NYCPT. For instance, Pulver had interviewed the several members of the prior Solnit Committee and told Strean that that committee, though divided in its opinions, was "predominantly negative" about what they had found, and that "even Al Solnit, for example, who was the most positive about NYCPT, did not feel that at the time of the site visit NYCPT could be recommended, though he did feel that the organization had the potential for qualification over a period of perhaps two or three years."

After citing Strean's letter to Hanly of October 14, 1991, in which Strean had acknowledged that a major NYCPT task would be that of demonstrating how the group had implemented all of the Solnit Committee recommendations, Pulver then launched into his reaction to the Strean response in the February 21 letter:

> Contrary to Solnit's recommendation of "keeping psychotherapy excluded from the psychoanalytic program," your February 21 letter makes it painfully obvious that the NYCPT has not excluded its "psychotherapy" students from its psychoanalytic program. Instead, your letter discloses that your "psychoanalytic" students are attending the same seminars and classes as your "psychotherapy" students. Moreover, your letter also makes it very clear that NYCPT feels that treatment done at the frequency of either 3 or 4 times a week is psychoanalysis and that all of your classes and teaching are based upon that conviction. You have done your best to accommodate the IPA by calling three times a week treatment "psychotherapy," but that is essentially a matter of changing a name in order to achieve compliance, rather than really changing your underlying philosophy.

In assessment of this, Pulver gave the Site Visit Committee response:

> To be quite frank, Herb, your February 21 letter indicates to . . . [us] that the NYCPT has not implemented Solnit's recommendations and has not been conducting a training program that meets IPA standards or is functionally equivalent to IPA sanctioned training. If NYCPT wishes to become a part of the IPA and to conduct an auxiliary psychotherapy teaching program, that is its privilege, but it must be separate and distinct

in all ways from the psychoanalytic educational process. That is, it must be taught as psychotherapy, with psychotherapy goals specified, the differences between the psychotherapeutic and psychoanalytic processes clearly defined, differences in technique spelled out, and no mingling of the two groups of students.

NYCPT was then confronted with two choices: "It may decide that such a modification of its present program is not what it wants and it can then drop its application for IPA membership. On the other hand, it may decide that it would like to modify its program as I have mentioned, with the hope of becoming eligible for IPA membership." If NYCPT were to choose the latter course, "we are prepared to work with you to help develop a transition plan to IPA standards"—though it was made quite clear that this would be a process that would take some time, at least a year. The Site Visit Committee was nonetheless prepared to go ahead with the March 14 meeting, "since it will give us a chance for discussion, clarification and an exchange of views, and we might even be able to make some specific plans for the future. On the other hand, if NYCPT decides that IPA membership is not worth the major organizational modification which is now clearly required then there would be no purpose to the meeting and we will understand if you call it off."

A new element had meanwhile entered into the IPA New Groups considerations. David Sachs (Philadelphia), as chair of the Subcommittee on New Groups in North America, received a letter dated February 27, 1992, from Anton Kris (Boston)—who had himself been a member of the original Site Visit Committee to IPTAR—written on behalf of himself and five colleagues, all but one psychiatrists, and three of them, in addition to himself, IPA members through their membership in the American. He was announcing the formation of the Massachusetts Psychoanalytic Study Group (MPSG) with the specific aim of becoming an IPA component organization: "The main aim of the MPSG is to foster postgraduate education and to provide a route to membership in the IPA for psychoanalysts in Massachusetts who are not eligible for membership through the American." In this connection he declared that the two members of his founding group of six who were not members of the American, "are trained, practicing psychoanalysts, whose credentials, in our opinion, meet the criteria for equivalency of training for full membership in the IPA." The group expected to have 10 members by the end of 1993, perhaps 50 by the end of the decade, "the majority holding doctoral degrees in psychology and related fields."

The scope of what was being proposed—and also its limitation—was stated as follows:

We propose that the MPSG make membership in the IPA available *over the next ten years only*, through the principle of functional equivalence of training, as it has been accorded to other groups previously excluded from participation in the IPA through the hegemony of the American Psychoanalytic Association. At the end of this period of ten years, the transition phase should have been accomplished and inequities set right. All who have been excluded in the past will have had ample time to complete training. . . . The MPSG does not propose now, or later, to become or to sponsor a training facility. It has no aim, therefore, to progress to the status of a provisional or full Society of the IPA [from Study Group status, that is]. Whether the Study Group would continue in existence long beyond the initial ten-year period is hard to foresee. Members might, for example, join one of the local IPA component Societies [one or the other of the two affiliate Societies of the American in Boston?] for which their membership in the IPA would make them eligible.

The intent of Kris and his colleagues in all this was clear, to provide a vehicle through which nonmedical mental health professionals in the Boston area, who had been trained outside the framework of the American, could now obtain access to IPA membership, just as their confreres in the New York and Los Angeles areas had been able to do, albeit with the difference that in those instances, this had been done through the channel of functioning (nonmedical) psychoanalytic training institutes that had been created over time and had established programs, histories, and track records. This was a proposal that came from someone within the heart of the psychoanalytic establishment—in both the American and the IPA.

The first response to the Kris letter was dated March 3, 1992, and was from Sandler, who had received a copy as the IPA President. It was friendly but guarded. Sandler stated that Kris was quite correct in not applying for recognition of the MPSG under the terms of the settlement agreement, because this was applicable only to analytic groups already in existence at the time of the settlement. The Study Group route, starting with a nucleus of at least four IPA members, as MPSG did, was therefore the only appropriate path available. Although the American had long had affiliated groups without training functions, that had never been the case with the IPA. Therefore this request would have to be considered, on a policy basis, by the IPA Executive Council, if the Committee on New Groups for North America (the Sachs Committee) felt that the MPSG application warranted processing. Of course, the two existing affiliate societies of the American in Boston would need to be consulted to see if the MPSG proposal posed any particular problems for them. Sandler ended, "I do not want to be negative about your idea, as I think that it has distinct possibilities. Let us see what the Committee on New Groups will have to say."

In his reply to Sandler of March 10, Kris thanked him for his interest, but expressed concern about a possible Catch-22 in his letter. If MPSG intended to start a training program and progress to component Society status in the IPA, it would have a more "normal" and acceptable pathway to IPA affiliation; but that would be exactly what would stir the opposition of the two institutes of the American in Boston, which would of course cripple MPSG's chances of obtaining approval. Kris could only state, "Since I feel sure you do not wish to imply such a Catch-22, I assume you are spelling out the argument *for* acceptance of this Study Group, that does not wish to become a Society, as much as you are stating the obstacles. The idea of a Study Group with a *temporary* charter for use of equivalency sets no awkward precedent as it solves a real, present problem."

On March 16, 1992, Sachs wrote his response to the Kris proposal. He had received both the letter from Kris and Sandler's response to it: "My first reaction to your proposal for an IPA Study Group that, 'does not propose now, or later, to become or to sponsor a training facility' was that it represents a creative solution to the difficult problem of making IPA membership available to people whom you believe are qualified but for whom no pathway to membership currently exists. And my second reaction was that it may not be as easy to implement as the straightforward simplicity of the idea suggests." Sachs then adumbrated several potential problems: (1) as mentioned by Sandler, the IPA had never had a Study Group of the type proposed, and this concept would need prior approval by the IPA Executive Council; (2) the IPA would need to consider how and when to invite the comments of the existing affiliate societies of the American in Boston; (3) the group might not be self-liquidating, because over ten years the leadership might well change and the new leadership might have a different vision of the group's purpose; (4) if the group were to truly dissolve within the specified time, where would its members go? Suppose other IPA groups didn't want them? Would they remain free-standing members of the IPA? and (5) the abiding concern about lawsuits: "You should be aware that whenever 'equivalency' is granted to someone, the possibility exists that someone else may believe he deserves the same benefit. This is fine when he does; but, it is also true that the undeserving do try to get benefits for which they do not qualify. And in the U.S., the way is through litigation."

Having said all this, Sachs indicated that he was putting the whole matter on the agenda for committee discussion in Washington in May, and he invited response by Kris to the issues he raised. He ended on an upbeat note: "I compliment you and your group for coming up with the kind of original idea that addresses a local problem in a way that might benefit both the IPA and those potential members who currently have no way to join it. I will do everything I can to give your proposal the thoughtful consideration it deserves." Sachs followed this letter with another to Kris just five days later, on March 21, 1992. The second letter followed his receipt of a copy of the Kris response to Sandler of March 10. He was not as sure as Kris that a Catch-22 situation might develop. For example, if MPSG were to elect to follow the usual Study Group to Provisional and then to full Society route to IPA membership, including the sponsoring of a training program through an institute it would create, possible objections by the two affiliate societies of the American in Boston would not necessarily be overriding. The IPA would need to take this into account, certainly, but the IPA also had an interest in the fate of people who would be eligible for membership but who currently had no way to join the IPA. He did, however, want to express disagreement with one of the last sentences in the Kris letter to Sandler: "Every action by the IPA *does* establish a precedent in the mind of someone. We have no control over our decisions having unintended (and awkward) potentials. For this reason we have to consider decisions such as this in terms of their precedent setting potential whether we want to or not." Again, he ended with a reassuring statement: "I trust you appreciate that raising questions does not imply any interest on my part to delay considering your request. On the contrary, it is to be construed as an interest in coming to grips with the problems your request raises as soon as possible."

In his response to both these letters by Sachs, dated March 25, 1992, Kris tried to deal with each of the many questions that had been raised about MPSG. He pointed out that whatever the custom to that point, nothing in the IPA constitution required a Study Group to pursue the course towards Provisional and full component Society status, and therefore the recognition of MPSG in the status requested would be a decision of the IPA Executive Council alone, not a constitutional matter. No objection from either of the American's two affiliate societies in the Boston area was anticipated, and MPSG had no concern about their being asked to review its proposal. That MPSG contemplated a life span limited to ten years was a misunderstanding. It might well go on longer; the ten-year span applied only to the right to make use of the functional equivalence standard for new membership in the IPA. MPSG did not foresee any need for a third IPA training facility in the Boston area, because "everything in the present manner of the IPA analysts and of BPSI and PINE [the two affiliates of the American in Boston] demonstrates an openness to non-physicians and to those who have been unfairly excluded in the past, and to those, whatever their background, who have something to offer to psychoanalysis. Though no one could predict its future, conditions might alter so that MPSG might disappear as a separate entity, folding into one of the local societies of the

American, if that would evolve into a welcoming and collegial environment, with the maintenance of IPA membership either through the American or directly with the IPA." With regard to potential lawsuits, Kris stated, "It would be unfortunate—comically unfair, in fact—to deny reasonable access to qualified individuals on the grounds that unqualified persons might sue for equal treatment." The precedent for functional equivalence had already been set, and Kris concluded that he should have said in his earlier letter, "no *adverse* precedent would be set by a charter for temporary use of functional equivalence, administered by the IPA Executive Council."

The last in this particular sequence was the response of Sachs, to Kris, dated April 3, 1992. The nub of his response was contained in this cautionary paragraph.

> Consider the possibility of analysts being trained in a "parallel fashion" that they claim is "equivalent" to those who were disadvantaged and who were accepted by the IPA under the concept of equivalency. Conceivably they could request a Study Group to evaluate their "equivalency" and an endless and extremely difficult task would confront the IPA both in the U.S. and elsewhere. As one who has evaluated people on the basis of equivalency in the litigious climate of the U.S. I can attest to the fact that the disqualification of anyone can be most difficult because they separately and together threaten to sue. Naturally, I am not implying that those people about whom you are concerned will belong to this group, but you can see my interest in considering negative consequences of separating the functions of a Study Group [separating off the intent to train and to progress to full institute and society status]. What we are learning is that there are people interested in taking advantage of the idea of "equivalency" that was created to redress a grievance and using that concept in a new context to legitimize training outside the IPA that is not equivalent. Then, they place the burden of proving that the training is not equivalent on the IPA and threaten to sue if the IPA disagrees with them.

On this basis, Sachs renewed his plea to Kris to consider going the regular Study Group route:

> I suggest that you could simply apply to become a Study Group like any other. If you only "qualify" and don't train, so be it. The IPA would not penalize you for not training and would not withdraw the right to train if you later decided to do it. No secondary application would need to be made if you did wish to train. . . . My concerns about the misuse of a special type of Study Group that only evaluates "equivalency" would be allayed

and we would all live happily ever after without creating new threats of lawsuits however unfair they might be.

From my own reading of these exchanges, the proposition Sachs was offering Kris would have been fraught with even more unhappy precedents and litigation-prone consequences than that of Kris. The so-called regular Study Group route depends on the viability and acceptance of a group (at least four) of IPA member analysts who, under IPA sponsorship, undertake to train new psychoanalytic candidates who, upon graduation, will qualify for membership in that group and in the IPA. Regular Study Groups do not qualify individuals trained outside the IPA structure on the "functional equivalency" basis. That option was created under the terms of the Settlement Agreement as a means of evaluating those who had been trained outside the IPA, in organized nonmedical institutes or even independently and informally, because such training had been denied by the American prior to the passage of the Gaskill proposal and the alteration of the Regional Association agreement. The MPSG proposal was designed to accomplish this same thing, for people already trained, by creating this new Study Group with four IPA members as its central cadre. Whether it undertook to train or not, the proposition—and the precedent—would be the same, and this was the issue posed for the Sachs Committee and the IPA Executive Council.

While these exchanges of correspondence over the MPSG proposal were taking place, the other New Groups concerns continued. On March 11, in an upbeat mood, Hanly wrote to thank me for a letter of support and appreciation I had just written to him regarding his myriad, often repetitive and tedious, activities, shepherding the entire New Groups process: "Your appreciation of my efforts is a great encouragement to carry on with what has become a very heavy burden (although a very interesting one)." He stated that Zuckerman was turning out to be a great person to work with, tough-minded and aggressive, while at the same time very careful and scholarly. On March 17, 1992, Hanly sent an equally upbeat letter to Sandler, beginning, "I am pleased to be the bearer of good news for a change." He went on:

> The letter to NYCPT [from Pulver to Strean, pointing out that the "changes" NYCPT had reported to this point were only cosmetic] followed by an excellent job done by Syd Pulver and his Committee seems to have produced, at least, the prospect of a breakthrough. They appear to have accepted that their "solution" for sorting out psychoanalysis from psychotherapy training is not viable and have decided to go back to their membership to discuss the impact of real changes, and their acceptability to their members. They acknowledge that these changes will need to be substantial and will require a new site

visit. They appear to have accepted that the Solnit Site Visit had not approved them and that there were serious reservations based on real problems that they had. Strean will no doubt be in touch with Stromberg, so we cannot be sure yet what further developments there will be, but, for the time being, there is the prospect of a workable site visit, the final outcome of which we cannot be sure of, but one which will enable us to discharge our responsibilities under the settlement and maintain our standards in doing so.

In the balance of the letter, Hanly passed on to Sandler the outcome of his inquiries into the recent meeting that Division 39 (Slavin and his associates) had had with the officers of the American. It seems to have been a friendly, congenial meeting. Hanly, however, was somewhat apprehensive that the new cordiality between the psychologists and the American also meant that the burden of recriminations was now directed more at the IPA, and he had some feeling that things had been said at that meeting that were not helpful to the IPA: "My present assessment is that it would be possible to make too much of it. What we need to do is make sure that all the top officials of the American understand our policies, the difficulties inherent in the legal situation, the current state of affairs, and the importance of our shared effort with the American to maintain training standards." There was no mention of the situation with the White Institute in this letter.

The next letter, however, from Hanly to Zuckerman, dated April 6, 1992, dealt at length with the situation with the White Institute. Kwawer had written to Hanly on April 1, and Hanly had drafted a reply for Sandler to make, which was being sent on to Zuckerman for legal comment together with an informational cover letter to Zuckerman. Hanly had found Kwawer's letter, asking for a meeting between IPA and White Institute members, encouraging and attributed this positive response to Zuckerman's letter of January 15, 1992, to Stromberg:

> For the first time the tone of Kwawer's letter is realistic and reasonable even if there is still a whiff of grandiosity.... But he has opted for a meeting without attorneys; he has acknowledged that there has thus far been no societal discussion of seeking affiliation with the IPA, let alone a decision to do so, and he has accepted that a meeting with us would be informational and not some attempt on their part to negotiate special status with the IPA. Conspicuous by their absence are all the threats of his past communications.

Hanly, of course, favored a positive response to Kwawer's request, and in the draft letter that he proposed for Sandler's consideration, attention was called to Zuckerman's call in his letter for an open meeting, off-the-record, and without attorneys, so as to encourage the frankest exchange of views and organizational positions.

Hanly added his suggestions to Sandler as to the composition of the IPA representation—second level representatives, so that appeal could then be made if needed to the higher level of the main IPA officers. He suggested Homer Curtis (Philadelphia) as his nominee to Sandler for the chairmanship of the Site Visit Committee, should a formal site visit process eventuate, and for the other representatives, David Sachs, Arnold Cooper, and himself. In this letter to Zuckerman (and Sandler) there was passing reference to the situation with NYCPT, where Pulver, "has been able to encourage some realism as well."

But by the time of the June 29, 1992, letter of six-month report from Zuckerman to Hanly, the situation with each of the applicant or potential applicant groups currently being considered—NYCPT, the White Institute, and MPSG—was as undecided as ever. Zuckerman could report his strong feeling that Stromberg (meaning Division 39, or GAPPP, or both) had backed off from the threat of renewed litigation. This risk, which had seemed to hover over matters ever since controversies first arose between the erstwhile plaintiffs and defendants over the "good faith" implementation of the settlement agreement (the American over the conduct of the CNMCT evaluation process, the IPA over a number of the site visit evaluation processes with LAISPS, the White Institute, and NYCPT) seemed to have substantially subsided.

However, matters were still unresolved with the several applicant groups: however unlikely, renewed litigation threats were always in the air, and Zuckerman dwelt in detail on the situation with NYCPT. After referring to the exchanges of correspondence I have cited, Zuckerman ended:

> As you also know, the relations between Dr. Pulver and Dr. Herbert Strean, the Director of NYCPT, became increasingly strained over the winter months. As a consequence, Dr. Pulver offered his resignation as Chair of the Site Visit Committee if Dr. Strean felt that he could no longer work with him; Strean's reply resulted in Dr. Pulver's resignation. Dr. Homer Curtis will be the new Chair of the Committee. The NYCPT is in the process of deciding whether or not to continue with the affiliation process or to engage in litigation.[1]

---

[1] This was evidence that Pulver's March 4, 1992, letter to Strean, in which he called the altered NYCPT training program only a cosmetic change designed to appear compliant with IPA requirements, which Hanly in his March 17, 1992, letter to Sandler had declared, "to have produced, at least, the prospect of a breakthrough," had rather led to an open rupture in the relationship between Pulver and Strean, which in turn had caused Pulver to resign from the Committee, so that the site visit process itself could perhaps be rescued via other hands.

The contretemps between George Allison, as President of the American, and Arnold Schneider and Harriette Kaley, representing the Settlement Enforcement Commission, was still continuing in the pages of *Psychologist Psychoanalyst*. The Spring 1992 issue contained another two letters in response to that interchange, one by Alan Sugarman (San Diego), a psychologist member of the American, and a reply to that by Schneider and Kaley. Sugarman took strong exception to the tone of the Schneider-Kaley letter of response to Allison, saying, "The hostility and paranoia so blatant in their letter can do nothing to promote a better working relationship with the American Psychoanalytic Association ... even a brief meeting with Dr. Allison makes it ridiculous to ascribe ulterior and solely self serving motives to his reaching out to Division 39." Sugarman applauded the American's increasing liberalization around policies of membership and certification and called it insulting to criticize its emphasis on high standards as "continuing the mythology of the American's omniscience." His central argument was:

> I have no support for legal attempts to force the International to modify its standards (in a direction many of us see as a lowering) so that Institutes using different standards may apply. It is one thing to insist on open opportunity for analytic training. It is another thing to say that we are now going to change the way in which the International or the American define what external criteria are most likely to result in a psychoanalytic process. . . . It seems grossly egocentric to expect an International accrediting body to change its standards to accommodate a particular Institute, rather than for that Institute to take some responsibility for meeting the standards of the organization which it wants to join.

The Schneider-Kaley letter followed immediately upon that of Sugarman. Basically they stood by their earlier letter and again sharply challenged Allison on his rendering of the concepts of standards and of legitimacy, to wit, that the American's criteria defined what constituted high standards, and that the American could presume to reach out to other organizations that it decided also provided legitimate psychoanalytic treatment.

> Given the American's and the International's continued unquestioning adherence to their so-called "high standards" (an issue which continues to threaten further legal action on the part of GAPPP against the International) and anti-scientific pre-judgment against diversity, we should not be surprised by the existence of obstacles to a true collaborative spirit. . . . It

would seem to us that to establish a real collaborative climate, the American would need to respect and be willing to study theoretically and technically diverse psychoanalytic practice and training systems in concert with such interested groups as are represented in Division 39 and other psychoanalytic organizations. And this process would need to be accomplished *before* "legitimacy" is bestowed on one psychoanalytic treatment or another. . . . While we respect the American's deep rooted belief in its own approach to psychoanalysis, we cannot bow to any effort to bestow legitimacy by fiat. Dr. Sugarman, in his letter, suggests that an empirical basis exists for such claims. What is needed is a comparison precisely of that type of data with that of the clinical data of other practitioners working out of different frameworks.

The succeeding issue of *Psychologist Psychoanalyst* (Summer 1992) continued the discussion of Division 39's relation with the American and the IPA, not in the Letters to the Editor column, but in Jonathan Slavin's final column, "From the President's Desk." The first part concerned relations with the American, and the next part, relations with the IPA. About the American—and in marked contrast to the Schneider-Kaley letters—the report was exceedingly friendly. Whatever the issues once had been over the CNMCT implementation of the Gaskill proposals, that controversy seemed to have subsided completely and was not even mentioned. The content was a report of a second meeting with the officers of the American, and a first with the Committee on Psychoanalysis of the National Federation of Societies of Clinical Social Work. The purpose was to explore common interests, and without sacrificing respective identities and goals, to seek out legitimate areas of cooperation. Issues of major shared concern were the establishment of a common external credentialing body for psychoanalysis to which they would all subscribe, cooperation in addressing the challenges of managed care and the rapid changes going on in the health care delivery system, and, in general, setting up a common information clearinghouse and consultative body, a Psychoanalytic Consortium, in which the three organizations, perhaps also the American Academy of Psychoanalysis, would participate as equals.

Slavin said that he was optimistic indeed about what had already been accomplished in this dialogue with the American (and the others). In this context he thanked Allison as President of the American—again in startling contrast to the diatribe by Schneider and Kaley in the immediately preceding issue of the same newsletter—and also Marvin Margolis, as Chairman of its Board on Professional Standards, for proposing the initial meeting: "I feel very gratified that this year, we may have witnessed the beginning of a new era in the thinking of psychoanalysts about their common professional future, regardless of the discipline in which they were trained. I have been very pleased to have been a participant in launching this process."

But concerning the IPA, Slavin spoke very differently: "I cannot report a similar change in the stance and attitude of the International Psychoanalytical Association. Here's a brief summary of where we are." He then reviewed the nature of the Settlement Agreement and the side-letter and asserted, "Unfortunately, the IPA has reneged on this agreement," and he reverted to the IPA demand that applicant institutes must implement four-times-per-week training even before being considered for admission. He then resurrected the threat of legal recourse.

> The reneging on a legal agreement by the IPA has occurred despite the fact that some of their accredited member Institutes train in three-times-per-week and have told the IPA that they have no intention of changing. It is only American Institutes . . . that are being discriminated against in this way. Unless there is substantial change, I believe it is inevitable that we will be returning to court to insure that the IPA is made to adhere to the legal agreements it entered into. It is unfortunate that a great deal more money may have to be spent in this process, but I believe that the Division should and will fully support this effort. Psychologists have worked too hard, for too long, to obtain the kind of professional equality and parity that they deserve, to be again excluded on the basis of truly trivial, as well as illegal, barriers.

This bellicose rhetoric thus offered an entirely different impression about the status of the IPA-Division 39 relationship and the likelihood of a return to legal action than the Zuckerman six-month report, which appeared almost simultaneously (the end of June 1992), with its optimistic assessment that the lawsuit danger had largely subsided.

Slavin turned his final paragraph into a judgment upon the "strange" character of the IPA. It was the only international professional organization he knew of that tried to regulate professional practice across national boundaries. It was also the only scientific body he knew that tried to specify the beliefs of its members, that all its component organizations must be "Freudian" in orientation, as if, a century after the foundation of psychoanalysis, Freud's work was still so vulnerable that it needed protection in the bylaws of an organization. In this sense, while he respected the wishes of those psychologists and those psychologist-run psychoanalytic institutes that wished to affiliate with the IPA, he himself could only "wonder whether the desire to affiliate with the IPA may sometimes be a result of the legacy of exclusion we have suffered for more than a half-century."

This was the summer of 1992, almost four years after the signing of the Settlement Agreement in October 1988, and a full three years after the joyous and triumphant entry of the first three applicant New Groups into Provisional Society status in the IPA at the Rome Congress in the summer of 1989. The summer of 1992 also marked the start of my own last year as a member of the IPA executive Council in my capacity as immediate past-President. Perhaps for that reason (being less in the information loop), or perhaps because the intense flow of correspondence, memoranda, newsletter articles, relating to the complex issues in the relationships between organized psychology on the one hand, and the American and the IPA on the other, actually slowed down, my personal detailed files on these matters abruptly dwindled. At the same time, the ongoing controversies, however heated and unresolved they still seemed, soon played themselves out, quietly and without any of the feared (or even expected?) tumult and with no effort to renew legal recourse, either by GAPPP or by any of the psychoanalytic groups struggling over the issues of the conditions for application for IPA affiliation.

I can best bring these various accounts up to the summer of 1996 by organizing the balance of this chapter sequentially under six headings. First is the IPA application processes of NYCPT, the White Institute, and MPSG. Second is the controversy that surfaced, then died away, involving IPTAR and LAISPS over the application of the "window of opportunity" policy, relating to the conditions under which fully trained, but organizationally unaffiliated, nonmedical analysts could now seek IPA membership through acceptance by one of the four New Groups that had achieved IPA affiliation (three of them in Rome in 1989, the fourth in Buenos Aires in 1991). Third is the organizational coalescence of the four new IPA groups in the United States—IPTAR, NYFS, PCC, and LAISPS—into the Coalition of Independent Psychoanalytic Societies (CIPS) in the IPA, with further group evolution thereafter. Fourth is the parallel organization of a loose Psycho-analytic Consortium, involving the American Psychoanalytic Association, Division 39 of the American Psychological Association, the Committee on Psychoanalysis of the National Federation of Societies of Clinical Social Work, and the American Academy of Psychoanalysis. Fifth is the gradual evolution of the structure and conditions of functioning of CNMCT, the American's Committee on Non-Medical Clinical Training. And sixth, the American's outreach effort towards the members of the new (predominantly nonmedical)[2] IPA Societies in the United States.

---

[2] It should be remembered that the smallest of the four new groups, Psychoanalytic Center of California (PCC), had been started outside the framework of the American by dissident members of the two affiliated societies of the American in Los Angeles, who had desired to create a more congenial home for their avowed more Kleinian theoretical orientation. From the start, the membership had been roughly 50% medical and 50% nonmedical.

Concerning the status of the several IPA application processes still undecided in the summer of 1992, in response to my inquiry, I received a letter of update from Charles Hanly, dated August 30, 1994. None of the applicants had undergone a further site visit in pursuit of IPA membership, and to the time of this writing—1996—that has not changed. Concerning NYCPT, after the debacle with Sidney Pulver, who had resigned as chair of the proposed IPA Site Visit Committee when Herbert Strean, Director of NYCPT, felt no longer able to work with him, Homer Curtis, also of Philadelphia, was named the successor chair of this Committee, which included Helen Meyers (Columbia) and Anna Wolff (Boston). Despite intensive correspondence initiated by Curtis, the NYCPT never agreed to institute the renewed site visit process. They finally became convinced that it would not be possible to maintain their psychoanalytic psychotherapy students and graduates in the same training and membership status as their psychoanalysis students and graduates if they were to become an IPA component organization. They initiated a process of internal discussion which resulted in a decision to discontinue that site visit process "for the present." Curtis informed them that the IPA would be happy to reconstitute the site visit process whenever they were ready to do so; they have not been heard from since on this matter.

The denouement with the White Institute was comparable. After all the intense (and almost cajoling) correspondence from the side of the IPA, the White Institute and Society never made formal application for an IPA Site Visit with its commitment to accommodate to IPA training standards. It has instead pursued its independent course, and some of its very prominent members—for example, Jay Greenberg, Edgar Levenson, Stephen Mitchell—have become regular contributors to the scientific programs and to the official journals of the American and the International. As for the MPSG, despite the detailed initial inquiries, the group never actually got off the ground or reached a point where IPA application could be considered. One of the six founding members (one of the two who were trained analytically outside the American and would have been provided IPA access through this group) died of cancer, and much of the group's impetus seemed lost after this. All in all, as of this writing, the count of independent and nonmedical New Groups admitted to the IPA since the Settlement Agreement and the American's relinquishing of the "exclusive franchise" it had held under its Regional Association Agreement with the IPA up to the revision of 1987 in Montreal, still remains at the original four—IPTAR, NYFS, PCC, and LAISPS—now all full component organizations. One lingering problem within LAISPS, the denial by the IPA Site Visit Committee of IPA training analyst status to one of its senior training analysts, was taken to court in a suit by that individual against the IPA. This was finally negotiated out of court through a cash settlement and an agreement that the involved individual would retire from that educational function.

Another set of issues that arose around two of these New Groups—IPTAR and LAISPS—had to do with a controversy over the application of the "window of opportunity" policy originally brought up by the IPTAR officers. Stanley Grand, then President of IPTAR, had written to Hanly on October 4, 1989.[3] He was protesting strongly against any move by the IPA to restrict the "window of opportunity" by which the New Groups, while still in Provisional Society status and under the supervision of the IPA through the continued involvement of the IPA Site Visit-Liaison Committee, could accept into membership qualified analysts who were trained outside the framework of the American and had been practicing independently without formal organizational membership. (It was understood that once the Provisional Society was voted into full component Society status, the window would be closed and that future membership in it could only be accorded to its institute's own graduates or to members from other IPA Societies.)

Under this policy, a small number of (mostly quite distinguished) individuals were evaluated and accorded membership in the four New Groups—all from the New York and Los Angeles areas. A new question arose around a person trained analytically in a psychoanalytic training program started in a similar manner in Mexico City, at a time when nonmedical candidates had been barred from training within the Institute of the Mexican Psychoanalytic Association. This person applied for IPA membership via IPTAR, with the understanding that because she had family reasons for visiting New York frequently, she would arrange her visits so as to be able to participate regularly in the scientific life of IPTAR on the same basis as the members resident in the New York area. Because the IPTAR evaluating committee found this applicant to be fully qualified and "functionally equivalent," and because the evaluation guidelines originally formulated by the Hanly New Groups Committee did not specifically require residence and practice in the same geographic locale for those to be admitted to a society under the "window of opportunity" policy, the applicant was voted into IPTAR membership with the concurrence of the IPA Site Visit-Liaison Committee, and her name appeared on the IPTAR roster when it was voted into full component Society status at the 1993 IPA Congress in Amsterdam.

---

[3] See the detailed discussion of Grand's letter, as well as the supporting letter by Bill Greenstadt, then President of NYFS, in chapter 15, pp. 345–346; and the response by Hanly, pp. 346–347.

This action became known to other colleagues in the same circumstance in Mexico City, and a total of 19 comparable inquiries about the possibility of IPA membership through a United States New Group came to LAISPS within the following year. These came to LAISPS rather than to IPTAR because, after July 1993, the latter was no longer a Provisional Society whereas LAISPS was (until summer 1995), and because Los Angeles is, after all, closer to Mexico City than New York is. Two of these 19 actually followed through with formal applications for LAISPS membership, and after consultation between the involved officers at LAISPS and IPTAR, they were admitted to LAISPS membership with the same stipulation about required regular participation in the scientific life of the society that took them in. By this time, however, the Mexican Psychoanalytic Association (APM) was very aware of this situation, especially because one of its members was a member of the original LAISPS Site Visit Committee. The APM objected strongly to the IPA at this jurisdictional invasion, in which an IPA society in one country admitted someone to membership who was barred from access to the APM by virtue of not having been trained officially under its auspices.[4]

The spectre raised, of course, beside that of geographic jurisdiction within national boundaries, was also the potential pressure for IPA admission by the graduates of so-called parallel training programs of variable quality that existed in many Latin American countries (some in Europe as well) where the issue had only been for some—like the three from Mexico—having been trained at a time when clinical psychoanalytic training in their country had been restricted to psychiatrists. Under these intense pressures from the APM, supported by others in Latin America, the IPA Executive Council, with a Latin American President (Horacio Etchegoyen) declared the actions by IPTAR and LAISPS to have been improper applications of the "window of opportunity" policy, which had only been intended for those who had suffered this inequity in the United States, even though it had not been formulated in a way to make this restriction explicit. The actions, however, had been taken and had been ratified by the IPA; on the advice of legal counsel, concerning the liability that would be incurred should the IPA try to reverse these membership approvals, those three were allowed to stand.

Since the full controversy arose around the LAISPS approval process, many of the recriminations about misunderstanding and misusing the "window of opportunity" policy came down on Brian Robertson (Montreal),

---

[4] This whole situation was, to an uncomfortable degree, an ironic replay of the half-century-long American struggle to bar from its ranks immigrant nonmedical analysts trained in IPA Institutes in Europe.

who had succeeded Charles Mangham as chair of the LAISPS Site Visit-Liaison Committee. Robertson responded to these allegations with a spirited defense, a 17-page report of the LAISPS IPA site visit, dated May 20, 1995, in which he detailed the whole history of the many confusions and ambiguities about the proper scope of the "window of opportunity" policy. He added, as appendices, three reports about "the Mexican Recruitment." One was by him, one by the four involved LAISPS officers, and one by Ramon Ganzarain (Atlanta), who had been sent by the IPA in January 1995 on a special "fact-finding inquiry" into the origins and the nature of the problem. The essence of the Robertson document was that "the main misunderstanding involved the belief that the Window was applicable internationally and not restricted to qualified United States analysts who had been disadvantaged, under the settlement terms of the lawsuit." He asked, "Why did this misunderstanding occur?" and drew on the shared (mis)understanding expressed in the June 12, 1994, LAISPS Board minutes that "the window of opportunity was established to redress discrimination policies and to establish a reparative time"—and this without mention of geographic limitation or restriction to the United States. Robertson rejected emphatically and categorically the imputation by the complainants, echoed to some extent within IPA official counsels, of malicious intentions to undermine the stability of IPA organizations in other countries. He declared it simply human misunderstanding and human error. With Robertson's document, the whole crisis around this issue was put to rest. With LAISPS itself being voted into full Component Society status in the IPA in July 1995, at the San Francisco Congress, the "window" is anyway now closed.

During these same years, the four New U.S. Groups, now admitted to the IPA and outside the framework of the American, formed their own collaborative working group, named the Coalition of Independent Psychoanalytic Societies in the U.S.A. (CIPS). Under the title *In Statu Nascendi*, Abby Adams-Silvan (NYFS) wrote an account of the group's development for the *IPA Newsletter* (vol. 2, no. 2, 1993). The CIPS purpose was

> to promote scientific exchange and collegial activity, and to maintain an active, cooperative, and facilitating dialogue in matters of mutual concern to the national and international institutional psychoanalytic communities. . . . these groups needed to communicate to the broader psychoanalytic community that there was a new IPA presence in the United States, and they needed to do this together. The idea of a joint entity emerged [p. 22].

The initiative was taken by Norbert Freedman, then President of IPTAR, and encouraged by Hanly, and a first meeting of the representatives of the four groups was held in conjunction with the Buenos Aires IPA Congress in 1991. A steering committee was created, initially cochaired by Freedman and Jean Sanville (LAISPS). The Coalition as an organized entity secured representation on the Arrangements Committee for the 1995 IPA Congress in San Francisco, and Ethel Person, editor of the *IPA Newsletter*, designated a contributing editor responsible for special coverage of news and notes from the Coalition and from its four member societies.

A major event in the evolution of the Coalition took place in 1992. The IPA President, Joseph Sandler, organized a working party designed to propose a restructuring of IPA governance to include a role for the component societies to fit somewhere into a governing structure that up to then had consisted of an elected (and partly appointed) Executive Council, responsible only to the Business Meeting of the individual members. The new structure proposed was a House of Delegates to represent the societies as organized entities, with nine members from each of the three main IPA geographic regions, three of whom (one from each region) would be elected to voting membership on the IPA Executive Council. Both Europe (the European Psychoanalytic Federation, EPF) and Latin America (FEPAL) already had constituted, and functioning, regional organizations of the component societies on their continents, through which election to the House of Delegates would be conducted. No such encompassing regional structure existed in North America, and talks were initiated involving the Coalition, the American, and the Canadian Psychoanalytic Society (CPS). An agreement was hammered out to allocate the nine North American places in the House of Delegates, two each to the Coalition and the CPS (each representing approximately 400 IPA members) and five to the American (with approximately 2500 IPA members). There was talk about creating a new North American entity, North American IPA Societies (NAIPAS),with a planning meeting scheduled for late fall 1993 in Montreal.

In the July 6, 1995, *NYFS News Briefs* there was a letter from the President, Emily Flint, which spoke of the activities of CIPS, now the *Confederation* of Independent Psychoanalytic Societies. To further update the evolution of these collaborative (or confederated) activities, Jean Sanville wrote an article on the history of the independent psychoanalytic societies in the Los Angeles area (LAISPS, PCC, and others that have not sought IPA affiliation) that appeared in issue 2, 1996, of *The American Psychoanalyst*. This described the actual birth of NAIPAG (North American IPA Groups; i.e., the American, the Canadian, and the Confederation of Independents) around the issue of agreeing on representation from North America to the IPA's House of Delegates, and then the organization of another collaborative endeavor on the local level in Los Angeles, the creation, in the fall of 1995, of FIPAS, the Federation of IPA Societies in Los Angeles, comprising the two affiliate societies of the American and the two independent IPA

Societies in Los Angeles, organized to promote shared scientific discourse and unified community outreach.

Parallel with these activities, drawing the IPA component organizations in North America into closer working collaboration through a variety of evolving confederated structures, there has been a comparable endeavor by the American to reach out to non-IPA psychoanalytic organizations in the United States, in the pursuit of common interests. These include the organization of external credentialing that could obtain accrediting approval from the United States Office of Education, the legislative pursuit of parity for mental health benefits within the rapidly altering healthcare system in America, the protection of the privacy and confidentiality of the therapeutic enterprise from the requirements of third-party insurance payers. Within the American, this development has been fostered most intensively by Marvin Margolis during his three-year stint as chairman of its Board on Professional Standards. The organizations involved with the American in these meetings were, first, Division 39 of the American Psychological Association and the Committee on Psychoanalysis of the National Federation of Societies of Clinical Social Work, with the American Academy of Psychoanalysis joining somewhat later.

This endeavor, named the Psychoanalytic Consortium, was hailed by Leopold Caligor, President of Division 39, in his President's column in the Spring 1993 issue of *Psychologist Psychoanalyst*. Gone was all the contentious talk of the difficult issues that had divided the American and Division 39 during the years of the lawsuit and the troubled post-settlement period, when charges of "bad faith" implementation and defensive responses continued to cloud relations between the two organizations. Caligor asserted of the Consortium, "A basic assumption is that all four groups are equal," and that the "Consortium is the collective voice for psychoanalysts of all disciplines" (p. 1). Interestingly, the first organizational meeting of the Consortium was held on October 9, 1992, at the William Alanson White Institute, with participants from the White in attendance. The Mission Statement for the consortium had been devised over a series of meetings in early 1993.

> The Psychoanalytic Consortium, composed of the major psychoanalytic organizations committed to high standards of training and practice in the United States, will be dedicated to the strengthening of psychoanalysis and psychoanalytic psychotherapy in this country. We will work cooperatively to assure the inclusion of psychoanalysis and psychoanalytic psychotherapy in the healthcare system as well as in the education of the public about the value of psychoanalytic treatment. The Consortium will promote joint cooperative

scientific and educational activities at national and local levels. The Consortium will organize itself on the basis of equality of its constituent organizations, and be respectful of the autonomy of each group's training and credentialing activities [p. 2].

This is not to say that all tensions and differences over policies and practices among the Consortium members have been finally and enduringly resolved. About such concepts as "high standards" and basic requirements for training and practice, should a shared, governmentally acknowledged external accrediting body come into being, there continue to be sharply discrepant conceptions, and these actual or potential differences have certainly been the subject of ongoing concern in the debates within the American over the American's participation in (and posture within) the Consortium. Nonetheless, the dynamic today seems all in the direction of enhanced cooperation and collaboration across disciplines and across psychoanalytic groups aligned within differing organizational structures. Among these, the American and the IPA are no longer the sole nor even necessarily the dominant voices.

During these same years, and going back to the passage of the "Gaskill proposal," the American had been very diligently, if at first somewhat contentiously, implementing its new mandate to (finally) admit nonmedical candidates from the array of mental health professions to full and equal psychoanalytic training for clinical practice, alongside the continuing pool of psychiatric applicants. As already recounted, the implementation committee, named the Committee on Non-Medical Clinical Training (CNMCT), started to function in May 1986 with Carl Davis (New Orleans) as the first chair.[5] A first overview of the history of CNMCT was in an article in *The American Psychoanalyst*, written for the first 1994 issue by Phyllis Tyson, who had by then succeeded to the chair of the committee. The first tasks of the committee had been to delineate the categories of individuals without medical training who would be appropriate for admission to institutes, and to forge a set of procedures for institutes to follow in applying the waiver process mandated in the original Gaskill proposal. By December 1986 the committee had decided that "individuals holding the highest clinical degree in their field and who had demonstrated excellence in clinical work, could be considered. In addition, the committee had in place a preliminary set of procedures, however flawed, for institutes

---

[5] The other members initially were Herbert Gaskill (Denver), Justin Krent (Cleveland), and Robert Gilliland (Houston), members of the original Gaskill Task Force, along with Gerald Adler (Boston), Dale Boesky (Detroit), Stanley Goodman (San Francisco), Stephan Levitan (New York), and Phyllis Tyson (San Diego). Tyson was the only psychologist member.

to follow" (p. 14). In the first round of applications, 24 requests for waivers were received, and in May 1987 the committee recommended that the Board grant waivers to 11 institutes to enroll 18 of those individuals in full analytic training.

What emerged rapidly was "the vast discrepancy among the assessment procedures used by the different Institutes, and the vast differences in what they required in the way of documentation from their interviewers" (p. 14). These discrepancies among the applications led, of course, to confusions and disagreements within the CNMCT.

> Although recognizing the important career implications for the individual on behalf of whom the waiver was requested and the pain that deferral would induce, in both the individual and the Institute, members were troubled by the incompleteness of certain applications, or by applications that presented contradictory information with no clues as to how the contradictions were resolved. This state of affairs often made it difficult for the committee to recommend waivers, and when they were not granted, tensions grew between BOPS [the Board on Professional Standards] and the local institutes. The continuing lawsuit added to the tension [p. 14].

This was precisely the state of affairs that led to the major contention between organized psychology (GAPPP and Division 39) and the American which emerged in Cliff Stromberg's letter of February 14, 1990, addressed to the "Directors and Faculty of Psychoanalytic Institutes," and his letter on February 21, 1990, addressed to Joel Klein as attorney for the American, in which Stromberg called so strongly, under threat of renewed legal action against the American, for the American to cease and desist from its central waiver oppositional practices and accord its unhappy and potentially rebellious local Institutes, who knew their applicants first-hand and in detail, full autonomy in processing waiver applications without obstructive second-guessing by CNMCT.[6]

In December 1988, after the first three groundbreaking years, the chairmanship of CNMCT passed from Davis to John MacLeod (Cincinnati), who moved swiftly to try to reunify the disparate views within the committee.

> Recognizing that CNMCT had by now gained considerable experience in processing waiver applications, he attempted to

---

[6] This contretemps has been fully recounted in chapter 15, pp. 351–354.

distill from that experience a more objective and explicit description of the types of documentation found most helpful and necessary in gaining a comprehensive view both of an applicant and of the Institute's processing of the application. Unfortunately, in asking for this documentation, and using its adequacy in evaluating applications, CNMCT only exacerbated tensions, which began to grow also between BOPS and CNMCT. Both BOPS and the Institutes began to suspect CNMCT of using the documentation to create and uphold a "national standard of excellence," thereby compromising Institute autonomy and second-guessing the Institutes' evaluations of their applicants. CNMCT came to be viewed by some as obstructing the very process it was created to facilitate [p. 15].

By this time, 101 waiver applications had been processed and 77 approved (more than 75%), but this evidence of a generally positive approval process did not allay the distress of Institutes whose applications had been deferred or turned down. Finally, "in December 1989, the issue was resolved by the passing of the Ross [Topeka] amendment to the Gaskill proposal, which more clearly defined suitability and eligibility. The amendment determined that local Institutes would be responsible for determining suitability and clinical aptitude, whereas CNMCT would be responsible for determining educational eligibility" (p. 15).

The next, even more far-reaching step, came a little more than a year later. By an overwhelming vote (771 to 146), the membership of the American approved a bylaw amendment dropping the central waiver requirement for full clinical training for nonmedical mental health professionals holding a Ph.D. or Psy.D. in clinical psychology, the doctorate in mental health (D.M.H.) from the University of California system, or the Ph.D. or D.S.W. in social work. As Tyson put it, "This historic step, effectively reversing a policy that had been in effect since 1938, was taken a scant five years after institution of the waiver program. Never before had change come so quickly within the American" (p. 15).[7]

In August 1991, Tyson succeeded MacLeod as chair of CNMCT. Passage of the bylaw amendment had sharply diminished the enormous burden of waiver applications to be processed, because they now were only required for proposed applicants without mental health doctoral degrees

---

[7] This is the change that Jonathan Slavin, president of Division 39, called "a landmark event in the history of psychoanalysis," in his November 18, 1991, statement, "What do Psychologists Want?" For a full statement of Slavin's (and presumably Division 39's) perspective, see chapter 17, pp. 391–393, and footnote 1, p. 391.

(like master's level social workers) or with other (nonclinical) educational backgrounds.

> In order to identify such individuals and come to a consensus about their eligibility, however, CNMCT had to find a different way of working with the Institutes. The committee wished to avoid, to the fullest extent possible, the tensions and hurt feelings of the past. It wished also to avoid the imposition of laborious efforts on Institutes preparing applications, long deliberations by CNMCT itself, and the disappointments and antagonisms arising in the event of unfavorable outcomes. Working more closely with Institutes to ensure that applicants are eligible and ready for psychoanalytic training at the time of the waiver application, and that applications are complete, became a priority [p. 15].

Toward that end, CNMCT initiated a liaison system with the applicant institutes. Consultations to discuss eligibility and potential problems were set up between the applicant groups and the CNMCT liaison member for those institutes, and this process quickly bore fruit. At the May 1993 meeting, for the first time ever, *all* applications were approved for waivers, and this was repeated in December.

In an overview of the seven-year history of CNMCT (1986–1993) to the time of her writing, Tyson stated that, in total, 188 waiver applications had been processed, of which 45 had been initially deferred, most of them in the early days when the committee was struggling to define its procedures. Of the 45 deferred, 30 were later granted waivers and one became eligible without waiver. Twenty-six institutes were participating in nonmedical clinical training and 50 of the nonmedical candidates (at 20 institutes) were social workers at the master's level. As of 1993, 23 of the candidates processed by CNMCT had already graduated. A survey of the involved institutes revealed that for the most part, this program was perceived as an overall enriching experience. Some concerns were still being expressed that waivers were being granted too freely, to the detriment of the American's training standards, and this concern centered mostly around master's level social worker candidates. The CNMCT had begun to work around this issue with the Committee on Psychoanalysis of the National Federation of Societies for Clinical Social Work. This group had been especially disappointed in having been omitted from the category of clinical specialties now exempted from the waiver procedure. Consultation had been ongoing over a two-year period between the psychoanalytic social work group and CNMCT, and CNMCT had come to see this group as "a dedicated group of highly trained and sophisticated clinicians specializing in the study and practice of psychoanalytically oriented clinical work" (p. 15). Some of them had been fully trained psychoanalytically, mostly in independent training groups outside the American. They had created an American Board of Examiners that granted a BCD (Board Certified Diplomate), "a credential that guarantees a certain level of clinical immersion, maturity, and expertise" (p. 15). The Federation hoped that social workers with a BCD would be made eligible for psychoanalytic training without a waiver. Of those accepted by the American to that point, 60% held a BCD.

All in all, Tyson felt that her chronicle reflected a rising gradient of positive changes in the work of CNMCT and the operation of the programs for nonmedical clinical psychoanalytic training in the American's institutes. Of the future of CNMCT, Tyson indicated that some institutes were calling for the dismantling of the committee and the reversion of all its responsibilities to the local institute level, while other institutes, less trustful in this regard, were of the opposite opinion, that eligibility criteria should not be further broadened, and that CNMCT (and the Board) should continue to exercise an oversight function. Clearly there was no consensus at that point to terminate CNMCT.

The further history of CNMCT was later updated (through December 1995) in a report on the Board meeting of December 13, 1995, by William Jeffrey in *The American Psychoanalyst*. About CNMCT, renamed the Committee on Preparedness and Progress (COPAP) in 1994, Jeffrey stated:

> Phyllis Tyson, chair of the Committee on Preparedness and Progress (successor to CNMCT), reported that the committee had now processed 208 applications for waiver and had recommended 194 on behalf of 25 of the 29 Institutes. Tyson commented that the Institutes have learned to evaluate nonmedical applicants effectively. She and her committee recommended a "local option" whereby institutes may accept, without requesting a waiver, candidates holding the highest clinical degree[8] generally awarded in any one of the traditional mental health disciplines. The Board, *without dissent*, authorized Tyson, in collaboration with other appropriate Board leaders, to present a specific proposal at the May meeting. She requested one waiver, which was approved by the Board [p. 7, italics added].

---

[8] This would effectively exempt master's degree social workers from the waiver requirement because very few schools of social work award clinical doctoral level degrees. Ph.D.s and D.S.W.s in schools of social work are generally granted for doctoral level graduate work with doctoral thesis requirements in the public policy and social policy arenas.

The final line of ongoing activity within the IPA and the American to be discussed here is the most recent outreach by the American toward the members of the four independent IPA psychoanalytic societies in the United States. In 1992, the American established an ad hoc joint committee (of the Board and the Executive Council) on Membership for Members of the IPA. The committee chair was Homer Curtis.[9] The committee mandate was to propose a plan that would expand eligibility for membership in the American to members of the newly approved IPA societies in the United States on a basis comparable to the long-existing eligibility for membership of IPA psychoanalysts trained outside the United States.

> An increasingly collaborative spirit has developed among the various organizations involved in training and professional activities in psychoanalysis, in recognition of the need for a stronger voice in determining the status and future of analysis scientifically and professionally. . . . We consider that providing eligibility and careful evaluation procedures for membership of qualified IPA members would be another way of unifying and strengthening analysis. It would provide a national membership organization for such IPA members, who could both gain from and contribute to our scientific and professional exchanges [Curtis, Report of Ad Hoc Committee, May 20, 1993].

The basic criterion for this eligibility would be membership in an IPA society. "In those cases where training preceded approval of the program by the IPA, or where the applicant was trained in a different program than that conducted by his or her present IPA Society, assessment of the training and of the IPA Site Visit evaluation would be utilized" (Curtis, May 20, 1993). Finally, it was suggested that application for membership by these analysts would not require prior membership in one of the American's affiliate societies, although that could be an open option. The Curtis committee stated that it would welcome comments and questions from the Board and all of the American's affiliated institutes and societies.

---

[9] The other members were Lawrence Chalfin (NYU), Richard Fox (Los Angeles), Maimon Leavitt (Los Angeles), and Edward Nersessian (New York). From his original appointment as chair of the Committee on Prerequisites for Training (1975–1981), the first in the sequence of four committees of the American appointed to consider the opening of the American to nonmedical candidates, through to this latest effort at outreach by the American to the members of the new independent IPA institutes in the United States, initiated in 1992, Curtis has played a signal role within the councils of the American, helping to spearhead and guide the process of major change on this once thorny issue, leading by now to a total undoing of the exclusionary policies that had marked the American since its initial organization in 1911.

A year later, on June 21, 1994, the Curtis committee sent a letter to all members of the American, notifying them that at the May meeting in Philadelphia, both the Board and the Executive Council had overwhelmingly approved the committee recommendation that the current bylaw allowing application for membership in the American from members of the IPA trained abroad be extended to include members of the newly approved IPA societies in the United States. The committee was not unmindful of the delicate, perhaps awkward feelings that might be aroused by this invitation.

> The Four IPA Societies in the United States have formed a coalition and rightly have a sense of independence and pride in their organizations. It is likely that many will not be interested in joining another psychoanalytic organization preferring to express their interests and loyalties in working within their own groups. Those who have had some part of their training with members of the American, as well as those who have professional and social ties with some of our members, may more likely be the ones interested in joining with us [Curtis, letter to members of American, June 21, 1994].

This proposed bylaw change subsequently passed without controversy, and the implementation of the change began. So far, a handful of these now eligible individuals have applied for membership in the American and been accepted.

This brings the story of "The Question of Lay Analysis" in the United States up to 1996. What began as a complete interdiction with the founding of the American Psychoanalytic Association in 1911, and then forced upon the IPA as the governing American stance at the fated 15th IPA Congress in Paris, 1938, with the American proclamation of the "1938 rule," subsequently ratified de facto by the IPA at the 16th IPA Congress in Zurich in 1949 and finally codified with the formalization of the Regional Association agreement in Stockholm in 1963, began gradually to weaken with the American's creation of the Committee on Training for Research in 1956. The situation was finally reversed—under the impetus of the lawsuit—with the passage of the "Gaskill proposal" by the American in 1986 and the alteration of the Regional Association agreement between the IPA and the American at the 35th IPA Congress in Montreal in 1987. Through all the years from 1911 to 1987, this was a highly contentious and divisive issue within the American and between the American and the rest of the psychoanalytic world organized within the IPA. The years of the lawsuit, from March 1985 to October 1988, were especially stressful and combative. Unhappily, even after the settlement of the lawsuit, the struggle between the defendant organizations and the erstwhile plaintiffs continued and at times seemed unabated in intensity. A quieting ultimately came as the IPA processed and accepted into component society status those nonmedical psychoanalytic training organizations in the United States that desired the IPA affiliation and were willing and able to bring their training practices into accord with IPA requirements, and as the American gradually made its procedures for evaluating and accepting into candidacy individuals from the nonmedical mental health professions less restrictive. At this writing, there are no active interorganizational tensions or conflicts over these issues, and the longstanding controversy over unfettered access to full clinical psychoanalytic training in the United States for qualified individuals in all the mental health professions seems finally and definitively put to rest.

The Meaning of the Controversy
The Identity of Psychoanalysis

T
he almost century-long struggle over nonmedical ("lay") analysis within the American and the International Psychoanalytical Associations is finally effectively over. As chronicled in this book, it has been a long, turbulent, and divisive contest that badly fractured organized worldwide psychoanalysis over much of its history, and that for periods—in the 20s and 30s around the functioning of the IPA's International Training Commission and in the 80s with the lawsuit—was the major focus of psychoanalytic organizational attention and energy. How can we account for the clamor of this struggle and the divisive polarization it created amongst individuals all equally devoted to the well-being of psychoanalysis as they conceived it? What was really at stake?

The lawsuit was initiated and fought on Sherman antitrust grounds, that is, on the economic stand that the American Psychoanalytic Association was operating an economic monopoly that deprived nonphysicians of access to training for, and practice of, this highly prestigious and lucrative means of livelihood. A suit could hardly have been filed on any other basis. However, I never accepted the argument, no matter how loudly bruited, that this was primarily a venal, "pocket-book," trade-union, and economic issue. Though self-serving economic entitlements and anxieties are hardly ever absent from human affairs, and though they could have been paramount for any one or any group of the involved individuals on either side of this long struggle, I have always experienced this primarily as a principled battle between people of conviction and goodwill who held very opposed visions of the nature of psychoanalysis as a discipline and a profession. In chapters 1 and 2, I traced the historical development and sociopolitical contexts of psychoanalysis in Europe and America in the early decades of the century that led to different—and on this issue of "lay analysis," diametrically opposed—positions being held by the earnest leaders of European and

American analysis concerning the proper training and qualification of the psychoanalytic practitioner. To the Americans, this meant the painful price of open defiance of Freud, the consummate genius who still shadowed the entire field he had singlehandedly brought into being and had given to them as a scientific and professional legacy.

I will not repeat here the arguments on both sides of that controversy. Rather, I want to emphasize that they all had to do—perhaps more than the leading protagonists in the struggle were able to formulate and articulate—with a major aspect of the nature, or more pointedly, the identity, of psychoanalysis as a discipline and a profession. Identity, of course, has been the central unifying theme of Erik Erikson's monumental contributions to the psychoanalytic corpus, first brought to the forefront of psychoanalytic consciousness in an evocative, clinical manner in his depth-psychological and anthropological explorations in *Childhood and Society* (1950), and somewhat later, more systematically and theoretically, in his monograph *Identity and the Life Cycle* (1959).

Leon Grinberg in his discussion paper (1983) at the first IPA Symposium, held at Haslemere, England in February 1976, traced this word and concept, *identity*,—though in a far more restricted context—to earlier analytic thinking and writing. Freud (or rather Strachey, as his translator) used the word 92 times in the English language Standard Edition according to the *Freud Concordance* (Guttman, Jones, and Parrish, 1980), although this was mostly in the sense of "identical," as in "perceptual identity," or of designating an individual whose identity was indicated. Grinberg declared that Freud used the term only once throughout his work in anything like the sense that Erikson later gave the word and concept. Even then, Grinberg stated, it was "in an incidental way and with a psychosocial connotation" (p. 52).[1] This was in Freud's address to B'Nai Brith (1926c) where he spoke of the meaning of his Jewishness and the "clear consciousness of inner identity" that marked it.[2] Grinberg also stated (p. 52) that it was Victor Tausk, (1933)

---

[1] This last phrase is a reflection of Grinberg's own bias, because the identity concept in its Eriksonian development always has a psychosocial as well as an intrapsychic dimension: who I am and what I am a part of, my uniqueness and continuity in time, but also my identifications and affiliations.

[2] Freud's complete statement was as follows:

> But plenty of other things remained over to make the attraction of Jewry and Jews irresistible—many obscure emotional forces, which were the more powerful the less they could be expressed in words, as well as a clear consciousness of inner identity, the safe privacy of a common mental construction. And beyond this there was a perception that it was to my Jewish nature alone that I owed two characteristics that had become indispensable to me in the difficult course of my life. Because I was a Jew I found myself free from many prejudices which restricted others in the use of their intellect; and as a Jew I was prepared to join the Opposition and to do without agreement with the "compact majority" [pp. 273–74].

who had introduced the word into the psychoanalytic literature in his classic paper on the origin of the influencing machine, but again with the very restricted meaning of the unity (or narcissistic omnipotence) of the newborn in a pre-objectal-relational mental world.[3]

Clearly it was Erikson who made the conception of identity, or "ego identity" as he sometimes called it—its developmental achievement as a vital life task; its susceptibility under adverse external and internal pressures to confusion and/or diffusion; its feared underside ("negative identity" formation); its role in affirming each individual's unique place in historic time and in geographic space while simultaneously locking that individual into the psychosocial surround (including all the collectivities in which he or she plays out a selected or required role), making possible the intergenerational cogwheeling of the life stages (the parents' and child's phase-specific interactions)—central to psychoanalytic thinking and such a major addition to the theoretical corpus bequeathed to us by Freud.

In turning the exploration of the identity theme upon our discipline itself, the focus has, however, been more on the identity of the psychoanalyst than explicitly of psychoanalysis itself. A major expression of this concern was the decision of Serge Lebovici, then President of the IPA, to make *The Identity of the Psychoanalyst* the topic of the historic first IPA week-long Symposium held in Haslemere, England, in February 1976 (Joseph and Widlocher, 1983). Forty-three of the IPA's leaders from around the world participated, and there were 17 formal presentations. The unifying theme that emerged had to do with the stability or the vulnerability of the psychoanalytic identity (the capacity to maintain an "internalized psycho-analytic point of view," in Sandler's felicitous phrase in one of the discussions) in the face of a widely perceived "crisis of psychoanalysis," both internally and externally, the latter in response to the constant flux and periodic crises in the sociopolitical and economic surround. During the course of that meeting, Edward Weinshel, in bringing what he called a "Message from a Past President" (1983), made a synthesized presentation of the writings of Max Gitelson upon the central theme of the Symposium. Anna Freud (1983) in her commentary, which she described as the voice of "a representative of the past" (p. 257), recounted how the same theme and the same concerns, in (different) earlier decades, had been articulated by Gitelson and experienced by her.

---

[3] The relevant quotation from Tausk (1933), on the psychic status of the infant, states "knows nothing of the outer world, not even that part of the world which he will soon discover within himself. It is this stage of *identity* that precedes the first projection for the purpose of object finding within one's own body . . . [a state of] absolute self-satisfaction, no outer world, no objects. Let us designate this stage as the innate narcissistic one."

Also expressed in the same meeting were Klauber's (1983) observations and mine (Wallerstein, 1983) on the problems created for psychoanalysis, or rather for the psychoanalyst, by the failure, still, then, 37 years after the death of Sigmund Freud, to have properly come to terms with the impact of that fateful event upon our identifications and activities as psychoanalysts. Klauber, in talking of the danger of "stultification of thought" in psychoanalytic work, stated: "We have never been able to come to terms with his death—nor, as a consequence, to assess the measure of transience which his ideas must share with all other scientific, philosophical, and religious ideas. This may lead to psychoanalytic rigidity and lifelessness, or to revolt. . . . We can no longer rely on our identification with Freud; and this is the main reason why we are here today" (pp. 46–47). I put it similarly (1983):

> Sigmund Freud, our founding genius, our paradigm-maker, is no longer with us, and we can no longer rely just on the momentum of our collective identification with him. In this context we are powerfully reminded that though Freud died in 1939, we have never come fully to terms with his transience and his death. . . . [He] remains our lost object, our unreachable genius, whose passing we have perhaps never properly mourned, at least not in the emotional fullness that leads to intellective accommodation [pp. 270–71].[4]

Finally, in recalling the 1976 Haslemere Symposium, I note how years before the initiation of the lawsuit in 1985, voices were raised by American participants in the Symposium—in this context of concern with our identity—in alliance with Freud's views on the nonmedical analysis issue. George Pollock (1983), a past-President of the American, asked, "Can we really justify excluding excellent and very gifted people from our field because they may not have the long and arduous antecedent medical training before applying for psychoanalytic education?" (p. 198). Weinshel (1983), in his presentation of the thoughts of Gitelson, a past President of both the American and the IPA, cited a paper by Gitelson (1964) titled "On the Identity Crisis in American Psychoanalysis," published more than a decade before the Haslemere Symposium: "*I think the time has come for psychoanalysis to accept its identity as a separate scientific discipline* whose practitioners can

---

[4] Of course, the whole, near century-long, struggle, so close to Freud's heart, over the status of "lay analysis" that has been depicted in this book, is an ironic reminder that on this, among other issues, many psychoanalysts have been far indeed from an identification with Freud.

be various kinds of intellectually qualified persons who are humanly qualified for the human experiment which is the psychoanalytic situation" (p. 474). Apropos this statement, Gitelson also remarked, "Perhaps it is necessary to cast a wider net for students of psychoanalysis" (p. 474), and also, forebodingly, "The nature of its [psychoanalysis'] beginnings in America, and the perpetuation of that in its statutory requirements for affiliation with psychiatry, have placed psychoanalysis in an impossible position for the untrammeled development of its intrinsic scientific possibilities" (p. 469).[5]

Far beyond the monograph stemming from the IPA Haslemere Symposium there have been a goodly number of other expressions in the psychoanalytic literature of the concern with the identity of the psychoanalyst. One of the earlier ones in the American psychoanalytic literature was the seminal article by Allen Wheelis (1956) on "The Vocational Hazards of Psycho-Analysis." Wheelis's theme is one that I picked up and elaborated further, using the language of "institutionalized countertransferences," in my own 1981 article, "The Psychoanalyst's Life: Expectations, Vicissitudes, and Reflections." Similar preoccupations can be found in the literature of each language area in worldwide psychoanalysis.

But it is Erikson (1956) who has articulated the most comprehensively multi-faceted conception of the intermingled complexities of what he called the "professional identity" (p. 109) of the psychoanalyst, as well as its inescapable linkages with the broader issues of the identity of psychoanalysis itself. His statement needs to be quoted in extenso:

> It may well be necessary for the individual psychoanalyst to ask himself what particular configuration of drives, defenses, capabilities and opportunities led him into the choice of this ever-expanding field . . . some of the most heated and stubborn answers to the question of what psychoanalysis *is* or *is not* [i.e., the identity of psychoanalysis] originate in another question of great urgency, namely: what psychoanalysis *must be* (or *must become* or *became*) to a particular worker because a particular psychoanalytic "identity" has become a cornerstone of his existence as a man, a professional, and a citizen [Erikson's linkage

---

[5] This explains the basis of Gitelson's final statement in his article: "We are caught in an identity conflict between psychiatry which is a therapeutic specialty of medicine and psychoanalysis which is a basic science" (p. 475). Of course *all* therapeutic specialties in medicine also have their basic science substrate, which in the case of psychiatry, includes psychoanalysis alongside neurobiology and social science; and psychoanalysis, besides being a basic science, is also a therapeutic, which is part of the reason for the conflations and confusions between psychiatry and psychoanalysis.

of the two conceptions of the identity of psychoanalysis and the identity of the psychoanalyst]. . . . psychoanalysis, in its young history, has offered rich opportunities for a variety of identities: it gave new function and scope to such divergent endeavors as natural philosophy and Talmudic argument; medical tradition and missionary teaching; literary demonstration and the building of theory; social reform and the making of money. Psychoanalysis as a movement has harbored a variety of world images and utopias which originated in the various states of its history in a variety of countries, and this as a result of the simple fact that man, in order to be able to interact efficiently with other human beings, must, at intervals, make a *total orientation out of a given stage of partial knowledge.* Individual students of Freud thus found their identity best suited to certain early theses of his which promised a particular sense of psychoanalytic identity, and with it, an inspiring ideology. Similarly, overstated antitheses to some of Freud's tentative and transient theses have served as bases for professional and scientific identities of other workers in the field. Such identities easily find elaboration in ideological schools and in irreversible systematizations which do not permit of argument or change. . . . Sooner or later, then, training analyses must encompass the varieties of professional identity formation in candidates-for-training while theoretical teaching must throw light also on the ideological background of principal differences in what is felt to be most practical, most true, and most right at various stages of this developing field" [pp. 108–109].

By contrast, except for the allusions in this quotation from Erikson and the even more explicit but very brief quotations from Gitelson cited by Weinshel, there has been little literature explicitly under the rubric of the identity of psychoanal*ysis* (as distinguished from the psychoanal*yst*), though clearly there has been a very substantial and impressive scholarly output— much of it marked by divisive and even rancorous debate—over a most important aspect of the identity of psychoanalysis, its nature or status as a science. Ernst Kris (1947), Heinz Hartmann (1959), Sidney Hook (1959), Paul Ricoeur (1970), Adolf Grunbaum (1984, 1993), Marshall Edelson (1984), and Carlos Strenger (1991) come to mind immediately as among the most active and important contributors to this half-century-long ongoing debate, or rather, multisided dialogue.

In my own contribution to this long controversy (Wallerstein, 1986b), I quoted what I called "the most succinct statement of the terms of this debate . . . in an opening paragraph of Holt's (1981) arrestingly titled article,

'The Death and Transfiguration of Metapsychology' (p. 417)." The statement was, "Beneath all the diversity may be discerned some strikingly different positions on basic methodological [I would say, "epistemological"] issues: Is psychoanalysis a science or one of the humanities, like history? If a science, is it or can it be a natural science or should it be a social-behavioral science, and what is the difference? Does it have one theory or two? If two, how do they differ, and what is the relation between them?" (p. 130).[6] My own overview was similar. After describing the efforts to construe psychoanalysis into an updated (information theory and cybernetic) natural science mold, and then the counterposed effort to conceive it as a humanistic discipline like history, or literary criticism, or the Biblical exegetical interpretation from which the term "hermeneutic" derived in the first place, I stated:

> Others like Gill (1976) and Klein (1976) and I think also Schafer (1976), have rather preferred to see psychoanalysis as still a science. They see it, however, as a science very different from the so-called natural sciences, bound and governed as it is by its own set of evidential standards. Its criteria for proof, they feel, are intrinsically related to the totally subjectivistic nature of its data base and are therefore putatively different from the usual canons of natural science. This is what Harrison (1970) called the tendency to describe psychoanalysis, in quotation marks, as "our science," implicitly our "peculiar" science or declaredly in some way our different *kind* of science [Wallerstein, 1986b, p. 420].

To this special and idiosyncratic status for psychoanalysis, Gill (1983) had appended the label "hermeneutic science" (p. 534).

But its status as a science, and if so, its kind of science, is not the only vantage point from which the identity of psychoanalysis has been at issue.

---

[6] At another point in my article I quoted a comparable assessment by Donald McIntosh:

> At the cost of some oversimplification, one can discern two main opposing trends in this new wave of revision. First there is the view that psychoanalysis is a purely interpretive discipline, dealing wholly with the contents of subjective experience. Some of those advancing this view hold that the clinical theory (the psychology derived from and used in clinical practice) is sound and scientific, but reject much of Freud's instinct theory and often also the structural theory as invalid. . . . Others in this [same] camp hold that psychoanalysis is [nothing but] a humanistic and hermeneutic, not a scientific discipline [at all]. . . . The other major trend seeks to purge psychoanalysis of its putative metaphysical, anthropomorphic, and metaphorical elements, and to put it on a sound footing as a full fledged natural science [McIntosh, 1979, pp. 405–406].

In Freud's well-known and oft-repeated dictum, psychoanalysis is three things: (1) a theory (or science) of the mind, of how the mind functions and how it got that way, and what comprises the range of disorder in its functioning; (2) a method for investigating the functioning of the mind in all its adaptive and maladaptive aspects; and (3) a therapy for the disorders of the mind designed to alter its functioning in desired directions.

As a therapy, its nature and identity has become as problematic and equally subject to controversy as its status as a science (or not). It was not always that way. Freud had labored heroically over his professional lifetime to establish and maintain a unified theoretical and technical-therapeutic structure for psychoanalysis against all the destructive or diluting pressures or seductions from without (and also against fractious human divisiveness from within). Over his lifetime, psychoanalysis as a therapy had been reasonably systematized into what Stone (1961) called an acknowledged "ensemble of techniques" that analytic practitioners more or less uniformly subscribed to, with the comfortable feeling that this adherence protected them well enough from the unhappy dangers of "wild analysis." When psychoanalytic psychotherapy—in all its expressive and supportive form variants—was crystallized during the 1940s and 1950s as a (primarily American) adaptation of the theoretical understandings of psychoanalytic psychology to the clinical exigencies of a wider array of patients than those amenable to the classical analytic treatment method, again, in relatively short order, a majority consensus was achieved on what constituted psychoanalysis and what constituted the various expressive and supportive modes of psychoanalytic psychotherapy. The indications, goals, and therapeutic techniques of each were specifically spelled out, as well as what comprised the similarities and differences amongst all these psychoanalytically based therapeutic approaches. These formulations, together with dissenting minority positions, were all presented in putatively definitive form in a series of three panel discussions published together in a single issue of the then new *Journal of the American Psychoanalytic Association* (Panels, 1954).

Since then, for a variety of reasons that I have adumbrated at book-length elsewhere (Wallerstein, 1995), the consensus on psychoanalysis and on the derived psychotherapies as distinct therapies, which seemed so clear in the 1950s, has fragmented utterly. Today we live in a pluralistic psychoanalytic theoretical world, with each theoretical perspective offering its own declaredly distinctive therapeutic approach, as well as a world in which the distinctions between proper psychoanalysis and the whole array of psychoanalytically based psychotherapies have become much more problematic and ambiguous on both clinical and theoretical grounds. This is so much so that what is today one person's proper psychoanalysis can be another's mere psychotherapy. I have reported this whole story in detail in *The Talking Cures* (1995). What is of moment here is that the same problematic that exists about the nature of psychoanalysis as theory (as science) pertains equally today about its nature as therapy. What distinguishes it, if it can or should be distinguished, from analytic psychotherapy? What, if anything, distinguishes the technical approaches within the various psychoanalytic theoretical perspectives from each other?

Even the third pillar of Freud's tripartite declaration about the nature of psychoanalysis, the method itself, has been questioned in its meaning and position. Most of us quite automatically still subscribe to the centrality of the free association method, as developed and elaborated by Freud, as the centerpiece of our distinctively psychoanalytic working method, and what presumably marks us off from the practitioners of all other psychotherapeutic approaches, whether analytically based or not. Anton Kris (1982), in his book reasserting the centrality of free association as both the unique method and the characteristic process of psychoanalytic work, after broadly describing the major shifts in the technical focus of psychoanalysis over time, felt the need to insert the following justification for his book into his preface: "Analysis of resistance and transference, now defined in terms of mental structures and their functions, is regarded as the major vehicle of the treatment, while free association serves as the somewhat neglected handmaiden to those theoretical stepsisters. In this book I illustrate an alternative approach to clinical formulation, which focuses on free association not only as the source of data but as the point of departure for formulation" (pp. x–xi). However much we may individually agree or disagree with Kris on the value of this reversion to the earlier days when free association was the unquestioned, and unique, method of psychoanalytic inquiry, a moment's reflection upon the technical literature of recent decades will serve as persuasive reminder that the major shift Kris describes away from the method of free association, Freud's method, has indeed characterized contemporary psychoanalysis. The overall point is that almost all of us accept Freud's tripartite compartmentalization of the essence (or rather, the multiple identities) of psychoanalysis; but we also live with major questions and significant, even though not always clearly articulated, controversies about each of them.

But these are not the only ways in which psychoanalysis has been characterized. In his famous history, Freud (1914) also called it a "movement." And the pejorative connotation of this word, with its image of a group of devout believers defending a propagandistic and quasi-religious orthodoxy, has often been invoked to buttress the assaults of the external enemies of psychoanalysis, and also to give comfort to dissidents within its ranks, as well as to create uneasiness among uncertain defenders. Gitelson (1964), however, in his elegant disquisition on what he called "the identity crisis" in American psychoanalysis—already referred to in Weinshel's exposition of Gitelson's thought at the Haslemere Symposium—challenged this negative conception of a "movement" head on. He did this by cogently developing the argument that all science, of whatever branch, is a "social enterprise" (p. 451) that always involves interaction, cooperation, and sharing. This is achieved through each scientific community's "way of life; its own ideals, standards, mores, conventions, signs and symbols, language and jargon; its ethics, sanctions, authority and control; its institutions and organizations" (p. 452). He further added, quoting from a 1955 talk to the AAAS meeting by physicist Harold Schilling, that each scientific community even has "its own creeds and beliefs, orthodoxies and heresies— and effective ways of dealing with the latter" (p. 452). Gitelson's point, of course, was that in this sense—in being a movement in the way Freud meant it—psychoanalysis was indeed a "normal" science, not singular in any way, and by example, no different from physics, that model "hard science."

This brings me to the perspective on the nature (or the identity) of psychoanalysis which is my own special focus here, and which, for want of a better defining and delimiting term, I call the "nature" of psychoanalysis as a discipline. I acknowledge that that word can be used as a descriptor for other of the perspectives upon psychoanalysis, what it constitutes and what constitutes it, that I have been describing in this chapter. However, I mean the connotation as a discipline, distinct from all other intellectual disciplines, yet necessarily related by bonds of varying intensity to all other disciplines that deal with our intelligence of man (meaning of humankind). This has been, to me, the heart of the long and bitter struggle over the legitimacy of nonmedical (lay) analysis—differing conceptions of what kind of discipline psychoanalysis is and how it fits into the entire hierarchy, or perhaps better, the mosaic, of disciplines that illuminate human functioning and human behavior.

Surprisingly to me, the struggle over this issue of lay analysis—despite all the fervent rhetoric on both sides of the question over the years—has almost never been articulated in precisely these terms. Freud did try to do so with his famous statement in *The Question of Lay Analysis* (1926b) that psychoanalysis is a psychology, not "medical psychology" but simply psychology, though not necessarily the whole of psychology, with the clear implication that its seeming derivation from, or connection with, medicine was simply the happenstance that Freud was a physician who had come to create psychoanalysis in his search for a cure for the hysterical illnesses that were crowding his neurological practice.[7] This definition has been regularly cited by those analysts, following Freud, who have separated psychoanalysis

---

[7] See chapter 1, p. 9–10, for the complete quotation from Freud as well as the exposition of its full context in the then already ongoing intense debate over the status of nonmedical analysts, and the litigation over whether Theodor Reik, in conducting psychoanalysis, was practicing medicine without a license.

as a distinct enterprise, apart from psychiatry and medicine. It was, for example, restated by Pontalis (1983) in the Haslemere Symposium. "Let us admit for a moment that psychoanalysis is a psychology: provided we understand the word as psychology, a logic of the psyche, composed of 'pairs of opposites' running through it" (p. 282).

Pontalis then went on to elaborate what he meant by psychology as comprised of "pairs of opposites": "It is, as I see it, the fundamental difference between the mental functioning according to the primary process and that of the secondary process, constantly at work: metamorphosed in the ego, displaced in the defense mechanisms, and repeated in the resistance to change in the structures of the imagination, of thought, and of character" (p. 282). This meaning of psychoanalysis as a particular kind of psychology—dealing with "pairs of opposites"—had been put much more tersely and more elegantly by Ernst Kris (1947) in his signal statement: "The subject matter of psychoanalysis was new in science when Freud started on his investigation; it is new and bewildering even today. That subject matter is *human behavior viewed as conflict*" (pp. 5–6; italics added). The clear implication here is that psychoanalysis is *nothing but* human behavior considered from the point of view of conflict, that is, a most substantial and important part, but nonetheless only a part, of the totality encompassed by human psychology. This, incidentally, was in sharp distinction from the grand agenda of Hartmann (1964), Kris's close collaborator, who aspired lifelong to make psychoanalysis into a comprehensive "general psychology" embracing the totality of psychology, in what he envisioned as the completion of Freud's agenda.

As a psychology then—a part of psychology—how can the discipline of psychoanalysis be viewed? What kind of identity does it have in Erikson's sense of distinctness yet connectedness? The one answer, the American answer for so many decades, leaned heavily on Freud's conjunction of the theory with the method and the practice and was based also on the derivation of psychoanalysis and the elaboration of its theory from the clinical therapeutic experiences with the hysterics who were its first patients. It declared psychoanalysis to be fundamentally only a branch of the medical healing arts that deals with a range of emotional and mental disorders, gradually extending far beyond the treatment of just hysterics: a subspecialty of psychiatry, itself a specialty of medicine. In this conception, the practice of psychoanalysis should, of course, be limited to the medically trained, the fate that Freud foresaw, to his distress, as the American path. The reasoning was that the proper practice of psychoanalysis might need to draw upon the full panoply of the practitioner's medical knowledge, especially when somatic complaints were intermingled with the psychological distresses.

The alternative conception, Freud's conception, and that shared from the start by most of the Europeans, has been of psychoanalysis as a fully independent discipline, not a part of medicine, but a general theory of the mind, a psychological theory, moving toward a full-fledged and established science of the mind. It had applications as a psychological therapy, to be sure, but also had ramifications into, and linkages with, all of the cognate disciplines that bear on mental functioning more narrowly, and on the entirety of the human condition more broadly. In this sense, psychoanalysis would have its interface with human biology, and thereby with medicine, in its concerns with health and disease, because clearly the mind exists within the body and functions by way of the activities of the brain. But psychoanalysis would also have its interface with the rest of psychology in purporting to a comprehensive understanding of mental functioning, because the focus of psychoanalysis is only on that aspect of the mind and mental functioning that is rooted in conflict, and unconscious conflict at that, but also with the whole array of social and behavioral sciences, sociology, anthropology, the law, as they deal with, and throw light upon, the meanings and motivations of the organized behaviors of humankind. And as still another aspect, psychoanalysis would have an impact on all of the humanities—philosophy, literature, religious studies, the arts—because each expresses and illuminates the functioning and the reach of the human mind in all its manifold meanings and complexities.

If this be the vision of psychoanalysis, what in essence it is, its fundamental identity as a human achievement, pioneered by Freud but now the collective responsibility of all of us who are its adherents, then it needs to be open to suitable individuals whose originating disciplines rest in any of the major interfaces that I have postulated for it, biological science, behavioral and social science, and even the humanities. In this way psychoanalysis can truly reflect the interaction and the comingling of all its component influences and refract them through the particular psychoanalytic way of looking at things bequeathed to us by Freud.

My thesis throughout this book has been that these two counterposed visions of what psychoanalysis is all about, a branch of the healing arts (a subspecialty of medicine) or an independent discipline, whether consciously made explicit or not, underlie the 50-year separation between the American and the world-wide position about analysis. As I have indicated throughout, both points of view have been strongly held over the years within each of these separated camps. It has only been the preponderant majority and the political power which has tipped, and not always stably, in the two opposed directions over the half-century span. With the final accommodation and reconciliation—with the settlement of the lawsuit and the changes in the American and in the IPA—the balance has tipped in the direction that Freud initially posed for us: psychoanalysis as a distinct discipline, a psychology with all the interfaces I have stated, rather than in the opposed direction of a therapeutic arm of medicine in a particular area of its domain. Put graphically, what has been altered fundamentally for American psychoanalysis over the course of these events has been the change in identity. It is no longer "I am a physician who has specialized in psychiatry and, within that, psychoanalysis, as a way of understanding and trying to ameliorate human mental and emotional distress," or that I am in the first instance a physician and secondarily a psychoanalyst. The fundamental shift has been to: "I am a psychoanalyst, devoted to understanding the human mind psychoanalytically, in all its dimensions and activities, who has come to this endeavor by way of prior training and study in medicine, or in psychology, or in whatever"; thus, I am in the first instance a psychoanalyst, and secondarily came to it by way of any of the variety of routes indicated.

The American Psychoanalytic Association has now made this choice, not entirely voluntarily on the part of all its members, but to my mind irrevocably, in reversing a 50-year-long historic stance and joining in the long-time historical position of its colleagues from all the other countries represented in the International Association. Its members have, in effect, taken on an altered psychoanalytic identity, though this was not necessarily explicitly perceived and articulated as such. In fact, many may still be only subliminally, if at all, aware of it. As chronicled in this book, this has been a difficult and often tormented process of change. But it is a fundamental change, and perhaps that is why it was so contested and took so long in coming.

References

References

Bergmann, M. S. (1988), Who is a lay analyst? *Psychoanal. Rev.*, 75:361–372.
———— (1993), Reflections on the history of psychoanalysis. *J. Amer. Psychoanal. Assn.*, 41:929–955.
Breuer, J. & Freud, S. (1893–95), Studies on hysteria. *Standard Edition*, 2:1–311. London: Hogarth Press, 1955.
Cocks, G. (1985), *Psychotherapy in the Third Reich: The Göring Institute*. New York & Oxford: Oxford University Press.
Edelson, M. (1984), *Hypothesis and Evidence in Psychoanalysis*. Chicago: University of Chicago Press.
Eissler, K. (1965), *Medical Orthodoxy and the Future of Psychoanalysis*. New York: International Universities Press.
Ekstein, R. & Wallerstein, R. S. (1958), *The Teaching and Learning of Psychotherapy*. New York: Basic Books. Revised and reprinted, New York: International Universities Press, 1972.
Erikson, E. H. (1950), *Childhood and Society*. New York: Norton.
———— (1956), The problem of ego identity. *J. Amer. Psychoanal. Assn.*, 4:56–121.
———— (1959), *Identity and the Life Cycle: Selected Papers*. Psychological Issues, Monogr. 1. New York: International Universities Press.
Etchegoyen, R. H. (1993), Psychoanalysis today and tomorrow. *Internat. J. Psycho-Anal.*, 74:1109–1115.
Fenichel, O. (1945), *The Psychoanalytic Theory of Neurosis*. New York: Norton.
Fine, R. (1982), On the history, theory and future of nonmedical psychoanalysis. *J. Psychohist.*, 9:501–527.
Fischer, N. (Panel Report) (1982), Beyond lay analysis: Pathways to a psychoanalytic career. *J. Amer. Psychoanal.*, 30:707–715.

Freud, A. (1983), Some observations. In: *The Identity of the Psychoanalyst,* ed. E. D. Joseph & D. Widlocher. IPA Monogr. 2. New York: International Universities Press, pp. 257–263.

Freud, S. (1888–92), Papers on hypnotism and suggestion. *Standard Edition,* 1:61–172. London: Hogarth Press, 1966.

——— (1893–99), Early psychoanalytic publications. *Standard Edition,* 3:1–322. London: Hogarth Press, 1962.

——— (1894), The neuro-psychoses of defence. *Standard Edition,* 3:41–68. London: Hogarth Press, 1962.

——— (1896a), Heredity and the aetiology of the neuroses. *Standard Edition,* 3:141–156. London: Hogarth Press, 1962.

——— (1896b), Further remarks on the neuro-psychoses of defence. *Standard Edition,* 3:157–161. London: Hogarth Press, 1962.

——— (1900), The interpretation of dreams (Second Part). *Standard Edition,* 5:339–627. London: Hogarth Press, 1953.

——— (1910), "Wild" psycho-analysis. *Standard Edition,* 11:219–227. London: Hogarth Press, 1957.

——— (1913a), Introduction to Pfister's "The Psychoanalytic Method." *Standard Edition,* 12:327–331. London: Hogarth Press, 1958.

——— (1913b), Totem and taboo. *Standard Edition,* 13:1–162. London: Hogarth Press, 1955.

——— (1914), On the history of the psycho-analytic movement. *Standard Edition,* 14:1–66. London: Hogarth Press, 1957.

——— (1916–17), Introductory lectures on psychoanalysis. *Standard Edition,* 15:1–239; 16:241–463. London: Hogarth Press, 1963.

——— (1926a), Letter to Paul Federn, March 27. Archives of the Sigmund Freud Gesellschaft, Vienna. Cited by H. Leupold-Lowenthal in "On the history of 'The question of lay analysis.'" *Psyche,* 38:97–120, 1984.

——— (1926b), The question of lay analysis. *Standard Edition,* 20:177–258. London: Hogarth Press, 1959.

——— (1926c), Address to the Society of B'Nai Brith. *Standard Edition,* 20:271–274. London: Hogarth Press, 1959.

——— (1930), Introduction to the special psychopathology number of *The Medical Review of Reviews. Standard Edition,* 21:254–255. London: Hogarth Press, 1961.

——— & Pfister, O. (1963), *Psychoanalysis and Faith.* London: Hogarth Press.

Gay, P. (1988), *Freud: A Life for Our Time.* New York: Norton.

Gill, M. M. (1976), Metapsychology is not psychology. In: *Psychology versus Metapsychology,* ed. M. M. Gill & P. S. Holzman. *Psychological Issues,* Monogr. 56. New York: International Universities Press, pp. 71–105.

——— (1983), The point of view of psychoanalysis: Energy discharge or person? *Psychoanal. & Contemp. Thought,* 6:523–551.

Gitelson, M. (1964), On the identity crisis in American psychoanalysis. *J. Amer. Psychoanal. Assn.*, 12:451–476.

Goodman, S., ed. (1977), *Psychoanalytic Education and Research*. New York: International Universities Press.

Grinberg, L. (1983), Discussion of Joseph and Widlocher. In: *The Identity of the Psychoanalyst*, ed. E. D. Joseph & D. Widlocher. IPA Monogr. 2. New York: International Universities Press, pp. 51–66.

Grubrich-Simitis, I. (1993), *Zurück zu Freuds Texten*. Frankfurt: S. Fischer.

Grunbaum, A. (1984), *The Foundations of Psychoanalysis*. Berkeley, CA: University of California Press.

———— (1993), *Validation in the Clinical Theory of Psychoanalysis. Psychological Issues*, Monogr. 61. Madison: CT: International Universities Press.

Guttman, S. A., Jones, R. L. & Parrish, S. M., eds. (1980), *Concordance to the Psychological Works of Sigmund Freud*, 6 vols. Boston: G. K. Hall.

Hale, N. (1993), Lay analysis, San Francisco and national policy. Presentation to Oral History Workshop, American Psychoanalytic Association Meeting, San Francisco, May 20.

Harrison, S. I. (1970), Is psychoanalysis *"our* science?" Reflections on the scientific status of psychoanalysis. *J. Amer. Psychoanal. Assn.*, 18:125–149.

Hartmann, H. (1959), Psychoanalysis as a scientific theory. In: *Psychoanalysis: Scientific Method and Philosophy*, ed. S. Hook. New York: Grove Press, pp. 3–37.

———— (1964), *Essays on Ego Psychology*. New York: International Universities Press.

Henry, W. E., Sims, J. H. & Spray, S. L. (1971), *The Fifth Profession*. San Francisco, CA: Jossey-Bass.

Holt, R. R., ed. (1971), *New Horizon for Psychotherapy*. New York: International Universities Press.

———— (1981), The death and transfiguration of metapsychology. *Internat. Rev. Psycho-Anal.*, 8:129–143.

Hook, S. (1959), Science and mythology in psychoanalysis. In: *Psychoanalysis: Scientific Method and Philosophy*, ed. S. Hook. New York: Grove Press, pp. 212–224.

Jones, E. (1927), Book review, *The Question of Lay Analysis. Internat. J. Psycho-Anal.*, 8:86–92.

———— (1957), *The Life and Work of Sigmund Freud, Vol. III. 1919–1939: The Last Phase*. New York: Basic Books.

———— et al. (1927), Discussion of lay analysis. *Internat. J. Psycho-Anal.*, 8:174–283, 392–401.

Joseph, E. D. & Widlocher, D., eds. (1983), *The Identity of the Psychoanalyst*. IPA Monogr. 2. New York: International Universities Press.

Kaplan, L. A. (1986), Brief to Federal Court, Southern District, NY—Motion for Summary Judgment to Dismiss the Complaint.

King, P. & Steiner, R., eds. (1991), *The Freud-Klein Controversies: 1941–45.* London: Tavistock/Routledge.

Klauber, J. (1983), The identity of the psychoanalyst. In: *The Identity of the Psychoanalyst*, ed. E. D. Joseph & D. Widlocher. IPA Monogr. 2. New York: International Universities Press, pp. 41–50.

Klein, G. S. (1976), *Psychoanalytic Theory.* New York: International Universities Press.

Kris, A. O. (1982), *Free Association.* New Haven, CT: Yale University Press.

Kris, E. (1947), The nature of psychoanalytic propositions and their validation. In: *Freedom and Experience,* ed. S. Hook & M. R. Konvitz. Ithaca, NY: Cornell University Press, pp. 239–259.

Kubie, L. S. (1954), The pros and cons of a new profession. *Texas Rep. Biol. & Med.,* 12:692–737.

Lane, R. C. & Meisels, M. (1994), *A History of the Division of Psychoanalysis of the American Psychological Association.* Hillsdale, NJ: Lawrence Erlbaum.

Lerner, L. (1988), The *Psychoanalytic Review* and lay analysis. *Psychoanal. Rev.,* 75:356–360.

Levine, F. J. (1989) The "research and special training" program: Toward a history of non-medical participation in the American Psychoanalytic Association. Unpublished manuscript.

Levine, M. (1942), *Psychotherapy in Medical Practice.* New York: Macmillan.

Lewin, B. D. & Ross, H. (1960), *Psychoanalytic Education in the United States.* New York: Norton.

Limentani, A. (1996), A brief history of the International Psychoanalytical Association. *Internat. J. Psycho-Anal.,* 77:149–156, continued by Robert S. Wallerstein, pp. 156–158.

McIntosh, D. (1979), The empirical bearing of psychoanalytic theory. *Internat. J. Psycho-Anal.,* 60:405–431.

Mahony, P. (1993), Book review: *Freud, Jung, and Hall the King-Maker: The Historic Expedition to America (1909). Internat. J. Psycho-Anal.,* 74:842–846.

Masson, J. M., ed. (1985), *The Complete Letters of Sigmund Freud to Wilhelm Fliess, 1887–1904.* Cambridge, MA: Harvard University Press.

Menaker, E. (1988), Early struggles in lay psychoanalysis: New York in the thirties, forties, and fifties. *Psychoanal. Rev.,* 75:373–379.

Nunberg, H. & Federn, E., eds. (1962), *Minutes of the Vienna Psychoanalytic Society, Vol. I: 1906–1908.* New York: International Universities Press.

Panels (1954), *J. Amer. Psychoanal. Assn.,* 2:563–797.

Paskauskas, A. R. (1993), *The Complete Correspondence of Sigmund Freud and Ernest Jones, 1908–1939.* Cambridge, MA: Harvard University Press.

Peck, M. W. (1940), A brief visit with Freud. *Psychoanal. Quart.*, 9:205–206.

Pollock, G. H. (1983), Self and identity: The psychoanalyst, psychoanalysis, and society. In: *The Identity of the Psychoanalyst*, ed. E. D. Joseph & D. Widlocher. IPA Monograph 2. New York: International Universities Press, pp. 195–206.

Pontalis, J.-B. (1983), Reflections. In: *The Identity of the Psychoanalyst*, ed. E. D. Joseph & D. Widlocher. IPA Monograph 2. New York: International Universities Press, pp. 277–287.

Reik, T. (1948), *Listening with the Third Ear*. New York: Farrar, Straus.

Ricoeur, P. (1970), *Freud and Philosophy*. New Haven, CT: Yale University Press.

Rubinstein, E. A. & Parloff, M. B., eds. (1959), *Research in Psychotherapy*. Washington, DC: American Psychological Association.

Sabshin, M. (1985), Psychoanalysis and psychiatry: Models for potential future relations. *J. Amer. Psychoanal. Assn.*, 33:473–491.

Schafer, R. (1976), *A New Language for Psychoanalysis*. New Haven, CT: Yale University Press.

Schlesinger, H. J. (1961), Report from the Topeka Institute for Psychoanalysis to the Committee on Training for Research of the Board on Professional Standards, American Psychoanalytic Association.

Schneider, A. Z. & Desmond, H. (1994), The psychoanalytic lawsuit: Expanding opportunities for psychoanalytic training and practice. In: *A History of the Division of Psychoanalysis of the American Psychological Association*, ed. R. C. Lane & M. Meisels. Hillsdale, NJ: Lawrence Erlbaum, pp. 313–335.

Sherman, M. H. (1988), Theodor Reik and lay analysis. *Psychoanal. Rev.*, 75:380–392.

Shershow, L. W. (1986), "10/40" celebration: The founders. *Los Angeles Psychoanal. Inst. Bull.*, Special Anniversary Issue, December: 4–9.

Shlien, J. M., ed. (1968), *Research in Psychotherapy, Vol. III*. Washington, DC: American Psychological Association.

Stanton, A. H. & Schwartz, M. S. (1954), *The Mental Hospital*. New York: Basic Books.

Stone, L. (1961), *The Psychoanalytic Situation*. New York: International Universities Press.

Strenger, C. (1991), *Between Hermeneutics and Science. Psychological Issues*, Monogr. 59. Madison, CT: International Universities Press.

Strupp, H. & Luborsky, L., eds. (1962), *Research in Psychotherapy, Vol. II*. Washington, DC: American Psychological Association.

Tausk, V. (1933), On the origin of the "influencing machine" in schizophrenia. *Psychoanal. Quart.*, 2:519–556.

Tyson, P. (1994), A widening stream: Nonmedical training in the American. *Amer. Psychoanalyst,* 28:14–15, 19.

Wallerstein, R. S. (1961), Recommendations to the faculty of the Topeka Institute for Psychoanalysis concerning the further development of our research training program in psychoanalysis.

——— (1966a), *Psychiatric Research and the Assessment of Change.* Group for the Advancement of Psychiatry (GAP) Report No. 63, New York, pp. 357–478.

——— (1966b), Report to the Board on Professional Standards of meetings with invited consultants to the Committee on Training for Research on some issues in research training in psychoanalysis.

——— (1966–1969), Semiannual reports from the Committee on Training for Research to the Board on Professional Standards.

——— (1968), The Psychotherapy Research Project of The Menninger Foundation. In: *Methods of Research in Psychotherapy,* ed. L. A. Gottschalk & A. H. Auerbach. New York: Appleton-Century-Crofts, pp. 500–516.

——— (1969), Introduction to panel on psychoanalysis and psychotherapy: Relationship of psychoanalysis to psychotherapy—Current issues. *Internat. J. Psycho-Anal.,* 50:117–126.

——— (1974), Herbert S. Gaskill and the history of American psychoanalysis in American psychiatry. *Denver Psychoanalytic Society Newsletter,* 1:1–9.

——— (1976), Summary of the 6th Pre-Congress Conference on Training: The contribution of child analysis to the training in adult analysis. *Internat. J. Psycho-Anal.,* 57:198–205.

——— (1977), Psychotherapy research: One paradigm. In: *Communication and Social Interaction,* ed. P. Ostwald. New York: Grune & Stratton, pp. 189–202.

——— (1978a), Perspectives on psychoanalytic training around the world. *Internat. J. Psycho-Anal.,* 59:477–503.

——— (1978b), The mental health professions: Conceptualization and reconceptualization of a new discipline. *Internat. Rev. Psycho-Anal.,* 5:377–392.

——— (1980), Psychoanalysis and academic psychiatry—Bridges. *The Psychoanalytic Study of the Child,* 35:419–448. New Haven, CT: Yale University Press.

——— (1981), The psychoanalyst's life: Expectations, vicissitudes and reflections. *Internat. Rev. Psycho-Anal.,* 8:285–298.

——— (1982), Education for psychotherapy and psychoanalysis: The questions. In: *Psychotherapy: Impact on Psychoanalytic Training,* ed. E. D. Joseph & R. S. Wallerstein. New York: International Universities Press, pp. 119–129.

——— (1983), Reflections. In: *The Identity of the Psychoanalyst*, ed. E. D. Joseph & D. Widlocher. IPA Monograph 2. New York: International Universities Press, pp. 265–276.

——— (1986a), *Forty-Two Lives in Treatment*. New York: Guilford Press.

——— (1986b), Psychoanalysis as a science: A response to the new challenges. *Psychoanal. Quart.*, 55:414–451.

——— (1988), Psychoanalysis and psychotherapy: Relative roles reconsidered. *The Annual of Psychoanalysis*, 16:129–151. Hillsdale, NJ: The Analytic Press.

——— (1989), The Psychotherapy Research Project of The Menninger Foundation: An overview. *J. Cons. & Clin. Psychol.*, 57:195–205.

——— ed. (1992), *The Doctorate in Mental Health*. Lanham, MD: University Press of America.

——— (1994), Psychotherapy research and its implications for a theory of therapeutic change: A forty-year overview. *The Psychoanalytic Study of the Child*, 49:120–141. New Haven, CT: Yale University Press.

——— (1995), *The Talking Cures: The Psychoanalyses and the Psychotherapies*. New Haven, CT: Yale University Press.

——— J. W. Chotlos, M. B. Friend, D. W. Hammersley, E. A. Perlswig & G. M. Winship (1957), *Hospital Treatment of Alcoholism*. New York: Basic Books.

Weinshel, E. M. (1983), Message from a Past President—Maxwell Gitelson, M.D. In: *The Identity of the Psychoanalyst*, ed. E. D. Joseph & D. Widlocher. IPA Monograph 2. New York: International Universities Press, pp. 67–83.

Wheelis, A. (1956), The vocational hazards of psycho-analysis. *Internat. J. Psycho-Anal.*, 37:171–184.

Archives, British Psychoanalytical Society
Chapters 2 and 3

Eitingon, Max (Jan. 16, 1929). Letter to Ernest Jones (German).

British Medical Association (June 29, 1929). Supplementary Report to Council. Published in *British Medical Journal*.

Freud, Sigmund (Oct. 19, 1929). Letter to Ernest Jones (German).

Jones, Ernest (Nov. 7, 1930). Letter to A. A. Brill.

Jones, Ernest (Sept. 19, 1933). Letter to Anna Freud.

Jones, Ernest (Dec. 20, 1933). Letter to Theodor Reik.

Oberndorf, C. P. (Jan. 28, 1935). Letter to Ernest Jones.

Simmel, Ernst (Sept. 2, 1935). Letter to Ernest Jones.

Simmel, Ernst (Sept. 2, 1935). Letter to A. A. Brill.

Jones, Ernest (Sept. 25, 1935). Letter to Ernst Simmel.

Jones, Ernest (Oct. 10, 1935). Letter to Members of Committee formed to draft Statutes of the American Psychoanalytic Association.

Oberndorf, C. P. (Jan. 14, 1936). Letter to Ernest Jones.

Jones, Ernest (Feb. 18, 1936). Letter to C. P. Oberndorf.

Berliner, Bernhard (Oct. 12, 1936). Letter to Ernest Jones.

Jones, Ernest (Oct. 26, 1936). Letter to Bernhard Berliner.

Freud, Anna (Feb. 20, 1938). Letter to Ernest Jones.

Freud, Anna (May 15, 1938). Letter to Ernest Jones.

Kubie, Lawrence (May 22, 1939). Letter to Ernest Jones.

Alexander, Franz (May 26, 1939). Letter to Ernest Jones.

Jones, Ernest (June 13, 1939). Letter to Franz Alexander.

Alexander, Franz (June 30, 1939). Letter to Ernest Jones.

Schnier, Jacques (Nov. 16, 1953). Letter to Ernest Jones.

Schnier, Jacques (June 20, 1938). Letter to Sigmund Freud.

Freud, Sigmund (July 5, 1938). Letter to Jacques Schnier.

British Psychoanalytical Society (Feb. 2, 1948). Minutes of Council.

British Psychoanalytical Society (March 10, 1948). Minutes of Council.

British Psychoanalytical Society (March 15, 1948). Minutes of Council.

British Psychoanalytical Society (May 31, 1948). Minutes of Council.

King, Pearl (undated). Notes on 1948 Meetings between the American and the British Analysts.

Hendrick, Ives (Nov. 23, 1953). Letter to Clifford M. Scott.

Bulletins of the International Psychoanalytical Association
Chapters 2 and 3

Eitingon, M. (1926), Report of 9th IPA Congress, Bad Homburg, Germany, 1925. *Internat. J. Psycho-Anal.*, 7:119–143.

Freud, A. (1928), Report of 10th IPA Congress, Innsbruck, Austria, 1927. *Internat. J. Psycho-Anal.*, 9:132–159.

Freud, A. (1929), Report of 11th IPA Congress, Oxford, England, 1929. *Internat. J. Psycho-Anal.*, 10:489–553.

Freud, A. (1933), Report of 12th IPA Congress, Wiesbaden, Germany, 1932. *Internat. J. Psycho-Anal.*, 14:138–182.

Glover, E. (1935), Report of 13th IPA Congress, Lucerne, Switzerland, 1934. *Internat. J. Psycho-Anal.*, 16:242–262.

Glover, E. (1937), Report of 14th IPA Congress, Marienbad, Czechoslovakia, 1936. *Internat. J. Psycho-Anal.*, 18:346–372.

Glover, E. (1939), Report of 15th IPA Congress, Paris, 1938. *Internat. J. Psycho-Anal.*, 20:116–136, 212–221.

Freud, A. (1949), Report of 16th IPA Congress, Zurich, 1949. *Internat. J. Psycho-Anal.*, 30:178–208.

Bibring, G. L. (1952), Report of 17th IPA Congress, Amsterdam, 1951. *Internat. J. Psycho-Anal.*, 33:249–272.

Eissler, R. S. (1954), Report of 18th IPA Congress, London, 1953. *Internat. J. Psycho-Anal.,* 35:267–290.

Eissler, R. S. (1956), Report of 19th IPA Congress, Geneva, 1955. *Internat. J. Psycho-Anal.,* 37:118–136.

Eissler, R. S. (1958), Report of 20th IPA Congress, Paris, 1957. *Internat. J. Psycho-Anal.,* 39:276–296.

King, P. (1960), Report of 21st IPA Congress, Copenhagen, 1959. *Internat. J. Psycho-Anal.,* 41:167–211.

Zetzel, E. R. (1962), Report of 22nd IPA Congress, Edinburgh, 1961. *Internat. J. Psycho-Anal.,* 43:362–375.

Zetzel, E. R. (1964), Report of 23rd IPA Congress, Stockholm, 1963. *Internat. J. Psycho-Anal.,* 45:457–482.

**Committee on the Prerequisites for Training (CPT)
of the Board on Professional Standards (BOPS)
Chapter 6**

Committee Minutes by Paula Bernstein, Secretary
  Dec. 19, 1975
  May 7, 1976
  Dec. 14, 1976
  April 26, 1977
  Dec. 13, 1977
  (No meeting of CPT in May 1978)
  Dec. 12, 1978
  May 12, 1979
  Dec. 14, 1979
  May 2, 1980
  Dec. 19, 1980
Reports from CPT to BOPS by Homer Curtis, Chair
  Dec. 15, 1976
  Dec. 14, 1977
  May 3, 1978
  Dec. 13, 1978
  April 30, 1980
  Dec. 17, 1980
  Dec. 16, 1981

Further Documentation: Chapter 6

Committee on Feasibility of Non-Medical Training. Amer. Psychoanal. Assn. *Newsletter,* 14:2, June 1980.
Minutes, Board of Professional Standards (BOPS), Dec. 16, 1981.
Minutes, Executive Council of the American, Dec. 17, 1981.

Minutes, BOPS, May 12, 1982.
Committee on Desirability of Non-Medical Training. Amer. Psychoanal. Assn. *Newsletter,* 16:1, May, 1982.
Minutes, Executive Council of the American, May 13, 1982.
Minutes, BOPS, Dec. 15, 1982.
Committee on Desirability of Non-Medical Training. Report to Executive Council, Dec. 16, 1982.
Reiser, Morton & Curtis, Homer C., Letter to Vann Spruiell, Feb. 3, 1983.
Spruiell, Vann, Planning Memorandum for Joint Ad-Hoc Committee on Non-Medical Training, April 23, 1983.
Fischer, Helen, Memorandum to Vann Spruiell, March 28, 1983.
Report of Meeting of Joint Ad-Hoc Committee on Non-Medical Training, April 26–27, 1983.
Spruiell, Vann, Personal Communication to Robert S. Wallerstein, May 28, 1994.
Joseph, Edward D. and Orgel, Shelley, Memorandum to Members of the American, October, 1985.

Documentation for Chapters 7 through 18

Chapter 7

Limentani, Adam, Private and Confidential Memorandum to IPA Executive Council, Apr. 19, 1985.
GAPPP, Letter to "Colleagues," May 7, 1985.
Stromberg, Clifford D., Draft of Proposed Settlement between Plaintiffs and IPA, May 23, 1985.
Limentani, Adam, Second Private and Confidential Memorandum to IPA Executive Council, May 29, 1985.
Saussure, Janice de, Letter of response to Limentani, May 14, 1985.
Chasseguet-Smirgel, Janine, Letter of response to Limentani, June 3, 1985.
Joseph, Edward D., Letter of response to Limentani, June 7, 1985.
Calder, Kenneth T., Letter of response to Limentani, June 9, 1985.
Villarreal, Inga, Letter of response to Limentani, June 9, 1985.
McLaughlin, Francis, Letter of response to Limentani, June 10, 1985.
Palacios, Agustin, Letter of response to Limentani, June 12, 1985.
Leupold-Lowenthal, Harald, Letter of response to Limentani, June 24, 1985.
Cannon, Lista M., Letter to Irene Auletta, June 13, 1985.
Auletta, Irene and Cannon, Lista M., Telephone conversation plus two letters, Auletta to Cannon, June 18, 1985.
Welch, Bryant, Deposition, July 15, 16, 1985.
GAPPP, Letter to "Colleagues," July 16, 1985.

Motion to Dismiss Complaint and/or Give Summary Judgment Dismissing the Complaint on Ground that There Is No Genuine Issue as to Any Material Fact, July 18, 1985.

Fisher, Clinton B., Memorandum to Lista M. Cannon, July 18, 1985.

Cannon, Lista M., Letter to Irene Auletta, July 30, 1985.

Chapter 8

Minutes, Executive Council IPA, Hamburg, Aug. 1, 1985.

Limentani, Adam, Letter to Richard C. Simons, Aug. 29, 1985.

Cannon, Lista M., Letter to Irene Auletta, Sept. 6, 1985.

Kaplan, Lewis A., et al., Reply Memorandum to U.S. District Court, Southern District, N.Y., in re Bryant Welch et al. against American Psychoanalytic Association et al., Sept. 27, 1985.

Joseph, Edward D. and Orgel, Shelley, Memorandum to Members of the American, plus the final Report of the Ad Hoc Advisory Committee to the Executive Committee of the American, plus the Summary by Austin Silber, Secretary of the American, of the Board and Council discussions in May, 1985, all sent Oct. 15, 1985.

Hearing Transcript, U.S. District Court, Southern District, N.Y., Bryant Welch et al. against American Psychoanalytic Association et al., before Judge John Keenan; Lewis A. Kaplan and Clifford D. Stromberg, Oct. 30, 1985.

Wallerstein, Robert S., Letter to Joseph J. Sandler, Nov. 25, 1985.

Wallerstein, Robert S., Letter to Joseph J. Sandler, Dec. 2, 1985.

Minutes, IPA Executive Council (partial meeting), New York, Dec. 20, 1985.

Stockhamer, Nathan, Letter to Edward D. Joseph, Dec. 31, 1985.

Joseph, Edward D., Letter to Nathan Stockhamer, Jan. 8, 1986.

Stockhamer, Nathan, Letter to Edward D. Joseph, Jan. 17, 1986.

Joseph, Edward D., Letter to Nathan Stockhamer, Feb. 5, 1986.

Dorkey, Charles E., III, Memorandum to Lista M. Cannon, Feb. 7, 1986.

Dorkey, Charles E., III, Letter to Robert S. Wallerstein, Feb. 5, 1986.

Joseph, Edward D. and Orgel, Shelley, Memorandum to Members, American Psychoanalytic Association, Feb. 13, 1986.

Freedman, Norbert, Letter to Robert S. Wallerstein, Feb. 13, 1986.

Auletta, Irene, Letter to Lista M. Cannon, Feb. 13, 1986.

Dorkey, Charles E., III, Memorandum to Lista M. Cannon, Mar. 7, 1986.

Dorkey, Charles E., III, Memorandum to Lista M. Cannon, Mar. 13, 1986.

Cannon, Lista M., Letter to Irene Auletta, Mar. 14, 1986.

Minutes, IPA Executive Council, Taunton, England, Mar. 23, 26, 27, 1986.

Levitan, Stephen J. and Hurwitz, Mervin, tellers, Memorandum announcing result of ballot on Gaskill Committee recommendations, Mar. 28, 1986.

Cannon, Lista M., Letter to Irene Auletta, Apr.8, 1986.

Chapter 9

Kaplan, Lewis A., Letter to Clifford D. Stromberg, Apr. 16, 1986.

Dorkey, Charles E., III, Letter to Robert S. Wallerstein, Apr. 17, 1986.

Auletta, Irene, Memorandum to IPA Executive Council, Apr. 18, 1986.

Cannon, Lista M., Letter to Irene Auletta, May 2, 1986.

Cannon, Lista M., Letter to Irene Auletta, May 6, 1986.

Minutes, IPA Executive Council (partial meeting), Washington, D.C., May 8, 1988.

Cannon, Lista M., Letter to Irene Auletta, May 21, 1986.

Cannon, Lista M., Letter to Irene Auletta, May 27, 1986.

Auletta, Irene, Letter to Robert S. Wallerstein, May 28, 1986.

Auletta, Irene, Memorandum to IPA Executive Council, May 28, 1986.

Stromberg, Clifford D., Letter to Lewis A. Kaplan and Charles E. Dorkey, III, May 29, 1986.

Kaplan, Lewis A., Letter to Judge John Keenan, plus proposed Stipulation and Protective Order for Confidential Information, and copies of two similar Orders issued in comparable cases, May 30, 1986.

Simons, Richard C., Letter to Members of Executive Council of the American, June 2, 1986.

Auletta, Irene, Memorandum to Charles E. Dorkey, III, June 3, 1986.

Cannon, Lista M., Letter to Irene Auletta, June 4, 1986.

Cannon, Lista M., three Letters to Irene Auletta, June 9, 1986.

Greenberg, Ira G., Letter to Judge John Keenan, June 9, 1986.

Wallerstein, Robert S. and Weinshel, Edward M., Quarterly Memorandum to Presidents of all IPA Component Organizations, June, 1986.

Cannon, Lista M., Letter to Irene Auletta, June 24, 1986.

Ten members of British Psychoanalytical Society, Memorandum and two Appended Letters to Officers of the IPA, July 8, 1986.

Auletta, Irene, Letter to Nina Coltart, July 16, 1986.

Cannon, Lista M., Letter to Irene Auletta, July 30, 1986.

Weinshel, Edward M., Letter to Nina Coltart, Sept. 19, 1986.

Simons, Richard C., Letter to Members of the American, July 15, 1986.

Stromberg, Clifford D., Letter to the Four Principal Attorneys for the Four Defendant Groups, Accompanying the Settlement Agreement Proposal Drafted by Stromberg, July 28, 1986.

Auletta, Irene, Letter to Lista M. Cannon, Aug. 1, 1986.

Wallerstein, Robert S., Response to Proposed "Settlement Agreement" Drafted by Plaintiffs in the Suit Against the American, the New York Institute, the Columbia Institute, and the International, Aug. 30, 1986, with cover letter, Sept. 4, 1986.

Simons, Richard C. and Orgel, Shelley, Letter to Members of the American, Sept. 8, 1986.

Kaplan, Lewis A., Stipulation of Settlement and Dismissal, Sept. 19, 1986.

Kaplan, Lewis A., Revised Stipulation of Settlement and Dismissal, Sept. 22, 1986.

Auletta, Irene, Letter to Lista M. Cannon, Sept. 24, 1986.

Person, Ethel S., Letter to Richard C. Simons, Sept. 26, 1986.

Fisher, Clinton B., Letter to Lewis A. Kaplan, Sept. 29, 1986.

Auspitz, Jack C., Letter to Lewis A. Kaplan, Mark Bunim, and Charles E. Dorkey III, Oct. 2, 1986.

Wallerstein, Robert S. and Weinshel, Edward M., Memorandum to Members of IPA Executive Council and to Presidents of IPA Component Organizations, Oct., 1986.

Chapter 10

Wallerstein, Robert S., Letter to Helen Fischer, Oct. 3, 1986.

Fischer, Helen, Memorandum to all Invited Participants in the Oct. 12 Meeting of the Defendant Parties to the Lawsuit, Oct. 3, 1986.

Silber, Austin, Memorandum to Members of the Executive Council of the American, Oct. 6, 1986.

Kaplan, Lewis A., Further Revised Stipulation of Settlement and Dismissal, Oct.15, 1986.

Wallerstein, Robert S., Letter to Richard C. Simons, Oct. 20, 1986.

Minutes, IPA Executive Council (partial meeting), Broomhills, London, Nov. 4, 1986.

Burrows, Karen B., Memorandum to IPA files, Broomhills, London, Nov. 5, 1986.

Davis, Carl L., Memorandum to Directors of Institutes of the American, Nov. 6, 1986.

Burrows, Karen B., Memorandum to IPA files, Broomhills, London, Nov. 12, 1986.

Cannon, Lista M., Letter to Irene Auletta, Nov. 17, 1986.

Schlesinger, Herbert J., Memorandum, "Paradoxical Scenarios," Nov. 17, 1986.

Pine, Fred, From the President's Desk, Division 39 *Newsletter,* Fall, 1986.

Welch, Bryant, Memorandum, as President of GAPPP, to the Members of the American, Nov. 26, 1986.

Cannon, Lista M., Letter to Irene Auletta, Nov. 26, 1986.

Peltz, Morris L., Letters to Richard C. Simons and Shelley Orgel, Dec. 8, 9, 10, 1986.

Minutes, Meeting of IPA Executive Council, New York, Dec. 17, 18, 20, 1986.

Orgel, Shelley, Letter to Robert S. Wallerstein, Dec. 22, 1986.

Wallerstein, Robert S., Letter to Shelley Orgel, Dec. 30, 1986.

Sachs, David M., Letter to Robert S. Wallerstein, Dec. 23, 1986.

Chapter 11

Peltz, Morris L., Letter to Richard C. Simons and Shelley Orgel, Dec. 27, 1986.

Wallerstein, Robert S., Letter to Nathan Stockhamer, Jan. 7, 1987.

Simons, Richard C., Letter to all Members of the American, Jan. 15, 1987.

Meisels, Murray, Letter to "Colleagues," Jan. 29, 1987.

Newsletter, American Psychoanalytic Association, Winter 1987.

Council News, Council of Psychoanalytic Psychotherapists, Feb. 1987.

The Monitor, American Psychological Association, Feb. 1987.

Fisher, Clinton B., Memorandum to Robert S. Wallerstein, Feb. 3, 1987.

Peltz, Morris L., Letter to Richard C. Simons and Shelley Orgel, Feb. 18, 1987.

Wallerstein, Robert S., Letter to Shelley Orgel, Mar. 10, 1987.

Orgel, Shelley, Letter to Robert S. Wallerstein, Mar. 18, 1987.

Fine, Reuben, Letter to Robert S. Wallerstein, Mar. 18, 1987.

Laufer, Moses, Letter to Edward M. Weinshel, Mar. 19, 1987.

Simons, Richard C., Letter to Members of the American, Mar. 30, 1987.

Wallerstein, Robert S. and Weinshel, Edward M., Memorandum to Presidents of all IPA Component Organizations, Apr. 1987.

Wallerstein, Robert S. and Weinshel, Edward M., Memorandum to Members of IPA Executive Council, Apr. 1987.

National Psychological Association for Psychoanalysis (NPAP), Announcement for All-day Scientific Conference, Apr. 18, 1987.

Orgel, Shelley, Memorandum to Fellows of Board on Professional Standards (BOPS), Apr. 23, 1987.

Weinshel, Edward M., Message to Meeting of BOPS, May 5, 1987.

Dorkey, Charles E., III, Memorandum to Robert S. Wallerstein, May 15, 1987.

Wallerstein, Robert S., Letter to Charles E. Dorkey, III, May 20, 1987.

Wallerstein, Robert S., Letter to Murray Meisels, May 18, 1987.

Meisels, Murray, Letter to Robert S. Wallerstein, June 2, 1987.

Wallerstein, Robert S., Letter to Murray Meisels, July 9, 1987.

Meisels, Murray, Letter to Robert S. Wallerstein, July 17, 1987.

Schafer, Roy and Frankiel, Rita, Letter to Robert S. Wallerstein, Dec. 10, 1987.

Smith, Sydney, Letter to Robert S. Wallerstein, Jan. 6, 1988.

Newsletter, *Behavior Today,* Vol. 18, No. 23, June 8, 1987.

Simons, Richard C., Letter to Members of the American, June 9, 1987.

Burrows, Karen B., Memorandum for IPA Files, Broomhills, London, June 18, 1987.

Fisher, Clinton B., Memorandum to Robert S. Wallerstein, June 30, 1987.

Stromberg, Clifford D. and Klein, Joel I., Petition to Judge Richard Daronco, July 21, 1987.

Minutes, IPA Executive Council, Rome, July 22, 1987.

Auletta, Irene, Letter to Lista M. Cannon, Aug. 7, 1987.

Chapter 12

Dorkey, Charles E., III, and Fisher, Clinton B., Responses of Defendant International Psychoanalytical Association to Plaintiffs' Request for Admissions, Aug. 21, 1987.

Stromberg, Clifford D. and Greenberg, Ira G., Counsel for Plaintiffs, Memorandum in Support of Plaintiffs' Motion for Class Certification, Oct. 14, 1987.

Fisher, Clinton B., Memorandum to Robert S. Wallerstein, Edward M. Weinshel, Irene Auletta, and Lista M. Cannon, Oct. 26, 1987.

Morrissey, Michael T., Memorandum to IPA Files, Broomhills, London, Nov. 4, 1987.

Minutes, IPA Executive Council (partial meeting), London, Nov. 5, 1987.

Morrissey, Michael T., Memorandum to IPA Files, Broomhills, London, Nov. 18, 1987.

Round Robin, Newsletter of Section 1, Division 39, Dec., 1987.

Meisels, Murray, Open Letter to N.Y. Psychoanalytic Institute, Dec. 4, 1987.

Simons, Richard C., Letter to Members of the American, Dec. 21, 1987.

Minutes, IPA Executive Council (partial meeting), New York, Dec. 16, 17, 1987.

Welch, Bryant, Affidavit to U.S. District Court, Southern District, New York, Dec. 22, 1987.

Fisher, Clinton B., Letter to Robert S. Wallerstein, Dec. 30, 1987.

Draft Report of IPA Ad Hoc Committee on Admission of New Groups, Jan., 1988.

Hanly, Charles, Some Initial Reflections, Nov., 1987.

Hanly, Charles, Letter to Robert S. Wallerstein, Jan. 12, 1988.

Meisels, Murray, Letter to Robert S. Wallerstein, Jan. 11, 1988.

Wallerstein, Robert S., Letter to Murray Meisels, Jan. 25, 1988.

Fisher, Clinton B., Letter to Robert S. Wallerstein, Jan. 25, 1988.

Fisher, Clinton B., Letter to Robert S. Wallerstein, Jan. 26, 1988.

Draft, Defendants' Brief in Opposition to Plaintiffs' Class Certification Motion, January, 1988.

Wallerstein, Robert S., Letter to Clinton B. Fisher, Jan. 28, 1988.

Defendants' Memorandum in Law in Opposition to the Motion for Class Certification, Feb. 12, 1988.

Simons, Richard C., Memorandum to Members of the American, Mar. 7, 1988.

Meisels, Murray, Letter to Robert S. Wallerstein, Jan. 26, 1988.

Wallerstein, Robert S., Letter to Murray Meisels, Feb. 3, 1988.

Chapter 13

Draft Report, IPA Committee on the Admission of New Groups, Mar., 1988.

Minutes, IPA Executive Council, Longhorsley, Northumberland, England, Mar. 31, 1988.

Fisher, Clinton B., Memorandum to Robert S. Wallerstein, Irene Auletta, and Lista M. Cannon, Apr. 6, 1988.

Fisher, Clinton B., Memorandum to Robert S. Wallerstein, Irene Auletta, and Lista M. Cannon, Apr. 7, 1988.

Simons, Richard C., Letter to Members of the American, Apr. 25, 1988.

Fisher, Clinton B., Memorandum to Robert S. Wallerstein, Irene Auletta, and Lista M. Cannon, May 3, 1988.

Goleman, Daniel, "Psychologists and Psychiatrists Clash over Hospital and Training Barriers," *The New York Times*, May 12, 1988.

Fisher, Clinton B., Memorandum to Robert S. Wallerstein, May 12, 1988.

Klein, Joel I., Letter to Jack C. Auspitz, Mark Bunim, and Clinton B. Fisher with enclosed Draft of Proposed Settlement Agreement, May 12, 1988.

Libbey, Mary, Letter to Robert S. Wallerstein, May 16, 1988.

Fisher, Clinton B., Memorandum to Robert S. Wallerstein, May 19, 1988.

Fisher, Clinton B., Memorandum to Robert S. Wallerstein, May 20, 1988.

Fisher, Clinton B., Memorandum to Robert S. Wallerstein, May 23, 1988.

Fisher, Clinton B., Memorandum to Robert S. Wallerstein, May 27, 1988.

Morrissey, Michael T., Memorandum to Robert S. Wallerstein, June 23, 1988.

Hitchcock, Christopher B., Letter to Allen R. Snyder, June 23, 1988.

Morrissey, Michael T., Memorandum to Robert S. Wallerstein, June 30, 1988.

Fisher, Clinton B., Memorandum to Robert S. Wallerstein, July 12, 1988.

Fisher, Clinton B., Letter to Allen R. Snyder, July 14, 1988.

Minutes, IPA Executive Council, London, July 29–31, 1988.

Fisher, Clinton B., Letter to Charles Hanly, Aug. 9, 1988.

Fisher, Clinton B., Memorandum to Robert S. Wallerstein, Aug. 10, 1988.

Snyder, Allen R., Letter to Joel I. Klein, Clinton B. Fisher, Mark Bunim, and Jack C. Auspitz, Aug. 10, 1988.

Fisher, Clinton B., Memorandum to Robert S. Wallerstein, Aug. 15, 1988.

Fisher, Clinton B., Draft of Letter to Allen R. Snyder, Aug. 15, 1988.

Fisher, Clinton B., Letter to Allen R. Snyder, Aug. 16, 1988.

Stromberg, Clifford D., Letter to Joel I. Klein, Clinton B. Fisher, Mark Bunim, and Jack C. Auspitz, Sept. 7, 1988.

Fisher, Clinton B., Memorandum to Robert S. Wallerstein, Sept. 8, 1988.

Klein, Joel I., Letter to Homer C. Curtis, Sept. 8, 1988.

Welch, Bryant, Lawsuit: Negotiated Settlement. *Psychologist Psychoanalyst*, Vol. VIII, No. 4, pp. 1–3, Fall 1988.

Liff, Zanvil A., From the President's Desk. *Psychologist Psychoanalyst*, Vol. VIII, No. 4, pp. 3–4, Fall 1988.

Snyder, Allen R., Letter to Joel I. Klein, Clinton B. Fisher, Mark Bunim, and Jack C. Auspitz, Oct. 6, 1988.

Draft of Notice of Proposed Class Settlement, Oct., 1988.

Fisher, Clinton B., Memorandum to Robert S. Wallerstein, Oct. 12, 1988.

Curtis, Homer C., Letter to Members of American, Oct. 13, 1988.

Wallerstein, Robert S., Letter to Clinton B. Fisher, Oct. 18, 1988.

Fisher, Clinton B., Letter to Robert S. Wallerstein, Nov. 2, 1988.

Dorkey, Charles E., III, Letter to Robert S. Wallerstein, Nov. 8, 1988.

Chapter 14

The Psychiatric Times, Vol. V, No. 11, pp. 1, 33, Nov., 1988.

Wallerstein, Robert S., Letter to John L. Schwartz, Nov. 9, 1988

Curtis, Homer C., Letter to Members of the American, Nov. 14, 1988.

Curtis, Homer C., Letter to *The New York Times*, Dec. 8, 1988.

Wallerstein, Robert S., Letter to *The New York Times*, Dec. 24, 1988.

Behavior Today, Vol. 19, No. 51, pp.3–4, Dec. 19, 1988.

Wallerstein, Robert S., Letter to Ira Rosofsky, Editor, *Behavior Today*, Jan. 10, 1989.

The Psychiatric Times, Vol. V, No. 11, pp. 1–2, 9, 18–20, Dec., 1988.

The Round Robin, pp. 8, 9, Dec., 1988.

Grand, Stanley, Letter to Robert S. Wallerstein, Dec. 21, 1988.

Wallerstein, Robert S., Letter to Homer C. Curtis, Dec. 22, 1988.

Wallerstein, Robert S., Letter to William Greenstadt, Dec. 22, 1988.

Wallerstein, Robert S., Letter to Mary Libbey, Jan. 11, 1989.

Libbey, Mary and Katz, Gil A., Letter to Robert S. Wallerstein, Jan. 19, 1989.

Wallerstein, Robert S., Letter to Mary Libbey, Jan. 24, 1989.

Libbey, Mary, Letter to Charles Hanly, Feb. 28, 1989.

Hanly, Charles, Letter to Robert S. Wallerstein, Mar. 25, 1989.

Wallerstein, Robert S., Letter to Mary Libbey, Apr. 6, 1989.

Slavin, Jonathan H., Letter to Robert S. Wallerstein, Feb. 23, 1989.

Wallerstein, Robert S., Letter to Jonathan H. Slavin, Mar. 1, 1989.

Council News of the Council of Psychoanalytic Psychotherapists, Feb. 1989.

Fisher, Clinton B., Memorandum to Robert S. Wallerstein, Apr. 17, 1989.

Curtis, Homer C., Letter to Members of the American, June 7, 1989.

Stromberg, Clifford D., Letter to Charles E. Dorkey, III, June 19, 1989.

Fisher, Clinton B., Letter to Robert S. Wallerstein, June 30, 1989.

Wallerstein, Robert S., Letter to Clinton B. Fisher, July 6, 1989.

Fisher, Clinton B., Letter to Clifford D. Stromberg, July 13, 1989.

Minutes, IPA Executive Council, Rome, July 27–29, Aug. 1, 1989.

154th *Bulletin of the IPA*, Fall, 1989.

Chapter 15

Newsletter, American Psychoanalytic Association, 18(3), p. 1, Dec. 1985.
Fisher, Clinton B., Letter to Robert S. Wallerstein, Aug. 23, 1989.
Wallerstein, Robert S., Letter to Clinton B. Fisher, Aug. 29, 1989.
Hanly, Charles, Letter to Robert S. Wallerstein, Sept. 6, 1989.
Sandler, Joseph J., Letter to Clifford D. Stromberg, Sept. 14, 1989.
Grand, Stanley, Letter to Charles Hanly, Oct. 4, 1989.
Greenstadt, William, Letter to Charles Hanly, Nov. 22, 1989.
Hanly, Charles, Memorandum to IPA Executive Committee, cochair Arnold
     M. Cooper, chair of IPA Site Visit Committees, Nov. 22, 1989.
Hanly, Charles, Letter to Robert S. Wallerstein, Jan. 3, 1990.
Wallerstein, Robert S., Letter to Joseph J. Sandler, Jan. 18, 1990.
Wallerstein, Robert S., Letter to Joseph J. Sandler, Jan. 29, 1990.
Sandler, Joseph J., Presidential Message, IPA *Newsletter*, Feb. 1990.
Wallerstein, Robert S., Letter to Joseph J. Sandler, Feb. 5, 1990.
Stromberg, Clifford D., Letter to Directors and Faculty of Psychoanalytic
     Institutes, Feb. 14, 1990.
Stromberg, Clifford D., Letter to Joel I. Klein, Feb. 21, 1990.
Fisher, Clinton B., Memorandum to IPA Officers, Feb. 28, 1990.
Wallerstein, Robert S., Letter to Clinton B. Fisher, March 12, 1990.
Rosica, Karen, Letter to "Dear Colleagues" on Murray Meisels's Stationery,
     Mar. 5, 1990.
Eisenbud, Ruth-Jean, Open Letter to the IPA from Division 39 on Murray
     Meisels' Stationery, Mar. 5, 1990.
Wallerstein, Robert S., Letter to Joseph J. Sandler, Mar. 29, 1990.
Lane, Robert C., President's Column in *Round Robin*, Newsletter of
     Section 1 of Division 39, Apr., 1990.
Wallerstein, Robert S., Letter to Joseph J. Sandler, May 14, 1990.
Sandler, Joseph J., Letter to Robert S. Wallerstein, May 16, 1990.
Wallerstein, Robert S., Letter to Joseph J. Sandler, May 17, 1990
Report of the New U.S. Groups Committee, July, 1990.

Chapter 16

Hanly, Charles, Memorandum to IPA Executive Committee, Aug. 7, 1990.
Stromberg, Clifford D., Letter to Charles E. Dorkey, III, and Clinton B.
     Fisher, Sept. 19, 1990.
Fisher, Clinton B., Letter to IPA Executive Committee, Sept. 20, 1990.
Hanly, Charles, Letter to Joseph J. Sandler, Sept. 24, 1990.
Wallerstein, Robert S., Letter to Joseph J. Sandler, Sept. 26, 1990.
Fisher, Clinton B., Letter to Clifford D. Stromberg, Oct. 19, 1990.
Policies and Procedures: IPA Evaluation of New U.S. Groups, Oct. 18, 1990.

Antonovsky, Anna, Letter to Arnold M. Cooper, Oct. 31, 1990.
Antonovsky, Anna, Report of the IPA Committee to the Council of Fellows, William Alanson White Society, Nov. 29, 1989.
Fisher, Clinton B., Letter to Joseph J. Sandler, Nov. 7, 1990.
Stromberg, Clifford D., Letter to Clinton B. Fisher, Oct. 31, 1990.
Wallerstein, Robert S., Letter to Valerie Tufnell, Nov. 8, 1990.
Fisher, Clinton B., Letter to Joseph J. Sandler, Nov. 29, 1990.
Kwawer, Jay S., Letter to the Editors, *Round Robin*, Dec. 1990.
Greenstadt, William, Letter to the Editors, *Round Robin*, Dec. 1990.
Sandler, Joseph J., Presidential Message, IPA *Newsletter*, Jan.1991.
Wallerstein, Robert S., Letter to Joseph J. Sandler, Jan. 7, 1991.
Sandler, Joseph J., Letter to Robert S. Wallerstein, Jan. 14, 1991.
Hanly, Charles, Memorandum to IPA Officers and Chairs of Site Visit Committees on Equivalency Procedures, Feb. 11, 1991.
Sandler, Joseph J., Letter to Jay S. Kwawer, Feb. 12, 1991.
Stromberg, Clifford D., Letter to Clinton B. Fisher, Mar. 4, 1991.
Fisher, Clinton B., Letter to Joseph J. Sandler, Mar. 12, 1991.
Wallerstein, Robert S., Letter to Joseph J. Sandler, Mar. 13, 1991.
Sandler, Joseph J., Letter to Robert S. Wallerstein, Mar. 14, 1991.
Hanly, Charles, Memorandum to IPA Officers and to Clinton B. Fisher, Mar. 21, 1991.
Hanly, Charles, Letter to Jay S. Kwawer, Mar. 25, 1991.
Fisher, Clinton B., Letter to Joseph J. Sandler, Mar. 28, 1991.
Hanly, Charles, Review of IPA New Groups Policy in the U.S., *Round Robin*, Apr. 1991.
Sandler, Joseph J., Letter to Clinton B. Fisher, Apr. 9, 1991.
Fisher, Clinton B., Letter to Joseph J. Sandler, Apr. 19, 1991.
Wallerstein, Robert S., Letter to Joseph J. Sandler, Apr. 19, 1991.
Hanly, Charles, Letter to Robert S. Wallerstein, Apr. 10, 1991.
Fisher, Clinton B., Letter to Joseph J. Sandler, May 1, 1991.
Stromberg, Clifford D., Letter to Clinton B. Fisher, June 6, 1991.
Fisher, Clinton B., Letter to Joseph J. Sandler, June 17, 1991.
Sandler, Joseph J., Letter to Clinton B. Fisher, June 18, 1991.
Wallerstein, Robert S., Letter to Joseph J. Sandler, June 19, 1991.
Sandler, Joseph J., Letter to Robert S. Wallerstein, June 21, 1991.
Wallerstein, Robert S., Letter to Joseph J. Sandler, June 24, 1991.
Fisher, Clinton B., Letter to Joseph J. Sandler, June 25, 1991.
Fisher, Clinton B., Letter to Joseph J. Sandler, June 28, 1991.

Chapter 17

Fisher, Clinton B., Letter to Joseph J. Sandler, Aug. 6, 1991.
Hanly, Charles, Letter to Charles A. Mangham, Aug. 10, 1991.

Hanly, Charles, Letter to Brian Robertson, Aug. 10, 1991.

Hanly, Charles, Letter to Herbert S. Strean, Aug. 12, 1991.

Fisher, Clinton B., Letter to Joseph J. Sandler, Aug. 14, 1991.

Fisher, Clinton B., Letter to Joseph J. Sandler, Aug. 28, 1991.

Slavin, Jonathan H., Memorandum to Board of Directors and Committee Chairs, Division 39, Sept. 13, 1991.

Hanly, Charles, Letter to Herbert S. Strean, Sept. 27, 1991.

Hanly, Charles, Memorandum to IPA Officers and New Groups Committee, Oct. 31, 1991.

Hanly, Charles, Letter to IPA Officers, Nov. 14, 1991.

Wallerstein, Robert S., Letter to Charles Hanly, Nov. 11, 1991.

Slavin, Jonathan H., What Do Psychologists Want? Nov. 18, 1991.

Minutes, North American Subcommittee of IPA New Groups Committee, New York, Dec. 17, 1991.

Minutes, International New Groups & Site Visit Committee, New York, Dec. 18, 1991.

Stromberg, Clifford D., Letter to Clinton B. Fisher, Dec. 17, 1991.

Fisher, Clinton B., Letter to Joseph J. Sandler, Dec. 17, 1991.

Slavin, Jonathan H., From the President's Desk, *Psychologist Psychoanalyst*, Newsletter of Division 39, Winter, 1992.

Schneider, Arnold Z. and Kaley, Harriette, Letter to Editor, *Psychologist Psychoanalyst*, Winter 1992.

Allison, George H., Letter to Editor, *Psychologist Psychoanalyst*, Winter 1992.

Hanly, Charles, Letter to Joseph Zuckerman, Jan. 5, 1992.

Hanly, Charles, Summary History of the IPA New Groups Policy in the U.S., Jan. 6, 1992.

Hanly, Charles, Memorandum to Joseph Zuckerman and IPA Officers, Jan. 7, 1992.

Zuckerman, Joseph, Letter to Joseph J. Sandler, Jan. 7, 1992.

Zuckerman, Joseph, Draft of Letter to Clifford D. Stromberg, Jan. 7, 1992.

Hanly, Charles, Memorandum to Joseph Zuckerman and IPA Officers, Jan. 9, 1992.

Hanly, Charles, Memorandum to Joseph Zuckerman and IPA Officers, Jan. 12, 1992.

Amati-Mehler, Jacqueline, Memorandum to Joseph Zuckerman and IPA Officers, Jan. 11, 1992.

Zuckerman, Joseph, Letter to Clifford D. Stromberg, Jan. 15, 1992.

Zuckerman, Joseph, Letter to Charles Hanly, June 29, 1992.

Chapter 18

Hanly, Charles, Letter to Joseph Zuckerman, Jan. 7, 1992.

Hanly, Charles, Letter to Joseph J. Sandler, Jan. 15, 1992.

Strean, Herbert S., Letter to Clifford D. Stromberg, Feb. 3, 1992.

Hanly, Charles, Letter to Sydney E. Pulver, Feb. 7, 1992.

Sandler, Joseph J., Letter to Joseph Zuckerman, Feb. 11, 1992.

Hanly, Charles, Letter to Joseph J. Sandler, Feb. 15, 1992.

Strean, Herbert S., Letter to Sydney E. Pulver, Feb. 21, 1992.

Pulver, Sydney E., Letter to Herbert S. Strean, Mar. 4, 1992.

Kris, Anton O., Letter to David M. Sachs, Feb. 27, 1992.

Sandler, Joseph J., Letter to Anton O. Kris, March 3, 1992.

Kris, Anton O., Letter to Joseph J. Sandler, Mar. 10, 1992.

Sachs, David M., Letter to Anton O. Kris, Mar. 16, 1992.

Sachs, David M., Letter to Anton O. Kris, Mar. 21, 1992.

Kris, Anton O., Letter to David M. Sachs, Mar. 25, 1992.

Sachs, David M., Letter to Anton O. Kris, Apr. 3, 1992.

Hanly, Charles, Letter to Robert S. Wallerstein, Mar. 11, 1992.

Hanly, Charles, Letter to Joseph J. Sandler, Mar. 17, 1992.

Hanly, Charles, Letter to Joseph Zuckerman, Apr. 6, 1992.

Zuckerman, Joseph, Letter to Charles Hanly, June 29, 1992.

Sugarman, Alan, Letter to Editor, *Psychologist Psychoanalyst*, Spring 1992.

Schneider, Arnold Z. and Kaley, Harriette, Letter to Editor, *Psychologist Psychoanalyst*, Spring 1992.

Slavin, Jonathan H., From the President's Desk, *Psychologist Psychoanalyst*, Summer 1992.

Hanly, Charles, Letter to Robert S. Wallerstein, Aug. 30, 1994.

Robertson, Brian M., 1995 Site Visit Report to LAISPS, May 20, 1995.

Adams-Silvan, Abby, In Statu Nascendi:The Coalition of Independent Psychoanalytic Societies in the U.S.A., IPA *Newsletter*, Vol. 2, No. 2, pp. 21–23, 1993.

Flint, Emily, Letter from the President, NYFS *News Briefs*, July 6, 1995.

Sanville, Jean B., Toward a History of the Independent Psychoanalytic Societies in Southern California, *The American Psychoanalyst*, Vol. 30, No. 2, pp. 13–14, 16, Vol. 1996.

Caligor, Leopold, From the President's Desk:The Psychoanalytic Consortium, *Psychologist Psychoanalyst*, Vol. 13, No. 2, Spring 1993.

Tyson, Phyllis, A Widening Stream:Nonmedical Training in the American. *The American Psychoanalyst*, Vol. 28, Issue 1, pp. 14–15, 19, 1994.

Jeffrey, William D., Board Approves Consortium Bylaws, Weighs External Credentialing, *The American Psychoanalyst*, Vol. 30, No. 1, pp. 6–7, 1996.

Curtis, Homer C., Report to BOPS of Ad Hoc Joint Committee to Consider Membership for Members of the IPA, May 20, 1993.

Curtis, Homer C., Letter to Members of the American from the Ad Hoc Joint Committee to Consider Membership for Members of the IPA, June 21, 1994.

List of Organizations Involved in the Lawsuit, Its Precursors, and Its Aftermath

Advisory Committee to the Executive Committee of the American, 1983–1984.

APsaA: American Psychoanalytic Association; The American.

American Psychological Association.

APM: Asociación Psicoanalítica Mexicana; Mexican Psychoanalytic Association.

BCD: Board Certified Diplomate, Committee on Psychoanalysis, National Federation of Societies of Clinical Social Work.

Behavior Today, weekly newsletter.

Boodle, Hatfield, and Co.: Attorneys for the IPA (London).

BOPS: Board on Professional Standards of the American Psychoanalytic Association; The Board.

CIPS: Confederation of Independent Psychoanalytic Societies (formerly Coalition of Independent Psychoanalytic Societies).

Columbia Institute: Columbia University Center for Psychoanalytic Training and Research.

CNMCT: Committee on Non-Medical Clinical Training, of the American.

Commission on Settlement Enforcement, Established by GAPPP, April, 1990.

Committee on Desirability of Non-Medical Training of the American (1981–1982).

Committee on Feasability of Non-Medical Training of the American (1978–1981).

Committee on Membership [in the American Psychoanalytic Association] for members of the IPA.

Committee on Psychoanalysis of the National Federation of Societies in Clinical Social Work.

COMPSED: Commission on Psychoanalytic Education of the IPA.

COPAP: Committee on Preparedness and Progress, of the American; successor to CNMCT.

COPE: Committee on Psychoanalytic Education, of the American.

COPER: Conference on Psychoanalytic Education and Research, of the American, 1974.

CORST: Committee on Research and Special Training, of the American; successor to CTR.

CPP: Council of Psychoanalytic Psychotherapists.

CPT: Committee on Prerequisites for Training of the American (1975–1981).

CTR: Committee on Training for Research of the American.

Division 39: the Division of Psychoanalysis of the American Psychological Association.

FIPAS: Federation of IPA Societies of Los Angeles.

GAPPP: Group for the Advancement of Psychotherapy and Psychoanalysis in Psychology.

Hogan and Hartson: Attorneys for the Plaintiffs (Washington).

IPA: International Psychoanalytical Association.

IPTAR: Institute for Psychoanalytic Training and Research (New York).

ITC: International Training Commission of the IPA.

LAISPS: Los Angeles Institute and Society for Psychoanalytic Studies.

Morrison and Foerster; Attorneys for the Columbia Institute (New York).

MPSG: Massachusetts Psychoanalytic Study Group.

NAIPAG: North American IPA Groups.

NAIPAS: North American IPA Societies.

NPAP: National Psychological Association for Psychoanalysis.

NYCPT: New York Center for Psychoanalytic Training.

NYFS: New York Freudian Society.

NYPI: New York Psychoanalytic Institute.

Ohrenstein and Bunim: Attorneys for the New York Institute (New York).

Onek, Klein, and Farr: second Attorneys for the American (Washington) (November 1986–).

Paul, Weiss, Rifkind, Wharton, and Garrison; first Attorneys for the American (New York) (1985–November 1986).

PCC: Psychoanalytic Center of California.

Psychiatric Times, newsletter, John Schwartz, Publisher and Editor-in-Chief.

Psychologist Psychoanalyst: Newsletter of Division 39.

Richards, O'Neill, and Allegaert: first Attorneys for the IPA (New York (1985–December 1991).

Round Robin: Newsletter of Section 1 (Psychoanalytic Practitioners) of Division 39.

Rosenman and Colin: second Attorneys for the IPA (New York) (January 1992–).

SVC: Site Visit Committee.

TAP: The American Psychoanalyst, Newsletter of the American.

WAW: William Alanson White Psychoanalytic Society.

List of Individuals Involved in the Lawsuit, Its Precursors, and Its Aftermath

Adams-Silvan, Abby: President, New York Freudian Society (NYFS).

Allison, George H.: President, American Psychoanalytic Association (1990–1992).

Amati-Mehler, Jacqueline: Secretary, International Psychoanalytical Association (1989–1993).

Antonovsky, Anna M.: Member, William Alanson White Society; then Member, Institute for Psychoanalytic Training and Research (IPTAR).

Aslan, Carlos Mario: Member, Executive Council of the International Psychoanalytical Association.

Auletta, Irene: Administrative Director, International Psychoanalytical Association (up to 1990).

Auspitz, Jack C.: Lead Attorney for Columbia Institute (from Morrison and Foerster).

Baker, Ronald: Secretary, British Psychoanalytical Society.

Beigler, Jerome S.: Chair, Constitution and By-Laws Committee, International Psychoanalytical Association.

Bernay, Toni: one of the four Plaintiffs in the Lawsuit.

Bolgar, Hedda: Member, Los Angeles Institute and Society for Psychoanalytic Studies (LAISPS).

Brodsky, Bernard: President, New York Psychoanalytic Institute.

Bunim, Mark: Lead Attorney for New York Institute (from Ohrenstein and Bunim).

Burrows, Karen B.: Attorney for International Psychoanalytical Association (from Richards, O'Neill, and Allegaert).

Calder, Kenneth T.: Chair, Committee on the Feasibility of Non-Medical Training, American Psychoanalytic Association.

Caligor, Leopold: President, Division 39, American Psychological Association, 1993.

Cannon, Lista M.: London Attorney for International Psychoanalytical Association (from Boodle and Hatfield).

Cerf, Chris: Attorney for American Psychoanalytic Association (from Onek, Klein, and Farr).

Chasseguet-Smirgel, Janine: Member, Executive Council of International Psychoanalytical Association.

Coltart, Nina: Vice-President and Chair of Council, British Psychoanalytical Society.

Cooper, Arnold M.: Member, Executive Council, International Psychoanalytical Association; Cochair, New U.S. Groups Committee, International Psychoanalytical Association.

Coopersmith, Sy: Editor, Council News of the Council of Psychoanalytic Psychotherapists.

Curtis, Homer C.: Chair, Committee on Prerequisites for Training (1975–1981); Chair, Board on Professional Standards (1982–1985); President (1988–1990); Chair, Joint Committee on Membership for Members of the IPA, all of the American Psychoanalytic Association; Third Chair, Site Visit Committee to New York Center for Psychoanalytic Training (NYCPT), International Psychoanalytical Association.

Daronco, Richard J.: Second Judge in the Lawsuit.

Davis, Carl L.: First Chair, Committee on Non-Medical Clinical Training, American Psychoanalytic Association (1986–1989).

Desmond, Helen: one of the four Plaintiffs in the Lawsuit.

Dollinger, Michael: Magistrate assisting Judge Daronco.

Dorkey, Charles E., III: Lead Attorney for the International Psychoanalytical Association (from Richards, O'Neill, and Allegaert) (1985–1991).

Dufresne, Roger: Member, Executive Council, International Psychoanalytical Association.

Eisenbud, Ruth-Jean: President, Division 39, American Psychological Association.

Eisnitz, Alan J.: Chair, Ethics Committee, American Psychoanalytic Association.

Ellman, Steven: Member, Division 39, American Psychological Assocation; Member, IPTAR.

Fine, Reuben: Founder and first President, Division 39 of the American Psychological Association; Founder and Member of New York Center for Psychoanalytic Training (NYCPT).

Fischer, Helen: Administrative Director, American Psychoanalytic Association.

Fisher, Clinton B.: Attorney for International Psychoanalytical Association (from Richards, O'Neill, and Allegaert).

Fliegel, Zenia O.: Member, Division 39, American Psychological Association; Member, IPTAR and NYFS.

Flint, Emily: President, New York Freudian Society (NYFS).

Frankiel, Rita: Member, Division 39, American Psychological Association; Member, NYFS.

Freedman, Norbert: President, Institute for Psychoanalytic Training and Research (IPTAR); Cochair, CIPS Steering Committee.

Ganzarain, Ramon C.: Member, American Psychoanalytic Association; IPA Fact Finder on "Mexican Recruitment" by LAISPS.

Gaskill, Herbert S.: Chair, Advisory Committee to the Executive Committee, American Psychoanalytic Association (the "Gaskill Committee," the "Gaskill Report"); First Chair, Site Visit Committee to Los Angeles Institute and Society for Psychoanalytic Studies (LAISPS), International Psychoanalytical Association.

Gilliland, Robert M.: Member of the "Gaskill Committee."

Goleman, Daniel: Science Reporter for *The New York Times*, psychology and mental health issues.

Gooch, James A.: President, Psychoanalytic Center of California (PCC); Member, American Psychoanalytic Association.

Goodstein, Leonard: Executive Vice-President, American Psychological Association.

Grand, Stanley: President, Institute for Psychoanalytic Training and Research (IPTAR); Member NYFS.

Greenberg, Ira G.: Attorney for the Plaintiffs (Hogan and Hartson).

Greenstadt, William: President, New York Freudian Society (NYFS); Member, IPTAR; President, Section 1, Division 39, American Psychological Association.

Gross, George E.: President, New York Psychoanalytic Institute.

Hanly, Charles: Chair, New U.S. Groups Committee, Chair, Site Visit Committee to the Institute for Psychoanalytic Training and Research (IPTAR), International Psychoanalytical Association.

Hitchcock, Christopher B.: Attorney for the New York Institute (Ohrenstein and Bunim).

Hoffman, Janet: Attorney for the American Psychoanalytic Association (Paul, Weiss, Rifkind, Wharton, and Garrison).

Hurwitz, Mervin: Teller for ballots on the "Gaskill Proposal."

Isay, Richard A.: Chair, Committee on the Desirability of Non-Medical Training, American Psychoanalytic Association.

Jeffrey, William D.: Editor, *The American Psychoanalyst*, Newsletter of the American Psychoanalytic Association.

Joseph, Edward D.: President, American Psychoanalytic Association (1984–1986); President, International Psychoanalytical Association (1977–1981).

Kaley, Harriette: Member, Board of Directors of the Group for the Advancement of Psychotherapy and Psychoanalysis in Psychology.

Kaplan, Donald: Member, Division 39, American Psychological Association; Member, NYFS and LAISPS.

Kaplan, Lewis A.: Lead Attorney for the American Psychoanalytic Association (Paul, Weiss, Rifkind, Wharton, and Garrison) (1985–November 1986).

Katz, Gil A.: Associate Editor, *Round Robin*, Newsletter of Section 1, Division 39, American Psychological Association; Member, IPTAR.

Katz, Jay: Chair, Committee on Psychoanalysis, Legal Issues, and Legal Review, American Psychoanalytic Association.

Keenan, John F.: First Judge in the Lawsuit.

Kernberg, Otto F.: Member, Executive Council, International Psychoanalytical Association.

Klein, Joel I.: Lead Attorney for the American Psychoanalytic Association (Onek, Klein, and Farr) (November 1986–).

Krent, Justin M.: Member of the "Gaskill Committee."

Kris, Anton O.: Organizer, Massachusetts Psychoanalytic Study Group (MPSG); Member, American Psychoanalytic Association.

Kuchenbuch, Albrecht: Member, Executive Council, International Psychoanalytical Association.

Kwawer, Jay S.: Chair, Ad Hoc Committee to the International Psychoanalytical Association, William Alanson White Institute.

Lane, Robert C.: President, Section 1 of Division 39, American Psychological Association; Coeditor, *A History of the Division of Psychoanalysis of the American Psychological Association.*

Laufer, Moses: Member, Executive Council, Member, New U.S. Groups Committee, International Psychoanalytical Association; President, British Psychoanalytical Society.

Lawrence, Ernest: Board of Directors, GAPPP.

Lebovici, Serge: President, International Psychoanalytical Association (1973–1977).

Leupold-Lowenthal, Harald: Member, Executive Council, International Psychoanalytical Association.

Levitan, Stephen J.: Teller for ballots on the "Gaskill Proposal."

Libbey, Mary: Editor, *Round Robin*, Newsletter of Section 1, Division 39, American Psychological Association; Member, IPTAR.

Liff, Zanvil A.: President, Division 39, 1988, American Psychological Association.

Limentani, Adam: President, International Psychoanalytical Association (1981–1985).

Loomie, Leo S.: President, New York Psychoanalytic Institute.

MacLeod, John A.: Second Chair, Committee on Non-Medical Clinical Training, American Psychoanalytic Association (1989–1991).

Mangham, Charles A.: Second Chair, Site Visit Committee to Los Angeles Institute and Society for Psychoanalytic Studies (LAISPS), International Psychoanalytical Association.

Margolis, Marvin: Chair, Board on Professional Standards, American Psychoanalytic Association (1990–1993).

McLaughlin, Francis: Treasurer, International Psychoanalytical Association (1981–1985); Secretary, International Psychoanalytical Association (1977–1981).

Meisels, Murray: President, Division 39, American Psychological Association, 1987; Coeditor, *A History of the Division of Psychoanalysis of the American Psychological Association.*

Michels, Robert: Member of three of the four Committees of the American Psychoanalytic Association (1975–1984).

Morrissey, Michael T.: Attorney, International Psychoanalytical Association (Richards, O'Neill, and Allegaert).

Mukasey, Michael B.: Third Judge in the Lawsuit.

Oberman, Norman: Member, Los Angeles Institute and Society for Psychoanalytic Studies (LAISPS).

Orgel, Shelley: Chair, Board on Professional Standards, American Psychoanalytic Association (1985–1989).

Pacella, Bernard L.: Treasurer, American Psychoanalytic Association (1983–1989).

Palacios, Agustin: Member, Executive Council, International Psychoanalytical Association.

Peltz, Morris L.: Director, San Francisco Psychoanalytic Institute.

Person, Ethel S.: Director, Columbia University Center for Psychoanalytic Training and Research; Editor, *Newsletter* of the International Psychoanalytical Association.

Pine, Fred: President, Division 39, American Psychological Association; Member, NYFS and American Psychoanalytic Association.

Pulver, Sydney E.: Second Chair, Site Visit Committee to the New York Center for Psychoanalytic Training (NYCPT), International Psychoanalytical Association.

Reiser, Morton F.: President, American Psychoanalytic Association (1982–1984).

Renik, Owen: Chair, Site Visit Committee to Psychoanalytic Center of California (PCC); First Chair, Successor North American New Groups Committee.

Robertson, Brian M.: Third Chair, Site Visit Committee to the Los Angeles Institute and Society for Psychoanalytic Studies (LAISPS), International Psychoanalytical Association.

Rosica, Karen: Member, Division 39, American Psychological Association.

Rosofsky, Ira: Editor, *Behavior Today*.

Sabshin, Melvin: Medical Director, American Psychiatric Association.

Sachs, David M.: Member, New U.S. Groups Committee, Second Chair, Successor North American New Groups Committee, Chair, Site Visit Committee to the New York Freudian Society (NYFS), International Psychoanalytical Association.

Sandler, Joseph J.: President, International Psychoanalytical Association (1989–1993).

Sanville, Jean L.: President, Los Angeles Institute and Society for Psychoanalytic Studies (LAISPS); Cochair, CIPS Steering Committee.

Saussure, Janice de: Member, Executive Council, Member, New U.S. Groups Committee, International Psychoanalytical Association.

Schafer, Roy: Member, Division 39, American Psychological Association; Member, American Psychoanalytic Association.

Schlesinger, Herbert J.: Liaison from American Psychoanalytic Association to Division 39, American Psychological Association.

Schlossman, Howard H.: Treasurer, International Psychoanalytical Association (1985–1991).

Schneider, Arnold Z.: one of the four Plaintiffs in the Lawsuit.

Schwartz, John L.: Publisher and Editor, *The Psychiatric Times*.

Shengold, Leonard L.: Member, Executive Council, International Psychoanalytical Association.

Silber, Austin: Secretary, American Psychoanalytic Association (1985–1990).

Simons, Richard C.: President, American Psychoanalytic Association (1986–1988).

Slavin, Jonathan H.: President, Division 39, American Psychological Association, 1991.

Smith, Sydney: President, Section 1, Division 39, American Psychological Association; Member, American Psychoanalytic Association.

Snyder, Allen R.: Attorney for Plaintiffs (Hogan and Hartson).

Solnit, Albert J.: First Chair, Site Visit Committee to New York Center for Psychoanalytic Training (NYCPT).

Spence, Janet: President, American Psychological Association, 1984.

Spezzano, Charles: Spokesman for Colorado Center for Psychoanalytic Studies.

Spruiell, Vann: Chair, Joint Committee of Board and Council on Non-Medical Training, American Psychoanalytic Association (1983–1984).

Steingart, Irving: Member, Division 39, American Psychological Association; Member, IPTAR and NYFS.

Stockhamer, Nathan: Director of Clinical Services, William Alanson White Institute; President, Division 39, American Psychological Association, Board of Directors, GAPPP.

Strean, Herbert S.: President, New York Center for Psychoanalytic Training (NYCPT).

Stromberg, Clifford D.: Lead Attorney for Plaintiffs (Hogan and Hartson).

Sugarman, Alan: Member, American Psychoanalytic Association.

Tufnell, Valerie: Administrative Director, International Psychoanalytical Association (1990–).

Tyson, Phyllis: Third Chair, Committee on Non-Medical Clinical Training, American Psychoanalytic Association (renamed Committee on Preparedness and Progress) (1991–).

Unwin, Dorothy: Associate Administrative Director, International Psychoanalytical Association.

Villarreal, Inga: Member, Executive Council, Member, New U.S. Groups Committee, International Psychoanalytical Association.

Wallerstein, Robert S.: President, International Psychoanalytical Association (1985–1989).

Weinshel, Edward M.: Secretary, International Psychoanalytical Association (1985–1989); First Chair, Site Visit Committee to the New York Center for Psychoanalytic Training (NYCPT).

Welch, Bryant: One of the four Plaintiffs in the Lawsuit; Executive Director, Office of Professional Practice, American Psychological Association, Board of Directors, GAPPP.

Widlocher, Daniel: Secretary, International Psychoanalytical Association (1973–1977).

Zuckerman, Joseph: Lead Attorney for the International Psychoanalytical Association (Rosenman and Colin) (1992–).

Index

487

For Product Safety Concerns and Information please contact our EU
representative GPSR@taylorandfrancis.com
Taylor & Francis Verlag GmbH, Kaufingerstraße 24, 80331 München, Germany

www.ingramcontent.com/pod-product-compliance
Lightning Source LLC
Chambersburg PA
CBHW070627270326
41926CB00011B/1842

9 781138 005426